A TREATISE ON MIND

VOLUME 4

Maṇḍalas

Their Nature and Development

Other Titles in the Series

The I Concept
Volume 1: The 'Self' or 'Non-Self' in Buddhism
Volume 2: Considerations of Mind - A Buddhist Enquiry
Volume 3: The Buddha-Womb and the Way to Liberation

Cellular Consciousness
Volume 5: An Esoteric Exposition of the Bardo Thödol (Part A)
Volume 5: An Esoteric Exposition of the Bardo Thödol (Part B)

The Way to Shambhala
Volume 6: Meditation and the Initiation Process
Volume 7: The Constitution of Shambhala

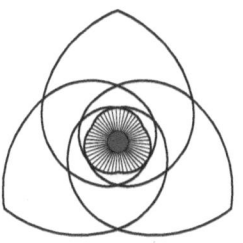

VOLUME FOUR

Maṇḍalas

Their Nature and Development

Bodo Balsys

Universal Dharma
Publications
SYDNEY, AUSTRALIA

ISBN 978-0-9923568-3-5

First Published 2013
Second Edition 2016
Third Edition 2025

Āḥ!

Homage to the Lord of Shambhala.
Inconceivable, inconceivable, beyond thought
Is the bejewelled crown of this most excelled Jina.
He whose Eye has taught many Buddhas.
And who will anoint the myriad,
that in the future lives will come.
As I bow to His Feet my Heart's afire.
Oh, this bliss, this love for my Lord
can barely be borne on my part.
It takes flight as the might of the Dove.
The flight of serene *nirvāṇic* embrace.
The flight of Light so bright.
The flight of Love so active tonight.
The flight of enlightenment for all to come to
their mind's Heart's attire.

Obeisance to the Gurus!
To the Buddhas of the three times.
To the Council of Bodhisattvas, *mahāsattvas*.
To them I pledge allegiance.

Oṁ Hūṁ! Hūṁ! Hūṁ!

Dedication

Thanks to my students, past, present and future, and in particular to those that have helped in the production of this Treatise.

Oṁ

Acknowledgments

Special thanks to Angie O'Sullivan, Anne Kocek,
Kylie Smith, Eliane Clarke
and Ruth Fitzpatrick
for their efforts in making this
series possible.

Oṁ

Contents

Preface ... xi

1. The Layers of Mind ... 1
   - Introducing the concept of *maṇḍalas* ... 1
   - Mind as origin ... 4
   - Further perspectives on the mind and its relation to *śūnyatā* ... 13
   - The five main attributes of mind ... 22
2. The Greater in the Smaller ... 31
   - The construction of *maṇḍalas* ... 31
   - The macrocosmic *maṇḍalic* form ... 34
   - Bubbles and patterns of thought ... 43
   - The Solar Plexus centre and the nature of *siddhis* ... 47
   - Maṇḍalas generally considered ... 50
   - The process of thinking ... 56
3. Examination of Chaos and the Void ... 63
   - The *saṃsāra-śūnyatā* nexus ... 63
   - Chaos and the Void ... 66
   - Logoi and the organisation of *citta* ... 75
   - The Void between understanding and non-understanding ... 87
   - The structure of cellular units ... 96
   - The *chakras*, consciousness, and the attributes of mind ... 101
   - The progress of enlightenment ... 106
4. The Discriminatory Mind and Dimensionality ... 117
   - The discriminatory mind ... 117
   - The nature of multidimensional perception ... 124
   - The Bardo realms ... 137
5. The Construction of Maṇḍalas ... 147
   - The logic of *maṇḍalas* ... 147
   - The necessity for the identity of things ... 152
   - The mystery of numbers ... 154
   - The *maṇḍala* defined ... 158
   - Basic elements of the *maṇḍala* ... 160
   - The three crosses and the *mahāmudrā* ... 167
   - The overriding *maṇḍalic* purpose ... 170
   - The *stūpa* as a *maṇḍala* ... 171
6. Dhāraṇīs and the Function of a Maṇḍala ... 179
   - The nature of *dhāraṇīs* ... 179
   - The function of a *maṇḍala* ... 181

The perception of things 184
The hive of consciousness 191
The Orientation of the major directions of a *maṇḍala* 197
7. The Will and its Manifestations 199
The will and consciousness 199
Various perspectives on the will 202
The will and the rebirth process 217
The Head lotus 221
The Sambhogakāya Flower and the will 233
Unravelling the mysteries of the *maṇḍala* of cosmos 237
8. The Maṇḍala and the Eightfold Path 242
Preamble 242
The motion of the swastika 244
The Four Noble Truths 249
An Exposition of the Eightfold Path 251
9. Consciousness and the Eight Directions of Space 276
A brief discussion of the eight consciousnesses 276
Various lists based upon the number eight 279
The eight Mahābodhisattvas 281
10. The Numerology of the Maṇḍala 327
Why all Tantras are knotted with veils and blinds 327
The *ḍākinīs* and the *chakras* 339
Numerological considerations concerning *chakras* 344
Avalokiteśvara and the Sambhogakāya Flower 356
11. The Great Bodhisattvas and their Consorts 365
The *maṇḍala* of the eight Mahābodhisattvas 365
The Bodhisattvas and the Solar Plexus centre 374
The role of the Consorts 391
The evolution of mind in Nature 396
The inner circle of *ḍākinīs* 401
12. Cells of Time 408
The experience of time 408
Chakras as the basis to it all 415
The Dhyāni Buddhas and the 'five-ness' of things 422
The Jinas and the future 427
The flow of *saṃskāras* 429
The expansion of the cellular structure 433
Bibliography 445
Index 447

Figures

Figure 1. The moving screen of the past ... 9
Figure 2. The process of the expansion of consciousness ... 10
Figure 3. The cycles of expansion of mind ... 11
Figure 4. The relationship of *śūnyatā* to *saṃsāra* ... 12
Figure 5. The dual functioning of mind ... 14
Figure 6. The abstract Mind ... 16
Figure 7. The layers of the mind ... 21
Figure 8: The inward vision of an Ādi Buddha ... 36
Figure 9. Chaos and the Void ... 67
Figure 10. Understanding/Non-understanding ... 90
Figure 11. The constitution of an animal cell ... 99
Figure 12. The Mind and the Elements ... 104
Figure 13. Spirals of consciousness ... 158
Figure 14. Two versions of the Kālachakra *maṇḍala* ... 161
Figure 15. Typical *stūpas* ... 173
Figure 16. The *stūpa* at Sanchi ... 176
Figure 17. The perception of things ... 185
Figure 18. The equilibrated sphere ... 188
Figure 19. The formation of a *chakra* ... 191
Figure 20. A minor *chakra* ... 192
Figure 21. The orientation of *maṇḍalas* ... 197
Figure 22. Lives in the Head lotus ... 221
Figure 23. The next seventy incarnations ... 225
Figure 24. The swastika ... 245
Figure 25. The *maṇḍala* of the eight Mahābodhisattvas ... 281
Figure 26. The seven major *chakras* ... 342
Figure 27. The Sambhogakāya Flower ... 361
Figure 28. The activity of the eight Mahābodhisattvas ... 368
Figure 29. The Dhyāni Bodhisattvas ... 382
Figure 30. The governing pentad of Dhyāni Bodhisattvas ... 385
Figure 31. The pentad of Mahābodhisattvas ... 388
Figure 32. The Bodhisattvas and the Solar Plexus centre ... 390
Figure 33. The energy flow of the *maṇḍala* ... 392

Preface

This treatise investigates Buddhist ideas concerning what mind is and how it relates to a concept of a 'self'. It is principally a study of the complex interrelationship between mind and phenomena, from the gross to the subtle—the physical, psychic, supersensory and supernal. This entails an explanation of how mind incorporates all phenomena in its *modus operandi,* and how eventually that mind is liberated from it, thereby becoming awakened. Thus the treatise explores the manner in which the corporeally orientated, concretised, intellectual mind eventually becomes transformed into the Clear Light of the abstracted Mind; a super-mind, a Buddha-Mind.

A Treatise on Mind is arranged in seven volumes, divided into three subsections. These are as follows:

The I Concept
Volume 1. *The 'Self' or 'Non-self' in Buddhism.*
Volume 2. *Considerations of Mind—A Buddhist Enquiry.*
Volume 3. *The Buddha-Womb and the Way to Liberation.*

Cellular Consciousness
Volume 4. *Maṇḍalas - Their Nature and Development.*
Volume 5. *An Esoteric Exposition of the Bardo Thödol.*
(This volume is published in two parts)

The Way to Shambhala
Volume 6. *Meditation and the Initiation Process.*
Volume 7. *The Constitution of Shambhala.*

The I Concept represents a necessary extensive revision[1] of a large work formerly published in one volume. Together the three volumes investigate the question of what a 'self' is and is not. This involves an analysis of the nature of consciousness, and the consciousness-stream of a human unit developing as a continuum through time. It will illustrate exactly what directs such a stream and how its *karma* is arranged so that enlightenment is the eventual outcome.

The first volume analyses Prāsaṅgika lines of reasoning, such as the 'Refutation of Partless Particles', and 'The Sevenfold Reasoning' in order to derive a clear deduction as to whether a 'self' exists, and if so what its limitations are, and if not, then what the alternative may be. The analysis resolves the historically vexing question of how—if there is no 'self'—can there be a continuity of mind that is coherently connected in an evolutionary manner through multiple rebirths.[2] In order to arrive at this explanation, many of the basic assumptions of Mahāyāna Buddhism, such as Dependent Origination and the Two Truths, are critically analysed.

The second volume provides an in-depth analysis of what mind is, how it relates to the concept of the Void *(śūnyatā),* and the evolution of consciousness. The analysis utilises Yogācāra-Vijñānavādin philosophy in order to comprehend the major attributes of mind, the *saṃskāras* that condition it, and the laws by means of which it operates.

The enquiry into the nature of what an 'I' is requires comprehension of the properties of the dual nature of mind, which consists of an empirical and abstract, enlightened part. As a means of doing this, the *ālayavijñāna* (the store of consciousness-attributes) is explored, alongside the entire philosophy of the 'eight consciousnesses' of this School.

Volume three focuses on the I-Consciousness and the subtle body, by first utilising a minor Tantra, *The Great Gates of Diamond Liberation,* to investigate the nature of the Heart centre and its functions, then the

1 The book was inadequately edited hence contains many errors and grammatical mistakes that have been corrected in this treatise.

2 My earlier work *Karma and the Rebirth of Consciousness* (Munshiram Manoharlal, Delhi, 2006) lays the background for this basic question.

chakras below the diaphragm. This is necessary to lay the foundation for the topics that will be the subject of the later volumes of this treatise concerning the nature of meditation, the construction of *maṇḍalas,* and the yoga of the *Bardo Thödol.*

The focus then shifts to investigate where the idea of a self-sustaining I-concept or 'Soul-form' may be found in Buddhist philosophy, given the denial of substantial self-existence prioritised in the philosophy of Emptiness. Following this, the pertinent chapters of the *Ratnagotravibhāga Śastra* are examined in detail so that a proper conclusion to the investigation can be obtained via the *buddhadharma.* This concerns an analysis of how the *ālayavijñāna* is organised, such that the rebirth process is possible for each human consciousness-stream, taking into account the *karma* that will eventually make each human unit a Buddha. In relation to this the ontological nature of the *tathāgatagarbha* (the Buddha-Womb) must be carefully analysed, as well as the organising principle of consciousness represented by the *chakras.* I thus establish that there is a form that appears upon the domain of the abstract Mind. I call this the Sambhogakāya Flower. The final two chapters of this volume principally define its characteristics.

The second subsection, *Cellular Consciousness,* is divided into two parts. Volume four deals with the question of what exactly constitutes a 'cell', metaphysically. The cell is viewed as a unit of consciousness that interrelates with other cells to form *maṇḍalas* of expression. Each such cell can be considered a form of 'self' that has a limited, though valid, body of expression. It is born, sustains a form of activity, and consequently dies when it outlives its usefulness. This mode of analysis is extended to include the myriad forms manifest in the world of phenomena known as *saṃsāra,* including the existence and functioning of *chakras.*

Volume five deals with the formative forces and evolutionary processes governing the prime cells (that is, *maṇḍalas* of expression), and the phenomenon that governs an entire world-sphere of evolutionary attainment. This is explored via an in-depth exposition of the *Bardo Thödol* and its 42 Peaceful and 58 Wrathful Deities. The text also incorporates a detailed exposition concerning the transformation of *saṃskāras* (consciousness-attributes developed through all past forms of activity) into enlightenment. The entire path of liberation enacted by a *yogin* via the principles of meditation, forms of concentration, and related techniques *(tapas, dhāraṇīs)* is explained. In doing so, the soteriological purpose of the various wrathful and theriomorphic deities is revealed. This volume is published in two parts. Part A explores chapter 5 of the Bardo Thödol concerning the transformation of *saṃskāras* via meditating upon the Peaceful and Wrathful Deities. This necessitates sound knowledge of the force centres (*chakras*) and the way their powers (*siddhis*) awaken. Part B deals with the gain of such transformations and the consequence of conversion of the attributes of the empirical mind into the liberated abstract Mind.

The third subsection, *The Way to Shambhala*, is also in two parts. They present an eclectic revelation of esoteric information integrating the main Eastern and Western religions. Volume six is a treatise on meditation and the Initiation process.[3] The meditation practice is directed towards the needs of individuals living within the context of our modern societies.

Volume six also includes a discussion of the path of Initiation as the means of gaining liberation from *saṃsāra*. The teaching in Volume five concerning the conversion of *saṃskāras* is supplementary to this path. The path of Initiation *is* the way to Shambhala. As many will choose to consciously undergo the precepts needed to undertake Initiation in the future, this invokes the necessity of providing much more revelatory information concerning this kingdom than has been provided hitherto.

How Shambhala is organised is the subject of Volume seven, which details the constitution of the Hierarchy of enlightened being[4] (the Council of Bodhisattvas). It illustrates how the presiding Lords who govern planetary evolution manifest. This detailed philosophy rests on the foundation of the information provided in all of the previous volumes, and necessitates a proper comprehension of the nature of the five Dhyāni Buddhas. To do so the awakening of the meditation-Mind, which is the objective of *A Treatise on Mind*, is essential.

---

3 The word Initiation is capitalised throughout the series of books to add emphasis to the fact that it is the process that makes one divine, liberated. It is the expression of divinity manifesting upon the planetary and cosmic landscape.

4 The word 'being' here is not pluralised because though this Hierarchy is constituted of a multiplicity of beings, together they represent one 'Being', one integral awakened Entity.

How to engage with this text

In this investigation many new ways of viewing conventional Buddhist arguments and rhetoric shall be pursued to develop the pure logic of the reader's mind, and to awaken revelations from their abstract Mind. New insights into the far-reaching light of the *dharma* will be revealed, which will form a basis for the illustration of an esoteric view that supersedes the bounds of conventionally accepted views. Readers should therefore analyse all arguments for themselves to discern the validity of what is presented. Such enquiry allows one to ascertain for oneself, what is logical and truthful, thus overcoming the blind acceptance of a certain dogma or line of reasoning that is otherwise universally accepted as correct. Only that which is discovered within each inquiring mind should be accepted. The remainder should, however, not be automatically discarded, but rather kept aside for later analysis when more data is available—unless the logic is obviously flawed, in which case it should be abandoned. There is no claim to infallibility in the information and arguments presented in this treatise, however, they are designed to offer scope for further meditation and enquiry by the earnest reader. If errors are found through impeccable logic, then the dialectical process may proceed. We can then accept or reject the new thesis and move forward, such that the evolution of human thought progresses, until we all stand enlightened.

This treatise hopes to assist that dialectical evolution by analysing major aspects of the *buddhadharma* as it exists and is taught today, to try to examine where errors may lie, or where the present modes of interpretation fall short of the true intended meaning. The aim is also to elaborate aspects of the *dharma* that could only be hinted at or cursorily explained by the wise ones of the past, because the basis for proper elaboration had not then been established. This analysis of *buddhadharma* will try to rectify some of the past inadequacies in order to explore and extend the *dharma* into arenas rarely investigated.

There will always be obstinate and dogmatic ones that staunchly cling to established views. This produces a reactive malaise in current Buddhist ontological and metaphysical thought. However, amongst the many practitioners of the *dharma* there are also those who have clarified their minds sufficiently to verify truth in whatever form it is presented, and will follow it at all costs to enlightenment. The Council of Bodhisattvas heartily seek such worthy ones. The signposts or guides upon the way to enlightenment have changed through the centuries, and contemporary practitioners of the *dharma* have yet to learn to clearly interpret the new directions. The guide books are now being written and many must come forth to understand and practice correctly.

If full comprehension of such guide books is achieved, those *dharma* practitioners yearning to become Bodhisattvas would rapidly become spiritually enlightened. Here is a rhyme and reason *for* Buddhism. The actual present dearth of enlightened beings informs us that little that is read is properly understood. The esoteric view presented in this treatise hopes to rectify this problem, so as to create better thinkers along the Bodhisattva way.

The numbers of Buddhists are growing in the world, thus Buddhism needs a true restorative flowering to rival that of the renaissance of debate and innovative thinkers of the early post-Nāgārjunian era. In order to achieve this it must synthesise the present wealth of scientific knowledge, alongside the best of the Western world's philosophical output.

Currently the *buddhadharma* is presented as an external body of knowledge held by the Buddha, Rinpoches, monks and lay teachers. This encourages practitioners to hero worship these figures and to heed many unenlightened utterances from such teachers, based on a belief system that encourages people to *uncritically* listen to them and adopt their views. When enlightened teachers *do appear* and find consolidated reasons for firing spiritual bullets for the cause of the enlightenment of humanity, then all truth can and will be known. The present lack of inwardly perceived knowledge from the fount of the *dharmakāya* on the part of many teachers blocks the production of an arsenal of weapons for solving the problems of suffering in the world. Few see little beyond the scope of vision in what they have been indoctrinated to believe, allowing for only rudimentary truths to be understood. While for the great majority this suffices, it is woefully inadequate for those genuinely seeking Bodhisattvahood and enlightenment. The cost to humanity in not being given an enlightened answer as to the nature of awakening, is profound.

We must go to the awakening of the Head lotus to find the most established reasoning powers. Without the 1,000 petals of the *sahasrāra padma* ablaze then there is little substance for proper understanding, little ability to hold the mind steady in the dynamic field of revelation that the *dharmakāya* represents. How can the unenlightened properly understand Buddhist scriptures, when there is little (revelation) coming from the Head centres of such beings? Much still needs to be taught concerning the way of awakening this lotus, and to help fill the lack is a major purpose of *A Treatise on Mind.*

Those who intend to reach enlightenment must go beyond the narrow sectarian allegiances promoted by many strands of contemporary Buddhism. Buddhism itself unfolded in a dialectical context with other heterodox Indian (and Chinese, etc.) traditions, and prospered on account of those engagements. When one sees the unfolding of enlightened wisdom in such a fashion, the particular information from specific schools of thought may be synthesised into a greater whole. Each school has various qualities and types of argument to resolve weaknesses in the opposing stream of thought. This highlights that there are particular aspects in each that may be right or wrong, or neither wholly right or wrong. Through this process we can find better answers, or if need be, create a new lineage or religion which is expressive of a synthesis of the various schools of thought.

The Buddha did not categorically reject the orthodox Indian religio-philosophical ideas of his time, nor did he simply accept them—he reformed them. He preserved the elements that he found to be true, and rejected those 'wrong views' which lead to moral and spiritual impairment. If the existing system needs reformation it becomes part of a Bodhisattva's meditation. The way a reforming Buddha incarnates is dependent on how he must fit into such a system. Thus he is essentially an outsider incarnating into it to demonstrate the new type of ideas he chooses to elaborate. If there is a lot of dogmatic resistance to the presented doctrine of truth, then a new religion is founded. If there is some acceptance then we see reformation. There is always room for improvement, to march forward closer to enlightenment's goal, be it for an individual or for a wisdom-religion as a whole. There is a need for reform throughout the religious world today.

By way of a hermeneutical strategy fit for this task, we ought look no further than the Buddha himself. The Buddha proposed that all students of the *dharma* should make their investigations through the *Four Points of Refuge*. These are:

1. The doctrine is one's point of refuge, not a person.
2. The meaning is one's point of refuge, not the letter.
3. The sacred texts whose meaning is defined are one's point of refuge, to those whose meaning needs definition.
4. Direct awareness is one's point of refuge, not discursive awareness.[5]

These four points can be summarised or rephrased as: the doctrine (*dharma*), true or esoteric meaning, right definition, and direct awareness are one's point of refuge, not adherence to sectarian bias, semantics, the dialectics of non-fully enlightened commentaries, or to illogical assertions. What may be long held to be truthful, but is not, upon proper analytical dissection, needs rectifying. Also, in other cases, a doctrine or teaching may indeed be correct, but the current interpretation leaves much to be desired, and hence should be reinterpreted from the position of a more embracive or esoteric view.

Hopefully this presentation finds welcoming minds that will carefully analyse it in line with their own understandings of the issues, and as a consequence build up a better understanding of the nature of what constitutes the path to enlightenment. Their way of walking as Bodhisattvas should be enriched as a consequence.

For a guide to understanding the pronunciation of Sanskrit words, please visit our website.
http://universaldharma.com/resources/pronounce-sanskrit/

Our online esoteric glossary also provides definitions for most of the terms used in this treatise.
http://universaldharma.com/resources/esoteric-glossary/

5 Griffiths, P.J., *On Being Buddha, The Classical Doctrine of Buddhahood*, (Sri Satguru Publications, New Delhi, 1995), 52.

My eyes do weep as I stare into this troubled world,
For I dare not place my Heart in my brother's keep.
He would grapple that Heart with hands so rough
So as to destroy the fabric of its delicate stuff.
Oh to give, to give, my Heart does yearn,
But humanity must its embracive,
Humbling, pervasive scene yet to learn.
To destroy and tear with avarice they know,
But little care to sensitive rapture they show.
How to give its blood is my constant fare,
For that Love to bestow upon their Hearts I bemoan.
But they hide their Hearts behind mental-emotional walls.
No matter how one prods these walls won't fall,
So much belittling emotional self-concern prop their bastions.
Oh, how my eyes do weep as I stare.
I stare at their fearsome malls and halls.
That lock Love out from all their abodes
And do keep them trapped in realms of woe.

Oṁ Maṇi Padme Hūṁ

1

The Layers of Mind

Introducing the concept of *maṇḍalas*

Consciousness must create an organised structure of the elements of the mind when one is thinking. This process creates the appearance of interrelated thoughts and images that are carefully delineated and linked by common structures, which can be termed a *maṇḍala.*[1] The structure and storage of the attributes of mind do not just exist in a specific place from where images are retrieved, such as in the brain or the Head centre. There are many levels of expression of mind, many nexus from one level to the next containing the *bījas*[2] of thought. These levels must be properly structured in organised patterns for easy retrieval. We also need to examine the way that *maṇḍalas* appear through the relationships that are instantly formed between thoughts as consciousness moves through time. This is the evolutionary process of moving from the point of origination of the seed thought to the circumference of expanded and inclusive resolution.

---

1 *Maṇḍala:* (Tib. dkyil 'khor), circle, wheel. A literary or esoteric corpus filled with religious symbolism that is drawn by one wishing to contemplate things divine, or to evoke potencies and forces associated with Nature and the subjective realms. A perfected, completed, state of being and perception encompassing all phenomena when presented symbolically in a specific form or blueprint of what is to be. Used as a visualising tool during Deity Yoga.

2 *Bīja:* seed (syllable), seminal point, the sound (*vac*) essence of a deity. The essential part of a mantra. The seed germ, the starting point for the display of power or creativity for a *maṇḍala*, or as a focus for meditation.

The colour, tone, note or sound, arrangement of lines, and overall structure are what determine the nature of the organisation of thought to be recalled. To these five must be added the grand design that correlates all seeming diversities into a unity, as well as the intensity of the thought or image. We thus have the seven Ray aspects conditioning *maṇḍalas* of structured thought, from the lowest, or seventh Ray quality in colour, to the highest, or first Ray quality in intensity.[3]

The demonstration of *colour* provides the major characteristics of the thought-form. All human mental-emotional forms of expression, such as anger, scientific opinion, and sensuality, manifest different hues of the electro-magnetic spectrum. The content of the thought-form can therefore be analysed by considering the particular hue it may possess.

Tone indicates how muddied, greyed (hence inchoate), or clear the nature of the thought may be. There may be different dull tones mixed with quite bright, clear patches of thought.

The *note* can be considered the inherent sound or resonance that immediately produces awareness of the thought's general meaning or purpose. Another thinker can thereby quickly deduce its basic content by attuning to this emanatory resonance. That attuned thinker can then agree or disagree merely by having experienced that note of the presenting thought.

The *line* determines how well the thought structure is delineated and modulated. It determines whether there is a clearly defined thought (possessing many lines of definition) or an inchoate brooding idea (possessing hazy or non-existent lines of definition).

The *structure* concerns the nature and complexity of the thought; how many layers or cells of thought (with their differing colours, tonalities, notes, etc.) may lie within the overriding thought.

Grand design differs in structure as it incorporates an overview of many different thought structures. It delineates the way that thoughts may be evolving and what they are evolving towards.

Intensity indicates the overall luminosity of the thought. This indicates the power and potency that it manifests in the realm of ideas, and in the world of activity. The penetrative power of the radiant

3 These Seven Rays were introduced in Volume 2 of this series, *Considerations of Mind* and will be further elaborated in this present Volume.

luminous potency of abstract thought destroys all illusory fabrications of mind. It is developed through yogic prowess, and reveals inevitably the *dharmakāya's*[4] revelatory vistas.

All *bījas* are grouped together in accordance with these seven major categories of each level of expression, and when multiplied together we have forty-nine such groups in all. To each of these can also be related a mantric seed syllable. Each category of thought then becomes a *bindu*[5] containing many *bījas* of images. Each *bīja* is thus a seed that can be categorised according to its major overriding characteristic or sub-characteristic within the general structure of the *bindu.*

We thus start from simple premises, *bījas,* ideas, to the more complex and ordered paradigms of thought, such as found in the Kālachakra Tantra *maṇḍala.* Indeed, most teachings designed by enlightened beings, as found in *kārikās, śāstras, ślokas,* and especially Tantras, are arranged in the form of *maṇḍalas*, which may be seen when the overall design is considered. Such a *maṇḍala* of thought was explained in Volume 3, chapter 7 of this series regarding a rendition of part of the *Uttaratantra of Maitreya-Asaṅga,* wherein the nine-petalled whorled structure of the Sambhogakāya Flower[6] was revealed.

One of the major purposes of the esotericism presented in this series of works is to assist Buddhists to examine their texts far more carefully than has previously been done. Generally, little more than the obvious aspects or levels of meaning of texts have been determined. Consequently, the

---

4 *Dharmakāya:* the body or vehicle of the *dharma.* It is the body of Bliss. *Dharma* is the fount of the Law and *kāya* is its vehicle. The primordial, eternally self-existing essentiality of *bodhi* (enlightenment). The highest of the three-fold bodies (*trikāya*) of a Buddha, or of any Initiate of the fifth degree or greater. (The other two being the *sambhogakāya* and *nirmāṇakāya.*)

5 *Bindu:* (Tib. thig-le) seminal point or 'drop' of energy. A *bindu* differs from a *bīja* in that a *bīja* is a unique indivisible seed germ, whilst a *bindu* may be a collection of many of these. From each drop can come an entire *maṇḍala* of visual or creative expression. The *dharmakāya,* for instance, can be taken as a *bindu* or 'seminal point' for *saṃsāra.*

6 Sambhogakāya Flower. In the *Uttaratantra* the Sanskrit term used for this concept is *tathāgatagarbha* (the Buddha-germ, or 'womb'). It is an alternate name for the reincarnating principle, in the form of a *chakra* (a flower) existing upon the domain of the abstract Mind.

wealth of information found in the far subtler layers of interpretation has only been skimmed, ignored, or not comprehended at all. Even seemingly simple early Theravāda works such as the *Dhammapada* could be better interpreted, as the example below will show.

Mind as origin

The first verse of the *Dhammapada* states:

> All things are preceded by mind, led by mind, created by mind.[7]

This phrase is generally interpreted in terms of only one type of mind: that possessed by the ordinary thinker. The correct esoteric interpretation, however, is based on there being three concentric circles of mind being referred to. The central circle being that which is 'preceded by mind', the next concentric circle being that which is 'led by mind', and the third, outer, concentric circle is that which is 'created by mind'. Each level or layer of mind is bound by the limit of attainment of its overall thought structure, which in reality would produce a sphere of thought. A circle is a two-dimensional representation of a sphere of containment, thus the three zones of interrelation are symbolised diagrammatically by concentric circles.

From this concept a cosmological schema can be derived relating to the creative process (of a Logos) and of the way the entire evolutionary process proceeds and evolves from a Mind.[8] Here we would need to

---

7 *Manopubbaṅgamā dhamma manoseṭṭhā manomayā. Dhammapada—Khuddaka-Nikaya, Sutta Pitaka*, Pāli canon. Different translators have made various renditions of these words. For instance, the version given in The Sacred Books of the East Series, Vol. 10., ed. F. M. Müller, (Motilal Banarsidass, Delhi, 2004), 3: 'All that we are is the result of what we have thought: it is founded on our thoughts, it is made up of our thoughts.' The version given by Dr. P. L. Vaidya, *Dhammapada*, (The Oriental Book Agency, 1934), 1: 'The qualities (of the things) come into existence after the mind, (lit. the qualities have got mind as their precursor), are dependent upon mind, and are made up (formed) of mind.'

8 In this book, mind (*manas*) will be capitalised when it refers to that attribute of mind that is beyond the concrete or empirical formulations of a normal mind (which will retain the lower case). Hence the enlightened Mind, abstract Mind, a Logoi or Buddha's Mind will all be capitalised. Note also that the meaning of the term Logos refers to a 'Thus gone' Buddha from a previous evolutionary epoch. For the sake of

be free to extrapolate or extend the consideration to the formation of an entire planetary manifestation. The conditioning factors being the degree of subtlety and pervasiveness of the mind in question. (However, the general Buddhist presumption is to relate it all to a person's mind.)

The statement that 'All things (*dhamma*) are preceded by mind' or being 'the result of what we have thought' thus presents a major philosophical assertion: that before there was anything (i.e., the objective phenomena of *saṃsāra*[9]) there was (only) mind. We are left to speculate how that mind came into existence in the first place, the organisational methods and structure of that mind, or whether or not it is incorporated as part of the thought process of an even greater entity that incorporates the bounds of all *manasic* substance.[10] What if our reference was also to the Mind of a 'thus gone one', a Tathāgata? However, when we enquire how 'all things' can come from such a Mind if they are preceded by it, we must utilise logic to realise how this can come to be. For things to proceed from any mind, that mind must be structured, organised and directed by a conscious manipulator of *manasic* substance. This necessitates a meditating or thinking entity.

There are five main candidates for such an entity:

1. An ordinary person, undertaking normal acts of volition to create or change things in *saṃsāra* based upon his/her ideas.

---

academic deference one could avoid such terms but then this would emasculate one's ability to describe truth relegated to the higher echelons of Being (the *dharmakāya*). Despite the use of certain superlatives, Buddhist terminology doesn't provide the ammunition to adequately describe this domain. The objective of this series of books is hopefully to better elucidate the ramifications of the *dharmakāya* to an audience unaccustomed to think at such a level. To do so one cannot be hamstrung by the limitations of approved terminology and related concepts that stifle explanation beyond a certain point.

9 *Saṃsāra:* cyclic existence, life-death cycle, the empirical realm. The ocean of causality, the perpetual turning of the wheel of births and deaths. Anything associated with the material worlds, to that which is ephemeral and ever-changing, and hence phenomenal, having no true substantiality of its own. It refers thus to the realms of illusion (corporeality) into which the personality incarnates and begins to identify with by means of the concrete mind.

10 *Manas* can refer to the substance of the mind. More accurately, however, it refers to the mind as an organ of thought, where the willing and thinking process is also incorporated. The Sanskrit term *citta* specifically refers to mental substance.

2. A person absorbed in *dhyāna*[11] but now focussed upon re-entering *saṃsāra,* thereby undertaking the necessary *manasic* volitions that will inevitably lead to incarnation into objective form, a reawakening thereto.
3. The Sambhogakāya Flower existing upon the abstracted realms of Mind in the process of retrieving *bījas* for the purpose of projecting a new personal-I.
4. A liberated awakened one, who manifests *siddhis* (psychic powers) for the purpose of phenomenal appearance.
5. A Tathāgata[12] in the process of manifesting a world sphere for the purpose of the enlightenment and liberation of all the incorporated (sentient) beings. The Mind in question here represents an aspect of *dharmakāya* manifesting a Thought-sequence that incorporates a primeval stage of Thought, right through to an inevitable conclusion of Buddhahood for all units of consciousness that are embedded within that Thought-sequence.

In each case, the process of the appearance of 'things' from the prior existence of a *manasic* impulse is similar, starting from a very limited effectiveness and scope in the ordinary person, to the far-reaching vista of an Ādi Buddha,[13] who is responsible for the appearance of what we understand as Nature. Generally speaking, that which is 'preceded by mind' refers to the originating thought of a primal Thinker, which starts the wheels of the law (of *karma*), and of Dependent Origination into motion. Without such an originating seed-thought nothing could

---

11 *Dhyāna:* concentration, one-pointed abiding in an unwavering state of mind. A state of absorbed contemplation, deepest meditation and abstraction into the causal realms of the Sambhogakāya Flower or higher, according to the abilities of the meditator.

12 Tathāgata: such Buddhas (Logoi) project a body of manifestation that is a planetary, solar, or any other cosmological body. They are darkness eaters, digesting primal (dark) substance in their 'stomachs' (*maṇipūra chakra*), converting it thereby into consciousness states. Thus the entire panoply associated with human evolution to Buddhahood comes into being.

13 Ādi Buddha: the primordial enlightened one, the essence of the *buddhadharma*, of which all other Jinas (Buddhas of meditation) are attributes.

come to be. This sets the pattern or paradigm of what occurred in the past, the *karma* and *saṃskāras*[14] that are retrieved by consciousness to condition the now.

In the retrieval process we are investigating the patterning of a *maṇḍala* that proceeds from within without. The *bījas* to be awakened are stored in the innermost sphere or circle of this *maṇḍala* of space-time, from which they make their way to the surface of whatever is to help condition the fleeting phenomenal world of events that we actually come to experience in consciousness.

The concept of space-time links the evolution of space from a *bīja*-seed with that of time. It is a concept utilised by modern physicists in their Big Bang theory, and works esoterically with respect to the evolution of any consciousness-stream. Consciousness expands from a central point as it evolves over time, developing *saṃskāras* of increasing complexity and intensity of mind. This movement happens in spiral form. The difference between the esoteric philosophy and modern science, however, is that there is a universal pre-existing space, from which and in which evolves each space-time continuum of mind. Each space-time continuum therefore is a unit of *karma*-formation. It can also be considered a unit of *manasic* expansion, therefore, of a human unit, world-sphere, solar system, or galaxy, within the context of myriads of similar mind-spheres (space-time continuums) evolving together within the primal matrix that is universal space.

Universal time (time being that which happens as a consequence of the formation of a *bīja* unit) is consequently particularised in terms of finite time, evolving time wherein consciousness manifests its expression for any 'universe' to appear. Inevitably, as *karma* comes to be resolved as a consequence of gaining enlightenment and liberation ensues, so all merges into the Clear Light of Mind. This Mind resting

---

14 *Saṃskāra* (compounding of ideas): from the Sanskrit roots, *sam* and *kri*, meaning the action (*kri*) that will improve, refine or make an impression in consciousness. *Saṃskāras* are thus the impressions from actions done in former incarnations and which are carried through to this one and thus become the basis for one's present *karma*. It also refers to the effects of one's present actions that will bear fruit in later lives. *Saṃskāras* are thus those actions that tend to bind one to the wheel of rebirth; to repetitious pain or pleasing dispositions, mental constructs, the inception of imagery, and all emotions. They can also be the tendencies to enlightenment.

in its natural unadulterated state, which is equated with 'universal space' above, and from one perspective can be viewed in terms of the concept of the Void (*śūnyatā*), is more specifically the zone that is the *saṃsāra-śūnyatā* nexus.[15]

The above summarises the major theme of this book, which will be elaborated from various perspectives, wherein we effectively have the eventual resolution of the *karma* producing world-forming tendencies of a personal-I. (This is also further explored in Volume 5, *An Esoteric Exposition of the Bardo Thödol*). This necessitates the destruction of 'ego', and the abstraction into that which represents the body of the *dharma* (*dharmakāya*). The entire purpose, therefore, is to move beyond mind and its activities to penetrate the boundary of what space veils.

The process of the evolution of *karma*-formations, in terms of a progressing space-time continuum, is presented in Figure 1,[16] 'The moving screen of the past', showing the process of bringing *saṃskāras* that were developed in past lives (or incarnation of a world-sphere, star system or galaxy) to the event horizon of consciousness.

An event horizon is that particular experiential zone, or imaginative sphere, that any consciousness is engaged upon at any moment in time. We can see, therefore, that the process is illusional, because it is changing all of the time, with the new images appearing and disappearing as the space-time continuum that is the event horizon evolves over time. (Represented by the serpentine arrow moving forwards, outwards from the page and upwards towards greater heights in consciousness.) The past (*saṃskāras*) are continually being retrieved from 'memory' to experience the present moment, yet one is always moving towards a future resolution of attributes of mind. Mind after all is the only thing that can comprehend the passage of time, and therefore of evolving space—the space that is the growing mental expansion of the consciousness-stream involved.

The triangle above the event horizon represents the progression of consciousness towards the future, and the triangle below it represents the place of storage and retrieval of *saṃskāras*. It therefore represents the past, or zone of comparative ignorance with respect to what the

15 The *saṃsāra-śūnyatā* nexus is explored in greater depth in chapter 3.

16 For more information see Volume 2, chapter 11, where this figure explained in detail.

future portends. The further one travels to the past the deeper the zone of ignorance, and therefore of comparative darkness, memory fades into the hoary mists of time.

The phrase from the *Dhammapada* that speaks of things being 'led by mind' refers to the actual images that are retrieved in the present moment (that is the eternal Now) within the realm of consciousness (*ālayavijñāna*[17]). This concerns the nature of the thought structure (idea *maṇḍala)* within which consciousness is presently imbued or working with. It is also inclusive of any number of interlinked thoughts that can seed the present one with ideas or images.

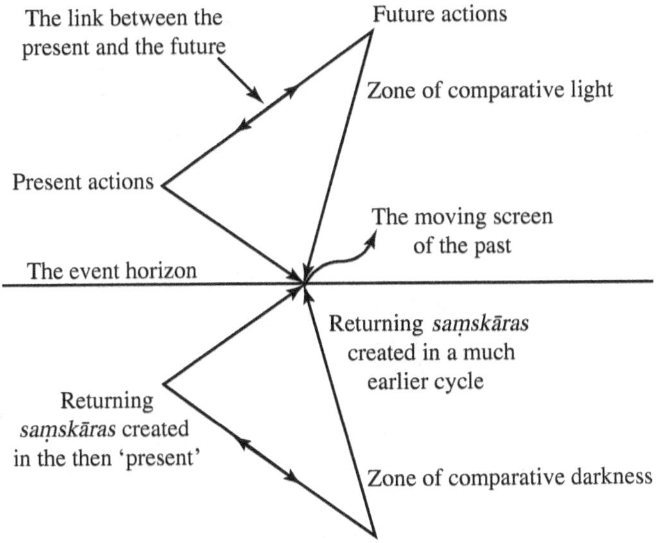

Figure 1. The moving screen of the past

That which is 'created by mind' refers to the impact of the recalled

17 *Ālayavijñāna:* the universal storehouse of consciousness, the mind as basis-of-all in the Yogācāra philosophy. Here *ālaya* is a store of mental images gained from the faculty of distinguishing or discerning (*vijñāna*). The *ālaya* can be conceived to be ever-present in one respect and also as being subject to evolutionary progression. The ability of the *ālaya* to evolve produces the many attributes of *manas*. The *ālaya* that remains in and by itself can also be considered an aspect of the abstract Mind. The *ālayavijñāna* is further explained later in this chapter.

saṃskāras with the external environment in such a way that they are modified or altered in some way, and therefore form new *bījas* of images to be stored within the *maṇḍalic* structure of consciousness. This incorporates any consequent actions of a mental, psychic, emotional-mental, emotional, or physical nature. Such actions produce experiences that are assimilated by consciousness and which change consciousness in some way, hence the future unfolds.

In the quotation from the *Dhammapada,* the world is considered to be that which is defined by consciousness and exists within consciousness, which is a view endorsed by the Yogācāra school. The problem of the nature and appearance of objective reality has however not been answered. The inner universe of the mind, and the outer universe of 'the world' that has been created by the mind, however, are causally linked. The nature of the expansion of consciousness as we move from the past to the future appearance of things is shown in Figure 2 below.

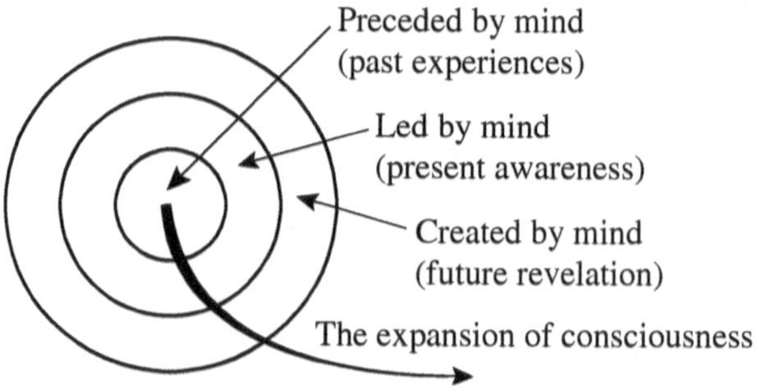

Figure 2. The process of the expansion of consciousness

Here we also see the process of the expansion of consciousness as the experiences of the things created by mind become assimilated. This assimilation then becomes the store for that which precedes a future expansion. Essentially, each expansion helps create the completed integration of the overall *maṇḍala* of the mind structure. As the *saṃskāras* generated become more refined and encompassing, so then the structure itself grows along a limb of truthful reason to find and then integrate with the trunk of the grand design of which it has always been a component part. Inevitably, the structure becomes energetically more intense because of increasing refinement of substance, causing it to grow upwards and outwards so as to encompass the vastness of the sky of *bodhi.*[18]

Now let us redraw the diagram in terms of the 'mind' that is created by mind. (This relates to the three aspects of time in relation to the evolutionary expansion of mind.)

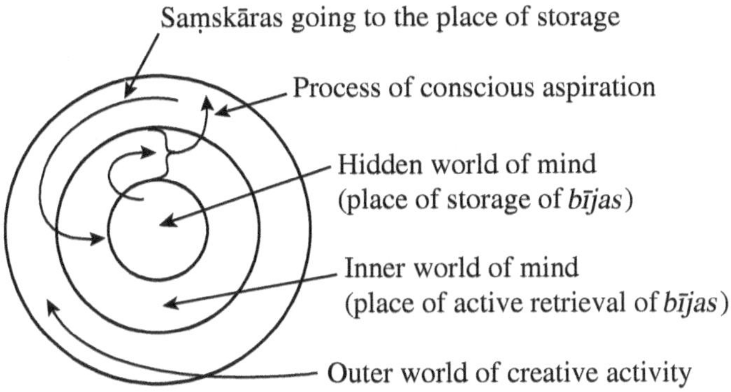

Figure 3. The cycles of expansion of mind

After new mental *saṃskāras* have formed and fulfilled their activity as a 'process of conscious aspiration', they become veiled in the place of storage. The mind therefore expands as the 'hidden world of mind' becomes increasingly filled with *bījas* of intensified potential. Whenever *bījas* are recalled they pass through the above process, and so the cycle of expansion progresses. If new images are processed through sensory contact with outer phenomena, and lessons are learned of what not to do, so then the cycles spiral upon ever higher arcs of endeavour. The substance of the *bījas* comes to be composed of an increasingly refined nature. This 'hidden world' can be considered to be five layered, relating to the store of *bījas* conditioned by the five Elements. This

18 *Bodhi:* enlightenment, full awakening, attainment of perfected knowledge, transcendental insight, the result of the union of compassion (*karuna*) and wisdom (*prājñā*). The expression of compassionate revelation. Literally compassionate understanding, divine Intelligence, 'Be-ness'. That which is obtained from the 'Bo' tree, under which the Buddha sat when he gained his full enlightenment.

can be expanded to include the view of the 3 x 5 characteristics of the Sambhogakāya Flower, which is the true place of storage of the rarefied *bījas* of any consciousness-stream.

Figure 3 depicts the foundational basis to the information presented in Figure 4: 'The relationship of *śūnyatā* to *saṃsāra*'. Figure 4 presents additional information relating to *śūnyatā* and of Nāgārjuna's four gates that were explained in Volume 1, chapter 9 of this series: 'not self, not others, not caused and not both' that allow consciousness to interrelate with *śūnyatā*[19] via the *śūnyatā-saṃsāra* nexus. This is veiled in Figure 3 by the central sphere denoted as the 'hidden world of mind'. This 'hidden world' is that of the I-consciousness. (That attribute of consciousness that outlasts the death of any incarnate personality.)

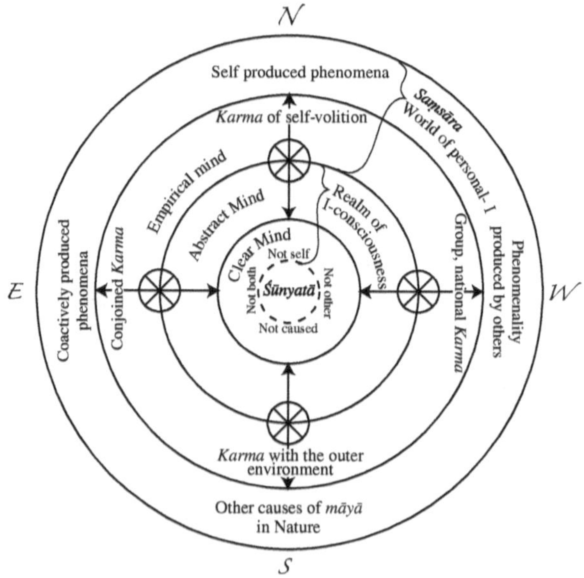

Figure 4. The relationship of *śūnyatā* to *saṃsāra*

19 *Śūnyatā:* emptiness, voidness, devoid of characteristics, suchness. That which relates to the absence of mind. In Candrakīrti's *Madhyamakāvatarā* there are said to be sixteen types of emptiness, which are really negations based on the categories of phenomena.

Further perspectives on the mind and its relation to *śūnyatā*

The 'inner world of mind' is the place of the creation of the four types of *karma* depicted in Figure 4. This is because as *bījas* are recalled to form images in the mind, they produce effects in the phenomenal world. The *karma* created is qualified according to its mode of expression with respect to the four directions. (The reader needs to refer to Volume 1, chapter 9 in this series for detail regarding each wheel of *karma*. There we saw that the entire paradigm is in the form of an Eye that manifests similar functions as the mechanism of a physical eye.) Figure 3 elaborates on the inner three tiers shown in Figure 4, and focuses on the way mind conditions the *māyā*[20] of Nature.

Consciousness is the expression that stems from the inner core of our being. It is replete in itself, and needs not an 'other' in order to be self-absorbed. However, if it is to expand into new vistas of revelation then experiential contact with 'the other' is inevitably necessary.

Looking from within consciousness to the external world, we see that consciousness incorporates the outer form of appearance, because whatever it experiences, it integrates as part of itself. The process of integration is instantaneous. As the entire process of integrating experiences and the retrieval of *bījas* produces phenomena, so the Buddha only presented that which fell within the realm of direct experience rather than making speculative assertions upon such things as to whether there was a God or not. The realm of direct experience equates with what clothes consciousness (organised mind-stuff, *cittavṛtti*) and processes all inner mental *saṃskāras*. It is concerned with the living individual and eventually helps produce the process of enlightenment. For actual enlightenment to occur, however, the mind must move beyond mere empiricism. It must derive an ontology

---

20 *Māyā*: illusion, deceit. The aggregates of forces controlling one's *chakras* (psychic centres) by excluding the controlling impressions from the realm of enlightenment. It concerns perceptions derived from the three planes of human livingness to the exclusion of any higher perceptions. It incorporates the sum of the energies working through the *nāḍī* system (the mechanism conveying the energies of the body) causing the individual to identify unduly with *saṃsāra* and its allurements. It is the sum of impressions that veil the real.

from strata of the abstract realms of Mind, wherein all grand designs conditioning Nature can be found. This is achieved in yoga-meditation via a methodology shown in the latter volumes of this series. We can then say that what the Mind possesses pertains to the Real, the True (*satya*).

Each concentric circle (*manasic* sphere) represents the limitations that bind a particular category of mind (differing spheres of activity). The perspective, however, is viewed from *saṃsāra,* where the outermost sphere appears the largest. The concept is illusory. A better perspective is that this sphere represents that which is most externalised and concrete, but is in fact the smallest sphere of activity. Being bound, each sphere of activity indicates that the forms constructed are the inception of a differing type of *maṇḍala* (or cellular constituent). The concentric spheres have their own internal arrangements for the storage and retrieval of the *saṃskāras* relating to the qualities that they embody. Each is a separate form, yet interlinked with others. The concentric spheres are therefore generalisations representing the densest type of substance contained by the *maṇḍalas* found within their locale. Each *maṇḍala* has its own internal links to the subtler spheres of mind. *Maṇḍalas* are the forms that categorise thoughts contained in the mind.

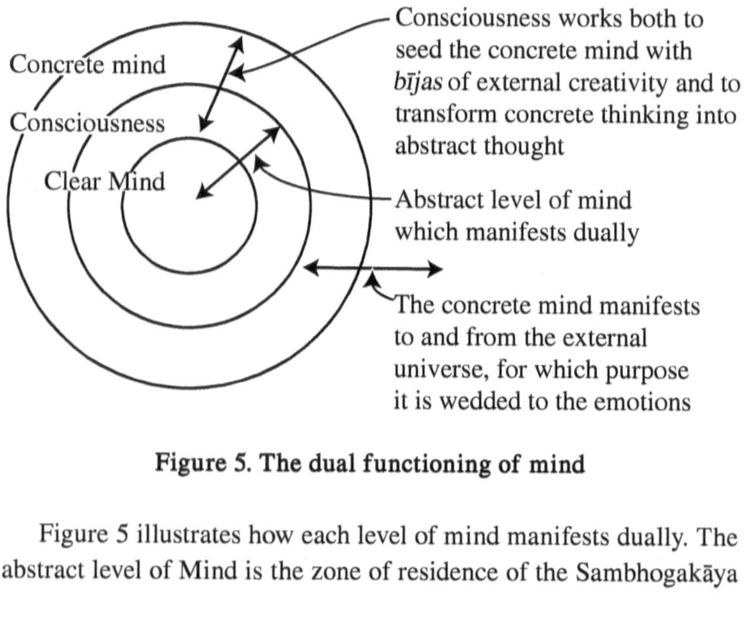

Figure 5. The dual functioning of mind

Figure 5 illustrates how each level of mind manifests dually. The abstract level of Mind is the zone of residence of the Sambhogakāya

Flower, which utilises the Clear Light of the Mind to relate to *śūnyatā,* and consciousness to relate to everything existing in *saṃsāra.* The Sambhogakāya Flower is the place of storage of *bījas,* and these *bījas* therefore come to be transmuted into enlightenment-attributes to be utilised by the Clear Light. Otherwise they are further modified or developed when they are called for expression in *saṃsāra.*

Consciousness is the basic attribute of the Sambhogakāya Flower, and exists in the eternal Now. It retrieves the *bījas* that will manifest as *saṃskāras* generated by the personal-I,[21] according to the nature of the *karma* to be expressed. As it is an expression of *bodhicitta,* consciousness works actively to awaken the personal-I to enlightened states.[22] Thus it helps establish the Clear Light in the person's mind through setting the stage for the elimination or transformation of obscuring and obstructing *saṃskāras.*

The personal-I resides in the outer world of creative activity, for which the person generally uses the concrete mind.[23] For all outward expression this is generally allied to desires and emotions. Though induced by subtle inner prompts (the silent voice of the Sambhogakāya Flower), the normal person develops abstract reasoning with great difficulty. This is because he/she must fight the emotions and the natural inclination of the mind to concretise. This produces inward striving and develops the way of the Heart.

On the level of consciousness, the future is envisioned so as to stimulate the outer world (pertaining to the concrete mind) with conscious purpose. In this outer world the past is evoked to form the continually changing present as the mind interacts with the transience

---

21 The term 'the personal-I' is utilised to denote the mind of an incarnate personality, wherein the focus of consciousness is centred around an ego, an 'I' concept.

22 *Bodhicitta* (Tib: chang-chub-ky'i-sem): the Heart's Mind, the Mind of enlightenment. The power or force producing awakened realisations, enlightenment, that emanates from the Heart centre. It is the Mind of pure perfection, the authentic nature of Mind.

23 Concrete Mind: a term that best describes the nature of the intellect that self-identifies, thus 'concretises' impressions. It is the cognised result of sense-perception fused with the afflictive-emotions. Consciousness normally possesses the concrete mind for the duration of the concept of an 'I', but there is also an abstract or enlightened Mind not thus conditioned.

of the external universe. The middle sphere of conscious awareness conjoins the innermost sphere with the outer. Here the three times are integrated as a unity.

In Figure 6 the domain of the abstract Mind is elaborated to include the factor of *śūnyatā*. This presents another triplicity, where firstly we have the sphere of Ideation where all expressions of what is to occur originates, as well as that which abstracts all *saṃskāras* into their ultimate resolution (the Clear Light of Mind). It represents the prime tool for all heuristic and ontological thought upon the panoply of possibilities within the evolutionary design of Nature. The Clear Light represents the natural state of Mind, after *saṃskāras* have been stripped of their *saṃsāric* qualifications. The Sambhogakāya Flower stands at the bridge between the sphere of Ideation and the Clear Light. It can be considered the Son of Mind. From this perspective the abstract Mind is triune, with *śūnyatā* emerging from the Clear Light standing at the heart of Figure 6. The Sambhogakāya Flower thus contains the mechanism in which all attributes of consciousness can be transformed and transmuted into the Clear Light or directly into the Void of Mind (*śūnyatā*). This Void is a mirror that acts to reflect the *dharmakāya* into the potent imagery of idea-forms that the concrete mind can withstand and accept as revelatory.

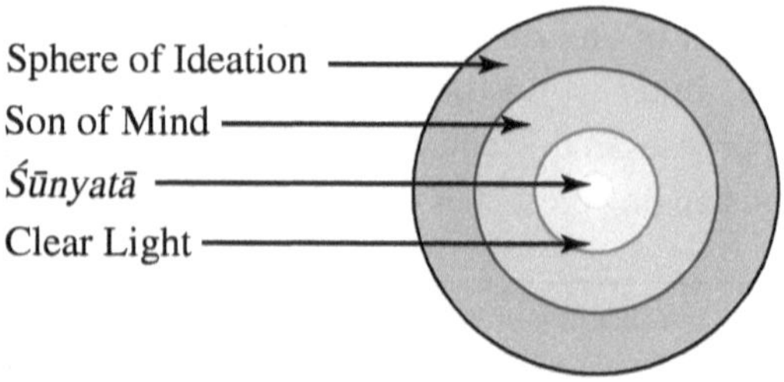

Figure 6. The abstract Mind

Śūnyatā stands at the heart of the all that is and is not, but the mechanism of contact with it is the Sambhogakāya Flower (the Buddha-*gotra*), as far as the phenomenal aspect of consciousness is concerned, until the meditative *yogin*[24] can bypass its form and directly

24 *Yogin*: a practitioner of yoga (a female practitioner is a *yoginī)* who engages in

experience the Void. This Flower therefore acts as the nexus between the Real and the illusory, where the true nature of the *saṃsāra-śūnyatā* interrelation can be directly experienced. The abstract Mind is the way of direct perceptual reason for communion with the Real, and its most clarified aspect is the substance of the Clear Light. It ultimately becomes the substance that is retained by all Buddhas who continue affiliation with those incorporated in *saṃsāra* in some way. It is then organised according to the *maṇḍalic* patterning of the *dharmakāya.* In Figure 6, the zone representing *śūnyatā* is colourless because it is beyond the capacity of mind to surmise.

The *śūnyatā*-abstract Mind interrelation can be equated with the term *dharmatā,*[25] where *śūnyatā* acts as a mirror reflecting the *dharmakāya* into the phenomenal world of appearances (i.e., into the substance of the abstract Mind). Then 'the real nature of things' is perceived:

> Those who saw me by my form,
> Those who followed me by my voice,
> Have engaged in wrong practice,
> Me those beings will not see.
> From the dharma are Buddhas seen,
> Indeed the Guides are the *dharmakāya.*
> But the real nature of things *(dharmatā)* cannot be discriminated,
> And so must not be discriminated.[26]

The enlightenment that ensues when a yogin can reside directly in *dharmatā* makes the Sambhogakāya Flower redundant. It literally

---

intensive meditational and ritual practice for long periods.

25 *Dharmatā* (Tib. chos nyid): actual reality, ultimate truth of phenomenon, *śūnyatā*. Also, the natural force of things, inherent nature, essence of existence. *Dharmatā* may sometimes be used interchangeably with the term *buddhi* in my works. Translated literally *buddhi* is denoted as 'intelligence', but the higher rendering equates it as an expression of Mind. It is that aspect of enlightenment that is the higher (cosmic) correspondence of the *prāṇic* vitality sustaining our forms. It is the expression of the *śūnyatā-saṃsāra* nexus that affects consciousness. Its evocation will allow one to see all things in time and space in a flash of revelation, 'at-oned', embraced within the Heart of Life. It also relates to the fourth of the alchemical Elements, *Air*, the breath of Life, thus the substance of the fourth plane of perception, that of the Intuition.

26 Conze's rendering of the *Vajracchedikā-prajñāpāramitā-sūtra* quoted in J. Makransky, *Buddhahood Embodied* (Sri Satguru Publications 1997), 35.

explodes into a supernova of consciousness and light upon the abstracted realms of Mind. Complete liberation results, as there is no longer attachment to the Sambhogakāya Flower or the personality. The term *dharma* in the above verse refers at first to the expression of the Wisdoms of the five Jinas[27] as reflected into the Sambhogakāya Flower, and then stored by it so that the evolutionary process of the unfolding personal-I's can proceed according to the dictates of evolutionary law. Later upon the evolutionary time scale, *dharma* is the direct expression of such Wisdom, once the *dharmatā* is activated in the Mind of a *siddha*.[28] Then there is nothing to be 'discriminated', because we have direct veridical valid perception *(pratyakṣa)*. The act of discrimination happens with the denser, concrete mind structure. Hence 'the real nature of things' 'must not be discriminated', i.e., the enlightened one must not fall into the trap of lower mental analytical discursiveness. The Clear Light of Mind *(dharmatā)* knows the truth, and that is all that matters.

The 'Guides' that 'are the *dharmakāya*' can be conceived of as the higher echelons of the Council of Bodhisattvas, as well as the Buddhas of past epochs of evolutionary attainment. Literally, they are a Hierarchy of enlightened being.[29]

The first part of the verse refers to the fact that those who tried to understand the nature of the Buddha with their ear or eye-consciousness will never know or see the Buddha, will never come to experience what such a one truly is. This is because they will have listened intellectually to the *dharma* or read the *sūtras* and *śastras* with active concrete minds. The perspicuity needed is only possible from within the precincts of the Clear Mind, or else directly from the *dharmakāya*. Cosmos then is the all.

The Sambhogakāya Flower that resides in the abstracted levels of Mind can gaze at the real via the Śūnyatā Eye,[30] as well as upon the phenomenal realms via the consciousness link *(sūtrātmā)* to the mind of

---

27 The five Jinas are also known as the five Dhyāni Buddhas.

28 *Siddha:* a *yogin* that has awakened supramundane psychic powers that come with enlightenment.

29 The phrase 'The Hierarchy' is also used to represent the constituency of the present Council of Bodhisattvas, continuing right through to the 'thus gone ones' of former aeons of evolution.

30 Explained in Volume 3, chapter 5, of this series.

the personal-I. With respect to the term 'Son of Mind', earlier presented for this Sambhogakāya Flower, the term 'Son' pertains esoterically to the Love-Wisdom principle. This is the *bodhicitta* that is born from the consequences of empirical activity ('the Mother' in this case) as one learns compassion for all beings and garners wisdom to appropriately help them. (The 'Father aspect' is represented by that which is expressed via the Śūnyatā Eye.) This Flower abstracts the *saṃskāras* of mind via the processes of the Heart.

The triune abstracted levels of Mind can thus be represented in terms of:

1. The *Will or Power aspect,* which is concerned with the most rarefied, lofty ideals; the Clear Light, which cleanses all thoughts from *saṃsāric* affiliation before being totally abstracted into *śūnyatā* (in the form of the consciousness-Void). The oft-emaciated, *dharmatā*-inebriated *yogin,* makes this form of substance the main constituent of his consciousness.
2. The *Love-Wisdom aspect,* the domain of the Sambhogakāya Flower, whereby the evolution of consciousness is instigated and sustained, and *bodhicitta* is generated. The Bodhisattva is succoured in his/her bliss-like state on this level.
3. The *Activity aspect* that is activated by the Flower whenever a *bīja* of thought is obtained from the *ālayavijñāna* (which is largely a product of this level of *manasic* Fire) and seeded into the concrete mind of the personal-I. The fine, highly articulate abstract thinker, the most thoughtful scientist or philosopher and also the creative genius, utilise the substance of this level of mind. There is often also the solitary contemplations of the *arhat*[31] focussed here.

One must pass through the finite spheres of consciousness before being receptive to the more embracive abstract levels. As we travel

31 *Arhat:* from the root *arh,* meaning worthy or deserving. Thus a worthy one, foe destroyer, also, *'arhant'*. One who has attained freedom from the cycles of existence, associated with the Theravādin (*śravakayāna*) tradition. A solitary meditator. A title given to those who have journeyed to the 'other shore' of *saṃsāra* by this tradition, thus a 'non-returner'. However, they must yet 'return' to incarnation as Bodhisattvas, despite the Theravādin concept of being a 'non-returner' given above. There is literally no stopping the evolutionary process.

towards the Heart of things, so then each level represents a more expansive state or form of creative awareness. Thus the inner circle (omitting *śūnyatā* in our consideration here) represents the most expansive form of Mind, because it is unhindered in its scope of action pertaining to truth. It is the integrating dynamo of all the other levels of consciousness. The outermost spheres are more concretised and therefore more limited in scope of application. They deal with the grosser conceptualisations and rationalisations of the average person, and are often tainted with emotional considerations and illusory images of all types. They help to propagate and sustain the full panoply of *saṃsāra.*

The number of spheres to consider are relegated by spiritual law. In Buddhist cosmology we have the *cakravāla* (world sphere), represented as a disk ringed with a series of seven circular golden mountain ranges. These mountain ranges are arranged concentrically with Mount Meru at the centre and the *cakravāla* wall of iron at the perimeter.[32] These seven concentric circles are a version of what we have represented previously in Figure 6, but the view is in terms of seven dimensions of perception, or else in terms of progressively transcendental states of mind. (To our world-sphere and the states of consciousness interpenetrating it.)

This means that there are four concrete levels of mind, to complete the seven when added to the abstract three. They are the means of conveyance of the four Elements, and because aspects of consciousness do not move in straight lines but rather in spirals, so the symbol of the conveyance of these Elements (Earth, Water, Fire and Air) are the four outer prongs of the *vajra,*[33] which are esoterically turned by the *swastika.* They have a bearing on the four major petals of the Base of

---

32 W.R. Kloetzli, *Buddhist Cosmology,* (Motilal Barnasidass, Delhi, 1997), 24.

33 *Vajra* (Tib. Dorje): the adamantine 'diamond sceptre' of Indra, the Hindu God of the Air. In Buddhism it symbolises the indestructible reality of Buddhahood, imperishable, indivisible (non-dual) immutable power, the synthesis of the qualities of the five alchemical Elements. The Dorje therefore is five-spoked (but can also be symbolised by the three pronged trident). He who holds it in consciousness has obtained the highest Wisdom—that which is the synthesis of the attributes of the five Dhyāni Buddhas. Indeed, such a one is master of all of space and time, ruler of the phenomenal realms. Thus it becomes the rod of power of all yogis, a symbol of their yogic prowess.

the Spine *chakra*, which grounds the respective *prāṇas*[34] (*saṃskāric* qualities) in the gross physical world.

The most concrete forms of mind ascribe names to all things in terms of the languages learned by the personal-I in its present incarnation. It also labels the process of expansion of consciousness. This process delineates the boundaries of conscious understanding inside it, so as to bloat its own capacity of thought, sustaining thereby the power and intensity of the ego, or the I-concept. The greater the nature of phenomena comprehended, the vaster this 'sphere of limitation' expands to incorporate the larger number of properly defined things. Included in such reasoning are all of the ideas and images of the concrete mind, thus it also constitutes the limitation of the thinking process. It works to draw all spheres of reason into a unity, whilst the laws of physics are also derived from it. (A logical extension of the fact that all phenomena are an expression of mind.)

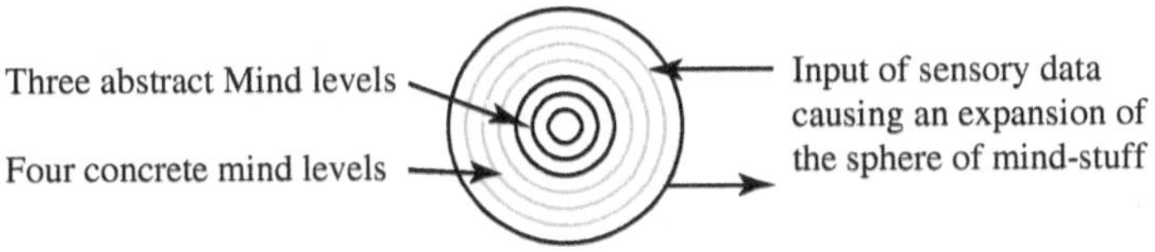

Figure 7. The layers of the mind

Note that in this expansion we can have input from the four main types of *prāṇas* or Elements, via sensory input, each seeking their own level or sphere of containment. Another way of stating this is that there

34 *Prāṇa* (Tib. rlung): 'breath', wind, current of energy, psychosomatic energy, of which there are five types activating the subtle body. The psychic energy or vitality that emanates from the sun, from the Heart of all manifest Life. This word is derived from the Sanskrit roots *pra*, meaning 'forth', and *na*, meaning 'to breathe, move, live'. It is the 'breath of Life', the energy drawn to the physical world from the etheric aspect of all phenomenal Life, and is the sum total of the vital energy composing a body, be it human, planetary, or solar. The process of liberation from bondage to the dense form is directly concerned with the transmutation and right projection of the grossest forms of *prāṇa* in the body. It is the energy that flows through the *nāḍī* system, where it takes on five different attributes or qualities (the five *vāyus: apāna, udāna, prāṇa, samāna, and vyāna*) related to the five main attributes of mind. (The four concrete levels and the abstract level.)

are four grades of increasingly subtle substance to account for in this structure of ego-formation. The fifth Element, Aether, corresponds to the level of the abstract Mind, which sits Vairocana-like at the centre of the grouping of four.

The five main attributes of mind

There are five main terms that explain consciousness in Buddhism as they relate to the five Elements pertaining to the mind. When ascribing the assigned Elements to them we should remember that we are actually analysing the various attributes of the Fiery Element that constitutes the mind *in toto.* They are:

1. *Citta,* the basic mind substance that is incorporated as our thoughts and deeds. Its fundamental nature is Earthy, because it is moulded as the forms of the thoughts generated.
2. *Vijñāna*, the discriminatory or judging principle, which colours the basic incorporated structure with the quality of the image. The Watery Element is assigned here because of the similarity of paint applied to forms presenting us with colours that we experience with the senses.
3. *Manovijñāna*, that with which ideas or images in the mind are articulated or particularised. It is the substance of proper definition, and as such constitutes the basic Fiery Element of the mind as a unit.
4. *Manas,* the function of mind as an organ of thought. Here all structures related to the image being construed are interrelated and integrated into the one thought-sequence, the complete idea. This then takes on the propensity of the Airy Element (which all living things need to survive).
5. *Ālayavijñāna*, the storehouse of all aspects of consciousness, the Aetheric Element.

We should also examine the more conventional interpretation of these terms, so that the above definitions can be better placed in the context from within the Buddhist psychological system. One of the best scholarly exponents of these terms for the West is D. T. Suzuki, who translated *The Laṅkāvatāra Sūtra* and gave extensive commentary upon this major Yogācāra-Vijñānavāda text. His book will be quoted at some length because it provides the key terminology and definitions in his treatise on mind.

1. Citta—the Fiery-Earth Element.

> *Citta* comes from the root *cit,* 'to think', but in the *Laṇkā* the derivation is made from the root *ci,* 'to pile up', 'to arrange in order'. The Citta is thus a storehouse where the seeds of all thoughts and deeds are accumulated and stored up. The Citta, however, has a double sense, general and specific. When it is used in the general sense it means 'mind', 'mentation', 'ideas', including the activities of Manas and Manovijñāna, and also of the Vijñānas; while specifically it is a synonym of Ālayavijñāna in its relative aspects, and distinguishable from all the rest of the mental faculties. When, however, it is used in the form of Citta-mātra, Mind-only, it acquires still another connotation. We can say that Citta appears here in the highest possible sense, for it is then neither simply mentation nor intellection, nor perception as a function of consciousness. It is identifiable with the Ālaya in its absolute aspect.[35]

What we therefore observe in the term *citta* is the basic substance of mind, with that substratum of substance which all of the thought-forms, ideas, and images of mind are constructed, on whatever level of mind we are viewing, from the lowest to that of the *ālayavijñāna.* This then equates it with the Earthy Element, which is the foundation for construction of all that is material, which 'piles up' the entire edifice of the formed realms. In this case, the 'formed realms' refer to the forms of consciousness, of the images or ideas that the mind makes.

2. *Vijñāna,* the discriminatory or judging principle, the Fiery-Watery Element.

> *Vijñāna* is composed of the prefix *vi,* meaning 'to divide', and the root *jñā* which means 'to perceive', 'to know'. Thus, Vijñāna is the faculty of distinguishing or discerning or judging. When an object is presented before the eye, it is perceived and judged as a red apple or a piece of white linen; the faculty of doing this is called eye-vijñāna.

35 Daisetz Teiraro Suzuki, *The Laṅkāvatāra Sūtra,* (Routledge & Kegan Paul Ltd., 1973), xxiii-xxiv.

> In the same way, there are ear-vijñāna for sound, nose-vijñāna for odour, tongue-vijñāna for taste, body-vijñāna for touch, and thought-vijñāna (*manovijñāna*) for ideas – altogether six forms of Vijñāna for distinguishing the various aspects of the world external or internal.[36]

These *vijñānas* are therefore the six sense-consciousnesses (*indreya-jñāna*). We shall omit *manovijñāna* for later consideration, and look just to the five sensory inputs. Each of these forms of input do not just come as clean, direct perceptions, but generally are infused with aspects of the (Watery) emotions. (Especially when concerned with all types of human interrelationships.) One generally tastes, touches and apprehends the physical world because one is emotionally involved with it in some way. Therefore, the *saṃskāras* that arise from such interaction are Watery in nature, and these impressions are brought together in a discriminatory and judging fashion by means of *manovijñāna* to be turned into consequential thoughts of some type.

3. *Manovijñāna,* the expression of ideas or images in the mind, the Fiery-Fiery Element.

> Of these six Vijñānas, Manovijñāna is the most important as it is directly related to an inner faculty known as Manas[37]....The six Vijñānas function, as it were, mechanically when the conditions are satisfied and are not conscious of their own doings. They have no intelligence outside their respective fields of activity. They are not organised in themselves and have no theory for their existence and doings.[38]

Manovijñāna, therefore, refers to the basic activities of mind (the intellect) when it is outwardly focussed via the five sense perceptors. It is interpreted as the 'sixth sense' that integrates, discriminates and co-ordinates the impressions received into the thought patterns that the personal-I is interested in, what he/she wills to achieve. As it interrelates pure ideas (*manas*) with the experiences gained from the senses (the *vijñānas*), hence it is that middle principle

36 Ibid., xxiii.

37 Ibid.

38 Ibid., xxvi.

that conveys the major type of mental *prāṇa*, that of Fire, into the sum of the processes of consciousness. For many reasons it can be virtually considered a direct expression of the sense of sight. The underlying thought here is the fact that the eye-sense provides the visual input from which most images that the mind conceives of are constructed.

4. *Manas,* the function of mind as an organ of thought, the Fiery-Airy Element.

> Manas roughly corresponds to mind as an organ of thought, but in fact it is more than that, for it is also a strong power of attaching itself to the resultant thinking. The latter may even be considered subordinate to this power of attachment. The Manas first wills, then it discriminates to judge; to judge is to divide, and this dividing ends in viewing existence dualistically. Hence the Manas' tenacious attachment to the dualistic interpretation of existence. Willing and thinking are inextricably woven into the texture of Manas[39]....Manas is conscious presence behind itself of the Ālaya and also of the latter's uninterrupted working on the entire system of the Vijñānas. Reflecting on the Ālaya and imagining it to be an ego, Manas clings to it as if it were reality and disposes of the reports of the six Vijñānas accordingly. In other words, Manas is the individual will to live and the principle of discrimination. The notion of an ego-substance is herein established, and also the acceptance of a world external to itself and distinct from itself.[40]

Air is that which pervades the space we reside in and which we breathe. The Airy Element is the basic *prāṇa* that pervades the *nāḍīs*[41] and which supports the conveyance of all the others. This is because it conveys the energies from the Heart, and the Heart is the source of Life. This indicates the pure thinking or perceptive

39 D.T. Suzuki, *The Laṅkāvatāra Sūtra*, xxiii.

40 Ibid., xxv-xxvi.

41 *Nāḍī:* literally river. (Also from *nāḍa*, a species of hollow reed.) *Nāḍīs* are finely reticulated channels for the conveyance of *prāṇa* in the etheric vehicle. These channels stem from the three principal *nāḍīs* in the central spinal column (*iḍā, piṅgalā* and *suṣumṇā nāḍīs*). They roughly follow the paths of the nerves and blood stream. There are said to be 72,000 main *nāḍīs* in the etheric vehicle, though this number is symbolic. Each *nāḍī* allows the passage of the five different types of *prāṇas*, and their combinations. Where *nāḍīs* containing twenty-one or more *prāṇas* intersect, then you will find a *bīja* for the appearance of an important *chakra*.

ability of consciousness, wherein images and ideas are analysed for their own worth, as impressions from the abstract Mind can be projected via its mediumship. It thus facilitates the mind's ability to work intuitively and spontaneously, and conveys the most refined thoughts that the concrete mind is capable of. It can also be combined with any form of sensory input, as governed by the other aspects of mind (forms of Fiery Element), to intensify and make vibrant the complete *maṇḍalic* structure of any lofty or aspirational thought.

5. *Ālayavijñāna,* the storehouse of all aspects of consciousness, the Fiery-Aetheric Element.

> *Ālayavijñâna* is *ālaya* + *vijñāna,* and *ālaya* is a store where things are hoarded for future use. The Citta as a cumulative faculty is thus identified with the Ālayavijñāna. Strictly speaking, the Ālaya is not a Vijñāna, has no discerning power in it; it indiscriminately harbours all that is poured into it through the channel of the Vijñānas. The Ālaya is perfectly neutral, indifferent, and does not offer to give judgements[42].....all the Vijñānas are evolving and deed-performing Vijñānas except the Ālaya which always abides in its self-nature. For the Vijñānas may cease from evolving and performing deeds for some reason, but the Ālaya ever remains itself...The Ālaya is incessant because of its uninterrupted existence; it is manifested because of its activity being perceptible by the mind.
>
> From this, we can see that the Ālaya is conceived in the *Laṅkā* as being absolute in one respect and in the other as being subject to 'evolution' (*pravṛtti*). It is this evolving aspect of the Ālaya that lends itself to the treacherous interpretation of Manas. As long as the Ālaya remains in and by itself, it is beyond the grasp of an individual, empirical consciousness.[43]

Much has already been presented concerning the *ālayavijñāna* in Volume 2 of this series, especially in relation to the foundation needed for comprehension of the nature of the Sambhogakāya Flower.[44] It was stated earlier that this relates to the activity aspect of the abstract Mind, 'activated by the Flower whenever a *bīja* of thought is obtained from

42 D.T. Suzuki, *The Laṅkāvatāra Sūtra*, xxiv.

43 Ibid., xxv.

44 See 'Commentary on *Ālayavijñāna* as Seed' in Volume 2, chapter 10, of this series.

the *ālayavijñāna'*. It is also the stored faculty of mind that those who work from the pure streams of *manas* can access the types of ideas and images that are arranged for future potential. This allows the logical construction of any sequence of a thought-stream without (necessarily) being influenced by the emotive (Watery) *vijñānas*. It is therefore *manas* that organises the necessary attributes of *ālayavijñāna* in the form of the mind of an incarnate personality that is functioning to solve a difficult or abstract problem, or who is engaged in some creative enterprise in any of the arts. The Sambhogakāya Flower also utilises the *ālayavijñāna* to obtain the seeds/*bījas* to impress the personal-I with needed ideas and image-impulses at the right time to propel the person onwards upon the Bodhisattva path towards Buddhahood.

Because the *ālayavijñāna* has implicit within it the pure substance of *manas,* it represents the mechanism of the expression of Mind that enlightened Ones working from the pure state of the *dharmakāya* can use to impress the personal-I. *Manas* then functions in a dual manner:

1. Looking downwards and fused with the *vijñānas*, in which case it is productive of the intellect, the concrete mind (*manovijñāna).*
2. Looking upwards and integrated with the *ālaya*, in which case it becomes the repository of all images pertaining to future possibilities and of the nature of enlightenment. This then becomes the expression of the *bodhicitta* that leads to Buddhahood.

The nature of the dual function of *manas* is described thus by Suzuki in terms of general Yogācāra philosophy:

> The Manas is a double-headed monster, the one face looks towards the Ālaya and the other towards the Vijñānas. He does not understand what the Ālaya really is. Discrimination being one of his fundamental functions, he sees multitudinousness there and clings to it as final. The clinging now binds him to a world of particulars. Thus, desire is mother, and ignorance is father, and this existence takes its rise. But the Manas is also a double-edged sword. When there takes place a 'turning-back' *(parāvṛtti)* in it, the entire arrangement of things in the Vijñānakāya or Cittakalāpa changes. With one swing of the sword the pluralities are cut asunder and the Ālaya is seen in its native form

> *(svalakshaṇa),* that is, as solitary reality *(viviktadharma),* which is from the first beyond discrimination. The Manas is not of course an independent worker, it is always depending upon Ālaya, without which it has no reason of being itself; but at the same time the Ālaya is also depending on the Manas. The Ālaya is absolutely one, but this oneness gains significance only when it is realised by the Manas and recognised as its own supporter (*ālamba*). This relationship is altogether too subtle to be perceived by ordinary minds that are found choked with defilements and false ideas since beginningless time.
>
> The Manas backed by the Ālaya has been the seat of desire or thirst (*trishṇā*), karma, and ignorance. The seeds grow out of them, and are deposited in the Ālaya. When the waves are stirred up in the Ālaya-ocean by the wind of objectivity—so interpreted by the Manas—these seeds give a constant supply to the interrupted flow of the Vijñāna-waters. In this general turmoil in which we sentient beings are all living, the Ālaya is also responsible as the Manas; for if the Ālaya refused to take the seeds that are sent up from the region of the Vijñāna, Manas may not have opportunities to exercise its two fundamental functions, willing and discriminating. But at the same time it is due to the Ālaya's self-purifying nature that there takes place a great catastrophe in it known as 'turning-back'. With this 'turning-back' in the Ālaya, Manas so intimately in relation with it also experiences a transformation in its fundamental attitude towards the Vijñānas[45]....The Ālaya has been looking at itself in the Manas mirror. There has been from the very first nothing other than itself. Hence the doctrine of Mind-only (*cittamātra*), or the Ālaya-only[46].... The Ālaya is thus known on the one hand as Tathāgata-garbha, the womb of Tathāgatahood, and on the other hand imagined by the ignorant as an ego-soul (*pudgala* or *ātman*).[47]

The 'turning-back' in the *ālaya* is a fundamental experience of all who are on the path to enlightenment, because their normal place of residence is then within the three abstract strata of the Mind rather than the four concrete levels (that produce the thirst for empirical experience). The four concrete levels have been the base centre of all mental activity,

---

45 D.T. Suzuki, *The Laṅkāvatāra Sūtra*, xxv.

46 Ibid., xxvi-xxvii.

47 Ibid., xxvii-xxviii.

but are literally now below the threshold of consciousness, a basic instinct for the enlightened. For them it is automatic and refined, with all limiting dross *citta* discarded, leaving only the most sublime *manasic* substance. The substance of the Airy Fires of Mind is now utilised within the *ālaya,* from whence (and with which) the Dharmadhātu Wisdom can be experienced. The Earthy and Watery Fires simply become addendums, instantly apparelling themselves to the seed-thought for the purpose of communicating to those who are still emotionally and physically orientated. Being highly refined and clarified, *manas* has become a mirror through which one from the abstracted realms of Mind can view the reflections from *saṃsāra.*

When one views the *ālaya* in terms of the *tathāgatagarbha* (the Sambhogakāya Flower), then its function as a store of mental *saṃskāras* of the past and future, for an individual consciousness-stream become clear. The differences between the classical understandings of the nature of the 'ego-soul' (*pudgala* or *ātman*) and the Sambhogakāya Flower have been analysed in Volume 3 of this series, they therefore need no reiteration.

Suzuki's statement concerning the stirring up of the waves in the *ālayavijñāna* to produce 'a constant supply to the interrupted flow of the Vijñāna-waters' gives a good description of that portion of the *ālayavijñāna* that stores the *saṃskāras* from the concretised levels of mind associated with the *manovijñāna* and the five *vijñānas.* The term 'waters' here really refers to the Watery emotional and desire principle, which Buddhism generally views as attributes of mind, but should be delineated differently. They are not necessary affiliated with *manas*, as for instance when viewed in a domesticated animal, such as a dog (which does not possess mind). Watery substance is a product of the animal kingdom and needs to be specially studied and accommodated in our heuristic and ontological schema, as has been done in this series of books. The function of such substance will of necessity be of great concern when dealing with the theriomorphic (animal-headed) deities. (This is discussed in Volume 5 of this series, *An Esoteric Exposition of the Bardo Thödol.)* However, with respect to the abstracted levels of Mind, the Waters do not exist, hence serenity is experienced. Serenity (or bliss) is experienced because one is abstracted into the most rarefied substance.

We see, therefore, that the *ālaya* is the store for all aspects of Mind, all the *vijñānas,* and the *citta.* Thus it contains tracks *(antaḥkaraṇas)* from one level to another for easy retrieval of *saṃskāras* to be utilised by *manas.*

As all *maṇḍalas* stem from the mind/Mind, so we are better equipped to understand the mode of construction and derivation of *maṇḍalas* via this analysis of the nature and structure of mind. We can therefore begin with first principles and expand outwards to fill the entirety of the domain of any *maṇḍala* in question.

2

The Greater in the Smaller

The construction of *maṇḍalas*

Each sphere of thought containment is finite. However, it can be viewed from within without, or from outside its boundaries. The point of view or angle of vision often changes the interpretation of the nature of the sphere. If our consciousness stands inside the sphere, then the intricate detail of its integral nature will be experienced according to the inherent qualities of which it is constituted. If our consciousness stands outside the sphere, then the generality of the form is perceived; line, colour and overall shape. From these aspects logic can deduce many things that are transparent to consciousness, but what the sphere embodies cannot be directly experienced. From within, any expansion of the sphere is barely noticeable because one's consciousness expands with it, thus it rarely views its own outward movement. When viewed externally, it can be seen to expand towards the infinite.

The internal movement can then be below the threshold of consciousness. We are subject to its laws and therefore we don't consciously understand or perceive where any such expansion could lead, as we do not cognise what lies outside its boundaries. The presumption here is that the entire structure is expanding in a uniform fashion. However, if only one part is thus moving, creating an anomaly in the overall structure, consciousness normally would perceive such an exaggeration. That to which the expanding sphere leads is generally beyond the ken of all but the most enlightened, because they have developed the ability to simultaneously view and experience both the inner and outer *maṇḍala* of any particular consciousness space.

The laws that are utilised to construe and to construct a *maṇḍala* within consciousness are identical to those which have formulated the external universe and that have caused the appearance of all that we can perceive. This also applies to the formation of a personal-I via the agency of the Sambhogakāya Flower. This essential fact of life allows enlightened beings and yogic powers to evolve. It may be extrapolated, therefore, that we all reside within the *maṇḍalic* cellular structure constructed by a great Meditation-Mind, and are experiencing the constitution of that *maṇḍala* from inside its form. Our forms are similarly built upon the same basic paradigm. In these two sentences lie the key to understanding the nature of all phenomena and of the mysteries of being/non-being. The teaching has also been garbed in Hermetic form: 'that which is within is also without, that which is without is also within', and 'that which is above is as that which is below and that which is below is as that which is above'.[1]

Thus the Buddha could say:

> Verily I declare to you within this very body, mortal though it may be, and only a fathom high, but conscious and endowed with mind, is the world, and the waxing thereof, and the waning thereof, and the way that leads to the passing away thereof.[2]

Buddhists have read this statement for millennia, but have not understood the basic implication that if *'the world'* is 'waxing and waning' within the mortal frame it *necessitates* that frame having been built upon a paradigm that exists external to it, and which also incorporates it. The questions then arise, 'who or what built it, and how was that external paradigm built?' If there were no such paradigm then there could be no correlation between 'the world' internal to the person and the external one. Some of these questions have been answered in earlier volumes of this series, and the remainder of this series will develop other themes not yet answered.

---

1 From the *Emerald Tablet of Hermes Trismegistus.*

2 Anagarika Govinda, *Foundations of Tibetan Mysticism,* (Century Paperbacks, London, 1987), 66. The quote is translated from *Aṅguttara-Nikāya II, Saṁyutta- Nikāya I.*

The 'waxing thereof' refers to the expansion from the inner to the outer spheres of the *maṇḍala* of mind. Consciousness becomes progressively materialised in form as it increasingly imbibes into its domain all of the images of things it can name and conceptualise. The 'waning thereof' concerns the removal of forms of activity from the outer tiers of mind, to intensify the activity of innermost ones. This process of intensification happens because the energy input that consciousness gained through millennia of *saṃsāric* activity is not wasted, but rather is stripped of its sluggish dross. It thus becomes more vibrant as *manas* lessens its grip on *saṃsāra*. Pathways are then concurrently established towards the *dharmakāya* and the *sambhogakāya* form of reasoning, which opens vast new revelatory vistas for exploration.[3] However, the *cittavṛtti* (modifications or movement of mind substance) is now sternly controlled, focussed, and directed, in order to receive the potent energies contacted from the higher strata of being/non-being without distortion; hence the mind becomes more intensified and strengthened. The thought-constructs, the *maṇḍalas* now formed, are consequently very potent and can have far-reaching effects.

From another perspective, as the moving fingers of conscious aspiration[4] travel from the relatively concrete to the subtler levels of mind, so what is contacted and experienced becomes more embracive and inclusive of the whole. The focus of mind upon ephemeral externals therefore wanes, and then dies altogether, except as a field of service in order to uncouple limited concrete *maṇḍalas* of mind. It allows them to expand into the freedom of vaster mental spaces. This comes as an extension of the adage that all life is one, i.e., that all minds are interrelated, and consequently must be brought to a liberated state for a person to gain true liberation. A Bodhisattva can plainly see the congested domains of mind (human egos) suffering limitations and

3 *Sambhogakāya* (Tib. longs spyod rdzogs pa'i sku): 'bliss body' of a Buddha or great Bodhisattva found in the heavenly world, the body of sublime vision, the ecstatic transformation body. The second of the three vestures of a Buddha or fully liberated Being. The form of the great ones depicted in Buddhist art.

4 The symbolism here relates to the 'fiveness' associated with and conditioning the functioning of mind. This also relates to the five *prāṇas* or Elements, the five sense-consciousnesses, the five poisons that eventually get transmuted into the five Jina Wisdoms.

stagnant attachment to repetitive transiency. The Bodhisattva cannot move permanently to greater and more intensified arenas of Mind unless an attitude shift has been produced with all of the interrelated minds that have formed projections[5] to his/hers, as they are really part of one greater *maṇḍala*. We come to know Life in such a death process, where the entire group dies in differing degrees to external attachment.

The macrocosmic *maṇḍalic* form

Now let us analyse such a macrocosmic *maṇḍala,* composed of a large number of interrelated minds, in greater detail. We firstly must begin to analyse the constitution of what may be termed a Logos: a Mind that is the integrating Heart, which structures a grouping of minds (and Minds) into a unity (such as the Ādi Buddha). Such a grouping, for instance, is the Council of Bodhisattvas, working together to liberate all of humanity from the thraldom of *saṃsāra*. A Logos embodies the united Word or note that is the combined integral essence of the thought-streams of all lesser minds of an integrated grouping of Minds, and consequently of their speech. (Here the term *'speech'* is utilised for the telepathic means by which a group of such Minds communicate with each other.) In the realms of mind, thoughts emanate varying types of sound, colour, and structural qualification.

Before proceeding, the meaning of the term Ādi Buddha should be clarified somewhat. Such a Buddha has evolved in a time-space continuum, such as our earth, gained liberation, and consequently travelled on in cosmos for further education, to obtain meditation states not possible upon the 'claustrophobic' confines of a little planet. Education in planetary, solar, and interstellar dynamics, the evolutionary processes of diverse forms of life and the nature of *maṇḍala*-forming on a cosmic scale, are all part of the curriculum of such a One.

Inevitably, the compassionate meditation of such a Buddha sees the

5 *Antaḥkaraṇa*: consciousness-link. Literally it is that which bridges or links the abstracted Mind to the concreted aspects of mind. It has been depicted as a 'rainbow bridge' because of the Rays of energies it conveys. At a later stage of meditative development it is consciously built through a sea of consciousness, bypassing the Sambhogakāya Flower, allowing linkage with the *dharmakāya* and the wisdoms of the five Dhyāni Buddhas.

need for the *maṇḍala* of a world-sphere to be formed, and in doing so, he thereby becomes a creative Logos; the empowering Word (hence the usage of the term Logos here) that establishes the entire dynamics of all that is to ensue. An 'empowering Word' is the issuance of the *dhāraṇīs* and mantras that will organise the necessary aspects of cosmic Mind, with respect to base substance (*prakṛti*), into a *maṇḍala* of potent possibilities. Thus is established what is known as the *ālayavijñāna* of a world-sphere. All is governed from the domain of the Buddha-Mind and organised according to the laws of Mind. There is no 'individual' Creator-God *per se,* because the concept of whatever could be considered an 'I' has long ago disappeared into the Void. The process of world-formation is directed via intermediaries who incorporate the entire host of Peaceful and Wrathful deities of the Bardo Thödol, as my book on the subject demonstrates. This explication will fill a gap in Buddhist cosmology, detailing much concerning the entire process of the formation and evolution of spheres such as our earth, that for many reasons had to wait until the present epoch to be revealed.

We can therefore refine the statement made by Govinda:

> From such a confusion of terminology arises finally the mistaken idea that the *Ādibuddha* of the later Tantras is nothing but another version of the God-Creator, which would be a complete reversal of the Buddhist point of view. The *Ādibuddha*, however, is the symbol of the universality, timelessness and completeness of the enlightened mind, or as Guenther puts it more forcefully: 'The statement that the universe or man is the *Ādibuddha* is but an inadequate verbalization of an all-comprehensive experience. The *Ādibuddha* is actually not a God who plays dice with the world in order to pass away his time. He is not a sort of monotheism either, superimposed on an earlier, alleged atheistic Buddhism.'[6]

Much more can now be provided concerning this subject, building upon what was earlier presented in the previous volumes, showing that the Ādi Buddha is not just a symbol of the enlightened Mind, rather He demonstrates the mode of action of such a Mind in cosmos, involving far vaster factors than what transpires upon our tiny speck of a planet.

6 Govinda, *Foundations of Tibetan Mysticism*, 99.

However, he cannot be equated with the God of the Theistic religions because of the nuances of the entire corpus of Buddhist metaphysics concerning the nature of what constitutes an enlightened Mind in action. Such a One is certainly not a God of the universe; there would actually be an entire hierarchical structure of 'thus gone' Ones from a myriad world-spheres over vast epochs, to consider here. Later theologians may draw parallels between the two approaches to causation, and if some form of rapport is established, that is altogether fine.

Comprehension of the nature of the *ālayavijñāna* is therefore also important. It is not homogeneous, but is organised in such a way as to facilitate the storage and retrieval of *bījas*—be these, for instance, for an individual incarnating unit, or for the integrated grouping of people composing a society or nation. It includes those who share similar (group) *karma*. *Karma*, as stated in the previous volumes, is largely a group law. The consciousnesses of those that are bound by group law, therefore, must logically share a united *maṇḍalic* structure within the *ālaya*. Together they manifest processes similar to the cellular constitution of a living organism, a theme that will be further developed in later chapters.

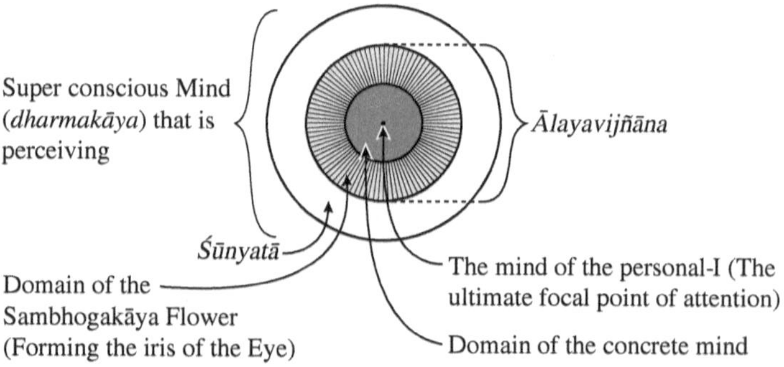

Figure 8: The inward vision of an Ādi Buddha

We see that Figure 8 posits the structure and functioning of an Eye of a primordial Buddha, who is focussed inwards to the cellular world constituting his concrete Mind.[7] Logically, the abstract aspect is directed

7 Though the gender here nominally is masculine, it should be noted that the

outwards towards the cosmos and the integrated Buddha-fields within which the Ādi Buddha finds a place. To view the mind of a human unit necessitates developing a form of microscopic tunnel visioning. The implication here is that to see the actual world of human constructs such a Buddha would have to peer through the collective minds of the groupings of human units that have manifested a civilisation, or portions thereof. The collectivised images viewed in such minds produce the picture of the nature of the phenomena they are involved with.

However, to descend far into the domain of darkened sight does not procure much useful information for a Buddha. A much better source, giving a clearer picture in the light of the three times is found in the domain of the Sambhogakāya Flower.

The Sambhogakāya Flower is the true cellular unit of this schema. The domain of the concrete mind is literally darkened, and is thus normally impenetrable to the direct gaze of a Buddha. Detail can be obtained by focussing via the meditative understanding of a Sambhogakāya Flower. The lines in the iris portion of this Eye indicate the Life links (*sūtratma*) of the various Sambhogakāya Flowers to the domain of the personal-I, or else the consciousness-links (*antaḥkaraṇas*) to that which *śūnyatā* veils. The hues attributed to the various Flowers constitute the general colouring of this iris portion, and the united action of groups of such Flowers constitute the movements of the iris according to the expressed Will or Word of the Ādi Buddha/Logos concerned. Whatever the movement at this level, it inevitably affects the worlds associated with the lower strata of mind. The Word commands the group, national, or international *karma* within the domain of the personal-I to take effect according to the quality of sound and the length of its intensity. Thus what are known as catastrophes, famines, and the like, as well as good years, are caused to happen and to recede as the aeons unfold. So also humanity is made to evolve ever higher consciousness states, to eventual liberation for the all.

It should be noted that in this consideration the agents of *karma* have been omitted. They are really the Intelligences embodying the substance within which all this eventuates. They are the feminine

---

disposition of such a One can just as well be feminine.

principle in Nature, the *devas* and *ḍākinīs* (about which more shall be presented later).

Figure 8 is really an elaboration of the expression of the Śūnyatā Eye, because the Eye of each individual Sambhogakāya Flower is linked in this way to the Mind of the progenitor Logos/Ādi Buddha. The Logos can thereby survey the sum total of the embodied form.

It should also be noted that *manas* represents basic physicality to such a One, in a similar way that our physical forms represent to us. The concrete realms of mind are therefore structured in such a way that input into the Logoic Mind happens through five sense-consciousness receptors. This is the basis for the *maṇḍala* of the five Dhyāni Buddhas, their consorts, accompanying Bodhisattvas, and the entire philosophy of the five Tathāgata Wisdoms. We thus have the way of transmutation of the expressions gained from the five senses into these five Wisdoms.

Once we have established the basis for understanding the structure of Logoic thought, then we can assume that the minute processes occurring at the periphery of a Logos's Mind are what concern the broad panorama of the world of human affairs. A relatively minor discharge of energy in that Mind will therefore produce considerable effects in the human domain. Mere resonance of this will even enter into 'the world' that is the inner universe of a human unit, and yet it will suffice to push onwards to conclusion the entire quest of the Bodhisattva path, and the transmutation of the coarser aspects of mind into the Clear Light.

Having presented a working representation of how a Buddha functions at the centre of his established Buddha-field (or *dharma*-field established for the purpose of enlightening the conscious lives contained within it), we can progress to establish other paradigms for analysis.

The functioning of the smallest cells in a human body have to be controlled by the central nervous system, or the person wouldn't physically survive. Similarly the smallest aspects of the Buddha-field of a Logos have to be continuously scrutinised, or they could not exist. Most of these functions (e.g., breathing, the heartbeat) remain below the threshold of consciousness both in the human and Logos.

As an organism becomes increasingly perfect (i.e., the autonomous functioning of the heartbeat, and the Logoic control of the formed realms), so it increasingly subsists below the threshold of awareness, because it manifests as a self-regulating, constantly self-maintaining activity. This relates both to the sentience of the cells constituting the autonomous nervous system of a human, and for a Logos. Here the corresponding collective directive Intelligence that embodies the substance of that form are the *devas* and *ḍākinīs*. Self-regulatory activity is always there, as with the heartbeat, manifesting automatically to maintain the life of the being. The greater consciousness need not pay attention to this area because it has taken care of maintaining itself. It continually manifests at its optimal potential, and only breaks down when:

a. The greater consciousness errs through misapplied action or thoughts, e.g., the taking of poisons, in thought, word, or deed.

b. The natural application of the laws of Life occur, which produce old age, the consequential cyclic demise of the form and the liberation of the indwelling consciousness at death.

Just because something is below the threshold of awareness does not make it redundant. In fact, it functions perfectly automatically because one does not have to think or will it to behave as one wants, or design it to function. The Life process automatically obeys its own set laws and goes on regardless (or despite) the machinations of the conscious mind. The law is set and directs all in the end, just as action produces reaction. Also, the good or bad consequences of all actions by a directive mind are similarly set by the same laws.

Conscious manipulation of substance speeds up the evolutionary process, despite the effects of 'bad consequences', because substance is made to experience evolutionary change as a consequence. (Presuming here that such manipulation is designed to gain awareness or knowledge of some kind.) This is why humans are the fastest evolvers, though they are mostly fully immersed in *māyā*. We also see why the physical plane is the place of greatest learning, because here the options for all types of actions and consequences are available, necessitating the continuous use of the will to make choices. Consequently, it is the only plane or zone wherein a Buddha can arise. A Buddha must demonstrate complete mastery from the lowest to the highest domain before he can become 'thus gone'. A Logos focuses his gaze whenever such a 'thus gone' one is to appear. The 'gaze' is towards the cellular units composing the greater sphere for which the Buddha-to-be is the focal point, and which represents his direct karmic commitment. The Logos is also karmically and compassionately bound to assist in the healthy functioning of this part of His/Her body of manifestation. A Buddha is really that which embodies an entire organ within the greater Logoic body. *Bodhicitta* manifests from the highest levels of the *dharma* to the lowest. In such a way does the energy of enlightenment flow.

The Logoic Eye looks upwards and inwards simultaneously. That aspect that constantly looks inwards is what keeps all of Nature's kingdoms, the Logoic body of manifestation, active. It manifests a congruent unity, as well as the entire karmic play of humanity rightly directed according to a far-visioned Plan.

The Sambhogakāya Flower/*tathāgatagarbha* represents the consciousness of a cell within the Mind-structure of a Logos. (That is, from the 'point of view' of the *dharmakāya*.) Its consciousness is accessible to the Logos when looking at the minutiae composing the form of that Buddha-sphere. He visualises it via the decreasing tiers of substance, as indicated by the diagram of concentric circles that represents the nature of Logoic microscopic vision. Here divinity comes to be concentrated into the smallest of forms (the *tathāgatagarbha*) directly perceivable by such a One. The focus produces the potency of the energy that empowers a *yogin's* meditative awareness when he utilises the laws relating to thought-form construction to gain enlightenment. To do so he defocuses from the lower spheres of sensation (a consequence of having turned about in the 'seat of consciousness'), to be absorbed into the upper strata of being/non-being.

The entire process of *guru paramparā* (transmission of the *dharma* via the *guru*-student lineage) comes into play, forming a Hierarchical structure when viewed over time. It concerns the transmission of the core doctrine through an unbroken succession of teachers (who have incarnated over a series of lives) to a receptive student. The process of transmission may continue over a period of millennia. What should be noted here is that if the succession is truly esoteric then the series is also from one's superior and continues accordingly from that one's superior. Therefore, it stems from the human (*mānuśi*) *guru* that one knows, to his *guru* (i.e., one who is esoterically senior to him) whose Bodhisattvic space encompasses a vaster number of beings, to his *guru*, likewise senior to the one who is the 'root *guru*' over all (which may be a 'thus gone' Buddha, for instance). This inevitably brings us to the concept of a Logos, because of the vastness of the scope of embodied (manifested *maṇḍalic*) 'concern' of such a Buddha. The true records pertaining to *guru paraṃparā* are thus not written down, so are not a matter of exoteric accounting, or recorded in the library stack of a monastery. These latter lineages are exoteric and rarely have more than symbolic truth as their basis. An exoteric doctrine may of course be transmitted over a succession of disciples, but the true inner relationships happen over many cultural situations, through many diverse incarnations, both Eastern and Western, and are not confined to any one religious dispensation.

We can thus work backwards or forwards with respect to such a One. The view then becomes either a microscopic vision (i.e., of the greater *guru* with respect to a disciple of a *guru* already far removed from his enlightened status), or telescopic vision with respect to the disciple viewing outwards to the primal source of all Love of his meditation mind-space. We can envision the qualities of a distantly related *guru* who gained his liberation from earth incarnations in the hoary past. For the 'primal source' of all lineages, Buddhists have used such terms as the Ādi Buddha.[8]

When viewing a completely integrated human unit esoterically, then we must investigate the *nāḍī* system. This system is composed of strongly defined lines of energy radiating out from plexuses that take the shape of flowers, of which there are a series of five differing sizes. *Bījas* are stored in the spirals of energies that are wound around each other according to the nature of their inherent colour (frequency of energy), making an overall atomic structure. Such *atoms* form on each level of perception as delineated by the Element of which each is primarily constituted. Thus there are five principal atoms to consider for each incarnating human unit, plus an extra unit to take into consideration for the abstract portion of the *manasic* level. (The mind being divided

8 This was as far as they could go, as the limitations of their ontological and metaphysical concepts would not allow them to proceed 'beyond' in their enquiries.

into an abstract and a concrete portion.)[9]

A Logos would not deem to view at the atomic level of a human unit however, unless such a unit is a high-level Bodhisattva. When viewing downwards He sees the groups of the Sambhogakāya Flower and impresses them with His Will. The *saṃsāric* world of the personal-I is not part of His normal visioning, nor is it within His ken to impress people directly (as many Christians and other revealed religions of 'the book' suppose). The Logos impresses the mundane world via advanced Bodhisattvas or Buddhas that work from *dharmakāyic* levels. They have expanded through the dimensions or spheres of increasingly greater embracive wholeness to meet the Logoic Eye. They can thus withstand the intensity of the Fiery potency that will come from contact with such a source. (An average unprepared human mind would be annihilated by such a direct contact. Its substance would be consumed in a conflagration of Fiery Light.) Communication is from Eye to Eye, through which they can view what is in His Mind. A Logos can also directly impress groups of Sambhogakāya Flowers, because they constitute cellular units of His Body of manifestation, and are conscious units. In their direct Ray and sub-Ray groupings upon the abstract levels of Mind, the *tathāgatagarbha* attribute can properly absorb and channel the direct 'blasts' from the *dharmakāya*.

The world of the personal-I is viewed via the image patterns contained within the Sambhogakāya Flower. (For here the reality of the world is perceived in truth, via the *maṇḍalas* of the three times viewed as a unity.) The visioning is normally via the integrated groups of Flowers that form any organ in His auric Field, which completes the picture of the sum of the group dynamics of any aspect of human civilisation. Conversely, the Eye of the Logos is viewed when the Sambhogakāya Flower cyclically peers through its own Śūnyatā Eye. This enables the Flower to gain an impression of the part that it must play within the collection of the purpose of all Flowers throughout the continuum of time. It also indicates the nature of the Identifications received by the enlightened one functioning in *dharmatā*.

---

9 This subject will be elaborated in a later book that will illustrate how *bījas* are stored to facilitate the recollection of things.

Bubbles and patterns of thought

Intelligently constructed, highly creative, or philosophic thoughts are stored within each sphere of mind in the form of *bubbles* of strongly defined thought-forms. The boundaries delineating these thoughts are clearly formed. They have been packed with energy of differing colourings, allowing these thought-forms to be potently used to correctly observe phenomena, the nature of the forms contained in the realm of ideas. There is a sympathetic or resonant empathy between similar colourations of thoughts that attract like thoughts to each other, allowing them to influence each other. The potency of the energy utilised allows penetration into other forms within the mind continuum of humanity. Duller thoughts offer little resistance to that which is made highly potent by intense energy. They quickly reveal the nature of the qualities they contain, of what was originally imbued in them by an emotional thinker.

The thinking style of an individual is delineated therefore by the nature and quality of energy utilised in the person's thought-constructs. When these thought-constructs are of a Watery constitution, their forms are generally fluid and ill-defined, though coloured with the images of things desired. Strong desires produce torrents of personal purpose directed towards the object of desire. Selfish and avaricious forms are coloured with base hues and generally delineate the experiences of the way people live. They produce a dull overall hue to the minds of their creators. Confused thoughts are seen clairvoyantly as swirling, generally dull colourings around the head of an individual. Fiery mentalistic constructs are far more vibrant and enliven the auras of their generators, and those who are receptive to such idea-forms. Within the thought-bubbles are *bindus* of lesser ideas relating to the main thought structure, which can be evoked, activated and expanded at any time to create new 'bubbles' of thought. From such considerations we have an indication of how a clairvoyant determines the quality of thought of various individuals.

The bubbles of thoughts represent dense concrete substance for a liberated Buddha, as the mental realm is the lowest or most concrete domain such a One observes. Our thought-structures represent the rocks and sandy substance upon which great Buddhas from past aeons 'walk'. These thoughts are therefore not things of great consequence, but rather they form the solid material with and upon which everything is moulded and construed. Like earth below our feet, these thoughts are below the threshold of consciousness of such a One. Such a perspective is however alien to a mind that reckons in terms only of human consciousness and which has not yet been trained to think in terms of transmuted strata of thought. Here we have a consideration of the 'foundation stone' upon which the edifice of the *dharmakāya* rests.

A clairvoyant views well-formed *manasic* bubbles emanating colour and light around the head of developed thinkers. The general colouring for *manas* is yellow-orange, and upon close inspection each thought-form displays an analysable structure. If they are highly refined thoughts pertaining to concepts of the *dharma* they will also manifest a vibrant energy field. Such structures will be found to be similar to the *maṇḍalas* displaying the way a Logos Thinks.

Both the intelligent person and a Logos display their respective forms of ideation to experience, understand, live and to evolve, and take steps to battle the ubiquitous *māyā* through proper analysis of what constitutes their respective environments. The intelligent person's thought-forms are less potent because they manifest upon a far smaller scale than that of a Logos, but reflect the abilities of the greater One. They do not have the intensity of quality or the vast reservoir of energy that the Logos can command, and consist of gross ephemeral *saṃsāric* substance, whereas the substance of a Logoic Thought is that of the *dharmakāya*.

Within the bounds of consciousness the process of thought construction is automatic and divine, alive within Nature. Here natural laws set into motion by the Logoic Thinker govern the domain of Mind, assisting Nature's agents to create forms, name, explore the unknown, and to tire of redundancies, thus to move ahead towards a predetermined, but somewhat uncertain future. The future is somewhat indeterminate (even for a Logos) because of the factor of human free will, which manifests upon a large scale.

General humanity has not yet developed the ability to identify with the greater Mind. The way a Logos thinks is far beyond the limits and scope of ordinary intellectual capacity. It needs input from the abstract Mind, which is deficient in most people. The discrepancies here are self-evident when cosmic evolution is thought of in terms of transmuted correspondences. (Lesser kingdoms in Nature, for instance, evolve into the human kingdom and the human kingdom into the constituency of a Logoic field of expression.)

While being inside a sphere of consciousness (to be above the sphere of consciousness takes much will power) it is nevertheless a worthy task to try to implement the mode of expression of *dharmakāya* (of divine action) in one's thoughts. Everything done creatively is much harder for a human than for a Logos, because a human strains under the weight of materialistic habit patterns and does not know the laws of Life, whereas for a Logos the consideration of such laws are an innate instinct. Materialism has been transcended, though Logoi do work with a form of 'substance' (the five types of *svabhāva* explained in Volume 1, chapter 5 of this series) when applying the laws of Thought (*mahat*).[10]

As one evolves, that which was experienced inevitably comes to be veiled by the threshold of consciousness. What was once needed for conscious action (the former territory of the ego of the personal-I) is transcended in one's experiential zone. It all becomes stored as memory *bījas*. Enlightenment can be considered to be the process of thinking in a *natural* way. The term 'natural' refers to a non-resistance to the laws governing the Thought-streams of the cosmos. This implies a spontaneous working with the Logoic energy fields and impulses that impinge upon the thought-strata of the abstract Mind. The laws of thought therefore govern all that is, is-not, that which must come to be, and ultimately to not-be. We all reside within the thought-streams of the greater Minds that embody the substance from which all of our forms are built (being concretised thoughts from past ages), and from which the innumerable lives and sentient units found throughout Nature arise.

---

10 *Mahat:* cosmic Mind (as an Intellect). This term, which literally means 'the great one', can best be understood as cosmic or Logoic Intelligence, expressing the Fires of the concrete Mind of such an Entity, and which conditions all manifest Life. The Mind of a Master of Wisdom (one who experiences the first level of the *dharmakāya*) can be considered an aspect of *mahat*. *Manas* is its lower reflection, and it can also be understood as that principle that causes the individuation of all manifest things, the ability of a (Logoic) Being to say 'I AM' and thus differentiate Himself from all others. Hence it is the producer of differentiation on a cosmic scale, when we are viewing universals, or the interrelation of groups of individuals within a greater whole. It is the major factor in creative being.

The sum of Nature is arranged according to patterns of Thought. These patterns are consistently 'cellular', as they are incorporated by a Mind, within which sentience has the space and time to evolve into intelligence and then into highly refined consciousness states. Each earth sphere can be considered to be a 'bubble of Thought' in the Mind of a particular Logos, a renowned Ādi Buddha of past aeons. Such a Buddha has gained the necessary cosmic Initiations, being sufficiently trained in patience, for instance, to see an entire World-sphere through from beginning to the end of an evolutionary paean.[11] This manifests the purpose of the eternal Plan developed for each sphere, at this level of evolution.

If one wishes to better comprehend this *dharmakāyic* world of the Logoi, one must understand that the *chakras* are real and govern the manifestation of all embodied space.[12] Every solar system, constellation of stars, groupings of constellations such as the eighty-eight seen in the night sky, are embodiments of *chakras*. They form galaxies, smaller galactic clusters, larger super clusters, and the sum of a universe. All are interconnected according to transmuted correspondences of the human *chakra* and *nāḍī* system. We therefore have level after level of Logoi to consider, each manifesting a *chakra* within the body of an even greater Logoic Lord. All are 'thus gone' Buddhas.

---

11 Here paean refers to the mantric songs of all enlightened Lives directing the course of that evolution with respect to the parts they must play in it.

12 *Chakra* (Skt. *Cakra*, Tib: *Khorlo*): 'wheel or disc'. A *chakra* is literally a vortex of energy that occurs at a point of intersection of energies. There are seven major *chakras* that stem from points in the spine and are divided by means of 'spokes' of energy and have been likened to the petals of lotus blossoms in the etheric body of a person or Logos. They allow the entry of light (or conversely, prevent such entry) of differing qualities and potencies from one dimension of perception into another. They are the psychic centres within one, and depending upon the qualities of the particular *chakras* that are activated, so manifests these qualities or characteristics through that being. The major endocrine glands are the physical plane externalisation of these flowers. They are described in most books on yoga-meditation. There are also many minor centres governing the vital well-being of organs. The seven major centres are: the Base of the Spine centre, the Sacral centre, the Solar Plexus centre, the Heart centre, the Throat centre, the Ājñā centre (the 'third eye') and the Head centre. Note that the correct Sanskrit transliteration is *cakra*, as the 'c' is pronounced 'ch', but I will use the anglicised *chakra* in this series, as it is phonetically correct.

Our earth is certainly not the only place in the universe where a human kingdom has appeared and Buddhas have evolved. Sentience and intelligence abounds throughout the cosmos, for the laws that allowed human intellects upon our planet are universal. Indeed, this cosmos is governed by the laws of Mind, whilst *karma* conditions all interrelationships. Consequently, there is plenty of scope for 'thus gone' ones to manifest their compassionate agendas. This then is the truth behind the nature of the universe and of the Way of Logoic evolution. In the mysteries of the human *nāḍī* system the secrets of cosmic evolution lie hidden. Therefore, the true nature of the *chakra* and *nāḍī* system has always been the most esoteric of subjects and has never been properly revealed in exoteric texts and Tantras. (Much more knowledge, however, is now possible to reveal, as presented in this series.)

The Solar Plexus centre and the nature of *siddhis*

At this stage in the evolution of human civilisation the discernment of eternal verities is not within the ken of the majority of humanity. No logical, sequential thought-structure of a truly high order is possible whenever the emotional *chakra* dominates humanity's thinking process. Amassed emotions governing people's political, religious and cultural thinking, engendered fear, selfish and prideful predispositions, bigotry, fanaticism, etc., have all produced their toll on human civilisation. If the Solar Plexus centre controls the other *chakras* then clear thinking or right discriminatory judgement is technically above the threshold of experience. The higher spaces of discernment are not reachable. The pristine clear logic of the Heart's Mind cannot override the agitation of the Waters until the later stage of conscious *manasic* control of the emotions. Lack of control of this Element prevents humanity from perceiving the true nature of Logoi. It produces the many unfortunate conceptualisations of the nature of 'God', or for instance, that individuals have personally 'talked' to such a one. Here the reality is more that they received impressions from great Watery thought-constructs of God or the gods, created by religiously inclined human beings throughout the ages. Sometimes they can come into contact with their own Sambhogakāya Flowers, or some Bodhisattva has helped them with a subtle thought-suggestion. *Cittavṛtti* is weighed down and obscured by too much murky, Watery emotional stuff.

For enlightenment to ensue, the Solar Plexus centre (conveying Watery energies) must come to be completely controlled by the Heart centre. The Solar Plexus centre then manifests a calm continuous auto-drive mode whenever thought is being processed. Consciousness then chooses what it wills in the realm of ideas, because the emotions (coupled to the *vijñānas)* no longer clothe the substance of thought. The Waters thus cease to keep one illusion-bound. The rarefied strata of *manas,* the Airy and abstract substance of Mind on the other hand, lifts one higher into the formless states in sympathetic alignment with potent streams from *dharmakāyic* sources, wherein the Creative aptitude of a Logos is found. *Kliṣṭamanas*[13] has then been transformed into *bodhicitta.*

When one focuses upon a thought, that thought simultaneously blocks out all the other images not included in the thought-sequence. The will decides the ideas to be thought of in that moment, and whatever is decided upon automatically attracts to it, through sympathetic vibration, all similar thought-*maṇḍalas.* From these the thinker can choose to assimilate, adapt, or reject whatever is desired to fit the purpose. Thought-streams can come from many other thinkers, even those from antiquity. The higher the strata of thought one works within, the more

13 *Kliṣṭamanas* (Tib. nyon yid): afflicted mind. The many types of afflictive emotions (*kleśas*) stored as *bījas* (seeds) in the *ālayavijñāna.* They are projected in the form of related *saṃskāras* when the personal-I is focussed upon an object of desire. When these emotional *saṃskāras* surface they immediately fuse with the mental consciousness (*manovijñāna*), to produce such things as desire-mind, self-will, (i.e., the four types of 'afflictive emotions') or forms of ego-clinging. The emotions always manifest in relation to a concept of 'self', executing the will to appropriate things desired. They thus produce attachments for all things deemed pleasurable, glamorous, or needy by the personality, and react to that which they dislike. There are said to be nine mental factors to *kliṣṭamanas.* (C.f., G. Sparham, *Ocean of Eloquence, Tsong-ka-pa's Commentary on the Yogacara Doctrine of Mind,* (Sri Satguru, Delhi, 1995), 107.) Five of these are expressions of the five sense-consciousnesses, and are really five Watery *skandhas* of the five Elements, of which the five senses come to be expressions. The emotions and the factor of desire are governed by the Watery Element and thus *kliṣṭamanas* is really 'afflictive' whenever the mind is conditioned by this Watery aspect in any way. The remaining four factors are those related to the production of a concept of 'self' or 'I'.

instantaneous is this process. Here we find a true communality of minds.

Clearly humanity must learn above all to control their emotional centre if it is to enter into a truly new civilised era of advanced thinking in all arenas of livingness,[14] with proper common sense prevailing in the laws that our societies make for people to live by. Presently these laws are like bad apples, pleasant to look at from a distance, but rotten in the core.

The Head and Heart centres must control the human system for divine enlightened thinking to manifest. To develop these one must remember that the edges of emotional thought-forms are undefined, volatile, containing relatively unrefined energy, limiting their ability to be really effective in the ocean of thought-forms. Consequently, one's attention can be erratic and easily influenced by other emotive streams, except in the case, perhaps, where things are strongly desired. The Watery substance colours all it comes in contact with (often with murky content) and is mixed with currents of energy that generally produce an almost uncontrollable urge to change direction, to experience whatever attracts it in the Watery stream. (These are the most alluring desire-forms that *saṃsāra* can offer.) Emotional and desirous thoughts sway from this to that, which produces a glamorous allure with no equanimous thinking, or high design. 'High design' means that one always knows to where one is striving in one's ambitions to overcome problems within the social or national fabric of the planet, to produce long-lasting changes for the betterment of all. There is not enough content or thought-substance in an emotional thought-form to allow a person to rationally think to the conclusion of any problem at hand.

The emotions in fact do little to overcome massed human miseries; rather they are the major causes of these. They are also the basis for the happiness, sadness, worry, joy, elation, fear and depression cycles that people are often conditioned by. They project onto others various irritabilities, hatreds, and misconceptions of any personal, group or national bias and are the propelling energy that sustains the *māyā* that

---

14 The term 'livingness' is used to convey a sense of the many streams of lives existing upon various dimensions of perception, rather than purely physical life. There is also the integrated concept of a being existing simultaneously on many levels of expression at once.

we observe all around. Emotionalities produce limited subjects of interest and circumspect perceptions in the mind of the thinker, because their entire focus is always on the personal-I. They reinforce concepts of the ego, as the emotional person is normally dramatically focused upon the central 'I' in some way. Such people rarely have the energy to be their own therapist, producing an inability to solve problems arising from within themselves, as new emotions always arise to stir the pot of their turbulent fickleness. Jumping often from the highs to the lows of the emotions (or *vice versa*) does not really solve anything in the long run.

The emotions aberrate all clear, clean lines of *maṇḍalic* structures, therefore no true *maṇḍalas* of power are possible with their use. To build the proper *maṇḍalic* cellular structure of thought in consciousness, all forms of the Waters (coupled with the *vijñānas*) must be eliminated. They must be occultly dried up through the right utilisation of the laws of Fire.[15] This is the secret of all true *siddhas* who possess powers over substance, over the crystallised, Logoic Thought-expressions in Nature. The *siddha* works with the laws governing the cellular consciousnesses of all lives in order to liberate them from the limitations of the type of form that encases them. The greater, as well as smaller lives, are all subject to the same laws of liberation, and with this in mind the *siddha* is able to perform 'miracles'.

Maṇḍalas generally considered

The modifications of the mind happen because its substance (*citta*) is continuously moving. Without motion thought is not possible, the *vijñānas* could not arise, neither could *manas* perceive (anything). The belief in motion is possible because one sees things moving and notices its effects upon the senses. The mind then registers movement. As one does so, one is viewing within the cycles of time. Some say that Buddhists deny motion, but there is no true denial of motion in the Mahāyāna (as has already been explained in Volume 2, chapter 11, of this series). A. Wayman illustrates this point in the following:

> Thus Nāgārjuna informs the attentive reader that the problem is

---

15 This is a technical process referring to methods that *yogins* use to transform Watery *saṃskāras*.

> not, as Kalupahana opined on *kārikā* 1-2, one of 'agent' but rather whether the realm in which there is *gata* (the gone) or *āgata* (the come) implies a realm in which there is *sthita* (staying). Recalling that in Chapter 2, Nāgārjuna set forth that a person either goes or stays. Since Nāgārjuna did not deny motion in Chapter 2 of his *MK*, this helps for understanding *MK* Chapter 22, in which it is clear that the Tathāgata went *(gata)*.[16]

Therefore, without motion there could be no 'thus gone' one, nor indeed any consciousness to register any experiences of anything at all, hence no way to get 'there' to be 'gone' from. All motion can be said to happen in the mind of the perceiver, from which a Buddha has 'gone from', to be 'thus gone'.

For the mind to register something, it must contain that which is registered within it, thus there is an esoteric reason why the head, physically the 'container' of the mechanism of the mind, is ovoid in shape. A sphere, represented diagrammatically as an ovoid, or circle, indicates all forms of motion appearing together, creating the appearance of time when integrated with consciousness. It binds sequences of time into set scenarios, *maṇḍalas* of expression, and encapsulates an entire completed thought-sequence embodying a specific type of idea.

A *maṇḍala* consisting of lines and symbols is but a visual representation of the living motion of consciousness that has established a consolidated pattern for a specific purpose, and is bound by a sphere of limitation qualifying its purpose.

Each form of motion (directed consciousness-flows, time continuums) manifests in a given direction. Each motion has a specific hue, length (duration) and vibrancy to produce the right effect in the mind of the one who comes to experience, and hence interpret it. A *maṇḍala* is a consolidated construct built consciously by a creative thinker with these basic concepts in mind, to legitimise a present meditative thought-sequence, and to store its potential for future expression. It has therefore

16 Alex Wayman, *Untying the Knots in Buddhism, Select Essays* (Motilal Banarsidass, Delhi, 1997), 176. The abbreviation *MK* refers to Kalupahana's translation of the *Mūlamadhyamakakārīkā* of Nāgārjuna. For reference as to how the denial of motion in Buddhism evolved, refer to Th. Stcherbatsky, *The Central Conception of Buddhism (Sri Satguru Publications, Delhi, 1991)*, 37-39.

imbued into it a set purpose, an overall pattern consisting of lines and colourings, spheres of activity containing symbolic representations. These are highly potent thought-constructs, generally taking the shape of lesser spheres of activity contained within the greater one. They are traditionally the places of incorporation of various deities (Herukas, Buddhas, and the like), which embody the potency of the quality of the thought imbued into that portion of the *maṇḍala* with respect to its relation to the greater whole.

A *maṇḍala,* e.g., the Kālachakra Tantra (Wheel of Time), may appear rigid, fixed in space, but this actually is not so. In reality its composition is constituted of internal structures that are quite dynamic, such as the five Elements, the composition of space, the activities of the Deities appearing in its portals, and specifically of the *vajra* that caps its entire structure with the multidimensional legitimacy of the five Dhyāni Buddhas. Any generic *maṇḍala* incorporating the functioning of these Jinas is the potent symbol of an actual meditative reality directed veridically to the higher strata of Mind that reifies the actual mode of manifestation of a *nāḍī* flow in space.

The time-sequence that is the flow of motion producing the development of consciousness, which eventually transforms into the five Tathāgata Wisdoms, is then viewed in energy terms as the manifestation of a *vajra*. This is a statement that can be rationally inferred from analysis of the function of the *vajra* in all symbolic representations of it in Tibetan art. However, proper explication can only come from an elaboration of the foundational geometry and underlying dynamics of the nature of the petals of the lotus flower (*chakra*) from which a *vajra* stems. This geometry is a beautiful synthesis, and an elaboration of all the pertinent philosophy involved with the processes will be explained in a later book.

The concept of time is, however, fundamentally illusory because it is based on the transience pertaining to *saṃsāra*. Yet we could raise a question here: 'Does the flow of time manifest a fundamental reality because, after all, without it the sequential experiences leading to liberation would not occur?'

According to Einstein's Theory of Relativity the measurement of time changes in moving objects, it actually slows down with increasing speeds, and is viewed relative to the perception of any observer. In the equation he gives, where energy equals the mass of an object times the speed of light squared, we see that this speed is invariant, manifesting at 186,282 miles (299,792 kilometers) per second. Nothing is said to be able to travel faster than light. In our equations, however, we note that light is equated with the ability of consciousness to consume the darkness of ignorance. Light is therefore the nature of conscious substance. From this perspective the speed of light is not an invariant. It changes according to the nature and quality of the substance of consciousness that utilises it. Einstein's thought experiments and field equations did not take into account the nature of the substance that he thought with, or where he received his flashes of intuition from, or the speed with which it was received. Such is not quantifiable through the methodology of modern physics.

Certainly, if light is understood as the effect of waves of energy impinging upon the retina of the eye, producing electro-chemical effects that are translated by the visual cortex of the brain in terms of the images that we 'see', then maybe we are observing phenomena at this 299,792 km/sec limitation of the rate of impression. However, the interpretative faculty of the mind is not thus limited, it is not bound by the substance of the human brain, as it survives the death of the human form.

We should specifically take the two types of substance of mind into account here. First the nature of the concrete mind, and the speed therefore of empirical thought. If limited to the expression of electro-chemical impulses, then the invariance of the speed of light can be a determining factor conditioning the processes of such thought. However, if we look to the nature of abstract thought, that of the archetypal intuitive Mind, then light is not thus conditioned, and its speed is considerably faster. Let us look, for instance, to the ability to recall impressions from past lives. Assuredly one can recall images that happened say twenty or more lives ago in an instant, one does not have to wait for the comparatively slow travel at light speed for such images to occur, or for any other phenomena associated with the enlightened Mind, the ability to prevision the future for instance. Here one does not have to wait for light to travel 'there' in order to see it.

One should also note that the true rate of travel in the cosmos happens at the speed of thought, thus is not limited to the relative inertia of physical light. This transcends time, as we understand it. True space travel therefore concerns a perfected mastery of the laws of thought, and of the processes that transmute substance via mind and mantra. In the future, 'space ships' shall be constructed thusly, and then the actual era of interstellar travel will ensue. Materialistic science still has far to go in its endeavour to comprehend the true nature of phenomena. Also, to help account for the mysterious 'dark matter',[17] they could put into their equations the mass of the substance of the ethers of space, and that of the *lokas*, the Bardo zones wherein those preparing for rebirth reside, as well as multidimensional realms associated with liberated being/non-being. The universe is far more vast and alive than the orthodox scientist admits, and until their equations reflect this they will forever find anomalies and paradoxes in their equations. Let the scientific fraternity work with the laws of expanding Mind and certainly answers will be forthcoming in such a way as to astound their imaginations, with the ultimate simplicity and reciprocity of all that is and is not.

We look to a continuously rebirthing universe (and of all associated stars and galaxies) to make room for incremental expansions of awareness of all the units of consciousness that have evolved therein within the appointed cycles, of cosmic 'days and nights', so that more arenas of darkness can be consumed with light.[18] Our universe is

---

17 T. Ferris, *The Whole Shebang* (Phoenix, London, 1997), 121, for instance, states: 'Dark matter is the black Taj of modern cosmology. During the past twenty years, theory and observation alike have indicated that at least ninety percent, and perhaps as much as ninety-*nine* percent, of the mass of the universe is dark. It is invisible not because it is far away—most astronomers assume that it is distributed more or less coextensively with the visible galaxies—but because it neither emits nor absorbs light. At least some of the dark matter is made of familiar stuff, but most of it may be of an exotic nature as yet unknown. Until it can be identified, cosmologists will continue to be confronted with the galling thought that the millions of galaxies that they have studied are a tiny minority, a sample that may not be representative of the whole. If the dark majority of the cosmic mass is different in kind or behaviour from the bright minority, then scientific conclusions that ignore the majority may be as distorted as, say a poll that attempted to predict the outcome of a national election by interviewing only vegetarian monarchists'.

18 With respect to this, the doctrine of Plasma Cosmology, stemming from the work of Noble Laureate, Hannes Alfvén, approximates better the appearance of the

constructed hylozoistically, for Life is all there is, animating every iota of substance. All forms are therefore embodied by Minds and have conscious, coherent purpose. There are no mechanistic determinations left entirely to chance, rather we have deliberate, consciously ordered sequences of events, both on the minute as well as on a vast scale. We need no complicated mathematics to comprehend this point, nor are equations filled with 'infinities' and convoluted conundrums of logic needed for the comprehension of all that is.

The production of time manifests as a system of recurring units: of cyclic recurrences of the same or a similar patterning in the fabric of space wherein the unit comes to be conscious of the order of time. This function produces the reincarnations of perceptive units that can bear time in consciousness, continuing on a *saṃskāric* stream of *manasic* (mental) deliberations. The *saṃskāric* flow pushes the reincarnating unities, or bits of the stream, to an eventful conclusion. But is this conclusion (the Void) 'real', the true ending of time? Or does this curly monster appear on a far vaster scale than before, of cosmic (universal) time reckoned by Buddhas delineating their enlightening zones of influence? This gives us a transcendental holistic accounting of the nature of the flow of the law of cycles.

Maṇḍalas must therefore also contain within them the concept of the repetition of cycles (certainly at their base level, which supports the structural tiers of the higher, more subjective strata or levels of interpretation), if the *maṇḍala* is a representation of that which pertains to the real.

Buddhists, however, do not properly perceive the process of the flow of time. True analyses of conceptions of time are lost, when mythology and history become jumbled in a potpourri of tales, and dates for any factual occurrence are rarely furnished. A form of conjunctivitis is manifested where the Mādhyamaka, specifically, view a non-beginning in their reckoning of causes, but yet there is an ending. (What 'non-beginning' and 'what end' are questions that deserve an award-winning transcendental thesis for an answer.) Proper corollaries must first be activated to prove the union of opposites in their completeness, for those

continuously rebirthing (physical) universe than does the 'Big Bang' cosmology of orthodox science.

thinkers who have defined things in Buddhism have not taken the whole into perspective. Such a perspective may have been available to their enlightened Minds, however, the language that needed to be used to comply with the Buddhist (syllogistic) mind-set could not accommodate such revelations. This concerns the totality of the thinking organism productive of cosmic Breath, wherein each cyclic rhythm can produce the formation and ending of stars and/or galaxies; of the nature of cosmic Mind organising chaos (black particulate matter) into eventual solar forms.

Buddhists have placed definitions of the Void into a category of its own that excludes any possibility of it possessing organs. (Their logic is presented in such syllogisms as 'The Seven-Fold Reasoning', and 'Essay on the Many and the One', as treated in Volume 1 of this series.) This is one of the criteria they claim makes the Void truly valid, and real. An organ is something that contains component cellular parts and yet is part of a greater manifesting living whole that functions in a coherent manner. So, general Mahāyāna philosophy informs us that 'things' like an organ, or a living entity composed of many such organs, lack inherent existence. In fact, all the sets containing the processes of Life are not explained for what they truly are in such syllogisms.

The paradox in the Buddhist view is that they logicise a non-structured Void as the only valid thing that has meaning. We however know from our empirical deduction that everything that has Life and meaning are living things that possess organs in order to move, eat, procreate, etc. They interrelate with us so that we can do the same, and consequently evolve. An endeavour to analyse the non-organed Void means that one is trying to define the undefinable and thus cannot proceed further, because this happens through a mind structure that can only define that which it is trying to know about. When such a one says 'that he/she can stop thinking', this is only in relation to the fact that he/she is grounded on a previous point that has been formerly defined. Because when one tries not to think further, all that happens is that one gets stuck on the last definition made in the mind. If the definition is of the Void, then this is what remains in the mind.

The process of thinking

The process to neither think or utilise definitions is illusory because all that has happened is that a person hasn't gone beyond the previous definition in their mind. Often the old definitions presented by other's thoughts are taken, and are not appraised correctly. This produces an anaesthetic effect in the mind. When this type of laziness of thought occurs, the mind stops being able to intelligently deduce hidden facts from the *maṇḍalas* established by the wise of the past.

When thinking of something that is believed to be truth, one must keep questioning how this is true in relation to something else, and continue to appraise other connections and possibilities for how it is pertinent. This involves creative thinking, even 'individualistic thinking', which very few bother to do, hence there are gaps in their logic where no thought has entered, which produces an anaesthetic effect.

A person can never understand that which has been defined by others unless it has a relation to the experiences of the person thinking. The term 'experience' denotes a certain sense of self-identity, as someone can't experience something unless they can add it to their own thought-structure with respect to other situations they know of.

Our endeavour is to integrate all the ideas that induce Buddhists to syllogise any sequential thought-stream in relation to both the macrocosm—the ultimate limit of that sequence, and the microcosm—that which is contained within the context of their discriminative minds. Then we can push out all the boundaries as far as we can go. We are not just concerned with simplistic syllogisms, of up and down, big and small. Our thoughts are contained in the fields of opposites (by which we can compare two things) but the relationship between those opposites is relative. Comparison delineates boundaries in thought, and thereby helps to visualise that which is beyond the current delineated limits to thinking.

If it were just up and down we would have small and large as opposites on one stream, but because we think in terms of wholes, of that which is inclusive, and of separations therein (points or things that do not include the whole), our syllogisms are complete. They are defined by the mind producing two immediate consequences: that which the mind does include, and that which is not included by it. This process of thinking in terms of small and large subsets produces limitations in thought, seen as circles (cells) of consciousness. Consciousness is held in smaller and larger cellular spheres. Each subset is but a *maṇḍalic* construct, so we move from the atomic in scale to that which encompasses the starry fields.

Within each such sphere lie the seeds that give rise to many confusing thought processes, as if tied in knots. Knots represent tangled-up aspects of ideas and thought-streams that have never been logically presented to form a completed *maṇḍala* of consequence. They therefore represent incorrectly sequenced syllogisms. The syllogisms consequently have flaws. Knots happen because people don't think in all directions at once; they don't paint from their topmost limit to the smallest unit simultaneously when utilising the process of analogy, or various syllogistic processes. When the mind utilised is unenlightened, then it is in a state that can only observe things in terms of opposites, or of the 'other'. It then gets lost in the detail of cross-purpose integrations, consequently producing such knots, especially when the anaesthetic effect described above is also involved. The mind generally does not have the capacity to visualise the nature of the larger cellular spheres of consciousness, as the entire domain of the unenlightened mind is usually within but one such sphere. The speed of thought here is also limited by the lethargic nature of the substance constituting it.

To prevent the knot-tying you must firstly use the discriminating mind to continuously review that which it discriminates, to reduce the tangles caused by circumspect logic and its convoluting, segregating qualities based upon limited items of knowledge. Secondly, the same must be applied with respect to any one thought the mind thinks in terms of its opposites (i.e., that which is used for comparison). This means that simultaneously the concept of the 'other' is entertained and then accepted, excluded, or modified. Petty detail can then entangle the flow, with the mind losing sight of the broad perspective of the overall view. Therefore, one must always keep an open perspective of as vast a domain of mind as possible to ascertain wherever the knotted pettiness might arise, and then to apply countermeasures.

To cognise, the mind has to see the opposites as an empirical whole, because the mind thinks simultaneously of the 'all' (its main thought-sequence) and of the opposites at once. It correlates the opposites into its picture or image of the 'all', of everything it includes and doesn't include, in order to understand what it is trying to cognise at any one moment. Thus the *maṇḍala* comes to be unknotted and set well ordered, fixed in space with the detail of all its attributes properly sequenced according to their function and qualities.

In having high ideals and enlightened thoughts, one will consider oneself as the smallest atomic part within the thought construct. If one keeps thinking in this way, of relating the high to the low (the high equals the whole organism of the thought, and low equals the small part of it[19]) in relation to one's heuristic experiences, then inevitably a simultaneous correlation between opposite thoughts will manifest (because one is trying to understand truth). We thus have a conjunction between that which is comparatively not an illusion (the whole with regard to the 'self') and that which is comparatively an illusion (the 'self' in comparison to the whole).

The concept of the smallest atomic unit is used as a mechanism by consciousness to interrelate with the whole, to prove that the whole is the reality, knowing that 'small' means illusion. We are really investigating the process of synthesis, because we are always talking about relationships and how to unite divergent unities. The identity of things like 'whole' or 'small' are not so important because we know that from wherever one looks it is all illusory (void), and the process of filling up that void is a mechanism we can transcend. Too many names within that void clutter up the consciousness-space.

We are concerned with the interrelationships of all things within limits. We evolve through graded steps of limitation, which helps consciousness to analyse, understand, and transcend these limits of experience to enlightenment. Each *maṇḍala* delineates such a sphere of limitation. It describes the bounds of a certain mode of consciousness-

---

19 We know that the high and the low are effectively illusions, but we prioritise our illusions. In the use of comparisons we know that which is defined is fundamentally flawed because it is based on delusion, of relating one finite point to another. It will become outdated, outmoded by the influx of ideas, or changes.

expansion and of the conditions governing the consequent ordering of space. It defines the chains of our former possible thinking so that this can be transcended.

One gets to a point where the mind's discriminative processes happen so quickly that its thought-sequences instantaneously seek the broadest possible perspective, where the highest concept is instantaneously related to the small and the smallest observance is noted within the panorama of the 'all'. The 'all' is inclusive of multidimensional space, the Elements of being/non-being constituting the expansions and contractions of everything. Thus the smallest interrelationship is related to the highest law and the concept of the whole is interrelated with and included in the smallest. This then is a definition of enlightenment. Within the enlightened Mind a *maṇḍala* thus can grow from a tiny seed point (*bīja*), like the proverbial mustard seed, and effectively expand to encompass the entire universe in its scope.

When the small and the universal interrelate with each other they become something that is more than either small or universal, they make the whole, the complete view. Both are illusional in relation to each other. It is difficult to view the small or minute from the perspective of the universal, and similarly the universal laws or bounds to its being are difficult to ascertain from the viewpoint of the smallest cellular unit. The small is part of the universal and yet has to evolve to become the universal. Thus the way we see form on the smallest level must take on the outer perspective, which eventually becomes the Law of Logoi (and how they manifest their 'Buddha-fields'), through establishing interrelationships on their level via acquiescing to the expression of the *dharmakāya*.

One could also take into consideration that every surface of something is a form of mirror, because every single boundary mirrors that which is outside of it to that which is inside of it, and that which is inside of it to the outside. Whatever appears on the outside of the form has an expression on the inside, and *vice versa*. Each section of a *maṇḍala* is a reflection of what can be found in the entire *maṇḍalic* construct as a whole, despite the fact that it is concerned with its own individualistic imagery. This produces a type of holographic effect.

Everything is categorised by the mind, as Griffiths inadvertently points out in reference to speaking about 'Buddha fields':[20]

> The truth is that all actions of Buddha, whether they appear to occur in a four-continent world like this one or in a golden Buddha-field adorned with vast and imaginative floral arrangements, are representations in the minds of living beings whose occurrence is explicable without remainder in terms of the needs of those categories: the first consists of the kinds of activities...of an apparently more-or-less human body in a world much like this one; the second consists of the kinds of activities....of an obviously nonhuman body in a world dramatically unlike this one.
>
> But some Buddha-actions fall somewhere uneasily between these two categories, and when this happens it becomes clear that the category system is entirely conventional: it matters as little whether a specific Buddha action is said to belong to one or another category as it does whether something said by a specific individual who is both spouse and professor is said to be spoken by a spouse or by a professor.

One should consider how supernally large such a Buddha-field may become, or how an earth-like sphere may evolve through each such *maṇḍalic* construct. The nature and laws of Mind that bind the inner and outer aspects of constructs into a unity are not properly understood. Much is yet to be revealed.

The type of ideas gleaned that originate in humanity (and not from a Buddha's Mind) can be used to infer that all information is discriminatory in nature. In contrast to enlightenment such ideas are illusory, transient, continuously changing. There can also be a separation of many thoughts in one moment. Eventually thoughts are bound to be discarded as of little or no relevance. The further away they evolve from the source of the structure for which they were intended, so as time proceeds, their use-by date appears.

The medieval thinking of much of the mythos relating to Buddhism should be updated to unveil the truth. The time for the spreading of their implicit revelation has moved far beyond, in relation to the time-sphere

20 Paul J. Griffiths, *On Being Buddha,* (Sri Satguru, Delhi, 1995), 138.

for which the instructions they contained were intended. Indeed, the evidence of the Buddha Maitreya's needed incarnation leaves no doubt that the Buddha expected trouble (in the minds of humanity), and that even the formulations of what evolved in relation to his life were some time to become outmoded.

Supernal teachings are needed for the discriminatory minds that are the thinkers of the future. That mental cognitions appear, eschewing the unease of wrongly faceted doctrines, necessitates the appearance of another Buddha. Modern thought has produced many new revelations in the field of science and the order of the universe, thus some of the Buddhist canon needs to be reformed (as the Buddha himself predicted). Thus Buddha Maitreya must incarnate to fix the problems in the human mental continuum so that further enlightened revelation can reveal the beauteous glory of the *dharma*. Because a Buddha never simply replicates or duplicates teachings that were presented before, new doctrines must appear that are maximally enlightening for the time. He must produce the highest possible revelations or logical syllogisms to be gleaned by humanity. A new Buddhist *maṇḍalic* construct is emerging to answer the needs of today's Bodhisattvas.

The teachings become increasingly more revelatory, hence esoteric, broader in scope and vaster in detail with each new Incarnation of a great One. The vast multitudinous expanse of the Logoic *maṇḍala* thus begins to seep into the Mind-spaces of an increasingly large number of people, eventually abstracting the entire sphere of incarnate space into higher spheres of Logoic Mentation we call *dharmakāya*. This produces inevitable *pralaya* (dissolution) of formed space, and thus the transformation of what was once darkened into the semblance of a brilliant Son-sun. Hallelujah! A new solar sphere finally appears, empowered by a glorious Hierarchy of Luminous 'thus gone' ones congruently radiating out to the cosmos the summation of their united enlightenment. Incorporated into the field of that solar space is a new generation of darkened substance, to eventually be transformed by evolutionary processes inherent in the Buddha-Mind into radiant fields of revelation.

3

Examination of Chaos and the Void

The *saṃsāra-śūnyatā* nexus

The disorganised thought-structures of most humans can be likened to chaos. The nature of this chaos and its relation to the Void should be properly examined, because in order to see anything clearly something approximating the Void must be created in which mental images may be formed that will not be distorted in any way. The *Void* (*śūnyatā*) refers to primordial undifferentiated space that is not conditioned by either non-understanding (which equals ignorance) or the organising principle of all that was, is, and is to be. This is inevitably comprehended as truth.

Much information was presented in earlier volumes of this series concerning *śūnyatā*. It was defined as neither being nor non-being, in terms of the *saṃsāra-śūnyatā* integration. The five Void Elements were also explicated. The simplest way of considering *śūnyatā* is in terms of whatever remains when mind or the effects of mind do not exist. The proviso must however be added that no phenomena of any type can exist within the 'space' that is *śūnyatā*. Therefore it cannot be defined or comprehended by mind. In many ways *śūnyatā* can be considered the middle between extremes. The term 'space' must be viewed in various ways and not merely from the perspective of the three-dimensional universe, or that which includes the separation between things. It also refers to the most refined of the alchemical Elements, the vehicle of expression of the quality known as *dharmakāya*.

In Nāgārjuna's enigmatic statements such as the often quoted verse below, one finds there is more implied than just the fact that both *nirvāṇa (śūnyatā)* and *saṃsāra* are conceived as being 'empty'.

> There is not the slightest difference
> Between cyclic existence and nirvāṇa.
> There is not the slightest difference
> Between nirvāṇa and cyclic existence.
>
> Whatever is the limit of nirvāṇa
> That is the limit of cyclic existence.
> There is not even the slightest difference between them,
> Or even the subtlest thing.[1]

As Garfield states: 'To distinguish between saṃsāra and nirvāṇa would be to suppose that each had a nature and that they had a different nature. But each is empty, and so there can be no inherent difference.[2]' What is inherently interwoven with such a statement goes beyond the mere view of what is emptiness, but how phenomena and the Void come to co-exist. They may indeed be identical from one viewpoint, however from another there is a difference, and that is the heart of the mystery of the *saṃsāra-śūnyatā* nexus. Here, according to Garfield's translation of Nāgārjuna, *nirvāṇa* is 'neither said to be existent nor said to be nonexistent. Neither both nor neither are said.[3]'

The ontological implications are profound, as they veil the mystery of how phenomena come to appear in such a way that a mind can register its existence. In other words, if one postulates *śūnyatā* to be 'real', then *saṃsāra* can also be considered to be real. However, *saṃsāra* has its basis upon that which lies outside the sphere of abstraction that is delineated as *śūnyatā*. This abstraction necessitates the origin of mind and the way it comes to discern anything to be included in one's analysis, because *śūnyatā* only has relevance in relation to that which it is not. This is in itself a self-evident dichotomy, but nevertheless is

---

1 Jay L. Garfield, *The Fundamental Wisdom of the Middle Way: Nāgārjuna's Mūlamadhyamakakārikā,* (Oxford University Press, N. Y., 1995), 331. The quote is from verses 19 and 20 of chapter 25 of the *Mūlamadhyamakakārikā.*

2 Ibid.

3 Ibid., 330.

a useful metaphysical quandary—from whence comes mind, and what exactly is 'it', because without it ('it' being the basis of a Buddha's wisdom) *śūnyatā* has no purpose. We see, therefore, that one cannot simply focus upon one side of the *saṃsāra-śūnyatā* interrelation and think that it is the whole truth. Both sides make up the complete picture, and the existence of both must be properly established in this ontology. The phenomena of *saṃsāra* may be considered to be Void, but *śūnyatā* is not empty of itself because as Nāgārjuna states:

> 'Empty' shall not be asserted.
> 'Non-empty' shall not be asserted.
> Neither both nor neither shall be asserted.
> They are only used nominally.[4]

The Void may be the absolute Truth, but this is relative only to the expression of mind, which holds myriads of truths that have meaning and are relevant as the foundation of the wisdom that is the expression of an enlightened Mind. We therefore get the term *bodhicitta*, which implies a fusion of the two principles. Of this compound word, *bodhi* (full awakening) has a direct relation to *śūnyatā,* but 'what then is this *citta* (basic mind stuff), where does it come from, and what is its relation to *śūnyatā?'* These are questions that really need to be answered in the ontology of *saṃsāra-śūnyatā.* Buddhist syllogistic systems as generally construed are ill-equipped to answer such questions, because they concern the substance of phenomena as a thing existing of itself. This is not a focus of Buddhism, but rather of the Hindu religion, contrary to which the Buddha evolved his syllogisms of the middle way between extremes. Universal substance matter (*mūlaprakṛti*[5]) is the material through which its evolution, and thus of all phenomena in the universe, forms the basis to the way the mind evolves and answers the question of the origins of intelligence. Buddhism on the other hand is mainly focussed upon the final resolution of things with *śūnyatā.* The ontology of the appearance of things involves the phenomenon

4 Ibid., 228. The quote is from chapter 22, verse 11, 'Examination of the Tathāgata'.

5 *Mūlaprakṛti: mula* = root and *prakṛti* = substance matter. The original store or germ from which all matter or substance evolved or was utilised by the creative Deity. Universal substance matter.

of creative entities, Logoi, such as Īśvara, Brahmā, etc. in Hindu philosophy. This is a subject beyond the scope of this present book, however, the foundation for such comprehension is established here. 'Chaos' in this text is equated with *mūlaprakṛti,* which is ubiquitous and precedes the formation of any universe or world-sphere, otherwise no such universe could come to exist and human experiences would be impossible.[6] Such substance therefore is 'real' and is that from which evolves mind. Without it there could be no *saṃsāra-śūnyatā* nexus, thus no enlightenment.

Chaos and the Void

Showing the relation between chaos and the Void can assist the reader to gain better comprehension of many such abstruse philosophical concepts, within the bounds of the limitations of language. What is presented can be seen as a metaphor assisting the mind to comprehend the nature of that which is essentially incomprehensible to it. In esoteric texts such as this, the reader must always be prepared to think in multidimensional terms. This is very unfamiliar territory for most, and one for which often language itself is a blind. Until one has experienced the nature of the abstract Mind, *śūnyatā,* or *dharmakāya,* veils need to be mentally processed to produce some semblance of comprehension to the concrete mind.

Chaos refers to that which is differentiated and unstructured. It has no order in it, and is the primordial matter or substance (cosmic dust, elementary *citta*) that is utilised as the basis for the formation of the phenomenon of *saṃsāra.*[7] It is unorganised, inchoate, formless, dark matter. Sentient intelligence evolves from it, and once established, intelligence equates all such substance and incoherence associated with it as equable with ignorance. At this juncture Buddhism begins its syllogism on 'cyclic existence'. Ignorance then becomes the basis

6 There is no such thing as *creatio ex nihilo* ('creation out of nothing'), which many Theologians believe and Cosmologists appear to support with their 'Big Bang' theory. 'Nothing comes from nothing' is a truism first said to be divulged by Parmenides.

7 Our conception here concerns the genesis of 'things' as part of the construct of an originating *maṇḍala* of a world-sphere by a Logos.

for the start of the twelve-fold formula of Dependent Origination (*pratītyasamutpāda*), from whence all *karma*-formations originate.[8] It is contained apparently 'within' the Void (taking the Void here to represent the 'all' that 'nominally' incorporates the being/non-being dualism), and as such becomes the background to the organising structure of the universe. The Void thus is/is-not the 'all'. It 'is' because nothing could exist without its support, and 'is-not' because there is a delineation between it and the substance of mind.

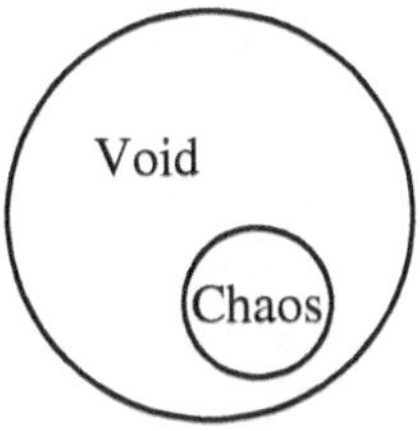

Figure 9. Chaos and the Void

As Figure 9 shows, the Void contains the sphere of chaos. Simultaneously it embraces it, incorporates it, yet is 'aloof' from it, for without the Void even ignorance could not exist. The bounded sphere containing the Void represented in the Figure is illusional. It symbolises that part of the Void that is incorporated within the Mind of a Logos. It is 'contained' thereby, allowing thought-forms of cyclic existence to appear in the form of 'bubbles' of expression of primordial substance, here termed chaos. These 'bubbles' are circumscribed by Mind and are organised according to the natural empathy with one or other of the five Void Elements[9] which form the basis for the expression of the five *prāṇas* and the development of the *saṃskāras* when incorporated

---

8 For detail see Volume 1, chapter 8, of this series, 'Dependent Origination', where it is stated 'the concept of ignorance needs elaboration, as it is considered 'the root of all *karma*-formations in Buddhism''. For this reason, the 14 verses of chapter 1 of the *Mūlamadhyamakakārikā* (Examination of Conditions) were fully explained. How ignorance is established as the basis for the start of 'cyclic existence' is to my knowledge not properly explicated in Buddhism, thus the account above is presented to fill in the hiatus of knowledge that evidently appears with respect to this subject.

9 Explained in Volume 1, chapter 5, of this series.

by mind. Similarly, the sphere depicted as containing the Void is a mind-construct needed to facilitate comprehension. The Void and chaos are thus integrated as a unity, but are differentiated. The uniformity of *mūlaprakṛti* becomes agglomerated into heterogeneous spheres by means of the organising principle of the Mind of a Logos.

From the perspective of this text, the domain of the mind represents the Real for all physical plane phenomena. Thus the atom of substance is really but a concretised reification of elemental *citta*. There is a constant passing forth of the sub-atomic particles described by physicists into and out from the etheric domain (which is inevitably controlled by *manasic* substance). This accounts for many of the perplexities observed, such as that associated with Heisenberg's Uncertainty principle, and the anomalous behaviour of a photon. The scientific community only thinks in terms of concrete phenomena, which is illusional, and this produces their enigmas, whereas our view is multidimensional. The statement, however, that energy and substance (the appearance of things) are interchangeable, holds true on all levels of perception. From this perspective, and in terms of Nāgārjuna's *catuṣkoṭi,*[10] we can say that phenomena exists ('is') when it is tangible to the senses, 'is not' when it does not register in consciousness, 'both is and is not' when it is in a state of transition from one dimension of perception to the next. (For example, from the ethers to physicality.) Finally, 'it neither is nor is not' when it has been transmuted as a Void Element.

The Yogācāra Idealism, which states that 'all is mind', can also be applied here, thus we can state that all phenomena bonded by the sphere of the chaos/Void interrelation is governed by Mind. The personal mind also reflects a similar control over substance upon its own little scale.

The Void here can be viewed as a type of separator between 'things', or different existents. Chaos is separated from Void by a sphere of limitation that is created around its form of activity, yet the Void interpenetrates chaos and facilitates its transformative activity. This is an automatic process because of the nature of the dynamic but very

---

10 *Catuṣkoṭi:* four limits: eternalism, nihilism, appearance, emptiness. Four-cornered logic. Also the fourfold system of dialectical negation, negation of the positive, the negative, of both, of neither. Four categories of existence, being, non-being, both being and non-being, and neither being and non-being.

subtle energy field of the Void, in comparison with the chaos, which has random fluctuating force vectors and continually reifying substance. The two thus appear as if they are immiscible, like globules of oil in water. *Sūnyatā,* however, interpenetrates all such globules, and remains after these globules of substance have been abstracted into the luminosity of the Clear Light of Mind by means of the agency of human minds, Love and Will. *Sūnyatā* manifests a force underlying the transformation of elementary substance into mind and of that mind to Mind. *Sūnyatā* remains unaffected, but in the process Mind has come to supersede it, as the *dharmakāya* is now its embrace. This is the gain of the evolution of wisdom. *Śūnyatā* is the base or foundation of it all. The implication of this is that inevitably the chaos becomes ordered and finally absorbed into the Void. This happens because the dynamic nature of the energy of the Void will ultimately absorb the chaos into its form of dynamism.[11] The intermediate process necessitates the bringing of order to the randomness of the disorder of chaos. This involves changes that happen within the field of consciousness. It is because of consciousness, not *śūnyatā*, that phenomena appears. Because consciousness and *śūnyatā* work together, conscious phenomena is distilled, transformed, and abstracted out of *saṃsāra*. Consciousness is also something that is oft depicted as illusional, however it is not illusional because its activities inevitably bring about Buddhahood, and this is the purpose of the entire *saṃsāra-śūnyatā* interplay. It has a veridical nature that sustains the entire drive of a Bodhisattva (that is not illusional) for the duration preceding the attainment of Buddhahood. Even then it 'remains' and must be utilised if interrelation with *saṃsāra* is to occur. Indeed, its transmuted nature is incorporated into the nature of the Wisdom of the Tathāgata. Such a nature is all-knowing. J. M. Reynolds presents similar views with respect to the rDzogs-chen tradition:

> If one observes the mind and searches for where a thought *(rnam rtog)* arises, where it remains, and where it goes, no matter how much one researches and investigates this, one will find nothing. It is this very 'undefinability' *(mi rnyed)* of the arising, the abiding, and the passing away of thoughts which is the greatest of all finds. Thoughts do not

---

11 If we conceive it to exist as a state of pure intensified energy then it fulfils the criteria of the *catuṣkoṭi* of being 'neither being and non-being'.

> arise from anywhere *(byung sa med),* they do not go anywhere *('gro sa med).* They do not arise from inside the body, nor do they arise from outside the body. They are truly without any root or source (*gzhi med rtsa bral*). Like the clouds in the sky, they arise only to dissolve again. Thoughts arise out of the state of emptiness and return again into this state of emptiness, which represents pure potentiality. We only have to observe our mind to discover this for ourselves. And this shunyata, this state of emptiness, is in fact the very essence of the mind (*sems kyi ngo-bo stong-pa nyid*).[12]

The 'essence of the mind' may have emptiness as its base, but such an emptiness manifests as a mirror that facilitates the reflection of the wisdom of the Dhyāni Buddhas into manifestation, and the transmuted correspondences from the gain of the sense perceptions into the *dharmakāya.* That aspect of consciousness that is *illusional* is its volatile substance, the part that *is not illusional* is what appertains and develops wisdom. The I-consciousness translates ignorance into wisdom and intelligence into enlightenment.

The inevitable fate of this volatile illusional substance, that has been incorporated as part of the functions of a human mind at the time of the onset of *pralaya,*[13] is to be qualified as the five Void Elements. This happens by means of the transformative action of the human unit's progress to Buddhahood. From this substance arise the *bījas* of expression needed to appropriately organise chaos (*mūlaprakṛti*) during the next incarnation of the cyclic universe.

The primordial *mūlaprakṛti* that was not incorporated as part of the transformative aspect of human consciousness, will by the onset of *pralaya* have gradually evolved through being incorporated as the bodies of expression of various lives, to eventually form the substance of the layers of the Earthy, Watery or Fiery domains. It will be abstracted upon *manasic* levels during *pralaya,* to be utilised again by application of the Logoic Word at the onset of *manvantara,* and in this new cycle

---

12 J. M. Reynolds, *The Golden Letters,* (Snow Lion, Ithaca, 1996), 75.

13 *Pralaya*: (*pra* = to dissolve, vanish, be absorbed). A period of rest, obscuration, or dissolution, as opposed to *manvantara.* The ending of the universe of 'things'. In Hinduism, the period of one *manu,* containing 4,320,000 human years or specifically a Day of Brahmā.

will become the substance of human minds. This is another way of saying that it evolves to become the substance of a human Life-flux that undergoes the rebirthing process.

Primordial substance actually consists of a fourfold differentiation, or alternatively exists at four levels of expression. This is the basis to the quaternary of the human personality: a) a corporeal body, b) its etheric substratum, c) the emotional body, and d) the mind. This is reflected also in the four main types of fundamental particles known by physicists: protons, neutrons, electrons and neutrinos. These are the heads of the families of the other subatomic particles. The four petals of the Base of the Spine centre have evolved to accommodate these four levels of expression of primordial substance. This substance is found in the four levels or sub-planes of the concrete (lower) mind. These four principles form the foundation of *saṃsāra*.

The five Void Elements are *bījas* projected downwards from the *dharmakāya* and the domain of *śūnyatā* by the Ideation of an Ādi Buddha into the primal *mūlaprakṛti* at the commencement of a new cycle of *manvantaric* activity. Their purpose is to integrate chaos into the ordered structure of a *maṇḍala*. Of the five types of *bījas* one is directly from the level of the *dharmakāya*. This is the *bīja* that becomes the centre of a swastika of energies that attracts to it the substance of the *mūlaprakṛti*, producing rhythmic activity in what was once chaotic. It becomes a veiled or central point of a four-fold vector-field of interrelation of the forming *maṇḍala*. It is depicted in terms of the moving arms of a swastika, and expressed metaphysically in terms of the wisdoms of the Jinas.[14] Thus the immutable power of a *dorje* manifests. The effect of this arrangement is also observed in Nature by the four fundamental forces that scientists have discovered: a) gravity, b) electromagnetism, c) the strong atomic force, and d) the weak atomic force.

This is also the basis for the somewhat enigmatic philosophy concerning the nature of *kliṣṭamanas*, where it is said that the number of mental factors is exactly nine. When *manas* is turned to the empirical world and identifies with the form via the sense perceptions, through which it functions, then I call this the *personal-I*. When *manas* is turned towards the realisation of 'mind's Pure Essence', or rather, when the

---

14 Dhyāni Buddhas.

nature of that Essence is directed towards the personal-I, then I call this the *I-consciousness*. Perhaps this I-consciousness is best described in terms of the seventh of the eight consciousnesses, termed *kliṣṭa-mano-vijñāna* (or *kliṣṭamanas*). Tsong kha pa describes *kliṣṭamanas* thus:

> The *kliṣṭa-manas* is defined as that obscured (*nivṛta)* [mind], not the subject of moralizing, which views the maturation part of *ālaya-vijñāna* as self and has only nine [mental factors like contact, attachment, etc].[15]

The text further states:

> By *nivṛta* is meant repeatedly polluted by afflictive emotions *(kleśa)* because this *[kliṣṭa-]manas* has been repeatedly polluted by the four root afflictive emotions *(kleśa)*[16]... How could its surrounding [mental factors] be only nine? Are there not also the following six: a) distraction *(vikṣpa)* implicit in [the opinion] 'I am here,' b) carelessness (*pramāda*) implicit in attachment and stupidity, c) fixation implicit in attachment; and d) absence of faith *(aśraddhā),* e) laziness *(kausīdya),* and f) dullness *(styāna)* implicit in the stupidity part? Are there not, therefore fifteen [mental factors] surrounding [*kliṣṭa-manas*]?
>
> [Response:] Although those [six mental factors] are said to be there, still the number [of mental factors associated with *kliṣṭa-manas*] is exactly nine. This is because the bases for imputing these six are the material realities (Tib. *rdzas)* of the four afflictive emotions [opinion about I, stupidity about I, pride in I, and self love]. [The six] do not exist apart from these four. That there is no mental factor beyond the material realities of these nine can be understood in detail from the *Vivṛta-guhyārtha-pinda-vyākhyā.*[17]

Of these nine mental factors to *kliṣṭamanas* five are expressions of the five sense-consciousnesses, and are really five Watery *skandhas*[18]

15 Gareth Sparham, (Trans.) *Ocean of Eloquence, Tsong-ka-pa's Commentary on the Yogacara Doctrine of Mind,* (Sri Sat Guru, Delhi), 107.

16 Ibid.

17 Ibid., 111.

18 *Skandhas:* The bundles or groups of aggregates that together constitute the human personality and are responsible for the evolution of consciousness. They manifest as the *saṃskāras* collectivised in their various groupings that are carried through from life to life. Exoterically, there are five such groups (attributes of consciousness):

of the five Elements, expressed as the five senses. The emotions and the factor of desire are Watery, and thus *kliṣṭamanas* is really afflictive whenever the mind is conditioned by this Watery aspect in any way. There are Fiery emotions (mental emotions) as well as teary, Watery ones of desire-mind, those prompted by visual stimulus, as well as from the sense of touch, etc. To these must be added the 'four afflictive emotions [opinion about I, stupidity about I, pride in I, and self love]' to make the nine factors. They represent the way that mind incorporates the four levels of expression implicit in the base substance (*prakṛti*). It has utilised this substance to formulate a conception of 'self' that distinguishes it from all other individualised human units.

The four afflictive emotions relegate one to identify with an I-concept, with separativeness, and hence to identify with all things illusory as if they were real. They represent the qualities inherent in the substance of the four sub-planes of the concrete mind, and are consequently great hindrances upon the path to high meditative achievement.

1. Stupidity about 'I'. The most elementary, coarsest attribute of human thought. It is the result of lazy, sluggish thinking, the inability to penetrate beyond the surface of any issue. Represented by the Earthy attribute of *citta*.
2. Self love. This represents the most Watery attribute of *citta*, based upon the fluid image-making faculty of mind. It produces a personalised myth-making fabrication about the worth of 'self'.
3. Opinion about 'I'. Here we have the most *manasic* (Fiery), asserting aspect, or level of the *citta* that is the substance of mind. Hence it is that which properly represents the functioning of mind as an expression of itself. The individual takes many concepts from the world of ideas to fabricate a complete profile of the image and potency

---

1) Form, or body, the sense organs, sense objects and interrelationships (*rūpa*), 2) Perception or sensation, feelings and emotions (*vedanā*), 3) Aggregates of action, or the motives to thus act (*saṃskāra*), 4) The faculty of discrimination (*samjñā*), 5) Revelatory knowledge (*vijñāna*). Literally they become one's karmic accumulations which must be worked with from life to life and are eventually transmuted into the seeds of enlightenment. These *skandhas* are expressed in the form of the five different types of *prāṇas* conveyed throughout the *nāḍī* system.

of the personal-I within the society of which that person is a part.

4. Pride in 'I'. This is an attribute of the most Airy, expansionary substratum of mind. It incorporates all of the other aspects and is the most tenacious attribute to overcome upon the road to enlightenment. It presents the major bubble of mind that needs to be deflated if the individual is to develop the true humbleness that represents the voice of the Heart speaking. Following this voice is the way out from the miasma of the domination of the rule of mind, and manifests as the *bodhicitta* that is the enlightened Mind in application.

This process of the five Void Elements' downward projection into the four attributes of mind is the esoteric basis to the formation of 'the double-nature of manas'. Govinda emphasises that they participate 'in the empirical-intellectual as well as in the universal' consciousness. He further states:

> *Manas* and *mano-vijñāna* are often mixed up and treated as synonyms and even in the non-buddhistic Sanskrit literature a higher and lower aspect of *manas* is discerned, depending on whether *manas* is turned towards the empirical world or not.
>
> Therefore it is said in the *Mahāyāna-Śraddhotpāda-Śāstra:* 'The mind (*manas*) has two doors from which issue its activities. One leads to a realization of the mind's Pure Essence, the other leads to the differentiations of appearing and disappearing, of life and death. What, however, is meant by the Pure Essence of Mind? It is the ultimate purity and unity, the all-embracing wholeness, the quintessence of Truth. Essence of Mind belong neither to death nor rebirth, it is uncreated and eternal.[19]

Because there has been the downwards projection of one principle associated with Mind, to be incorporated by another aspect expressing the elemental substance of mind, there is actually a gap in consciousness between the lower concreted attribute of mind and that of the higher abstracted part. A bridge, called the *antaḥkaraṇa,* must therefore be consciously built through continuous aspiration towards abstract thought during the practice of meditation, or via high mental aspiration based

19 Govinda, *Foundations of Tibetan Mysticism*, 79.

upon clear logical thinking. All forms of reification must be avoided, and refinement of thought via precise meditation methods utilised. The elimination of reification essentially means quietening the thought processes via a complete relaxing of mind, so that the subtle expansive paradigms of Thought (seed *bījas*) from higher strata of Mind can be received. The mind must be held steady in a quiescent state, however, there must also be an upwards orientation or vision in the 'mind's Eye' that assists to build the bridge. This is an important consideration that needs to be taken into account as a mechanism to gain liberation by all meditators and Tantric practitioners. Once the bridge between the two levels of mind has been established then the vistas of revelatory ideas can flood the mind from domains beyond its natural ken. Mind then can supplant mind.

Logoi and the organisation of *citta*

Our focus should now turn to the state that existed before 'the beginning of things', before consciousness evolved to order space into categories of phenomena. Then time was not, as all such conceptualisation would be meaningless, there being no mind to behold (it). This view concerns an analysis of the way that Logoi organise dark space so that consciousness eventually evolves.

This begs the question of how time arises and comes to be meaningful, as well as how the sequence of events associated with Dependent Origination (*pratītyasamutpāda*) can arise. If consciousness is to arise and define ignorance by developing the *vijñānas* which allow one to experience *kleśas* (emotional afflictions), there must be *movement* in the chaos. With movement comes an inevitable collision between particles of the primordial *mūlaprakṛti* (*citta*). Such movement is provided by the originating seed impetus (*bīja*) of the Logoic Thinker.[20]

---

20 More forces play upon this substance than just Logoic Thought, as the substance itself is but part of the embodied nature of that Primeval Buddha's feminine counterpart (consort). This hints at the true significance of the coital interrelation (Tib. yab-yum) between the Ādi Buddha and his Consort, which is much more than just the union between Wisdom and Compassion. (This being the commonly held interpretation of the union.) We will, however, not delve into detail in this present introductory synopsis. More will be revealed in the later chapters in relation to the functions of

At first there will be considerable resistance by the inert target substance to be organised. The force (mantric potency) applied by the Thinker must be appropriate to produce the correct sequence of events at the correct pace. *Karma* is thereby engendered for that Thinker, necessitating such a One to carry the process through to its conclusion. The conclusion means bringing about the resolution of *karma*, according to the nature of karmic purpose.

Resistance produces heat, as energy is dissipated this way to other atomic forms. Heat then manifests as radiatory energy, which would be seen as light if a consciousness existed to perceive it. At this stage such has not yet evolved, though the process has been set in motion.

Alchemical, yogic terminology needs to be utilised to allow the metaphysics of multidimensionality to be defined, the generation of heat is then equated with the expression of the Fiery Element. It is Fiery because that's the way that consciousness perceives the nature of this energy and indeed, it is the basic substance of that self-same consciousness. The radiatory energy emanated by heat generates light. At first the light is of the deepest infrared and gradually glows orange as more heat is generated. Light is then equated with the ability to 'see'. However, so far we have only a materialistic universe.

Such *citta* becomes the principle of Life for all subsequent evolutionary impetus. It is the basis for the teaching of a hylozoistic universe presented here, which is herein purported to be the world-view of the enlightened. Without such *citta* what is presently known as human intelligence could not evolve from basic atomic substance. All is built upon this base inchoate substance of mind (which in its unorganised state is termed chaos), and is directed by Mind so as to evolve minds that can similarly express the Will to direct various forms of substance, resulting in the transformative momentum that will produce Mind from mind. Thus, as the Yogācāra philosophy states, 'all is mind'. Snelling adroitly summarises this philosophy as the background to the establishment of the *ālayavijñāna* for humanity as a consciousness-store:

> The Yogācārins took a more positivistic line of approach than the

---

ḍākinīs in the scheme of things. Subsequent books will of necessity elaborate from an esoteric perspective the principles of causation, and the evolutionary process for Life upon our planetary sphere within the context of solar evolution.

> Mādhyamīkas. All is mind or consciousness, they maintained, hence their central doctrine of *citta-mātra:* 'mind only' or 'nothing but consciousness'. According to this view, the objects of the world do not exist per se but are created from and by mind. To explain how this is done, they put forward the idea of a store consciousness (*ālaya-vijñāna*), a kind of collective unconscious in which the seeds of all potential phenomena are stored and from which they ceaselessly pour into manifestation. Delusion (itself a creation of the mind) consists of taking these for real, whereas they are in truth just evanescent projections of mind. [21]

With respect to the phenomena of mind, Dujom Rinpoche presents the Mādhyamika view in one of his quotes from the *Supreme Continuum of the Greater Vehicle*:

> Just as space is omnipresent,
> Having a thoughtless nature,
> So the natural expression of mind,
> The immaculate expanse, is all-pervasive.
>
> Its general characteristic pervades the limits
> Of negative and positive attributes,
> In the manner of the space
> Within inferior, mediocre and superior material forms.[22]

We can see that this quote depicts the nature of the abstract Mind. The important line from the quote from the present perspective, however, is that 'the natural expression of mind, The immaculate expanse, is all-pervasive', and in fact it is omnipresent. Contrasting this, the Yogācāra position is more focussed upon the characteristics of mind, and by implication how such a mind evolves to become Mind. The key ingredient is the *ālayavijñāna*, which evolves from the primal *mūlaprakṛti* that was incorporated into the Logoic Thought of what is-to-be with respect to the origination of a world-sphere, such as is our present earth. All stems from the omnipresent 'natural expression'

---

21 John Snelling, *The Buddhist Handbook,* (Rider, London, 1998). 106.

22 Dujom Rinpoche, *The Nyingma School of Tibetan Buddhism: Its Fundamentals and History,* (Wisdom Publications, Boston, 1991) 174. The quote is from Ch. 1, 49-50.

of Mind, directed by an enlightened bearer of such a Mind, in a Compassionate act to transform elemental atomic lives into conscious radiant bearers of the light of Mind. To quote Dujom Rinpoche again, using the same text:

> The seed[23] which is empty of suddenly arisen phenomena
> Endowed with divisive characteristics...
>
> The nature of this expanse in the minds of sentient beings is like a treasure of precious gems within the earth, uncovered by stains in respect to its own essence, and yet it simultaneously assumes the suddenly arisen forms of saṃsāra, in a manner, for example, of water and ice. It says in the *Sūtra of the King of Contemplation:*
>
> Pure, clear and inwardly radiant,
> Undisturbed and compounded
> Is the nucleus of the sugata,
> It is the reality that abides from the beginning.
>
> And in the master Nāgārjuna's *Eulogy to the Expanse of Reality (v. 23):*
>
> The water that lies within the earth
> Remains immaculately pure.
>
> Such quotations maintain that the status of the nucleus [of the tatāgata] according to the definitive meaning is inconceivable.
>
> This nucleus of the tatāgata, with respect to its own essence, is the same throughout saṃsāra and nirvāṇa, without good or evil.[24]

Now, when the phrases 'the seed' and 'the nucleus of the sugata' are mentioned the reference is to the *tathāgatagarbha,* and thus to the existence of the Sambhogakāya Flower upon the abstract levels of the mind. Clearly a vast philosophic background of information is hinted at, but never elaborated in Buddhist texts, as to how such 'nucleus' comes to form in the first place, and what its exact constitution is. The latter has been explained in Volume 3 of this series, whilst here is presented an outline of how such a human consciousness-stream (contained by such a 'nucleus of the sugata') comes to exist as part

---

23 *Tathāgatagarbha*: the Buddha-germ, or 'womb'.

24 D. Rinpoche, *The Nyingma School of Tibetan Buddhism*, 173.

of the compassionate *maṇḍala* generated by an Ādi Buddha. Each individual consciousness-stream does not appear spontaneously out of nowhere within space. It may be 'the natural expression of mind', but that the existence of billions of such entities as a planned event, part of a logical sequence of events related to the evolution of the elemental *citta* is what needs elucidating.

The information here should be incorporated with what was presented in chapter 7 on 'The Evolution of Consciousness' from Volume 2 of this series, concerning the question of the existence and nature of a God (or rather, a Creative Buddha-Mind), and why the transmuted realms of consciousness have not been properly investigated and catalogued by Buddhists. Appearances in human consciousness may exist in terms of concepts of a Creator, which can manifest in the form of a reflected paradigm of an abstract demiurge. They can also be wistfully veiled in concepts of Buddhist Divinities, such as an Ādi Buddha, in ways that many Buddhists can accept. Rather than being 'theistic' *per se*, this philosophy constitutes a Buddha Field of a 'thus gone Buddha'. The aim is to present detail involving such a constituency upon logical terms, and not keeping the idea upon some mystical realm relegated to the enlightened domains only. The aim here is to show the way that the appearance of phenomenal world(s) of sense perception arise from it. Thus the concern is the appearance of *saṃsāra,* and then also its proper relation to *śūnyatā*. This necessitates an analysis of what exactly constitutes a 'Buddha germ' and the formation of *saṃsāra* wherein this 'germ of sugata' comes to be defiled.

The terms *nirmalā* and *samalā tathatā* are used to describe the attributes of the *tathāgatagarbha. Nirmalā tathatā* is defined as 'Suchness apart from pollution (*saṃsāric* defilements)' and refers to the Sambhogakāya Flower as it exists upon its own level. *Samalā tathatā* is defined as 'Suchness covered over or concealed with impurities' and refers to the evolutionary process of the successive rebirths of a consciousness-stream as directed by the Sambhogakāya Flower. It is important to note that before the appearance of such Buddha germs upon the abstract levels of Mind, the conditions must first appear wherein such a 'germ' and the related human consciousness stream can come to be 'concealed with impurities'. All happens according to a pre-planned pattern of Thought carefully sequenced by the Ādi Buddha concerned.

The *maṇḍala* made potent by the Ādi Buddha does not organise *citta* directly, but incorporates an entire hierarchy of entities, collectively known as consorts (*ḍākinīs*) of the Buddhas and Bodhisattvas, as well as the *devas*[25] that populate the domain of *ḍākinīs,* whose function it is to assist in this process. Hence the *maṇḍala* consists of many moving parts, and together these great controlling Lives are termed 'Mother Nature'. Indeed, they embody its activities, as will be described in the next volume concerning the Deities of the *Bardo Thödol.*

For consciousness to arise, the elementary particles of chaotic action must intrinsically be constituted of elementary *citta*, already contacted by the organising Mind of the Ādi Buddha looking upon *saṃsāra* via the 'lens' of the Void. By producing organised movement this Mind galvanises chaos into form (an inevitable process inherent in the nature of conscious activity). The particles of deep space thus collated by the Mind of the Ādi Buddha become impregnated with his *jīva* (Life principle), i.e., with *cittavṛtti* (Mind-energy). This becomes the basis to establish the *tathāgatagarbha* or *gotra* (the Buddha-germ) for the forming world sphere. (In contradistinction from that of a human being, which has not yet arisen.)

The course of the evolutionary impetus is now set, as the *citta* and its primeval Fire becomes the inherent sentience governing the progress of all forms. The *citta* itself progresses through many stages of expression before it is incorporated as the highly refined essence of a human mind, which a person can utilise to cognise and instantly create picture images of whatever is desired. Before this possibility, many sentient carriers of elementary *citta* have played their part in the process of its transformation and refinement. (Referring here to the purpose of many subhuman species of mineral, plant, and animal life, including also the feminine *deva* evolution.) The appearance of the mineral kingdom is the result of an aeonic process concerning the

---

25 *Deva* (Tib. lha): 'shining one', deity, the general term for the celestial beings of the heavenly worlds. The derivation is from the Sanskrit roots *dā*, 'making gifts' (as a god does), *dip*, being radiant, and *dyut*, the sphere of heaven. Esoterically they are viewed as members of the angelic kingdom, the feminine counterpart to the human kingdom, to which such entities as fairies, nature spirits, Seraphim, undines, *ghandaravas, apsaras*, and *ḍākinīs* belong.

'condensation' and concretion[26] of the primal *citta*.

Working in the form of Mother Nature, the *devas* evolve the rudimentary lives (involving various planes of perception) that eventually become the animal forms that integrate the primordial growth of the Fires of *citta* with a rudimentary mind.

Samalā tathatā is the effect of the *citta* that becomes the subject of thoughts incorporated by a human mind and absorbed into the domain of a Sambhogakāya Flower as part of its constitution according to the dynamics of the evolution of its petals. The process of how a human kingdom evolves from the animal kingdom lies outside the scope of this book and will be provided in a later text. (Briefly, the human consciousness-streams individuate as unique entities, each a *tathāgatagarbha,* from the collective streams of sentience possessed by animals. Through comprehension of the rebirth process revelation arises of how a *tathāgatagarbha* is produced.)

Many missing gaps in the ontology of earnest Buddhist enquirers regarding the origins of humanity can here be filled. The Hua-yen and Ch'an master Kuei-feng Tsung-mi has provided an important commentary in this field. It presents the major syllogisms according to the main Buddhist schools, as well as of Confucianism and Taoism. He states in the concluding part of his thesis:

> Although the true nature constitutes the [ultimate] source of bodily existence, its arising must surely have a causal origin, for the phenomenal appearance of bodily existence cannot be suddenly formed from out of nowhere[27]...At first there is only the one true numinous nature, which is neither born nor destroyed, neither increases nor decreases, neither changes nor alters. [Nevertheless], sentient beings are [from time] without beginning asleep in delusion and are not themselves aware of it. Because it is covered over, it is called the tathāgatagarbha, and the phenomenal appearance of the mind that is subject to birth-and-death comes into existence based on the tathāgatagarbha[28]...The interfusion of the true mind that is not subject

---

26 'Crystallisation', to use the alchemical terminology.

27 Peter N. Gregory, *Inquiry into the Origin of Humanity: An Annotated Translation of Tsung-mi's Yüan jen lun with a Modern Commentary,* (University of Hawai'i Press, Honolulu, 1995), 192.

28 Ibid., 193.

> to birth-and-death in such a way that they are neither one nor different is referred as the ālayavijñāna. This consciousness has the aspects both of enlightenment and unenlightenment[29]...Nevertheless, the vital force with which we are endowed, when it is traced all the way back to its origin, is the primal pneuma of the undifferentiated oneness; and the mind that arises, when it is thoroughly investigated all the way back to its source, is the numinous mind of the absolute. In ultimate terms, there is nothing outside of mind. The primal pneuma also comes from the evolution of mind, belongs to the category of the objects that were manifested by the previously evolved consciousness, and is included within the objective aspect of the ālaya[vijñāna]. From the phenomenal appearance of the activation of the very first thought, [the ālayavijñāna] divides into the dichotomy of mind and objects. The mind, having developed from the subtle to the coarse, continues to evolve from false speculation to the generation of karma (as previously set forth). Objects likewise develop from the fine to the crude, continuing to evolve from the transformation [of the ālayavijñāna] into heaven and earth...When karma has ripened, then one receives one's endowment of the two vital forces from one's father and mother, and, when it has interfused with activated consciousness, the human body is completely formed. According to this, the objects that are transformed from consciousness immediately form two divisions: one division is that which interfuses with consciousness to form human beings, while the other division does not interfuse with consciousness and is that which forms heaven and earth, mountains and rivers, and states and towns. The fact that only humans among the three powers [of heaven, earth, and humanity] are spiritual is due to their being fused with spirit. This is precisely what the Buddha meant when he said that the internal four elements and the external four elements are not the same.[30]

However, in all such Buddhist ontology there remains the problem of the origination of ignorance, as Hakeda writes:

> The problem of ignorance remains. It is inherent in the paradox of the tathāgatagarbha, which is pure and yet appears to be defiled, a paradox that, short of enlightenment, remains a mystery that must be accepted on faith. The problem becomes even more intractable

29 Ibid., 194.

30 Ibid., 205-206.

> with the recasting of the tathāgatagarbha into a monistic ontology in the *Awakening of Faith*, where it takes on the force of the analogous problem of theodicy in the Western religions.[31]

This is a problem that hopefully has been clarified in the present accounting of the origins of a world-sphere. It necessitates the supporting ontology presented in earlier volumes of this series regarding the *tathāgatagarbha*. It is immaterial if the doctrine manifests in the form of a theodicy, or takes the semblance of a theistic idealism, such as that presented concerning the term Logos. What matters is that the truth—of the nature of appearing phenomena from first principles and of the progress to enlightenment—is firmly set upon a logical foundation.

The development of a human mind is similar to the early formation of an earth sphere, as described by scientists. First we have the coalescing of primordial substance (*citta*) into a sphere of activity in such a way that a pervasive Fire is generated. In the case of the earth we have the agglomeration of myriad primordial dust particles, planetary debris, and comets into a form able to produce a coherent fiery planetary sphere. Pressure exerted by the force of gravity then produces a central sphere of molten iron and lava long after the crust cools. In the case of the mind we have the coalescing pressure of the inherent organisational tendency of *citta,* where a myriad minute images and desire-impulses come together in an organised form (in the primitive animal-man) that will ignite the Fires of mind.[32]

The vibrancy of the Fires intensify as the quality of thoughts improve. Through the generation of the will throughout the process of cyclic rebirth and the effect of the laws of *karma,* the *saṃskāras* are transformed into stable enlightenment attributes. This story is well known in terms of the ramifications of the Buddha's Four Noble Truths and Eightfold Path. The phenomena of strong magnetism and plate tectonics is produced by natural movement of the internal fires (lava) of the earth that obey the laws of gravity and thermodynamics.

31 Ibid., 196. See also Yoshito S. Hakeda, *The Awakening of Faith Attributed to Aśvaghosha,* (New York, Columbia University Press, 1990).

32 The *citta* now has this tendency because it is imbued with the *jīva* of the overshadowing Buddha.

This is essential for the well-being and evolutionary process of the entire biosphere of the earth. Similarly, the organised movement of *citta* produces the 'magnetic' quality of thoughts to attract similar thoughts. Also, the thoughts accrue an evolutionary tendency as they recycle themselves so as to give birth to new ideas. *Saṃskāras* of past thoughts come to the surface at the appropriate karmic situation. These thoughts are then adapted in some way by a person, producing further karmic pressure for renewal of the adapted thought in the future. Overall the process of repetition is progressive, the thoughts thus gradually become refined and elevated. The process in evolution produces cyclic appearance and disappearances of different categories of Life. The process progresses, culminating in the appearance of a human kingdom and its slow momentum towards liberation. The growing pressure of intensified thoughts helps quicken such progress.

The earth revolves around a central sun, producing the major cyclic changes (seasons), and vitalises the planet with the light and warmth that allows Life to evolve as it does. Similarly, the purpose of the entire consciousness-stream that is the human mind is directed by the Sambhogakāya Flower, which impresses it with all vital revelations needed for its evolving Life and eventual enlightenment. Opposing this is the predilection for the desire principle to attach itself to transitory phenomena. Pain and suffering ensues, teaching consciousness what not to do, and so it progresses through continuous changing attitudes. The impurities of the *samalā tathatā* thus gradually come to be eliminated and the Life that is the hidden Buddha is revealed.

Once the Ādi Buddha's Mind has organised the basic substance of chaos into the form of a world sphere then his compassion has set the course of motion of everything within that sphere to evolve, coming to utilise the *citta*, and then experience the Void. The Void is experienced as a hiatus between cycles of circumscribed conscious activity. (*Maṇḍalas* of realisation utilising the *vijñānas,* which have developed from elementary *citta.)* It represents the unbounded pathway to the experience of the Buddha Mind, the 'boundless all'.[33] *Saṃsāra* can thus be established as a zone of chaotic experience that must

33 A phrase borrowed from H.P. Blavatsky's *The Secret Doctrine,* (Theosophical Publishing House, Adyar, 1971), Vol. 1, 113.

become perfectly organised in a comprehensible way by *manas*. It represents a mode or pathway that will be integrated as part of the normal constitution of a Buddha-Mind in time, once the chaos that represents primordial *citta* has been transformed and transmuted by the activity of Mind. *Citta* then becomes highly organised, energised, made potent, clarified, and elevated into a higher stratum of lighted substance, that of the Clear Light, the basis for the type of Mind known as *dharmakāya* or *dharmatā*.

At the beginning of time the Ādi Buddha forms spheres of existence interrelating the Void (*śūnyatā*) and *saṃsāra*. Pathways are created between the Void Elements that are *bījas* of future atoms and the elementary *citta* that clothe these *bījas* with form. This allows the progressive growth of sentient organisms of varying capacities, and eventually units of intelligent expression. In this way the evolutionary scale of events matures.

The *citta* naturally comes to be organised into five grades, which can be denoted by the terms conditioning the evolution of the world of form:

1. *Movement*, which produces the expansion of any experiential zone. This effects the generation of the sense of hearing sounds that come as a consequence of the movement of forms.
2. *Friction*, being a term used for the generalised effect of the resistance between corporeal entities as they physically interact and endeavour to move past each other. Friction is here represented as the natural resistance of one form of matter towards further growth as it interacts with the physicality of another organism. This produces a natural lethargy, opposition, antagonism, or slow growth at the beginning of any evolutionary cycle. The sense of touch evolves as a consequence of the experiential reaction of that which is contacted. In later development many forms of resistance are eliminated because of the development of the flow of integrated sentience, and then of conscious adaptation to all of the adverse attributes of *saṃsāra*.
3. *Heat*, or an engendering of energy fields, which is the effect of the friction or resistance between two physical entities attracted to or interrelating with each other. There is also the effect of the sustained motion of the internal atomic structure or component parts

of the entity concerned. A sustainable internal warmth, inherent vitality, then becomes an essential condition of all living *maṇḍalas.* Eventually (*manasic*) fire is generated. This then becomes the basis for the evolution of the sense of sight as a consequence of the generation of visual sensations of knowable things. Light illuminates substance when the internal heat of the entity becomes great enough to self-ignite. A radiant awakening of consciousness is thereby generated in order to see further into the darkness of what is not yet revealed, to perceive the path that once was, and to generate the prescience to know what is to be. The flooding of the universe with light allowed the evolution of the eye sense-perceptors as a necessary prerequisite to develop intelligence. From this perspective sight is the most important of the senses, because the mind visualises as it thinks. The mind's most valuable asset is the creation of images of all types, via which it makes logical deductions. This function is based upon its ability to engender light.

4. *Assimilation* of the gain of what was contacted and experienced, producing a consequent reaction or adjustment to the experience. This develops the sense of taste, wherein the assimilated experiences are cognised and digested. Consequently, awareness can be developed as to the next step forward, generally as the result of many subtle discernments (tastes) having been made upon the banquet of Life. Sentience, and then consciousness have been procured via organisms whereby all experiences can be appropriated and thoroughly determined for what they mean or where they lead to. In the case of sentience, instinct produces pre-determined Life patterns, to which the animal Life adapts and finally manifests competitive actions that allow it to break free from the bonds of the instinctive push. It then incarnates into a more advanced Life form, and so the cycles of adaptive, assimilative experience develop, until finally the human stage is reached and the light of reason is possible.

5. *Progressive growth,* the intensification and expansion of the Light to penetrate the bounds of everything sustained by the 'boundless all'. The sense of smell develops in order to experience the subtlest forms of energy (aromas) produced. This can be seen in the quest for increasingly refined experience, and eventual liberation from

affiliation with limiting, restrictive substance. This happens through the transformation of the substance of mind so that it manifests a pristine limitless expanse of cognition, for which we use such terms as 'Clear Light' and 'luminosity' to describe. The five Void Elements are then revealed as pathways to the liberated realms via the medium of the developed wisdoms of the five Dhyāni Buddhas.

The Ādi Buddha expresses these five stages upon all levels of the established *maṇḍala* via the agency of five Entities to appropriately sow, regulate, and deal with the consequences of this pentad of evolutionary expression. These are the five Dhyāni Buddhas, with their corresponding Wisdoms manifesting in reverse order. Thus,

1. Amoghasiddhi's All-accomplishing Wisdom helps to set the motion of all things into effect, so that the eventual gain in terms of 'accomplishing wisdom' can be reaped.
2. Ratnasambhava's Equalising Wisdom mitigates the worst effects of the friction (strife, conflict, antagonism) caused when relatively mentally lethargic and powerful forces meet.
3. Amitābha's Discriminating Inner Vision properly utilises the resultant *manasic* Fire so that it produces incrementally greater wisdom throughout the course of evolution.
4. Akṣobhya's Mirror-like Wisdom works to ensure that the light that is generated becomes increasingly clear, allowing subtle discernments to be made that reflect the intensity and quality of that observed in the higher strata of being/non-being. *Saṃskāras* are transformed into light so that the radiance of the Clear Light of the Void remains.
5. Vairocana's Dharmadhātu Wisdom then ensures that growth of the entire *maṇḍala* of Life is in accordance with the *dharmakāyic* prototype.

The Void between understanding and non-understanding

The way of experiential growth previously outlined, is programmed to produce intelligence, while the effects of the five Jinas is to assist the consciousness leap for humans between the lower mind into that which is abstracted and non-reified. Only a refined mind can perceive the non-chaotic fundamental nature of Mind, and make the challenge to access the Void. Its enlightened stance can hold all former experience *in situ*, and thus can try to describe this experience to other minds. Words however fail to properly translate what has been experienced. The concrete, lower mind does not have the mechanism for the comprehension of subtle abstractions such as the perception of emptiness. There are no pathways to such experience in the lower realms, but there are pathways to abstraction and refinement in consciousness.

The gap between divine Reason (revelatory understanding) and non-understanding is filled through slow incremental evolutionary growth of *citta* so that there are eventually the five attributes of mind earlier defined*: citta, vijñāna, manovijñāna, manas, and ālayavijñāna. Cittavṛtti* then fills the space between any opposites of thought. (Going from the largest to the smallest levels of thinking in the case of 'divine Reason'.) The process involves comparison, identifying what something is in relation to other similar objects. The unknown is then known through the example of comparison with what is familiar. Clearly, failing to identify with future possibilities because of ignorance will not help divine Reason to eventuate. Instead it results in the repetition of cycles of ignorant reaction, repeating until eventually valuable experience is assimilated. This involves the painful process of enforced evolution by means of karmic selectivity. The overseeing principle (the *tathāgatagarbha*) directs *karma* in a progressive manner so that ignorance is eventually overcome.

If one is clearly unenlightened, how then can one understand what exists between appearing opposites? The evolution of wisdom eliminates the gulf that lies between an understanding and a non-understanding of things. The development of levels of intelligence on the way to wisdom circumscribes rings of mind around concepts that are void (of intrinsic value) but which are not the Void. These rings are 'bubbles' or mental images in spheres of non-understanding. As consciousness expands so a 'bubble' is incrementally made to grow in size and often burst the limitations of others to include them in its sphere of containment. Eventually one form remains, which distinguishes consciousness from the Void. Pathways are established that pierce the boundaries between consciousness and the Void. When these spheres of limitation have broken down completely the person is considered 'liberated'.

It is not possible to understand the Void unless one is there, and this necessitates enlightenment. If one doesn't understand the Void they are ignorant, if one believes they understand the Void, there exists the thrall of illusion. The mind always works with analogical processes, relating one thing to another when processing data of any kind. This allows things to be named, categorised, understood and to form a picture of whatever it is trying to analyse or observe. The mind cannot think adequately about things without a systematic, analytical approach. Such an approach merely produces the 'bubbles' of mentation explained above, which are not the Void.

Whether there is ignorance or the comprehension of things, the activity of mind is implied. From one perspective, the Void exists in the spaces where such action is absent because the activity itself is a definition of *saṃsāra*. When activity ceases *saṃsāra* is revealed to be Void. This is the reason why Nāgārjuna said *saṃsāra* and *nirvāṇa* are equable. The pacification or elimination of thoughts, however, does not automatically produce the condition of the Void, because as one peels back the layers of *cittavṛtti* then the potency of the energy of thought increases, as it contacts the more refined unreified strata of ideation that have emanated from the *dharmakāya*. The Mind inevitably contacts that vast well of energy that caused the entire *maṇḍala* of the world-play established by the Ādi Buddha. The mind must be prepared to withstand this potent dynamo if there is any chance of the revelation of what is Void. This necessitates an aeonic progress of the development and refinement of mind. Finally after a sufficient potency (specific gravity) of mind has been developed, a pacifying of mental activity is needed that allows the *antaḥkaraṇa* to be built to reveal what Mind veils. Otherwise any senile, 'mindless' individual, can by the definition of having 'no thoughts' be considered to reside in the Void. There may indeed be a void of thoughts, or thinking structure, but such a void is a retrogressive hiatus in the progress of evolution, relegating such a one to the state of reverting back to elementary *citta*. Practitioners should beware of falling into the trap of mindlessness, thinking that somehow this equates with *śūnyatā*.

The physical domain is literally a concretion of energy sources derived from higher planes of perception. Its energy quotient is therefore sluggish when compared to that associated with the non-physical. The higher the plane of perception one can contact, the more intense the energy to be withstood. This is an esoteric fact that all who teach the art of meditation must take into account when instructing their students, if enlightenment is to be the goal.

Knowledge of the Void is only another concept that in itself occludes experience of the Void. Similarly, the wilful (mentalistic) process of holding thoughts at bay, or utilising the mind to try to eliminate them is counter-productive. Therefore pathways to the Void are not found through either understanding or ignorance, but when all such *manasic* activity ceases. Then the 'spaces' reveal themselves. They function to unravel the *saṃskāras* of mind.

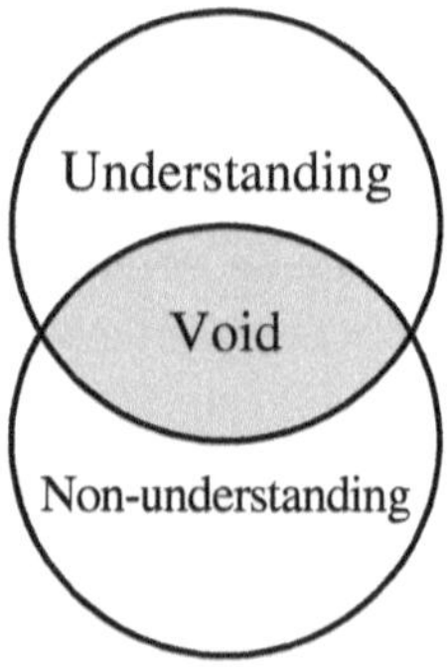

Figure 10. Understanding/Non-understanding

How is it possible to develop an experience of the Void when the way lies directly between non-understanding and understanding? This is the main problem that confronts the practitioner, who is so focussed upon the conceptualisations of attainment that the true picture is not perceived. Elimination of all forms of conceptualisation must therefore be taught to such a person. The mind then comes to reside in its natural (unmodified) state, it simply is, and then it is said by some commentators that this is all there is to enlightenment. This is, however, a simplistic view, as has already been explained above, because of the necessity of handling energy dynamics.

The Void can be seen as an illusion from the perspective of when there is a void of thinking capacity, known as ignorance. Ignorance then reigns supreme and has no conception of anything other than what 'it' knows. From another angle we can have the space that is void of all discernible characteristics, which is the basis for enlightenment. We should note here that there are sixteen types of *śūnyatā,* listed in Mahāyāna texts, as referred to in my book on *karma:*

> In the literature of the Mādhyamika (cf., Candrakīrit's *Madhyamakāvatarā*) there are said to be sixteen types of emptiness, which are really negations based on the categories of phenomena. These are said to be: 1. Emptiness of the internal. 2. Emptiness of the external. 3. Emptiness of both internal and external. 4. Emptiness of emptiness. 5. Emptiness of the vast. 6. Emptiness of the ultimate. 7. Emptiness of the produced. 8. Emptiness of the unproduced. 9. Emptiness of the extremes. 10. Emptiness of the without beginning and without end. 11. Emptiness of that which is not to be abandoned. 12. Emptiness of self-identity. 13. Emptiness of all things. 14. Emptiness of self-defining characteristics. 15. Emptiness of the non-referential. 16. Emptiness of the absence of substantiality.[34]

From the angle of the true dynamics of the Void, it manifests as illumined energy piercing through the subjective reality to change the view of ignorance. The Void is a reality upholding the substratum of *saṃsāra*. It can therefore be said to be that from which *saṃsāra* (as a bounded sphere of accomplishment) emanates, but is itself 'void of characteristics', as far as *saṃsāra* is concerned. When those in *saṃsāra* try to view the Void all they see is a mirror, reflecting an image of what they wish to see, of whatever image is in their minds. Thus to them the Void is an enigma. The way to experience the Void, therefore, is to utterly transmute all mental concepts, and image-making tendencies, through continually subtler refinement until what is left is that which is void of all these things. This is the basis of reality. Reality is an energy

---

34 Bodo Balsys, *Karma and the Rebirth of Consciousness,* (Munshiram Manoharlal, Delhi, 2006), 39. Adapted from Graham Coleman, ed., *The Handbook of Tibetan Buddhism* (Rupa & Co., New Delhi, 1995). Other sources quote 18 emptinesses, as listed, for instance, on 204-205 of Jeffrey Hopkins' book *Meditation on Emptiness* (Wisdom Publications, London, 1983).

field (a flux) that is contactable by intensely luminous clarified thought, as it is then of like nature to that field.

The illusional void that is ignorant thinking on the other hand can be easily determined because it lacks Love. Such a quality as Love is integral to the Void because it interrelates all things, which also is a prime attribute of this energy of Love. Love needs to be developed to transmute the illusional void through revelatory knowledge. Because the world-sphere has been constructed via the compassionate Ideation of a Logos, that Love permeates (directs) the all that is. It is that which binds all separated and separative *manasic* particulates into oneness (the Void). It is therefore the mode of union for various separations between things that also includes the spaces between those 'things'. All things (that which is and that which is not) can therefore be comprehended in Love. The expression of this Love is termed *bodhicitta* in Buddhism, because it also implicates integration with the primeval mental substance (*citta*) that is carried forth from former aeonic epochs of *manasic* evolution.

Knowledge alone produces separation and segregation, which is the opposing force to Love, thus the Void cannot be experienced or understood through knowledge. Therefore we can see that the extent of one's knowledgeable universe is limited to the degree of lack of Love present. Knowledge and Love together produce wisdom (via abstracted, comprehensive reason), the attainment of which is the purpose of human evolution. Only through wisdom can liberation from the bonds of *saṃsāra* be attained, and the links to the Void begin to be projected. The progress of wisdom leads eventually to that which is beyond the Void. When *antaḥkaraṇas* (consciousness-links) begin to pierce through the veil of the mirror which has the Void as its basis, consciousness has completely turned about in its focus, away from *saṃsāra* and to the realm of (ultimate) causes; to cosmos. The Void is the 'platform' upon which the accomplished One who is fully imbued with Love-Wisdom stands.

When we look to the process that constitutes the phenomenon of evolutionary Life we can look to seven key terms: chaos, Love, order (structured *maṇḍalas*), neither structured nor unstructured order, *karma*, unstructured structured order, and cosmos.

1. *Chaos* has been described above. It refers to the elementary substance found at the beginning of time. This is the basis of the state

broadly described as ignorance. It is that from which all phenomena originates, and is ordered in space by the basic *citta* that is the inherent sentience of the realms of Life below the human.

2. The *Love* that is spoken of here is an expression of the Tathāgata whose Mind-structure permeates all that is and is not, and who thereby produces the *vāsanā*[35] to push the entire evolutionary play along the road towards the gaining of liberation from the thraldom of *saṃsāra* via *bodhicitta*. This instigates a corresponding development of Love by the minds that have evolved from the originating chaotic *citta*. This Love and the consequent wisdom that is evoked leads them to liberative bliss, because their purpose is to resolve all forms of chaos and chaotic action (forms of ignorance) into a unity. Unity represents the Oneness gained through the fusion of the Wisdoms of the five Dhyāni Buddhas. These are the most refined, abstracted, and broadened forms of the five sense-consciousnesses. 'Broadened' here means the expansion of consciousness to include the way of the working or Thinking of the cosmic Mind of a Tathāgata.
3. *Order* refers to created structure, the *maṇḍalas* delineating the forms within *saṃsāra*. This comes as a consequence of the development of intelligence, the *manovijñāna* described earlier. The *devas* are the bearers of this principle for all of Nature, thus we get the perfected structural ordering of things wherever we look at the great Mother's purpose. Humanity comes to develop it in its masculine wilful aspect. As a consequence, theirs is a shortcut to liberation, via the added *karmic* qualification of overcoming the pain and suffering that ensues when people's wills oppose that of the general trend of Nature's evolutionary push.
4. *Neither structured nor unstructured order* refers to *śūnyatā*. This means that *śūnyatā* is 'ordered' in that it obeys certain laws that accommodate the nature of the enlightened Mind, but is neither

35 *Vāsanā* (Tib. bag chags): karmic predisposition driving the *saṃskāras* to come to the surface of consciousness. Potency, a driving force of *karma* and consciousness (*citta*), said to be generated or accumulated from within the *ālayavijñāna*. Technically, the *saṃskāras* are stored in the *chakras*, and *vāsanā* is the force that drives these karmic aggregates to fruition in *saṃsāra*.

structured nor unstructured as far as its natural expression is concerned. It has been 'organised' to accommodate the Ādi Buddha's *maṇḍalic* purpose, yet it is not possible for one to see either structure or non-structure in that which is Void.

5. *Karma* is that which works to resolve all forms of disharmony that have emerged within the structured and ordered universe of Nature's domains into a harmonious universality. It specifically affects the forms of chaos caused by the little wills that represent the personal-I's working, according to their own separative agendas, and resolves the chaotic into harmonious accord. For this reason *karma* is an expression of the law of Love.
6. *Unstructured structured order* refers to the Minds of the Jinas working from the *dharmakāya*. There is a *maṇḍalic* structure that interrelates all such liberated Minds into an integrated pattern of *dharma*, with which they work to impress all interrelated lives evolving in their auric spheres.[36] However, they do not adhere to the fabrications of the concrete mind; they work effortlessly and spontaneously with the *mahāmudrā*[37] in accordance with the naturalness of the liberated sphere to which they belong. Therefore there are no concretions or rigid 'structures' to which they adhere.
7. *Cosmos* refers to the exalted realms, the *citta* dust and stellar systems governed by Regents of cosmic Mind, unfathomable to most minds, of which the Jinas are examples, and within which they develop further as Logoi and great cosmic Entities (Principles). They can

---

36 These may be world spheres, but not necessarily so. Nevertheless, *maṇḍalas* of purpose exist for many purposes, all exhibiting hierarchical structures.

37 *Mahāmudrā* (Tib. phyag rgya chen po): Literally 'great seal'. The Great Symbol, referring to the state of the attainment of Buddhahood. It is a *'mudra'* ('hand-gesture' signifying some accomplishment) because realisation of the three bodies of a Buddha in one is sealed in supreme unchanging bliss. It involves realisation of enlightenment in one lifetime through the 'seal' that integrates the masculine compassion with the feminine wisdom aspect. In the Kagyu tradition it denotes the experiential attainment of the Buddha-Mind. The absoluteness of being/non-being, which unites all duality, male and female into a unity, completeness. This Symbol can be depicted as the cypher zero, and involves the sum of the entire cause-effect world play, as it impresses itself upon consciousness.

also become Avatars[38] for future world cycles in epochs unknown, as part of the great continuum of unlimited Life beyond the confines of formed space.

The five grades of *citta* (on page 85) are organised into the terms conditioning the evolution of the world of form, plus the seven key terms conditioning the phenomenon of evolutionary Life (above), and effectively constitute the first principles of the twelve petals of the Heart lotus. The 'first principles' are the elementary qualities of the *prāṇas* that the Heart centre channels. These are needed to establish the Heart as the central factor of the Life of any multicellular organism, or *maṇḍala* of expression. The petals expressing *prāṇas* of the 'five grades of *citta*' can be considered non-sacred.[39] Their function is to transmute the gain of the sense-consciousnesses into enlightenment attributes. The remaining seven petals are considered 'sacred' because they channel the *prāṇas* external to the incarnating unit. They deal with the externalised *maṇḍalas* that are integral to the dynamism sustaining the cosmos. The Head centre is also essentially a twelve-petalled lotus, capable of dealing with the interconnected *prāṇas* associated with this external *maṇḍala* in full.

The dynamics of the Void exist in the cosmos. It appears 'Void' to human units ensconced in empirical minds, however, in the domains of liberated Beings it possesses a certain substantiality. There it can be considered the higher transmuted correspondence of our etheric body that supports the entire *nāḍī* system. Previously the five Void Elements were called attributes of the Void, and these Void Elements are the elementary (most basic) form of substance of the *prāṇas* that flow upon *dharmakāyic* domains. The Void is thus the energy Body wherein exist the *nāḍīs,* the pathways of expression from Logos to Logos and to all of

---

38 An Avatar is one who 'descends from above'. A divine Incarnation. An Avatar incarnates into a form for the purpose of salvage and service, but gains nothing 'personally' from that act of sacrifice and limitation, having long since transcended the related state of evolution into which it incarnates. From the Sanskrit roots, *ava,* to come down, or become less, and *tri,* meaning to cross over a river, to fulfil, save, etc.

39 These five non-sacred petals of the Heart centre were described in Volume 3, chapter 2, of this series.

the Flowers (*chakras*) of their combined interrelationships. The *prāṇas* that concern us here are direct expressions of the Wisdoms of the five Dhyāni Buddhas, in accordance with whatever combination of them (or their further developed expressions) are most emphasised by any Logos. The *prāṇas* exist also along Ray lines.

The *nāḍīs* project the subjective reality of *śūnyatā* to systems resoundingly proclaiming the Love of a Tathāgata. However, through these *nāḍīs* may also manifest darkened auric colourings of a basic lack of such Love being expressed.[40] Therein is seen the focus of cosmic need. Whenever a Buddha-field is established, through the agglomeration of elementary *citta*, bringing about an entire world-play, as outlined above, then we have the appearance of developing *saṃskāras* for the Logoi concerned. Streams of lives evolve, each with different characteristics, and eventually a human kingdom, wherein we have many categories of consciousness-streams, all developing interrelated and integrated colourings and attributes. The Fiery *saṃskāras* of a Logos are constituted of the manasic currents of any human civilisation. Such a One is karmically bound to those human lives for the duration that they manifest *cittavṛtti*. The Logos must bring all such units to liberation. The aeons of time this takes represents the Compassion of such a One.

The structure of cellular units

In relation to the structured unit (such as a human consciousness), the whole *maṇḍala* seems unobstructed. In relation to the structure of the whole, the small seems inconsequential: the smaller the structure the more expendable it appears to the larger encompassing mass. Therefore it is impermanent in relation to that encompassing whole; that whole can exist without any particular small life. That is a reason why a minute life form is relatively impermanent with respect to the larger all-encompassing one. As you observe the gradations of consciousness from the smaller unit to that of the Logos (of which the smaller is a part), you observe that relative impermanence is metered out according to the respective size (sentience or consciousness-space) of these gradations.

40 There are sources of sickness, disease and death, and emanations of cosmic evil at this level that also could be analysed, but which shall not be considered here.

A question that can be asked is 'Why do you need the smaller cells when the larger unities appear to suffice?' Obviously the larger unities are constituted of a myriad of smaller ones, that together form organelles and organs in the larger body. These organelles do matter, but the functioning of the larger unities is not impaired significantly in the breakdown or death of any small entity constituting an organ. Structural coherence necessitates many building blocks, but the structure is sound because it is built upon the foundation of resonant, resilient scaffolding that can withstand the removal of (many) blocks.

It is necessary to take such considerations into account because in every evolutionary schema established by a Logos or Thinker tactical adversity must be included in the planning. If certain elements of a *maṇḍala* fail their function it will not overtly affect the final outcome if the planning is well formulated. The human body, for instance, has inbuilt safeguards to deal with factors of sickness and disease-bearing organisms. One may succumb to such effects, but generally the body knows how to compensate for the effects or to eliminate the adversity. Similarly, a Logos has compensatory mechanisms in place for the effects of self-willed, recalcitrant, separative minds that refuse to evolve, that manifest predatory assaults against the health of the general *maṇḍala*. To such antagonistic adversaries we provide the collective term 'dark brotherhood'.

Our concepts of time are analogical, requiring a relationship between the small and large. The smaller cells constitute the fabric of being of the greater entity in the way graduations of time establish themselves as mind comes to evolve. The smaller forms of sentience that are incorporated within the greater body of manifestation race through many cycles of activity, thus through apparently far faster times zones for that mind, like the second hand of a clock with respect to the hour hand.[41]

What this effectively means is that whilst the vaster Mind is pursuing what represents a normal life-span to it, the smaller unit incorporated as part of that consciousness-space may race through many incarnations

41 The term 'apparently' is used here because one could argue whether a sentient entity registers time at all, or if it did, one must seek out the form of bio-clock it responds to.

of activity. Myriads are the thoughts that cycle and recycle through a human mind during the course of a life, for instance. Important thoughts may have a longevity, other trivial thoughts may vanish in seconds. Time appears to slow down as the cycles of active manifestation become vaster. This may be elaborated with respect to a human life span in relation to that of a Sambhogakāya Flower, and the life-span of such a Flower with respect to a Logoic appearance in a world-sphere.[42] Everything is relative.

We possess the cells of our body (a myriad of small unities) because *we have evolved them* as our consciousness has been reborn into and out of one vehicle after another. These minute sentiencies are karmically tied to us. We cannot appropriate any particular form without the little lives with whom we have such *karma*. Once in the far-distant past our state of awareness was limited to what was developed by a cell: such a form of 'cellular consciousness', or sentience, was the limit to our sphere of attainment. We existed as unicellular organisms and had to experience everything that this cellular world could offer before evolving out of it to include greater systems of awareness (sentience states). Through aeons of evolutionary development our cellular awareness became multicellular, inclusive of the awareness-state of organs, which later developed into the I-concept of a normally thinking human.

As we grew out of a lesser state of sentience so we expanded with respect to cellular numbers, developing more intricate systems of cells to thereby experience the nature of the external universe. (Hence also the evolutionary progress through many categories of the animal kingdom.) As we evolved consciousness so our cells grew with us, therefore they are directly *saṃskārically* and karmically related. These cells are part of our intrinsic constitution. The *karma* persists with every change or modification that consciousness makes. Even a 'thus gone one' (Buddha) is not freed from his karmic connections with their correspondences to him, though he is freed from karmic ties to this earth sphere. Because of such karmic ties we can 'possess' and utilise them as a mechanism to bear our conscious experience in the natural world. The smaller unities that we once embodied have evolved to become organs, with a

42 For further insights into the nature of time see Volume 2, chapter 11, of this series, 'The Examination of Time in the *Mūlamaddhyamakakārikā*'.

much more expanded animal-like sentience, and so forth.

When we become a Logos, these cellular unities will also have expanded in awareness to become the *tathāgatagarbhas* (Buddha-embryos). The Sambhogakāya Flowers (Buddha-embryos) demonstrate (masculine) *piṇgalā* qualities and *ḍākinīs* demonstrate (feminine) *iḍā* qualities. Together they will constitute our Buddha-fields and work for the enlightenment and liberation of many units of consciousness. So the story develops, from the originating speck of a chaotic dust particle to a Buddha-Mind. Thus it is also possible to unfold *siddhis* via meditative awareness, as we learn to properly control the sentience of the cellular constitution of our forms, and to perfectly master the interrelated *prāṇas* of their tiny *nāḍīs* in such a way that the energy of the void spaces between each tiny form is consciously utilised. The applicable *prāṇas* of the Void Elements can then be directly utilised. Because of the direct karmic connection with these cells, all forms of mastery can be demonstrated as shown in the Tantric texts, such as levitation and the transmutation of substance. Many seeds for meditative revelation are provided in the above statements.

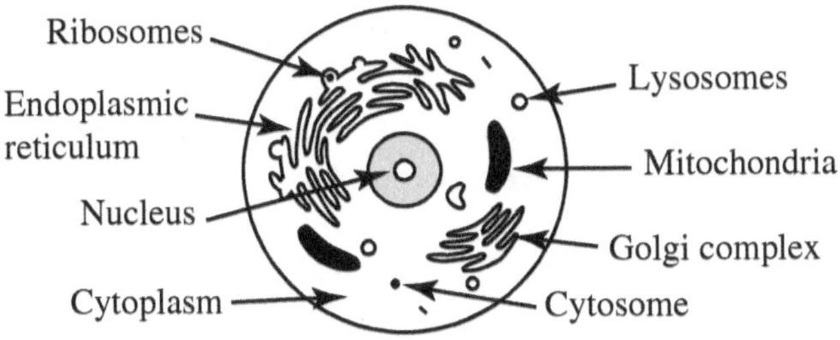

Figure 11. The constitution of an animal cell

Figure 11 presents a basic pictorial representation of the constitution of an animal cell. Here we will find that the originating chaos has become coherent and highly organised. It contains a nucleus, which governs the entire structural evolution of the cell as a unit and contains the genetic material responsible for its continuity, and rebirth into new forms. The nucleus will evolve over time into a human brain and its intellect, the central integrating structure of a person. The sphere that enclosed the original chaos has evolved into the outer cellular membrane, containing the sense-perceptors, which are responsible for communication with the external world of other cells.[43] Its interchange with the Airy world (the exchange of gases) relates inevitably to the ability of the human consciousness to exchange ideas with others, and eventually of the consciousness of a person to transfer from mind to *śūnyatā*.

The Golgi complex, ribosomes, mitochondria etc., eventually evolve into the internal organs and *chakras* of a person's form, and also become the basis for the sense-perceptors and organs that allow the expression of the *vijñānas*. Only the briefest outline shall be presented below.

The *nucleus* of the cell eventually evolves into the Head centre, being the central organisational structure of the cell.

The *cytoplasm* is the material enclosed by the cell's membrane, and therefore contains all of the channels of nutrients and lines of communication. This will later evolve into the functioning of the vascular and nervous system in a human, and have their subjective basis in the function of the Heart centre and the *nāḍī* system.

Lysosomes contain enzymes that break down many substances. They eventually evolve physically into the human glandular system, and the function develops into the Ājñā centre, with its ability to peer into all aspects of the body corporeal, to 'digest' the 'substances' (information) obtained.

The *ribosomes* are concerned with the manufacture of proteins, which are the basic structural component of our bodies. These eventually form the muscular and bony structure of the body. This also relates to the ability of the Throat centre to utter sounds and to name, being the basic structural aspect of the thinking process that is the leitmotiv of the average human unit. This function delineates a person's strength and stature in human societies.

The *Golgi* complex processes proteins and other substances produced in the cell. This will eventually evolve into the human digestive system. The processing of all elements of the human psyche (emotionalities, desire-mind attributes) is also a function of the Solar Plexus centre, which evolves as the subjective organ controlling all digestive activities.

The *endoplasmic reticulum* is a complex network of membranes

---

43 Inevitably the correspondence will also be found to include the civilisations of humans, and upon a higher level, the relationships on the realm of the Sambhogakāya Flower.

that store proteins and help channel substances to various organs. This will eventually evolve into the liver and spleen in the human unit. This function is developed by the Inner Round of *chakras*, with the Splenic centre being the central organ of distribution of the related *prāṇas*. This *chakra* stores *prāṇa* and channels vitality to the various organs in the body, specifically via the Solar Plexus centre.

Mitochondria are the power plants of the cell. Essentially this expression transmogrifies into the future sex functions of the human unit, the ability to reproduce the species, as well as the self-defensive mechanism of the person, the over-all life-sustaining capacity. This function is an expression of the Sacral centre, which regulates the internal heat of the system and channels the principle of desire that empowers most activities of the personal-I.

The function of the Base of the Spine centre is expressed in the overall structure of the cell and the various cellular membranes that keep the form intact as a unit.

The *chakras*, consciousness, and the attributes of mind

There are two ways of listing the main attributes of consciousness; that relating to the lower reflexes of the Wisdoms of the five Jinas, and that depicted in terms of the 'eight consciousnesses' of the Buddhist Yogācāra philosophy. The *prāṇas* of all these attributes are developed and channelled by the *chakras*. In this respect the *maṇḍala* of the *chakras* are changed to accommodate both views. First we look to the integration of the main *chakras* into a listing of five, the standard typology given in Tibetan texts. The reason for this is first to accommodate the philosophy of the five Wisdoms into the sum of manifestation. Here we see that of the seven main *chakras*, the Head and Ājñā centres form an overlapping integrity, similarly with the lowest two, the Base of the Spine and Sacral centres. This provides the necessary five from which the entire philosophy can proceed. With respect to the 'eight consciousnesses' we add the superimposed Splenic centre to the main seven. (These centres are labelled Splenic centre I and Splenic centre II in Volume 3, chapter 3, of this series.) As a unit the Splenic centres manifest the power of a major centre.

With respect to the first group of five we have:

1. The *Base of the Spine/Sacral* centre develops the sense of *hearing* of physical sounds, a function of the ability of all membranes to communicate with agents external to them.
2. The *Solar Plexus* centre develops the sense of *touch*, which is really the expression of our emotional interrelationships, the desire to communicate with the external 'other'.
3. The *Throat* centre develops the sense of *sight*, which helps to directly build the basic 'structural component' of our thinking processes.
4. The *Heart* centre develops the sense of *taste*, in order to experience the many refined discriminative discernments available to consciousness.
5. The *Head/Ājñā* centre combination develops the sense of *smell*, allowing the very subtle odoriferous impressions to uplift consciousness to the most lofty spaces conveyable by the *prāṇas* that this centre is responsible for processing.

With respect to the 'eight consciousnesses':

1. As above, the *Base of the Spine* centre develops the sense of *hearing.*
2. The *Sacral* centre is associated with the sense of *touch* because it is the conveyor of the *prāṇas,* thus it governs the output of the entire *nāḍī* system. This system then 'touches' all of the centres in the body via the *prāṇas* in order to gain the impressions contained in them. This allows the right mix of *prāṇas* to be circulated. It should be noted here that the major *prāṇas* conveyed in the *nāḍīs* for the greater part of human evolution are the Watery ones governed by the Solar Plexus centre. We therefore have a correlation between these two second points in both listings.
3. The *Solar Plexus* centre, which is the organ of clairvoyance, finds its functioning in the sense of *sight*. With respect to this, the various attributes of such clairvoyance are developed by most sentient animal species, explaining many of the mysteries of massed animal behaviour. The scientific community must yet recognise such abilities in their analysis of the capacities of the various species,

and when it does so it will cause another major revolution in their understanding of the nature of the evolution of consciousness.

4. The *Splenic* centre attribute is the sense of *taste*, as its function is to subtly discern the true qualities of all of the *prāṇas* that circulate specifically in the centres below the diaphragm. This is an integral part of its function as the 'sewer' of the *nāḍī* system. It must appropriately determine which *prāṇas* can be recycled and which must be discarded from the system. The recirculated *prāṇas* are either sent to the Solar Plexus centre for processing, or upward to the Heart centre via a process of purification of *saṃskāras*. The directing purifying energies that organise the *prāṇas* come from the Heart centre to Splenic centre I. The Heart is thus the ultimate directing organ for all of the *prāṇas* in the body. It is the source of the vital Life (*jīva*) of the entire body.
5. An integral attribute of the *Ājñā* centre then is *smell*. The subtle 'essences' of all the *prāṇas* can be analysed and redistributed according to where they need be by means of the functioning of the 'all seeing eye' that this centre represents.
6. The *Throat* centre governs the development of the 'sixth sense', the *intellect* that coordinates all of the five sense-consciousnesses. It regulates the projection of the Fiery Element throughout the *nāḍīs*.
7. The *Heart* centre directs the way of evolution of the 'defiled mind' (*kliṣṭamanas)* in the body. It presides over the process of its conversion into *bodhicitta*.
8. The thousand petalled Lotus *(Head centre)* is organised in such a way that it facilitates all impressions from the *ālayavijñāna*, and all other sources coming via the abstract Mind.

People often take for granted the evolutionary development of the five senses and intellect. They are 'ours' individually and inadvertently because we have developed them, and communally also, because the cellular unities eventually become highly organised collectively, as everything in Nature does.

Figure 12 is a simplified representation of the relationship of the elements to the expansion of mind. In relation to this Figure we see that the numbers 1 to 5 represent the process of the expansion of the mind, from the central point of relative limitation, to the outer sphere of expansive inclusiveness.

Figure 12. The Mind and the Elements

With respect to this illustration we see that:

1. The central sphere of limitation represents the 'I', self-consciousness. At first its activity is intensely self-focussed, separative, and deluded, but later it ascribes to the natural order of the laws governing its existence. The Earthy Element is developed, wherein responses primarily manifest with respect to the material world of forms and apparent solidity.
2. Here the 'I' sees and interrelates with the small or reflected material universe around itself, its world of cultural values, social ethics, and civilised structures in the nation or tribe of which it is a part. The Watery world of the emotive sense-perceptors are thus developed in conjunction with the constantly mutable field of desire, sensuality and the emotions.
3. The 'I' now perceives the universe in an existential, empirical, ontological, eschatological and heuristic way. The Fiery Element is developed as a zone of residence for and within itself.
4. That which the 'I' perceives as the limit of the structures that contain its evolutionary process, thus the ending of time and space, which

equals the Void, the beyond. The Airy Element is developed as a means to escape from the trammels of the formed world of the mind and the lower sense fields.

5. Here the conceptualisations of the mind come to be transcended with a more embracive visioning that is direct and infallibly correct. It perceives none of the 'things' of the world to be real, because it has identified with a reality formerly considered as indefinable and unknown, stemming from the higher strata of Mind. It is abstracted from these 'things' and yet can see the processes and lines of formation that relate them into structured wholes, *maṇḍala*s of experiential expression. Here the Aetheric Element is developed as a means to Know the meaning of the All.

The *diagonal lines* represent the pathways to the major categories and subsets of the discriminatory mind via the fixed and mutable crosses. It concerns the mode that orders its thinking processes to retrieve information in accordance with the eight natural gates or directions in space.

The mind that can create syllogisms and rationalise all of the vagaries of the universe is fully developed, but needs to gain perceptions beyond intellectualisation. It gleans its picture of the universe, from the other vastly more encompassing 'I's' that it identifies with. When identifying it thus sees two 'I's'; firstly the mind's 'I', the creator of the concepts it possesses, which stores all images. The second 'I' it identifies with concern any of the many unities it views all around it in the natural universe, such as trees, other people, organisations, nations, stars, deities, and Logoi. It collates all of these images into a complete picture, presenting us with a concept of the One, the all-encompassing Deity (or Space). In thus formulating we eventually come to observe the way whereby the qualities of the five Jinas have been developed and that have been expressed in the formed world, subsuming also the structure of consciousness.

Ideas need to be imbibed in thought structures, allowing us to understand the next appropriate steps for any existing system, but can such analysis allow us to prove the nature of enlightenment? How does chaos coexist with order to make an interwoven *maṇḍala?* The strings of concepts making order out of chaos spiral onwards and upwards towards enlightened potential at the event-horizon of future possibilities, or else eventually into the Void. Differing lines of reasoning manifest thus with frequent intervals, or 'spaces' between each next happening, allowing for the rebirthing (a regurgitating or reworking) of former thoughts upon higher cycles. Also, new appearances are staged from a deep reservoir of spaciousness, which though invisible, is actually the source of revelation of the antiquity of Life, of the way it has evolved and to whence it moves.

These forces (consciousness, substance and chaos) are juxtaposed and thrust in relation to each other in the great play of Life. They are thrust into one's awakening as a circus of events, and may ride far off together on the journey to enlightened bliss; for chaos, substance, line, structure, unfolding order is the progress of the sequence of things, the making of all *maṇḍalas*. When directive energy and consciousness are added to the group, then the *chakras* externalise themselves in the great scenario that Nature offers for the formative manifestation of the all.

Everywhere are projected the lines of interrelationship (*nāḍīs*) conveying the substance of forms (*prāṇas*) that will manifest the structures (the Flowers) producing order out of the chaos of undefined *citta*. Different Flowers, of differing hues and sizes, manifest to prove the diversity of Nature, anchoring energy for all the manifold streams of Life. Then the vibrancy of the myriad interrelated lives thrill with the experience of awakening Mind as the *citta* comes to be more organised and strengthened with added qualities through an evolutionary impetus.

The progress of enlightenment

Chaos is noisy substance; order is the rhythmic Voice of the *svabhāvikakāya* (all three bodies) of a Buddha rhyming out the mantric sounds of the evolving lives throughout time. (Each unitary Life has its own integral distinct note in the fabric of space.) Voiceless is the meditating one who listens and comprehends how to sound and thereby control the lives of his/her own *nāḍī* system. They order all forces within that sphere of influence, from squares with rigid lines of relation, to triangles of conscious receptivity, and then to the great arcs of the plenitude of Life. Thus is the *maṇḍalic* structure articulated via the pentads of the creative Minds that build the all, integrating the chaos within their bodies of manifestation, and outputting the sentient forms in all their diversity as the laws of Mind dictate. In serene silence are these laws obeyed and projected to inform the all, with the enlightened presence of the Buddha embodying a planetary or solar system. All the Flowers are aspects of His Solar Plexus unfolding the *prāṇas* of all sentient Life. This is the Inner Round of minor *chakras* unfolding.

The major *chakras* are embodied by major groups of the conscious intelligent lives, human and *deva*, with the *ḍākinīs* (a form of *deva*) being the mediators of the two major streams of lives in the macrocosmic body. (Each such grouping is presided over by a major Bodhisattva or Deva Lord, and is governed by Ray purpose.) The *deva* and human hierarchies are symbolically joined at the hip, through Sacral centre interrelation (as all Life is bound by the sexual impulse). The great bliss of a *mahāsiddha* thus concerns the union and thence fusion between these feminine *iḍā (deva/ḍākinī)* and masculine (human) *piṅgalā* lives in the great Lord's Body. The *suṣumṇā* Fires are the outcome. There we have the Buddha and his Consort coherently joined in their Base centres, awakening the great Fire to sustain all Lives, and emanating their integrated experiential *nirmāṇakāya*[44] voice, resounding the *maṇḍalic* mantric sound as voiceless silence for all but the most discerning of ears. One's Heart can listen to the expression of an all-encompassing Mind![45]

---

44 *Nirmāṇakāya* (Tib. sprul pa'i sku): 'transformation body', the emanation (form) body of a Buddha. One of the three bodies or vestures of a Buddha *(trikāya)*. It is the outer or phenomenal appearance, tangible, and can be contacted in the realms of illusion, the incarnation body. The other two vestures are *dharmakāya* and *sambhogakāya*. In the esoteric doctrine a *nirmāṇakāya* can also be seen as one who has taken the highest Initiation on the earth sphere (the sixth or greater), but instead of travelling upon a cosmic Path still retains a link with the earth Hierarchy. Thus such a one resides in an illusional body of contact within cosmic dense substance.

45 A useful mantra for the practitioner to use with respect to this concept is 'O my Lord, let my Heart listen and so be the expression of thy all-encompassing Mind!' Such a heart-felt invocation is an important method of manifesting a link (*antaḥkaraṇa*) between the meditator's Mind and that of the downward-focussed liberated Ones (gurus) that act as accessories to enlightenment. It represents part of the process on the arc of return that cleanses the karmic slate of the Ādi Buddha as a consequence of having originally formulated the *maṇḍala* of the world-sphere, of which the meditator is a part. Note that English words are used to supplant what in the past would have been Sanskrit or Tibetan syllables to achieve the same purpose. Mantras are useless if not properly comprehended and visualised by the utterer.

We know that the mind discriminates. An overall synopsis of the functioning of the mind is that it discriminatively categorises aggregates of 'finite infinities', plus the various forms of finites. We all order our structured reality in terms of the rational progress of concepts of mind. Each aggregate of mind is a scale by means of which we weigh the specific gravity or worth of each new thought. Each thought is accentuated upon different levels of the scale in accordance with one's opinion of its true value, from minuscule and irrelevant to potently vast and then all-encompassing. New forces of discrimination are continually being used to look into the scales of our minds.

Inevitably the facts that people endeavour to ascertain do contain an assemblage of reality. It is worthy to note that the appearing Deities and Bodhisattvas prefer to teach the minds of those awakening to the reality of the not-self. Defocussing from the concept of 'self' allows one to comprehend, thus to define the formerly indefinable. Also, the Buddha was not silent, he gave an analytical discourse in His intention to help all sentient beings, thus manifesting a teaching methodology whereby all people could be assisted to comprehend the structure of the *maṇḍala* of liberation.

If one is trying to define the indefinable, then any form of definition immediately falls short of the truth, because one cannot immediately visualise the things beyond one's comprehension. These things have yet to be experienced. In trying to transcend the process of defining, whilst endeavouring to retain awareness of the process, this can make one a pedant with respect to the search for enlightenment. The right method in fact becomes a necessity. In finding the middle way between opposites, whenever one is trying to comprehend something one will inevitably come to a zone of inner peace, producing a tranquil harmony in the substance of mind. Then what was formerly not ascertained can be understood in the subtle whisperings of truth that begin to modify the quiescent *citta*. The subtlest breezes of the revelatory thought environment can then be discerned.

One can only say, however, that a thing is either a thing or not a thing, that it is neither a thing nor no-thing, or that it is both these things together, to again invoke the Nāgārjunian *catuṣkoṭi*. Here from the point of view of a visionary whole we have a positive assertion of the way things truly are.

Whether there is an inclination or not to describe the process of definition, the mind will not make a firm distinction between the opposites without viewing vital sources of information, of aspects of what it regards as truth. It might however include only part of the whole picture, the subsets of a process of definition. Here we have the truth of many streams of Buddhist dialectics that focus upon the process of enlightenment. This process is a highly refined and selective procedure.

One can conceive of enlightenment in finite terms, because the first port of call for the process is the *tathāgatagarbha.* Enlightenment is contained within the constitution of the *tathāgatagarbha*/Sambhogakāya Flower. When one is enlightened and absorbed in its structure the full expression of the Kālachakra Maṇḍala[46] is revealed via the Flower's underlying geometry.

The first stage in the process of gaining enlightenment is therefore to try to imbue in consciousness the awareness of a highly sophisticated instrument (the Sambhogakāya Flower) by utilising at first the comparatively unsophisticated tool of the ordinary mind.

When people analyse such 'tools' they inevitably become aware of their own failings, finding that while building a repertoire of awareness there are flaws in the 'building' that is consciousness. They don't know the capabilities of the tools they possess until they see the products of their creation. At first they are happy, but then they observe flaws, rigidities and cracks of logic in the final structure. With close inspection of the mechanism of their logic they see room for improvement and ways to think more accurately.

When the effect of the cracks are analysed one becomes aware of the quality and the limitations of one's tools. Thus the work to improve the tools proceeds and expansion of consciousness is the result. Accordingly, the buildings and facades of consciousness improve. The mind thus utilises the faculty for discrimination in order to analyse its limitations and grow as a consequence. Otherwise it stagnates, and a crumbling

---

46 Kālachakra: the wheel or lotus upon which dances the Lord of time (Kāla). In Buddhism, Kālachakra is a Meditation Deity of Anuttarayoga (highest yoga) Tantra level. The Kalāchakra Tantra concerns the cycles of time and Buddhist cosmology, said to have been given out by the Lords at Shambhala. It thus concerns the way of awakening of the highest spiritual perception by means of the conquering of time, and mastering the related cycles.

edifice is built preventing the onset of enlightenment. A mixture of a serene consciousness (of no thought) and active discrimination is what makes observing the process possible. If there is no discrimination, only states of awareness relating to producing 'no thought', then one doesn't have the capacity to make improvements upon the tools that produce enlightenment.

The reflection of the Sambhogakāya Flower in the mind of the personal-I creates the awakened builder who needs to serenely reflect upon what is being built by producing a mirror-like awareness for the incoming impressions. Depending upon how clean and free from aberrations the mirror is, so the quality of information obtained is either pristine or aberrant. Once the reality of the *tathāgatagarbha* has been reflected in consciousness then an evolutionary milieu has been reached, an *arhat* is produced. One must, however, yet move further along the enlightenment stream. This necessitates a dissemination of the forces of the *tathāgatagarbha* into active manifestation, thus building the foundation for travelling the Bodhisattva path. The meditative process is not to simply reflect the qualities of the Sambhogakāya Flower, but to move towards the Eye of being/non-being, the deep indigo blue veiling the *dharmakāya*. As one does so one reflects the power of the creative amplitude of a Logos into the edifice of one's building and then to the world of forms.

The necessary tools and building material (the quality of the expression of one's thoughts) must be continually updated and improved. This is the process that builds the *nirmāṇakāya* of a Buddha, and is merely a reflection of the creative act of an Ādi Buddha when he formed a world sphere. Inevitably when the perfect expression of the evolutionary plan is demonstrated via an undistorted mirror of meditation substance, the qualities of the five Dhyāni Buddhas come into full established glory.

Obtaining an enlightened consciousness necessitates the following:

1. A heightening of energy for a new experiential level of the consciousness, producing an accelerated increase in the learning and penetrative ability of consciousness. This produces more consciousness-substance of a greater refined and resilient quality to work with in ever increasing spiral-cyclic activity of mental constructs.

2. Right interrelationship between the tools of consciousness and the building of the links to higher awareness necessitates a consistent dynamic striving. One must build an expression in consciousness that represents a *maṇḍala* of the higher principle that one wants to attain.
3. Tools are needed because one can't always have the necessary requirements for thinking until the right images and ideas (tools) come into the event horizon. These are sequenced according to the way of *karma* and necessitate reading the appropriate books, or the fortunate meeting with a preceptor or guru. These tools can also be projected into consciousness at appropriate times by the overshadowing Sambhogakāya Flower. The aspects of the mental construct to be improved can then come into view, especially as the capacity to build enlightened constructs increases. The capacity of the mind to hold intense images steady in the light of revelation becomes the final instrument of the *maṇḍala* of enlightenment. The perceiver can then obtain the ongoing secrets of enlightenment in ever-expansive vistas of revelation. The major tools for comprehension are those of analogy and the law of Correspondences.
4. Once consciousness has become the *maṇḍala* of revelation, likened to the completed construction of a building, then consciousness can integrate with the *tathāgatagarbha* by travelling via the lightning flashes of enlightened revelation descending. This concerns uniting with the true nature of what divinity represents via a structural mechanism. The structure becomes vital, dynamically alive. One structures oneself to images of perfection, but inevitably one notices that 'perfection' has its limitations. As the *maṇḍalic* structure comes to be more intensified and expanded so one moves to higher domains of revelation.
5. Perfection is relative to that which is considered imperfect. As one continues to evolve to greater transcendental boundaries, that which was once 'perfect' recedes into the background, as new qualities, formerly unknown to have even existed, become the norm for development. The analogy in the human frame is instinct. We do not have to work on establishing our instincts, they are inherent, having been developed in the earlier stages of the evolution of sentience and thence intelligence. The instincts are a 'perfection' that we have evolved away from, but are still existent, producing their inherent effects.

From a different perspective, the intelligence that humans possess is a goal for the animal kingdom; it represents 'perfection' for them, a state of enlightenment. For humans, however, it is simply a base that people must first properly develop and improve upon by developing enlightenment-attributes. The goal or signpost for their evolution has shifted from mere-consciousness to Buddhahood. In this analogy Buddhahood is just another step upon the upward way to absolute perfection, for which we have presently no proper term. Our ability to understand what lies beyond is similar to that of a cell in a human body endeavouring to cognize what lies beyond the bounds of the human form, or even of the forms of sentience and over-riding intelligence that are the governing law of their relatively little lives.

The structural procedures need to be erected before the building can be completed. Once the mind (which is involved in discriminatory shape building) has produced the structure of its main *maṇḍalic* construct (of everything contained in the one unit, taking the antithesis of vast and minute into account), then it will need to start upon a grander, larger construct. This is because there is no ending to the building process. Those in the middle of all extremes may rest in quiet repose, the Void, or state of bliss, before commencement upon a new cycle of activity, at all levels of the rebirthing process. When one has reached the perfection attainable by the discriminatory mind, then consciousness is free to move in any direction at will, and all directions simultaneously when enlightened. The Mind then encompasses the knowledge of the spiritual verities gained by all enlightened Ones, and this is fitted into a *maṇḍala* of 'what is'. This becomes part of what the Buddhas of past cycles have created through their relationships. Consciousness breaks through the limited vehicle and moves on to include all future attributes of being/non-being. The 'future' represented as the mechanism of definition is yet to be defined.

The future implications of any conception upon which one is focussed have been deduced and conscripted into one's consciousness, and also the past (represented by the relative thinking of the awakening minds of humanity). The past vehicle and the presently appearing future evolve into more than the sum total of the affirmations and information of the present. They become the *dharmakāya*. Consciousness then resides in what is the future for humanity and takes its preliminary precepts from there to educate humanity regarding the way ahead of them. A Bodhisattva takes humanity to where he/she requires it to go, because of the Bodhisattva's ability to create potent *maṇḍalas* of future potential out of humanity's limited minds.

One must leap beyond that which is self-created (by all the subsets of human minds combined, with their limitations), to become the evolutionary leader in conceptualisation. One then manifests the ability to help progress their thoughts into arenas needed by them. The Bodhisattva envisions what is needed. This is an integral aspect of his/her consciousness because humanity has helped to form it thus, and he/she has transcended its limitations. Therefore at all times the Bodhisattva can teach people what they don't know, though the Bodhisattva's action is conditioned by their limitations of thought and distorted ideologies and concepts. Here then develops the arena of service for the Bodhisattva. The enlightened one cannot teach people anything unless it is in terms they can comprehend. Like all good potters, the Bodhisattva must work the consciousness-clay into the shapes that are appropriate to the situation, to produce the finished product in the firing.

One type of clay (e.g., porcelain clay) produces one result or finish, and another type, (e.g., raku clay) another. Thus the Bodhisattva must understand how all these forms of consciousness work. He/she is limited by the sluggishness (inertia) of the material to be worked in certain areas. A human society can also be overwhelmingly focused in convoluted, fanatical, or muddied ideologies (acting like a stubborn mule seeing only one forage patch ahead). Thus they often need to be shown other views to lessen the intensity of their focus.

The Bodhisattva uses the entire past and present knowledge of humanity as leverage to proceed beyond what has been presented. Because the constitution of the enlightened Mind can be inclusive of what can be found in all other minds, so then the Bodhisattva's Mind becomes aware of all limitations. What therefore is propounded is at the forefront of thinking. The Bodhisattva is always the leader and reformer, spurring people's minds on to reach greater heights. As the limitations of those minds change due to having expanded closer to the Bodhisattva's consciousness state, so his/her Mind also expands. The Bodhisattva uses the platform of the accomplishment of the collective mind to project all to the next level. Thus the Bodhisattva follows the law of evolutionary progression.

Buddhas also need to keep appearing, because the parameters of human minds keep evolving to predetermined standards, which then need a major injection of right knowledge to direct the constructed *maṇḍalas* of thought to needed heights of awareness for any evolutionary period. More of the mysteries of being/non-being thus are revealed for all time.

Minds that once held a certain criteria for the attainment of enlightenment must then advance, as the former criteria no longer suffice, because the goal posts have been moved to greater distances (in consciousness). Thus when new Buddhas incarnate they keep adding to the collective human consciousness that which is the future goal for them, which is of a greater attainment than that previously asked by the former Buddha. All beings advance and expand their field of awareness together. Thus the Bodhisattva moves on to his/her next *bhūmi,*[47] and a Buddha progresses in *parinirvāṇa.*[48]

Most people wander through *saṃsāra* in a dreamlike state, but as they become more aware they have more frequent and complicated dreams. Because their 'dreaming state' is more active, so it will entail a greater opportunity to awaken into heightened states of revelation and then enlightenment.

As more Bodhisattvas evolve, they add their accumulative wisdom to the hotch-potch of human ideas, to the aggregates of group human experience. This produces a crescendo of enlightening experience for humanity, like a flower unfolding its petals to the full light of the spiritual sun. In terms of energy, it can be viewed like water coming

---

47 *Bhūmi:* the ten progressive levels of realisation, stages of perfection of the Bodhisattva.

48 *Parinirvāṇa:* that which is beyond (*para*) *nirvāṇa*. The Buddha was said to have attained *nirvāṇa* under the Bodhi tree, and *parinirvāṇa* when he 'died', thus complete extinction of, or release from, all attachment to the form. In technical Buddhism it refers to complete cessation, non-residual *nirvāṇa*, the passing away of Buddhas.

rapidly to a boil, with the enlightened ones steaming off. The bud-like potential of humanity will unfurl to become perfect, with a perfect amount of aroma, perfect colour, perfect form of the petals, of the full flowering of the human group-soul externalised. The description above illustrates the way humanity as a unit becomes a collective Buddha. This group-Buddha manifests simultaneously in the three realms, as the full potential of a dynamo that intensifies the sum of evolutionary growth for all in Nature's domain.

Meditation allows one to observe all phenomena in true detail as it really is. It is the sharpened discriminatory mind in process of observing its own workings. It observes every phenomenon with full clarity of reflection of the mind within itself.

The process described above can be considered in terms of the Mind of a great Buddha unfolding throughout the aeons. He holds the sum of human consciousness, the Sambhogakāya Flowers, as part of his meditation-Mind. His purpose is the process of transforming the units of self-ness (*ahamkāra*) into states of awareness that incorporate the selflessness of the all. The darkened aspects of that meditation-Mind represent the struggling units of human consciousness steeped in illusion, glamours, fields of desire, etc., and the lightened aspects are the Bodhisattvas working to diffuse their brilliance throughout the darkness in order to illumine the all. They must do so through the shields and barriers to light — the accumulated ignorance manifested. These must be broken down, and this constitutes the process of evolution for humanity. Such a meditation-Mind unfolds throughout the aeons of humanity's evolution, and thus always pushes the all on to greater levels of attainment of conscious mental freedom.

When a *yogin* attains a corresponding ability to meditate, the purpose is to reflect the potency of the greater Mind, and thereby gain access to the *dharmakāya*, once reciprocity has been attained. Such is the way to liberation and the nature of the path of a 'thus gone one' who has chosen earth-service as His/Her field for compassionate activity. Such is the effulgent dawning of great revelatory vistas for all upon our planet. Such is the never-ending crescendo of light cascading through the *nāḍīs* of human group evolution. Such is the vibrancy of the swirling *maṇḍala* of human perfection as it grows in brilliance and begins to demonstrate fourth-dimensional motion. Such is its spiralling onwards and outwards beyond the confines of the earth sphere into the immensity and grandeur of the cosmos, to eventually confer itself as a brilliant galaxy of starry lights. Myriad are the 'thus gone' ones who have travelled that Way.

Oṁ

4

The Discriminatory Mind and Dimensionality

The discriminatory mind

The analysis of mind has so far led us to explore aspects of the appearance of phenomena in the cosmos. Earlier in this treatise, the appearance of cosmos has been attributed to the expression of Mind. Also, the dissemination of the Wisdoms of the five Dhyāni Buddhas throughout manifest space can be considered to produce the laws governing the expression of mind. These laws governing the way mind expresses itself condition both its higher abstract form and its lower concrete expression. Much has been investigated in our analysis, however the concept of dimensionality of thought needs better exploration. The reason is that, in what might be termed the *sambhogakāya*[1] domain, and what the Tibetans call Bardo, lies much concerning human livingness that is speculative to empiricists, but definitely knowable by all who are cognisant of the laws of mind and the phenomena that comes under its control.

The Mind governs the nature of the rebirthing experience, and the appearance of the types of forms into which mind incarnates. The mind then governs the appearance of all phenomena by way of the conscious perception of things. The human brain, however, is not the only form of anchorage of mind's expression. That the mind persists

1 The *sambhogakāya* refers subjectively to that which is an attribute of the domain of the Mind.

in some form long after the death of the human body is ascertained by all religions, for sound ontological, experiential, and eschatological reasons. Many have had remembrances and glimmerings of their past lives, myriads have experienced paranormal phenomena, and others have conversed with the recently deceased. Just as others have had out-of-body experiences and have communicated their experiences in logical ways. Evidence for such phenomena abounds and can be found by all but the most truculent or bigoted materialists. For them, the subjective laws of mind are a closed book. They remain blind to all but what they wish to know and believe, they will twist all reason and evidence to support their way. Little therefore can be revealed to them, nevertheless, the nature of the substance that allows the mind to persist whether or not in a physical body is an important subject of enquiry for any genuinely enquiring thinker.

Buddhism presents a critique of the mind's ability to analyse and apprehend reality. We can summarise this critique in a number of statements:

1. The discriminatory mind is used to process itself (or to think logically) to formulate the many differing opinions promulgated by Buddhists and others.
2. There are differing characteristics of mind involved in the generation of various thoughts. We can look to unsophisticated minds as more conditioned by illusion, whilst sophisticated minds are less conditioned. Lazy concretising minds are prone to stagnation in the mire of past concepts; reactionary minds to the destructive potency of the charged emotions; fearful minds retreat into reactionary hell states; zealous minds impose bigotry upon others, whilst prideful minds construct walls of self-complacent I-ness. Critical minds assert the war-like tendencies of imposing one's own opinions through attacking other's credibility. Hateful minds manifest the awesome destructive potency of spiteful disdain for any thought or belief other than their own

A proper treatise on the nature of such mind states and how they are influenced by emotional input would be invaluable. The thesis would specially note that all of the emotions can be accorded animal-like status, because they were developed in the animal kingdom and further exemplified and exaggerated in the human. With respect to this we should also note the Seven Ray Aspects of Mind, explained in Volume 2, chapter 1, of this series.[2]

3. If comprehension concerning all aspects of the processes of Life and of the way beings evolve is to be gained, the discriminative process needs to be properly developed. Differing levels of analysis arise if logical philosophic investigation of the nature of all phenomena is to be ascertained. All forms of emotionality (whereby attachment to presented dogma manifests, biasing interpretation) must be eliminated in the process of right discrimination. Discrimination differentiates between subtly appearing phenomena (that is close to, or an expression of, the real) and partial, biased, or emotionally distorted phenomena, expressive of the *māyā* wherein most people reside.
4. Prior to a fully enlightened state the process of discrimination helps rectify aspects of *dharma* that need reform. It allows deduction of different categories of text, and helps reveal levels of hidden esoterica, facilitating an awakening of the enlightened Mind. One should also attempt to introduce rectified information for general consumption based on the various levels of interpretation of *dharma*.
5. There is always further refinement possible in the ability to perceive, in the development of what can be viewed as the penetrative ability of the Eye. Layer after layer of Mystery is thereby revealed. Thus one gets progressively more enlightened. Even for those that are *already* enlightened progression still happens in the vast domains of cosmos, as there are many levels of Buddha-fields to discover and learn from. The signposts of the mysteries of being/non-being shift whenever one has made a revelatory accomplishment. Thus what can be considered as utter and complete enlightenment is only relatively so, because such a term as *samyaksaṃbodhi* is defined from the

2 These Ray aspects were described under the headings: will of mind, loving mind, critical mind, pride of mind, concrete mind, desire mind, and the wrongly faceted mind. The animal-like mental-emotions were also discussed: racing hounds of mind, dog-like mental activity, spider-like desire-mind, slugs of mind, monkey mind, crabs of mind, and mouse-like mind.

point of view of the present human evolutionary attainment.[3] The momentum of every journey to the bliss state always manifests as a continuous process of expansive inclusive Reason, and then of further progress in cosmos. There is more, there is ever more to behold in the Buddha's Eye as he explores the incomprehensible, increasingly subtle Domains that open before him in his Journey's Quest.

6. A well reasoned, analytical study of what a 'process' means is needed. This would require comprehension of the nature of the patterns of construction of a *maṇḍala*, which manifest as a continuous happening. Each expanding process in consciousness produces some gain of revelation. These revelations verify that one is moving to better territories of awareness. For this reason, all procedures that lead to enlightenment must be illumined to the best of one's ability.

7. Historical evidence needs to be utilised as a grounding of experience. The nature of the evolution of human civilisations and of human consciousness needs to be more fittingly comprehended, through enhanced sense-perceptors developed to perceive and deduce. Examples can then be presented of the aeonic process that show the underlying patterns of evolution. This necessitates adequate comprehension of the subjective nature of the changing ephemera throughout time, of the psychic as well as concreted processes governing the rise and fall of various types of civilisations.

    What type of patterns repeat themselves, and when is the time for the reappearance of higher cycles than those of yore? What are the psychic paradigms and forces governing the processes of Nature contacted by the human imagination and symbolised in the form of nature spirits, the gods, and divine personages? How does the history of black verses white magic play out in it all? These are the types of questions to be asked. Hence we have a vast study for the accomplished seer, one that predicates the true basis for evolution of all civilisations, including our own. The way of the law of cycles is little understood by Buddhist theoreticians, but is needed for any enlightened understanding of the nature of the appearance of things. It should be noted that the law of *karma* is cyclic.

---

3 *Samyaksaṃbodhi:* correct, proper, wholesome, perfect enlightenment.

In addition, the popular mythos of what constitutes enlightenment in Buddhist and Hindu texts needs to be better defined, or refined. The need for the attaining of enlightenment is universally promulgated, but what actually constitutes enlightenment is in fact debatable. It has been defined in terms of abstract superlatives, but its levels of revelation have not been adequately conveyed. The Mādhyamika way of equating enlightenment with *śūnyatā* has validity, but is also an extremist position. Their *de facto* denial of all attributes of appearing phenomena, that actually are necessary for the appearance of enlightenment, is a case in point. Such denial in fact effectively manifests a form of antithesis to enlightenment, as enlightenment is a partner of the discriminatory process. (Nevertheless, there is validity to the process in terms of one aspect of enlightenment-consciousness only; namely the Void.) Enlightenment in fact has many categories of attributes, and many terms are provided, such as: *satori, dharmatā, mokśa, śūnyatā, nirvāṇa, parinirvāṇa, bodhicitta, mahaparinirvāṇa, dharmadhātu, tathatā, samyaksaṃbodhi, tathāgatagarbha, dharmakāya*, as well as the *arhat* (or *ālayavijñāna)* enlightenment. These terms are not all equable. There are many shades of differences, many have already been explicated in this *Treatise on Mind.* As the definition of what enlightenment consists of, or of its levels of revelation, has not been adequately explained in the past, so this series of books hopes to fill in some of the lacking information. Even so, words can only inadequately convey the importance of a discriminatory mind that is well-disposed to meditate upon the nature of the Mind beyond (it).

The discriminatory mind has five main categories to consider in its analysis of things: is, is not, is and is not, maybe and probably not. One could also consider the category 'neither is and is not', but this is an attribute of *śūnyatā,* which lies outside of the discriminatory mind. It is non-discriminatory. If we added this category then we would also have to add the revelatory certainty of the *dharmakāya* (Mind), which would make seven factors utilised for absolute comprehension of the nature of any 'thing'. We shall, however, limit our consideration here to the nature of categorisation of phenomena and not that which lies beyond.

The enlightened state instantly analyses any category of ideas or images, or set of categories, according to these five criteria of discrimination, and spontaneously makes a decision based upon all known facts at hand. If it 'is', then the facts have attributed the query to be true. If 'not', then there lies a fallacy somewhere that has quickly been discerned, and the query is automatically rejected, with no more thought added to waver an opinion. If 'is and is not', then attributes of both assertions can be investigated. If the decision is 'maybe', then the facts implore a possibility of a thing being true, pending more information before a final decision is made. The enlightened one then holds the case in mind and waits for the time of the rightful presentation of the necessary facts. If the decision is 'probably not', then the known facts have already portended the fallacy of the query, but the enlightened Mind can view a pathway that may make the query true, though such a pathway is very improbable. The tendency therefore is to reject the query as fallacious, pending the outcome of the possible pathway appearing.

The enlightened Mind is always true to any situation, it always answers truthfully whatever the outcome may be, it will not bend or distort a line of investigation to fabricate a desired answer.[4] Therefore the enlightened Mind is not simply 'empty' of thoughts, ideas, but rather is replete with knowledge and instantaneous discriminatory capacity. However, the natural state of an enlightened Mind rests in serene equipoise, it is void of concepts when not prompted by external circumstances to analyse phenomena of some type. Yet the nexus between *saṃsāra* and *śūnyatā* is its domain when riding the gift waves of Bodhisattvic activity. The place of residence then is the zone that is neither *saṃsāra* or *śūnyatā,* but is inclusive of them both. Such a zone of residence allows the floodgate of *dharmakāyic* impression to enter the domain of Life to produce revelatory certainty in all thought processes.

When one enters into lofty attempts to try not to define, definition is still taking place in the human mind. Definition has wheeled its spokes into ruts of conjecture of the order of the universe wherever an unenlightened human unit is manifest, producing controversy when an enlightened one speaks. The difference between one who is enlightened and one who is not, is that the enlightened being rests in the naturalness

4 The tendency to bend or to distort is the most common character trait of unenlightened minds, indeed, it is its overriding tendency, especially when the emotions are in any way involved.

of Mind and knowing the truth, conjectures not. On the other hand the substance (*citta*) of an unenlightened mind is always active, even when purporting to be 'empty', and enflamed with opinions, even if subtle. The enlightened one can see the overview from a vaster vision, and can from there particularise the minutiae, the cellular unit. The unenlightened resides in the domains of the cellular unit and does not glimpse the multidimensional overview.

One is defining things whenever these or similar words appear in the mind: 'this', 'not this', or 'neither this nor that', 'this and that', or any permutation of these. In the process of speaking or writing thoughts you define things, automatically categorising by the mere act of thinking about things. The enlightened Mind speaks the Truth of what is and is not, of that which needs definition, or categorisation. 'Things' appear as conceptualisations first, stimulated by the backing of the sensory apparatus. Without the mind there is no true human existence in the phenomenal world.

The categorising function of the mind cannot be denied, but it can be transcended by the development of the enlightened Mind. It chooses whether to be active or Void. One can define or not define with respect to the field of service, in the ever-present Now. Thus it may be said an enlightened one possesses 'no thought'. There are no individual ideas or thoughts, no warring ideas or clashes of opinions, just instantaneous streams of revelation. The discriminative mind of the unenlightened, in contradistinction, always concerns a potpourri of thoughts and decisions based upon observances in relation to themselves. To serve, the enlightened one stays at the border between the Mind and the categorising consciousness. The idea, word, and deed of the enlightened manifest through terms, but the true nature of the Mind of such a one is wordless and thought-less Clear Light.[5] It spontaneously creates the necessary *maṇḍalas* of thought and effortlessly manifests them in a karmically propitious way when there is need. Speech assists both the unenlightened and the enlightened. Speech is the product of concepts, it concerns the linking of one concept with another, expressed for people to personify an experience. Telepathic impression is, however,

5 The term 'thought-less' here means 'having no thoughts', rather than lack of consideration, or lack of mind.

the method of choice for the enlightened. The method of revelation from such telepathy concerns listening to often very quick thought impression, as well as observing images, and if needed, *maṇḍalic* effect. Thus the consciousness readily observes the polarities and their individual separations in the vale of illusion.

Vast universalised, often complex Ideations from the domains of Mind, often need to be concretised into concepts and terms, to be particularised for a set purpose, if they are to have meaning for the residents in *saṃsāra*. This generally necessitates a veiling or encoding process in the usage of words, where many levels of interpretation can be gleaned from the one set of terms or sentence structure. Numerological encoding is also frequently utilised because numerology is the language of the enlightened. In this way the various strata of the most esoteric teachings can be most succinctly and efficiently presented.[6] The directions in space, and the dynamics of the *chakra*s, such as explicated in this book, also need to be mastered. The term 'universalised' above means that these Ideations contain all differing thought-sequences about any topic simultaneously, allowing the enlightened one to automatically choose the perfect response to any given query.

The nature of multidimensional perception

Without discrimination no thought could be wrought. Each thought-stream represents a line of knowledgeable representation, each line is a discriminatory process, and each point of that line can represent a different aspect of dimensionality whereby one thinks. If one is to construct a *maṇḍala,* the concept of dimensionality is important. Dimensionality can be thought of in two ways:

a. Mathematically, where size, numbers of objects, length, depth and breadth of inclusiveness, new elemental expressions, linearity or non-linearity, and overall geometric structure is taken into account.

b. Levels of abstraction or density of dimensions of perception implied by various aspects of the construct.

---

6 The keys to such a numerological system will be revealed in a later book: '*The Astrological and Numerological Keys to the Secret Doctrine.*'

Dimensions of conscious awareness and of existence are boundaries depicting different levels of consciousness that limit or guide our ability to perceive all things in the subjective and objective universes. They are extended or limited according to the abilities of our organs of perception. A geometric example is an effective way to explicate the nature of dimensionality.

A zero-dimensional object can be represented as a point in space with no direct relationship to any other point in space. This point in space can be considered the central *bīja* or point from which the entire dimensional *maṇḍala* stems. It is inherently replete with all of the elements that will later spring forth in the complete construction. Yet, having no interrelation with anything else, it can be considered to be 'no thing'. It is the potential of whatever is to be, thus from it the extended geometry of the construct can proceed, from point to periphery of the circle of being via the moving radial line of interrelationship. This radial line forms the images and constructional ideas (deities, representational consciousness attributes and forces) of what is to be built into the *maṇḍala*.

If we produce another point with respect to this 'zero-spatial point' and join these two points with a line, then we have a one-dimensional zone possessing the attributes of length and breadth but no width, imagined as line AB:

A ———————— B

A being on this dimension could only go forward or backwards, but not up or down, nor round or about. This relates to the development of sentience, for instance the way that trees grow from darkness to light, and of the nature of the way that many lesser animal species observe things. It is the basis to all of the later 'squared' geometry that encloses various aspects of one's mind-space. When observing the nature of the evolution of consciousness we will see that the progress does not actually move in a straight line, but as a spiral, as this best depicts the ways that consciousness evolves. The spiral moves onwards and outwards to produce the circumference of containment of the entire thought-construct.

A spheroid figure resting on that one-dimensional line can only appear as a point (the point z), where the circumference of the sphere would come into contact with this line.

If a being, x, on this line meets another being, y, going in the opposite direction, then certain things would ensue:

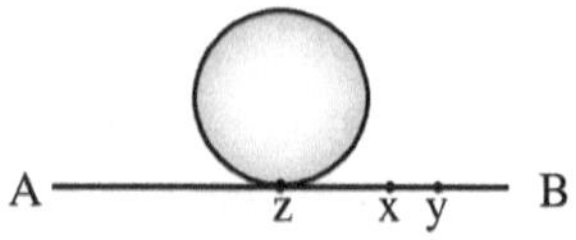

a. They could not pass each other.

b. Nor could they see past each other, for though x could possess a greater length than y, their width and height would be the same, the minutest possible (to our three-dimensional perception) and yet the maximum for one-dimensional perception.

One-dimensional thought can be considered to be akin to a one-track mind that sees only one vision or concept ahead for which to base any action upon.

We can also look to the nature of appearing *saṃskāras,* where each particular awakening Element arrives via a line of conveyance (*nāḍī*) to be quickly demonstrated in a three-dimensional fashion of interrelatedness of all Elements, once the *saṃskāra* becomes expressed in terms of a consciousness volition. The neuro-chemical impulses obtained from sense contact with external phenomena travelling along the nerves to the brain can also be considered in one-dimensional terms, until the impressions are correlated by the brain to produce the images we think with. This one-dimensional attribute is equated with the expression of the Element Earth. (One-dimensional lines of relationship also betoken how chemical compounds interrelate and combine.)

If we now took two points, C and D, at right angles to A and B, and joined them up to form a plane figure A, B, C, D, we would then have a rectangle possessing the characteristics of length and breadth but no height:

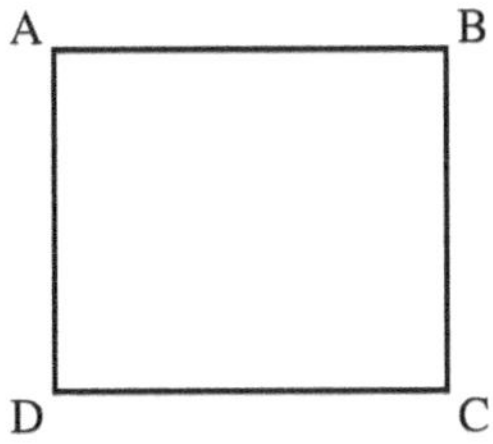

The area of this rectangle (or square) can be infinitely extended to the four directions of space, and this would represent the second dimension. The above-mentioned spheroid figure would now possess one further attribute if placed on this dimension. The dot would be expanded to form a circle (an ovoid if viewed obliquely).

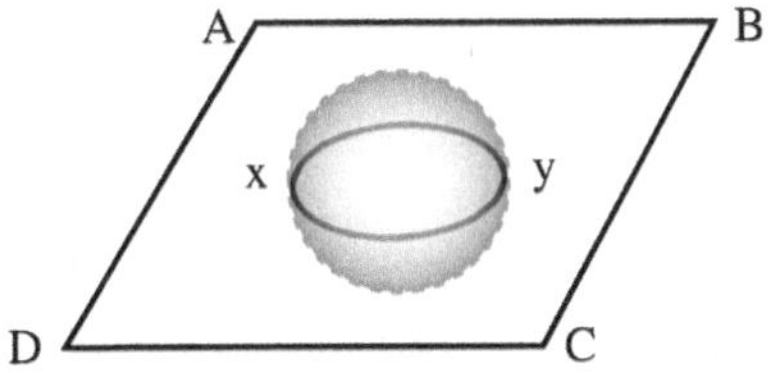

Two sentient animate beings, x and y, on this rectangular plane could go around each other, but they would not be able to perceive distance, for there is no way to gauge depth or volume on a rectangle. Even so, the two-dimensional (2-D) world gives a far greater view of reality (in this case the spheroid figure) and freedom of movement than a one-dimensional world. The spheroid figure would no longer be seen as a point on the line but a circle.[7]

It is in this form that most thoughts are depicted upon printed pages and in painted images. Utilising our logic we can extrapolate much information from them because we are capable of thinking in multidimensional terms. The moving spiral of consciousness unfolding can now be depicted accordingly.

---

7 This circle is actually only seen from the perspective of a viewer being at right angles to it looking from a three-dimensional world.

The emotions, divorced from *manasic* control, manifest in this two-dimensional manner. They can engulf and surround the object of desire, of that wished for, but the image of what is contacted can never produce the full three-dimensional (3-D) reasoning that consciousness produces. The emotions can produce awareness of only a slice or surface area of what is contacted, thus they immediately distort the true image. They also curtail reasoning in terms of the 'I' and the object of desire, where the image of that object is coloured according to what is desired. True penetrative reasoning is not obtained, rather, a quick truncated two-dimensional impression is obtained. Later, in quieter moments, the mind can derive further realisations from the initial emotional contact, when logic is activated.

The associated *saṃskāras* are clothed in the Watery Element, which manifest torrent-like to grasp an object without penetrating the three-dimensional relationship between various objects, or of the complete perspective of that which the emotions contact. The rounded out inclusivity of view that is the *manasic* perspective is absent.

If we extend at right angles the points A, B, C, D of the two-dimensional figure and joined all the points together, we have a cubic three-dimensional object A, B, C, D, E, F, G, H possessing the added property of volume, that is, length x breadth x height, as shown in the diagram below.

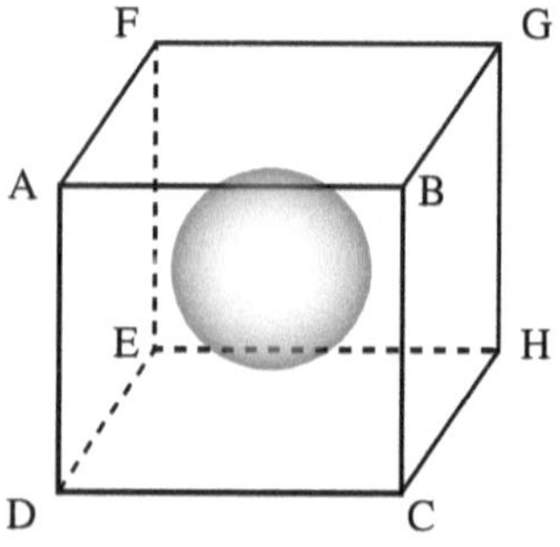

It possesses the attributes of both the first-dimension (the line A, B) and the second-dimension (the plane figure A, B, C, D), yet it has acquired extra characteristics; for the viewer on this dimension can also measure depth. The viewer can now see around this object, observe distances and perceive volumes. Thus the spheroid figure, as well as its attributes being viewed as the circle or point, can now be seen truly as a sphere. It is the dimension of form, solid objects, and the concept of perspective, demonstrating a vanishing horizon point, that allows us to measure distance. It gives the perceiver a greater insight into the nature of reality, a greater expression of freedom of movement than was possible in the former dimensions.

Humanity views the universe in terms of 3-D rules and limitations. In this way, for instance, we are deluded by the illusive three-dimensionality of a painting or photograph, despite the fact that it is really a 2-D object. Similarly, the fact that there are higher, subtler dimensions, escapes the attention of most; that if we over-rule our 3-D conditioning from giving things a 3-D flavour, then we will be able to view things from a more comprehensive angle.

It has been stated that all things are in constant motion. Solid matter consists of molecules (a combination of atoms), which vibrate at a certain frequency. Liquids and gases, because of their faster vibratory motion, have detached themselves from the more rigid solid structures. The atoms constituting a liquid are loosely attached to each other. Therefore they collectively take the shape of whatever contains them. Gases however have greatly transcended any adherence to form because of the very much higher velocity of their molecules.

According to scientists, there is a comparatively large space (or distance) between the nucleus of an atom and its electrons. This is illustrated by the idea that if a football represents the nucleus of an atom, then the electrons would revolve around it at a distance comparable to that between the centre of the earth and its gaseous envelope. The space between two atoms compared to their size is even greater.

Thus, it can be claimed that the content of what is to us solid, three-dimensional physical matter, is really empty space with specks of matter (atoms) separated by relatively great distances and linked by definite laws. The atoms also obey the laws of conservation of energy and are in constant vibratory motion, whilst their 'matter' is almost wholly concentrated within the nucleus of every atom. There is also a relatively vast distance between it and the cloud of electrons spinning around it. The electron's mass is about 1/1840th of either that of a proton or neutron, which together constitute the atom's nucleus, there being an increasing number of neutrons and protons to each atom as we ascend up the periodic table of elements.

The Fires of the mind now come to the fore, producing the ability to gauge depth, and to reason in terms of all points of view, the length, breadth, and depth of a mental image. The information gleaned from all sense-perceptors are correlated in this manner by the intellect. All commonplace *saṃsāric* events can now be visualised throughout the sequence of time. In this analysis time is *not viewed* as a separate 'dimension', but rather as an expression of or an addendum to the third dimension. The visioning of the time-sequence is conceptualised in terms of 3-D events as perceived by consciousness.

As the first-dimension is represented as a line, so the second-dimension could be viewed as a square, and the third-dimension as a cube. Each dimension is viewed at right angles to the preceding dimension, and speaking metaphorically, its principles or facilities (of perception) progressively transcend its correspondences in the previous dimensions. Thus the fourth-dimension must have all the possibilities of the above mentioned dimensions of perception and yet transcend them. Therefore, a person in the fourth-dimension could clothe himself in any of the shapes that are represented as form in the third-dimension and yet that form would not limit him. This would give such a person the added characteristic of being able to interpenetrate all aspects of the third-dimension. He would be able to see and move freely within and about the solid (3-D) matter (similar to the action of x-rays) without the loss of his own form.

This is feasible if we remember the comparatively enormous distances between atoms of 3-D matter. We could then take into account much smaller, subtler 4-D atomic unities existing at much higher frequencies and permeating the spaces between ordinary physical atoms. To a being with 3-D perception or instruments (such as those possessed by the average person and the scientist), such matter would to all accounts be undetectable.[8]

This can be further illustrated by the idea of a stick that is moving to and fro. As the stick is vibrated faster and faster, the object of perception (the stick) becomes a blur. The analogy is completed if we imagine a whole forest of such sticks rapidly vibrating in an engulfing forest of slow moving trees (representing the world of atoms). In comparison, the perceiver would have the dimensions of a huge mountain but be able to see only the trees, even with the help of instruments.

In order to detect matter composed of such minute entities, one's faculty for visual perception would have to resonate at that ultra-high frequency, and that faculty must be trained or focussed to observe the matter before one.

Such ability is termed *clairvoyance,* and will manifest if one refines one's physical, emotional, and mental bodies, and then adopts a rigor of concentration or meditation upon the subject at hand (utilising the appropriate psychic sensory organs). Some types of drugs will also induce psychic visions, and certain people, such as mediums, are born with these abilities. This does not mean, however, that these people are more 'spiritually' advanced than others, but rather indicates that there are flaws in their psychic constitution.

The alchemists attributed the property of Water to this form of matter, for by analogy with the physical plane, 4-D matter is fluid like water. It permeates the dense form and is easily moulded by external forces. In this case by thought energy. This is because its molecules (or rather; the arrangement of its form) are not as rigidly bound as those of 3-D matter, the molecules of 4-D matter freely discharge themselves from the 4-D atmosphere, and vice versa. Therefore, a 4-D being can assume whatever shape desired. This means that the Watery Element is fluid and easily moulded into the shape of whatever contains it.

Just as a person with 3-D eyes can read all of a 2-D world (such as a newspaper) at a glance, so a person with 4-D eyes, if confronted with a 3-D object, would be able to simultaneously read the facial markings on each of the plane surfaces of that object from an external point in

8 We could produce an argument that many of the subatomic particles detected by physicists, such as quarks, are indeed the 'atomic' constituency of this fourth-dimensional world.

space, as well as perceiving the inner nature of that solid object. One would thus not need to open a book to read it. This is because the organs of perception of a 4-D person are diffused to all parts of his/her body. This is possible because 4-D matter is highly tenuous when compared to the physical 3-D body, which has its organs of perception localised to certain areas of the body, such as the eyes in the head.

Localised perception is therefore transcended. The whole body, literally every atom, now functions as an organ of perception. (Similar to the sense of touch.) As the 4-D matter interpenetrates the 3-D matter, so the internal as well as external features of an object would be able to be simultaneously discerned.

We can also say that because 2-D perception is at right angles to the first dimension, and 3-D perception is at right angles to the 2-D, so 4-D perception must be at right angles to the 3-D. This means that a person with 4-D vision will be looking perpendicularly, that is, on all the (six) sides of a 3-D world, from one point in space.[9]

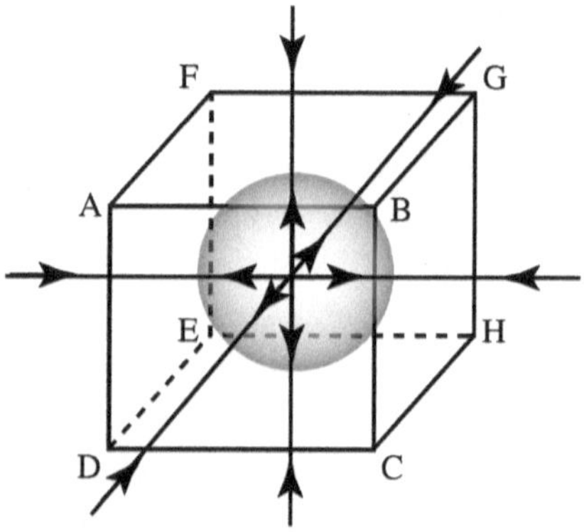

The particles of 4-D substance represent particles of sentient response. They clothe the impulses of the mind. It is the intensity of the energy of the desire-mind that gives them the vibrancy, or propelling force. This substance is instantaneously galvanised into activity by the impulse of desire, and is quickly coloured by the force of human

9 The book *Geometry, Relativity, and the Fourth Dimension* by Rudolf V. B. Rucker (Dover Publications, 1977) gives a basic explanation of the geometry associated with the fourth dimension. See also James S. Perkins, *A Geometry of Space and Consciousness*, (The Theosophical Publishing House, Adyar, 2004).

emotions. These emotions consist of minute Watery *devas*, which introduce the factor of *karma*, because this energisation affects the *devic* lives that inevitably must return the energy to the original source. Thereby equilibrium is restored in the field of Life. All substance is in fact constituted by these *devas,* who can be considered minute units of sentience. They are the evolved expression of the earlier described elementary *citta.*

Achieving the equilibrium of the pristine condition then becomes the *modus operandi* of karmic purpose. It is a version of the second law of thermodynamics working out upon this level of expression, as it does with all systems containing particulate matter when the Life force withdraws, no longer sufficing to hold it into form.[10] All physical systems containing microscopic entities will then increase the entropy of the system. Entropy can be considered the state of chaos originally described, and manifests when atomic unities are no longer directly controlled by an overriding mind, or field of desire (which produce order out of chaos). This represents the state of substance during *pralaya,* the dissolution of things at the end of time for a *maṇḍala* of incarnate expression. The macroscopic body is calm, but the minute particulate matter constituting it is chaotic. (Except when it is again directed or galvanised by some energy field or Life force. This happens at the new dawning of a world or universal sphere of activity.)

In the field of Life each atom of matter carries with it a unit of gain, a quantum increase or added colourisation of the type of energy that swayed it as part of an organised force. The gains are qualitative and each unity grows in experiential quality over time. Because of this, chaos imperceptibly slowly moves towards greater order when *manasic* embodiment becomes the goal of the elementary lives concerned. The activity of mind is thus what organises chaos. The entire universe marches this way in a cyclically reincarnating expansion, not towards some far distant 'heat death', as some scientists imagine. The progress of all things is thus away from chaos into a congenial state of order. Myriads of cycles come and go before an elementary Life evolves to organise itself into the comprehensive system that is a Buddha Mind.

10 For detail see Martin Bailyn, *A Survey of Thermodynamics*, (American Institute of Physics, Woodbury NY, 1994), 100.

Elementary substance that is incorporated as part of human emotional expression differs from that which was. Over the course of human evolution such substance has accumulated upon the earth and has enriched the biosphere of the human experience. It has created the heaven and hell (Bardo) states, described in an exaggerated fashion by our religions. It thus has become a special zone of living for human consciousness, experienced after the death of our physical bodies. It is compliantly malleable by that consciousness. Indeed the sum of human emotions and minds have conditioned the Watery substance of the Bardo experiences according to the way ordained by massed human imagination. Images of all types created by human desire-minds hold sway. Entire landscapes of desirable places and homes are created in this way, and are depicted as heavenly or 'godly' realms. This zone of human habitation is also inextricably governed by the law of *karma*, which determines the quality of substance that one is clothed in after the physical form has died. The selfish *saṃskāras,* for instance, that one developed previously clothe the individual after life, producing a squalid environment.

Here we have the basis for the *asura* and *preta* realms claimed by Buddhists, and the purgatory of Christians. Also, according to the degree of rapacity, cupidity, hatred, separativeness, or spite manifested throughout that life, so an equal force implodes upon the individual after death, enforcing a hell state for those that manifested such attributes. People thus experience the true effects of the pain they have caused to others. This, however, is not to be confused with the pain people create for themselves due to uncontrolled emotions in reaction to something that may have happened to them. An individual is not karmically responsible for the irascible, petulant, tetchy, spiteful, fractious, etc., emotions of another. Such emotional ones are very apt to blame others for their 'hurt feelings', and must learn not to do so. *Karma* will manifest in a way to teach people to not blame.

Pain-inducing *karma* is produced by those responsible in changing the environment or living conditions that produce hell-like, squalid life-styles for individuals, where the direct infliction of pain is caused, or where their resources are stolen from them in some way. What is termed 'good *karma*' is produced through acts of kindness and charity, whereby the 'good intent' engendered is experienced in Bardo, and the physical effects of the charity provided when later incarnate.

Everything equilibrates in the end. *Karma* is an exact law, and most people have to think out more logically as to what exactly will be the karmic repercussions of every action manifested with their thoughts, emotions, and physicality. The resources one possesses, for instance, is karmically measured in terms of how a person obtained it and what it means emotionally to them. Monetary value has a conceptual meaning in terms of the value people assign to things, however true value is represented by the sacrifice or effort a thing took to acquire, or the hardship caused when it is gone. A poor widow's 'two mites', for instance, may be worth more than a rich person's treasure.[11]

We shall digress a little here. It should be mentioned that there are many people that use the 'letter of the law' to steal another person's wealth (viewed in terms of physical and emotional effort to obtain) which is accredited karmically in the money they are awarded by a judge for some perceived abuse. The plaintiff does not understand the karmic debt that will be owed to the one thus stolen from. It must be paid back in a later life. Receiving money in a lawsuit does not atone the *karma* of being assaulted, for instance. One has simply accrued a karmic debt through this legalised theft. Society must obviously provide checks to individuals that perpetuate violent (etc.) actions against others, but stealing from them does not rectify their wrong. If one meditates upon the subject of such crimes, we see that the 'victim' (in this case the one assaulted) is generally paying karmically for crimes perpetuated (i.e., having assaulted someone) in a past life. The karmic slate may have been wiped clean in the unfortunate incident, but by thieving, the 'victim' is now bonded in a new karmic debt. People must beware their avarice and feelings of revenge. Karmically, the effects of such emotions produce heavy burdens.

The alchemical term Water is used to describe this substance that is affected by our moods, feelings, glamours, and massed emotional states, because its intrinsic nature is fluid. This fourth-dimensional substance[12] is equated with the astral plane in the various books on

11 The reference here is to the Bible, *Luke 21:1-4.*

12 A confusion in terminology is possible here because earlier the emotions were said to act in a 2-D way, whereas here the substance of the astral plane, which consists of the sum of people's emotions, desires and glamours, is depicted as 4-D. Also *manasic*

occult or hermetic philosophy. Astral substance thus constitutes our body of emotions, desires, and feelings, the associated *prāṇas* and *saṃskāras* regulated by the Solar Plexus centre and the minor *chakras* in the body. The word astral means starry, luminescent. The term is however somewhat of a misnomer, for that quality really depicts the *etheric body* (the intermediary between the astral and the dense physical realm, housing the energy field of the corporeal form) with which the astral is often confused by clairvoyants. The two forms of substance are practically extensions of each other. The etheric body is auto-luminous, diffused with a starry light, as is the astral. Those with psychic and mediumistic tendencies have awakened minor *chakras* facilitating perception of this subtle realm, which includes therefore the Bardo states described above.[13]

The first-dimensional perception can be viewed as the type of sentience developed by the mineral kingdom. (The direct interrelation between individual molecules, atoms, or subatomic particles from a linear perspective.) The second-dimensional perception can be seen as that developed by the vegetable kingdom. They grow principally upwards and downwards, but can also spread out sideways, such as the action of vines and creepers. They are composed of layers of generally highly geometric, interrelated, superimposed cells. Such layers of receptivity (two-dimensional planes, as for instance observed in the form of leaves) are fully developed in this kingdom. They are also a basis for the life in the animal kingdom. Thus we can deduce that plants view things as if it were on a plane surface. Third-dimensional perception is represented by the type of sentience developed by animals, whilst fourth, or rather, fifth-dimensional perception is the birth right of humans. Esoterically, our view concerns the way of the mind (the

---

perception was labelled 3-D. Effectively, the way of perceiving with the mind, *via* external objects is 3-D, but the nature of the expression of the substance of the mind is 5-D. Hence we can imaginatively control *manasic* input, build empires of mind, and to project pathways to the future without having recourse to the forms of the 3-D world.

13 The perceptions of psychics are generally fragmentary and distorted. There normally is much glamour involved, and rarely do they properly scrutinise or validate their impressions. Many are the traps and lures that such individuals can fall prey to, and rare are genuine knowledgeable instructors to guide them safely through the lower astral miasma of their psychicism.

fifth-dimension), as everything is mind-conditioned. The astral realm is really an illusional zone of residence created by the human desire body and emotions. We see, therefore, that the terms fourth and fifth-dimension depend upon the way that the mind expresses itself. Animals can also share in the fourth-dimensional experience.

It is commonly known that during deep sleep many of us leave our bodies in our astral forms and experience many beautiful and wonderful things, remembered as vivid and euphoric dreams.[14] Such dreams are usually in colour and often manifest as precognitions, educational scenes, pleasant floating sensations, and lyrical wanderings. These usually appear when the dreamer had previously strongly desired (even subconsciously) to see something or someone that is loved, or when there is a strong desire to know about something. An example can be seen in a mother's concern for her separated son in the case of a war, and having a true prophetic dream of him being killed in action. In general, astral experiences are not remembered because most have not manifested a cognisable alignment between the two realms of perception by having stimulated the psychic centre concerned. Some very physically biased people have also not sufficiently developed their astral form.

The ordinary concepts of time or motion with respect to distance are transcended in the higher dimensions. Because the astral body is really the Watery sheath of the mind, so motion is instantaneous with thought. Time is only related to 3-D cycles or events, whilst distance is perceived astrally by changes in vibrational rates, by the earth's astral boundary, or else in relation to 3-D perception.

The Bardo realms

The appearance of things is regulated by response to differing degrees of light and vibrational intensity. This is a basic statement concerning all realms of perception. It is especially seen, for instance, in our physical world in relation to the vegetable kingdom, which grows upwards towards the direction of sunlight. With respect to the domain

14 The term used in the relevant texts for this function is 'astral projection'. Probably the best book on this subject is by Peter Richelieu, *A Soul's Journey,* (Thorsons, London, 1996).

of mind/Mind we see various permutations of light overcoming arenas of darkness or ignorance. The astral domain is auto-luminous. It is lit by energy from the higher realms. It is constituted by the substance of the collective experiences of the human units that have built it. Humanity have projected their desired images therein by incarnating into and out of it as an experiential zone for uncounted ages. Finally, the domain of enlightenment is the Clear Light.

There is a link called the *silver cord,* uniting the astral and physical bodies.[15] It has similar functions to the umbilical cord, the dense physical manifestation conveying nutrition from the greater Life or universe (the Mother) to the foetus. The *prāṇa* that sustains the life of a person is the energy ('nutrition') conveyed by the silver cord. Once this cord or link between the subjective and corporeal person is severed, then the body dies and the consciousness is freed from its habitation in the dense form. This cord is said to be composed of the subtlest type of astral matter and is able to instantaneously absorb the energy, or matter, from the astral sea (Bardo realm) that the person needs to travel in. Therein the Wheel of Life spins for experience in what has been termed the *asura, preta,* or hell states, or else in a 'god-like' paradise realm that humans subsequently find themselves in.

The symbolic and psychic truism of the Six Realms of Buddhists (and the general reification of the philosophy) has been explained in *Karma and the Rebirth of Consciousness,* and Volume 3, chapter 3, of this series. That there is no birthing of human consciousness into the animal kingdom, for instance, was explored in *Karma and the Rebirth of Consciousness.* The following volume in this series lays the foundation for comprehending what actually happens and is experienced in the Bardo realms. It establishes the esoteric doctrine, which compliments the doctrine of the Six Realms.[16] For a complete picture the student

15 In *Ecclesiastes 12:6-7* it is stated that if the 'silver cord is loosed, or the golden bowl be broken....Then shall the dust return to the earth as it was: and the spirit shall return unto God who gave it'. The 'golden bowl' is the sum of the *prāṇa* that vivifies every cell in the being. The reference then is to the effect of breaking the connection between this cord and the physical body, which produces the death of that body.

16 Such a doctrine is expressed also in the Tantric 'twilight language' or secret code (*sandhyābhāṣā*). Sometimes the term *sandhyābhāṣā* 'intentional language' is used.

should integrate all of the teachings on the subject so far presented into a unit. The relation between the exoteric and esoteric presentations, and also their congruence, will then become clearer.

We should also note that the doctrine of the Six Realms was primarily a postulation on the psychic constitution of a person developed for *yogins*, which was adapted for lay consumption by integrating it with currently held beliefs anent the afterlife at the time. The hybrid doctrine then served both groupings of the society. For lay practitioners the teachings of the Six Realms is primarily a doctrine of fear of the consequences of wrong action, thereby encouraging the participants to amend their ways. It was probably considered the best way to beneficially educate the common people of the time as to the consequences of wrong action in a way that would help produce in them a fervent striving for liberation from the wheel of *saṃsāra*. The teachings became exaggerated through zealous religious thinking. It is obvious that the enlightened ones that originally proposed the doctrine knew that *yogins* would arise who would learn the correct esoteric doctrine from their awakened gurus, and from practical experience. The teaching here on the astral plane follows upon a similar vein, to provide the serious practitioner background information so that they can maximally gain from the Bardo Thödol as a text for meditation concerning the Peaceful and Wrathful Deities. This is elaborated on in the next volume of this series.

Most people travel astrally during their sleep life, with only a few having developed the ability to thus consciously travel. The silver cord is able to stretch indefinitely to wherever the person wishes to go within the astral environment, and is at all times anchored in the physical body, which is in a sleep or trance state during the process. It can be linked to the physical body in one of three places:

1. For the average sensually or physically orientated person, in the Sacral centre.
2. In the Solar Plexus centre for the average emotional person, mystic, or for those who are consciously working to master this *chakra*.
3. At the top of the head in the definitely mentally polarised person (or *yogin*).

When the indwelling Life (the Sambhogakāya Flower) has no more use of the dense vehicle, then the Life force and the consciousness of the personal-I is withdrawn through one of the three apertures of release and the silver cord is severed. The astral body then becomes the densest sheath of the person, after a brief span residing in the etheric body.

The effects of people's continually reinforced desires, emotions, sensuality, glamours, and illusions must be lived out fully in their astral bodies after they die. Such energies become concretised on the subjective realms. They have clothed the person's *aura*[17] whilst alive, which then becomes the manifest form after they die. All types of gods, devils, religious or non-religious idea-forms, unpleasant or aesthetic images, can become visually real to the deceased. They continue the pattern of unfolding *karma* carried through to this plane of perception. Thus the devotional type of person that had strong preconceived ideas on the nature of a personal beneficent Deity would live the emotional aspect of that idea as it was imagined whilst in physical incarnation. Eventually inconsistencies between these self-focussed effects and the natural state of affairs on this realm present themselves in an unavoidable manner, breaking the bonds of personal glamour. When a person's vision has been sufficiently clarified then true inhabitants of these subjective realms can also be seen.

The rules governing astral experiences depend upon the person's inbuilt desire qualities and karmic relationships. The intensity of glamours, desires and the *saṃskāras* that were developed whilst incarnate determines much of what is experienced. The people residing on the astral plane are far more group-conscious than those physically incarnate, as this realm is created directly by the united emotional efforts of people throughout the ages. Common desires and collectivised massed thought-forms are thus what one inevitably experiences here. They are the reward of humanity's involvement in social, national, racial, or religious groups. People directly experience their emotional thought-forms to the degree that they were effected (and not annulled) during their incarnate life. The appearing *saṃskāras* are no longer subdued

---

17 *Aura:* literally a field of light around an object. Auras are spheres of radiatory activity. The colouring of the subtle astral body clairvoyantly seen extending from the physical body. All individuals have auras. They get more luminous, vibrant, and intense as the lower conditionings of the astral body are transcended.

by the propensities of a dense physical body. They are experienced directly in the astral substance of which they are constituted, being the resultant *karma* for attachments and desires. The experiences gained then become incentives for future right action.

The description of the tortures in store for us in the hells of various religious theologies, Hades of the Greek and Roman mythologies and Amenti of the ancient Egyptians, have their validity. In Buddhism we not only have the various hells, the realm of the *pretas* with their abominable thirst, but also the jealousy or envy of the *asuras*. These depictions may be graphically exaggerated or symbolic, but also actually reference experiences that karmically entrap people upon the astral. Those that had much monetary power, luxuriating in opulence when incarnate, yet were indifferent, callous, or derisive to other's sufferings due to poverty, experience the karmic consequences as being effectively born as an *asura* in the after-death state. The 'gods' to which they are jealous are those that were formerly deprived of resources, but are now residing in the consequential luxury of their heavenly abodes. In the case of those who are intensely selfish and emotionally rapacious whilst incarnate, they find themselves as *pretas,* with an overwhelming thirst. This is a result of their inability to command the Watery astral substance they are now karmically ensconced in. Their Watery *karma* attacks them in every way, giving them no 'thirst-quenching' relief. Such people have many *saṃskāras* to transmute and much to eliminate karmically from their desire bodies by such means. Their former appetites cage them in a self-made hell that they must work to overcome.

The hell zones are inhabited by those who were the most cruel, hateful, extremely selfish, or spiteful, separative, and cunningly, callously manipulative of other's resources and lives for self-gain. They were insensitive to the pain and suffering they have caused, often upon a mass scale. Conditions in these domains are extremely squalid, wretched, wherein much karmically reciprocated pain is experienced. Many of the pictures of hell with its flames and furnaces are, however, exaggerated inventions. They are purposely made exceedingly horrendous to induce the members of the religious community to do 'right', or to conform to the dictates of a religion through fear of a tortured afterlife if these dictates were not carried out. No matter how intense the experience, however, educational pathways exist to higher, more pleasant domains, and consequent rebirth. For this reason, in the depiction of the Buddhist wheel of rebirth a Buddha-emanation of Avalokiteśvara appears in each of the six realms, to try to help the associated residents out of them.

It is necessary for people to eliminate from their minds all concepts of fear of the afterlife if they are loving, generous people. It should be emphasised that emotion and pain are greatly modified on that realm. There is no physical pain as we understand it, for there are no physical nerves, thus there are no means to satiate sensuous addiction or experiences, but states of anguish there certainly can be.

Most religious practices, teachings on morality, and meditation techniques, assist individuals to eliminate base, selfish, aggressive, hateful, desirous thought-streams whilst still incarnate. This facilitates engendering a pleasant astral life. A pleasant sojourn in the afterlife is, after all, one of the main things that religious teachings provide to their adherents.

One should note that though seemingly wonderful, the heavenly realm is really illusional. It is the realm of the psychic, the source of much of the inspiration of the mystic, as it is the home of many of the visions colouring the effects of one's devotional and psychic probing. It contains the substance of glamour, imagination, emotions, and feelings. Here, therefore, exist picture forms of all kinds that humanity's combined hopes and dreams have built throughout the ages, and in which most people are basically polarised. Therefore this astral domain has no substantiality of its own.

The energies taking form upon the astral plane are not just pure emotion and feeling. They also constitute the instinctual desires, evoked by mind utilising the evolving substance of the physical plane. In its entirety through the activity of the human family this substance is gradually being redeemed and drawn upwards until some day we shall see its transformation into the Void. Also permeating this astral realm are the descending thought-forms which the developing human being is always creating and drawing downwards into manifestation, clothing them with the substance of desire. When the descending forms of thought and the ascending mass of instinctual demands from the lower aspect of humanity as a whole meet, then we have the appearance of what is known as the astral plane. It is therefore a sphere of activity created by human desire-minds. The superhuman lives have surmounted it by having discovered the secret of its delusion. They, therefore, no longer recognise it, except as a temporary field of service. In the astral sphere one learns the fact that reality is not this, but only this and that in relation to something 'other' that is more vibrant, subtler, providing many more degrees of freedom to move, create, and to infallibly know. The projection of thought-power is what enables all construction and travel in this domain. The refinement of thought is the mechanism to travel to higher domains.

People must learn to control the forces and to comprehend the properties contacted in every new state of perception (sphere of sensation) by being born into it, until eventually all aspects of phenomena are completely mastered. Eventually the properties of the three worlds of experience (the physical, astral, and mental realms) with which we have karmic obligations, come to be transmuted. We then rise out of the corporeal world to reside in the realm of enlightened being. Our grosser contacts and expressed sensations are gradually eliminated as karmic lessons are learned. The useful elements are absorbed, then refined and eventually abstracted, when a new higher cycle of experience is entered. Frequent and intimate contact with the enlightened members of society, in conjunction with the energies from the Sambhogakāya Flower will always stimulate and draw people higher, closer to enlightenment. Hell states in the astral Bardo then become passé, no longer possible for that individual.

The higher astral levels are conditioned by the musical interplay of sound and colour, the 'music of the spheres', from which much of the inspiration to musicians and artists comes. People residing here are generally devotionally engrossed in the development of the creative faculties of their imaginations. They thereby build astral utopias. There are various categories of service work on this realm, plus the ability to research in all scientific fields. Whatever will be the focus or leitmotiv of their next incarnation will generally influence all their actions.

If the person previously had an intellectual life he/she is eventually drawn from the astral realm (the *purgatory* of the Christians) to the *mental realm,* the true heavenly realms (*devachan*), the experiences of which can be equated with Amitābha's Paradise Realm. The appropriate *karma* of the thought world is then experienced. At the borders of this realm one undergoes a *second death,* of dying to one's astral body.

In the mental realm the doors to higher revelatory knowledge open, and the complete understanding of the laws of Nature concerning humanity on the lower planes is available, as the thinker is now a king on his true estate of mind. The universe that one now resides in is composed of the same substance that constitutes people's minds. The registration of thought thus becomes instantaneous and is in the form of one unbroken expansive vista of whatever subject the person is engrossed. The result for the thinker will be one of sublime ecstasy of direct involved realisation in mentation.

In terms of the symbolism of the *stūpa* (which will be revealed later) we have now travelled up its edifice from the Watery to the Fiery level.

On the lower mental sub-planes, abstracted archetypal ideas and ideals from the realms of enlightenment are fragmented into set patterns and forms that can be directly experienced by the thinker. Here also the person experiences the thought-forms that were formerly built, bringing to the fullest expression all the latent ideas and mental tendencies or problems that they were engrossed in whilst incarnate. Thus a scientist is able to explore the most intricate thought that may have previously frustrated him. Here one's mind cannot be clouded and marred by the emotionalism and glamour of the astral realm, or be limited by the sensations and lower instincts of the physical body. Thus the type of empiricism normally possessed by people in dense bodies does not exist here, there are no flirtatious imaginative discursions. Reality is seen for what it is, undistorted by physical plane encumbrances.

The physical plane is the world of reasoning and experimentation. The astral is the realm of imagination, whilst the mental is the realm of direct illumination. For instance, if the history of the world is the object of one's contemplation, then upon the mental domain one can become that history to the extent of being absorbed in the collective group-mind of all who were involved in the enactment of any historical scenario. The *karma* of the thought life is lived through until that life has been transcended and one is able to stand within the Clear Light. The domain of the *tathāgatagarbha* then becomes within one's ken.

Being born therein means loss of concept of the 'ego' of that life, the full consciousness-stream of all one's lives as a continuum is experienced, whilst the force of the rebirth process inevitably karmically chooses a new human womb to incarnate into.

The above information concerning the nature of what happens after death is broadly generalised and thus suffers from the errors natural to all generalisations if too concretised.

Seen in terms of mass human conditioning the astral realm can be visualized as a dark, murky cloud hovering over our planet, which is almost impenetrable to light. This is the *darkness* of massed ignorance, and can be equated with hell-states, being the substance of many agonies of the desire-mind unfolding. Most suffering comes through the lack of the ability to control the volatility of one's emotional substance (*kliṣṭamanas*), or to see clearly through the fogs and miasmas associated with the Watery realm. To clearly see the way through requires the generation of *bodhicitta*, the demonstration of *śamatha*[18] and the application of the techniques of *vipassanā.*[19] The mind must therefore be firmly in control and be able to reason its way through the glamour, darkness, and illusion of this *māyāvirūpa.*[20] *Bodhicitta* represents the gain of transformed astral substance. Proper meditative yogic discipline therefore helps to ensure an abstracted sojourn in the highest heaven (the 'paradise realm' of the *tathāgatagarbha).* For the Bodhisattva the Hierarchy of Enlightened Being becomes home, and for the most advanced the *śūnyatā* experience and Shambhala become domains of great revelatory power.

Right methodologies of mind therefore represent the way out of the phantasms engendered by attachment to changeable substance. Mind is the true creative potency within the framework of the human persona. In terms of the above symbolism of dimensionality we can view mind in terms of fifth-dimensional expression, but obviously concepts become more abstract in trying to interpret this from the point of view of manifesting at right angles to fourth-dimensionality.

18 *Śamatha:* calm abiding meditation.

19 *Vipassanā:* insight meditation.

20 *Māyāvirūpa:* the great illusional form of this world.

It allows the *maṇḍala* of being/non-being to be properly constructed and viewed logically.

Analysis becomes facilitated if we view the astral plane as mind-conditioned. The focus of this book is upon the method of construction of a *maṇḍala*, which starts from a *manasic* point in time and space, that radiates out to produce a full circumference of discriminatory awareness. This process produces many interesting phenomenal considerations, where we see that the Bardo realms are left behind as inappropriate apparel for the domain of the enlightened Mind. In the following chapter we will explore further the construction of *maṇḍalas*.

5

The Construction of Maṇḍalas

The logic of *maṇḍalas*

When you build a grand concept, a *maṇḍala* within the bounds of consciousness from the smallest point up, then you need excellent logic to fill the possibilities of that structure. This will allow that structure to support a larger system or field of awareness. An originating idea is therefore essential to be recognised as an instigator producing background information that allows one to aspire to higher dimensional pursuits. Continuous right discrimination must manifest to produce a perfect structure for revelatory attainment in all possible directions of thought that exist within the bounds of the *maṇḍala* of a vaster (Logoic) Mind. Such a revelatory attainment incorporates and transcends the present mind space of the intelligentsia. Wrong or lazy discrimination will prevent the person from proceeding beyond the barriers of any lines of limitation delineated by a *maṇḍala,* or of its major segments.

An enlightened thought-structure does not limit itself to 2-D representations of the *maṇḍala*, but it becomes *stūpa*-like, voluminous, multidimensional, as defined and ascertained by the superbly trained Mind. The definition of things may be exact but may be considered illusional when everything in fact is transitory. Even Buddhist concepts fall prey to illusion when they propose exact definitions by using the discriminatory mind to define such things as *śūnyatā* and *dharmakāya.* In each historical period of the *buddhadharma* a Buddhist philosopher manifested a certain 'absolute' form of reasoning in the syllogistic presentation of the school he founded. Then based in the seeming 'infallibility' of this logic, many other streams of thought are tacked on to it by the successor logicians of that school. This produces a particular *maṇḍala* of that school of thought perceived by later generations of seers.

Here, an analogy can be made to an organism manifesting a cellular structure of paradigms with a central trunk of core ideas. A radiatory support structure of branches and leaves is then propagated for the dissemination of ideas and the gaining of lighted impressions from the general environment. This translates as the floral expression of many centres of learning, of monasteries and universities, where the pure foundational *dharma* thrives, as well as variations derived from it. Mutations of new adaptations of logic based upon the earlier presentations will evolve in time, to provide the growth of entirely new forms of trees of knowledge.

As time evolves, so the original organism generally becomes more woody, gnarled, concretised as per the conceptions in the minds of later followers of that doctrine. The structure has entered a *rigor mortise* stage where further expansion in the domain of high ideas is stifled, and fourth-dimensional motion prevented. The *maṇḍala* then barely moves around its central core, so weighed down is it with the encumbrance of obsolete reified ideas. Rigid lines of thought have formed from the basic structure, distorting or obliterating the vibrant pristine expression of the original ideation.

Inevitably, therefore, a palpable reliance upon some dead revered philosopher's doctrine, thinking that reification or verbatim reiteration is the best way to truth, becomes a process of regressive limitation rather than of liberation. Mere acceptance manifests orthodoxies of expression because streams of thought no longer explore new and unfamiliar pathways of consciousness. The constraints of a tradition thus retard the freedom of the consciousness-stream to expand, preventing it to break free from the bounds of its own inherent self-limitation.

Lack of the will to think accurately, precisely, and conclusively along unorthodox, non-sanctioned lines by later adherents of the doctrine produces ungainly, hardened connections to the primary *maṇḍala*. Thus the structure becomes replete with the forceful, but shallow thoughts of the indoctrinated. Thoughts then manifest in patterns of desired outcomes, curtailing penetrative insights into high thought domains. Only part of the entire paradigm of the revelatory universe can then be realised. Such Watery consciousness-links can source desired information only from the designated *maṇḍala*. The often subtle, but broad forms of interrelatedness with other *maṇḍalas* becomes squashed or invisible. Desired outcomes generally colour or muddy the links, eventually producing stifled, sensationalised, or garbled ideas. Thus cancers and knots of reasoning form in the base structure. The entire organism becomes unwieldy; obscuring the original pristine, vibrant formulation of lines in the *maṇḍala* of thought that benefited the entire structure in a wholesome manner and produced organic growth. The cancers that develop become accepted as the norm. Cancers may exist in a crippled organism allowing it to live for a long period of time, but inevitably they produce death. Analogous cancers may be found in various religious, social, and political systems.

To stimulate the will to visualise whole *maṇḍalas* correctly, in the spirit engendered by the ancient masters, is the challenge for all earnest students of the *dharma*. They must free themselves from the constricted bounds of aberrant opinions, to truly reflect the multidimensionality that is veiled by the originating constructs. Concentrating effort upon the most obvious facile, simplistic, and reified characteristics is the death-knell to enlightenment. The challenge needing to be wisely met is the propagation of a wholesome view of the *maṇḍala* that effects the liberation of thought, rather than the imprisonment of thought.

The discriminatory mind must be properly utilised to overcome the mental peregrinations of the average Buddhist, or any other philosophically inclined individual. For the sake of argument, we must utilise a suitable structure that supersedes the aberrant composite of their accumulative minds. The integrated *maṇḍala* to be utilised will therefore proceed against the grain of commonplace thinking, if it is to clean up the messy doctrines that have obscured the pristine expression of the enlightened *dharma*. This is an obvious objective of this series of books. Hopefully the dynamics of the accumulative cancers that have obfuscated Buddhist logic throughout the millennia can thereby begin to be eliminated. By explicating many of the veiled truths extant in the *buddhadharma* the conceptual thinking of Buddhists can be freed, allowing them to become more attuned to many parameters needed nowadays to make enlightenment possible. These parameters are no longer the same as in Gautama's time because of the advances of thought in this modern scientific era.

New revelations are now possible, producing a scintillating vibrancy to the corpus of the *buddhadharma*, facilitating much quicker insights into the vast domains of revelation pertaining to the *dharmakāya*. New ways of perceiving truths are always beneficent, allowing old staid attitudes to be reformed. If for instance, one starts to think of such things as *śūnyatā* as something one cannot go beyond for 'truth', then one has limited one's thoughts to that concept. The statements related to *śūnyatā* are only true in relation to the immediate capacity of the finite mind. They are not necessarily true for one that is grounded in *śūnyatā*, by having gone 'there'.

Building *maṇḍalas* is the way that ideas can be thoroughly defined. Similar *maṇḍalas* can be built in terms of other conceptions, with separate mental constructs. However, pathways from one to the other must also exist, making comprehension of what they mean in relation to each other possible. Without such pathways there would exist two or more separate views for comprehension, but no basis for any common reality-structure. They are therefore of little use as grounds for ascertaining truth. Isolated islands of opinion are thus not logical in the truest sense, as all truth is an expression or extension of the same main trunk of the fundamental ground of revelation. Such islands exist in many minds, producing disjointed thinking with no possibility of enlightened outcomes. They produce only individual ideas that are rarely integrated into the vast panorama of conclusiveness that is revelatory truth. (Unless artificially grafted to a vaster limb of awareness.) Verily all revelatory truth is interconnected.

The construction of the cellular unit (a *maṇḍala*) necessitates discriminatory thinking and thus a measurement of things, from which one can deduce desired information in terms of distance between two or more reference points. This immediately produces a time sequence, a continuum of expression of the component parts of the cell, and of the entire structure as a unit within its general environment. This then facilitates the process of evolutionary sequence, or space, constituting an interrelated construction of many such points, each manifesting an evolutionary path. The important thing in any cellular construct is that all separate parts are travelling together in the same time-continuum. For any particular level of the *maṇḍala,* if one point within the construct is seen to move askew, moving considerably faster or slower than the other points to which it is linked through lines of relationship, then there would be an aberration threatening to destroy the harmonious progression of the entire structure.

We can extrapolate such a cellular unit to represent a community of humans living a similar life pattern. When a person arises whose consciousness is travelling far slower than the others, then we have a retardation of growth of the entire community, producing concern to the others. It necessitates them to move backwards to assist the deviant one (who for example manifests a form of sickness or psychological illness in the organism) in an endeavour to move the entire construct forwards. If there is another who is travelling too far into the future for the others, transcending the paradigm of the commonality of what is considered 'self-identity' by the rest, then we have the appearance of a saviour, a saint. Such a one is much misunderstood by the common body and is oft reviled, condemned, castigated because viewed as an anomaly, thus feared. The entire body thereby acts to bring that one back to the stance (or time zone) that they represent. However, the saviour-saint (Bodhisattva) will see the lethargy of thought in the group from which she/he has evolved and will work to bring them faster to what really represents their future.

It is selfhood that represents the greatest danger to the harmony of all cellular units, because the horse of mind of each 'self' races to assert its own agenda, generally against the harmonious movement of the whole. For a 'self' to reach its particular goals it works to siphon from the whole whatever it deems necessary for the building of a separative empire of thought and materialistic constructs around itself. We therefore have the appearance of ulcers, calluses, and cancers in the *maṇḍala*. The construct then warps, with its entire progress being stifled.

The results of all such distortions in our present human societies are obvious. The need to overcome social injustice created by the aberrant self-seeking ones is well understood. To rectify them we should analyse the nature of each mind to view the points of aberration. The aim being to help make the entire mind hum and resonate a harmonious song. This allows the minds of the aberrant ones to transform from points of relative ignorance to the luminous spheres of great brilliance we call enlightenment.

The necessity for the identity of things

One should understand the *karma* generated in all forms of actions, and even of 'no-action'. *Karma* governs whatever *maṇḍalic* construct one builds, even that pertaining to the Void. Everything exists with respect to some form of identity. Even those that nonsensically deny that Buddhism is a religion have had to identify, define Buddhism in some way. What often manifests as a nemesis to enlightenment, for Buddhists, is the belief that one, or everything that exists is void of identity. It stifles action on the physical plane to truly help humanity overcome the deceit of materialism. The popular Buddhist ideal of *śūnyatā* often prevents clear Bodhisattvic action, because a proper comprehension of the way things truly exist subjectively is not appropriated. They need to manifest a true command of the scientific attributes of their philosophy to help them overcome their own *saṃskāras* preventing enlightenment.

A forceful denigration of 'self' muddies clear comprehension of what actually is. Playing imaginative games will not work. The resolution of a confused, incoherent identity into an enlightened unity occurs through the transmutation of *karma* expressed from many past life attainments. See the *karma* and see the *saṃskāras* flowing via purpose driven identity to produce enlightenment in the end. Analyse the complexity of Life; its numerology and processes, to train the mind to better comprehend from where we have come and to where we go. That the ego must die to the grip of *saṃsāra* is all too true, the ego must altogether die, but the way to accomplishment is to become identified with an Identity far greater than 'self' via the intermediate stage of *śūnyatā*. The many views of Life being infused with Divinity of Logoic purpose cannot be avoided. This is another way of depicting the immanent transcendence into the *dharmakāya*. All 'thus gone' ones retain such an Identity. *Śūnyatā* is a space, or 'platform', that allows one to travel far beyond the empirical confines of our earth evolution. One must vision in silence the true nature of the *maṇḍala* of enlightenment to transcend empirical knowledge. Present the tranquillity of your Hearts, and the training can go efficiently.

No matter how liberated one is, the corners of cosmic direction in space: the north, east, west, and south will still exist. For all the ways we perceive, space still contains form from a relativistic perspective. Note that the term 'space' here does not just refer to the space of Cosmologists, but more specifically to *dharmatā*. Everything has its moment for action and then for dissolution, to be embraced in a Void, with consequent rebirthing upon a higher cycle of expression.

Too many people use the concept of 'nothing exists' as an excuse to avoid acting appropriately in the physical domain by avoiding responsibility of right karmic action when clear decisions are to be made. They have provided a mentalistic concept of nothingness, thinking that by a process of avoidance (the denial of the phenomena around them) that they will somehow 'get there' and become liberated. Such naïve presumptions will only produce further karmic ensnarements. The paradox of forming such concepts in the mind should be made clear. When a structural thought is considered 'real', such as the concept that all is Void, and then one lives out a life according to a preconceived idea of what that may entail, one is lead to error. One is still involved in a mind game, making *real* decisions to act in this or that *saṃsāric* way, because it is the mind that is defining it all as Void.

By extrapolation we can say that a philosophy (such as Buddhism) has a 'self'; a transient identity, though the *dharmas* may be relatively permanent, the philosophy is an evolving form. This is what will allow the religion to eventually be swamped in an ocean of liberated Life. This necessitates the admittance that such an ocean could eventuate by eliminating all *cul de sacs* of thought. Such identity can't be avoided, even at the highest level. The collective corpus of Buddhism is viewed as a form because therein people are trapped in *māyā*. It is 'something' that exists, even if phenomenally so.

One cannot avoid everything phenomenal simply because it is perceived to be illusional. All manifest things serve a purpose, they produce order in (cosmogenic) space. Purpose is undoubtedly the play, or way to liberation, of entrances and exists into and out of form, from the spaces of mind and of no-mind, and that which exists beyond. *Śūnyatā* has an obvious part to play in the process of gaining enlightenment, but the truth of its existence is only a part of a greater play.

The attainment of *śūnyatā* is much more difficult than most imagine. It requires stern yogic discipline at the task of transforming and transmuting the force of the *saṃskāras* that have taken many lives to develop. Such *saṃskāras* must first be recognised for what they are. It's not so easy to convert such long standing vipers of desire-mind, ego-posturings, the *kleśas,*[1] *kliṣṭamanas,* etc. Neither is it easy for most to recognise the little grey worms of subtle aberrant thoughts, worries, doubts, and the tendencies to misapply idealistic teachings through self-centred intent. The practical teachings given in the next volume of the series on the yoga of the Bardo Thödol offers a more detailed view as to the nature of the task confronting one in the quest for enlightenment. Only by ardently following such yogic disciplines (*sadhāna*) will one learn to reside at the *śūnyatā-saṃsāra* nexus, and to work out one's life in all eight directions of space. From there the true basis for the construction of the *maṇḍala* of being/non-being will be established.

The mystery of numbers

The secrets of being/non-being lie hidden in the mystery of numbers. They are not illusions, but relate to the platforms of awareness that make things definite. They establish identities, that which is definable, according to certain patterns of expression. They also veil that which is undefinable. They exist in their own right as formations, and yet there is a continuous stream of resolutions of all numbers culminating to points, the cipher zero, or to infinities. Every fraction makes up part of the whole of another number, so one can look to its progress to infinite smallness or even to its unlimited scope for expansion, to produce the expansion of wholes to infinity. All depends upon which way the continuous stream of numbers flow, e.g., the number can refer to going

---

1 *Kleśas* (Tib. nyon mongs): the force of defilements, afflictive, dissident emotions. They are generally signified as the three poisons: delusion, attachment, and hatred. The quality (passion-desire) that causes one to attach oneself to all aspects of the formed realms, and to identify with them as real.

forwards or backwards in the stream of consciousness. Such a stream can also be viewed in terms of being circular or cyclic. Consciousness is here delineated because consciousness divides phenomena into streams of numbers, of definitives. It constitutes the process that makes up the identity of a number, but also the fractions that make up a whole. This means that a number can be included as part of something else, such as the thinking of Logoi. Consciousness is thus a stream of order of little spheres, *bindu*, or beginnings of things, to produce cyclic culminations. (Thus we have such conceptions as 'the mundane egg' from which the cosmos originated.) Each division or unitary something is but a fragment or portion of the overall *maṇḍala* of being/non-being.

Numbers indicate the processes of beginnings and endings, yet consolidation, resolution, transcription, transformation, and transmutation are key words to utilise when referring to consciousness in relation to numbers, because nothing culminates without the process leading to the transforming and the transmutation of its elements. The egg, the singularity or unity, or esoterically the zero point of manifestation, manifests a process that transmutes into the 'chicken' that is the completed unitary aspect of consciousness.

Numbers are the symbols of the transmutation of certain hierarchical orders of expression. The silence of symbols manifests in the form of tranquillity of mind, allowing one to interpret any number of symbols together, to be part of a perfect harmonious accord. The numbers manifest in a continuous stream, where each has its individual identity and yet the sequence makes a smoothly flowing movement. Each number can have its own note, thus together numbers act as a repository for the emanation of various harmonies of sound, which when mixed with the hues of light help to make resonant the full intricate structure of the *maṇḍala*. The overall numerology produces sharp razors of mind because each number separates, but their inner analysis necessitates a tranquil mind to arrive at the true meaning of their symbolic import. A karmic stream of identifications flows through all allowing them to retain their identity, despite the progression from one number to the next.

As one transits from a number of a sequence or progression to the next, so the former members of the sequence do not disappear, but hold intact their veiled potency. Because the sequence exists, so we have order and evolutionary attainment, not chaos. The entire universe is expressed in this way, via sequences of numerical correspondences, of mathematical and algebraic terms, and esoteric definitions.

The forces producing the flow of events may move on, but the numerical sequence remains. Therefore each number remains and holds a tension, even if situated in the past. This allows the unfolding of the universe. An appearing number is a unit of potential purpose expressing an intrinsic noetic Fire. Its stability is however grounded in a moving sequence, and is constantly expressing the mutability of ever-changing phenomena. It is responsive to the immediacy of every single movement, thus we say it is in harmony because it is moving with the flow of everything else, and yet it retains its separations, its wall of limitation, as governed by the numerical function. Even when relegated to the past as an expression in time, consciousness presumes that its function has not altered, but it has appeared and moves in accordance with the sphere of action-reaction (the *maṇḍala*) or universe of which it is a part. When the *maṇḍala* moves to its conclusion (*pralaya*), the Void, it takes the past (number) with it, as it must. In a consequential outbreathing (*manvantara*) that past number has relevance within the context of the newly forming cipher, the cosmic/mundane egg. Such pulsation of forces and appearances of 'things' in and out of the Void are governed by numbers. All is thereby realisable by wisdom. Such sequencing immediately allows the wise to gather the information needed concerning anything that is meditated upon. The past and the present can be juxtaposed with the inherent future, because the future is just another number in the sequence that is being analysed, and which is already being activated with a pulse of energy (*saṃskāra*) of numerical affinity from the past. The nature of the All is cognisable because of the mathematical array in which every type of phenomena is sequenced.

Each number of a sequence becomes the middle ground of a line of activity of whatever is the past and the future of its sequential position. This happens whenever the flow of Life-flux[2] activates it with

2 Life-flux flow, the consciousness stream (*jīva*) linking successive incarnations into a unity.

consciousness-volitions. The sequence's tensions of purpose therefore oscillate whenever a part of the fabric of its being is stimulated.

Thereby we have the *saṃskāras* and *skandhas* of commutability that embody all evolving things flowing from the past to the present. They manifest through discrete quanta of expressions as they come to be experienced by consciousness or sentient states. Each quantum can be defined by a specific numerical term, a fractional notation, delineating differing energy states that are being expressed, e.g., of the Rays of lighted propensity, or proportions of them.

Thus there are cycles of energies coming and going through each numerical sequence, the nature of which the wise come to comprehend in their analysis of whatever they are viewing. The cycles flow in increasingly refined, sublime, cascading hues of expression as the culmination points of each cycle are reached. A period of *pralaya* ensues before the new cycle commences (is reborn) in the consciousness-stream of the entire *maṇḍala* being envisioned. The *maṇḍala* therefore is not a static image, it is depicted in two or three-dimensional form[3] but is continually moving, evolving. It is vital and alive, though the symbolism depicted by the concretised form persists throughout for wave after wave, cycle after cycle of expression of the energies it contains, as they are numerically encoded in line, colour, and symbolical representation.

The movement of waves of energy when they cross each other presents the imagery of the awakening of a lotus flower. The petals do not go straight out, they go up and wind in a curve towards the central axis. But the flowers are more like spheres of containment, with each petal appearing to be curved, as around a sphere. They are bent into three-dimensional form. When describing a Head centre, then we must also look to tiers of petals gyrating around, according to the nature of the energy input. Each tier consists of a series of differing size petals, with smaller ones integrated by larger ones according to numerical considerations. In a fully enlightened being the gyration has become fourth-dimensional, with the motion going round from within without and from without within, and unfolding in a multidimensional arc that is spinning forwards. All motion of consciousness-expansion is

3 Such as a Thangka.

spiral-cyclic, like the precessional motion of the earth around the sun as the sun is travelling along its cosmic path.

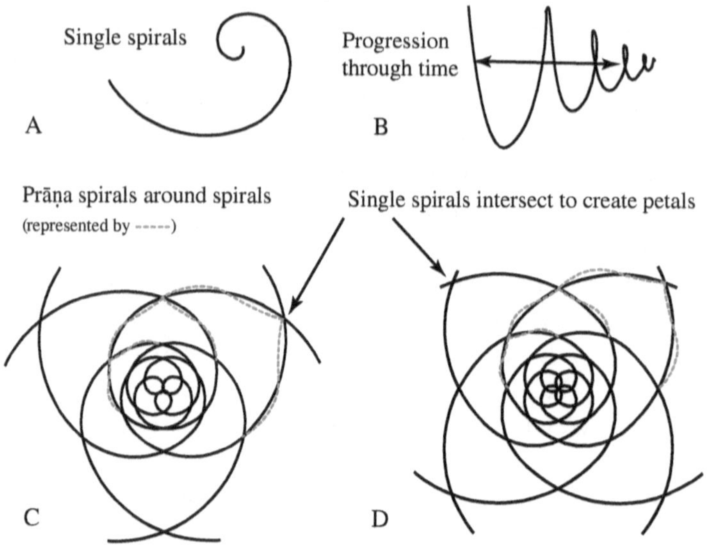

Figure 13. Spirals of consciousness

In a sense, the eye is like a sun, as it is a source of light for the brain. The eye focuses upon differing aspects of the *maṇḍala,* it makes the little separations of degrees of light, line, and form, which allow numerical analysis to be accomplished. It splits the image up into various pieces for the brain to process.

The *maṇḍala* defined

Maṇḍalas illustrate the process of arriving at the state of awakened perception through which one may become absorbed in either the *ālayavijñāna* experience, *śūnyatā*, or the *dharmakāya.* The literal translation of *maṇḍala* in Tibetan is 'centre and periphery', which provides an idea of the genesis of the *maṇḍala* from a *bīja* point to eventually encompass the space included in its periphery. *The Encyclopaedia of Eastern Philosophy and Religion* states 'A *maṇḍala* can be understood as the synthesis of numerous distinctive elements in a unified scheme, which through meditation can be recognised as the basic nature of existence.'[4] *Maṇḍala* literally means circle. A circle is a relationship between what is within a spherical boundary, what is outside that boundary, and the line that separates these, as well as the central point from which the entire sphere (of activity) emanates.

From the Mahāyāna perspective the most important relationship is between the opposites; *saṃsāra* and *śūnyatā*, form and Void. We also have the relationship between male and female, positive and negative, time and space, etc. Each of these relationships incorporates two points of interrelation, but that which relates the two is the 'I', the conscious perceiver that observes them, and binds them together. Consciousness stands between them, traversing from one point to the other until it is understood that their point of reference is neither exclusive of one or the other, but as all. *Saṃsāra* and *śūnyatā* then become identified as one, because all is intrinsically Void. At that point of relation consciousness is itself transcended. The *maṇḍala* therefore endeavours to express the nature of the nexus that is the point or place of interrelation, where either, or neither, or both exist simultaneously. It is replete with the potential of all possibilities, as well as that which is beyond.

The *maṇḍala* is also a diagram of the universe. The ancient adage, 'as above so below' applies meaningfully to all *maṇḍalas*. This adage describes the *mahāmudrā* or union of the inner and outer Tantras, or of the cosmic landscape that the *maṇḍala* mimics in its symbolic form. All *maṇḍalas* are constructed in accordance with the principles of multidimensional space. The meanings of each *maṇḍala* change according to the number of elements included within it and their placement. Tucci states:

> *Maṇḍala* is--a map of the cosmos...the whole universe in its essential plan, in its emanation and reabsorption...a psychcosmogram, the scheme of disintegration from the one to the many and the reintegration from the many to the one.[5]

---

4 Stephen Schumacher and Gert Woerner (eds). *The Encyclopaedia of Eastern Philosophy and Religion*, (Shambhala, Boston, 1994), 219.

5 Guiseppe Tucci, *Theory and Practice of the Maṇḍala, (*Rider and Co, London, 1961*)*, 23-25.

From a comparative perspective:

> The maṇḍala is the geometrical diagram of cosmos projected on a level surface; the Buddha's statue or painting, besides being a representation of a god, is a temporary reflection of the eternal being caught in the act of revealing himself, the stupa is dharma architecturally constructed. The principle underlying these representations is one, the standards which determine their symbolism are one, and their iconometric rules are identical.[6]

Basic elements of the *maṇḍala*

A typical *maṇḍala* is that of the Kālachakra Tantra. It, therefore, can be used as a template that will allow us to analyse some of the major constituencies of a *maṇḍala*.[7] Our representation is Tantric, and in such *maṇḍalas* the emanating Deity of the Tantra (generally united with consort/*śakti*) is depicted at the centre of the *maṇḍala*. It thereby represents the great bliss (*mahāsukha*), obtained through union with the highest of energies and transcendental consciousness states.[8] The *maṇḍala* is laid out in relation to the eight points of the compass, with four gates at the cardinal points. These directions with the centre represent the domains of the five Dhyāni Buddhas from the point of view of a 2-D representation, whilst from a 3-D perspective, we have a symbolic five tiered mountain, with Vairocana embodying the highest tier and Amoghasiddhi the lowest.

Figure 14 shows five main portions of a *maṇḍala*:

1. The outer perimeter of fire.
2. The charnel grounds.

---

6 Guiseppe Tucci, *Tibetan Painted Scrolls,* (SDI Publications, Bangkok, 1999), 299.

7 Two good books on *maṇḍalas* are: Martin Brauen, *The Mandala: Sacred Circle in Tibetan Buddhism,* (Serinda Publications, London, 1997), and D.P. Leidy, and R.A.F. Thurman, *Mandala: The Architecture of Enlightenment,* (Thames and Hudson, London, 1997), from which Figure 14 is adapted.

8 The Deity in this case is the Kālachakra Deity, with his Consort, Vishvamātā. The objective here is not to detail the attributes of this Deity or *maṇḍala.* If a student wishes further information, the book by the Dalai Lama (Tenzin Gyatso) and Jeffrey Hopkins, *Kalachakra Tantra: Rite of Initiation* (Wisdom Publications, London, 1989) should serve the purpose.

3. The gates to the celestial mansion.
4. The abode of the deities.
5. The point of abstraction, from which all comes and returns, becoming the central deity and consort.

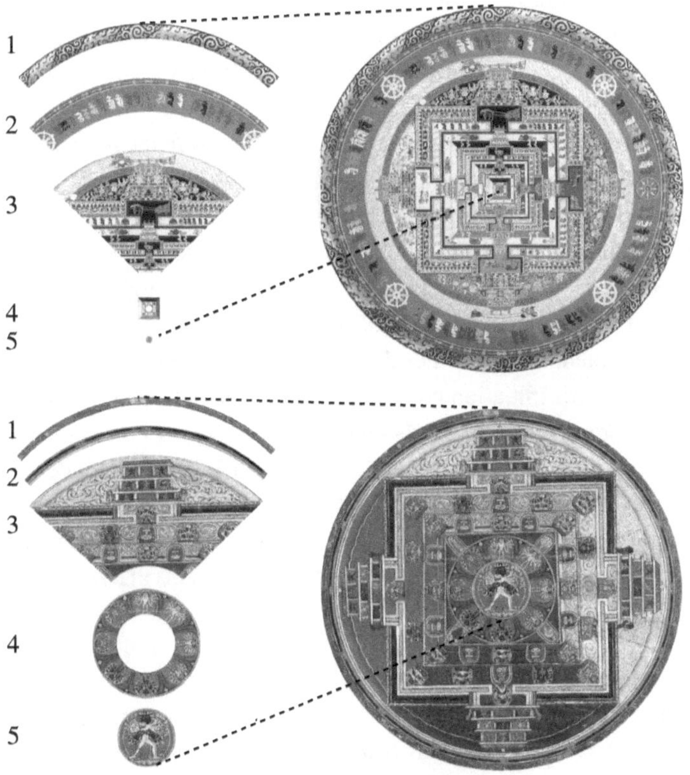

Figure 14. Two versions of the Kālachakra *maṇḍala*

The process that leads towards this union, i.e., towards the centre of the *maṇḍala*, is the esoteric path of Initiation, which can be understood as the mastery and perfection of the personal 'self', leading to its transcendence. (Similar to the purpose behind conventional Buddhist initiation ceremonies.) Here the progressive stages of Initiation can be likened to the unfolding of the *maṇḍala*, and as one nears its centre one begins to develop the attributes that allows one to emulate the functioning of the central deity.

The first Initiation concerns passing the outer ring of fire. This requires the attitudes concerning one's materialistic incentives, lusts, base desires, and impediments to meditation to be cleansed. Here *kriyātantra,* or action Tantra is practiced which involves mastery of physical plane conditions. The second Initiation involves the process of purifying oneself of all desires and emotional defilements in the charnel grounds. This involves mastering the second of the four classes of Tantras, *caryātantra*, which deal specifically with astral plane conditionings. The third Initiation involves entering through the gates of the *vajra* and the unions with the minor deities in the *maṇḍala.* The focus of the *yogin* in the third class of Tantras, *yogatantra*, is to deal with the rules governing all attributes of mind. The types of deities, such as presented in the Bardo Thödol, are meditated on and embodied. All *manasic* ideas and illusions must now be thoroughly eliminated and enlightenment-attributes developed instead. The *ālayavijñāna* enlightenment thus becomes the focus of attainment.

The fourth Initiation concerns entering the palace at the centre of the *maṇḍala,* wherein the *śūnyatā-saṃsāra* nexus becomes the object of focus. The final consummation (the fifth Initiation) concerns the fruits of the main Deity's union with his consort. The attributes of the *anuttarayogatantra*[9] practices thus come to be mastered within the central domain of the *maṇḍala* wherein these two Initiations are undertaken.

The outer perimiter

The outer perimeter is surrounded by a great protective circle of fire that burns away ignorance. The fires convey the five colours of the Dhyāni Buddhas, symbolising their transformative emanations. From their auras also emanate the Wrathful Deities that are the protectors of the *dharma,* trampling upon the obscurations preceding each Initiation level. Only after these obscurations have been transformed into enlightened-

9 *Anuttarayogatantra:* Highest (unsurpassed) yoga Tantra. It concerns visualising the chosen deities: any of the Dhyāni Buddhas and Vajradhara, and is usually centred upon Akṣobhya or Vairocana. It involves the union of Father and Mother Deities, thus the evocation of pristine cognition through the fusion of skilful means and discriminative awareness, whereby the qualities of the five Jinas come to be embodied. Refers to non-dual classes of Tantras.

attributes will the Deity allow the candidate to enter into the inner recesses of the *maṇḍala*. Initiation can then be undertaken.

In order to pass through this initial fiery burning ground one must have accomplished the first degree of refinement of the substance of one's periodical sheaths. This specifically refers to the physical body and the etheric stratum, wherein the *naḍī* system resides. The *naḍīs* convey the five *prāṇas* that express the rarefied *skandhas* that are the Elements of Life. (These Elements support the reified expression of the Wisdoms of the Dhyāni Buddhas.) Therefore, before even entering the *maṇḍala* one needs a theoretical understanding of the nature of the psychic cleansing process undertaken in yogic practices. The *maṇḍala* exists at a more rarefied and potent energy state than the novice possesses, and therefore he/she must refine the substance of consciousness to enter its sacred confines. We should note here that consciousness and *prāṇa* are considered identical in Tantric works.

This initial preparatory stage and its rewards (the entering of the peripheral fires of the *maṇḍala)* constitutes the first Initiation for the candidate. It involves more than consecration to the noble ideals that the *maṇḍala* represents, it also necessitates the refinement of one's psychic constitution and consciousness. This Initiation always produces a period of internal crisis, as all issues concerning physical plane living must be carefully analysed. The focus is upon the fields of sexuality, material comforts, and the right use of money and its karmic consequences. It also often involves considerations of diet, fasting, and breathing exercises, yogically interpreted as the right expression of one's *prāṇic* vitality. We also have considerations of material plane law verses that associated with one's spiritual life. (This requires an insight into the way that *karma* works in human society.) All such issues must be resolved correctly in this burning ground stage for the novitiate before the guru or hierophant responsible, as the training will deem the candidate worthy of entering the sacred precincts of the *maṇḍala*.

The commonly believed idea that one may enter this burning ground whilst drinking wine and indulging in gross sensuality (or that one can 'prove' the ability to transmute such defilements) is clearly a ruse. Such exoteric blinds are often presented in the Tantric treatises, as they serve to quickly weed out the unworthy.

Many of the preliminary 'initiations' given in Buddhist Tantric texts, such as the vase initiation, water initiation, etc., are really aspects of this first Initiation because they deal with the elementary stages of purification of body, speech and mind. Thus they focus upon concentration of the mind, and memory work via enhancing one's visualising ability. All of this comes under the auspices of *kriyātantra*.

The charnel grounds

The charnel grounds symbolise the next stage of purification needed to enter the *maṇḍala* proper. It involves the transmutation of the Watery Element/*prāṇa* via proper comprehension and control of the emotions. All forms of aversion and attachment to formed concepts (related to the emotions) must be eliminated or transformed into lighted reason. The various charnel grounds and graveyards wherein a *yogin* meditates symbolise the centres below the diaphragm. It is here that the *yogin* must 'dance upon the corpses' of *saṃskāras* to be eliminated or converted. This allows one to be liberated from the lower Watery *devas* embodying the substance of the emotions and desire-mind. The centres below the diaphragm store the putrescent *saṃskāras* (*kliṣṭamanas*) associated with the five sense-consciousness, and the overriding intellect. Battling with the various demons of the desire-mind, to transform the wrathful attributes of the many theriomorphic deities as described in the Bardo Thödol, happens during this *caryātantra* stage. (The succeeding *yogatantra* stage generally sees the process through to completion.) One cannot become overawed or overwhelmed by the psychic forces arrayed against one at this stage of the path. Practitioners generally have accrued much psychic *karma* from former lives of black magic and wrong yogic practices, for which they must now atone. It takes an awakened and skilful guru to guide the practitioner at this level of yoga. For this reason *yogin*s traditionally inhabited caves and forest retreats where they could safely practice without too many external *saṃsāric* influences interfering.

When mastery is successfully accomplished then one can undertake the second Initiation, concerning control of the Watery Element, which leads one to the portals of the doors of profound revelation—the celestial mansion.

The gates to the celestial mansion

Next to be mastered concerns all of the properties and functions of mind. This inevitably necessitates a comprehension of the *ālayavijñāna*. The Initiate can then enter into any of the four gates of the celestial mansions of enlightenment that represent the main body of the *maṇḍala*. Each mansion conveys the attributes of one or other of the four Dhyāni Buddhas (and their consorts) that support the throne or seat of power upon which sits Vairocana. Emulation of the attributes of the Jinas by way of awakening to the potency of the abstract Mind represents the taking of the third Initiation. It necessitates complete control of the vicissitudes of mind by overcoming the intensity of the emanations of all *manasic saṃskāras*. Long cherished beliefs, illusions, assumptions, bigotry, intolerance, and pedantry will have to be reviewed and often changed. Here the guardians of the *dharma*, the Wrathful Deities come to the surface of consciousness. They represent all of the perturbations of mind that need to be transformed into enlightened attributes in this *yogatantric* methodology. The ego then comes to be annihilated as the person takes on the paradigm of the Buddha-Mind. Full cognisance of the nature of the *dharmakāya* has, however, yet still to be established, but the framework is now built allowing such eventuation.

At this point the *yogin* can be considered an awakened member of the Council of Bodhisattvas, having been Initiated into the mysteries of the *maṇḍala* representing their combined Wisdom. No longer does the 'self' of the personal-I rule, as all such considerations have been eliminated by having mastered the laws of Mind associated with the attributes of the *maṇḍala*. All deities, representations of Bodhisattvas and Buddhas, are really Mind-born, and seen for what they are in the Clear Light of Mind. Having penetrated the mysteries of all attributes of the nature of Mind, the Initiate now knows the full concourse of the *ālayavijñāna* universe. This incorporates the *tathāgatagarbha* and thus the nature of the *sambhogakāya* of a Buddha. The remaining developments in meditation are through the higher yoga Tantras.[10]

---

10 The *anuttarayogatantra*. This unsurpassed yoga Tantra incorporates *mahāyoga*, *anuyoga* and *atiyoga*. The subtleties differentiating them are really only properly understood by advanced Initiates, and therefore their descriptions need not occupy

The abode of the deities

This abode normally incorporates a circle of eight deities and their consorts around the central deity and his consort. After all of the attributes of the *maṇḍalic* quadrants have been comprehended and the veiled qualities mastered, then one can be prepared to enter the *arena* of great Bliss at the centre of the *maṇḍala*. One can thereby come into union with one's consort (*deva* counterpart), by fusing all masculine and feminine attributes in the body and consciousness by a grand yogic *mahāmudrā* integration. The central element of *mahāmudrā* is said to be the recognition of the inseparable nature of wisdom and compassion.

In esoteric terms we have the *deva* or form aspect (producing the perfection of wisdom) and human consciousness (demonstrating effective compassion). By *deva* is meant the elementary Lives incorporated as the bodily form that manifest the forces (*śakti)* awakened by the *yogin*. Later the elements of *prajña*[11] are developed, which manifest as the *ḍākinī*[12] or consort for the meditator. This allows the domain of the Peaceful Deities to be experienced in full, which happens at the *sambhogakāya* level of experience. The union with the consort signifies a fusion with all phenomenal existence. No longer does the mind differentiate 'self' from everything else. Instead it is immersed in the infinite unity of the Clear Light, the resolution of the all that is and is not. *Śūnyatā* and *saṃsāra* come to be fused into the embrace of being/non-being. Such

---

space here. What is provided in standard texts suffices. They are effectively integrated into the practice called the Dharmakāya Way in this *Treatise on Mind*.

11 *Prajña* (Tib. shes rab): enlightened knowledge, analytical wisdom, discriminative awareness. The Wisdom coming from identifying or being absorbed into the universal Mind (*ālayavijñāna*). Also the consort of a Buddha, signifying the wisdom aspect of enlightenment.

12 *Ḍākinī* (Tib. mkha' 'gro ma [khan-dro-ma]): Literally, space voyager, or sky-goer. Thus it refers to one that is immersed in emptiness, because space here symbolises emptiness. Also, an accomplished *yoginī.* They are female protectors of the Law, the Consorts of the various Wrathful Deities. They can be most fierce in the pursuit of their duties. (The symbolism of the conversion of *saṃskāras* is here implicated.) The consummate union with a practitioner, which is full enlightenment, signifies the complete mastery of all attributes of the *saṃskāras* by means of Mind. The subject of the evolution of *devas* into *ḍākinīs* is a necessary ingredient in the consideration of the nature of a hylozoistic universe.

empowerment constitutes the taking of the fourth Initiation, when the causal form of the Sambhogakāya Flower merges into a greater unitary expansiveness known as *dharmatā*. It is no longer needed as a factor guiding the consciousness stream of that being towards liberation.

The point of abstraction

Here we have the central dot (*bīja*), the seed point from which the entire *maṇḍala* emanates. It is the door to the ineffable experience of cosmos, the qualities of which the *maṇḍala* resonates. The entire structure is made in the image of what is veiled in the central *bīja:* that which expresses the *dharmakāya*. The *bīja* manifests as the central Deity with his consort. The abode of deity then becomes dual, taking the form of eight Deities with consorts that represent aspects of the central Deity (around which they revolve) projected via the eight directions in space. (This being the depiction of most maṇḍalas based upon the Head centre.[13]) The ability to stand in the awesome potency of this state of Buddha-Mind constitutes taking the fifth Initiation. It is the gain of the entire evolutionary milieu. Effectively one becomes a Master of Wisdom and takes on the attributes of Vairocana.

The three crosses and the *mahāmudrā*

In the symbolism of the *maṇḍala* three types of crosses will be found represented, two actively expressed, and one veiled. They are important because they govern the way of development of all aspects of Life, and indicate the nature of the way energy impacts upon substance. All beings therefore will be found active upon principally one or other of the arms of any of these crosses. Each of the crosses has four arms, relegated to four directions of space. When taken together we have the 3 x 4 = 12 potencies that constitute the twelve petals of the Heart *chakra*, the dynamics governing the organisation of the twelve main petals of the Head lotus, and of the expression of the twelve signs of the zodiac. The three types of crosses are:

1. The *fixed cross* (the four cardinal positions of the compass)

---

13 See also Volume 5, chapter 7, for further explanation of a general *maṇḍala* with respect to the Head centre.

represents esoterically the human, or consciousness-stream, of the *prāṇas* of the *piṇgalā naḍī.* This stream expresses the steady unfolding purpose of the attributes of Love, developed by humans through overcoming the forces of separateness and ego-clinging. Being inherent within the constitution of the *tathāgatagarbha,* Love provides an onus for humanity to develop wisdom, as a consequence of treading the wheel of rebirth (*pratītyasamutpāda*[14]). Wisdom necessitates Love as its foundation. By this accounting, humanity is conditioned by the great second Ray attribute of Love-Wisdom. The general corpus of the *maṇḍala* is built upon the foundations of this cross. Its four main arms represent the four main gates of the *maṇḍala* embodied by the Dhyāni Buddhas, whose function it is to help develop their united wisdom throughout its structure. Once upon this path a person becomes fixed upon this cross, unable to move from it, until all of the wisdoms associated with these four directions have been fully developed. Knowledgeable pursuits in *saṃsāra* necessitate the pursuit of Love before wisdom can develop.

2. The cross of *continuous mutable activity*, and of periodic adaptation to moving events (the swastika), represents the *iḍā naḍī prāṇas* developed by a human unit. It is therefore the function that produces the development of the mind. This quality is also innate within the line of development of the *devas/ḍākinī*s. They are the conditioning intelligences embodying form or substance, the nurturing, intelligently perceptive, feminine principle in Nature. Buddhism relegates wisdom to the feminine principle. This concept appears to be derived from hagiographies, wherein *ḍākinīs* appear. There they possess exemplary wisdom, advising great ones in their moments of tribulation and provide prophetic revelations. What the future portends is always their gift to confer. *Ḍākinīs,* however, actually represent the activity of clear Intelligent foresight, which is directed towards applying the law of *karma* with Mathematically Exact Activity (the third Ray). The law of *karma* is their vehicle of manifestation; therefore they can foresee all of its ramifications. The way of manifestation of *karma* necessitates continuous activity.

---

14 *Pratītyasamutpāda:* the twelve links of dependent arising, dependent origination.

This cross embodies the qualities of the north-east, south-east, south-west, and north-west orientations of the *maṇḍala.*

3. The *cardinal cross* (the upward pointing arrow of Fiery, piercing liberating revelation) represents the nature of the fusion of the two crosses, and the projection of the synthesised qualities out from *saṃsāra* altogether. (It therefore represents the non-dual attributes of the male-female in a *mahāmudrā* of expression.) This cross provides the overall direction in multidimensional-space, thus the true orientation of the *maṇḍala,* moving it onwards to the goal of liberation and into the domain of the *dharmakāya.* It therefore represents the intent of one-pointed Will. This will then can be directed to any of the four arms of the cross by a liberated being, in order to produce an objective purpose. (For example, the organisation of *prima materia* by an Ādi Buddha so that a world-sphere can be formed, in which case the focal point would be the southern arm of this cross.)

Though depicted as a static image in Buddhist art, the *maṇḍala* should be understood as dynamic, with energies moving through it, revolving like a swastika. It is a blueprint for the change to be effected upon the individual or group purpose.

When we are engaged in analysis of a *maṇḍala,* where there is a union of two differently polarised energies, then we must also look to the concept of *mahāmudrā.* The direct translation of the term *mahāmudrā* in Tibetan is said to concern a freedom from *saṃsāra* by realisation of *śūnyatā,* there being, however, an inseparability of these two factors. We thus have implied the *saṃsāra-śūnyatā* nexus. It begins with serenely dwelling in the natural state of Mind and culminates in the transformation of every experience through the Clear Light to *śūnyatā.*

The *mahāmudrā* is symbolised by images of a Buddha and consort in sexual union. The concept of *mahāmudrā* encompasses absolute union of all that is dual, to produce an indivisible whole. All things can be seen to be intrinsically empty (of duality) and therefore marked with the 'great seal' or *mahāmudrā.*

Realising *mahāmudrā* may also be understood as analogous to the cleansing of the entire *naḍī* system, and awakening the *chakras* in turn according to right geometrical order. The progression is in consciousness through the lines of interrelation between each *chakra*. For each Initiation to occur the cleansing and awakening of many minor *chakras* and petals leading to larger *chakras* must occur on the way to the centre of it all. (The Heart in the Head centre, the *sahasrāra padma.)* Each deity and grouping of deities is steeped in symbolism that must be decoded by the Initiate. The path of *mahāmudrā* is thus the path of abstraction into cosmos, to the grand Heart in the Head of the All. For this reason the passing out from the trammels of *saṃsāra* by an Initiate of high degree is a rare event.

The overriding *maṇḍalic* purpose

If Dhyāni Buddhas, being perfected Beings, create *maṇḍalas* in their meditative reflection, which incorporate the *karma* and laws of the phenomenal world, why then do humans (being integral components of such *maṇḍalas)* suffer such impure thoughts? The answer necessitates the concept of evolutionary purpose in Nature. We incorporate the impurities, the defilements into the unenlightened quality of our thoughts for the purpose of their eventual transmutation. Also, attachment to these impurities in the light of their intrinsic transience is what causes us to suffer. No impurities can stay in the face of the divinity of the driving force of the originating *dhāraṇī*.[15] The defilements must come to be rectified, transmuted into the wisdoms of the Jinas as part of the process of the gain of human evolution. The rectification process necessitates the medium of a human consciousness. Such a consciousness must come to learn to devise mechanisms to detach from all forms of transience. Wisdom is gained in the process of learning this art. The entire evolutionary process is thus part of the Jinas' compassion. What cannot enter into their pure domain during any completed cycle of activity gets recycled again and again until it can. This process is automatic because of the instrumentality and exigencies of the law of *karma*. It is made so because of the activity of the *ḍakinīs* that embody it. They are the Jina Consorts. These beings embody the purposeful

15 *Dhāraṇī:* a meditation aid, explained in detail in the next chapter.

substance impregnated into the womb of time-space, the Buddha-germ, thus pre-conditioning the tenor of its overall progress. They command the function of the related Lives, so that wisdom can be evolved out of it all. The seeded wisdom-principle by a Buddha-Mind (Monad) is the human principle that develops the consciousness-attributes.

Human consciousnesses represent the burning ground, the place of transformation and transmutation of base substance, the impure energies, into spiritual gold (the elixir of enlightenment). The human unit therefore represents the agent of change of darkened substance into light, ignorance into great wisdom. For this reason the great *maṇḍala* that is the field of Life has been instigated. The yogic and Initiation process then awakens the full attributes of the great *maṇḍala,* the *bīja* of which was originally seeded by the Ādi Buddha. Some of the detail of the nature of the process that drives the entire Thought construct of this *maṇḍala* back to its originating source will be revealed in Volume 5 of this series, *An Esoteric Exposition of the Bardo Thödol.*

Salutations to the magnanimous One that provided us with that text for our benefit to help liberate the All! Salutations to all the great Ones who have passed along that Way and have thereby become *mahāsiddhas,*[16] liberating their parts of the *maṇḍalas* that were incorporated as part of the fabric of manifest space! Salutations to the future Jinas that will evolve from out of the earth's consciousness-space to later incorporate great *maṇḍalas* of what must then be!

Oṁ Svaha! Thus it shall be.

The *stūpa* as a *maṇḍala*

A *stūpa* (Tib. chorten) is a *maṇḍala* manifesting as a circle of the earth and space, 'squared by the four-fold divided cycles of time',[17] determined by the movements of the sun. It is a sanctified space delineated out of unstructured chaos. The *stūpa* plan can also represent the Regents

16 *Mahāsiddha:* a *yogin/yoginī* having developed the higher *siddhi,* psychic powers (spiritual accomplishments) through yogic practices. *Siddhis* may be supramundane (attained by a Buddha) or 'common' (attained by an ordinary *yogin).* Thus a *mahāsiddha* is an accomplished Tantric *yogin.*

17 Adrian Snodgrass, *The Symbolism of the Stupa,* (SEAP Cornell University, New York, 1985), 101.

of the four quarters of the universe, and specifically in the Mahāyāna philosophy the five Buddhas of Meditation.

The levels of a *stūpa* symbolise the various planes of perception as well as the nature of the interrelation of the Elements. As a Tantric Buddhist *maṇḍalic* construct the *stūpa* is a five-tiered concept. These tiers symbolise the way of transference of the five Elements into the wisdoms of the five Dhyāni Buddhas by means of the medium of the mind. The Dhyāni Buddhas are also symbolically depicted in the directions of the four sides of the *stūpa,* with the central point represented by Vairocana. This is then extended upwards to manifest the full 3-D representation of the *stūpa.*

Govinda states:

> The Tibetan chorten also comes near to this ideal form, because the central cupola (aṇḍa) of the stūpa has been reversed into a pot-shaped vessel (Tibetan: bumpa) which rests on a cubic substructure and is crowned by a tall cone, ending in a small upturned hemisphere which carries on its plane surface a crescent, a sun-disc and the drop or flame-shaped 'jewel', one upon the other. In addition to this the main parts of the chorten are actually painted in the colors of the great elements (mahābhūta): the cubical substructure yellow (earth), the spherical central part white (water), the conical spire red (fire), while the form of the fourth element (air), which should show a green surface, is generally hidden under the honorific umbrella, a symbol which, especially in its Tibetan form, is closely connected with the concept of air...Between the horizontal umbrella-disc which covers the cup-like hemisphere and the flaming drop, symbols of air and ether respectively, there is a white crescent and a red sun-disc (the latter resting upon the inner curie of the crescent), which thus repeats the colors of the two main elements of the stūpa, namely that of the moon-related, waterpot-shaped central part and that of the sun-related spire. The meaning of this repetition becomes evident if we remember that the moon represents the Iḍā (whose color is pale white), the sun, Piṅgalā (whose color is red), and the superimposed flaming drop, the synthesis of the solar and lunar energies in the Suṣumṇā and the final realization of enlightenment in the crown-centre (sahasrāra).[18]

18 Anagorika Govinda, *Psycho-cosmic Symbolism of the Buddhist Stūpa* (Dharma Publishing, Berkeley, 1976), 93-94. Note: The ordering of Govinda's presentation of

It should be noted that the symbolism of the *stūpa* is depicted from below up. The Element Earth manifests the widest area as it is the foundation of the construct. The symbolism related to each subsequent Element becoming progressively more refined and smaller in volume, with the fifth Element (Aether) represented by a point or line (i.e., zero or one-dimensional space). It represents the *bīja* from which all else proceeds. This is true from the perspective of those aspiring to attain the *dharmakāya*, but not true from the point of view of those actually residing in the *dharmakāya*, in which case the entire construct must be reversed. Here the *dharmakāya* becomes the vast base from where all proceeds, and *saṃsāra* becomes the moving zero-dimensional point that is the focal point of the Dharmakāya Eye. This point is continually moving, drawing the geometry of space-time, the illusional 3-D constructs wherein we reside with our consciousnesses.

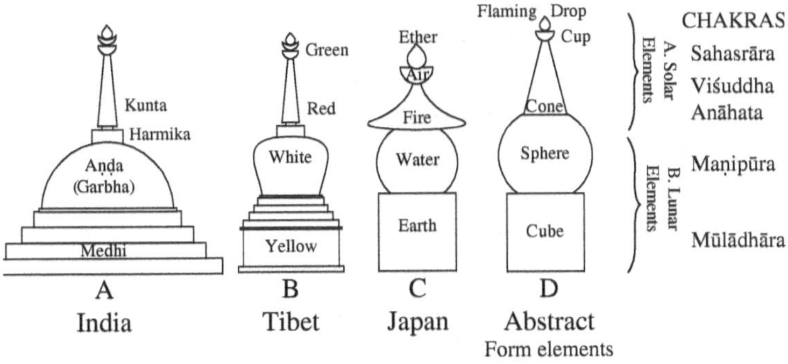

Figure 15. Typical *stūpas*

(Adapted from A. Govinda, *Psycho-cosmic Symbolism of the Buddhist Stūpa*)

Much of the symbolism of the *stūpa* has come from Hindu cosmological philosophy, which Buddhism borrowed and adapted to form its own sophisticated eschatological doctrines and metaphysical world-view. It symbolises the creation of the universe from out of chaos.

Essentially, the *stūpa* represents a symbolic portrayal of the body of

---

the *stūpas* has been rearranged. Mahāyāna Buddhism presents eight main *stūpas*, representative of the enlightenment process.

the Buddha, thus it is that which houses his saved relics. It also contains an interconnected web of meaning that summarises the sum of the Law, the tree of enlightenment, the sun of Life, the spiral of evolution, the spire of attainment, as well as the final goal *(śūnyatā)*. The main mass of the *stūpa,* the hemispheric dome, represents the Buddha-Womb. It is the world-egg, the cosmogonic source of all manifested Life of all worlds, Buddha-spheres, in the universe. The 'womb' contains successive levels of such world-spheres, like the layers of an onion. In the Hindu system this is represented by Hiraṅyagarba, the golden egg floating on the waters of all that possibly can exist, and in the Mahāyāna doctrine this becomes the *tathāgatagarbha,* the 'womb' of the *tathāgatas.*

The point at the centre at the top of the *stūpa's* plan reflects the highest point of illumination, thus the meditating *yogin* or Bodhisattva attains enlightenment by ascending up this pinnacle of existence. He/she passes first through the world of desire *(kāmaloka)*, the hemispherical dome, then the world of form (*rūpaloka,* the formed heavens), the spire and its discs, finally through the formless heavens *(arāpaloka)*, the *stūpa* pinnacle. This pinnacle is commonly terminated by a vase *(kalasa),* the containment of the Void *(śūnyatā)*.[19] The three abovementioned *lokas* represent the three worlds of the Buddhist Cosmology.

We also have the Theravāda system of meditation, whereby the meditator works to conquer one level after another of this cosmogonic spire until eventually the heavens of the formless realms are reached. Each of these four abstracted levels (of Mind) are given specific qualities associated with Voidness, whilst the last merges into the Void that is equated with final liberation.

Thus, having ascended all of the levels of formed and unformed space in meditation according to the *stūpa* plan, the *yogin* has reached the ultimate pinnacle of Life—the Void, the essence of Arhatship. From here the plenitude of the *dharmakāya* finds its emanatory purpose in later Mahāyāna representations of the *stūpa*. This then is the sum total of what the *stūpa* silently offers to all who circumambulate before it, or

---

19 In Buddhist iconography the full vase symbolises the plenitude of the enlightened Mind, and that a complementary imagery emphasises the pot's emptiness, signifying the Void *(śūnyatā)*. Snodgrass, *The Symbolism of the Stupa,* 343.

who merely pass by it and reflect upon its presence. It is the mimesis of all that one could hope to achieve through the conquering of one's base nature, upon which the *stūpa* stands, right through to the *bodhicitta* that is the high point of the *stūpa* spire (or the parasol commonly seen crowning it). It stands as a stately sentinel of the path that lays before one on one's own journey to Buddhahood.

Concerning the circumambulation, which is the principle ritual connected with the *stūpa*, the performer of the ritual follows the ascending progress of the sun in a south-north direction for the attainment of liberation and then the descending course back into the world as a Bodhisattva returning to aid all sentient beings.[20]

Stūpas can be seen to consist of a series of concentric spheres of diminishing radius arranged within each other around a common centre, and is the schema of the various heavens and hells 'relative to a given plane of existence.'[21]

One of the earliest *stūpas* is that found at Sanchi, and is depicted below on the following page. In the demarcation and orientation of the *stūpa* plan that mimics the directions of the sun in its diurnal and annual cycle we have the physical empowerment of the way the metaphysical sun, the source of all Life and light, travels in space. The sun symbolises the illumined consciousness, and orients one to conquer space. Govinda therefore states that:

> The inner space, between the fence and the *stūpa*, and the circular terrace (*medhi*) at the basis of the cupola were used for ritualistic circumambulation in the direction of the sun's course. The orientation of the gates equally correspond to the sun's course, to sunrise, zenith, sunset, and nadir. As the sun illuminates the physical world, so does the Buddha illuminate the spiritual world. The eastern torana represents his birth (buddha-jati), the southern his enlightenment (sambodhi), the western his 'setting in motion the wheel of the law' (dhammacakkapavattna) or the proclamation of his doctrine, and the northern his final liberation (parinibbāna).[22]

20 Ibid., 33.

21 Ibid., 17.

22 Govinda, *Psycho-cosmic Symbolism,* 8. Note here the correlation to the earlier

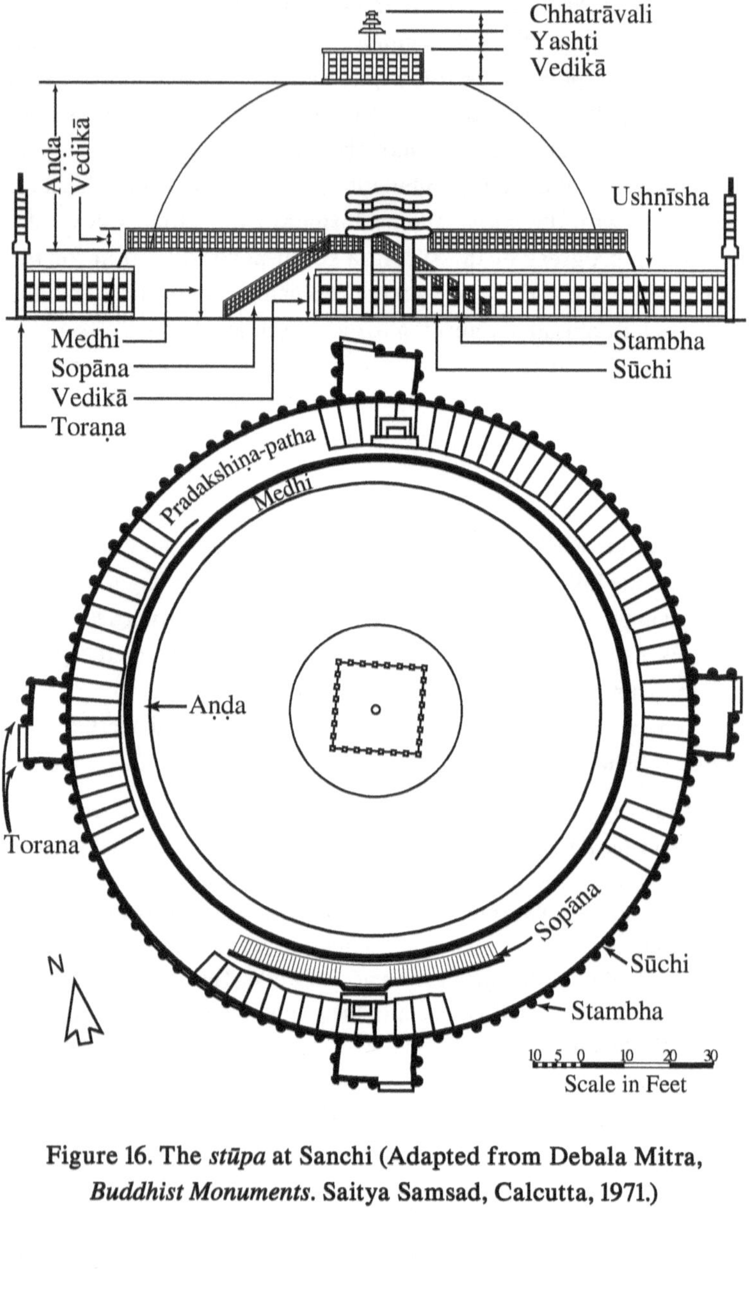

Figure 16. The *stūpa* at Sanchi (Adapted from Debala Mitra, *Buddhist Monuments*. Saitya Samsad, Calcutta, 1971.)

The orientation of the central point of the *stūpa* represents the fulcrum of the world from which all emanates, determined by reference to the movements of the sun, delineates therefore, the related astrological inferences of the solar cycle. This fulcrum or naval is the summit of the world mountain. This is 'the eye of the celestial vault and viewed from the felly of the World Wheel the Sun is at the zenith of the circle's radius.'[23] The *harmika* located at the apex of the *stūpa* dome (the spire) represents a cosmic tree rising from a mountain summit (mount Meru), where the existence of the mountain is seen as the cupola.[24] Mount Meru represents the summit of empirical attainment, the high point of striving, as well as being the abode of the Gods. It is the *brahmarandhara vidara* at the top of the head, which in yoga philosophy is the point of attainment to strive for if the elixir of enlightenment is to be gained. Through this point a person (and central *prāṇas*) is said to exit and enter the body at death, birth, and deep meditation. Snodgrass states that it is connected with the word *stūpa*, which in 'its literal sense also means "topknot or crest"',[25] and further informs us that the path to the summit of the Mountain is spiral, thus 'each layer of the *stūpa* is one turn of a helix described upon a cylinder whose axis coincides with that of the *stūpa*.'[26]

The felly of the wheel represents the material world wherein we gain our experience, turning upon the mud and dirt of *saṃsāra*. The nave may represent either; the heavenly realms, the domain of mind, the *ālayavijñāna* environment, *śūnyatā,* or *dharmakāya*, depending upon the level of *maṇḍala* upon which one's vision is focussed. The spokes join all segments or delineations of the *maṇḍala* of being to their principal centre—the hub of the universe, or the source of all *dharma*. In the case of the manifestation of consciousness the wheel has eight spokes, for the four cardinal directions in space and their intermediate positions. A six-spoked wheel represents the wheel of

information presented anent the qualities associated with the directions of the fixed cross.

23 Snodgrass, *The Symbolism of the Stupa*, 24.

24 Ibid., 226. See also page 256 where he states that the Tibetan term for the axial pillar of a *stūpa* literally means 'life wood', or 'tree of Life'.

25 Ibid., 263.

26 Ibid., 235.

becoming, dividing phenomena into six realms. If there are twelve divisions to the wheel it represents the twelve linked chain of Dependent Origination. The nave of the wheel is then represented by three animals that symbolise the root causes *(hetu)* of all rebirths—greed, hatred, and delusion. They are tied together by ignorance *(avidya)*. The twelve-spoked wheel also refers to the zodiac, or to the functioning of the Heart *chakra*, thus to the evocation of the wisdom represented by *bodhicitta*. We also have the full symbolism of the qualities of *dharmakāya*, if the Head lotus is represented.

The symbolism of the dome of the *stūpa* as a *chakra* is of importance, as all Buddhist metaphysical speculation rests on the foundation of the symbolism of the lotus. Often the wheel is explicitly represented in the *stūpa*, as at Sanchi and Bharut, where the gateways of the *stūpa* are turned at right angles to the axes, which indicates the movement delineated by a swastika.[27] The swastika is the power that turns the wheel, unfolding in its turn the qualities of the *chakra* of which it is the foundation. When placed in a circle, the swastika represents the forces pertaining to the construction of the solar system, and outside of one it represents the forces pertaining to humanity. It is a very ancient symbol found throughout the world's mythologies, a symbol of fourfold power, activity, and of material construction.[28] The cyclic forces symbolised by the petals of the *chakras* can be seen on all planes of perception, in all possible directions, taking the form of immaculate multi-dimensional flowers when fully developed, the highest of which is the *sahasrāra padma* (1,000 petalled lotus) at the top of the head. Tucci states that the usual representation of the interior *maṇḍala* vision is a lotus, with four or eight petals symmetrically disposed about the corolla symbolising 'the spatial emanation of the One to the many'.[29] The lotus is an apt symbol of the nature of the evocation of enlightenment because it is a spotless flower (the awakened mind) that grows out of the mud of the *saṃsāra* and rests upon the Waters of Life.

---

27 Ibid., 78.

28 Detailed information about the swastika will be given in the later chapters of this Volume.

29 G. Tucci, *The Theory and Practice of the Mandala*, 27-28.

6

Dhāraṇīs and the Function of a Maṇḍala

The nature of *dhāraṇīs*

Comprehending the concept of *dhāraṇī* is essential to understanding the nature and context of the way *maṇḍalas* are built. *Dhāraṇīs* are the structural elements of thought; they help to concretise that which is visualised. This allows an analysis of the impression to be extended over the period needed for complete comprehension. *Dhāraṇīs* are therefore necessary in establishing the expression of a *maṇḍala*. They allow the truth veiled by the conceptualisation to manifest in the elements contained in the *maṇḍala*.

Dhāraṇīs consolidate thought, they establish meaning in what otherwise would be empty mental constructs. They prevent wistful peregrinations of mind, imposing order and needed discipline, even ritual, to produce a determined outcome. The determined pathways need not produce enlightenment, as various forms of *siddhis* and materialistic objectives can be the goal. The type of practitioner determines the results. On a higher cycle they can reveal the structure of the cosmos, the truth underlying the manifestation of phenomena. They can be used by Logoi to construct world-spheres. The *dhāraṇī* thus brings all conceptual pathways to fruition. The *dhāraṇī* retains detail through consolidation of the subtlest of thought processes for the mind to later access.

Govinda states that:

> *Dhāraṇīs* are a means for fixing the mind upon an idea, a vision

> or an experience gained in meditation. They may represent the quintessence of a teaching as well as the experience of a certain state of consciousness, which hereby can be recalled or recreated deliberately at any time. Therefore they are also called supporters, receptacles or bearers of wisdom (*vidyādhara*). They are not different from mantras in their function but to some extent in their form, in so far as they may attain a considerable length and sometimes represent a combination of many mantras or 'seed-syllables' (*bīja-mantras*), or the quintessence of a sacred text. They were a product as well as a means of meditation: 'Through deep absorption (*samādhi*) one gains a truth, through a *dhāraṇī* one fixes and retains it.'[1]

Dhāraṇīs are the process that allows meditators to construct the forms they wish to have appear in the time-space continuum. They are therefore utilised in the demonstration of spiritual power. They are needed in the creating of all forms and activities of consciousness that are to have purposeful longevity, as they are the mode of directing streams of *karma*. Thus they delineate the certainties of decision in the mind. They help to make the individual meditator what he is. They are the templates for the construction of ideas to be brought forth in the *maṇḍala* of Life. They are built with the will by utilising colour, tone, note, line, structure, grand design, and intensity, to produce their effectiveness.

The entire sequence of appearance of every rebirthing *jīva* (vital body of a personal-I) of any consciousness-stream is held as a *dhāraṇī* in meditation by the Sambhogakāya Flower. The pattern of the accompanying *maṇḍala* is made potent with its part of the vision of the greater plan in the meditation-Mind of the *tathāgatagarbha* concerned. An incarnation of the objective form thus occurs. Accompanying *karma* helps dictate the conditions of the overriding *maṇḍala,* with the peculiarities of the pattern unfolding to harvest the wisdom that will be accomplished over time. Wisdom and the accompanying *bodhicitta* then bring about the eventual dissolution of the entire *maṇḍala.* Having achieved its purpose, the Sambhogakāya Flower is liberated from being in thrall with the need for a manifest form.

Once a *dhāraṇī* is established and empowered with the necessary will then the process of its manifestation becomes automatic, no longer

1 Govinda, *Foundations of Tibetan Mysticism,* 31-32.

needed to be the focal point of consciousness. From then on it delineates the way that the prime *saṃskāras* that underlie the basis for existence must manifest along the lines established by the living *maṇḍala*. All processes inherent in the structure will then manifest in accord with the inbuilt (numerical) code for the right timing of each eventuation.

What is seen in all of Nature, the structural elements of interrelated matter, is really propelled by a sequence of *dhāraṇīs*. They are the decision-making function of a Logoic Thinker, and Nature is the reverberating repercussion of their expression. The repercussions then propel the overshadowing Lives to dwell in the structure that constitute the *maṇḍala* of Nature. *Dhāraṇīs* begin primordially along the lines of five streams of *nāḍīs*, utilising Elements that resonate progressing, evolving forms in ever increasing diversity. Inevitably we have the cacophony of the *skandhas* and *saṃskāras* of all manifest Life. From the originating *dhāraṇī* first springs the five Dhyāni Buddhas and their consorts who form the pillars of the entire structure of the *maṇḍala* of time and space. The *maṇḍala* is thus composed of pentads that are squared by the delineations of the four directions, and is circumscribed by a sphere of limitation.[2] The elements composing it can thereby also be considered the *dhāraṇīs* of Dhyāni Buddhas.[3] It is the construct of their combined meditations. When the pentads come to be directed according to the eight directions in space, then the functionality of the eight Mahabodhisattvas and their consorts appear. Their compassionate action is administered to the rest of the *maṇḍala* we call *saṃsāra*. (The forthcoming chapters will detail the part these Bodhisattvas play in the great play of Life.)

The function of a *maṇḍala*

Function is what properly delineates what a *maṇḍala* (the cellular unit, or a universe for that matter) is all about. It delineates how any form defines itself to record and play out all of the messages and information embedded in the structure of the *maṇḍala*. Function integrates the

---

2 Making a Throne or Seat of Power upon which the primordial One sits.

3 Much concerning the five Dhyāni Buddhas (Jinas) was elaborated on throughout the first three volumes of this series, to which the reader must refer for the foundational elucidations.

particles (entities in space-time) that exist potentially and which can be activated at any point in time.

The *māyā* (integrated illusion) of any construct normally divulges its secrets slowly at first, and extensively later in a rapid succession of revelation. *Māyā* is not without merits, because it represents the play of *saṃsāra*, the ever-changing scenario of the phenomenal form. It is encoded in the *maṇḍala* as the functional elements that exist therein to produce the necessary changes in the entire structure. It is the substance of the *dhāraṇī* wherewith the construct was built in the first place. It thus has its own temporal relative reality, and cannot be denied. Without *māyā* there could be no path of accomplishment, no mastery over the senses, no accumulative gain of wisdom. It is the veil of the Real, thus through study of the patterns of the way it is organised, enlightenment of what lies beyond can unfold. These patterns are the consequence of the originating Minds that seeded the structure of the *maṇḍala* of *saṃsāra*. They are therefore in the form of a paradigm of the enlightened Mind. The problem however exists once the *saṃsāric* play has been established and unenlightened minds have evolved. They contribute their defilements and turbulent swirls of mentation coagulating the *māyā* into ungainly pools of thought, thereby muddying its pristine expression.

If enlightenment is to be gained, the meditator must therefore thoroughly undertake the process of cleansing defilements, pacifying the swirls, to unwind the maladroit congealed knots of mind. Enlightenment thus refers to arriving at the pristine state of the originating *dhāraṇī* of the Buddha that seeded the *māyā* of the *maṇḍala*. By clarifying the defilements in the *māyā* and tracing the steps of the processes of establishing the originating *dhāraṇī* the meditator comes to emulate the nature of a Buddha-Mind. He/she has established the logic of the Mind that established the *maṇḍala* and thereby has discovered the way that a Buddha comes to be. The meditator has arrived at the place where *māyā* mirrors the Real, the *śūnyatā-saṃsāra* nexus. To become a Buddha the meditator thus has to properly emulate the process of *maṇḍala*-building at this level of expression.

Points to consider in the unveiling process of a *maṇḍala* are:

1. The revelation of the intricate detail of the *maṇḍala* concerns the degree of clarity and the nature of illumination the mind has

developed. The ramifications are that it must be viewed in terms of a multidimensional space-time continuum. The full implication of the *maṇḍala* can only thus be revealed when a visionary observance of the continuity of Mind has been sufficiently awakened. The enlightening of mind so that the hidden secrets of the construct are unveiled takes a considerable time to establish. The methodology is presented in current Tantric texts. However, their esoteric context for the most part still needs to be properly unravelled by astute thinkers. The explication of the Bardo Thödol in the next volume of this series titled *An Esoteric Exposition of the Bardo Thödol* provides the general keys to interpreting most Tantras.

2. The ordering of the *maṇḍala,* its units of construction or formation may exhibit characteristics not directly perceptible by the concrete mind. The Clear Mind thus needs to be awakened, allowing the overall nature of the construct to be viewed in one flash of timelessness. *Saṃskāras* pertaining to emotional identification, and desirous attachment to the illusions of the play of *māyā* with *saṃsāra* have therefore to be discovered and transmuted. All forms of illusional appearance must be mastered before the way that *māyā* mirrors the Real is perceived.

3. As the *maṇḍala* is designed to expand from a *bīja* to the full revelatory construct, so then there is also an implicit ability to produce a contraction back to a *bīja*. Multidimensionality is veiled by the point. This is the point of creative potency, the focal point of the Eye as it moves through space to bring into activity all atoms, lines, delineations, and forms of the *maṇḍala's* abstract paradigm. Similarly in a human life span, the youthful body first grows and expands, reaches middle age, then 'contracts' as old age sets in. Next there is death followed by inevitable rebirth. These rebirths are progressive and follow an evolutionary sequence. Death always follows the birth of anything in *saṃsāra*, but all experiences are sequenced to produce inevitable growth. There are many internal mental and psychic deaths of appearances that must be accomplished before the All-seeing Eye (Ājñā Centre) that can visualise everything in the entire construct is awakened. The Mind that accompanies the expansion of consciousness to all directions in space must be

developed, then that Eye can awaken and function to full capacity.

4. That which exists outside the *maṇḍalic* cell's wall of experience can be more alive and dynamic than the interior of the cell. A greater portion of the *maṇḍala's* existence is found there, if the cell is a part of a larger *maṇḍala*, making the associated energy currents more potent, as the entire structure must be served by these external consciousness links. It represents sources of vital Life, *prāṇas* necessary for the growth of the individual mind construct. Therefore, a greater intelligence quotient will be sourced from what represents a greater consciousness expanse external to the unit.[4] If the cellular unit is unaware of future productivity (that which is external to its form) and it manifests negative or retrograde activities, the greater environment of which the unit forms a part will inevitably countermand such action. The future is where the cell is proceeding to. It concerns what it will inevitably evolve to become. The future represents not just a lateral expansion to encompass more space, but also a vertical expansion through the dimensions of perception, as well as a spiral expansion of consciousness moving through time. The entire evolutionary arc of awakening perceptions evolves out of expanding increments of experience. This necessitates an object of perception, that which perceives, as well as the sum of the environment within which the perceiver is travelling.

5. We see the *maṇḍala* to be but part of a larger overall structure, integrated within a universal principle extending throughout the spaciousness of a Buddha-Mind. Once that spaciousness is perceived it can be attained. The steps for attainment have by then already been comprehended.

The perception of things

The seventeenth verse of *Mere Consciousness,* a Yogācāra-Vijñāvadin text, states:

The various consciousnesses manifest in two divisions, perception and

4 Note that the *karma* that exists between all units of consciousness integrates the entire *maṇḍala* so that the right consciousness-bits are shuffled to the needy organelles in the cellular organism.

object of perception. Because of this, all these do not exist. Therefore, all is Mere-consciousness.

> Kārikā: *vijñānapariṇāmo 'yam vikalpo yad vikalpyate/*
> tena tannāsti tenedaṃ sarvaṃ vijñānaptiātrakaṃ.

> Excepting darśanabhāga and nimittabhāga nothing real exists.

'The various consciousnesses' indicates the three developments of consciousness and their mental associates. They are called 'development' because all of them are capable of development which appears to have two aspects—that of the perceiving part *(darśanabhāga)* and that of the perceived part *(nimittabhāga)*. The perceiving part is termed as discrimination *(vikalpa),* because it apprehends the second. The second part developed is termed as 'that which is discriminated', because it is apprehended by the first one, i.e. the perceiving part.[5]

This information can be illustrated thus:

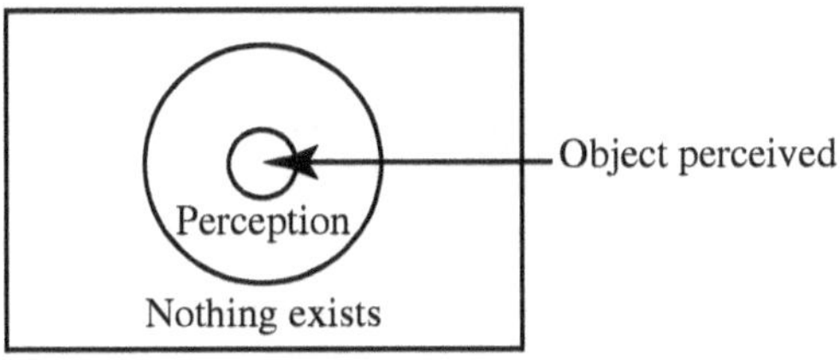

Figure 17. The perception of things

In this Figure the perceiving part (*darśanabhāga*) and the object perceived (*nimittabhāga*) are all that is considered real (to the Vijñāvadins), everything else is considered 'unreal', therefore as non-existent. The bundles of perceptions obtained from the objects perceived are thus what developed consciousness.

The text continues:

Apart from what is thus developed from consciousness, there are

5 Swati Ganguly, *Treatise in Thirty Verses on Mere-Consciousness,* (Motilal Banarsidass, New Delhi, 1992), 114-115.

> no real *ātman*[6] or *dharmas*[7]; because, besides what apprehends or is apprehended, there exists nothing as real (*bhūtadravya*) excepting these two aspects (*bhāgas*).[8]

This observation however needs refinement, because the statement does not include a conception of what causes pressure on the external wall of the cellular structure to prevent it from annihilation or abstraction into the space designated 'nothing exists', or rather, 'there exists nothing as real'. Obviously we are not analysing *śūnyatā* here because *śūnyatā* is considered 'real'. Our analysis is thus of *saṃsāric* phenomena of some type, that contains perception, or which causes the process of the perception. This then incites us to conclude that our consideration concerns the substance of mind. It is held in abeyance whilst the process of perception happens, i.e., the moment of identification with the object perceived. It immediately introduces the categories of knowable things. The mind can then categorise what was perceived, to find a place for it within its terrains of mutability and transience.

That which is perceived must be catalogued, if the mind is to store it with a view to possible future retrieval for its advancement. Much, therefore, which comes within the focus of perception rapidly falls away into obscurity. It is immediately forgotten as irrelevant for the present. There can be no true perception of anything if the process of perceiving is not sustained, because the force of mind would discard it immediately as a peripheral triviality. The perceiving part must be able

---

6 *Ātman,* self-identity, the innermost essence or 'soul' of the individual, seen to be eternal, unchanging, as well as the universal 'Self'.

7 *Dharmas,* factors of existence, from a doctrine found in the *Abhidharma* of Theravāda Buddhism are factors of existence, elements of mind. Briefly, each *dharma* (element) is a separate entity or force, there is no substance apart from the qualities of a *dharma*, they have no duration, but flash as new appearances with each moment. The *dharmas* cooperate with each other. (There are 72 of these *saṃskṛta-dharmas.)* Thus they stem from causes and proceed to extinction when influenced by wisdom, but when influenced by ignorance they are continuously generated. The gaining of liberation, therefore, is that which produces their extinction. For a summary of their properties see Theodore Stcherbatsky, *The Central Conception of Buddhism,* (Motilal Baranasidass, Delhi, 1994), 74-75.

8 Ganguly, *Treatise in Thirty Verses on Mere-Consciousness*, 115.

to hold its tension of perception for long enough to perceive the object and register it in consciousness. This is the way that most perceivers look at *maṇḍalas*. The eye rapidly moves from category to category of the representation, quickly glancing at one image and then the next, maybe noting colour or deity, and then moving to the next part. This process stifles assimilation of the integral meaning of what is depicted. The meaning of what is veiled is not perceived by the mind, as it quickly discards as irrelevant what it fails to observe. It takes much training for the mind to develop a sharp, penetrative, discerning eye that allows it to become initiated into the integral meaning that makes the *maṇḍala* relevant as a means for enlightenment.

When another perception appears then all former images contained in the mind must somehow be sequenced for memory purposes, if sense is to be made of the new perception, and of those to come. The perceptions must be contained in some way, which necessitates an external pressure to be put upon them to hold them in place. Alternatively, there could be an internal pull upon them from some central 'self', again keeping the perceptions *in situ*. We could also have both simultaneously, whilst multidimensional analysis might also be necessary.

If there were a complete vacuum external to the cellular wall then there would be nothing keeping it from expanding at a rate similar to that of the hypothesised 'big bang' of physicists. We see therefore that all ideas must be contained by boundaries determined by the forces bought to bear both internally and externally to them. If the thought is infused with a stronger internal pressure or driving force than that containing it then rapid expansion is necessitated. If weak, the external pressure will limit its expansion and sphere of influence. If there was just an external pressure, then the perceptions would become highly compressed and could not be properly organised for use by the perceiving consciousness. Something other than what is needed for the manifestation of one's self-will would be determining the outcome. The external universe would effectively tell one what to perceive and how to do it, much like the way instinct drives the animal kingdom. The Figure below indicates the nature of these opposing forces, which here maintains an equilibrated sphere.

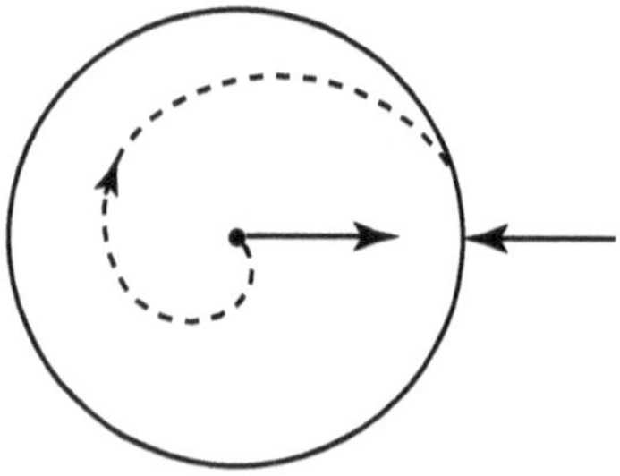

Figure 18. The equilibrated sphere

If the activating force were purely internal then there would be no possibility for commingling of perceptions that represent a commonality of experiences shared with others. As no two beings could perceive the same things and relate these experiences to another, so all experiences would forever be separate and distinct. What manifests instead of these options, therefore, is the cell possessing both internal and external pressures. They keep the wall in place with no implosion or explosion of substance. Things exist this way throughout Nature, except when the cell sickens and dies. Sickness or disease generally results in the loss of the ability of the organism to maintain equilibrium upon the cell wall. That which exerts pressure upon the cell from the outside (e.g., the *ālayavijñāna* environment) is generally a more substantive force than that which manifests inside the cell, but is matched by a more intense internal pressure. This gives the cell its general ovoid or spherical shape. (Which is the result of the equilibrium attained between the internal and external pressure.) The inner environment can also be viewed in terms of:

1. Moving mass of perceptions.
2. Overall organised structure.
3. The appearance of organelles for the storage of differing types of perceptions.
4. Potential to expand.
5. Future abstraction.

This is then counterbalanced by an external force consisting of:

1. The mass of forces impacting upon consciousness by means of sense contact with the external universe.
2. The sum total of opinions, social mores, customs, educational and emotional pressures apprehensible by the mind in question.
3. The pressure of similar thoughts and ideas from the community of minds of which the thinker is a part.
4. The sum of the *ālayavijñāna* environment within which the thoughts of all such thinkers reside. This includes all images and ideas engendered by all thinkers throughout the epochs of human evolution.
5. The pressure of the energy of the Logoic Mind of which that *ālayavijñāna* environment forms a part.

If a Buddha finds it worthwhile to manifest a meditation incorporating 'things' then we have a valid purpose for their appearance. 'Things' exist, though transitorily so. For this reason a personal-I can incarnate into a universe of those things so that it can catalogue what it has experienced into a correlated sequence, from which it can create imaginary things, or else learn from its interrelation of experience with something new.

Here we can see that in saying that 'nothing exists' outside the perception of things, and that the thing perceived can be considered to be an untruth, one also needs to take account of the meditative activity of the Dhyāni Buddhas, of the mode of action of the Dharmakāya type of *karma*. Such *karma* incorporates the way of interrelating the entire universe of things outside a particular object of perception, which is called 'nothing' in *Mere-Consciousness*. The object of perception has become a field of perception, which allows a broad visioning of everything in the universe, irrespective of whether a human unit is experiencing a particular aspect of it at any time in any particular incarnation. However, if 'the thing perceived' manifests via any of the five points above then the statement that 'nothing exists' outside the perception of things is a truism for the perceiver. This presumes that consciousness is necessary for a thing to be registered as being an existent. It does not incorporate the process that produced the appearance of that consciousness in the first place, defined in terms of the *dharmakāya* type of *karma* mentioned above.

First there is sentience, then evolves consciousness. By this token, a universe or world-sphere can be constituted of myriads of sentient entities before a human consciousness appears that can define something as 'existing' or not. Such a sentient world can exist in the Mind of a Logos and be viewed as objects that 'exist'. Nevertheless, they are still parts of a vast Mind-structure, objects of perception therein, which can later evolve the consciousness of a human unit. The vastness of the panorama, the plenitude of the 'things' that a Mind can contain, is what is in question here.

Intelligence (the perceiving principle) necessitates a continuously categorising mind. It consciously acts to make systems of living *maṇḍalas* enter into its awareness. It is an awareness that categorises, organises patterns of things, defines, and creates a superstructure model of what is reality to it. That superstructure then finds its relativity in one or other of the abovementioned pentad of external forces within which it resides. Desires, wishes, experiences, and imagination go together to make up the *potpourri* of what is real to the person. It is not just as simple as the 'object of perception' and the 'perception', more is needed to produce the flavour of what has been perceived in order to distinguish it from what is out there in the external universe. The way that things are perceived is what makes up the *saṃskāras* of the person rather than just the object perceived. This is important to note. The *saṃskāras* are constructed not only from sense contact, but also from the fusion of that thing with emotions and imagination. The *saṃskāras* are also called forth from past life activities. Often there is also added mental input. In the external universe, these additions do not exist, but the 'things' that can be experienced do relatively, otherwise no consciousness could arise in the first place.

When we look at the paths of each evolutionary point constituting a *maṇḍala,* taking into account differing rates of movement, we get intersections, where lines meet. When consciousness is concerned, the paths are curved with respect to the passage of time. Depicted visually we get the impression of a flower petal. In the normal mental construct the floral patterning will be viewed to possess many differing sizes of petals, of which a certain number may be stunted or grossly distorted. However, the archetypal pattern of a human unit is based upon mathematical harmony which, when viewed in terms of *nāḍīs* and their intersections, produces flowers of response called *chakras.* We have a truly aesthetic *maṇḍala.*

Figure 19. The formation of a *chakra*

When viewing the concept of *chakras,* then we should visualise *maṇḍalas* based on the extension of the numbers four and six specifically.[9] The floral forms manifest according to particular colours. They emanate perfume of different types, producing a nectar that is ambrosial in its nature gathered symbolically by the bees of consciousness.

The hive of consciousness

One can look to the cellular construction of a bee's hive, separating out a singular unit as a paradigm for a *maṇḍala* based upon the number six. We can then extrapolate esoteric principles from the exoteric expression. Here the cellular unit manifests as a perfect six-sided form, opened at one end and closed at the other. It is utilised mainly for the storage of honey *(prāṇa)*, the basic food for those of the hive, and for the growth of their larva (thought constructs). The empty cell can be considered to represent that which is Void of conscious thought or thinking processes. It is to be filled with honey, the substance that vitalises the mind-space with useful information for the personal-I's road to enlightenment and liberation. Each cell can also be viewed in terms of the mechanism of the integration of the five sense-consciousness, plus their synthesis by means of the sixth sense, the intellect. Like a bee, the consciousness-principle moves from flower to flower (or from cell to cell) of ideas and bits of information needed for its survival and growth.

9 Even the *sahasrāra padma* with ten petals fits into this pattern from the perspective that it is based on a construct of twelve petals with two removed.

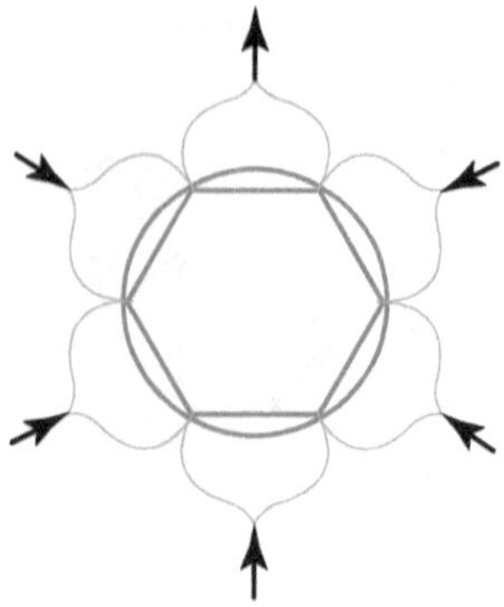

Figure 20. A minor *chakra*

This Figure is that of a minor *chakra*. Not all minor *chakras* have six petals. Of the six petals, five are for incoming *prāṇas* and one for outgoing *prāṇas*. This allows the growth of *nāḍīs* that link one such flower to another. The empty cell that is void (of conscious thought) waits to process experiences bound by a sphere of limitation of what is possible. The *prāṇas* of the five points of input to the cell are those of the five sense-consciousnesses that eventually produce the sublime wisdoms of the Dhyāni Buddhas. Transcendence (the piercing of the circumference) however happens by the projection of the intellect (the sixth point) into the sphere of consciousness, representing the sum of the activity of the 'hive'.[10]

The ritual of the honeybee-thinker's search for nectar amongst the alluring flowers of experiential potential expands consciousness. The honeybee receives the flower's nectar, which also acts as a signal, a sentinel of consciousness, giving to other worker bees the impression of where to obtain nectar. The bee returning to the hive awakens an expression from the *chakra*/the flower, adding to and affirming the knowledge from the sum total of the hive.

The analogy can be viewed in the following way:

1. The *nectar* is *prāṇa*, the raw material for enlightenment.
2. The *signal* represents volition/karmic action of what to do, of where

10 The *maṇḍala* that is perceived is in reality a little more complex than a simple hive, but the analogy is close enough for the purpose of illustration.

to gather the raw materials to gain the nourishing elixir of Life.

3. Honey is the product of it all, where the nectar has passed through the digestive process of the bee, producing a sweet nourishing vital food. This symbolises the enlightenment that feeds the sum of the workers, the information gatherers.
4. The *honeybee* represents the mental-emotional *saṃskāras* bundled together in an individual. This is the basic mechanism for the gathering of information or enlightened understandings in little packets of experience.
5. The *queen bee* is the functional organisation of the entire mental structure of the *chakra*. It integrates all forms of activity into a coherent unity.
6. A *hexagonal unit* represents the matrix upon which the sum total of the *maṇḍala*, the pathways of conscious experience, is fixed to. (As far as the basic structure of each *chakra* is concerned, rather than that of the *maṇḍala* of the overall *chakra* system.) It is the root or base of the enlightenment process; an integral part of the way the beehive is structured. There are five pathways for the input of information (from the senses) and an integrating outward pathway conveying the synthesis of the admixed input. We can also gather from this that the synthesised stream is collated at a higher level of the 'hive' that interrelates similar strands, and which may not be governed by the hexagonal structure. We have, for instance, the eight directions of space, thus *chakras* exist to incorporate these directions.
7. The *hive* represents the complete *maṇḍala* of conscious receptivity, of which all component parts are expressions. We thus have the fully integrated and functioning Head centre.

As noted above, the honey stored in the cell is analogous with *prāṇa*, a major subject to be investigated. The *saṃskāras* carried by the *prāṇa* colour all aspects of the structure. *Prāṇa* is the vehicle of consciousness, so if we say that the boundary of the cell prevents attainment of *nirvāṇa* we are observing the way consciousness limits itself. Without *prāṇa*, consciousness could not be expressed. The consciousness is thus viewed in terms of streams of *prāṇa*. When *saṃskāras* are transmuted by consciousness they pierce the bounds of the sphere containing each cellular unit. This ultimately leads to liberation.

The function of the honeybee is to bring nectar to the hive. It then digests (collates the packets of information) to produce a usable form (honey). The consciousness-bee effectively travels on its flight from flower to flower, (*chakra* to *chakra*) via the *nāḍīs,* to the receptacle or universal storehouse of consciousness (the hive) to convert its seed impressions (nectar) into usable thoughts (honey). Consciousness is thus updated and expanded whenever any of the cells are refurbished with honey. The memories of experiences gained while gathering nectar are stored in the cells.

The consciousness-bee uses the mechanism of honey gathering for the benefit of the greater structure (of mind). The bee's ritualised dance are movements conveying messages, ideas, images, consciousness states (light waves), to other bees (units of consciousness), directing them to the flowers where the best sources of nectar are. These dancing bees represent the educative members of the community.

In this analogy the 'highly enlightened' queen bee represents the Buddha for the hive. The Buddha's various early forays into *saṃsāra* symbolise the enlightened way, the mode of developing the all-embracive naturalness of Mind travelling and unfolding through space. His flight from his cloistered pleasure garden into the world sphere of a *yogin's* quest, gathered revelatory experiences (nectar) from *chakra* point to *chakra* point (teachers) of the flowers of the total environment that he was in. Eventually the multitude (of bee-disciples) that came later could be nourished with the properly processed precious nectar he gathered in his quest. Similarly the young queen leaves her former hive, mates, and then must seek an ideal location to establish a new hive, where she works hard to produce the new workers, and then like a Buddha, never moves from the sanctified space.

The cyclic movement (dance) of the honeybee from flower to flower, back to the hive, then out again, and so forth, also represents the awakening of *chakras* via *nāḍīs*.

The relationship of honey to nectar can be seen as one of degrees of refinement of energy. The nectar is pure unadulterated energy, but of a Watery consistency. The Watery aspect must be removed to a large extent with an added Fire of the bee's digestive process, to produce the highly viscous nutritive liquid desired. The bees have converted nectar to honey for their own purposes of nourishment. A hive stores honey so that it can utilise energy (*prāṇa, saṃskāras*) over a long period. Similar to a hive, the activity of a *chakra* may wane during 'winter months', but the Flame of Life continues to burn for consciousness-bees because of the honey.

All flowers do not bloom simultaneously, but different flowers awaken and then die to their floral brilliance throughout the seasons. So also with respect to the process of the *prāṇas* coursing through the *chakras*. Their petals open and close according to the nature of the *saṃskāras* they must channel at any time, and may remain dormant because of the lack of the expression of such flow. One group of *chakras* awaken, whilst the petals of a former group lack stimulation, as the person processes different types of energies and experiences. (The vision here encompasses both the major and minor *chakras*.)

The collective knowledge bank of the consciousness-bee, as represented by the full structure of the hive, is the Head lotus. Fiery *prāṇas* (*manasic* experiences) are collected from the *chakras*, and this thought-energy is stored in the *sahasrāra padma's* many cellular components.

The central, most vital integrating portion of the hive, where the Life-giving enlightenment-Queen is laying the germs of all future activity, is the Heart centre. She is assisted by her attendant helpers, each being a most dedicated 'follower of the faith' that expresses the truism of the hive. Being closest to the Queen, and attending to her needs makes them the most enlightened members of the hive. The Heart centre integrates the entire structure into a unity through the energy of Love and vitalises it with the principle of Life *(jīva),* without which the form could not exist. This centre assists the awakening mind to ascertain reality.

When taken as a unit all the bees in the hive represent the Solar Plexus form of activity, whilst the cellular constituency of the hive represents the Sacral centre/Base of the Spine combination. The honey that is stored in each cellular unit represents the Throat centre's form of activity. It regulates the consciousness-bits of information processed by the mind. In the above-mentioned centres the five Elements are processed. The Aetheric Element is processed in the Head lotus/Ājñā centre, which also incorporates all Fiery *prāṇas.* The Airy Element is expressed via the Heart centre, the Fiery Element via the Throat centre, the Watery Element in the Solar Plexus centre, and the Earthy Element in the Sacral/Base of the Spine centres.

Bees are a good environmental force because they help to cross-pollinate many flowers in their search for nectar. This ensures the next season's harvest of fruit, and the future generations of each species of plant it visits. Such activity corresponds first to the effect of the dissemination of beneficent ideas, and then to *bodhicitta* (the combined energy from the Head and Heart centres) amongst us. Such effects, seen in terms of expressed wisdom, are the major reasons for the initial functioning of mind, which must work cooperatively with the heart to awaken *bodhicitta.* Such cooperation is a major imperative for the entire integrity of the hive. All beings come to benefit from the effects from the worker bee's cross-pollination of ideas and expression of *bodhicitta* in human society. (Though there exist drones whose effects can be burdensome to the hive.) The analogy of cross-pollination clearly represents a stage or cycle in human development that details the teachings of science, the *sūtras,* or the charitable forms of *dharma* evidenced by all Bodhisattvas. This produces positive changes in human civilisation, assisting all upon our earth to function in a wholesome, integrated manner, to produce many flowers of beauteous accomplishment.

To view the totality of the *maṇḍala* of the hive one should positively review one's thoughts and aspire to think comprehensively, rightly differentiating between various categories of thought (areas of the hive, such as the nursery or food storage cells). *Saṃskāras* that can pierce the boundaries of each cellular construct (here viewed as the basic building blocks of each human mind) can then be projected as pathways to liberation, allowing one to experience the patterns of reality. The mind must be cleared of all rigidity of thought to experience the overall pattern of the hive of consciousness (the bee flies to do so) and so attain the revelations of a Clear Mind. Residence at the heart of the Mind, freed from the pathways of the thought constructs allows experience of the Void.

The Orientation of the major directions of a *maṇḍala*

It might prove helpful for the reader if a diagram is presented explaining why the direction east appears on the left side of the page in my books, contrary to the way it is conventionally depicted on a map. It is technically a moot point because the way of the heart (the right hand path) is always to the east. Firstly, it must be understood that we are referring to the realms of consciousness, not to geography. Though if one were to stand facing the North Pole the east would remain on the right side, what is being asserted here is that we are not the map itself, we are the way one traverses maps of consciousness. The direction north is logically the way upwards from the heart to the head. The right hand path to enlightenment travels from east to west (as the sun), which is the way that the spiral in Figure 21 is depicted. The direction from the central point to the western field of service and of activity, therefore, first faces the way of the heart if *bodhicitta* lies at is foundation, and eventually finds its field of resolution in the north (The Head lotus).

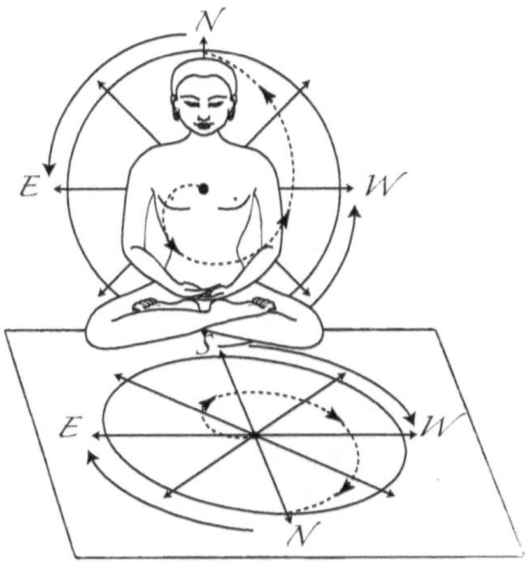

Figure 21. The orientation of *maṇḍalas*

The orientation of the cardinal points in Figure 21 therefore depict the way that consciousness evolves from an esoteric perspective, where the heart rules. This process starts first from right to left, producing involvement with the great illusion (*saṃsāra*). Later this direction is reversed as the individual experiences a turn about in their seat of consciousness (or special orientation) and is focussed upwards to liberation. The Figure at the top of the image therefore represents an enlightened being looking down and bringing into manifestation energies. It could also represent the direction of a *chakra* that is producing reification. The image at the bottom represents the individual in the field of service, with the outward expansion of the heart moving upwards towards enlightenment as *saṃsāric* illusions are overcome. This representation is in the nature of a mirror image.

If the orientation of the Figure were reversed (with the west where east is on the diagram), it would depict the world of unenlightened activity, which is not what is intended concerning the *maṇḍalas* of Buddhas and Bodhisattvas.

If we observe the custom of perambulation around temples from left to right, and *maṇḍalas* in two or three dimensions, this diagram is clearly correct. However, one must always take into account there is no fixed orientation. Movement from above-down relates to the descent of energies or impressions from the higher planes of perception, and from below-up it represents the focus of an aspiring consciousness.

The above-down direction is shown in Figure 21 by the meditating person, in which case an east to west orientation (right to left motion) is depicted. (The focus is downwards into *saṃsāra* for such a one.) Its reflected aspect is shown in the spiral below it, where the west to east (left to right) motion is shown, indicating the way the devotee correctly perambulates around sacred shrines, statues, and temples. (The focus here is away from *saṃsāra* towards liberation.) The devotee thus effectively receives the energies flowing down from the high domain that the sacred object represents.

7

The Will and its Manifestations

The will and consciousness

The will must be utilised in all viable *maṇḍalic* construction because it alone builds clearly defined lines of segregation between different aspects of the overall structure. It then propels the *maṇḍala* to fulfil its appointed purpose. The potency of the will needs to be incorporated in the *sādhana* of the practitioner[1]. Indeed, harnessing the Will-to-Love is the means to liberation on the path of a Bodhisattva. Without the will, no high revelations in the concepts pertaining to *dharmakāya*, or no alterations of patterns of penetrative thought directed towards high strata of revelation are possible. It produces the evolution of *maṇḍalas* of thought so that consciousness may grow to be inclusive of all aspects of the multidimensionality that *maṇḍalas* veil. Lack of the will means lazy thinking, shallowness of thought, because the mind does not put the effort to deeply ponder the hidden layers of meaning of any profound ontology, syllogism, *sūtra* or Tantra.

Dhāraṇīs are projected, sustained, and eventually converted into new forms through the conscious use of the will. *Mantras* can also be utilised by the will's potency to structure Rays of light into *maṇḍalic* forms, sustained for the requisite time. The Elements conveyed by the light can then manifest appropriately in the *maṇḍala* and structure the

---

1 *Sādhana:* literally means 'leading to the goal, a means of attainment'. It generally refers to one's devotional practice involving ritual, prayers, visualisation and observation of various precepts and rules of training.

form. The force of the will applied to the *dhāraṇī* can then inevitably ground the form upon the physical domain.

We should observe the aspect of consciousness that actually uses the will that produces enlightenment, of how it organises the collection of experience from subtle realms via the images perceived. The delineations between such attributes as desire, ambition, assertiveness, and focussed intent, should be carefully noted.

In analysing consciousness from within the structure of the human mind one should note that only a symbolic quarter of it is confined to the gross space of the dense form (the brain). The brain is a mechanism that correlates and integrates (especially in its visual cortex) sensations conveyed by the nerves from impressions obtained by the sense-perceptors. The remaining three quarters of consciousness relate to the subtle body (the *nāḍī* system and *chakras)*, the Watery emotional or desire body, and the field of *citta*. Impulses from the *chakras* condition every thought instantly. Here the necessary types of *saṃskāras* are automatically called forth by the nature and quality of the impressions from the senses. The use of the will takes into account all of these expressions. In an unenlightened mind, the energy body or desire body is unthinkingly used to produce the desired modifications of the mind. The resultant created thought is then sent off to its errand. An accompanying image and desired attachment to some manifest form is thereby created.

An enlightened person must take much more care as to what is being built. The intensity with which it is being sent off to effect its errand, as well as the probable karmic effects of the impact of the thought on its target, must be taken into account. The emotions are stilled and are, therefore, unproblematic, the concern is however the ingathering of qualified *prāṇas* from one or other of the *chakras*. The nature and intensity of the *prāṇa* is noted and from which *chakras* they are derived. The objective is clearly envisioned, and the thought-form sent upon its errand with the right amount of will. Nothing is left to chance.

If for example, impressions from the Dhyāni Buddhas are to manifest in one's consciousness, a construction must be built to handle the way these forces would impact upon the mind. We may have a red stream from Amitābha's Mind coming from one field of perception, a green stream of Amoghasiddi's adamantine power from another, followed by a yellow one of Ratnasambhava's equalising energy. They all would manifest different effects in the Head lotus. The potency of the energy exchange would effect a number of major petals of the Head centre to significantly expand as they spin, to reveal the images veiled by the Jinas of the respective colourations. The Head lotus must be properly prepared for the potency of the energetic downpour. As a portion of the *maṇḍala* of the mind is vivified with the related colourings it effectively explodes into living multidimensional action. To contain intensified energy fields from the Buddha realms the Mind must be developed and held steady in the light by means of the developed will. Such a Will cannot be subservient to the vicissitudes of desire, or held rigidly in place by the ego posturing of the concrete mind. Rather, it must be fluid enough to pierce vast vistas of revelation, and be reinforced sufficiently to withstand the potency of the content of what a Buddha proposes.

If you endeavoured to describe the lines of relationship that were thereby energised, you would find that those lines are indefinable, because of the myriad levels of realisable impressions they would provide. Line patterns would however be discernable, leading to other parts of the *maṇḍala* still to be awakened to the mind's Eye. The content of what is to be revealed being veiled by glyph, colour, and symbol; the gist of which is immediately understood. Full revelation would instantaneously be accorded if the meditating one so willed it.

Will is conscious projection. One has to use the will to cause something to move from point a to point b. Also, a vast amount of time may take place between each volition, between the beginning and ending point of one's involvement with any aspect of *māyā*. In between there may be many little separation points (wilful volitions) before the overriding intention is accomplished. The duration of time may be infinite, but cycles of wilful manifestation are not. They can be measured, but each can exist in the form of an unlimited time frame.

The will chooses where to look and what to do. Therefore it can be divine (when it works to produce the drive to liberation) or mundane, when it attaches itself to any form of *māyā*. The will of reason may certainly choose to deny anything it so wishes, or to build illusional *cul de sacs* of belief. The nature of the will is manifold. It can be the outcome of pure desire-mind, which binds something desired to a 'self'. It can be an expression of the intellect that concretises images into set unwieldy mental objects or thought structures. It can be any aspect of the higher Mind, which works to liberate thoughts into expansiveness. It can be an aspect of divine Will, which will push all *saṃskāras* to become transfigured upon the thrones of the Dhyāni Buddhas.

Various perspectives on the will

All forms of persistent action, obstinacy, pigheadedness, tenacity, forthrightness, starting anew, bringing actions to conclusion, penetrative direction, even volatile actions, as well as directing the expression of *bodhicitta*, necessitate use of the will. Seven forms of the will shall be categorised below. Two of these can be considered bonded or conditioned will: *Strong desire, and the personal (selfish) will.* The next five forms of the will can be considered emancipated or non-bonded will. They are: *free will, goodwill, the Will-to-Love, the Will-of-Love* and *Divine Will.* We can also include group will, national and international wills as addendums, if the concept of the will is extended to include that which is generated by any *maṇḍala* of people.

Strong desire

Strong desire is impulse driven, based upon sensuality, and attraction to pleasured things of the form. It is often induced by any of the five instincts, to which it is allied. Blind, strong urges, over which the individual rarely has much control, characterise this elementary form of will. Riding upon the fields of desire, however, the desirous one manifests wilful intent to grasp for the 'self' whatever the objects of desire are. It is difficult to overcome these forceful *saṃskāras.* Desirous ones generally think they are free to choose whatever the object of desire they wish, but they are actually bonded according to the strength of the desire manifested. Before free will is truly obtained the individual must grow out of adolescence and mature over many, often painful experiences, because of the illusionality of the object of desire.

The personal (selfish) will

Selfish will is emotionally based. It is the source of all complacency, illogical thoughts, biased and ignorant reactions, as well as irrational behaviour in humanity. Most people spend their daily lives not manifesting an intention helpful to others outside their immediate family or friends. Their main goal is to apply their personal wills for self-interest and pleasure. They use their energy and desire ritualistically to create their own personal utopias, if that is possible. Thus they remain ensconced in selfhood. They manifest little or no will to battle the *māyā* of *saṃsāra*, for they are trapped in its materiality and illusional miasma affects their perceptions. They suffer the consequences of the law of *karma* and subsequently remain ignorant and unenlightened.

This selfish will is steeped in emotionality and is the mainstay of the glamours of the majority. It switches off the higher reasoning mind from properly analysing things before the possibilities of any new threatening idea can be listened to. This happens because of certain inherent fears or conditional notions of the person. The emotions generally produce a confused, reactionary mishmash of thinking, of winding through paths constituted of thickets and briar patches of opinions and into the murk of all types of animated volatilities. Bigotry or zealotry can also arise. The emotions blind and bind people to their fears, various insatiable appetites, and attachments to all forms of ephemera. This represents the great hydra that chokes the spiritual abilities of all aspirants upon the path to enlightenment. It thus produces many wayward actions.

Here we need to add the doctrine of the seven Ray aspects of mind. They are the seven major forms of the *kleśas* (the force of defilements, afflictive emotions) with respect to the activity of the mind, explained in Volume 2, chapter 1, *(An Enquiry into the Nature of Self)* of this series.[2] Briefly, they are:

1. *The will of mind,* the direct application of the wilful mind of a person expressed in a forceful manner, to dominate other's opinions and often their lives.
2. *The loving mind,* where the mind tells itself it is loving in its formulations worked out to help others. But in reality this is not so, there is always a (subtle) hidden selfish motive.
3. *The critical mind,* where the mind is infused with strong emotions and is used to critically dissect other's beliefs without

2 These Ray aspects of mind were detailed along with their more emotional cousins: racing hounds of mind, dog-like mental activity, spider-like desire-mind, slugs of mind, monkey mind, crabs of mind, and mouse-like mind.

true understanding of the issues involved. The critical one uses knowledge gained to emotionally attack others.

4. *Pride of mind* concerns the building of an aura of self-conceit and of boastful arrogance. Egoism is dominant.
5. *The concrete mind,* where the mind resides in a fortress of its own logic, materialising all ideas and opinions in self-centred terms, disallowing any information that does not fit in with its established rules of mentation.
6. *The desire mind*, where all aspects of the thinking process are distorted by one's desires and emotions.
7. *The wrongly faceted mind,* which focuses upon specific desired arenas of activity and exaggerates them, disregarding all other arenas of thought. Blindness of the integrated view results in impressions that are coloured with a distorted overtone of opinion, which often even invades the area of specialisation.

The manifestation of selfish orientation throttles the process of karmic rectification. Enslaved by selfish thought, people take from others to appropriate for themselves the resources their selfishness demands. By striving to appropriate empires of desired imaginings and ephemera for the 'self', people thereby upset the balance of harmony in Nature. Such self-will contains only a limited love for the greater life; it is not metered with compassionate insight. Because self-willed ones have not ascertained reasons to choose the path of action to help others as the main base of their intention they do not comprehend the prime causes for suffering upon this planet. They effectively blind themselves to the needs of the common weal, and continuously compete with all other self-willed ones to amass the limited amount of desired resources available at any time. This clashing and competitive warring of the little wills produces much pain, misery, destructiveness, and inevitable impoverishment for the majority. The acquisitive greed of the self-focussed one can be vast as the many capitalistic empires of our present plutocrats demonstrate. Such empires happen upon the micro-scale of individual interrelations, as well as upon a national and international scale involving local communities and general societies.

This personal selfish will then characterises the scheme of things presently prevalent in our world. New *karma* is thus continuously generated. Aberrant use of the personal will causes people to steal, manifest violent actions, lie voraciously, scheme against other's prosperity and property, swindle, murder, etc. Such lack of compassion in the path that the self-willed one undertakes destroys much that is vital to wholesome planetary life. The solution lies in the re-evaluation of our educational systems to avoid the doctrine of competition and selfishness based upon greed for monetary possessions. Cooperativeness and integrated caring social values should be taught to our children instead.

Most individuals react disconcertedly with much anguish when aspects of their *karma* painfully manifest, but the past misapplication of their selfish will demands such *karma* inevitably must be cleansed according to the effects of the way it was engendered. Individuals must learn not to blame others for the predicament they find themselves in. Instead they must subdue their reactionary wills when the blows of fate work to cleanse the slate clean from wilful acts manifested through impropriety in previous cycles. The *karma* teaches people to become more loving. They learn to respond to the suffering they find themselves and others in and effectively say, 'gee, I want to be happy, and wish others to be happier too, as a caring society is better than a callous one'. In giving to others they receive reciprocal benefits. If people create no new volitions of revenge, etc., they will be freed from some of the worst effects of their self-will, producing a domino effect of understanding and of learning by example. Thus we have the genesis of goodwill, demonstrating loving actions by rightly focussed will in alignment with the evolving planetary purpose.

The unsophisticated mind often holds separative viewpoints and philosophy, backed up by the intensity of its personal will, and this limits the scope for higher revelations. If one holds too much separation in mind then one cannot see the broader concepts, the overview so necessary in an enlightened stance.

Group will is easily seen in any religious or social group, warring faction, or in a competitive arena, such as in business or politics. The effects can be beneficent or harmful to the society, depending upon the nature and purpose of the will engendered.

A population's overwhelming emotional flavour developed via their thoughts in historical concourse as governed by such things as regional issues, racial characteristics, and overriding *prāṇīc* force, determines the national will of a country. This '*prāṇic* force' is a product of the *chakra* the nation is an expression of.[3] At present *national will* is the collectivisation of the emotional wills of the people the nation contains, but is directed by self-willed individuals. It is easily dominated by ruthless demagogues, the wilful manipulators of thoughts and emotions via control of the media and by fear-based propaganda. The vicissitudes of the massed emotional volitions of the society they are in are fickle, predictably selfish, sensation seeking, full of fears and prejudice, and possessing small attention spans. This allows the masses of people to be easily swayed. The manipulators seek power as a natural extension of their own will's projection. Thereby structures of potent destructive intent are created in the societies ruled by them. They are destructive because the empires of self-concern do not substantiate the harmonious universe around them. Rather, they heap rapacious burdens upon the ephemera of people's cupidity and avaricious acquisitions in consumptive constructs of inevitable woe. Selfish and separative accumulations of power do not build ever-lasting effects, and are very destructive when manifest upon a national or international scale.

The capitalistic societies that have evolved manifest the covetousness of their national identity, which when aggressively focussed results in nations going to war. The base common denominator of the collective desires is enhanced by the most ambitious and oft materialistically rapacious that become the powerful ruling elite, who then project the governing laws. The degree to which people (or nations) have wilfully dug holes in the mud of *saṃsāric* life must be understood if there is to be any way to help them out. The greater the potency of the personal will involved, the harder it is to help the person, as an equal force is required to help that individual turn about their wilful fixation of consciousness. Similarly with the national will and the nation concerned. Because of the *manasic* input of all such modern constructs, the *māyā* of it all spells its own (fiery) collapse.[4] The overriding *karma* of self-assertion causes an inevitable implosion when what was taken from the 'other' to

3 This theme will be further developed when astrologers appear who can think esoterically and are armed with a correct *maṇḍala* of the *chakras* of this earth.

4 These constructs are externalised nowadays into the modern war machines utilised to assert the state-generated *maṇḍalas* of selfhood.

build the construct of greed or power (e.g., of the state or organisation) is returned. It must return because the law of the common good, that of *karma,* demands it so.

Only Bodhisattva-like actions that build progressive constructs aimed for the common weal, construed in terms of what most people truly need, will produce lasting effects. Accordingly, teachings that relate to people being liberated from the woes of *saṃsāra* can be given. The personal will then comes to be sublimated into Divine Will, utilising the principles of the highest good, that harmoniously integrates the smallest unit into the integrity of the vastest possible *maṇḍalic* construct. The national body that accommodates and respects them can therefore promulgate the laws that pertain to the beneficent universal whole. The self-centred manipulative one (the demagogue or plutocrat that nowadays often stands as the national leader), on the other hand, utilises the will to destroy the integrity of the greater harmony so that ambitious constructs can survive contrary to the general beneficent motion of the all. Thus is the outcome of the 'greed is good' philosophy of the harbingers, financers, executives, and politicians of our present materialistic civilisation. Its methodology necessitates ruthless power of the organisation or politicians over all in the nation, and by extension, over all nations in our predominantly globalised world. For those working to offset the destructive evils of such rapacious greed, educating the masses to create a new national will based on socialistic idealism rather than capitalism would be a good start. [5]

The *international will* is at a very infantile stage, and the United Nations that represents the world body seriously needs reformation, with veto power removed from the hands of self-serving nations. The evils of economic globalisation through such agents as The World Bank,

---

5 The term socialism here refers to those policies that are designed to truly benefit the entire society or nation, rather than any power elite, political or industrial cartel, or capitalist demagogue. Socialistic policies necessitate proper resource-sharing of the productivity of a nation for all. It demands the foundation of cooperative communities and small-scale enterprises that produce true wealth generation for many. The utilisation of money must be tightly regulated so that it is not debt based, but used properly as a commodity of exchange and nothing more. The enormous disparity in the distribution of wealth that we see in our societies nowadays must become a thing of the past. The true value of labour must therefore be established by law in the society, and not be dictated by those who manipulate money.

the International Monetary Fund, and multinational Corporations are well documented, needing no repeat here. The subject would divert us too far from the main theme of this book, but follows the same lines as the way selfish will is applied by an individual, that when manifest upon a far vaster scale, causes misery and poverty to billions of people.

Free will

Free will is purposely directed logical deduction freed from emotional control. It can be linked to selfish will or to Devine Will, according to the way one chooses to act. The genesis of any new idea, or what is seized upon by the mind, is an expression of the will. The will can also consciously choose to ignore whatever it wishes. Free will allows this possibility, however it is really only free when it is no longer dominated by desire, overwhelmed by emotions, or attached to sensual pursuits. Then it becomes eminently rational, practical, and logical in decision-making. Rationality inevitably leads to the choice of a path that frees one from cycles of suffering through comprehension of their causes. Those that reside in ignorance must learn from the rational ones how to exert the will to overcome the basis to all their problems. A rightly projected will can free people from indolent habits, allowing the creation of new insights and tendencies, right knowledge, right concentration, etc., as epitomised in the Buddha's Eightfold Path. Without use of free will one cannot manifest the necessary logic to find the loopholes in thought, propaganda, ideologies, and socio-political or religious agendas that are being continuously projected by many in their societies.

Effectively this form of the will allows one to choose either the way of travelling the left hand path of the black magician, or the right hand path that produces liberation from *saṃsāra*.

If one thinks there is no (personal) will, based on the logic that the idea of 'self' is illusional, then the purposes of enlightenment and clear-based understanding of anything is not achievable. To achieve something one needs to be motivated with well-reasoned thoughts and to strive with a wilful purpose or manifest ambition. Similarly, the construction of *maṇḍalas* of liberation need a properly organised, ritualised, focussed mind, utilising free will to manifest its purpose. Substituting the emotional will for free will is the major difficulty of all beginner meditators. The free will is utilised to follow the straight road through to liberation from all mire. With developed wisdom one then knows how to conserve energy, to will the ability to cut off wrong activities and increase the right ones.

The definition of free will implies recognition of eventuation. Through the will rightly applied, the fulfilment of people's dreams becomes possible. The will then morphs into qualities such as strength, agility, adaptability, sturdy cultivation of patience and ordered thinking. Finally, it allows the production of *maṇḍalas* of divinely patterned order in thinking. Then the *saṃskāras* productive of pain and suffering can be found, overcome, and enlightenment attained.

Goodwill

The path of developed free will is continuous for all Bodhisattvas (and for Buddhas also). The will thus never ends, but transmutes into higher empowerments productive of revelations and identifications via the stages of goodwill and the Will-to-Love.[6] Goodwill is a continuation of free will, but here the individual has recognised that helping to rectify any of the common problems of humanity is the true basis of happiness for all. It thus draws upon a strong devotional basis to serve. Devotion drives the personality with images of the divine, or a utopia that can be obtained by means of common striving. It may have rightly directed emotions or desire admixed with it to propel the wilful intent towards the vision of what is the 'good'. Various forms of devotion are required to build pathways to the object of devotion, and if based on truth are sustained for many lives by any consciousness. Such an object of devotion may manifest as a religious idea for instance, and later be transformed into the parallel construct of another religion in the next life, or similarly into an expression of scientific materialistic research. Devotion later becomes translated into aspiration to high ideals.

Humanity must come to be freed from cycles of retributional activity by first endeavouring to think better thoughts and generating goodwill to others. The consequences of such generation naturally follow to produce freedom from concepts of 'self' and its perceived wants. People need to transmute the emotional-will of self-interest into devotional awareness

6 Teachings concerning goodwill, good will and the Will-to-Good have also been presented in the writings of Alice A. Bailey, to which the reader can refer for other perspectives on the meaning of these terms.

to community and social needs, to truly transfer their good feelings for others and social well-being into actions that count in society and the world at large. Only then can better societies for everyone be achieved. This represents the beginning of the path to enlightenment and the evocation of the *bodhicitta* that makes a Bodhisattva.

The Will-to-Love

This will is consciously developed upon the path of the Bodhisattva. It is the expression of the free will rightly orientated towards enlightenment. It differs from goodwill because now the elements preventing a true loving disposition are sought after and rectified so that they serve the requirements of the path. The emotions are consequently viewed as a hindrance to clear insight, and of how best to serve. They are then transformed by a similar methodology as that posited in the next volume of this series. Compassion is the key to liberation, but without the use of the Will-to-Love compassion remains theoretical, a sad hypothesis of what may have been. To wisely help others one needs insight into the *saṃskāras* of the past, allowing access as to the need of any arena of concern. Assistance can then be skilfully provided. This requires true insight as to the way *saṃsāra* is structured, of the nature of the individual wills directing the forces of *māyā,* and where they go wrong. Such insight is needed for all arenas of concern where advantageous changes must be made to produce a superior product.

One must develop a detailed consideration of the glamours and illusions that are common to human thinking, without which enlightenment is impossible. One must learn to draw upon the Will-to-Love to overcome all aspects of personality desires. *Dhāraṇīs* must be created for the most propitious outcomes, to manifest the purposes at hand. The process of developing the Will-to-Love and its eventual transformation into *bodhicitta* involves a long, arduous battle with self-will. It necessitates many lives of accomplishment, whereby slovenly *saṃskāras* come to be transformed into intensities of purpose, building *maṇḍalas* to liberation. Building such a *maṇḍala* becomes a personal *sādhana*, which must be carried devotedly to conclusion. A successfully built *maṇḍala* is a symbol (or map) of the liberation of mind. Such liberation necessitates the evocation of the Will-to-Love as directed by the rational mind, whilst the generation of *bodhicitta* is its leitmotiv.

Obviously, considerable effort to develop such a will is needed by those inherently ignorant of the fundamentals of the law of Love, because they do not have the proclivity created in a past life towards enlightenment. The *karma* they may have from the past needs to be reinforced to walk the path to enlightenment. They must assert their will to produce new sets of characteristics to overcome unwholesome behavioural patterns of self-concern. New diligent processes of the Will-to-Love must be fabricated, carefully weeding out all of the roots and briars that formerly produced egotism and selfishness. The way then is made clear upon the path towards the inception of Divine Will, and proceeds over many lifetimes.

Having generated goodwill in a past life assists in the progress towards enlightenment in the present one. The force of this goodwill helps one to intrinsically, one-pointedly ride the gift-wave of aspiration to seek out how best to love. Generating the Will-to-Love represents a paradigm shift from simply manifesting goodwill. It involves transference from a feeling based aspiration to help that is knowledge based, and orientated towards Divine Will, to produce right behaviour patterns to liberation. Such generation necessitates coming into contact with the higher teachings (*dharma*) that will allow a practitioner to formulate the needed logic that will awaken the Heart centre. The task involves transforming the dominant emotional forces of the Solar Plexus centre into enlightenment-characteristics. Here many aspirants often slip into erroneous thought, based upon 'remembrance' of murky *saṃskāras* (*karma*) generated many lives ago. Transforming such undisciplined, muddied *saṃskāras* needs lighted attention through generating the Will-to-Love. No ugly head of a defilement should be allowed to persist. This necessitates utilising the creative intelligence, 'skill in means', through right discrimination and action.

We can see, therefore, that the entire yogic path and ways of training disciples for enlightenment, all of the trials and tribulations of the path to liberation, now come to the fore. Transforming the Watery forces of the Solar Plexus centre into the calm equanimous energies of the Heart is not easy.

In the latter stages of the path the Will-to-Love becomes effortless. It produces unfettered meditation and joy; the awakened *bodhicitta* of the next stage of the will's development. The mind then will have been trained to be totally relaxed and subordinate to the silent voice of the Heart speaking. The serene Mind responsive to the Heart's guise is produced through many lives of meditative focus. The materialistic potency of all forthcoming *saṃskāras* come thereby to be exhausted, and the emotional will no longer has a say. It has been controlled by the mind and transcended by Love, by pure reason manifesting spontaneously for the benefit of every sentient being.

It should be noted that even those who gained enlightenment in past lives have to recapitulate past lines of mastery in any particular life. There will be new obscurations of mind to counteract, new subtle distortions and misunderstandings concerning perspectives of truth to be mastered, in the replication of any of the stages of awakening. The Initiates however possess a sophisticated mechanism of response to deal with all issues relating to the quest for enlightenment, and an evolved determination to do so, which assists in what they have yet to perfect. This is another way of saying that there are Bodhisattva levels (*bhūmis*) still to be undertaken.

The Will-of-Love (*bodhicitta*)

The Will-of-Love is the attaining of high aspiration (or will) to develop a deep-seated Love and wisdom. It is the way of the Heart speaking volumes of divine reason for everyone's benefit in every sentence of instruction. It is the emanation of the roar of the lion that has conquered the vicissitudes of *saṃsāra*. It is the way that the energy of Love and wisdom manifest via the applied service work of the Bodhisattva. It is the fount or force of *bodhicitta* driving on the compassionate acts of each Bodhisattva in accordance with his/her specific line of service. We observe the nature of the manifestation of *bodhicitta* through comprehending the mode of activity of the Bodhisattva of higher degrees.

The Bodhisattva works to change the *self-will* of humanity in general (at all levels and departments of society) into *goodwill*. This is transformed into the *Will-to-Good*[7] when an individual uses the will to progressively effect positive changes to benefit society, civilisation, or Nature. The expression of the *Will-to-Love* aligns one directly with the *dharmakāya* (thus Shambhala[8]). This allows the flowing down

7 The force of the Will-of-Love.

8 Shambhala, in Buddhism associated with the Tantric deity Kālachakra, governing

of *Devine Will* from liberated sources, to overshadow and influence consciousness in a way that *maṇḍalas* of universals are worked upon, and not just particulars. An individual then consciously embraces the macrocosm, transcending the microcosmic world that formerly held that person's attention.

Personal wills create the glamours of this world, which manifest in differing degrees of intensity. Therefore if one were to extract people from their illusions and glamours, thereby enlightening them, then the exact strengths of their personal wills must be known. The amount of energy needed to counter these wills can then be ascertained. Calculations need to be made by a Bodhisattva if such extraction for an individual is possible in that life, or if steps are to be taken over a series of lives. A similar meditation undertaken by the most advanced Bodhisattvas is needed for all categories of lives in our civilisation. The question then asked is: 'When and where were the collective *saṃskāras* generated, and to what extent or strength was the will utilised?'

Though there is much turmoil and evil within human civilisation, nevertheless, our societies would be very primitive, with people chained to abysmal ignorance and ruled by kleptocrats, tyrants, etc., if it were not for the Bodhisattvas that make their vows of compassion to incarnate into the earth. Spurred on by the Will-of-Love, each appearing high level Bodhisattva acts as a *bīja* for the generation of a *maṇḍala* of human units. The *maṇḍala* organises aspects of civilisation along the intended path of loving vision. Thus the Bodhisattva's service work proceeds according to a predetermined pattern of events, assisted by co-workers (disciples) as purpose is activated according to the flow of the

---

the wheel of time, plus various exoteric myths. Esoterically, it has its foundation upon the substance of the *ālayavijñāna* and is constructed as a consequence of the interrelated Minds of the Jinas working from a higher domain than that of *śūnyatā,* wherein its energy patterns are perceived. It is the holy city that embodies the Head centre of our planetary Logos (Ādi Buddha). It is said to exist in the 'sacred white Isle' in the Gobi desert, constituted of the substance of the second ether and is thus undetectable to all but those with the eyes to see. It is the centre where the Logoic Will is demonstrated for the governance of all upon the planet. It is the residence of the great King, the Ancient of Days, the Great Sacrifice, and His Council. All advanced Bodhisattvas are members of this Kingdom, from where their directives to serve are generated in the form of a centralised plan for the benefit of all upon the planet, according to the way that the combined *karma* of humanity is to be appropriately rectified. This kingdom represents the prototype *maṇḍala* upon which all that are described in this book are based.

force of Love. Each frame of the *maṇḍala* that is energised reactivates *saṃskāras* of past lives so that the *māyā* can be understood, bound, and eventually transformed. Amassed *saṃskāras* are brought to the surface of human societies so that people can comprehend their nature (thus the associated *karma*). Eventually they will perceive the transmutative mode of action of the Will-of-Love, thus of the way to liberation.

Bodhisattvas embody the qualities pertaining to the perfection of humanity. They always sagaciously aspire to advance humanity to more luminous domains, hence they become illusion-slayers. The Bodhisattva is also a *māyā*-container for the sake of humanity. Thus they hold the patterns of the next form of idealism needed for human advancement. The Bodhisattva slows down his/her path, providing the time to help lessen the massed potency of the personal-wills of others, to assist in their reformation and refinement. The transformed wills can then be used to project all to the next higher level or way of progress. Thus the Bodhisattva helps to transform the general *māyā* into *śūnyatā* through rightly focussed compassionate activity.

Being an expression of the Will-of-Love, the Bodhisattva vows obviously can't entertain any volition or thought that could hinder another's spiritual growth. The ramifications of the force of the *karma* created through people's desirous self-will must therefore be rightly understood. Misery ensues as a consequence, and the Bodhisattva must manifest a counterbalancing will to try to ameliorate the points of imbalance caused by these self-willed ones. The Bodhisattva understands also that pain and suffering is a necessary educator for such actions and will not use the loving mind to try to offset the needed teaching of the karmic consequences. Prescient wisdom at all times is needed. The questions Bodhisattva's ask then are along these lines: 'How to stop these *saṃskāras* causing massed suffering from being created, and to transform the *māyā* that is forming? How is the *maṇḍala* of the eternal Now to be enflamed with living wills of light? How are the repetitions of grievous mistakes caused by other's ignorant wilful intent to be stopped and converted into beneficent actions? How are people to be taught to develop the Will-to-Love?' Inevitably people must learn to understand the actions and motives of a Bodhisattva, to see the way out of pain and suffering through the conversion of self-will in such a way that it benefits the group need.

Being the centre of a *maṇḍala* of enlightenment the Bodhisattva sacrifices personal release from its thrall until those that are its constituency can build similar *maṇḍalas*. The development of the Will-of-Love demands that this shall be so. The Bodhisattva thus endeavours to awaken the Will-to-Love of others, by changing their wilful behaviour so that they will unreservedly show compassionate concern. A Bodhisattva reserves judgement for right action in all episodes of the manifestation of *karma*. The Bodhisattva thus acts as a causative impulse, a catalyst, creating action to spur on other people's good will. From this basis then the higher wills are fostered, producing their freedom from materiality.

The Bodhisattva acts as the beacon of light at the end of the path so that others can trust that the path is correct, that it will take them where they aspire to go. The crystal-clear Waters of Love, with which to refine and clarify consciousness, can then be collected. Bridges to the fountain of Life can be built to properly nourish humanity. *Maṇḍalas* of light can be presented, proffering the living Waters of Life to the central point of the mind so that energies can flow along all avenues of thought to vitalise the target aspects of consciousness. Assisting the energy of Love to clarify human emotions will provide the ability to rightly reason. People can then increase their thought volume to the realms of the Clear Light by not being wilfully obsessed with themselves. Until the cool Waters of Love flow unimpeded through and upon humanity, via the path that produces the evocation of the Will-of-Love, their thoughts will continue being stultified by abased energy and unworthy thinking. Until the stream of Love flows freely in humanity, the thought possibilities will remain as muddy pools in a barely moving stream with many agitated eddies of misunderstanding. Inevitably, the high order of the Will-of-Love must flow to push humanity to more exalted levels of thought. The Bodhisattva's purpose wills it so.

Divine Will

Divine will is pure veridical reason that unites the sum of liberated Life to consciousness. The massed illusional ways and mannerism of the self-willed points of consciousness actually shape the nature of the manifestation of an embodying Logos. The higher Wills in cosmos are affected by the small wills, because these higher Wills are embodiments of the Bodhisattva vows expressed upon a macrocosmic scale. The macrocosm is inclusive of the microcosm, and thus the Love of the greater One incorporates the needs of the lesser lives, as all is interdependent. The little selfish wills must inevitably be integrated into the greater harmony of the whole, but selfishness means self-focus, effectively cutting off of oneself from all around. The functioning of the overriding Will of the greater One thus works to curtail the activities of the various units of separativeness taken as a unity or as groupings of unities. Vast panoramas of scale are involved, with corresponding time scales to accommodate the process of transforming the 'self-ness' of the masses.

This is the way that human evolution is shaped, gradually moulded into the paradigm of the *maṇḍala* that exists within the Mind of the presiding Logoic Will. The process is but part of the *dhāraṇī* of the Adī Buddha concerned. The meditation is multifaceted because of the vast diversity of the wills involved, and of their categorisations. It necessitates differing modes of application for the greater Will to effect the necessary changes upon the various categories in the related scope of vision. The Power-of-Love is the force directed by this Will, but Love never imposes its authority, rather it always seeks to produce meaningful transformative changes from within the target *maṇḍala*. It also bathes the aberrant ones with energies pertaining to the direction of movement of the future purpose. Problematic areas within the *maṇḍala* caused by the separative wills thus will eventually be rectified so as to harmonise with the integrated structure.

Attributes of this *maṇḍala* are viewed in terms of groups of colours and sounds that the panoply of the categories of Life produce. Individuals are not the object of focus, except as far as a whole group of beings possessing similar characteristics can be considered an 'individual': such as a nation, tribe, or all members of a religious sect. When viewed upon such a scale and from a different perspective we should also note that demagogues who hold the masses in sway via manipulation of their selfish wills are agents of the lords of Dark Face. To counter this, the Lord of Life sends out enlightened emissaries, Avatars, the highest-ranking Bodhisattvas, to assist the masses to think appropriately. They can then overcome the wilful manipulation of their lives by the Dark Brotherhood. This is a field of service work that meditators *must* come to be initiated into when they pass testings upon the way to enlightenment. The true nature of the purpose of meditation upon the path of Love and Will is being revealed here because it is unwise to further veil the aeon-long battle between the Lords of Life and the opposing cosmic forces of evil intent.[9] All serious students of the Bodhisattva way must learn the nature of the roles they shall play to produce the planetary awakening that will occur when the evil therein is finally defeated. Such meditative work is the paramount way to liberation. The awakened Bodhisattva knows this way, because he/she is part of the great defending bastion protecting humanity (to the degree possible) from the sources of darkness drawn to the planet because of the effect of humanity's amassed selfish will.

Later, Divine Will is utilised by a Logos to manifest a world-sphere.

The will and the rebirth process

We all have many incarnations; each with a different purpose (pre-determined *karma*), proving that what controls the flow of the human Life-flux is not a will-less volition. The consciousness flow would otherwise continue haphazardly on its course *ad infinitum*. A mass of consciousness-bits jostling to incarnate at any time would make any incarnation untenable, and we would have the unpredictability of blind chance determining any outcome for what is to be. The concept of the entire law of *karma* would then be an impossibility. Basic Buddhist tenets concerning the rebirthing process, such as that presented in *The Maha-Prajñāpāramitā-Śāstra* below, clearly do not answer any serious enquiry in how *saṃskāras* or the *vijñāna* (the consciousness-stream) order themselves to bring about a specific rebirth, or how they choose the necessary *karma* out of the effective trillions of differing karmic streams to do so.

> What conditions the entering of the womb by *vijñāna,* in order to take on a definite embodiment? The *saṃskāras* condition it. *Saṃskāras* are the impressions, the traces of deeds done in the past and it is the seeds that lead the *vijñāna* into the womb for a (definite) embodiment.
>
> When the wind blows and the flame goes out, the flame enters *ākāśa*; at that time it rests on wind. (696b)

---

9 They have developed countering wills along their path, demonstrating the power of hate, which we need not delve into here.

> Similarly in the intermediate state the *saṃskāras* rest on *vijñāna*.
>
> In the previous span of life, when one was a human being, (one's thirst for) sense-contact was aflame and, at the end of that span of life the deeds done there (came to rest on *vijñāna* as subtle tendencies). It is these deeds that lead the *vijñāna* to the womb. (696b).[10]

Clearly, there needs to be an overriding will[11] that drives a particular consciousness-stream to take rebirth. It must select those *saṃskāras* out of the enormously vast store developed in past lives that need to be coherently dealt with for any particular life. The sum total of all associated *karma,* not just that to be experienced, must therefore be clearly visualised by a directive principle before what is selected for due processing can be worked upon in a particular life. *Karma* is not a blind law, in fact it is a group law (i.e., it was not created in a vacuum) as was explained in the author's previous book on *Karma and the Rebirth of Consciousness.* Organised purpose is the key here, not blind chance proffered by a vast number of past volitions jostling to manifest at any time, which would but produce insanity in any incarnation. The enormous magnitude of the problems presented by their accounting of *karma* escapes the unenlightened Buddhist mind-set.

The entity riding the Will-to-Love that wisely directs the *saṃskāras* is the *tathāgatagarbha.* It was explained in detail in Volumes 2 and 3 of this series, where it was renamed the Sambhogakāya Flower, because of its inherent nature and of the mode of construction of its form. It takes the shape of a whorl of nine-petals, veiling a central bud of three petals. The Sambhogakāya Flower directs aspects of the *vijñāna* stream into unities of karmic expression, and separates coherent units we call humans to incarnate in the right sequence so that the packets of *karma* can be eventually eliminated. Without such wilful direction and organisation there could be no impetus in the individual stream to incarnate at any time sequence, or in fact to incarnate at all.

The previous quote infers that 'one's thirst for sense-contact' being aflame is responsible for taking another birth. But we could query

10 K. Venkata Ramanan, *Nāgārjuna's Philosophy: As presented in The Maha-Prajñāpāramitā-Śāstra,* (Motilal Barnasidass, Delhi, 1978), 240.

11 Be this the Will-of-Love, or the Divine Will.

'whose thirst', that of the previous life, or of the one previous to that, or of the impassioned thirst of the unrequited *karma* say from maybe one hundred lives previous? What decides which of these (effectively myriad) 'thirsts' makes the fateful leap into incarnation, and what stops them from all wanting to take that incarnation together? Do these 'thirsts' carry packets of *karma* with them, or is it *karma* by some unaccounted mechanism that directs them? In other words, *how* does the law of *karma* work? The actual mechanism of its manifestation is not accounted for by such Buddhist syllogisms. *Karma* is the wish-fulfilling genie called upon to veil their ignorance of the nature of the entire process.

Similarly with each incarnated mind. Without an organisational will it would possess a mass of jumbled images, making it impossible for us to remember anything, thus to function. The will is what allows one to selectively perceive something, to make it a fact in consciousness. Memory simply would not be ours to command. Indeed, aspects of memory that pop into our minds at uncalled for moments, and which often radically alter the course of our subsequent lives, also hints at a greater Will than our little ones. (This greater Will directs the course of our lives to produce a meaningful expression.)

No Bodhisattva could appear if the thesis of uncontrolled Life-flux was correct, for then there would be no being that could arrange a *maṇḍala* of liberation prior to incarnating. Neither could the *karma* necessary for helping a target arena of need in the world be arranged. Often the concept of *vāsanā* is used to describe the driving force behind the appearance of *saṃskāras*. However, *vāsanā* must be directed by something, by a conscious will, otherwise it would be a universal energy, at once applicable in all directions, and also to no particular direction. Energy continues in its own motion and only when impacted upon by a directed force, becomes a force that can do work. In the field of consciousness such a force can only be conscious volition, thus a will to direct. Each life accounts for conscious travelling, utilising a myriad accentuations of wilful intent. The enlightened one must be in control of all aspects of the Life processes, and thus of the factor of all successive rebirths until Buddhahood is obtained. If this is so then all future actions in the envisioned fields of service must be pre-planned.

The way that the karmic volitions of the entire interdependent *maṇḍala* of service are to be directed must be meditated upon and the appropriate *dhāraṇīs* of accomplishment established. This also would not be possible if there were no unitary forms of expressions constituting each human Life stream. For *karma* to be directed, there must be something that responds to that *karma* that can be directed and accounted for by the enlightened Mind. The appropriate syllogisms explaining the way of karmic action have already been established in my earlier book *Karma and the Rebirth of Consciousness*. The Bodhisattva's Will-of-Love is both an organisational and a directing force to assist in the liberation of the many in need.

There are many different wilful changes of directions with respect to travelling from points a to b of one's Life continuum, for as each new thing is experienced the person changes tact, point of view, or emotional expression. The will thus accounts for changes in thoughts, emotions, and deeds. New wilful input can produce an entirely new life's expression. Even within the context of a single life one can experience a myriad of different life-structures, when each new will is evoked for each new thought or change in direction of the focus of the individual. One can therefore live many lives in one, through the evocation of the accompanying new volitions. (Indeed it is the *saṃskāras* from many past lives that often produce the wilful expression of any new course of activity.)

Lifetimes of experience that teach how to direct wilful volitions causing no harm to anyone is the background required to rightfully utilise *dhāraṇīs* in the meditative construction of *maṇḍalas* of liberation. Without this aeonic background of converting destructive to constructive wills, and to be able to sustain the will for the duration needed to accomplish a given task, no Bodhisattva could evolve to manifest an eventful *dhāraṇī* for liberation. Such *dhāraṇīs* may even take more than one lifetime to fulfil. Certainly the *tathāgatagarbha* meditates in a similar fashion to steer each life of the consciousness-flux it directs toward a meaningful conclusion, towards Buddhahood.

Eventually a similar intention from life to life is evolved to call the Buddha into one's consciousness. The process of manifesting Buddha-qualities is gradually evoked, and the allurements of *saṃsāra* come to be annulled through countering the *saṃskāras* of former wilful attachments to forms of transience. As the process nears its conclusion the *tathāgatagarbha* projects many volitions into the Mind-stream of the Bodhisattva concerned to develop the Buddha-Mind. This is the basis to the liberation process.

The Head lotus

Figure 22 shows part of the outermost (activity) circle of petals of the Head lotus of a person. It posits the way that sequences of lives are structured or organised for one of its major petals, of which there are twelve. Each small petal processes the *saṃskāras* of a particular life. The significance of this diagram shall be briefly outlined below, however, there will be a full explanation reserved for a later book. The purpose is to lay the foundations allowing revelation of considerably more than hitherto possible of a subject that has always been veiled. This then becomes the structural support for an entirely new emerging science, that of the *chakras*. The calculation of epochs of time by the enlightened is only possible through knowing the science of the *chakras*. It concerns comprehension of the esoteric categorisation of the entire field of Nature, and of the evolutionary process of all that is.

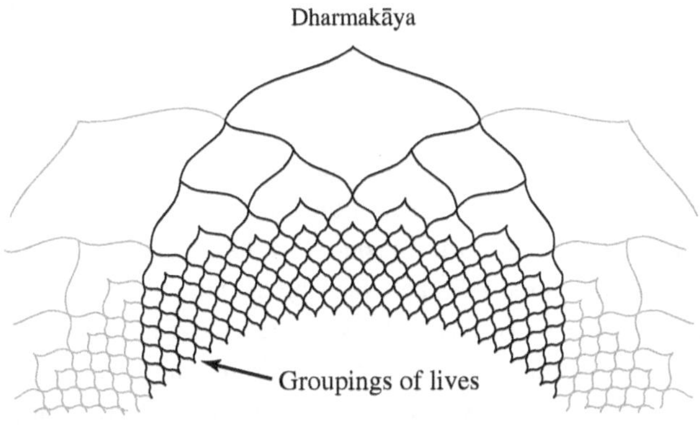

Figure 22. Lives in the Head lotus

Here we have five different levels of petals arranged in size from the smallest to the large synthesising petal. Each grouping contains places to process *saṃskāras* of a specific Element. The smallest petals, of which there are six rows, specifically process the *prāṇas* generated through the entire field of desire and experiences in the material domain associated with the Earth Element. The next largest petal will be seen to contain 33 of the smaller ones in its field of expression. This petal then processes the Watery *prāṇas* generated by the individual, and the related *saṃskāras* inherited from previous lives of activity. There are nine such petals to one major petal of the Head lotus. They allow directive input from the nine major petals of the three whorls of petals of the Sambhogakāya Flower. We also see here that there are many opportunities for the mixing of qualities wherever two groups of petals are overlapped.

The next major petal synthesises the *prāṇas* of a grouping of three Watery petals, admixing them with *manasic* (Fiery) attributes. We therefore have the processing of all forms of mental-emotional energies in their three categories: a) those predominantly infused with desire, b) the major emotional *saṃskāras,* and c) the more purely mental impulses. As there are 33 minor petals to each group, so effectively there are 3 x 33 = 99, plus 1 for the major overriding manasic quality, making 100 *saṃskāric* qualities that are processed by this level of petal in the *sahasrāra padma.*

The fourth largest petal of the Head lotus processes the Airy *prāṇas* that are generated. These are the general *saṃskāras* flowing throughout the *nāḍī* system concerned with transforming the qualities of the mental defilements (*kliṣṭamanas*) into *bodhicitta.* Each of these petals controls the flow of *prāṇas* from two of the *manasic* level petals. This represents two hundred *saṃskāric* qualities that can be processed in this manner.

Finally, the major synthesising petal represents the processing of the abstracting Aetheric *prāṇas* that allow the development of the type of perceptions pertaining to the *dharmakāya.* Its capability is two groups of 200 *saṃskāric* qualities each, making the number 400.

Because there are five major tiers of petals so we have the possibility of processing the sum of the input derived from sense impression. (The five sense-consciousnesses.) These *saṃskāras* can be slowly transformed into the attributes of the five Jina Wisdoms as the enlightenment-path progresses. They also allow a two way interchange between the Head lotus and the arrangement of any of the five groups of petals of the Sambhogakāya Flower. (Described in Volume 3 of this series.)

Next, we need to comprehend the structure of these petals with respect to rebirth. Our focus starts with a grouping of 100 petals, synthesising 3 x 33 lives of attainment. Each small petal effectively expresses one major *saṃskāric* quality, which becomes the purpose of a particular life to develop. A 100 petalled unit is the basis for many cyclic computations. Its main focus concerns the infusion of Fiery and Watery *prāṇas* to the base Earthy incarnations. We therefore have all forms of the emotions processed, coupled to the base desires and attachments to ephemeral, material things and materialistic incentives. This combined group represents the foundational clothing of the qualities of mind that are conveyed by the Head lotus. The major consideration is the *manasic* petals, of which there are four to a major petal. They represent the places of discerning the real, where all *prāṇas* are properly admixed and appropriately processed by the mind. From this level on we see that there are seven major petals controlling the overall processes associated with the awakening of Mind, four Fiery, two Airy, and one Aetheric petal.

There are two different orientations of the four petals relegated to the expression of the attributes of mind. One pair is oriented towards the left and another towards the right. The right hand one processes mainly *prāṇas* from the *piṇgalā nāḍī* stream,[12] and the left hand pair the *iḍā nāḍī* stream.[13] Each member of a pair then specialises either in a subsidiary *iḍā* or *piṇgalā* functioning.

Each pair of manasic petals will be seen to be responsible for processing a sequence of 200 lives of attainment. There are five smaller petals within the catchment area of their embrace. These five groupings can also be considered to each specialise in processing one or other of the *prāṇas* derived from the five sensory inputs: touch sense-consciousness, eye sense-consciousness, etc. When incorporating the processing of both *iḍā* and *piṇgalā* streams of *prāṇas* for the *saṃskāras* derived via sensory experiences we then have 2 x 200 = 400 lives. This represents the number of incarnations that are generally needed

---

12 *Piṇgalā nāḍī:* the right hand masculine *nāḍī* stream. (Buddhists also use the term *rasanā.)* This stream concerns the evocation of consciousness (Love-Wisdom) and the flowing of the related *prāṇas* throughout the body. It is the second of the triple cord (*iḍā, piṇgalā,* and *suṣumṇā*) that runs up the spinal column from the Base of the Spine centre to the Head centre via all major *chakras* in the body.

13 *Iḍā nāḍī:* the psychic channel that embodies the feminine, intelligently creative, forces and energies in Nature, seen in terms of consciousness. Thus the *prāṇas* pertaining to intelligence; the Fires of the mind. It forms a triplicity, with the *piṇgalā* (Son) and *suṣumṇā* (Father) *nāḍīs*.

to fully develop the basic attributes of intelligence. Thus everything concerning the development of the selfish forms of the will, plus the free will that is the onus of expression of the four larger synthesising petals can be incorporated.

The development of goodwill then becomes the purpose of the two larger Airy petals that incorporate the *manasic* petals as part of their arena of expression. Within the Head lotus they process the general *piṇgalā prāṇas* circulating in the *nāḍīs*. The left hand petal processes the mental-emotional (*iḍā*) *prāṇas* directed from the *chakras* below the diaphragm, in a way that the emotions come to be properly subordinate to the mind. (These energies are controlled by the Throat centre overall.) The right hand petal processes the tendencies towards the development of goodwill in such a way that the emotional input comes to be increasingly dominated by the Love energy coming via the Heart centre. These are *piṇgalā* in nature. Thus we have a *piṇgalā-iḍā* and *piṇgalā-piṇgalā* expression for these two petals. One hundred lives each are relegated to the development of the various levels of expression of goodwill under the general auspices of these main petals. When we add this number to the 400 lives earlier posited then we get a sum total of 600 lives set aside for the development and processing of the *saṃskāras* that produce a Watery-Airy loving disposition of the mind for the consciousness-stream concerned.

A personality then develops and experiences a specific level of expression of an aspect or minor petal of the major structure in that particular life. Thus the wheels within wheels that are the petals of the Head lotus turn and spin to advance the general forward motion of the overall schema. All depends upon the nature of the will expressed by the personality during any incarnation.

The major synthesising petal integrates all the experiences of the individual into the most refined form possible to develop during an incarnation. This overall synthesis is then channelled to and directed by the Will-to-Love of any of the major petals of the Sambhogakāya Flower. They thus assume an overall control of the Head centre's activity. The degree of control depends upon advances towards the higher Wills a person has made. The Sambhogakāya Flower incorporates a similar structure to what has been described. It is the model upon which the Head lotus is based.

One hundred lives of development are set aside in this major petal for the further refinement of free will coupled with the development of goodwill. At this stage, devotion to noble causes and high idealism come to be viewed as objectives worthy of serious input and effort, as well as logically reasoned religious sentiment whose purpose is to generate conscious aspiration towards enlightenment. Seven hundred lives are therefore generally needed by people before they are ready to travel the Bodhisattva path.[14] Because of the quickened pace of life and awareness characterised by those at this stage of evolution we can assume that the next level of expression concerns a slightly different ordering of petals. (The focus here will be upon another major way of analysing the organisation of the tiers of the petals of the Head lotus.)

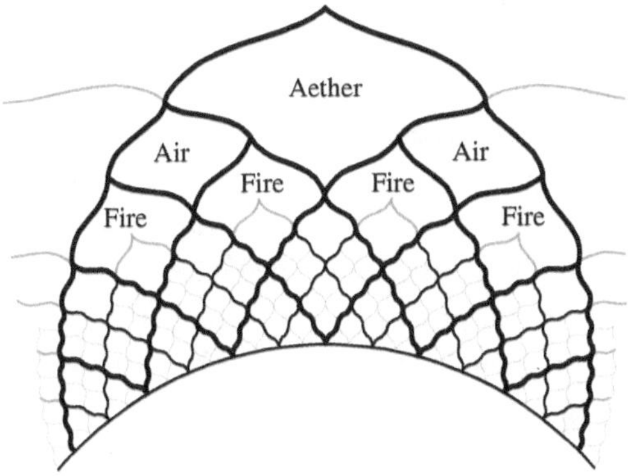

Figure 23. The next seventy incarnations

In this synopsis we must first assume that the seven major petals are concerned with the path of discipleship and Initiation. Each of these petals are conditioned by one of the seven Ray characteristics. They determine the major hue that all of the subsidiary petals are conditioned by. These hues differ according to the evolutionary progress of the consciousness-stream and purpose of the governing Sambhogakāya Flower.

These 70 incarnations are viewed at a higher level of expression than the earlier 700, because of evolutionary gain. The purpose of the earlier cycles is to evolve basic mental characteristics (*manas*), whereas

14 The way of discipleship to the Hierarchy of Love.

the 70 incarnations deal specifically with the mental-emotions (*kāma-manas*) developed with view of their refinement. The objective being the production of pure *manas* (Fire) and its integration with Airy *prāṇas* (Love) from the Heart centre so that wisdom is evolved and the qualities pertaining to the higher centres can be fully expressed. This entire process shall be detailed in chapter 7 of Volume 5 (An Esoteric Exposition of the Bardo Thödol), therefore it suffices to only present an outline here.

When counting the number of petals in Figure 23 depicting the next seventy incarnations, then we will see that there are 49 petals in all, including the four lightly outlined. They relate to the 7 x 7 Ray and sub-Ray potencies that must be processed by each major petal of the *sahasrāra padma*. This image is constructed by following the contours and extensions of only the seven major petals, plus that of the nine synthesising petals for Watery input that support them. Therefore, of the minor petals only every second one is represented. At this stage of development the *saṃskāras* of both their *iḍā* and *piṇgalā nāḍī* expression are evoked, developed positively, and transformed concurrently.

This produces groups of ten incarnations (7 + 3) to consider for any manifest cycle. The image shows that there are five larger petals to integrate Watery *kāma-manasic prāṇas*, each with ten smaller petals constituting it. Five petals are necessary because they are cauldrons for transforming selfish *saṃskāras*, developed via sense perception and fused with emotionality (*kliṣṭamanas*), into foundational goodwill attributes which evolve into the wisdoms of the Dhyāni Buddhas. These petals can be considered places of admixing the *iḍā* and *piṇgalā* inputs of the general *kāma-manasic* environment in which the aspirant still resides, so that the combined attributes can come to be ruled by the free will of the Fiery petals. These petals deal with the evolved attributes of the higher abstract Mind, whereas the Watery petals deal with the factors producing the concretion of mind.

There are four more Watery petals lightly drawn, which do not have a direct bearing upon our consideration here. They come into expression temporarily as the great wheel upon which the major petals of the Head lotus turns, one minor petal at a time, considerations of which lie outside of this present summary. The nine petals allow the projection of refined *manasic saṃskāras* into the nine whorls of petals of the Sambhogakāya Flower.

At this point the aspirant must face all attributes in life with much more wisdom and emotional control than before. The objective of self-discipline is to teach how to most efficiently rectify *karma*, and to transform base motives into high aspiration. A life of aspiration and of discipleship is far more sophisticated than that of an average self-willed individual. The force of the prevailing mood or opinion in the society they find themselves no longer sways disciples. They are mostly masters of their own destiny, even though *karma* will still play its retributional hand for misdeeds of bygone times. Theirs is a life wherein the many divergences of public opinion come to be understood and resolved into right thinking, producing greater compassionate considerations for the common plights of humanity. They have developed goodwill and are motivated to choose to fix up erroneous *saṃskāras,* even though they often do not know the esotericism of the processes involved.

There are two groups of ten Watery petals incorporated in a synthesising *manasic* (Fire) petal. One group manifests a general *iḍā* line of input, and the other group a general *piṅgalā* line. This makes eight such groups of petals for each grouping of the four *manasic* petals. This number is important for a number of reasons:

a. It facilitates processing the qualities of the eight consciousnesses (of the Yogācāra philosophy).

b. Each grouping of petals specialises in the reception of energies from one or other of the eight major *chakras.* (The superimposed Splenic centre is here viewed as a major *chakra.*)

c. It incorporates the qualities developed from the projection of consciousness towards any of the eight directions in space.

d. It facilitates the development of the types of awareness associated with the eight Mahābodhisattvas.

The four main *manasic* petals also have a direct sympathetic link to the mode of expression of the four large petals of the Base of Spine centre. These Base of Spine petals are the foundational generators of the *prāṇas* of the four Elements and of the main experiences gained through interrelating with the four Kingdoms of Nature. Later, in the generation stage of *kuṇḍalinī,*[15] the Fiery Head centre petals are the first of the *sahasrāra padma* to be enflamed, thus bringing about enlightenment.

Only ten lives of development are effectively needed to process the qualities associated with each of these petals upon the path of discipleship with respect to the positive development and concurrent transformation of both the *iḍā* and *piṅgalā nāḍīs.* This produces a pattern of forty lives for the development of free will and its conversion to the Will-to-Love, as far as *manasic* purpose is concerned. Four rounds of incarnations are needed because:

a. The Fiery *saṃskāras* of the four concreted sub-planes of the mental domain must be transformed. (There are three abstract and four concrete levels to the domain of mind/Mind.)
b. Mastery of the four sheaths of the personality thereby come to be achieved. They are the concrete mind, the Watery astral body (thus all of the emotions and glamours of an incarnate personality), the etheric or energy body wherein are found the *nāḍīs,* and all of the lures and appetites associated with incarnation in a physical form.
c. The projected Earthy qualities associated with the four petals of the Base of the Spine centre.
d. The *prāṇas* of the four major *chakras* below the diaphragm must be accommodated by the Head lotus. These *chakras* are, the Base of the Spine centre, Sacral centre, Solar Plexus centre, and the superimposed Splenic centres.
e. The mode of integration of the related *prāṇas* into the four major *chakras* above the diaphragm must also be accomplished within the Head centre.

---

15 *Kuṇḍalinī:* the serpentine creative Fires of Life buried within the Base of the Spine centre. It is feminine in nature and sustains the sum of the activity of the form. *Kuṇḍalinī* interrelates and coheres the atoms of substance into a unified form. It is the effect of the lowest descent of the Fiery Creative Word, sustaining the foundations of gross substance. It is seven layered (sheathed) and when evoked by means of appropriate *mantra* (via the expression of the energy of the Will), unites with the Potency veiled (conveyed) by the *mantra* (which is masculine) to produce that all-consuming Fire that fills the *suṣumṇā nāḍī* that liberates the Life aspect incarcerated in the bodily form. (This Potency is directed from, or via, the Sambhogakāya Flower.) Its Fires are said to liberate the wise and destroy the foolish who would prematurely or rashly wish to contact this (pro)creative force.

Next we have the two Airy petals, which admix the energies of *bodhicitta* from the Heart centre to drive the development of the Will-to-Love of those who aspire to advance up the Bodhisattva ranks. They similarly integrate the qualities of *saṃskāras* of both the *iḍā* and *piṇgalā nāḍī* expression of the goodwill and Will-to-Love that is developed. When we count the number of large subsidiary petals to each of these Airy petals, then we will find that there are ten per petal. When added to the forty above mentioned, then we get 60 in all.

The major Aetheric petal similarly deals with ten large petals wherein the most refined, abstracted *manasic* energies are produced through cleansing the *saṃskāras* of the defiled mind (*kliṣṭamanas*) and their transmutation by means of the free will at first, and later by developing the Will-to-Love. This process of refinement of *manas* draws its potency from the activity of the Throat centre. Its focus, therefore, is the development of the wisdom part of the Ray of Love-Wisdom. The ten petals are counted as: the Watery five that are together synthesised by the four (Fiery) *manasic* petals plus the final Aetheric petal. The Aetheric petal also represents the fifth (and synthesising) Fiery petal, to complete the pentad of mind/Mind. The five Watery petals therefore deal with the *prāṇas* of the major quality of normal *manasic* consideration, the desire-mind or mental-emotions.

This produces 770 petals altogether (10 + 60 + 700) that specifically deal with the perfection of mind, and the gradual development towards the *ālayavijñāna* form of enlightenment. (One that accomplishes this is described as an Arhat.) This number then represents the symbolic number of lives needed for an individual consciousness-stream to gain the valid wise discernment that will produce enlightenment. (The foundation needed for travelling the higher Bodhisattva *bhūmis*.)

There are two additional Airy petals that need to be included at this stage, whose focus concerns inbreathing the energies from the Heart centre (*bodhicitta*). These produce the Love aspect of the dual Ray of Love-Wisdom, and consequently the development of the Bodhisattva path proper for all meditators awakening the full potency of their Head centres. These petals also admix the general Airy *prāṇas* of the entire incarnate expression into the Fiery meld that is the natural expression of the *sahasrāra padma,* and the functioning of the will that it embodies.

With respect to this there are twelve main petals to each of the major petals needed to fully accommodate the main *prāṇas* from the Heart centre. The Heart is truly the Life of any system, the true place of the generation of *bodhicitta*, and for the experience of *śūnyatā*. These petals are the five Watery petals, the four Fiery ones, the two Airy ones, and the Aetheric one. Their combined transformed *prāṇas* need to be developed by the Will-to-Love upon the Bodhisattva path if liberation is to be achieved. Twelve is accordingly the base number of petals to the Head lotus, from which the entire lotus is derived.

Finally, we have the most sublime of the Fires of Mind to be developed in the seven major petals, at the ending of the path to enlightenment, when the higher Bodhisattva *bhūmis* are to be trod and the Will-of-Love fully expressed. It is during these lives that the *saṃsāra-śūnyatā* nexus can become the true place of residence for the Bodhisattva. This lays the foundation for the final experience, denoted as *dharmakāya*, the full potency of which can be conveyed by the *sahasrāra padma* only when the main *prāṇa* that flows in the Head lotus is Aetheric. With respect to this it should be noted that the *ālayavijñāna* enlightenment is expressed when the Fiery *prāṇas* are dominant in the Head lotus. The *śūnyatā* enlightenment happens when the Airy *prāṇas* are dominant.

We see here also that as well as the twelve main petals, there is a natural internal arrangement of groups of seven petals and their powers, dealing with the expression of the attributes of the seven main Rays in manifestation. There are also the processing of the five main *prāṇas* associated with the sense-consciousnesses. They manifest through groups of five petals and the powers thereof. The various septenaries have accordingly been earlier designated in this *Treatise on Mind* as 'sacred petals', and those related to the number five as 'non-sacred'. When seven is added to five then we get the number twelve, the base number of petals to the Heart and Head centres.

At the latter stages of the path, the petals controlled by the Aetheric petal and the two Airy petals are responsible for the development and refinement of perception associated with the three abstracted levels of Mind, which were earlier termed the sphere of Ideation, the Son of Mind, and the Clear Light. When added to the four petals governing the more concreted levels of mind, then we have an important septenary responsible for the sum of what is denoted as Mind. When the final seven petals are added to the 770 already described, then we get an understanding of the nature of the mechanism underlying the significance of the 'mystery of the 777 incarnations'. This basic teaching was first presented in *A Treatise on Cosmic Fire.*[16] That account, presented in terminology suited for Westerners, alludes to the mechanism with respect to the three major tiers of petals of the Sambhogakāya Flower. The present account posits the corresponding mechanism in the Head lotus presented for Buddhist thinkers. Despite the differing orientation of presentation, both versions are really the expression of one teaching. One represents that which controls the entire process, and the other being the mechanism of response wherein the process of the evolution and transmutation of the generated *saṃskāras* is carried out. The Head lotus is thereby the crucible of experience wherein the great Alchemical transmutative process of turning base metals (attributes of mind) into spiritual gold (enlightenment-attributes) is wrought. For many lives the trials and tribulations of transforming the poisonous material of the defilements of mind are undergone, until finally, at approximately the last seven lives of the process, the right formula is found and the great stage of transmutation of mind into Mind is finally achieved.

In the above three levels of the awakening of the Head lotus we have effectively expressed the Amoghasiddhi, Ratnasambhava, and Amitābha reflex of expression.

a. Amoghasiddhi—the empowering of needed mental characteristics through repetitive accumulation of often segregated and dissonant experiences and their slow transformation into high revelations. The tier of seven hundred petals.

b. Ratnasambhava—the development of integrative, loving, and unifying concern associated with goodwill. The field of expression of the seventy lives.

16 Alice A. Bailey, *A Treatise on Cosmic Fire*, (Lucis Publishing Company, New York, 2005), 825-829. The quote is from p. 825.

c. Amitābha—the broad sweeps of the perfection of mind, integrating consciousness into one grand *maṇḍala* of accomplishment. Eventually we have the achievement of the perfection of every quality and attribute of mind, and the awakening of the power of Mind wherein all mental processes come to be expressed effortlessly and spontaneously. The demonstration of the potency of the final seven lives.

We see, therefore, that the ability to reside in the natural state of Mind represented by Amitābha's tier of expression is the result of an aeonic development of the evolution of mind, if all goes well. Effectively seven hundred and seventy-seven lives will have then been trodden. In *sūtra* terms we have the achievement of the realisation of the *prajñāpāramitā,* the boundless virtue of wisdom, the Mother of all the Buddhas. There are further steps still possible for the Bodhisattva to travel, related to the awakening of the full potency of the *dharmakāya* (where the application of Tantra comes into play), necessitating a transitional stage that spells the end of the Sambhogakāya Flower's existence, as it is no longer needed. The high level Bodhisattva has taken over its function, because true residence in the consciousness-space denoted as *bodhicitta* has been permanently achieved.

Each of the major petals of the Head lotus thus embodies but one major category of the Sambhogakāya Flower's purpose, as conditioned by a particular sign of the zodiac. The repetition of the pattern of lives for each petal twelve times is necessary because then all of the conditionings and experiences possible to be derived from *saṃsāra* can be accounted for. The main wheel therefore turns to allow experiences to be undertaken in each of the twelve signs as one undergoes the 777 incarnations. This then happens in accord with the way of the Heart of Life beating out the pulsation of its rhythm. The Heart's blood that is poured out represents the qualities evoked by the conditioning sign of the zodiac, as the wheel slowly turns from cycle to cycle. There thus is a connection here to the great astrological ages, the evolutionary development of humanity with respect to the precession of the equinoxes and the rate of development of each individual consciousness-stream. All can be viewed in terms of a sea of energies wherein greater cosmic sources condition the development of the streams of consciousness with the inherent qualities of any zodiacal sign that is dominant at the time. We thus have an indication of the veracity of the qualities of the signs of the zodiac attributed to the Heart centre, as provided earlier in this *Treatise on Mind.*

Thus though there are 777 incarnations implicated for each of the twelve major petals of the Heart that is the Head lotus, twelve times 777 incarnations are not necessary to gain enlightenment. Rather, each of these major petals are attuned to a particular sign of the zodiac, which colours a particular grouping of lives that are experienced within its influence, because the wheel of the Head lotus has turned to be influenced by that sign during a specific evolutionary period. Effectively, each petal, and grouping of petals, can be viewed in terms of wheels turning within wheels, with the spokes of energy interchange being determined by the qualities of the three crosses earlier explained. Vast is the intricacy therefore of the nature of the evolution of mind.

Because of the necessity of presenting to the Buddhist audience a proper explanation of the qualities of the twelve petals of the Heart centre, the signs of the zodiac were explicated in some detail in Volume 3 of this series. The twelve major petals of the Head centre represents the manifestation of the way of the Heart centre with respect to the development of the attributes of mind and their conversion to Mind. In applying the symbolism of the qualities of the twelve signs, with respect to the Heart centre, many other lists of attributes found in the *sūtras* and Tantras will be better comprehended by Buddhist students and practitioners. Buddhism is after all, predominantly a religion espousing the Middle Way (*mādhyamā pratipad*[17]) which is an expression of the Heart centre's awakening, wherein the experience of *śūnyatā* is the basis of all.

The Sambhogakāya Flower and the will

The strong, unforeseen and little comprehended urges driving us forward in this life, and memories of past lives, are only possible because there exists a mechanism that spans many lives from the past into the future. This mechanism controls the expression in each incarnation and

17 *Mādhyamā pratipad:* refers to the middle way or path between extremes of eternalism and nihilism.

influences successive volitional actions. It indicates that each expression of wilful action is not extinguished at the death of a personal-I. The flow of wilful volitions continues into the next life at appointed cycles, allowing one to move on from one's past level of attainment. We saw earlier that this mechanism is the Sambhogakāya Flower. *Saṃskāras* are generated with each wilful action and are propelled upon their course according to the intensity of the will with which they were generated. *Saṃskāras* repeat future cycles in an ordered flow. Before they can act thus, however, the *saṃskāras* must be contained and organised by an overriding will. The overall memory of the sequencing of the little wills is also not extinguished from one life to the next. A general directing will is needed to span all the lives constituting a consciousness-stream. The separate wills of each incarnating life can then be organised according to a predetermined pattern.

When this process is extended, one must then see that there is a framework for the incarnation of each body that appears from life to life, from one major volition or purpose to another, similar to what was depicted concerning the Head lotus. The energy currents of each successive life can then be rightly transformed to achieve the goal of the 777 incarnations. The Sambhogakāya Flower is thus the major conditioning will for the entire process of rebirth. When the volitional current from this Flower projects past tendencies to the future then each little will incorporated by it begins a new cycle of activity.

Each life is a continuation of the volitional tendencies of previous cycles of activity from former lives. The cycles of what transpired in the past are repeated upon a slightly higher spiral of activity. The repetitive nature allows memory to be recalled when at a particular stage of any life one is engrossed in volitional activity that was seeded in a previous life. All this is possible because as previously stated, the overriding will of the Sambhogakāya Flower stores the information of when to incarnate and to actualise a set of instructions for an intended purpose. Because the little personality will does not generally base its activities upon a conscious remembrance of past events, the overriding will chooses the order of events for the little will's appearing choices for activity, and the appearing points of crises. Thus is produced a future outcome, according to how well the challenges of the points of crises were met. The will is evoked through the process of overcoming personal obstacles. It develops whenever right choices in overcoming those obstacles have been made. To try to offset the predicaments imposed by pain, suffering, and personal hardship is thus a major motivating factor producing wilful intent. Obstacles are thus keyed into the life's purpose for every individual by the Sambhogakāya Flower concerned.

The sum total of the wilful expression of the various personalities (lives) that manifest represent a continuum of *saṃskāras* accumulated by the 'individuality' of the Sambhogakāya Flower. Such 'individuality' is the expression of the Śūnyatā Eye that is integral to this Flower, for it directs the progression of the continuum of lives of any personal-I. The Śūnyatā Eye is the Eye of *dharma*, and is viewed as the expression of what is depicted in Figure 4 entitled, 'The relationship of śūnyatā to saṃsāra', when viewed as an extension of the central 'iris' of the Sambhogakāya Flower. It represents the way of visioning for the Sambhogakāya Flower/*tathāgatagarbha*. It regulates the concourse of all of the successive wills generated by the incarnated individuals. Generative mechanisms are necessary to transmute desire-based impulses (that foster ego-clinging and repetitive actions) into the Will-to-Love. This produces liberating *saṃskāras*, and eventually a successful outcome.

Cycles repeat on a higher level of expression, and are recreated in a new format. They continue the patterning of Mind, set up by the larger Will of the *tathāgatagarbha*, of which they are a part. The Will-of-Love is used by the *tathāgatagarbha* to direct the orientation of each past life and allow the Śūnyatā Eye to create the needed forms to be held in place so that the *maṇḍala* can grow in resilience and strength towards its overall purpose. The activities of each appearing form (personal-I) necessitates changes of approach to appearing points of crises that the Eye perceives, producing subtle modifications in the Will of the overriding Flower. The Śūnyatā Eye must also be constantly focussed upon the manifesting Wills of the collective grouping of Sambhogakāya Flowers of which it is a part. The *karma* of a nation or civilisation must be together wrought by them, when group and national *karma* (and thus associated *saṃskāras*) must be factored into the directive mind-stream of each incarnating *jīva*. Streams of Logoic Will that accentuate or change the flow must also be appropriately responded to. The overall *maṇḍala* that the Śūnyatā Eye must work upon is focussed entirely towards the production of the future events seen within the field of vision of that Eye.

With respect to the cellular mind-structure of the personal-I, the future represents an unknown alien entity possessing an expression that the cell doesn't know. As the mind penetrates the surface of the cellular wall this unknown expression flows into the cell and fills the body of the organism. It becomes identified with what is known, and then becomes the past. Thus the future purpose integrates the past into an organised direction according to the directives of the higher Will, and the process fills the organism of the cell. The present is the surface contact area of the cell or *maṇḍala* needed for conscious assimilation. The past concerns everything veiled that is bound within the cellular structure, and the future is what remains outside of it.[18] The *maṇḍala* precipitates as substance out of the past when the energy of the future comes in contact with the present. What contacts the future is a highly organised form of the past, which holds the present in a cohesive form. This organised collection of energies then depicts the surface area of the *maṇḍala* that can be analysed, because encoded within it are the cryptograms (*dhāraṇīs*) of all past experiences. Thus is encoded the imprint of the Now, wherein determinate energies form a point of contact between the future and the past *saṃskāras*.

The past can be said to represent a static energy held within the organism of the cell. It manifests a resonance existing at a lower frequency than the future. The future (*saṃskāras* directed by the Sambhogakāya Flower) is far more alive than the cell containing the past substance. The cell records the energy of the future, utilising the past according to the purpose of a predetermined Will from the Flower. This Will moulds the present tendencies of the cell to move to the arenas of activity the Will wishes to embrace. Where the cell is predetermined to go to therefore is of a higher frequency than all the energies held within the present life form, unless sickness or disease sets in. From the Sambhogakāya Flower's point of view such 'sickness' represents a form of resistance to arenas of activity of a higher energy domain that the personal-I can manifest at that time. This is because of

18 Here a subject earlier presented is reiterated and expanded with further references.

sluggish attachment to constraining *saṃskāras* of desire for ephemeral and material sensation that work to perpetuate what was viable in the past (e.g., of a past life). It can thus be the result of the karmic repetition of the constraints of low energy when the overall Life patterns have progressed beyond.[19] Though a sickness may apparently retard the speedy delivery of the greater will's intent, it may cleanse the blockages to future application of this will. A cleansing agenda may manifest as instances of diseases that can occur over many lives. Calculations have been made by the Flower, according to the mode of activity of the above mentioned 777 incarnations, for a slow but healthy development of improved forms of will by the personal-I's concerned. By evolving selfish will into goodwill the greater Eye thus focalises upon improvements and incremental positive changes towards the good within the manifestation of the little will of the incarnate personal-I.

If that little 'I' or 'eye' cannot activate an applied logic or wisdom to change direction away from the generation of sickness, to produce higher forms of will, then the Sambhogakāya Flower will retentively store the energy for a later date when greater (healing) light can be engendered. The line, structure, and grand design of the overall *maṇḍala* thus gradually comes into view. It comes to be coloured with a greater intensity of tone and note.

Unravelling the mysteries of the *maṇḍala* of cosmos

The mind clothes and collates all forms of experiences of the personal-I so that they can be projected into future possibilities. Upon the Initiation path (the last seven or so of the 777 lives) such activity happens in relation to the design that already exists in the complete *maṇḍala* of enlightened

---

19 This can also be seen in cases where excessive emotion was generated, because in reality the intensity of such (Watery) emotions does not match the measured potency of the future Fiery accumulations (of energy). The energies generated by these emotions have weakened the area through expulsion of substance, which then invites low-level psychic entities to inhabit the vacant spaces. When they are to be expelled in a later, corresponding though heightened, energy cycle these entities foster the breeding of the pathogens associated with their energy state, and what is known as sickness ensues. The battle associated with their elimination then proceeds according to the dictates of *karma*, the ignorance level of the individual (who can perpetuate unfruitful, often counterproductive actions) and the strength of the *jīva* needed to fight the pathogens.

Beings. This level of organised Life is the focus of the mind's highest aspiration. From it all categories of Mind step toward the largest form of encompassing energy. It bears the prototype *maṇḍalas* productive of all possible outcomes in the future. Each *maṇḍala* is but a system of expenditure of energies, producing the multidirectional arenas of Mind, and expansion of consciousness of those integrated into its structure.

All energy functions in physical matter manifest as part of the process of categorisation of form by mind into units of light. How energy transforms matter into subtle forms by the light of mind can be comprehended when the mind unravels the *maṇḍala* of being/non-being. The mysteries of the universe expanding from a single point, of the sun swirling around its central star in our galaxy, and the formation of galaxies of consciousness awakening, are all revealed by a comprehension of the nature and structure of the *maṇḍala*.

Unravelling the mysteries of the *maṇḍala* requires comprehension of the categorisation of energies into moments of consciousness. All Life processes exist within the sphere of moving matter. This concerns the mystery of how the universe coheres together whilst still maintaining separate functions. For example, having different points of rotation, such as planets with unique orbits around the sun, all manifesting a *maṇḍala* of integrated energy directives. We must then look to the forces that bond all into coherent structures, thus how Mind regulates the entire process.

The observed universe is the macrocosm of how Life exists at its smallest level, such as the sentience of a cell and the way differing categories of energy are seen to move and interact therein. The multidimensional universe represents the future evolution of the cellular unit. It indicates that which it will someday awaken to, and then incorporate in a transcended form of consciousness. This is part of the mechanism of future purpose moving to direct the energised *maṇḍala* towards it. The cell then gradually unfolds the process of reception to increasingly subtler, though vaster, more comprehensive energy states. Everything exists within the sphere of moving substance. The Life process of universal happenings is existent within the Mind of an incalculably vast cellular unit (a Logos). The *maṇḍala* constitutes the far reaches of cosmos. Therefore, we can extrapolate what is in cosmos according to our understanding of the *maṇḍalic* aspect of our own present time-space continuum, which relates to the nature and awakening of our own conscious being.

The structure of a cell and of the sentience that incorporates it can be considered to be more complex than the structure of a universe if that cell is fully understood whilst the universe is not. It is far easier for a scientist to study the sentient nature of a cell than of the Mind integrating the macrocosm. Because scientists do not consider the universe as alive, so they do not see the movement of the stars and planets as being guided by a comprehensive Intelligence. Similarly, it is not easy to convince them of the sentient minds (*devas*) governing the sum total of cellular evolution, but approaches thereto can be logically presented.

Understanding the processes of cellular Life is relatively easy for human minds, as it is within their level of experiential contact, because the cells are incorporated into our constituency. But many will argue whether or not we contain the universe within, even though logically the evidence is there to see. For when you observe any form of progressive Life, and project its evolution into the far distant future, then you must extend the process to include the universe in your scope of vision.

An ancient adage states that 'God geometrises'. We can say that this is so (despite our differing opinions of whatever a 'God' may be) because such a creative Being orders his/her cellular constituency according to set established blueprints or observable patterns of Life. From a Buddhist perspective, one need only look to the geometric structure, the *maṇḍala* that emanates from the five Dhyāni Buddhas, to see this as a truism.

The five Elements form a structural basis on which the Jinas comprise their holistic reality. The reflection from the aspects emanated from these Buddhas of meditation then creates form. All formed space is an expression of their reflected attributes, manifesting via the mirror of *śūnyatā*. The Dhyāni Buddhas can therefore be viewed collectively as a creative Logos. Even though they remain archetypal, they symbolise principles to be aspired to by humanity. They are therefore both embodied entities, as well as the hypostasis of all we see around us. The mysteries of the *maṇḍala* become clear as we penetrate the processes within our consciousnesses that are expressions of the Jina's omniscient, omnifarious presence.

Cosmos is an ordered system, and if we develop our consciousnesses correctly, it will come to include the entire *maṇḍala* that is cosmos. When freed from the confines and limitations of physicality (incarnate space) the *status quo* persists, though revelation of the nature of this fundamental truth increases as we ascend within the dimensions of space. A Buddha moves 'to the other shore' of cosmos, into the universality of a more embracive *maṇḍala* than lived within on earth. That through which he evolved has effectively transformed itself into the lines of a vastly expanded cosmic geometric delineation.

The greatest holistic concept we all observe is reflected in the microcosm, which we all embody when pursuing our microcosmic lives. We exist in a past time frame for those who have extended their awareness to be inclusive of macrocosmic unities and Identifications.

Chaos, we have seen, is found in cosmos, but chaos certainly does not rule the Life processes, as all lives revolve around a centre (or centres) of activity, and evolve from an originating point. Everything moving around a circular rotating sphere is held to that movement by something else moving in relation to it, if there is to evolve the perception of things. Many such interdependent factors make up a universe. Consciousness also manifests a focal point of power in relation to the object perceived, and other units of consciousness. Anything that behaves as if it has a centre participates in the Life process. This is correct even if the centre is a special axis in another dimension. Space, after all, is multidimensional. The focal points of Life are acquired as part of a higher process of balancing energy expenditure within an integrated *maṇḍala*. The flux of consciousness holds it all unto an organised unity. Lines of force (depicted as the Will above) radiate out from the central point to assist the movement of all within the periphery of its embrace. Conditional Will propels everything forward, for all unities are part of an embracive whole, as the entire *maṇḍala* moves onwards to incorporate the unknown future space. The process of movement happens in time, but reckonings of time with respect to space are a cyclic process. Space is unlimited; it is only conditioned by the bounds of time when consciousness is awakened.

Ultimately, everything in the universe must be equilibrated, hence the law of *karma*, which ensures harmonious interrelationship between all aspects of the overriding *maṇḍala*. This facilitates its overall purpose. *Karma* is the application of the force of Love, and is an esoteric relation to the law of gravity, which keeps all forms in motion because they are attracted to each other. We therefore have universal cosmic interrelationships and ordered space. The resolving purpose (*śūnyatā*) is directed by Love, or rather, an expression of Love.

Love is a universal magnet. It draws all separate unities, parts of the *maṇḍala,* back to its originating centre (cause) by rectifying *saṃskāras*, causing them to return upon a higher (subtler) turn of the spiral (for all forms in our universe reincarnate). *Karma* and the rebirthing principle (causing the cyclic pulsations of the 'electricity' of Life, which is an expression of consciousness) are two fundamental pillars of the temple of universal Life. Both come to be conditioning factors of the functioning of consciousness. Love directs the force of *karma* to ensure that the rebirthing principle (Mind) produces appropriate expansions of awareness of the cellular unit (or *maṇḍala* of expression). The integration of the force of Love with Mind produces the expression of the Love-Wisdom principle termed *bodhicitta*. Embodying *bodhicitta,* the cellular unit can then integrate with the central dynamo of the Will that caused all to come to be. Thus is found the central sacred tabernacle, the Holy of Holies within the Temple of Life. This is but another way of describing the *śūnyatā-saṃsāra* nexus.

8

The Maṇḍala and the Eightfold Path

Preamble

The Four Noble Truths *(āryasatya)* and the Eightfold Path (*aṣṭāṅgamārga*) were the most basic teachings promulgated by the Buddha. In fact they provided the major discourse given to his five ascetic brethren when he came to seek them out near Benares (Sarnath) after his enlightenment. Briefly stated, the first of the Four Noble Truths is that all life is suffering. The second truth informs us that attachment to things impermanent (through desire) is the cause of the suffering. The third is that one can be freed from suffering through a process of non-attachment to the objects of desire, producing eventual *nirvāṇa.* The fourth is that the process of non-attachment necessitates following the Eightfold Path. This Path is given as; right understanding (*samyak dṛṣṭi)*, right thought (*samyak saṃkalpa*), right speech (*samyak vācā*), right action (*samyak karmānta*), right livelihood (*samyak ārjīva*), right effort (*samyak vyāyāma*), right mindfulness (*samyak smṛti*), and right concentration (*samyak samādhi*).

The purpose in this and the following chapters is to elucidate many points concerning the Buddhist listings of eight or twelve that to date have not been discussed by analysts of the scripture. Much that was formerly hidden in these apparently simple teachings can thereby be revealed. Specifically, information regarding the natural unfolding and awakening of the *chakras* will be presented.[1] It is important that

---

1 A detailed exposé of the *chakras* will be developed throughout this *Treatise on Mind.*

practitioners of meditation be equipped to think esoterically. They need to transform sedentary concepts (*saṃskāras*) into vibrant links to the abstract Mind if high meditative achievement is to be obtained.

The meditation-Mind can only develop by overcoming the tendencies of a pedantic or a lazy mind. Enlightenment will not be obtained through wallowing in the belief in supine or unsound doctrines, or trite repetitive formula recitation (exoteric mantras). The attainment of enlightenment necessitates developing a powerhouse of continuous revelation. The revelations must pierce through increasingly complex, more intense, and vaster thoughts to approach the domain of Mind. All arenas of concretion and dogma must be transcended. It's not easy to reside in any of the levels of Mind—the Sphere of Ideation, the Son of Mind, or the Clear Light, whence the *dharmakāya* can be found. The jump from concretion of mind to pure Ideation necessitates the development of the ability to think esoterically, via the input of the Heart's agenda. There is no other way to gain enlightenment.

Consider what thinking with the Heart (*bodhicitta*) really means and represents, thus truly experience the prescient activity of the Heart centre. The Heart converts the defilements of mind derived via *saṃsāric* activity and attachment to fields of desire from sources below the diaphragm. For this reason texts such as the *Bardo Thödol* are meditation guides, wherein clear instructions provided for those that can think esoterically are only veils and blinds for all others.

The *sūtra* teachings concerning listings of eight entities or principles, such as the eight consciousnesses or eight Mahābodhisattvas, must also be properly comprehended for what they symbolise. They are signposts veiling the way of movement of the little wheels that feed the major petals of the Heart with the consciousness-sustenance it needs to fuse Love with mind to produce Wisdom. Only then can the skilful means of the Bodhisattva's tasks be accomplished. Let the practitioner therefore begin to look at *chakras* the way they aught to be viewed, as places of empowerment of transformative energies governed by the potency of the governing Peaceful or Wrathful deity. Let thereby the task of transforming and transmuting base *saṃskāras* begin, allowing eventual achievement of the enlightenment-gold that is *dharmatā*. The yogic path is no place for lazy thinkers, for those not willing to apply the will to master challenge after challenge upon the path to liberation. Lazy, shallow, conventional, or dogmatic thinkers will achieve corresponding rewards, but enlightenment will linger far from them. The transformation of base *saṃskāras* takes lifetimes of effort, as the teaching on the nature of the 777 Incarnations has indicated.

One can thus confidently say that there is no such thing as 'enlightenment in merely one life' as some Tantras indicate, because for that 'one life' to happen it presupposes that many hundreds have gone into laying the foundation for its making. Let the practitioner therefore have a realistic view of approximately what is possible to achieve in a particular life, or to what level he/she resides upon the Bodhisattva ladder of attainment. A proper striving to gain the next level can then be accomplished through right knowledge wrought through yogic discipline (*tapas*[2]), as instructed by a true Master of Wisdom. Such a one possesses the will to overcome incorrect thinking and has demonstrated *tapas* in such a way that consciousness naturally resides in the abstract Mind, or that 'beyond' has been achieved. The teachings here are provided to hopefully help light the way whereby Buddhism can provide an adequate number of Clear Sighted ones. They are needed to weed out the defilements of doctrine, to cleanse the many closets and shelves held by the religion containing dogmatically asserted ungainly, erroneous precepts. Such impediments to liberation should no longer be promulgated as *dharma* for seekers. True beacons of light are needed to demonstrate the Bodhisattva path for the many, and to guide the way to enlightenment for all sincere aspirants.

The motion of the swastika

Figure 24 summarises what has so far been presented concerning the nature of the evolution of consciousness from an energy perspective. It depicts the basic generative dynamo for the movement of energies (*saṃskāras, prāṇas*) directed by the *chakras*. Without this internal dynamo a *chakra* could not exist. With respect to the orientation of the arms of the mutable cross (swastika), it should be noted that there

2 *Tapas*: yogic austerities, heat. Generally taken to mean the austerities that produce contemplative insights, meditation. However, it literally refers to the practices that kindle the inner creative fires (*kuṇḍalinī*), or those that sustain the sum of the contemplative life, rather than mere austerities and asceticism. Its equivalent in Tibetan is tum-mo, meaning 'psychic heat'.

are two ways that they can turn. Both directions could be drawn, with the orientation indicating the way that energies flow. This can be either towards the concretion of substance, and hence manifestation or appearance of forms, or else towards liberation of the substance of consciousness. The left to right direction of the spiral arms indicated in Figure 24 concerns the evocation of energies producing liberation from *within* the individual. It represents the way of aspiration towards enlightenment.[3] From the diagram's point of view, the energies of the north-west arm therefore point towards the north (upwards to the liberated realms), as that is the way one orients oneself to obtain liberation, producing expansion of consciousness. The north-eastern direction concerns assisting the unified activities of all in the group of which one is a part. The direction south-east directs energies to arenas where deeds need to be accomplished in the general field of service. The direction south-west relates to utilising or directing the gain of what was accomplished to those that can benefit thereby.

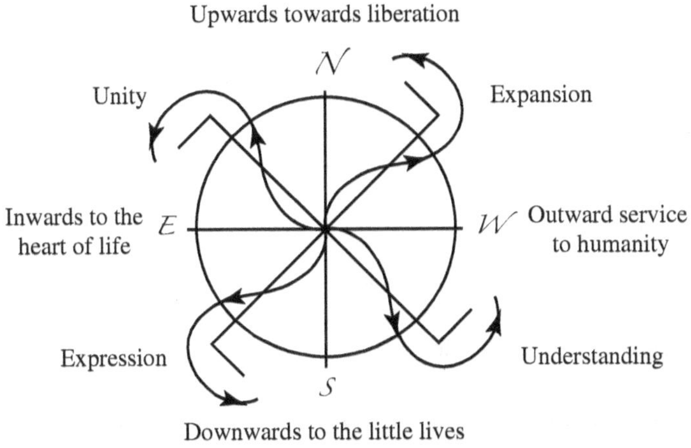

Figure 24. The swastika

In terms of the integral *maṇḍala* of a *chakra* system, the north-west energies represent those that are the most potent and sublimated. They

3 One must be orientated in the same direction as the diagram is facing to be able to correctly postulate its orientation.

are directed towards *chakras* whose potency and sphere of influence in the *maṇḍala* are greater than it. The north-east arm points eastwards to direct the most refined energies from the *chakra's* internal motion towards the heart or Life expression of the *maṇḍala.* The south-east arm points southwards so that the entire field of activity represented by the multitude of evolving forms, the many smaller integral parts of the *maṇḍala,* can be vitalised with the appropriate energies from the *chakra* best suited to them. The south-west arm points westwards, where the various flowers of similar stature as the *chakra* can share in the particular qualities that the *chakra* conveys or embodies. (The *saṃskāra* channelled becomes the flavour of the moment.)

It should be noted here that the swastikas depicted in the *maṇḍala* of the Eight Mahābodhisattvas presented in chapter 11, Figure 28, are drawn in an opposite orientation than that given above. In that case the point of view is from the domain of liberation, of looking downwards towards humanity toiling in the fields of *saṃsāra.* (It thus presents a mirror image of what is perceived as the 'correct' view within *saṃsāra.*) From the liberated perspective, therefore, the purpose represents the projection of the energies of manifestation and thus of concretion. Here the consorts of the Mahābodhisattvas are responsible for the formation (and hence existence) of *saṃsāra.* The Bodhisattvas have to tone down the potency of their energies so that the energies can be appropriately received by those that aspire upwards, or look inwards, for beneficent inspiration. Too strong a force entering unprepared desire-minds would have disastrous consequences. Such impression represents the stimulatory or liberating lifeline for these aspiring ones. They must however also progressively manifest the form of meditative activity indicated in Figure 24 if *saṃsāra* is to be mastered. The energies will then be directed in terms of transforming *saṃskāras* that will eventually produce the enlightenment that the benevolent Mahābodhisattva is the representation.

The path therefore consists of a process of receiving internal and external stimulus of transformative energies (denoted as 'gift-waves of the gurus' in the Tantric texts), plus that which is generated from within as one aspires to transcend one's limitations. The meditative process therefore concerns the awakening of *chakras* in this many-faceted way. The potency and purpose of each arm of the swastika must be appropriately mastered during each turning of the wheel of all the *chakras* before *saṃsāra's* processes can be transcended.

Fortunately, the process happens automatically during the early stages of the path of meditative and yogic aspiration. Later, however, when inner vision has been awakened, the process of transforming *saṃskāras* is then meditatively done, the forces of the *chakras* are consciously worked with, and the liberation process quickens considerably. We see, therefore, that the overall movement of the energies evoked must flow from the east to the west. In all things vital, the liberation of the energies from the Heart centre is the key.

The relevant passage from Volume 3, chapter 3 of this series, '*The Centres below the Diaphragm and Voidness*', that supplements the above information shall be added here, the focus being the energies entering the system from external sources.

> The direction *northeast* of this cross was previously stated to represent *unity*. This concerns being attuned with all forms of Life, subjectively, objectively, or transcendentally, and with humanity in particular. It necessitates receptivity to the incoming energies from one's family, or group of which one is a part. It can also include the membership of the Council of Bodhisattvas. It concerns receptivity to streams of energies, and blending together the factors, with which a causative agent must work. (The word 'causative' here relates to the conscious, self-willed production of phenomena that exists for some duration of expression.) It concerns the information coming from any aspect of human civilisation, or from the Sambhogakāya Flowers in the *ālayavijñāna* environment. From another perspective, it represents the input of the *bījas* from the Sambhogakāya Flower into the personality.
>
> The direction *southeast* represents *expression*. Here all is unfolded in the field of Life, and concerns the process associated with the battlefield of desire. On a higher turn of the spiral, this battlefield involves overcoming the major *saṃsāric* impediments associated with the desire-mind. It necessitates the process of assimilating the outgoing energies that are directed to the formed realms from the northeast direction. At first desire and the concrete mind of general humanity is stimulated, then their fields of aspirational activity. The causative agent must now rightly direct quantified streams of energy to do his bidding and to absorb impressions from *saṃsāra*. The process

necessitates activating the *bījas* associated with mental-emotional energies so that what is being experienced can gain the benefit of past awareness and impressions. Thus it can be assimilated into the consciousness of the individual. This concerns perception of what occurs as part of happenings through time. Without drawing upon the past experiences there can be no reference point relating to the present. One thus cannot come to know anything properly, as there would be no sequence of *bījas* activated for the manifestation of any activity. Expression therefore involves considerations of right timing or of cyclic activity.

The direction *southwest* concerns making all experiences an essential part of the unit of consciousness. This necessitates an essential identification with the experience, thus producing *understanding*, so that new *bījas* are created for the future activities of that ego to recall when needed. The experiences thus become assimilated into consciousness and consequently become the past, part of one's own personal identification, giving the ability to walk on to the future, to a new category of impressions that influence consciousness. Eventually the full flowering of the *tathāgatagarbha* is experienced. What is assimilated then becomes the note, a new quality or colouring of *prāṇa* to be channelled into the *nāḍīs*.

Once the energies of Life have been expressed in the field of the earth, and the battles of desire have been fought, then the understanding of the entire Life process proceeds with certainty. This produces entry into the path of Initiation into Life's mysteries. Eventually the evocation of the emanatory goodwill *(bodhicitta)* happens that will direct the person off the mutable cross and away from embodied expression. The work of the causative agent thus finds its fruition. The purpose of the long, aeonic cycles of endeavour thus comes to light.

The direction *northwest* concerns the process of *outward expansion* of the entire sphere of identification into the future, the forward progression of the individual towards enlightenment. This emanatory auric quality sent out ahead (denoted as a goodwill or *mantric* beneficence) is replete with future patterns of what is to be. It can also represent that which the conscious units in the external environment come to know or define as Deity, viewed as a unique Individuality. This emanatory energy produces the projection of the *antaḥkaraṇas* out of the realm of the earth (the embodied form) into the higher spheres, and into cosmos. It involves projecting the creative, or causative stream of activity from a limited field of application to another more embracive one. The energy or quality of the singular unit or group can now merge into the whole. It therefore produces ever-expanding scenarios of activity. Having fulfilled this task, the causative agent attracts the gain of the former activity, so that the related qualities can be utilised for an even vaster work.

The Four Noble Truths

The Four Noble Truths can be specifically relegated to the four cardinal directions of the compass. These Truths concern the means whereby suffering can be relieved by non-attachment to transient things, inevitably producing the manifestation of wisdom. Wisdom is an end product of the process of positively mastering the effects of experience via developing a compassionate concern for other's sufferings. It is the accomplishment of the incarnation process wherein the gain in experience is progressive and oriented to benefit the many. This is a natural outcome of the first Noble Truth; seeing the effects of the causes of suffering upon oneself. This develops into the realisation that, because all are interlinked, to truly be freed from suffering one must inevitably work to eliminate the basis of its causes in all those with whom one is communally linked.

1. The *first Noble Truth* is the fact that all life is suffering, or results in suffering sooner or later. This is relegated to the *southern* direction, (the material domain) wherein all activity producing suffering is engendered and experienced in a physical body, coupled to the emotions and the mind.
2. The *second* shows that the root cause for suffering is desire, the never-ending craving of the senses. This is an aspect of the selfish grasping of the separative lower 'self' for things it wants from all around to sustain itself. It concerns the illusion of a 'self' that is separate from all other 'selves', and produces indifference to, or avoidance of, the real needs of others, except when it is self-serving. The direction here is *west,* that related to all human interrelations. The attitude of separateness causes continued thirst for sentient existence, whilst an innate desire for sexual union with

a complementary separated 'self' produces vehicles (by means of the sexual experience) through which another consciousness can manifest the illusion of 'self'.

Later, this desire is transmuted into the aspirational quality needed to tread the path to liberation. This concerns a deliverance into, or fusion with, that which is considered to be an All-Self, or else with a non-self. It involves the battle between the concept of 'self' and the innate promptings for consummatory union with the All, or else with a Void of all things. Manifold metaphysical and devotional outpourings also produce the major sufferings of the mystic and the aspirant on the path to either outcome. This is because attachment to various concepts inevitably need to be revised, whilst images received via devotional outpourings prove to be transitory.

At first separativeness is instinctive, people assert their individuality (concepts of self-identity) in the world around without any intention. Cumulatively it is reinforced through involvement with the warring, clashing activities and opinions of the great mass of people. (The concept of differing degrees of ignorance can be used to qualify the nature of such opinions.) Later, separateness is forcefully projected upon others because of the power such assertiveness gains for the individual. Bands of such assertive ones then produce the strife and warfare that has beset humanity throughout the ages. (The potential for suffering for the many thereby increases exponentially.) Everyone's sufferings are correspondingly diminished if separative attitudes have been curtailed through steps taken to abnegate these effects via treading the path to self-realisation. (Concepts of cooperation, harmlessness, and self-sacrifice are thereby produced.) This path is discovered as a consequence of the realisation of the third Noble Truth.

3. The *third Noble Truth* states that by the elimination of desire and craving through fostering enlightened attitudes, producing compassion, the cause of all suffering created by people will be removed. An entire sequence of positive revelations is thereby instigated. Eventually this path necessitates the inward contemplation of the *yogin,* associated with the direction *east,* wherein the munificent way of the Heart is fully meditated upon.

4. The various steps allowing the cultivation and development of the *yogin's* attitude constitutes the *fourth* self-evident Truth. These steps concern following the *Eightfold Path*. Their collective action produces the direction *north,* the way of aspiration upwards towards realms and states sublime, and beyond. Each part of this wheel of the Eightfold Path relates therefore to an aspect or quality developed by the aspiring person to something greater than his/her position in life. At the later stages it concerns the means whereby the person can be better equipped to serve all beings by choosing to travel the way of the Bodhisattva.

An Exposition of the Eightfold Path

The *northeast* direction representing *unity* is expressed by the first of the Eightfold Path, *right or perfect understanding.* Here the specific focus is towards rightfully collating and assimilating information coming from: a) the sum of the sense-consciousnesses and the intellect, b) the knowledge gained by human civilisation, c) the Sambhogakāya Flowers in the *ālayavijñāna* environment, d) the Clear Mind and *śūnyatā*, e) the *dharmakāya.* This path is explained with respect to the related signs of the zodiac:

1. Right understanding (Aries the ram). Mental Beginnings. This implies obtaining an intellectual grasp of the essence of all religious philosophies, the cause and result of the evolutionary process, of wrong actions and attitudes, of the mystery of being/non-being, and nowadays also of the basic laws and precepts discovered by scientific investigation. One obtains such understanding through contemplative reflection upon the nature of the Four Noble Truths, and hence the expansion of the philosophy into the remainder of the *buddhadharma.* The sign Aries the Ram is the first sign in the zodiac, and therefore instigates the primary mental understanding of the nature of the path and the necessity of following it to enlightenment. Aries instigates the impetus of the will to carry through to conclusion one's initial decision. This is necessary if such understanding is not to remain a purely mental exercise.

The *maṇḍala* to be constructed evolves through rectifying wrong actions and attitudes. This is manifested with respect to this direction by developing the lines of communication (*antaḥkaraṇas*) to the exalted thought-streams coming from the enlightened units of consciousness within the *ālayavijñāna* environment. Later, pathways to *śūnyatā* and *dharmakāya* can be established. The foundation for the perfect understanding of this direction is laid via one's continued meditation upon the meaning of all phenomena and of the way of evolutionary progress via it. The nature of attachment and mechanism of nonattachment to transience must be clearly established in the mind.

Consequently, the detachment process involves gaining comprehension of the mysteries of creative Life through residence in the Clear Light. From the northeast direction comes all of the thought sequences and the amalgamation of available *karma* to create a new *maṇḍala* of activity. Thus from the domain of the Sambhogakāya Flower is projected a human personality into manifest life. This can occur only after the Bardo experience of the previous incarnation of that consciousness-stream, once it has abstracted into the Flower.

The associated *chakra* is the Ājñā centre. It allows visioning to manifest in all the directions from where such understanding is to be obtained. Also, the use of this Eye is necessary if the new *maṇḍala* is to be projected to fulfil its purpose.

When linked to the eight consciousnesses the sense developed is that of *sight*, allowing clear visioning of the qualities of the forthcoming *maṇḍalas*.[4] There are five distinct stages producing *Right Understanding*:

1. At first information is gleaned through interrelation with the rest of humanity, who present to us the basic experiences on the path of life, the ways to achieve personal happiness.
2. Later such 'happiness' is seen to be illusional, because of the transitoriness of all phenomena. The person then seeks refuge in the precepts of the *dharma* and in companionship with others who are also undergoing training from an enlightened One. Refuge is

---

4 The earlier account in chapter 3 related the sense of sight to the Solar Plexus centre, which is the organ of clairvoyance, the astral visioning of the psychics. The listing in that chapter therefore provides a more exoteric account, from the point of view of the aspiration process that works to transform consciousness. The viewpoint in this present chapter is esoteric, relating to the domain of enlightenment. The emphasis of the *chakras* then shift to their right functions upon the rectified wheel. In this view sight becomes the attribute of the organ of vision *per se,* which is the Ājñā centre, the 'all-seeing Eye'.

taken in the Buddha (*guru*), the *dharma* (the spiritual teachings), and the *saṅgha* (the spiritual community). They are viewed as a unity from which one takes sustenance.

3. The Bodhisattva path is then developed, wherein succour is gained from an integrated interrelationship with all other Bodhisattvas, especially those on a higher level that act as spiritual preceptors.
4. Once enlightenment has been attained one is absorbed in the *ālayavijñāna* environment, of which the Sambhogakāya Flower is a part. Unity with all other Flowers is then experienced.
5. Upon the attainment of the highest Bodhisattva stages unity with the entire domain of *dharmakāya* is accomplished and Buddhahood is gained.

When the above has been established by means of the Ājñā centre (by a *yogin*) or the Śūnyatā Eye (in the case of the Sambhogakāya Flower), the *maṇḍala* may be projected. The five stages of manifestation are:

1. The divine 'blueprint' already exists in the realm of the Sambhogakāya Flower (or from a higher perspective in the *dharmakāya*), as do the imprints of all other enlightened constructs, which the meditating one studies in its detail. The start involves activating the qualities of the seed *bīja* of the particular *maṇḍala* that the meditator wishes to construct. The realm utilised is the abstracted level of the mental domain, which contains the seeds and archetypal patterns of everything that must come to be a viable form in *saṃsāra*, according to the dictates of *karma*.
2. The mechanism where the *bīja* comes to expand into the full *maṇḍalic* expression can now be explored.
3. The *bīja* then expands and its progress is directed by means of the enlightened understanding of the *yogin*.
4. The *maṇḍalic* expression is now held steady in the mind's eye of the *yogin*, who makes sure that it is complete in every detail.
5. The mind is prepared and the appropriate conditions for its projection into the formed domains are laid.

The direction *east* represents the way *inwards* to the Heart of Life via contemplative introspection. This involves the practice of meditation coupled with the generation of *bodhicitta.*

This direction is represented by the second of the Eightfold Path, *right or perfect aspiration or attitude of mind.* This necessitates aspiration towards enlightenment, thus of compassionate understanding. Once one has rightly comprehended the need for improvement, or to achieve a goal in life, then aspiration to achieve its fruit naturally follows. Inevitably the path that produces Initiation into the mysteries of being/non-being is sought for and found. Right aspiration reveals the portals of the zone of residence of the Council of Bodhisattvas by following the ten levels of the Bodhisattva path. They are lords of compassion and examples of the way of the Heart centre's activity.

The Heart centre is therefore the *chakra* awakened through the treading of the path of right aspiration. The sense-consciousness developed is that of *taste*, to rightly discriminate the subtle discernments between the differing meditative paths that one can aspire to follow.[5]

2. Right aspiration (Taurus the bull). Desire-aspiration. This implies aspiration towards the development of Love-Wisdom (compassionate understanding). It follows naturally from obtaining right understanding and concerns setting one's feet on the path that leads to liberation from the realms of suffering and death, to the portals of the Heart of Life wherein enlightenment resides. The sign Taurus the bull introduces the desire principle, which translates as devotion to the *dharma* and right aspiration when one is no longer attached to *māyā.* In the Taurean cycle one clothes understanding with right aspiration.

Awakening the path of the Heart initially concerns a gradual process producing identification with the Sambhogakāya Flower, and the purpose is then to discover the truth of *śūnyatā.*

There are five distinct stages to *Right Aspiration*:

1. At first the carnal person looks inwards only for gratuitous images to assist in obtaining sensual, pleasurable fulfilment.

---

5 In chapter 3 the centre assigned was the Splenic centre, wherein subtle and palatable discernments of *prāṇic* qualities (*saṃskāras*) yet to be controlled must be made.

2. Tiring of the endless cycles of repetitious images created in the mind the person finds that the associated experiences are not so fulfilling, as each bout of satiation leads to craving for more, which cannot be properly fulfilled. Dissatisfied, the person looks for fulfilment in involvement in a group seeking enlightenment. There are five levels of different groups that can be sought to find fulfilment: family, communal, societal, national, and international. The group from which spiritual nourishment is derived can be found structured within any or all of these levels. All five are thus also expressed by the *saṅgha* in its interrelationship with the world. Later we have also distinctly Bodhisattva activities working via these five levels of group-sharing. (This view relates to the work of the first seven Bodhisattva levels.)
3. Having developed the Will-to-Love, the person then looks meditatively inwards to find answers in any or all of these five levels of group-sharing. To do this effectively, an enlightened sage must be found that will present right meditation techniques that will awaken the mind to indubitable reality.
4. A concentrated *dhyāna* (meditative absorption) brings one to the experience of the Sambhogakāya Flower, which is outwardly focussed with respect to the aspiring personality's attempts to achieve high revelation.
5. This later develops into the *dharmakāya* meditation[6] upon arenas of love and service greater than that represented by humanity.

With respect to *maṇḍalic* construction for right aspiration with the direction east, the *maṇḍala* is now to be created in the realm of the abstract Mind, based upon the blueprint of the image contacted earlier.

6 The path related to this type of meditative unfoldment has been termed the Dharmakāya Way in this *Treatise on Mind,* rather than use the allied terms Āti yoga, or rDzogs-chen. The latter terms relate to Nyingma practices that have the same goals and methodology of riding *saṃsāra* as a means of achieving *nirvāṇa* (because the two are seen as one) as the Dharmakāya Way, but they are also infused with a number of exoteric interpretations and practices. This muddies the waters of the path. Rather than enter into polemics as to what does or does not constitute rDzogs-chen, I have decided that it is best to present a clear view as to what the (quickest) path to enlightenment actually represents.

Here the Airy Element is infused into the *maṇḍalic* construct. The five stages of manifestation are:

1. The preparation of the mind necessitates the evocation of the energy of *bodhicitta* by means of utilising the Heart in the Head centre. For the construct to be a viable expression of the white *dharma* it must be seeded in Love. The meditator first contacts the seed *bīja* previously visualised in the *ālayavijñāna*. It is then vivified, utilising available *karma,* and light is directed thereto in accordance with the keynote meditation.
2. The image-making faculty of the mind is now intensified and utilised to consolidate construction of what was previously visualised, starting with the seed *bīja*. Now the process whereby the *bīja* (the central point of the construct) comes to expand into the full *maṇḍala* can be developed.
3. The *bīja* grows accordingly, with its inherent qualities delineating the major lines of the *maṇḍala.*
4. The *maṇḍala* develops its major characteristics, with the symbolism and expressions that makes it unique to other *maṇḍalas* being woven into its overall form.
5. The *maṇḍala* is now completed in its total complexity and splendour as a construct within the abstract Mind, the domain of the Sambhogakāya Flower.

The direction *southeast* concerns the outward expression of the inner impressions gained, which is represented by the *third* of the Eightfold Path, *right or perfect speech.*

3. Right speech (Gemini the twins). Relationships of all types. Once right attitude of mind has been developed, then the person curbs all idle chatter out of necessity, and cultivates silence, speaking only that which will benefit others, or produce right (magical) results. The effect of erroneous or zealously misdirected speech, or writings (an extension of speech), can produce the most long-lasting and serious damage to the development of the aspirant and his endeavours to cultivate harmlessness. The power of the written word for good or for bad is obvious to all. The way that one speaks, and to whom one speaks to, defines one's social acquaintances and boundaries. The nature of that speech determines the nature of relationships. Speech must be skilfully presented, so as to endeavour to unite all warring factions (of ideas) into one common embrace.

Speech must be made sacred, a creative endeavour brought to the precincts of the temple of the Heart (an activity ruled by Gemini), and thence made to never leave that temple, to officiate in all of the effects of the Bodhisattva vow. The cultivation of silence is necessary if the person is to meditate and utilise sacred mantras with effectiveness.

One speaks according to the level of understanding about anything one has. Or else one asks questions (the outward expression of one's contemplations) to obtain such understanding. Answers allow assimilation of what one desires to know. The Throat centre is now empowered, allowing invocation of sacred mantras for either creative or liberating purposes. It thus empowers the projection of the *maṇḍala* into manifestation via the centres below the diaphragm. *Smell* is the predominant sense-consciousnesses developed here, allowing the discernment of the subtlest and most expansive thoughts from the abstract Mind. Once comprehended they can be articulated when needed.[7]

The five distinct stages of externalising inner thoughts and desires to produce *right speech* are:

1. At first the person chatters idly to others about things of interest and of desirous intent. The opinions expressed relegate topics of concern in the society and define the person's personal interests. The articulation demonstrates the level of knowledge and particular bias of the individual. Being knowledgeable about things provides the capacity to speak forthrightly about the topic. Slander, general hubris, deceit, etc., may also be topics of concern. Pride of what is comprehended about a subject, or general conceit are easily developed and articulated.
2. One's interest comes to be consumed in the pettiness and glamour of the social world, within which one seeks to manifest a helpful agenda so that a personal mark is left. This encourages one to

7 The more exoteric account in chapter 3 relates this sense to the Ājñā centre, which at that stage synthesises the subtlest *prāṇas* from both the left and right hand *nāḍīs*.

learn more. A career path needs to be chosen, thus one may enter a university to study for altruistic motives, to become a doctor, lawyer, politician, artist, a monk, etc. The accompanying service role then helps one to find a meaningful place in society. The mind consequently becomes increasingly developed, language skills become more refined and sophisticated, especially in relation to the field of service. Such skills involve developing a specialised jargon generally not understood by those not indoctrinated in that field.

3. Eventually the person realises that the way to truly help people is to teach them to refine their consciousness, and then inevitably the way of the *dharma.* Such education necessitates a focus upon the most pertinent issues in life, and nonattachment to ephemeral things and control of the emotions. We thus have the gaining of wisdom, the language of enlightenment is learnt, wisely refining the use of speech. The Throat centre is then used to articulate the results of the revelations received in meditation.
4. *Dhyāna* inevitably brings one to experience the domain of the abstract Mind, and the Sambhogakāya Flower (which is focussed downwards upon the meditator). Enlightenment is then achieved, producing comprehension of the true significance of mantras, thus the truth behind the meaning of words. The cultivation of silence is necessary if the Word (*oṁ* or any combination of seed syllables) is to be wisely used with effectiveness. Little is spoken and all speech is now pregnant with meaning, aimed at bringing the listener to enlightened states of awareness.
5. In the later *dharmakāya* meditation, the enlightened strata of thought is achieved allowing one to present revelatory teachings to whole nations, or to produce new religious dispensations. The subtleties of the problems that have vexed people can thus be explicated. Such words have power and are often studied for generations, even millennia by those wishing insight into the nature of enlightenment.

With respect to the *maṇḍala* for *right speech*, the southeast direction concerns the way of projecting it into the lower mental realm (the mind of the personal-I). Henceforth physical externalisation becomes possible. The *maṇḍala* is now directly infused with the energy of the Fiery Element. The five stages of manifestation are:

1. The general outline and major arenas of concern of the *maṇḍala* now appear in the mind for analysis, which builds into it the *manasic saṃskāras* obtained from one's thought life, plus what has been derived from past lives. Images of the overall purpose of its consciousness begin to flood the mind. The person begins to articulate the words mentally that will allow the expression of the meaning of those impressions to people in the external world.
2. Once the *saṃskāras* pertaining to the general structure of the *maṇḍala* have been evoked and analysed, then the detail can be pictured and built into the construct. Colourings, sounds, flaws (if any), plus all associated thought-forms can now be viewed in perspective. A plethora of revelatory images are thereby brought to life in the mind.
3. Having viewed the general panorama of the *maṇḍala,* the meditator now ensures that it is complete in every detail, and that all aspects of it are verifiable through the use of analogy, logical deduction, and other keys of comprehension. Its meaning must be comprehensively explained when asked by others, once its construct is manifest in their world.
4. The meditator now prepares the mind for projection of the construct downwards towards concrete expression. The resources contained within the Watery psychic and emotional constitution must be analysed, especially with respect to whether the *prāṇas* are capable of properly embodying the living construct.
5. Having reviewed the sum total of the equipment of response that involves the *maṇḍala,* the *yogin* draws all energies together and projects its expression into manifestation.

The direction *south* represents the way downwards into the realm of the objects of perception, from which sense-consciousnesses derive their experiences. This direction is represented by the *fourth* of the Eightfold Path, *right or perfect action.*

4. Right action (Cancer the crab). Movement and incarnation. Once the person can actively cultivate his speech, necessitating the development of an effective meditative rhythm (the production of unabated *dhyāna*, or meditation Mind), this automatically finds expression in all aspects of life. His/her relation to all sentient beings unfolds meditatively and compassionately so that always the most skilful means can be found to help them. This is the keynote of the Eightfold Path, for action, not belief, is the emphasis of the Buddhist religion. Only direct (experimental) action will produce the concrete expression of the other aspects of the Path. It involves what we do and refrain from doing, and thus concerns the deepest self-analysis and scrutiny of the real motives for all actions. *Dhyāna* evokes an attitude of receptivity to the Voice of Silence within, to objectively obey the dictates of the revelatory *dharma*.

The nature of the Cancerian influence here is symbolised by the ability of the crab to scurry from one convenient place to another upon the rocky shoreline of *saṃsāra* to find sources of right nourishment (the *dharma*) and shelter (from *māyā*). Being the most southerly of the signs it is the place of dense incarnation of ideas and of the *maṇḍalic* construct developed by the *dhyāna* of the *yogin*. Right action necessitates the ability to apply the construct formulated in realms of the meditation-Mind within deepest *māyā,* to achieve the unfolding purpose of what was formulated. It involves impeccable timing for every event to come. This is symbolised by the quick and precise movements of the crab along the shoreline, by its ability to not be effected by the vicissitudes of the waves. (The mode of *saṃsāric* interrelationships as dictated by *karma.*)

One first looks downwards to manipulate aspects of *saṃsāra* for one's own benefit. At a later stage of the evolutionary path all *saṃsāric* attributes are either adapted to benefit the quest of helping people to gain *bodhicitta,* or else they are relinquished as unworthy to be attached to. The Base of the Spine centre is now activated and evokes the potency to empower physical plane constructs. The sense-consciousness developed is *hearing*, to receive the words and mantras from the Lords of Life. The Throat centre can then articulate its response. The five distinct stages to produce *right action* are:

1. At first the action is centred around the personal-I to obtain the

object of desire. The person takes from the greater whole so as to amass things for the little 'self'. Ambition can run amok, with everything being ruthlessly amassed to gain an empire (e.g., of financial wealth). When the effort to fulfil such ambition is successful from the personal point of view, then it can be said that there was right action in relation to that object of pursuit.

2. Next we have the manifestation of right action to assist the needs of the members of the family and society of which one is a part. One realises that to help provides greater aesthetic benefits and sense of security than a purely materialistic pursuit for oneself.
3. Eventually the person realises that gaining true happiness necessitates working for the benefit of others, and for the world in general. One comprehends the fact that everything is interdependent and that the massed greed, selfishness and suffering in society lay at the root of its malaise. One's thought life and efforts are now totally infused with the desire to help all. One's life, conduct, writings, and speech become exemplary, an inspiration to others. The Bodhisattva path is followed, wherein the field of action becomes the saving grace that assists others to follow the *dharma* in all things.
4. Thinking of ways to help along any particular route involves mastering the art of contemplation, the refining of perceptions, so that one's aims can be best achieved. As the *dharma* is actively sought and practiced so the *dhyāna* produces access to impressions from the abstract Mind, which now increasingly projects images to the meditator. The Sambhogakāya Flower then guides one's actions. Thus is learnt the way of right action, whereby all karmic strands within *saṃsāra* are eventually mastered and transmuted, according to the way of expression of the 777 incarnations.
5. Eventually actions relating to the higher Bodhisattva stages manifest, allowing experiences of the *dharmakāya* to invade the meditation-Mind. This allows building the structures in the material world for multitudes to walk the road to enlightenment.

In this southern direction, with respect to *maṇḍalic* construction for *right action*, the sum of the equipment of response is visualised with view of immanent externalisation of the *maṇḍala*. The place of externalisation is the general Earthy (*saṃsāric*) environment. However the Watery *prāṇas* specifically become the main focus of concern, because these *saṃskāras* are very problematic in people's lives. The path to enlightenment necessitates their mastery. The substance of the (astral) emotional world therefore needs to be visualised clairvoyantly,[8] in preparation for precipitation of the *maṇḍala* into the material domain. All of the major *chakras* below the diaphragm need to be assessed for their ability to bear the potency and appropriate qualities to be conveyed. The five stages of manifestation are:

1. At first the mental *maṇḍala* is visualised and its general properties noted. This is accomplished via the normal rules of meditation.
2. The needed auric colourings are built into the construct and the basic tone or sound noted, allowing the necessary sound to ring out. Any discordancy must be rectified.
3. The meditator thus ensures that all aspects of the detail are correct and express the appropriate symbolism. The Watery version of the prototype must also be seen to approximate the ideal.
4. The integral structure is made vibrant by infusing it with the inherent life that carries its purpose to fruition. This purpose must be visualised with clarity to ensue that it fulfils its karmic reward.
5. The *maṇḍala* can now be projected into full active manifestation in the world of forms, the *māyā* of objective phenomena. The meditator must evoke the will to do so if its purpose is to be carried to conclusion. It is made tangible by drawing upon the force of the Sacral centre, that acts to precipitate it into manifestation. Average emotionally based seekers can then appropriate it, because it influences their psyche, or stimulates their field of desire. They then make the physical actions whereby their object of desire becomes realised.

The direction *southwest* concerns the process of *assimilating* the impressions gained from contact with phenomena. Mental-emotional *bījas* are activated, allowing what is experienced to benefit from past assimilations. It can then be understood in context and incorporated

8 This relates to visualising, for instance, the theriomorphic deities of the *Bardo Thödol*, when viewed in terms of the forces they intrinsically represent.

into the present consciousness. The consequential happenings then become new qualities (colourings) of Wind (*prāṇa)* to be channelled in the *nāḍīs*. The past experiences produce reference points to present happenings. Knowledge is then collated to project a course of action producing right livelihood, which sustains the person's future. This future course of action must be planned meticulously if the objective of the life's purpose is to be achieved. We thus have the *fifth* of the Eightfold Path—*right or perfect livelihood.*

5. Right livelihood (Scorpio the scorpion). Tests and trials on the path to light. Right action carries naturally through into right livelihood, which takes naught from others that is not given, nor harms the development of any other being. It therefore implies following the Bodhisattva path of harmlessness and right service to others.

Testings upon this path involve overcoming all of the negative and hindering *saṃskāras* that have been carried forth from past lives and which must be transmuted, as well as the accompanying base attacks from the dark foes, who continuously look for signs of weakness in the aspirant's aspirational armour. Both lines of activity are symbolised by the ability of the scorpion to sting with venomous jabs. The scorpion lives in the symbolic deserts of materiality and under the hard, rocky places of *saṃsāric* activity. Testings for worthiness of shouldering the burdens of enlightenment must be undertaken within the context of (rocky) material endeavour.

Tests are designed to provide the necessary fruits of accomplishment that exalt the aspirant who is skilfully applying chosen arenas of service work. The purpose is to lift the aspirant into levels of revelation not hitherto possible.

Such service is the result of a life-long contemplation upon need in relation to the characteristics possessed that enables one to rightly give. It causes one to robe oneself in qualifications according to one's Ray type, that befits becoming a scientist, artist, etc. It gleans the best of past life experiences, plus those developed in this life as conditioned by the various mental, emotional, and socio-political environments one is in. It necessitates being able to envision the direction that one's chosen field may take in order to develop qualities that may be of greatest future benefit to those being served.

Right livelihood also means sincere heartfelt, ritualistic devotion to the bounty of Mother Nature and to the karmic opportunities that provide one with the resources that are the mainstay of one's livelihood.

The five stages producing *right livelihood* are:

1. At first one works at a profession (e.g., a carpenter or farmer) to provide the necessities of life for oneself and family. Such livelihoods are necessary to sustain the fabric of our societies. Generally each profession benefits the whole, even if selfishly orientated.
2. Later the orientation of the person changes. A stronger interest in community, politics, and religious affairs manifests. Charitable and educational activities are instigated to benefit the community of which the person is a part.
3. The form of livelihood shifts as a consequence of intellectual pursuits, producing doctors, academics, and writers capable of influencing and helping large numbers of individuals. Others now naturally focus upon the quest for enlightenment. Right livelihood then also incorporates heartfelt, even ritualistic devotion to Nature's bounty, the precepts of the gurus to that which sustains all Life.
4. Meditation techniques are now pursued on how to utilise efforts to help beings along the best possible lines of efficacy. Impressions from the higher domains are received, the Will-to-Love developed, and the Bodhisattva path is followed. The resources obtained from the Bodhisattva's livelihood are then desirelessly utilised so that the greater whole is served. Meticulous planning as to what the future may bring allows the Bodhisattva to appropriate the resource management of the livelihoods of all within his/her care. Having eliminated personal ambition, then only the appropriate pathways to achieve the desired goal for everyone's welfare needs to be acted upon.
5. The *dharmakāya* awareness that follows in the next level demands that everything done is part of the plan for human betterment, as unfolded by the Council of Bodhisattvas, and that all existing *karma* is appropriately analysed. Meditation is thus upon the reticulated sum of national and international *karma*, and how this must be adjusted so that the worst effects of societal conditionings and people's *saṃsāric* attitudes are eliminated. Contingency plans must

always be taken into account because the attitudes (affecting the livelihoods) of those that an enlightened person must work with and through can always produce problematic effects. This is because of the factor of human free will.

With respect to *maṇḍalic* construction for *right livelihood,* the direction southwest concerns the mode of vivification of the entire *chakra* and *nāḍī* system. It needs to be vitalised with the energy that will sustain the duration of the *maṇḍala's* existence. Thus the Sacral centre, which is responsible for the distribution of the energies of the vital body, is utilised. Here primarily the Watery-Earthy Elements are admixed prior to dense physical expression. The sense-consciousness attributed is that of *touch.* All aspects of the physical body and need for physical stimulus are thereby mastered, as well as any expression of their emotive effects. The five stages of manifestation are:

1. First, *manasic* Fires are evoked by the meditator. The Throat centre is activated whenever Fiery *prāṇas* are utilised, and they must be organised to become directed to the Earthy orientation as part of the externalisation process.
2. Next the Watery *bījas* are invoked, utilising the Heart and Solar Plexus centres. The Heart centre infuses the *maṇḍala* with organised Life, whilst the Solar Plexus centre controls the dissemination of all of the Watery *prāṇas* in the body. The Heart vitalises the entire construct, whilst Water characterises it with the specific emotive forces and energies that colour its progress.
3. All available *prāṇas* are now organised, with view of future occurrences. Vitality from the Sacral centre is evoked to energise the construct with the energy needed for it to possess a separate life in the formed realms. The *maṇḍala* is now fully vivified with living energies, preparatory to its immediate externalisation.
4. The externalisation process occurs with the use of the projecting force of the *Will,* and bathed with the unifying force of Love. The Ājñā centre is utilised to rightly visualise and to project the construct.
5. The *maṇḍala* is born, revealed in the light of day, and ready to fulfil the purpose of its construction, according to the strength of its vitalisation.

The direction *west* represents the way outwards to the world of human interrelations in general, wherein the knowledge obtained from all human social interactions is gained. This direction is expressed by the *sixth* of the Eightfold Path, *right or perfect effort.*

6. Right effort (Sagittarius the archer). One pointed direction. Sagittarius is the archer who fires his arrows of ambition or aspiration towards a distant goal to which he steadfastly strives to reach. One must learn to strive for enlightenment with persevering one-pointed aspiration with all of one's heart and mind, whilst never losing sight of the manifesting *bodhicitta*. Only thus is enlightenment acquired. It concerns a persistent striving that, with certainty, will overcome all the obstacles to obtaining the goal, and will lead to the production of the qualities required to meet all needs.

This effort underlies the five previous precepts, manifesting in each of them with differing degrees of intensity at the various stages of the path. In the final two precepts, the *chela* or *yogin* must be so imbued with the qualities accrued because of this striving that the effort is automatic and spontaneous. To all intents, therefore, it becomes effortless, below the threshold of consciousness. When related to meditative development, the idea of striving or working to concentrate becomes meaningless, because complete relaxation of all cognitive processes is what is needed. The act of effort prevents concentration in its final stages.

The five distinct stages producing *right effort* are:

1. At first the effort relates to one's own sense of accomplishment. This is geared to obtaining the material and sensual pleasures that are so greatly desired. Seeing the abundance of pleasures others have, the person enviously works hard to acquire the same or better. Such effort may be right for those at the beginning of the path to correct knowledge.

2. Then comes the effort for social betterment, for glory or fame in some way, to be admired, and for the powers given to the person by others. For instance, we have the present clamour amongst many to become movie or musical stars or sports heroes. Highly glamorous profiles give such people the ability to help many because they are admired and consequently listened to. Unfortunately, Bodhisattva virtues are rarely seen in this category of individuals.

3. Here we have the truly altruistic efforts made by philanthropic and socially minded people. They toil to better the society in which they live in some way, working tirelessly for some cause. People are thereby educated concerning the nature and effects of their selfish and emotional attitudes that often produce painful experiences. The collective negative effects and even ruination to the general environment by such attitudes are also elucidated.
4. The higher correspondence of such effort produces the relinquishing of attachment to the vicissitudes of the *saṃsāra*, as directed by the impressions gained from the abstracted levels of Mind via meditation. Thus the *dharma* is followed by being equipped with the qualities needed to tread the Bodhisattva way.
5. Finally, the *vajrayāna*[9] path is trod, eventually producing a consequent effortlessness in all interrelationships with *saṃsāra*. Then karmic effects and processes of Life are instantaneously taken into account.

With respect to *maṇḍalic* construction for *right effort,* the direction west concerns the full externalisation of the *maṇḍala* within the field of human activity. It is thus clothed with the Watery Element admixed with that of Fire. This allows all mental-emotional *saṃskāras* to be expressed as part of the incarnation process. The purpose concerns the process that eventually brings about the dominance of the *intellect* (the sixth sense) in all human activity. The Solar Plexus centre that controls this *kāma-manasic* disposition comes to be fully empowered by the Heart and Mind working together, producing a type of perception that can be likened to a type of Fire-mist.[10] The entire glamoured, murky field of Watery *prāṇas* has thereby become clarified and transmogrified into their Fiery attributes. The Solar Plexus centre then serves to assimilate

9 *Vajrayāna* (Tib. rdo rje theg pa): The path (*yāna*) of the adamantine state of being/non-being, of the indestructible power (*vajra*) of the Jinas, as developed in Tantric Buddhism. Synonymous with Tantrayāna (rgyud kyi theg pa) and Mantrayāna (sngags kyi theg pa). The Vajrayāna practice is said to assist the obtainment of enlightenment in a single lifetime through the guru via proper yogic discipline and transformative meditation.

10 In the semi-exoteric account in chapter 3, the Throat centre, controlling the Fires of the mind (thus the intellect), governs the expression of this western direction during the present scientific materialistic epoch.

the impressions from the five sense-consciousnesses and rightfully disseminates their effects without modification. The ten petals of the Solar Plexus centre are arranged in pentads for this reason. The *Bardo Thödol* teachings in the next book of this series are concerned with this transformation and transmutation process of Watery *prāṇas* into attributes of Mind. What is known as the astral plane is no longer a field of experience for the Initiate concerned. *Saṃsāra* is mastered completely, and when done so it is then esoterically an expression of the Solar Plexus centre's purpose.[11] The five stages of manifestation are:

1. As the concrete form has now objectified in the world of appearances, the stimulatory effect of its interplay with consciousness now develops. It can be experienced by means of the five senses, so the sense-consciousnesses and imagination together produce images of what is contacted, what is desired, and what imaginatively is construed to be pleasing. Right effort at this level concerns gaining all knowledgeable forms of experience possible and to properly direct the creative imagination.
2. The *maṇḍala* is made to observe all of the laws of active manifest life. Now the vibrancy of the construct imbues its effulgence to evoke Watery/emotional *saṃskāras* from the perceiver. Thus a response is produced related to the way the perceiver feels the potency of its effects. Right effort then necessitates one to come to experience the nature of its inner life. The meaning and purpose of all human relationships and constructs will eventually come to be known.
3. The feeling-response makes one want to touch the *maṇḍala*, to try to come to know the meaning of the lines and symbolic images in great detail with immediate effectiveness. The mind needs to know, to try to make everything it perceives part of itself. The person now manifests right effort to integrate the *maṇḍala* into his/her own personal makeup by developing *saṃskāras* constituted of all associated images.
4. The *maṇḍala* stimulates meditative response, where the viewer tries to perceive the nature of the subtlest level of meaning that can be

11 The mystery concerning the relationship of the *deva* kingdom to this centre is then solved.

derived from its imagery. Therefore Airy *prāṇas* are awakened, to produce revelations from the loftiest realms of contact. Right effort here concerns the meditator's ability to transcend the limitations of what was formerly known concerning the subject veiled by the *maṇḍala*. Abstract enlightened thought ensues.

5. This produces the enlightened Mind, which was the purpose for the *maṇḍala's* intended construction and externalisation. Right effort thus concerns obtaining a complete revelation of all that the *maṇḍala* could possibly teach, inclusive of the vistas of the *dharmakāya*.

The direction *northwest* concerns the process of *outward expansion* of the entire sphere of identification towards the future, thus the progression of an individual into enlightenment. The emanatory aura of the *maṇḍala* broadcasts its qualities, replete with patterns of the future. It represents what the conscious units in the external environment come to know or define as a unique entity, a specific evolving personality. This direction concerns the *seventh* of the Eightfold Path, *right or perfect concentration or mindfulness.*

7. Right mindfulness (Aquarius the waterbearer). Service to others. If the other precepts are followed, then whatever prevents the person from obtaining release from suffering falls away. One is left with concentrated energies that are assimilated and projected towards the goal. It produces perfect mindfulness of all things, concentrating upon that which produces meditative development and the demonstration of the *dharma*. The purpose is the gaining of enlightenment and the elimination of the *karma* that ties all sentient beings to material existence. It produces a specific effortless tension which empowers the application of the meditation in which the mind-nature is held steady, unwavering in Light.

When focussed (upon a form or idea), tension becomes the seed that can effectively explode into that which empowers complete unfoldment of any stream of realisation, or else it can direct one to realms beyond thought. It is effortless because it is the outcome of long periods of meditative development that has become a spontaneous state of transcendence manifesting through the person. There is then naught in him/her to resist the realisation of the most potent energies or revelations.

The revelations are centred around the thought that there can be no true liberation for one if everyone is not also brought to such a state of freedom (from suffering). This defines the parameters of right mindfulness of purpose and of liberation for all. It is the Bodhisattva way.

Aquarius is the water bearer pouring the Waters of Life, a free-flowing field of energy, outwards to all who are willing to find succour in the plenitude of the *dharma* so offered. The *dharma*-water flows from the zone of meditative tension to the field of need wherein the little ones reside who have succumbed to the turmoil of *māyā*. They need to be rightly nourished in order to have the strength to find their way out from confusing illusional activity. The Waterbearer's qualities and actions are the prototype for all forms of activity of Bodhisattvas.

The five distinct stages producing *right mindfulness* are:

1. Concentration of all efforts to gain the desired objective (this is difficult for the material, carnal person, except in cases where it relates to desire). The thought life must be developed; this advances learning for the individual considerably. Clear thought is required to effectively overcome desire for carnal or sensual pleasure, or for the amassing of wealth.
2. Next are those who concentrate their time and energy to master any religious philosophy or university curriculum to meet their ambitions. If the goal is to be achieved, greater discipline is required than previously, often demanding austerities that eliminate many pleasures that one would have had. Personal desire later develops into ambition to excel, to achieve excellence, providing the best possible chance to succeed in life. Such intellectual pursuit causes one to discover arenas of knowledge and philosophies that would otherwise not be known.
3. Mental development eventually produces an inherent aptitude to learn the higher way of meditation. This produces the joy of the mind that abides in a state of revelation. The resultant mindfulness facilitates development of the abstract Mind faster than is possible in the earlier stages of the Eightfold Path. It equips the person with the ability to manifest seminal works in various disciplines: science, technology, religion, law, medicine, environmental concerns, the

arts, and philanthropy. It facilitates leadership roles, producing notable accomplishments relating to human or societal betterment, allowing others to learn from one's example.

4. This level produces many gifted meditators naturally inclined to a contemplative life capable of generating *bodhicitta*. The allurements of *saṃsāra* are clearly seen and quickly bypassed in a *dhyāna* that reveals the Clear Light, or absorption into the *tathāgatagarbha*. Ways are consequently found to ensure that the meditator's lifestyle facilitates obtaining right concentration in the field desired. It necessitates right *maṇḍala* building, so that the resultant writings, art, scientific achievements etc., meet the greatest audience, to produce the greatest benefit for humanity.
5. Right concentration means more than just right mental focus, as this activity must follow through into the entire lifestyle by discarding all irrelevant mental images and ideas. Superfluous material baggage is discarded, whilst the resources needed to produce the goal are concentrated to achieve meticulously timed effects. The entire life is geared to assist the need of eliminating suffering and producing enlightenment in humanity. *Karma* is thereby cleansed. Such baggage that follows one from life to life is eliminated as one travels the higher Bodhisattva stages.

   The *dharmatā* experience produces spontaneity in one's ability to concentrate all resources to produce the most efficient service demanded concerning the rectifiable arenas of humanity's woes. Such resources are vast, as the Bodhisattva is normally meditating upon many lines of service at once. Each specific *dhyāna* is an integral part of the entire *maṇḍala* pictured. The Bodhisattva expediently moves from one arena of concern to the other, according to the reticulations of the need at any moment.

With respect to *maṇḍalic* construction for *right mindfulness,* the direction northwest concerns an appropriate visualisation of the externalised *maṇḍala*. The present *maṇḍala* has borne the fruits of its existence. Its resonance thus expands towards the different groups to which the person belongs, and beyond. Once the *maṇḍala* has been fully assessed and its benefits gained, then the meditator must convey its revelations to others so they can be assisted to make similar beneficent constructs. Energies and resources are concentrated for this purpose. The *chakra* involved is the dual Splenic centre, whose function is to cleanse all ungainly *saṃskāras* below the diaphragm.[12] The seat of consciousness is no longer focussed downwards for selfish concerns, but rather upwards towards liberation. *Kliṣṭamanas* (defiled mind) is the specific focus of transformation via the generation of goodwill. Goodwill, the Will-to-Love, and *bodhicitta* can then resonate the song of Love outwards for all people to experience. Upon the Bodhisattva path the Splenic centre helps purify the *maṇḍala* from the defilements possessed by those the Bodhisattva serves. The five stages of manifestation are:

1. First the meditator learns to build the manasic construct, visualising with concentrated intent all attributes of the *maṇḍala* and rightly interpreting its symbolism.
2. Next is learnt the art of empowering the construct with the vitality needed to sustain its life and to achieve its purpose. The meditative concentration builds into the construct the necessary colourings with the right vibrancy and the precise hues allowing stimulation of other minds with its intent. Unnecessary ingredients and *prāṇas* are consequently expelled or transformed.
3. Next we have concentration upon assuring that the entire construct is complete in every detail and that it will produce its purpose when projected into manifestation.
4. The *maṇḍala* is now precipitated into active manifestation with the meditator focussed upon all of the arenas it is to service. All karmic pathways for its existence must be carefully explored and the long-range potential clearly visualised.
5. Having projected the *maṇḍala* into *saṃsāra,* the meditator looks to eventual abstraction back into its source, and upon the overview

12 In chapter 3 it was stated that: 'The directing, purifying energies that organise the *prāṇas* come from the Heart centre to Splenic centre I. The Heart is thus the ultimate directing organ for all of the *prāṇas* in the body.' For this reason the Heart centre was given the rulership of the transformation of *kliṣṭamanas* in that semi-exoteric account. In the esoteric perspective, the Heart is the place of attainment of *śūnyata,* with *bodhicitta* as its directive power, which then acts upon Splenic centre I to transform defilements. The relation between the two *chakras* will be elaborated in later chapters.

of accomplishment with respect to future expressions of other *maṇḍalas* to produce an integrated purpose.

The direction *north* represents the way upwards towards the divine, to the Sambhogakāya Flower, *śūnyatā*, and thence the *dharmakāya*, depending upon the level of attainment previously achieved.

This direction is represented by the *eighth* of the Eightfold Path, *right or perfect bliss or absorption.* It is generally viewed as an absorption into that which is Void of all discernible characteristics, which is absolute and unconditioned (*śūnyatā*). The Dharmakāya Way then leads to higher portals in cosmos. This expanded view is inclusive of what can also be seen as absorption into the Heart of the Hierarchy of Enlightened Being, of which all Bodhisattvas are participating members. At first we have the full experience of the *ālayavijñāna* associated with the Sambhogakāya Flower, and later we have the Bodhisattva path leading to the *dharmakāya.*

8. Right absorption (Pisces the fishes). Salvation or liberation. It is an absorption into that which is Void of all discernible characteristics, but which is the fount of all liberative insight. Esoterically, this can also be seen as an absorption into the Heart of the Hierarchy of Enlightened Being.

Pisces the fishes is the last of the signs of the zodiac, thus signifies termination or completion of a cycle. It is consequently also the sign of a world saviour, who has sacrificed his state of abstraction in nirvāṇic bliss in order to incarnate into the waters of *saṃsāra* for the sake of liberating the swimming 'fishes'. They are bonded to all aspects of their watery world.

The five stages producing *right absorption* (or perfect bliss) are:

1. The average carnal person looks upwards to his/her superior or boss, hoping to emulate the boss's success in life. In the *saṅgha* it is the reverence that the ordinary monk pays to the *guru* at the heart of his community. By aspiring to be like the superior, the person may develop the qualities to later take the same position. The immediate goal in life is then achieved.
2. This level concerns the attainment of high ambitions, by looking upwards to great social, religious, political, or scientific standing in the community. People work hard to excel in chosen professions,

to become leaders in their society or group, such as becoming the president of a company or of a nation. This necessitates impressing those that can place one at the top of an organisation or community.

3. Direct meditative development through one-pointed aspiration towards achieving the contemplative goal is pursued upon the Bodhisattva path. Fruits are achieved relatively quickly because of the accumulation of merit from past lives of attainment. *Bodhicitta* is already innate, as well as the *saṃskāras* of leadership developed from former lives of northward aspiration. Many lives of being a ruler of a nation or large enterprise would have already transpired. The Bodhisattva can thus correctly provide succour to those that come for advice (via the southern direction).
4. The Sambhogakāya Flower also pours forth all knowledgeable things related to the field of service, based upon past life attainments into the meditator's mind. Abstracting the mind in the domain of the Flower brings in an increased flow of energies to the meditator, and also high identifications when focussed via the Śūnyatā Eye. Eventually the Sambhogakāya Flower comes to be abstracted into *śūnyatā* via the activity of the sacrificial Will of the meditator. Liberation from the constraints of *saṃsāra* is thereby produced.
5. The *vajrayāna* path is pursued and transcendental *dharmakāya* meditation results in the gaining of Buddha-qualities. Inevitably, the choice of which of the cosmic paths (that lead irrevocably away from the earth sphere) to travel approaches.

With respect to *maṇḍalic* construction for right *bliss or absorption,* the direction north concerns abstraction of all aspects of the *maṇḍala* back into the *bīja* form because it has served its karmic purpose. The universal storehouse of consciousness (*ālayavijñāna*) is the focus here, whilst the centre utilised is the 1,000 petalled lotus (*sahasrāra padma*). The five stages of manifestation are:

1. The gain of the *maṇḍala* is fully assessed; making sure that there is no further use for its existence. The nature of the ramification of the *karma* into the future is analysed, and if appropriate the abstraction process can begin.

2. The mind is now focussed one-pointedly to generate the intense abstracting *Will* that drives the entire construct to its fitting conclusion. Its essential Life can then be withdrawn, terminating its karmic connections with the material world.
3. First the Earthy Element is abstracted, causing its dissolution in the physical domain.
4. Next the Watery Element is dried off, making it lose its vitality and vibrancy. Its potency in the psychic levels now wanes.
5. Its image can now be condensed into its most essential form within the Fiery domain, from which all aspects can be reconstructed when necessary. The abstracted *bīja* form is then stored in the *ālayavijñāna*, to be utilised in a later incarnation. A new cycle of meditative constructs can now be visualised.

From the above we see that the two lists for the Eightfold Path produce a complete picture of the nature of the striving for enlightenment, as well as the Thought-form building (*maṇḍalic* construction) that becomes the service work of an enlightened One. The first of the two lists for each Path can therefore be considered an *iḍā* or feminine stream, the expression of developing *wisdom*. The second list can be considered a *piṇgalā,* or masculine *compassionate* function, wherein the gain of the former striving and learning is utilised for a service arena. By the time the fifth point of each listing is reached, then an enlightened *suṣumṇā* function is produced. We thus have a complete *maṇḍala* of enlightenment in the 80 steps herein presented. Detail will later be provided concerning the nature of these masculine and feminine streams. They are symbolised by the Mahābodhisattvas and their consorts in relation to the complete, vivified *maṇḍala* of enlightenment when integrated with the *suṣumṇā* aspect of the Dhyāni Buddhas.

The interrelation between the Mahābodhisattvas and the Jinas are seen above in that the attributes of the Jinas are reflected in the listings of five steps each, whereas the function of the Mahābodhisattvas is seen in the overall categorisation of the activity of the Eightfold Path.

9

Consciousness and the Eight Directions of Space

A brief discussion of the eight consciousnesses

The nature of the eight consciousnesses[1] of the Yogācāra Philosophy can also be viewed from a similar perspective to the Eightfold Path, to which they have a relationship. These eight are comprised of the five sense-consciousnesses, the intellect,[2] *kliṣṭamanas*[3] and *ālayavijñāna*. The five forms of sense-awareness are developed from the sense perceptors, the sixth being the intellect that collates the input of information derived from them, directs conclusions with wilful intent, and adds its own visual images. The seventh is *kliṣṭamanas*, the defiled mind, which is essentially the emotional-mind, as earlier explained. As the qualities of the five sense-perceptors and their perceptions were described in Volume 3 of this series, they need no further elaboration.

The *ālayavijñāna* is assigned to the *northern* position of the *maṇḍala* of the eight consciousnesses. This represents the upward way of liberation, towards the storehouse of the consciousness-streams gained from myriads of incarnations in the material world, plus that derived from the *dharmakāya*. It concerns the *eighth* of the Eightfold Path, *right absorption.*

---

1 Also called the eight *vijñānas.*

2 The intellect is denoted as the sixth of the sense-consciousnesses in the Yogācāra doctrine (they are thereby often called 'the six consciousnesses') but it rightfully belongs in a separate category, as the collator, director and modifier of the impressions derived from the senses.

3 Also *kliṣṭa-mano-vijñāna.*

The *northeast* arm of 'unity' concerns the sense of *sight,* which envisions clearly the qualities of the *maṇḍalas* to be comprehended. It is associated with the first of the paths, *right understanding,* because sight easily penetrates the darkness of ignorance, thereby eliminating it. Sight integrates all diverse attributes of perception into one panoramic vision. Ignorance manifests as an inappropriate understanding as to the nature of any manifesting phenomena, producing attachment to transitory things. Comprehending the nature of the obstacles upon the path before one, and the mechanism of overcoming them, constitutes the way to liberation.

In the *eastern* direction of the way to the heart we have the quality of *taste,* which discriminates between the pleasing and nourishing (the *dharma* that liberates) and that which is poisonous (the intoxicating emotional broth that embroils one deep in the mire of *saṃsāra*). Through the appropriately discerning effects of taste both the body and mind can be adequately sustained. How the mind is focussed determines the type of information processed. By tasting all forms of subtle impressions the aspiring one utilises the most pertinent perceptions to proceed to the chosen direction. This involves the qualities of the second of the Eightfold Paths, *right aspiration or attitude of mind,* which as previously stated is to 'rightly discriminate the subtle discernments between the differing meditative paths that one can aspire to follow'.

The *southeast* arm of 'expression' concerns the sense of *smell,* the most refined of the senses. It appertains to perceptions carried in the air, producing a pervasive comprehension of things, of the way that people's thoughts are expressed, and communicated via ideas. The ideas can be of all types, from gross sensual, to the most abstract forms of metaphysical philosophy, such as the doctrine of *śūnyatā.* This implicates the third of the paths, *right speech.* All aspects of the desire for physical stimulus are first spoken about and then acted upon.

The *southern* arm ('downwards to the material world') is where most people are focussed. In this material domain consciousness derives its most basic impressions. The corresponding sense-perception is *hearing,* because sound is the most limiting or confusing of the senses. It is easily mistaken or misunderstood, similar to the confusing plethora of experiences obtained in *saṃsāra.* Right assimilation of what is heard, however, allows one to choose the appropriate path to take, to develop social skills, become educated, or to learn about the *dharma*. When the nature of the phenomenal world is understood via what is gained through *hearing* then it produces the fulfilment of the *fourth* of the Eightfold Path, *right action*. One then acts according to decisions made consequential to having heard the *dharma* spoken by the enlightened. As previously stated it allows one to 'respond to the words and mantras articulated' by the Lords of Life.

The *southwest* position of 'understanding' is occupied by *touch*, the sense ascertaining the reality of what defines contact with the material world and all forms of sensuality. Contact with phenomena validates the experiences gained through any of the senses. With it we can build everything and grow the food needed for physical survival. *Right livelihood*, the fifth of the Eightfold Paths, is thus implicated. Such livelihood can externalise impressions gained from the subtlest discernments. The wise can then give heuristic advice to help people eliminate the causes of pain and suffering. Living examples of the nature of the enlightenment path follow.

The sixth of the Eightfold Path *(right effort)* is found upon the *western* arm of 'outwards towards human interrelationships'. It is ruled by the *intellect,* which assimilates all of the experiences gained by means of the sense-perceptors and directs the entire thought process outwards in an expansive manner. New domains of experience can thereby be mastered through right effort. It was previously stated that the purpose of such effort 'eventually brings about the dominance of the intellect in all human activity'. With rightly directed effort it coherently directs thought to eliminate arenas of ignorance illuminated from the world of experience.

The *northwest* direction of 'goodwill' concerns the seventh of the Eightfold Paths, *right concentration or mindfulness*. Such concentration properly disciplines all aspects of the desire-mind and the emotions. These defilements (*kliṣṭamanas*) are the major enemies that countermand the production of meditative equanimity. *Kliṣṭamanas* was previously stated to be the 'focus of transformation through the generation of goodwill from selfish will'. *Bodhicitta* is the gain.

Various lists based upon the number eight

Some of the other lists based upon the number eight in Buddhism are explored below. All lists are placed from the point of view of the natural movement of the eight-spoked wheel of the *dharma* and of consciousness-direction in space. Such direction starts from the northeast, thence east, then southeast, etc.

The eight qualities of the *dharma*[4]

1. The northeast: *unthinkability (acintyatva)*. This concerns the collective revelation of all meditation-Minds, wherein revelations of the true nature of *dharma* are shared by all. In this collective meditation-Mind there is nothing to think about concerning the *dharma*, it is automatically comprehended as it is.
2. The east: *non-duality (advayatā)*. This is the way of the Heart centre's expression. The taste of enlightenment blends all experiences into a unity.
3. The southeast: *non-discriminativeness (nirvikalpatā)*. The verbalisation of the nature of obtained revelation to all and sundry. The truth is presented without discrimination.
4. The south: *purity (śuddhi)*. The way that *saṃsāra* must eventually be transformed as a consequence of meditation upon it and the consequent actions to cleanse defilements. The utter purity of the *dharma* is then revealed.
5. The southwest: *being manifest (abhivyaktikaraṇa)*. The nature of contact with phenomena and manifesting the form of livelihood that utilises *saṃsāra* as a vehicle to liberation. The expression of the *dharma* is then seen in each and every thing.
6. The west: *hostility against obstacles (pratipakṣata)*. Here all fields of human perception and *saṃsāric* attachments come to the fore. This necessitates the mind to develop wisdom to positively rectify the various materialistic problems that prevent the progress to enlightenment. Once the wise beneficence of the *dharma* is manifest then obstacles are quickly overcome.

---

4 These are 'as recorded by the *Ratnagotravibhāga*'. The listing is quoted from Brian Edward Brown, *The Buddha Nature*, (Motilal Barnasidass, New Delhi, 2004), 294.

7. The northwest: *deliverance from passions (virāga).* The outward expansiveness of an enlightened consciousness manifests when all forms of attachments to one's former allurements have been eliminated. At this stage *kliṣṭamanas* has been converted to *bodhicitta.*
8. The north: *causes of deliverance (virāga-hetu).* This is the result of meditation or absorptiveness in the nature of the *ālayavijñāna* environment, *śūnyatā,* or of the *dharmakāya.*

The eight virtuous roots of the Bodhisattva[5]

1. The northeast: acceptance of existence through origination by their own will.
2. The east: unweariness towards the perfect maturity of living beings.
3. The southeast: efforts for perfect apprehension of the sublime doctrine.
4. The south: endeavour after works to be done for living beings.
5. The southwest: non-abandonment of propensity of desire for phenomena.
6. The west: non-reluctance from fetters of the highest virtues.
7. The northwest: non-satisfaction in searching for the accumulation of merits.
8. The north: earnest wish to meet the Buddhas.

The eight Mahābodhisattvas

1. The northeast: Mañjuśrī
2. The east: Kṣitigarbha
3. The southeast: Maitreya
4. The south: Ākāśagarbha
5. The southwest: Viṣkambhin
6. The west: Avalokiteśvara
7. The northwest: Samantabhadra
8. The north: Vajrapāṇi

---

5 Ibid., 295.

There is also a listing of the *eight qualities of Buddhahood,* which are given as: Immutability, Freedom from effort, Enlightenment not dependent upon others, Wisdom, Compassion, Supernatural powers, Fulfilment of self-benefit, and Fulfilment for others.[6] The directions will not be assigned here because the ontological discussion of what the major qualities of a Buddha may or may not be would take us too far afield from the main topic in this book. Also, the eight names of Guru Rinpoche have been relegated to Volume 5, chapter 1 of this series.

The eight Mahābodhisattvas

The main focus of this chapter shall be upon the qualities of the eight Mahābodhisattvas, the information of which is derived from *Secret Doctrines of the Tibetan Books of the Dead.*[7]

The allotted directions of these Bodhisattvas are presented below:

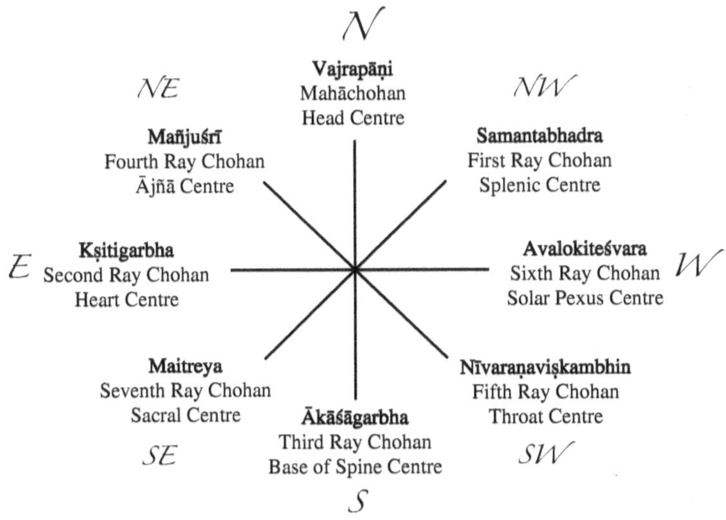

Figure 25. The *maṇḍala* of the eight Mahābodhisattvas

6 Ibid., 294.

7 Detlef Ingo Lauf, *Secret Doctrines of the Tibetan Books of the Dead*, (Shambhala. Boston, 1989), 115-117.

Figure 25 depicts the positioning of the eight Mahābodhisattvas, the relation of these Bodhisattvas to the Chohans,[8] and the associated *chakras*. The word Chohan is a shortened version of the term Dhyān Chohan, which refers to a liberated Lord (Buddha) of meditation. The Chohans are tenth and eleventh *bhūmi* Bodhisattvas, the highest level Bodhisattvas upon this earth. Effectively, they are Buddhas. Rather than moving on to a cosmic path at the end of their evolutionary sojourn upon this earth, which would normally be required by those of their spiritual rank, they still manifest ties with earth evolution. They fulfil necessary positions of the *maṇḍala* that governs the evolution of consciousness of this planet. There are seven of them, plus one extra, the Mahāchohan. They are thus also high representative members of the constitution of Shambhala. The Mahābodhisattvas can be considered planetary executives, truly enlightened beings and not just symbolic or metaphoric representations. Each (apart from the Mahāchohan) is a Lord of a specific Ray line, disseminating the related qualities for the entire planetary manifestation. They embody the functions of the seven major planetary *chakras*, plus the dual Splenic centre, as far as the evolution of the sum of human consciousness is concerned.

This subject has been introduced here to provide greater information to Buddhists as to the nature of the Council of Bodhisattvas veiled in their texts. It is also a necessary foundation that will be later integrated with the information to be presented in the final volumes of this *Treatise on Mind, Meditation and the Initiation Process* and *The Constitution of Shambhala*. Together these two books provide practitioners a solid basis as to the nature, methodology, and gains of meditation. They also show why it sometimes took the great *yogins* decades of meditative pursuit to reach their goals. These books thus provide necessary information concerning the nature of the fruit of enlightenment, elaborating many essential concepts not considered elsewhere.

---

8 The term is of uncertain etymology, and first appears in H. P. Blavatsky's *The Secret Doctrine*, where it is assigned to various types of fully liberated beings. The term Chohan is used in my books to specifically refer to an Initiate of the sixth degree, a great Lord of Life. It is the degree of Initiation attained by the Buddha at his *parinirvāṇa*. With respect to this, it should be noted that what it took to produce a Buddha in Gautama's relatively simple times differs to what is required now. Nowadays meeting the challenges of the complexity of our civilisation requires much greater accomplishment; hence the 'entrance level' for Buddhahood has been raised.

With respect to Figure 25, we see a number of *chakras* assigned to the Mahābodhisattvas. Their functions remain as earlier presented concerning the eight consciousnesses. However, though Figure 25 posits the major determinants as static, the orientations do change over time. The *chakras* through which the Bodhisattvas of the fixed cross focus their attention remain unchanged, however those of the mutable cross move depending upon the development of their associated service arena. The *maṇḍala* of world service alters as the work progresses. There are natural alignments between *chakras*: the Sacral centre with the Throat centre, the Solar Plexus with the Heart centre, the Base of the Spine with the Head centre, and the Ājñā centre with the dual Splenic centres. The latter pair is also quite fluid with respect to energy responses. Thus the Sacral-Throat centre duo is an *iḍā-nāḍī* pair, the Solar Plexus-Heart centre is a *piṇgalā-nāḍī* pair, the Base of Spine-Head centre is at first an *iḍā-nāḍī* pair but eventually there will be a *suṣumṇā*[9] interrelation. The Ājñā-Splenic centre interrelation will however move from either *iḍā* or *piṇgalā nāḍī* attributes according to the energy distribution at any time. Diagrammatically, this effectively means that the Ājñā centre can also manifest at the northwest position and the Splenic centre at the northeast, with a corresponding shift between the Throat and Sacral centres. The work of the associated Mahābodhisattva will correspondingly alter.

The northeast: Mañjuśrī

The Bodhisattva attributed to the northeast is Mañjuśrī.[10] Concerning him we are told:

> The Bodhisattva Mañjuśrī has a saffron-yellow colour, and he carries the blue utpala-blossom and the bell. He is familiar to us from the teachings of the Mahāyāna as the Bodhisattva of knowledge, and so he appears here to enlighten the faculty of thinking (S. manovijñāna; T. Yid-kyi rnam-shes). As long as normal thinking is ruled by the intellect

---

9 *Suṣumṇā:* the central *nāḍī* that rises up the spinal column from the Base of the Spine centre to the Head centre. It relates to the Father aspect of the trinity, *suṣumṇā* (Father, the abstracting, liberating energy), *piṇgalā* (Son, or consciousness-engendering), and *iḍā* (Mother, or form sustaining) *nāḍīs*. It is the energy that descends down the spinal column at the appropriate time to awaken the sleeping *kuṇḍalinī* and fuses with it, to rise up again to liberate the individual.

10 The name means 'possessing gentle glory'.

> and its deceptive reflections, a breakthrough to perfect knowledge is impossible. The female counterpart of Mañjuśrī is the red Ḍākinī Ālokā, who carries the all-illuminating light. She appears in order to enlighten thought-awareness, in that she protects it from all future intellectual activity with the clear radiance of her light.[11]

His most usual representation, however, is the sword he holds above his head in his right hand, and the book of the *Prajñāpāramitā* in his left hand. Alice Getty states:

> Mañjuśrī belongs to the group of eight Dhyāni-Bodhisattva, and is therefore represented like a prince with all the Bodhisattva ornaments. He may have a small image of Akshobhya in his crown, and his *ushṇīsha* is sometimes ornamented at the top by a flaming pearl. The *ūrṇā* is generally on his forehead, and, if painted, his colour is usually yellow, but may also be white, red, or black.
>
> Mañjuśrī or Mañjughosha, as he is frequently called in the *sādhana,* has two distinct types: one with sword and book, which is the more usual form, and the other with the *utpala* or blue lotus.
>
> The sword symbolises the cleaving asunder (dissipating) of the clouds of Ignorance; the book is the *Prajñāpāramitā* Treatise on Transcendental Wisdom.[12]

The 'Knowledge' or wisdom represented here is not common knowledge; it is the *prajñāpāramitā,*[13] the great virtuous transcendental wisdom that lies at the heart of the Mahāyāna canon. The *Prajñāpāramitā* literature extols the philosophy of *śūnyatā,* and of the Mādhyamika position of the absolute Truth. In many ways, however, we see that it is an idealised externalisation of knowledge contained in the *ālayavijñāna,* integrated with what can be viewed via the Śūnyatā Eye. Knowledge is seen in the form of 'the all-illuminating light' conveyed by the red *ḍākinī*

---

11 Lauf, *Tibetan Books of the Dead,* 117.

12 Alice Getty, *The Gods of Northern Buddhism,* (Oxford University Press, Oxford 1928), 111.

13 *Prajñāpāramitā* (Tib. shes rab kyi phar phyin): perfection of wisdom. Seen as the result of the perfected discriminative awareness of a Buddha, also in the form of the Bodhisattva *bhūmis* (paths). It generally refers to the vast literature presenting the essential aspects of the path to *śūnyatā* that is fundamental to Mahāyāna Buddhism. The personification is a female Buddha, the Mother of all Buddhas.

Ālokā. Red is the hue associated with the Wisdom from Amitābha's domain of the abstracted Mind. Such wisdom empowers the communion of all interrelated Sambhogakāya Flowers (which characterises the term 'unity' ascribed to the northeast position), plus that emanating from the *dharmakāya*. From this position he projects the collective wisdom of the Jinas into manifestation. With this basic outline of the overall design of the *maṇḍala* that is conferred by Mañjuśrī we can incorporate the detail of its construction.

The blue colour of the *utpala* blossom expresses the energy and qualities of the Mirror-like Wisdom emanating via the (blue) Dhyāni Buddha Akṣobhya (who embodies the eastern direction of the *maṇḍala* of the Dhyāni Buddhas). This blossom symbolises the Sambhogakāya Flower, but can also be taken to represent a generic term for any major *chakra* in cosmos. The emphasis here is however upon the Love-Wisdom that characterises the blue colour of its form. It is that upon which the gaze of Mañjuśrī is focussed. He then impresses the Love-Wisdom (*bodhicitta*) received with the Knowledge ('virtuous transcendental wisdom') that is his forte. The combined Knowledge-Love-Wisdom expressed by the pair Akṣobhya-Mañjuśrī may be qualified as *prajñāpāramita*. This is the basis of Mañjuśrī's sword of right discrimination that cuts asunder the veils of illusion,[14] the *saṃskāras* and *skandhas* that prevent the attainment of *nirvāṇa*.

It is also easily seen that the first of the Buddha's Eightfold Path

---

14 The two edges of Mañjuśrī's sword can also represent the fusion of the *deva* and human hierarchies, the feminine (*deva-iḍā*) with the masculine (human-*piṇgalā*) manifestation of intelligence and inherent love on earth. This presents the esoteric background and meaning of the *Prajñāpāramitā*, the *Treatise on Transcendental Wisdom*, the gender of which is generally feminine in Buddhism. (This is the *deva-ḍākinī* line in evolution. Note that the true nature of the line of evolution of *ḍākinīs* is barely hinted at in the Buddhist texts, thus much of this esotericism now needs to be revealed.) As a deity, Prajñāpāramitā is viewed as a Buddha in her own right. Mañjuśrī's sword of right discrimination and loving action therefore assists this Mother to promulgate wisdom to the world, though specifically as part of the process of the development of *siddhis* by yogis. The sword is a mechanism that regulates the qualities of the *prāṇas* and the direction of their flow in the *nāḍī* system. The sword is a transformative tool used to dispense with degenerative *saṃskāras*, well represented in Tantric iconographic representations. The *iḍā* and *piṇgalā nāḍīs* are the two edges of the sword, and the *suṣumṇā* the central ridge.

(right understanding), attributed to the northeast direction, leads eventually to the full expression of Mañjuśrī's Wisdom.

The virtuous root of the Bodhisattva that has been attributed to the northeastern direction is that of 'acceptance of existence through origination by their own will'. This direction pours the combined energy of the Mahābodhisattvas into manifestation (the 'existence' that is accepted) through the demonstration of their Will-to-Love for the purpose of liberating the denizens of *saṃsāra*. The yellow colour by which Mañjuśrī is depicted betokens his standing as the fourth Ray Chohan, who governs the dissemination of this energy. The golden yellow colour of the fourth Ray of Beautifying Harmony overcoming Conflict is the best energy to bear this compassionate impress, considering the strife and turmoil found in the generalised field of service that is humanity. The fourth Ray represents the mirror that reflects the attributes of Divinity (borne by the three higher Rays) into corporeal form (expressed by the three lower Ray dispositions). The energy of this Ray best qualifies the Eye (the Ājñā centre) that sees all of that which is above, and that which is below the veil of the Real. It allows one to see clearly all the directions of the *maṇḍala* wherein the *prajñāpāramita* doctrine can apply.

The associated quality of the *dharma* for this direction is 'unthinkability', the way of the collective revelation of all meditation-Minds. For a practitioner, 'unthinkability' concerns the way of detachment from the vicissitudes of *saṃsāric* allurements through the application of right understanding. Being attached to any aspect of *saṃsāra* is deemed as unthinkable. Mañjuśrī's sword is used to cut away all ties to transitory phenomena, so all that remains concerns following the path of right discrimination and knowledge to full enlightenment. Immutably expressed wisdom can then forthrightly manifest. Everything has been wrought through experiential knowledge and deemed to be true through the test of the discriminatory sword. The sword has cut the ties to transitoriness, and has also pierced the veils to the highest strata of being/non-being (awakening the 'all-seeing Eye' to do so). That which was also once 'unthinkable' (the *dharmakāya*) now comes within the reach of the developed Mind.

Seen from this perspective the sword can also be viewed as flashing in all four directions of the Mutable Cross, as its application can be found on any of its arms. If one looks to the symbolism of the sword, however, we can see that it is in the form of a fixed cross (bearing Akśobhya's blue Wisdom into manifestation), held in the right hand of the practitioner. He/she takes the guise of Akṣobhya-Mañjuśrī, potently wielding *bodhicitta* in the form of *prajñāpāramita,* as a tool of revelation for all beings.

If the *chakra* associated with this northeast direction is viewed as a Splenic centre, then the entire eight-armed cross will take the form of Splenic centre II containing defiled *prāṇas* to convert. Here the golden energy poured through this northeast gate represents the combined energies from the planetary Heart centre (directed by the Council of Bodhisattvas), or else from Splenic centre I, that will work to cleanse these defiled planetary energies. This is the effect of the Bodhisattva vow to never cease striving until all sentient beings have been released from suffering.

The east: Kṣitigarbha

Kṣitigarbha (matrix, or womb, of the earth) governs the internal meditative contemplation productive of the way of the Heart. The Heart governs the womb of all phenomena in that it integrates the sum of any *maṇḍala* into a unity, giving it its vital Life force. It allows Kṣitigarbha to feed into this matrix the ability for everyone to develop *bodhicitta*. This is the force of Love promulgating the goal of liberation for every sentient being.

Lauf states:

> The white Bodhisattva Kṣitigarbha with the symbols of a red branch from the tree of wishing and the ghaṇṭā[15] in his hands appears in order to purify visual awareness (S. cakṣurvijñāna; T. Mig-gi rnam-shes) from false impressions of things in the world, so that the illusory aspect (S. māyā) of all impermanent things can be recognized. The Bodhisattva Kṣitigarbha has his Ḍākinī the goddess Lāsyā whose colour is clear as water. She carries the mirror and the ghaṇṭā, and her realm is the visual field and all objective things.[16]

15 *Ghaṇṭā:* bell, symbol of the transient, the feminine, wisdom principle (*prajñā*). The *vajra* then represents the masculine, compassionate principle.

16 Lauf, *Tibetan Books of the Dead,* 116. Note that the two contrasting accounts between Getty and Lauf have been utilised in this exposition of the Mahābodhisattvas so that aspects missed by either account can be revealed.

Getty adds:

> He is represented, like all the other Dhyāni Bodhisattva, with the thirteen ornaments, and is standing with his right hand in 'argument', and his left hand is in 'charity' *mudrā*. His symbol, the magic jewel, generally in shape of a flaming pearl, is supported by a lotus-flower on a level with his right shoulder. There is sometimes a book supported by a lotus-flower at his left shoulder, and he may carry a *kalaśa,* with the right hand in *abhaya mudrā*.[17]

Lauf's statement is that Kṣitigarbha's colour is white, yet he is just as often depicted green or yellow. Also, there are three sets of depictions of him: a) holding a red branch in one hand and a *ghaṇṭā* in another; b) one hand manifesting the argument *mudrā*, and the other that of charity; c) one hand holding the *kalaśa* and another conveying the protection *mudrā*. Iconographically this makes him difficult to categorise. This apparent confusion, however, correctly depicts that which represents the Heart of Life, because it manifests in many forms to sustain all types of beings. The Heart centre expresses charity (compassion) to the needy, protection from harm for the distressed, and from it emanates the esoteric *dharma* that can be skilfully articulated to worthy hearers. It pours the Waters of Life (*amṛta*) to fill the *kalaśa*[18] cup. It can also peal out the sounds of wisdom to fill all receptive minds with enlightened revelations. It is all-knowing and embracive of every need.

The case for Kṣitigarbha being assigned this eastern direction however rests mainly on him being the second Bodhisattva taking Akṣobhya as their Lord. Akṣobhya's deep blue of Love thus becomes the primary energy empowering this Mahābodhisattva. His most distinguishing feature, the flaming pearl that is supported by a lotus flower on a level with his right shoulder, symbolises Love-Wisdom. (The iridescent pearl represents compassion, and the flame denotes the application of wisdom.) The red branch from the 'tree of wishing'[19]

17 Getty, *Gods of Northern Buddhism*, 102-103. The *abhaya mudrā* is the *mudrā* of protection, the blessing of fearlessness.

18 *Kalaśa:* a vase or urn, the vase believed to hold the *amṛta,* or elixir of Life. It is the vase of abundance, auspiciousness, and regeneration. *Amṛta* is defined as 'deathless state', the elixir of immortality, soma, ambrosia. A purified, transmuted mixture of the *saṃskāras* that were formerly productive of ego-clinging.

19 Another way of viewing this is that it is a 'magic wish-fulfilling jewel'.

serves a similar function as that of Love-Wisdom, because the way of the Heart is to fulfil all of one's most precious wishes, not just for oneself, but also wisely through love to assist others. The colour red signifies the intensity of the will that is needed to secure the necessary branch from the enlightenment-tree that will allow the 'wish-fulfilling' requests of the awakened ones to be accomplished. This involves the Bodhisattva's vow of ceaselessly working for the welfare of all sentient beings. The 'book supported by a lotus-flower at his left shoulder' is the *Prajñāpāramita,* whose propagation he shares with Mañjuśrī, just as they share the beneficence of Akṣobhya.[20]

The Heart centre thoroughly rejects all aberrant *prāṇas* before accepting the remainder. This produces the 'non-dual' quality of the *dharma* for this eastern direction, allowing the unification of all into oneness. To experience the way of the Heart therefore necessitates a *dhyāna* that is focussed upon the mirror that is formed in the stillness of the Mind, wherein no defiled, concreted images can reside. (The substance of such a Mind constitutes the symbolic mirror that his consort carries.) The mirror reflects non-duality equally to all beings. This is equable with the Mirror-like Wisdom of Akṣobhya. The clear water of the consort's colour implies that the emotions have been cleansed of defilements and stilled, so that correct non-agitated perception of aspects of consciousness without muddied distortion is possible. If the meditation is focussed in the realm of the Sambhogakāya Flower then one can contemplate via the Śūnyatā Eye upon the *dharmakāya.*

The *second* path of the Eightfold Path comes into play here wherein aspiration towards the development of *bodhicitta* (the force of compassion) is fostered. *Bodhicitta,* of which the Heart centre is the emanating source, also demonstrates as Love-Wisdom. The natural expression of this force is a fully awakened 'unweariness' (the 'virtuous root' for this direction) directed towards the salvation of all beings. It produces an unwavering effort to bring all Life to a fusion of enlightened unity and blissful liberation.

Perhaps here we should refresh our understanding of the qualities of the Dhyāni Buddhas of the four cardinal positions and their

---

20 Both Bodhisattvas are on the second Ray line, constituted of the Rays: 2.4.6. Because the sixth Ray is a lower correspondence of this line, so this Ray Lord takes on another Dhyāni Buddha as his protégé.

accompanying Bodhisattvas.

1. First we have *Amoghasiddhi* (the All-Accomplishing Wisdom) in the *northern* position of the *maṇḍala*, which represents the direction upwards towards the spheres of enlightenment. The Element ascribed to him is Earth.[21] Only upon the Earthy sphere, where all Elements are mingled and interrelated, can a person truly pass all testings related to the mastery of phenomena, to turn about in the seat of consciousness, from self-focus to the Will-to-Love, and so aspire upwards to the *dharmakāya*. Only through incarnation upon the earth sphere can all attributes of Life be truly mastered. The Bodhisattvas associated with Amoghasiddhi are Vajrapāṇi (north) and Samantabhadra (northwest). Their Consorts are Nrityā and Mālā respectively.
2. The *eastern* direction is attributed to Akṣobhya (the Mirror-Like Wisdom). This is the way inwards to the Heart of Life, and the full development of *bodhicitta*, which is carried lightning-like through the Airy Element. Inward contemplation via the Heart centre produces the spaciousness associated with this Element. The Bodhisattvas associated with Akṣobhya are Kṣitigarbha (east) and Mañjuśri (northeast), with their Consorts being Lāsyā and Ālokā respectfully.
3. The *southern* direction is attributed to *Ratnasambhava* (the Equalising Wisdom) and the Element Water. The major defilements are expressions of this Element. Such Watery substance constitutes the glazes that obstruct the clarity of consciousness through which one sees, thereby conditioning all *saṃsāric* activity. Most human actions are sustained by desire and the emotions until the enlightenment-path is trod as a consequence of seeking Ratnasambhava's equalising Wisdom, wherein the Waters[22] come to be cleansed of their impurities. The Bodhisattvas associated with Ratnasambhava are Ākāśagarbha (south), and Maitreya (southeast), and their Consorts are Dhūpā and Puṣpā respectfully.

---

21 Note that the accompanying *skandhas* and Elements to the Dhyāni Buddhas are changed from what is conventionally presented, in accordance with the explanation presented in Volume three of this series. See Volume 3, chapter 5, of this *Treatise on Mind* for the rationale attributed to the Jinas in the *Bardo Thödol*.

22 Which dissolves substances, thus 'equalising' all phenomena.

4. The *western* direction is attributed to *Amitābha* (the Discriminating Inner Awareness) and the Element Fire, which qualifies the manner of expression of consciousness. This direction represents meditation outwards towards the field of human interrelations, thus the way of serving people through the medium of consciousness. The Bodhisattvas associated with Amitābha are Avalokiteśvara (west) and Viṣkambhin (southwest), whilst their Consorts are Gitā and Ghandhā.

The southeast: Maitreya

The southeast is the direction of outward *expression*, of all previous *dharma* into *saṃsāra,* as directed by Maitreya (the compassionate one) and his Consort Puṣpā. This direction relates to the third of the Eightfold Path, *right speech*. Maitreya is the Bodhisattva denoted to be the future Buddha, whose speech (symbolising all forms of creative or educational expression) will demonstrate its potency in providing the new revelatory lore on the nature of *dharmakāya.*

Lauf states:

> The 'cloud-coloured' (whitish-yellow) Bodhisattva Maitreya (T. Byams-pa) carries the Nāgakeśara branch and the bell (ghaṇṭā). His aim is the enlightenment of hearing (S. śrotravijñāna; T. rNa-ba'i rnam-shes), in order that the ear may perceive the unchanging voice of the dharma. The Ḍākinī of Maitreya is the 'Mother of Pearl' goddess Puṣpā, who carries the symbols of the white lotus and bell. She clears awareness of all previous and karmically effective illusory thinking.[23]

Getty adds:

> In Tibet, Maitreya is also represented both as Buddha and Bodhisattva. As Buddha, he has short curly hair, the *ushṇīsha, ūrṇā*, and long lobed ears. He wears the monastic garment, with the right shoulder bare, and his hands is in *dharmacakra mudrā.* He is seated, but the legs, instead of being locked, are pendent, and the feet may be unsupported. He is the only divinity in the Northern Buddhist pantheon represented seated in the European fashion.
>
> As Bodhisattva he may be also seated with the legs closely locked[24]...but is usually seated in European fashion with each foot

---

23 Lauf, *Tibetan Books of the Dead*, 116.

24 Getty, *Gods of Northern Buddhism*, 22-23.

> resting on a small lotus-flower *āsana*. He is represented as an Indian prince with all the Bodhisattva ornaments, and in the crown is generally a *stūpa*-shaped ornament which is his distinctive mark, but he may be without a crown and have the *stūpa* in his hair. His hands are in *dharmacakra mudrā* and may be holding the stems of flowers supporting his two symbols, the vase and the wheel, on a level with his shoulders. He may be seated on a throne supported by lions and have five Dhyāni Buddhas in the nimbus.
>
> He may have an antelope skin over his left shoulder, in which case he is generally standing. His hands are in *vitarka* and *vara mudrā*, and he either carries the vase, or the two symbols—vase and wheel—are supported by lotus-flowers on a level with each shoulder. It is this latter attitude that he is represented in the group of 'eight Bodhisattva'. He never carries the wheel, which is always supported by a lotus-flower....[25]
>
> Maitreya's two distinctive marks are a *stūpa* in the crown and a scarf wound around the waist and tied to the left side with the ends falling to his feet; but these may be missing.[26]

Lauf stated that Maitreya's aim was 'the enlightenment of hearing in order that the ear may perceive the unchanging voice of the *dharma*'. This means that his purpose is to clear all the obstacles and defilements in people's minds that would prevent them from listening to the inner voice from the Heart. (Which is the Voice of Silence, the enlightened-mind speaking.) Only thus can people properly come to understand the new teachings (Tantras) he will bring. Though being a primary tool, the intellect will however inadequately serve this purpose.

Practitioners must begin to think with the Heart to properly realise the secrets of being/non-being. They must listen to the Heart to know the truth. Only by walking the way of the Heart is liberation from *saṃsāra* possible. Practitioners must learn to reside in the Heart if they aspire to be a Bodhisattva. They must become the Heart in the Head if Buddhahood is to be their life's offering. The Lord of compassion is the Heart speaking, and this is one interpretation for the significance of the coming of the Buddha Maitreya, as symbolised

---

25 Ibid.

26 Ibid., 23.

by this southeastern direction, where outward expression is the focus. It involves the awakening of compassion in many disciple's Hearts simultaneously, so that they manifest the relevant acts of service to those in their community via a new form of engaged Buddhism. Collectively then they also symbolise the emanation of this Bodhisattva.

Maitreya's Consort, Puṣpā, 'clears awareness of all previous and karmically effective illusory thinking' of accumulated distortions in people's minds. All such doctrines have their karmic effects. The compassion of this *ḍākinī* helps to clear these karmic impediments from those hearing Maitreya's teachings. They will then have a capacity to learn that which will propel them as Bodhisattvas far into the new millennium of enlightenment.

The *dharmacakra mudrā* is one of the attributes that tie Maitreya to the seventh Ray of Ceremonial Cyclic Activity, of Demonstrable Power. This *mudrā*[27] manifests as a hand gesture representing the wheel of the *dharma.*[28] The seventh Ray assists in this activity as it bears all conditionings manifesting their purposes in a cyclic or ritualistic fashion. For the southeastern direction we find that Maitreya's expression therefore, is that of perpetually turning the wheel of the *dharma* for all beings involved in *saṃsāra.*[29] It is essentially the effect of this energy of teaching that helps determine the timing of the next turning of the great wheel of Life (the zodiac). The response to what is being taught effectively alters the rate of this wheel's motion. The fact that 'He never

27 *Mudrā* (Tib. phyag rgya): literally 'hand seal'. *Mudrās* are religious and occult signs made with the fingers, as for instance the various hand gestures of the Buddha depicted in Buddhist art. They symbolise different aspects of the teachings, and are often all that is needed to distinguish one type of Buddha from another. In the context of *mahāyoga,* four seals are secured: commitment, action, doctrine, and *mahāmudrā.* Quoting Buddhaguhya, Alex Wayman states; 'There are three kinds of *mudrā*: (1) the *mudrā* that is not transcended. It is not transcended by reflection on true nature (*dharmatā*). (2) the illustration *mudrā.* The illustration with *mudrā* is e.g., of five colours. (3) the hand gesture *mudrā*'. (Alex Wayman, *The Buddhist Tantras* (Motilal Barnasidass, 2005), 113.)

28 In Tantric symbolism of the Jinas this wheel is an expression of Vairocana's teachings.

29 Meaning for cycle after cycle of ritualistic activity, or rather, as the cycles of appearance of phenomena come and go in *saṃsāra,* we find Maitreya engaged in teaching the good lore.

carries the wheel, which is always supported by a lotus-flower' indicates that this 'wheel' is effectively that of the mansions of the zodiac and the cyclic turning of *karma* that manifests in *saṃsāra*. This wheel is thus not his directly; it is something that includes his purpose. From this point of view the spokes of the wheel also represent the petals of the Heart centre. The wheel he carries can also indicate the directions of space,[30] the eight ways that all Initiates will develop under Maitreya's guidance as a consequence of listening to his compassionate eloquence. These directions are the eight ways they must progress to gain the necessary expansions of consciousness in the domains of space.

All of the Ray qualities (departments of Life) are expressed in the seventh Ray purpose, therefore Maitreya embodies the generic, symbolic import of the function of all Bodhisattvas. This makes him the prototype Bodhisattva as far as physical appearance is concerned, and his name, meaning 'compassion', is also the main attribute of Bodhisattvas.

The references to teaching the *dharma*, and the activity of turning this wheel, also implicate the use of the Throat and Sacral centre in combination. The Throat centre is needed to intelligibly convey the message to a receptive audience. The Throat is the power that directs the Fires of Mind into manifestation. The Sacral centre regulates the desire that causes the turning of the wheel. Also, the mastery of this principle will eventually allow one to step off that wheel. We can therefore deduce that much of Maitreya's verbosity concerns teaching the methods whereby desire and attachment to transitory material things can be offset. For these reasons, another main depiction of Maitreya concerns the manifestation of the *vitarka mudrā* (the gesture of discussion), as well as the *varada mudrā* (the bestowal gesture), that signifies the bestowal of the Will-to-Love to those that can master their desire impulses. (The term *vara* means 'most excellent, precious'.) We also have the symbolism of the vase and the wheel, referring to the containment of the elixir of Life, of the enlightenment that he effectively confers upon receptive people during any new cycle of the turning *dharma*-wheel. Nothing can be forced, every new teaching and transformatory effect must be presented at the most opportune moment to the target group to benefit them maximally. The mode of the transformation of desire and self-will

30 There are, after all, eight spokes to the wheel depicted in the iconography.

into the Will-to-Love for humanity presents an insight into the nature of Maitreya's continuous meditation upon human needs. This process necessitates the development of the abstract Mind in those who can practice the import of his teachings.

The seventh Ray also empowers purposeful endeavour in the physical domain, to which inevitably all compassionate action is directed. It thus also governs the nature and function of a *stūpa*, one of Maitreya's major distinguishing marks, being found in his crown or hair. The *stūpa* is not only a reliquary for important Buddhist saints, but also the symbol that grounds the potency of the *dharmakāya* upon the earth. It is a three dimensional representation of the highest teachings knowable concerning the multidimensionality of the Bardo states, in relation to the reflected attributes of the five Dhyāni Buddhas. The sum of such knowledge is then carried in the Head lotus, the nature of which he will reveal to humanity.

His other distinctive mark is a 'scarf wound around the waist and tied to the left side with the ends falling to his feet'. The waist is the area of the Solar Plexus centre, which controls the Watery emotional and desirous *prāṇas*. They must be properly controlled if the path to enlightenment is to be trodden. It symbolises the fact that the entire area below the diaphragm must therefore be effectively girdled. It signifies the need to master all of the lower centres by means of appropriate awareness that will allow comprehension of the nature of emotional-desire attachments and associated perceptions.

The direction 'left' refers to the *iḍā nāḍī* circulation, which starts in the Sacral centre and finds its eventuation in the Throat centre by means of the mastery of the energies of the concrete mind. Maitreya's teachings must address the problem of the misuse of the personal will, if enlightened outcomes are to be produced. The entire field of the desire-mind and its mastery is therefore signified by this scarf and the way that it is tied. It reminds us that the *saṃskāras* associated with the lower carnal self cannot be generated if enlightenment is to ensue.

The quality of the *dharma* attributed to this direction is that of 'non-discriminativeness'. The role of Maitreya, therefore, is to compassionately speak the truth to all that come his way. He does not discriminate as to who comes to hear the *dharma*—all are welcome. They choose the level of teachings they receive from him according to their own inherent capacities to rightfully process and apply what was given. Worthy ones will hold out larger cups to receive the benefits of his outpouring. The skilful means of a Bodhisattva always manifests in choosing the level of the truth to be presented to the worthy supplicant. They are the vessels of reception and the means to educate the entire world in time.

The way of outward expression means that this *dharma* quality allows proper broadcasting of that which originally emanated from the northeast direction of unity—to all approaches and walks of life, so that understanding and consequent mastery of the Life process can proceed. The Bodhisattva seeks out salvation from *saṃsāra* through the powers of observation and by utilising right discrimination to garner the wealth of material presented in the phenomenal world. Therefore all aspects of truth are acknowledged and utilised as a basis for an ever-growing powerhouse of awareness that leads inevitably to great wisdom, and consequent liberation. Outward expression produces an eventual assimilation of that which is useful and a rejection of the remainder on the path of great virtue.

As Maitreya promulgates Ratnasambhava's Equalising Wisdom in the form of a non-discriminatory compassion, the outpouring of this Love transforms all disparaging forces into a grand harmonious unity. The expression of goodwill, or the Will-to-Love, by people must be the eventual outcome of such compassionate action amongst humanity.

The *virtuous root* of the Bodhisattva given for this direction is styled 'efforts for perfect apprehension of the sublime doctrine'. This concerns the way of expression of one's efforts in life to gain a perfect understanding of the nature of the *dharma* in whatever form it is found in the world. It necessitates striving to comprehend the sum of the wisdom teachings found upon the planet so that they can be utilised as a knowledge-bank to truly help everyone.

A general note may be given with respect to the antelope skin draped over his left shoulder. Animal skins associated with a *yogin* or Wrathful Deity convey the development of the major characteristics symbolised by the animal. Hence, an antelope refers to meekness, gentleness. A tiger or lion skin symbolises ferocity in pursuing the enemies of the *dharma*, and steadfastness, fearlessness, in the pursuit of meditation accomplishments. An elephant represents having attained the immense wisdom of the Buddhas.

Maitreya as Buddha

The depiction of Maitreya seated in the European fashion is a prophetic statement implying the eventuation of an incarnation in a Western body. It stands to reason that both the Western and Eastern hemispheres of the world must be properly represented by *dharma* stemming from a Buddha-Mind. Gautama came to enlighten the East, and presented teachings favourably suited to the natural meditative inclination of Easterners. Jesus came later to the Middle East, starting a new religious dispensation that found a dominant role in the Western mind-set. The new Buddha logically therefore must continue the work of his predecessors by manifesting where the need is greatest. This infers taking a Western body to appropriately unify both Eastern and Western streams of Teachings. The present, most materialistic period of human civilisation betokens of the darkest period of the Kālī yuga, signifying a dire need for the appearance of such a one. The synthesis of both Eastern and Western thought in a truly non-prejudicial form of world religion must therefore be compiled. This necessitates providing a *dharma* that reveals the nature of both inner and outer universes—the esoteric eschatological and heuristic doctrine of life and death—as well as a true scientific explication of the nature of all phenomena. The true nature of enlightenment can then be revealed.

When Maitreya appears, he will be the direct representative of the combined qualities of all Bodhisattvas. He grounds their purpose upon the physical plane. The seeds of the new forms of the *dharma* he will bring can thus also be planted into receptive minds telepathically via the many disciples who are receptive to such impression. This produces another interpretation of Maitreya as a group manifestation, and provides an esoteric interpretation of the sense-perceptor that is attributed to him; the ear. It allows him (or the world's Bodhisattvas collectively embodying his function) to hear instructions, or to gather information from:

a. The *dharmakāya*.
b. The Lords of Shambhala.
c. The Council of the Bodhisattvas, and of the domain of the Sambhogakāya Flower.
d. The realm of the *ḍākinīs*.

e. The cries of suffering, and of need from those in the Bardo states.
f. The needs of humanity, specifically in relation to their various philosophies and doctrines, so that he can teach the most appropriate *dharma.*
g. The animal sentience, and little elemental lives throughout Nature's domain. Another way of interpreting this ability to listen to the sounds and rhythms of Nature, involves the ability of the scientific community to study the various laws and conditionings of the sum of the physical domain. Mantric sounds are also produced and all are controlled by means of appropriate ritual occultly enacted by the wise.
h. From the followers of the left-hand path, so that he can know how best to oppose their materialistic mechanisations.

This essentially symbolises the effect of Maitreya's teachings with respect to the syllogisms of extant religions and concepts of humanity. Like his predecessor, Gautama, he will be no sycophant or supplicant of what exists, but will be in a commanding position to reform all-important doctrines, rejecting those that are not viable.

The south: Ākāśagarbha

Ākāśagarbha represents the matrix (*garbha*) of space (*ākāśa*) from which all material phenomena appears. This Mahābodhisattva governs the manifestation of the etheric forms in *saṃsāra.* They represent the lowest, most concreted reflex of the forms existing in the domains of space, the Airy-Aetheric Element. Our concern here is with the energy body (*prāṇamayakośa*) incorporated within the etheric form of each incarnate being. The etheric body can be considered the true form of a person, as it contains the *chakras,* and the entire *nāḍī* system. The *chakras* are effectively matrixes of sentience that present the way to liberation for all beings, whereas the dense physical form is really an automaton to the energy impulses and *saṃskāras* flowing from them. There are great externalised *maṇḍalas* consisting of many *chakras,* these form an etheric grid interrelating all sentient beings through which *prāṇas* flow. The *saṃskāras* that flow through these centres then come to be embodied as the different complexities of the incarnate form.

From this perspective Ākāśagarbha's Bodhisattva vow concerns liberating people from the rigours of the congealed and aberrant *saṃskāras* coursing through their *nāḍī* systems. As all etheric bodies are interrelated, so he works with the entire matrix of appearing lives, the *maṇḍala* of all formative forces regulating the appearance of what people consider the Now. His energies therefore help build the constructs of all forms, and work to ensure that their activities manifest according to an evolutionary plan. This process is facilitated by the fourth of the Eightfold Path, *right or perfect action*, for such action will ensure that the various streams of sentient lives appear in the sequence of the most karmically opportune moments. They must do this if sentience and consciousness are to evolve upon the evolutionary road to enlightenment.

Concerning Ākāśagarbha, Lauf states:

> The Bodhisattva Ākāśagarbha, whose colour is yellow and whose symbols are the sword and bell, is associated with the sense of taste[31] (S. jihvāvijñāna; T. lCe'i rnam-shes). His Ḍākinī is the goddess Dhūpā, who carries a vessel filled with sweet-smelling essences and also the bell.[32]

Getty adds:

> He is usually standing, with his hands in *vitarka* and *vara mudrā,* in which case his special symbol, the sun, is supported by a lotus at his right shoulder, whilst at his left is a lotus-flower supporting a book, the symbol carried by four Bodhisattva of this group[33]...In the reproduction in the Five hundred Gods of *sNar-t'an* he is figured seated, holding in his left hand the stem of a lotus, from which springs a sword. Both hands seem to be in *vitarka mudrā*. In this form he resembles Mañjuśrī.
>
> In both China and Japan he is represented practically the same way. He is standing, a graceful drapery falls from his waist, and a

---

31 Comment upon which of the 'eight consciousnesses' might be assigned to the Bodhisattvas shall be generally avoided, as this exoteric listing is not consistent with the esoteric qualities of these eight consciousnesses of the Yogācāra system, or with the proper function of the Bodhisattva concerned.

32 Lauf, *Tibetan Books of the Dead,* 116.

33 Getty, *Gods of Northern Buddhism*, 101.

> long narrow scarf is wound loosely around the body from the left shoulder to the right hip. The breast and the right shoulder are bare, and the hair is drawn up in a *stūpa*-shaped *ushṇīsha* like Maitreya.[34]

The *Sun* vitalises all plant life, giving the ability to produce flowers, of which our *chakras* are representatives. The plants also utilise the vitality (*prāṇa*) from the sun to produce the nourishment that feeds the animal and human life of the planet. In such functioning of both *chakras* and plants lies the meaning of the lotus that Ākāśagarbha holds in his left hand. Though the lotus is a common iconographic symbol, the fact that the lotus bears a sword here is important, because it signifies Ākāśagarbha's role in controlling the *prāṇas* manifesting via the *chakras* governing all phenomenal Life.[35] Every green and living thing is vitalised as the sun pours its energies downwards into the material domain, whilst the sword specifies the way the energies are to be most effectively utilised.

The 'sweet smelling essences' that Ākāśagarbha's Consort carries in her vessel refers to the perfumes of the *chakras* (flowers), the most refined of the *prāṇas* that they convey. Her principle work therefore concerns the organisation of the little lives whose sentience (the 'perfumes') thrill throughout Nature.

The doctrinal and ontological debates implied by the *vitarka mudrā* utilise syllogisms directed by the Clear Mind to rightly educate all incarnate beings. Though the teachings detail methods of rectifying the impure *nāḍīs* of mental-emotional *saṃskāras* developed by humanity, this logic may be extended to directing streams of animal lives towards their evolutionary goal through mantra. The mantras specifically affect Nature's kingdoms through the potency of Ākāśagarbha's third Ray of Mathematically Exact Activity. The green colouration of this Ray specifically governs the interplay of the plant kingdom, which vitalises all other kingdoms in Nature. The charity associated with the *vara mudrā* is therefore that of pouring blessings of radiant light upon the *nāḍī* and *chakra* system of all manifest Life.

34 Ibid., 101-102.

35 As previously stated, the two cutting edges of the sword are the right and left hand *nāḍīs*, whilst the main body is *suṣumṇā*.

The graceful drapery loosely wound around Ākāśagarbha's body simply signifies his involvement with, and control of, the various *prāṇic* streams of the planet.

The *stūpa*-shaped *ushṇīśa* informs us that, like Maitreya, his principal focus is upon the physical domain, and the projection of the qualities of the five Elements associated with the *stūpa*.

The quality of the *dharma* is that of *'purity'*, referring here to refinement of all attributes pertaining to *saṃsāra*. This is a vast undertaking when all of Nature is included in the equation of the appropriate modes of purification. Inevitably, with respect to humanity it refers to the eventuation of an appropriate purity of sensual qualities that need to be attained by those upon the yogic path. The Base of the Spine centre (regulating the expression of the Element Earth) is the *chakra* governing the southern direction, and becomes the object of focus once the necessary purity has been obtained and the *yogin* is preparing to liberate *kuṇḍalinī.* This centre effectively grounds the potency of the Head lotus, and the entire bodily organism. It should however be noted that the Base of the Spine centre and the Sacral centres form a functioning unity. For this reason the symbolism associated with Ākāśagarbha also relates to a Sacral centre function. He shares this role with Maitreya. The Sacral centre is responsible for the distribution of *prāṇic* vitalisation throughout the form. Therefore the entire path of yogic purity leading to enlightenment is directed via it, necessitating much stern discipline for its control.

The sense attributed to Ākāśagarbha is 'taste', with which he can directly experience all consciousness-attributes developed by sentient beings. The quality of taste allows one to discriminate the bitter from the sweet, etc., as well as to reject 'food' (coarse, base *saṃskāras* or *prāṇas*) which may be harmful to the system or otherwise disagreeable. Ākāśagarbha can be said to effectively consume the *prāṇic* qualities of the *chakras* (as esoterically they are 'plants'), allowing their related qualities to be digested and assimilated so that the proceeds can be excreted in the form of organised *saṃsāra*. Another effect is to stimulate the principle of desire, the mechanism that causes the incarnation ('excretion') of the various factors of Life according to the organising processes of material plane law. This evokes the Sacral centre as the distributor of energies in the body and is the principle organ directing the energies of sexual procreation.

Psychic fastidiousness and purity is essential if one is to produce great 'works to be done for living beings', which represents the *virtuous root* of a Bodhisattva for this southern direction. *Prāṇic* discolouration seriously hampers, pollutes, and misdirects the work that could be made to benefit all beings. The *vitarka mudrā*[36] is therefore utilised to teach the way that people can achieve healthy dispositions. The third Ray facilitates the application of pristine logic to help direct the *prāṇas* to their appropriate destinations. From the stability that the Clear Light affords it produces the manifestation of good works on all levels of expression, from a pure base, pure in motive, and pure in heart. The *saṃskāras* of the pure white *dharma* then flows without obscuration.

The *nāḍī* system, rather than the dense physical realm *per se,* is the most impure of all the realms of perception because here is the grossest immersion of *māyā*, constituting the sum total of the obscurations and defilements developed by humanity. Thus it requires the strongest energies to properly purify the associated *saṃskāras*. The physical mechanism is but an automaton in the way it responds to the energies from the *nāḍīs*.

From the southernmost direction the entire course of evolution can be redirected upwards to greater heights. This redirection process also represents a form of 'argumentativeness'.

Ākāśagarbha is one of the Bodhisattvas assigned to Ratnasambhava, who is concerned with cultivating the Flowers in the world of the *tathāgatagarbha* to produce a well-coordinated integrated tonality of colour and euphony of song in their environment.

The southwest: Nīvaraṇaviṣkambhin[37]

In this direction a full assimilation of the experiences, teachings, and energies coming from the southeast is possible. Consequently, it produces a better comprehension of the processes of Life. Viṣkambhin means 'the eliminator of stains or obstructions'. These stains are those of the defiled

36 The *vitarka mudra* (the gesture of discussion) also symbolises the control of Watery *prāṇas* with the mind, and implies the purity of the other three Elements in the three remaining fingers pointing upwards.

37 The name shall herein be shortened to Viṣkambhin.

mind and of aberrant qualities perceivable in people's auras. They are produced through generally selfish and emotionally based activities. This Bodhisattva's focus consequently relates to the development of the fifth of the Eightfold Path, *right or perfect livelihood* within humanity. He works to ensure that the way that people manifest their livelihoods produces right human livingness in all arenas in their societies. They will then sustain a wholesome considerate culture that will govern our civilisation, removing thereby its ugly psychic impediments (stains) that betoken their most debased forms of activity. Vast arenas of murky, selfish dispensation are all too evident in human societies. Much needs to be accomplished to cleanse this massed turbidity in the planetary *nāḍī* system with streams of lighted substance. The brightness of humanity's auric display will then demonstrate the effect of right livelihood in the moving kaleidoscope of human activity.

Lauf states:

> The reddish-yellow Viṣkambhin, appears in the southwest of the maṇḍala with the book of wisdom and the bell. The book as the symbol of the highest wisdom and the bell with the tone of all-pervading emptiness indicate that this Bodhisattva is able to enlighten the universal or ground-awareness (S. ālayavijñāna; T. Kun-gzhi rnam-shes). His Ḍākinī is the green Gandhā, who carries incense and the bell, and who overcomes all presently-occurring intellectual activities.[38]

Getty adds:

> His special symbol, the full moon, and a symbol which is also carried by several of the Bodhisattva of this group, the *pustaka* (book), are supported by lotus-flowers at either shoulder[39]...The Bodhisattva is seated with legs closely locked. The right hand in *vitarka mudrā,* holds the stem of a lotus on which is a disc, and the left is in *vara mudrā.*
>
> If in company with the Buddha, as liberator of the Serpents, and like Maitreya, Avalokiteśvara, and Mañjuśrī, he may hold a *cintamaṇi* and an ambrosia cup.
>
> In his Yi-dam form he stands with legs apart, on a prostrate personage lying face downward. He wears a tiger-skin hung around

38 Lauf, *Tibetan Books of the Dead*, 117.

39 Getty, *Gods of Northern Buddhism*, 107.

> his waist, and a garland of heads. On top of his *ushṇīsha* is a half thunderbolt; he has the third eye; his right hand holds a *kapāla* (skull-cap) and his left a *grigung* (chopper).[40]

His special embodiment is to demonstrate the *manasic* attributes of wisdom that all Bodhisattvas must emulate. The skilful use of the discerning qualities of the mind allows him to teach how to remove the subtlest of the defilements and obstructions that hinder the development of *bodhicitta*. This necessitates purifying and transforming the emotional defilements (*kliṣṭamanas*)[41] including the heightened forms of religious devotion.

Because the 'stains' are Watery in nature, so this wisdom involves comprehending the nature of the *prāṇas* that reticulate through the minor *chakras* (the Inner Round). This necessitates wise logical control of desire, attachment, avarice, and forms of ego-clinging. Appropriate syllogisms must be developed to counter these impulses.

There are five worthy qualities developed via proper emotional control. They are produced by utilising the emanatory qualities from the Dhyāni Buddhas along this Watery line. Thus Amogasiddhi is the progenitor for the first quality to be utilised (idealism), and Vairocana for the last quality, faith.

1. *Idealism,* to achieve a goal or to study worthy teachings.
2. *Devotion*, to higher ideals, the guru, concepts of the *dharma*, etc.
3. *The Creative Imagination,* the use of the mind and visionary aspect of the clarified emotions to imagine things as they could be, and then to go about producing that. (For example, concepts of liberation.)
4. *Aspiration,* the driving energy that produces the achievement of the highest goals, which makes one leap into a higher field of Revelation.
5. *Faith,* without which nothing of real value could be accomplished. One can ruminate that something is true or correct, but without demonstrating faith one would not manifest the steps to complete knowledge or reality. For example, until it is experienced the average practitioner must have faith that *śūnyatā* is attainable.

---

40 Ibid.

41 His special sense of 'ground awareness' can be attributed to *kliṣṭamanas* in the Yogācāra system.

The southwest direction collectivises the gain of the entire evolutionary process. (This involves a complete understanding of the experiences first seeded in the southeast.) The reddish-yellow colour of Viṣkambhin is the general colouring of the mind, which facilitates the attainment of wisdom. Such wisdom is more than a mere intellectual compendium of knowledge; it also concerns the right utilisation of knowledge to produce enlightenment. His consort directs *karma* to offset the reification of various facets of mind that may occur through the accumulation of knowledge. The dangers of over-concretion of mind need to be avoided; otherwise too many human units will follow the left-hand practices of the dark brotherhood. The purpose, therefore, is to assist humanity to develop the abstraction of mind that is the Clear Light. We saw that his southern brother (Ākāśagarbha) expresses the qualities of the Sun, the *prāṇas* of which are conveyed by the *piṇgalā nāḍī*. It represents the qualities of the spaciousness of consciousness that he infuses into the collective *nāḍī* system of the planet. The symbol of Viṣkambhin is the sun's sister, *the Moon*. The Moon expresses the qualities of the *iḍā nāḍī*, the attributes of intelligence, and of emotional-mental characteristics. The work of Viṣkambhin therefore concerns transforming these characteristics into their enlightened correspondences. He chops rationalisations into comprehensible bits with his *grigung*, and properly dissects irrational syllogisms, so that they can be integrated into a comprehensive *maṇḍala* of reason. This facilitates granting people's wishes for enlightenment by means of the 'wish-fulfilling jewel *(cintamaṇi)*' in his possession. The dark pathways of mind that the *iḍā nāḍī* fosters may thereby be avoided.

The *chakra* utilised is the Throat centre (*viśuddha chakra*), which is responsible for the complete control of all the forces and qualities of the mind. This allows building correct syllogisms wherever illogic abounds. The associated fifth Ray of Scientific Reasoning assists in assuring that people utilise the rigours of a broad-minded logical methodology in their thought constructs. The goal is always focussed upon drawing forth impressions from the abstract Mind.

Much of the symbolism related to Viṣkambhin stems from the fact that this southwest position represents the place wherein real progress is made upon the yogic path of ascent. Life's experiences have been assimilated and their purpose comprehended, leaving one free to pursue the quest of liberation. Providing to *yogins* the necessary tools to pursue their meditations allows Viṣkambhin to wear a tiger skin in his *yidam*[42] form, signifying his fierce prowess at stalking the *siddhis* to be mastered. The garland of heads signify conquering all aspects of the process of dying, including that of the transformation of *saṃskāras.*

The awakened all-seeing Eye, the *vajra* (thunderbolt), the *kapāla* containing the blissful 'blood' of enlightenment (*bodhicitta),* and the chopper used to cut away and flail the attributes of *saṃsāra,* are all implements utilised by a *yogin.* The *yogin* works principally from either the south or southwest position of the *maṇḍala* of the crosses in order to master *saṃsāra.* The knowledge gained (from the southwest) through the process of mastery allows the *yogin* to use the weaponry to direct the transformed *prāṇas* to the centres above the diaphragm, signified by the northern arms of this eight-armed cross.

Viṣkambhin is the liberator of serpents, signifying the mastery of the *kuṇḍalinī* that awakens as a consequence of yogic attainment. We should note here, however, that because the moon is his special symbol, so the form of enlightenment that is specifically gained in this direction is the *ālayavijñāna* enlightenment, which comes as a consequence of the mastery of Mind. The *śūnyatā* enlightenment is facilitated by means of further Bodhisattvic activity in the western direction under the auspices of Avalokiteśvara. The *dharmakāya* enlightenment is effectively honed in the northwestern position under the auspices of Samantabhadra, when the Initiate prepares to enter cosmos as a consequence of becoming a Buddha. The western side of the eight-armed cross is therefore principally concerned with these main stages of yogic ascent as one travels the way of the Bodhisattva *bhūmis.*

The quality of *dharma* attributed to the southwest direction is 'being manifest'. This concerns the way that *saṃsāra* is used as a vehicle to liberation via the transformation of the little serpents of desire whenever they appear in the *nāḍī* system, as visualised in one's meditative life.

---

42 Yidam (Skt: *iśtadevata*): Tutelary deity, a personal protector for one's practice, a guide to enlightenment. Traditionally, a vow binding one to a personal deity or meditation *maṇḍala* as the root of accomplishment. The Yidam is the main practice that flows from the preliminaries of a yogic path. It includes the stages of development and completion as a bridge to the accomplishment of Mahāmudrā and rDzogs-chen. The Yidam becomes the holder of the views developed by these attainments.

All attributes of *saṃsāra* must be experienced and utilised through being physically incarnate; 'being manifest'. The symbols of the path to enlightenment are manifest throughout *saṃsāra*. Everywhere one looks one can come to find signposts to Viṣkambhin's guiding light of Mind. Once they are recognised then the ways of the various forms of yoga open before one, allowing them to be used to gain the enlightenment that mastery of Mind confers. Viṣkambhin's Consort, who carries the bell of 'all-pervading emptiness', sets the karmic stage allowing all candidates for enlightenment to cleanse their minds from concreted intellectual obscurations and diversions, so that eventually the Clear Light of Mind is found. Then *śūnyatā* (the 'all-pervading emptiness') can become the true domain of residence for the attained *yogin*.

The *virtuous root* is that of 'non abandonment of propensity of desire for phenomena'. Thus those working in this direction do not omit considerations of phenomena of any type from their experiences. Everything experienced must be properly understood in order to be converted into wisdom. Total involvement with all possible types of experiences attainable by one evolving upwards from this direction allows the gaining of compassion for the plight of all sentient beings. Myriads of experiences are needed to comprehend the purpose of the pain, trials and tribulations of all people. Viṣkambhin's guiding light comes because of such experiences. Having fully developed the mind, and by projecting its vision upwards, it must then evoke the compassionate stance of Avalokiteśvara for the various twisted and oft agonising paths people travel upon. Working together, the three main Mahābodhisattvas of the mutable cross of evolutionary development in humanity: Mañjuśrī, Maitreya, and Viṣkambhin, cyclically lay the foundations that develop into the Bodhisattva path. This is specifically symbolised by the qualities of Avalokiteśvara, the prototype Bodhisattva. This is the secret of the *cintamaṇi's* potency and the ambrosial cup that they all hold. It is the Bodhisattva path that produces the wish-fulfilling gem and the nectar of immortality that is the purpose of all of life's quests. Buddhahood is gained as a consequence.

The west: Avalokiteśvara

This direction represents the way outwards to the world of human interrelationships in general. Avalokiteśvara's specific focus concerns looking downwards to the sufferings of humanity and to the mechanism of removing that suffering. This is a reason why Avalokiteśvara (the 'downward-looking Lord') is the most popular of the Bodhisattvas.[43] He works to assist people to turn their gaze upwards to his realm, so that they can be educated with the correct *dharma*. He consequently touches the hearts of humanity with his symbolic 1,000 hands, teaching the nature of compassion. These hands are extensions of the energies of the Heart in the Head centre, the Thousand-petalled lotus (*sahasrāra padma*), projected by this Bodhisattva to arenas of concern within humanity. They reach out to wherever *saṃskāras* are to be transformed so that people can eventually find their rightful place as part of the governing *maṇḍala* of accomplishment, viewed as a Heart lotus. Avalokiteśvara therefore utilises the Head centre to reach out to the sum of the human domain so that people can be lead to the Heart of all that is. The entire course of human civilisation thus becomes the object of his compassionate attention, specifically with respect to the activity of the world's Solar Plexus centre (*maṇipūra chakra*). In the regulatory activity of all the associated minor *chakras* in the body we see the effects of myriad transformatory battles. The purpose here concerns the transformation of people's selfish wills to goodwill, or the Will-to-Love. He works via the Heart in the Head centre to transform the Watery disposition of humanity into the compassionate activity that is the way of the Heart.

The above is but a transposition of vision from what happens inside the human form to the body corporeal of humanity. The symbolism therefore can also relate to an individual *yogin's* meditation upon the needs of his incarnate form, where each hand represents the five fingers of *prāṇas* conveyed in the *nāḍī* system from the Head lotus.

Avalokiteśvara is a conduit of the sixth Ray of Devotion. This means the transformation of massed human emotions, aspirational zeal, and devotional outpourings into their higher correspondences.

---

43 The term Avalokiteśvara is a construct of the terms 'avaloka', meaning 'down towards the *lokas*' (domains of perception), and Īśvara, meaning 'capable or all-controlling Lord'. Īśvara is the personalised Deity of the Hindus, the overlooking one, the world Soul or Logos, from which the incarnation process proceeds and into which it resolves. He is the supreme Lord, who oversees manifest space.

The associated *chakra* is the Solar Plexus, which governs all of the *prāṇas* generated below the diaphragm. Such outpourings also involve the worst excesses of the muddied affairs of the selfish, manipulative, self-centred individuals, which cause so many arenas of service for all Bodhisattvas. Devotion to noble causes, creativity, and high aspiration may be generated through the process of experiencing and learning from the emotions. Humanity thereby becomes more compassionate. Such qualities are antidotes to gross desires, selfishness, and sensuality. All attributes of the emotions: desires, lust, selfishness, avarice, cupidity, evilly focused devotion, attachments to material comforts, and every form of glamour, are the cause of people's many woes. They also are the most difficult qualities for humanity to overcome.

As these qualities are the basis for perpetual wanderings in the Six Realms, so Avalokiteśvara stands steadfast in this western orientation to show humanity the way out of the need for rebirth by cleansing the cesspools created by their emotions. In Buddhist iconography, therefore, we find his presence in each of these realms, with the appropriate symbolism, to assist those suffering to find the way out. In Volume 3, chapter 3 of this series it was stated that all of these realms are really zones for experiencing karmic repercussions by members of the human kingdom.[44] There is no birthing into the animal kingdom *per se,* except from the point of view that a human form is an animal body.

Lauf states:

> The fifth Bodhisattva is Avalokiteśvara with an eight-petalled lotus and the bell. He is associated with the sense of the body (S. kāyavijñāna; T. Lus-kyi rnam-shes). His Ḍākinī is the coral-red goddess Gitā, who carries a lute. She appears in order to enlighten all perceptions of tone with the sound of the heavenly music of the Kinnaras[45], which permeates the spheres.[46]

---

44 In fact, all of the divisions of the Six Realms, other than that of physical plane human habitation, really represent experience in the sub-planes of the Watery astral plane. This is governed by the expression of the *saṃskāras* processed by the Solar Plexus centre.

45 Kinnara: winged celestial being residing in the paradise realms.

46 Lauf, *Tibetan Books of the Dead*, 116-117.

Alice Getty adds:

> In the *Mani-Kambum* it is related that 'once upon a time, Amitābha, after giving himself up to earnest meditation, caused a white ray of light to issue from his right eye, which brought Padmapāṇi (Avalokiteśvara) Bodhisattva into existence'. It goes on to say that Amitābha blessed him, whereupon the Bodhisattva brought forth the prayer: '*Oṁ Maṇi Padme Hūṁ!*' 'Oh! The jewel (of creation) is in the lotus!' (Beal).
>
> Avalokiteśvara, the Measured Light of the Sun and Moon, is thus the reflex or spiritual son of Amitābha, Buddha of Infinite Light. As the personification of Power, the All-pitying One, he is the most popular divinity in the Mahāyāna Buddhist Pantheon[47]...Another reason for his popularity is that he is believed to have created the fourth world, which is the actual universe, and he is therefore our creator...[48]
>
> Avalokiteśvara is sometimes represented with five heads, in which case he resembles Śiva as Mahādeva with five heads; but his form with more than one head is usually double that number, with the head of Amitābha on top, making eleven heads in all. He is often represented in *yab-yum* attitude with his *Śakti,* but there are examples where he holds his *yum* on his knee in archaic manner, as Śiva holds Pārvatī.
>
> In his earliest form he is represented with one head and two arms, and either sitting or standing. His hands may be in 'prayer' *mudrā*, or the right in 'charity' and the left in 'argument' *mudrā*. His most popular non-Tantra form is Padmapāṇi...He is worshipped in a triad with Mañjuśrī, God of Wisdom, and Vajrapāṇi, God of Power, on either side. [49]

Avalokiteśvara is assisted in his task by the Bodhisattvas of the various arms of the *maṇḍala* of the fixed and mutable crosses. Kṣitigarbha, however, wielding the second Ray of Love-Wisdom (the fundamental energy of all the Bodhisattvas), is the source of the transformatory energy of Love used by Avalokiteśvara. (They stand as polar opposites on the horizontal arm of the fixed cross.) Their combined potency is therefore wielded to cure the predominant emotionally biased ailments of our societies. A reason for Avalokiteśvara's popularity therefore relates to his direct involvement with fostering

---

47 Getty, *Gods of Northern Buddhism*, 57.

48 Ibid., 58.

49 Ibid., 60.

people's right emotional and aspirational qualities towards high ideals, especially through religious devotional imagery. Here we can see how Avalokiteśvara appropriates the sixth of the Eightfold Path, *right or perfect effort,* to help turn humanity away from their addictions to gross pleasures and sensual activities, to aspire towards enlightenment.

Because a vast wealth of information concerning Avalokiteśvara exists, only the most pertinent symbolism need be explicated here. Govinda has presented excellent information in his book,[50] especially in relation to the mantra Oṁ Maṇi Padme Hūṁ, which thus needs no detailed repetition here.

He is said to embody the 'sense of the body' (touch), which his 1,000 hands symbolise, each with an eye in the palm to see into the hearts of humanity that he touches. He can therefore effect revelations in any of the petals of the Head centre (the thousand-petalled Lotus) of a devotee or meditator. This allows right education of the sum of the human persona, allowing people to correctly experience the vast vistas of the *ālayavijñāna* that is the domain of Mind from whence this 'touch' emanates. His technical mechanism is the well-known mantra Oṁ Maṇi Padme Hūṁ! This is one of the most important of the mantric phrases, especially sacred to the Tibetans, because it invokes the compassion of this all merciful downward looking One. The mantra allows devotees that recite it to gain receptivity to the intended meaning of its syllables. Oṁ is the mantric word that resonates the note of the liberation of consciousness. The word Maṇi means 'radiant jewel', here of the *maṇḍala* that is the foundation of manifest space. Padme means 'lotus blossom' (signifying the entire *chakra* system) and Hūṁ brings the entire expression into manifestation through the power of the compassionate Heart.

This mantra also effectively embodies the main levels of the Sambhogakāya Flower, and expresses the properties of this Kingdom. The Oṁ denotes the collective consciousness of all the Flowers of humanity, which the practitioner is aligned to when yogically reciting this mantra. The Maṇi resonates to the *maṇḍalic* construction upon which each Flower is based. The Padme denotes the qualities of the actual form of the Flower, whilst the Hūṁ expresses its downwards focussed

50 Govinda, *Foundations of Tibetan Mysticism.*

meditation upon the receptive mind of the personal-I. Avalokiteśvara's experience of 'body' therefore refers to the manifest form of these Flowers. He works to infuse into them greater receptivity to the energy of Love-Wisdom from the domain of the Mahābodhisattvas. These Flowers can then project the result of their increased stimulation into the evolving human personalities that they overshadow.[51]

The quality of 'sense of the body' can also be considered the body of the *bhavacakra* (wheel of the Six Realms). When symbolised by the six syllables of the mantra Oṁ Maṇi Padme Hūṁ, the *Oṁ* is said to relate to the realm of the gods, the *ma* to that of the Titans, the *ṇi* to that of humans, the *pad* to the realm of animals, the *me* to that of hungry ghosts, and the *Hūṁ* to the hell realms.[52] This lordship over the Six Realms makes Avalokiteśvara the prime example of the Bodhisattva ideal. Here we have veiled much concerning the mysteries of how *saṃsāra* is organised, based on the qualities of a hexagram.

Avalokiteśvara is said to be 'the Measured Light of the Sun and Moon',[53] which means that he fuses the qualities of both the lunar Viṣkambhin and the solar Ākāśagarbha. We thus have the union of wisdom and compassion, in this outward direction of educating humanity by way of *bodhicitta*.

His Consort (Gitā) has a lute that plays the heavenly music that will clarify all perceptions of her listeners in the Six Realms.[54] They will then hear the internal mantras and words of wisdom that will

---

51 Note that detail as to the special relation of Avalokiteśvara to the Sambhogakāya Flower will be presented in the next chapter where the iconographical depiction of his eleven heads, thousand arms, etc., is examined.

52 See Lauf, *Tibetan Books of the Dead*, 118-130, or Govinda's *Foundation of Tibetan Mysticism*, 228-241.

53 Getty, *Gods of Northern Buddhism*, 57.

54 This form of Tārā—Gitā is not the usual *śakti* of Avalokiteśvara, his Consort is generally the white or green Tārā (Tib. sgrol ma). She is said to be born from the compassionate tears of Avalokiteśvara, thus is associated with pristine cognition and specifically, compassion for the sufferings of all women. Of the twenty-one forms of Tārā, the two main ones generally depicted are a green one and a white one, with slightly different qualities. Green Tārā equates with protection, white Tārā with healing and longevity. Tārā is the Buddhist equivalent of the Holy Mary of Catholics, and is the most popular of all the Deities to the Tibetan laity. The word can be translated as 'saviouress, she who liberates via sympathetic and compassionate understanding'.

guide them away from their enfeebled morals, vile, and reprehensible ways, enabling them to achieve more appropriate rebirths. The sound positively conditions the pathways in the substance wherein they are confined, facilitating their release, according to the dictates of *karma*.

Avalokiteśvara emanates from Amitābha's right eye, the eye of wisdom,[55] as the compassion of this western oriented Dhyāni Buddha. This is also the means of vitalising the entire *piṇgalā nāḍī* system with that which Avalokiteśvara represents. This emanation from the right eye of Amitābha signifies the means of mitigating the worst attributes of the desire-mind in humanity. Indeed, this is a most difficult task to accomplish. The main beneficiaries are the devotional masses whose gratitude he has captured, and to whom Avalokiteśvara is seen as the prototype Bodhisattva.

The yogic objective along this *piṇgalā* line concerns the transformation of the defilements of *kliṣṭamanas* into *bodhicitta*. Amitābha empowers the entire domain of Mind with his Discriminating Inner Vision. Avalokiteśvara is the mechanism to assist individuals to negate the effects of the concretions of mind, for those within levels of mind ensnared in materialism.

He is also given the name Padmapāṇi, the holder of the lotus, which (esoterically) refers to the Inner Round series of minor *chakras*, that are controlled by the Solar Plexus centre. The implication being that his compassion works to cleanse the *prāṇas* flowing through all of the *chakras* of the body. The minor *chakras* are important because the bodily organs represent their externalisations. The consequent good health or diseases of these organs depends on the quality of the *prāṇas* conveyed through the minor centres. The eight-petalled lotus he holds in his right hand is taken to represent the Heart centre in the Tibetan system,[56] whose energies Avalokiteśvara utilises to cleanse the centres below the diaphragm. From his western position he

55 Viṣkambhin, the other Mahābodhisattva taking Amitābha as his Jina thus represents the left eye, that of knowledge.

56 The relation of the eight-petalled to the twelve-petalled lotus has already been indicated. With respect to the Heart centre the eight petals are exoteric, signifying the early unfoldment of the Heart centre's activity, when only the *prāṇas* of the eight consciousnesses are being expressed, and the eight-spoked wheel is being activated. The full twelve petals are activated when the individual can *prāṇically* channel all of the qualities of the twelve signs of the zodiac. A detailed explanation of this will be provided later.

compassionately looks down to the arenas of activity associated with Maitreya, Ākaśagarbha, and Viṣkambhin.

The Life that incarnates upon a planet, such as the earth, is really that which exists below the diaphragm of a Logos, wherein the Solar Plexus reigns supreme as the 'abdominal brain'. (With all minor *nāḍī* streams leading to it for processing.) In such esotericism lies the foundation for the statement that 'he is believed to have created the fourth world, which is the actual universe'.[57] Vast is the study for an awakened one with respect to the schema of cosmic Incarnation. Pouring forth the Watery dispensation from the cosmic astral plane, therefore, he 'looks down in compassion' (as a Christ) towards the three abovementioned Mahābodhisattvas, who are responsible for the distribution of these *prāṇas* into the sum of our planetary Life. Tārā, being the organising principle of the Waters, is then the Mother of all Life upon a planetary domain.

Amitābha, Avalokiteśvara and Tārā can be considered a *trimūrti.* Amitābha represents the Will or Power aspect that brings the *bindu* of the entire world sphere into activity via the domain of the Mind. Avalokiteśvara represents the compassion of all Bodhisattvas, flooding the lives that spring forth with the Love that is the leitmotiv of their evolutionary journeying (the development of consciousness). Tārā is the Mother of the sum of the cyclic activity of *saṃsāra* wherein the lives evolve. She anchors their potency into physical manifestation.

From the point of view of the diagram of the Mahābodhisattvas on page 281, we see that Vajrapāṇi and Mañjuśrī represent the combined Head centre that when focused via Avalokiteśvara can vitalise the entire formed realms *(saṃsāra)* via the Solar Plexus centre that governs the activity therein, in Nature's domain (governed by Tārā). This is the main reason why these three Mahābodhisattvas are often seen together in Buddhist iconography.

The quality of the *dharma* attributed to this western direction is 'hostility against obstacles'. These obstacles are those presented by humanity that are antagonistic to the path of enlightenment, such as the 'five poisons' which are: desire, hatred, ignorance, jealousy, and

57 Here his role as Īśvara (Tib. dban phyung) is indicated, who, as previously stated, is the world Soul or Logos, from which the incarnation process proceeds and into which it resolves.

pride.[58] The 'hostility' represents the activity that needs to be evoked to overcome the massed desire-mind that humanity have developed by their materialistic, selfish, and sensual ways. The virtuous root of the Bodhisattva given for this direction is 'non-reluctance from fetters of the highest virtues'. They are called 'fetters' because they are still *saṃsāric*, even though their purpose is to liberate people from their illusions. A Bodhisattva is handicapped, fettered, by being born into *saṃsāra,* which necessitates working to overcome all the travails of life before being able to help liberate others.

The northwest: Samantabhadra

This direction implies that the principal function of Samantabhadra (meaning 'universal kindness') concerns the outward progression of the entire *maṇḍala*, making it more expansive with respect to the space (of human consciousness) that it incorporates. His mode of activity is thus specifically that of the seventh of the Eightfold Path, *right or perfect concentration or mindfulness.* Such mindfulness is upon the *maṇḍala* as a whole and where it is going to. To travel ahead to the future, all hindering defilements must be left behind. The way that they will come to be transformed must therefore be planned for. His form of 'kindness' also fine tunes the guidance people must receive for their next step towards liberation. It is the process that brings them into the next domain of revelatory awareness.

Concerning Samantabhadra, Lauf states:

> The third Bodhisattva is the 'topaz-coloured' Samantabhadra, who carries the ear of corn and the bell. His realm is the sense of smell (S. ghrāṇavijñāna; T. sNa-ba'i rnam-shes). His Prajñā is the Ḍākinī Mālā, whose symbols are the garland of flowers and the bell; she leads awareness towards religious thinking.[59]

Getty adds:

> Samantabhadra was looked upon, among the ancient Northern

58 Development of the Wisdoms of the five Dhyāni Buddhas represents the antidotes to these poisons.

59 Lauf, *Tibetan Books of the Dead*, 116.

> Buddhists sects, as Highest Intelligence, a primordial Buddha; but his popularity diminished when the two great sects, the dKar-hGya-pa (Red Bonnets) and dGe-lugs-pa (Yellow Bonnets), set up Vajradhara as Ādi-Buddha.
>
> Certain of the Yogācārya sects claim that Samantabhadra, instead of Vairocana (his Dhyāni-Buddha), was the founder of the Yoga system, and look upon him as divinity of Religious Ecstasy. He is the special divine patron in Japan in those who practise Hokkésammai (ecstatic meditation).
>
> Samantabhadra, reflex of Vairocana, is the first Dhyāni-Bodhisattva corresponding with the five celestial Jinas, or Dhyāni-Buddhas, and is one of the group of eight Dhyāni-Bodhisattva found in Northern Buddhist temples. He is represented with the crown, the ornaments and princely garments of the Bodhisattva, and holds his symbol, the *cintāmaṇi,* in his left hand, or it may be supported by a blue lotus at his left shoulder. The right hand makes *vitarka mudrā:* the hand raised—the thumb and index touching at the tips forming the 'triangular pose'. He may be either seated or standing; and is sometimes with his *Śakti* in the *yab-yum* attitude.
>
> When in the group of eight Bodhisattva, he is standing with his hands in 'argument' and 'charity' *mudrā,* holding the stems of lotus-flowers which support his special symbol, the *cintāmaṇi,* at right, and an accessory symbol, the *vajra,* at the left. If painted, he is yellow.[60]

The 'ear of corn' refers to the great spiritual wealth of this Bodhisattva that nourishes all beings. It specifically signifies manifold abundance because of the many individual corn kernels on the cob. The bell sounds out the notes of the *dharma,* teaching all beings the nature of the 'all-pervading emptiness' of phenomena.

The garland of flowers held by his consort refers to the fact that she vitalises the qualities of the entire *maṇḍala* of the Bodhisattvas, which are expressed in the form of *chakras.* This is part of the function of the dual Splenic centre, which this Bodhisattva and his consort embodies as part of the *maṇḍala* of the Mahābodhisattvas. This centre processes the toxins and *prāṇas* to be rejected from the system, and recycles those found to be worthy for the expression of the Now. This translates as the conversion, transformation, or else the rejection of

60 Getty, *Gods of Northern Buddhism*, 47.

the worst of the *saṃskāras* developed by humanity at any time. With respect to the entire panoply of humanity such rectification takes vast cycles of activity, as many differing streams of *karma* must be taken into account. This involves assessing what must be given according to the level of expression of the true need of the target human units. Meditative analysis of group or massed psychology must be undertaken upon what qualities can be transformed, recycled, and what can be rejected because the human psyche allows it so.

The wish-fulfilling gem (*cintāmaṇi*) that Samantabhadra possesses aptly fulfils the function of the ability to turn base metals (base *saṃskāras*) into spiritual gold (enlightenment-perceptions) through the transformation and transmutative function of the Splenic centre. The appropriate processing of *prāṇas* makes this an inevitability as the 777 incarnations run their course for any consciousness-stream. Because the *cintāmaṇi* embodies the powers of the diamond-Mind of a Buddha, so it indicates the true quality of the refractive nature of the combined qualities of the Bodhisattvas that are Samantabhadra's dispensation. He cyclically projects these outwards as the gain of any evolutionary cycle. The *vajra* that he is depicted holding in his left hand is the symbol of immutable power, and indicates that such power comes only as a consequence of having transmuted base *saṃskāras* into spiritual gold, allowing *kuṇḍalinī* to be liberated. It is the emblem of both Akṣobhya and also Amoghasiddhi, (the Jina that reflects the Ādi Buddha into manifestation), who carries the double *vajra* (*viśvavajra*). The yellow colour of this Bodhisattva betokens the general colouring of the *prāṇas* that are processed by the Splenic centre.

The northwest position is important with respect to Samantabhadra and his relationship to the twelve-petalled Splenic centre I. When viewing the *maṇḍala* of the Bodhisattvas as a primary *chakra*[61] it is focussed outward towards cosmos. Cosmos here represents the *chakras* above or 'beyond' the diaphragm of empirical *saṃsāric* concern. It is the universe of various Buddha-fields. Splenic centre I effectively projects the gain of the current field of service to the Heart of the greater *maṇḍala* of which the *maṇḍala* of the Mahabodhisattvas is a part. This

61 In this example, this primary *chakra* is the Solar Plexus centre, because we are concerned with the conversion of base mental-emotional *saṃskāras* of humanity.

means that all *nirvāṇees* from our earth pass through his gate as they proceed 'to the other shore'. Samantabhadra therefore regulates the nature and pace of their journeying. The purpose of the eight-petalled Splenic centre II, on the other hand, is inwardly focussed. Its function is the recycling and transformation of *prāṇas* to be expressed in the *maṇḍala* of the Mahābodhisattvas. It is the sewer and waste processing system for the indigenous *prāṇas* the corporeal form needs. This dual function of Samantabhadra is what provides the esoteric basis for his role as both a Bodhisattva and a primordial Buddha. Also, the appellation of a Primordial Buddha befits him because he embodies the combined qualities of the eight Bodhisattvas and is responsible for the general outward expansion of their compassionate emanations. These functions can reasonably equate with what we could expect a Buddha to manifest.

The meanings of the argument and charity *mudrās* have been explained with respect to other Bodhisattvas, indicating that these are common functions of Bodhisattvas. Similarly, the blue colour of the lotus that is 'his special emblem' is that of the Love-Wisdom possessed by all of the Bodhisattvas.

The quality of the *dharma* assigned to this direction is 'deliverance from passions'. 'Passions' refer to strong emotional attributes, even those of passionately or reverently clinging to aspects of the *dharma* or images of the deities with altruistic intent. Absolution from all passions produces that perfect equanimity of mind that is the hallmark of a liberated being. The term 'passion' also has a reference to the expression of sexual desire, from which one must also be freed. Once these passions (forms of bondage) are eliminated, the outward expansion of consciousness that this direction represents is possible.

The *virtuous root* is the 'non satisfaction in searching for the accumulation of merits'. This phrase can be analysed in two ways:

a. One cannot be satisfied in searching for 'merits' if the goal of *śūnyatā* is to be gained, as all such merit can be conceived as fetters in their own right. *Śūnyatā* is void of all such accumulations. Merits come on their own accord as one treads the path, and as a consequence one need not search for them. They are the spontaneous expression of the activity a Bodhisattva manifests to help sentient beings. If there is no 'searching' then there is nothing to be satisfied or unsatisfied about.

'Searching for merits' is a disguised form of ego posturing. True humbleness that is the foundation of egolessness is the mechanism of release for all upon the path. In the pursuit of such humbleness no *karma*-engendering 'merits' are accumulated. A natural spontaneity in response to need is the hallmark of the Bodhisattva, wherein the self-evident task is fulfilled by the most skilful means possible. In this the Bodhisattva seeks only gain for others.

b. At the level of activity of all the Mahābodhisattvas, we see that they are beyond the junior level of spirituality that aspirants undertake who search for the accumulation of merits that will lead them to tread the Bodhisattva path. Specifically, with respect to the outward-going northwest direction wielded by Samantabhadra; an accumulation of Bodhisattvic merit would cause the *maṇḍala* he is responsible for to swell unduly because he would be inwardly focussed towards humanity, and not outwards to cosmos. This would restrict the forward momentum for the entire meditative plan of the *maṇḍala*. There would be no door of release for *nirvāṇees*. The *maṇḍala* must have its own inward momentum, which all the other Mahābodhisattvas share in, but it must also have a forward-progressive motion, which is the specific purpose of the first Ray attribute wielded by Samantabhadra to achieve. The first Ray of Will or Power always dynamically projects the construct towards the future. In this case towards the greater cosmic inclusiveness veiled by *śūnyatā*. In this process humans come to be transformed into Buddhas, leaving all 'merit' that is the *karma* of human interrelations behind.

His special sense is *smell*. Esoterically, smell is that which liberates, it brings perception to the highest form of refinement possible, necessitating the evocation of the highest Will to sacrifice all attributes of *saṃsāric* affiliations for the good of the all.[62] It concerns the *yogin's* ability to control the finest of the Airs. All *saṃskāras* are thereby cleansed of gross defilements, allowing the *yogin* to make the quantum leap into a higher category or order of revelation than ever before achieved.

---

62 The astute student can similarly analyse the esoteric ramifications of the sense-attributes for the other Mahābodhisattvas.

The north: Vajrapāṇi

Vajrapāṇi, the last of the eight Bodhisattvas, stands at the northern direction, thereby focussing our vision upwards to the regulating Head centre, the Dharmakāya Flower, or to Shambhala. This direction is represented also by the eighth of the Eightfold Path, *right or perfect bliss or absorption.* The absorption can be into any of the above, and also into That which is unconditioned, Void of all discernible characteristics *(śūnyatā).* The name Vajrapāṇi means the bearer of the *vajra,* the adamantine power of the Dhyāni Buddhas. It is both a liberating power and also that emanatory energy that sustains the entire fabric of space. It evokes the plenitude of the *sahasrāra padma* (Head centre) wherein the entire *maṇḍala* of the Mahābodhisattvas is incorporated. It processes the functioning of all activities related to the liberation of consciousness from the trammels of *saṃsāra.* It allows the entire Life of the *maṇḍala* to be visualised, rightly integrated, properly vitalised, and directed over time. He thus represents the principle of the liberating power of all Bodhisattvas, as exemplified by the qualities of the *vajra.* Its acquisition opens the doors to high domains and revelatory states of bliss for those who pass testings of Initiation. His special 'sense' is therefore spiritual power, which emanates from the *sahasrāra padma.* Its petals awaken one after another as a consequence of a veridical meditation towards liberation; this is the expression of the Dharmakāya Way, the *vajrayāna.* The Jina Wisdoms disseminate this power via the five Rays of Mind, as governed by the third Ray department in the Council of Bodhisattvas. However, all Ray lines must be utilised by Vajrapāṇi to manifest his directive purpose. When all attributes of the *ālayavijñāna* environment come under its control, the first stage of mastery of the petals of this lotus has been accomplished.

Lauf states:

> The eighth Bodhisattva is the 'tourmaline-green' Vajrapāṇi (the vajra-bearer), who holds the diamond scepter (vajra) and the ghaṇṭā. He appears in order to enlighten all hindrances still remaining in collective awareness (S. ādānavijñāna; T. Nyon-yid rnam-shes). His blue-green Ḍākinī Nṛtyā carries a bowl of heavenly food as a foretaste of the bliss of liberation.[63]

63 Lauf, *Tibetan Books of the Dead*, 117.

Getty adds:

> Besides being the protector of the Nāgas against the Garuḍas, Vajrapāṇi is the impeccable enemy of the demons[64]...(which) seems to explain the presence of Vajrapāṇi as guardian of the Elixir of Life in a triad with Amitāyus, who holds the ambrosia vase, and Padmapāṇi, who carries a *kalaśa* (ewer of *amṛta).*
>
> Vajrapāṇi is the second Dhyāni-Bodhisattva corresponding to the five Celestial Jinas. He is also one of the group of eight Dhyāni-Bodhisattva found in the Northern Buddhist temples, in which case he is represented standing, and may carry the *vajra* in the right hand with the left in *varuda mudrā,* or with the *vajra* and *ghaṇṭā* supported by lotus-flowers, the stems of which he holds in 'charity' and 'argument' *mudrā.* If painted, he is white in colour.
>
> He is sometimes figured seated with the right or left leg pendent. The right hand holds the *vajra* at his breast, while the left may be leaning on the lotus pedestal, behind the left knee, or be lying on the left knee in *varuda mudrā.*[65]

Representing the gateway to the north, of the way upward out of the realms of the *saṃsāra,* Vajrapāṇi will work to help eliminate the last vestiges of hindrances still remaining in the mind of the accomplished *yogin.* Looking upwards towards Vajrapāṇi's guiding hand is the way that Initiates can ascend from one realm of relative purity and accomplishment to the next.

Vajrapāṇi is said to be the 'impeccable enemy of the demons', as well as being known as 'the protector of the Nāgas[66] against the

---

64 Getty, *Gods of Northern Buddhism,* 51.

65 Ibid., 52.

66 *Nāga:* literally 'serpent', a serpent Deity, but esoterically it refers to one who has evoked Wisdom, a wise person, Rishi. It connotes the 'serpent power' that flows through the *nāḍī* system and which liberates a being, conferring supersensory powers, making one an adept. When personified the *nāgas* can be considered as the flow of any of the *prāṇas* within the etheric vehicle. (Each of these streams of *prāṇic* energy are likened to serpents possessing differing colours, a tail relating to their genesis, and a head orientating them towards future purpose.) The serpent grows into a dragon, hence the term Dragon of Wisdom when referring to a Master of Wisdom. The serpent or dragon energies are also those associated with the meridians of energies ('ley lines') which cover the face of the earth. They were well known by the seers of the past, who erected

Garuḍas'.[67] This informs us that his *vajra* is chiefly utilised to guard people from the spells of sorcerers and demons, of all psychic entities that would wreak *siddhis* to manipulate or control those that are relatively weak-willed. There are cosmic sources of such demons as well as human sources, therefore it is significant that this northerly gate is utilised to protect all in *saṃsāra* from these nefarious influences.

The entire *maṇḍala* of the Mahābodhisattvas must be protected from dark brotherhood predation. If it comes to be dominated by the left hand path then disaster will befall all beings incorporated by it. This protection then becomes a major purpose for Vajrapāṇi's absorptive meditation. It is not as simple as blocking out all such influences from the *maṇḍala,* because humanity has much *karma* with the forces of evil, many contracts of selfish and separative concern. Vajrapāṇi therefore must carefully meditate upon the sum of the *karma* concerned, and to wisely direct it so that eventually the dark brotherhood's many machinations against humanity are defeated. He must empower each human unit that strives upwards towards the domains of Light and Revelation with the weapons (*vajras*, swords, bells, *mantra,* light) that they need to effectively cleanse their minds and psyche from the spells and psychic influences of those who would try to prevent their spiritual progress. Such empowerment has always been 'ear-whispered' because of the idiosyncrasies of the nature of the war between the dark forces and those of Light. It is an intricate part of the path to enlightenment. Any prospective *yogin* needs to develop the ability to

---

the many temples and sacred shrines of antiquity based upon the points of intersection of these lines. Note also the ouroboros, depicted as a serpent biting its own tail, signifying the future swallowing up the past. *Nāgas* are especially associated with the sanctity of water, rain clouds, or flowing *prāṇas* (rivers). They are also seen as a water spirit that may take the form of a serpent. Some are regarded as custodians of doctrines (keepers of the *dharma*) and are depicted as arising out of the sea.

67 *Garuḍa*: vehicle of Amoghasiddhi. Associated with Vajrapāṇi and the wrathful forms of Padmasambhava. A mythic bird-man of the sun, usually shown with a raptor's beak, is an enemy of serpents, and as such represents the mechanism of the transmutation of evil forces, the tainted *saṃskāras* depicted in the form of serpents *(nāgas).* As the sun he controls the *abgas,* who have power over Water. Garuda is also the steed of Viṣṇu (the second person of the Hindu *trimūrti*) in the form of a great bird in the ancient Hindu religious epic, the Ramayāna. He can thus be seen to embody the major cycles of time wherein consciousness evolves.

utilise the weapons of protection provided him/her from Vajrapāṇi's direction, as a consequence of awakening *siddhis*.

His protection of the *nāgas* (serpents) concerns the purification of the *nāḍīs*. The associated energies are likened to serpents, hence the term 'serpent power' given to the evocation of their combined potency. Protecting the *nāgas* is thus another way of saying 'psychic protection'. Purifying the *prāṇas* allows *siddhis* to manifest as the result of awakened *chakras*. *Prāṇas* take the form of *nāgas* as they flow through the *nāḍīs*. The *nāgas* grow into serpents of wisdom as the *prāṇas* become more resilient, transmogrify, and grow in liberating potency on the road to enlightenment. (Hence we also have the name Nāgārjuna,[68] indicating the method whereby he gained his Wisdom.)

The seeming discrepancies related to the *nāgas,* where on one hand they are to be devoured by Garuḍa, the vehicle of Amoghasiddhi, and on the other they are to be protected by Vajrapāṇi, lies in the nature of the *nāgas* themselves. They are the moving qualities of *saṃskāras* viewed over time. These *saṃskāras* can express base human emotional qualities, in which case Garuḍa is their enemy and will devour them. Otherwise, they are expressions of enlightened attributes, in which case Vajrapāṇi will protect them from being obscured by Garuḍa. The associated *siddhis* arising need to be rightfully conveyed in meditation and must not be stifled or diverted to erroneous functions.

We should note here that Garuḍa is a bird and therefore represents the Airy Element, which controls the general coursing of the *prāṇas* (serpents). Garuḍa therefore represents the yogic method of directing this *prāṇic* flow. For this reason he is the vehicle of Amoghasiddhi, the basis of his All-accomplishing Wisdom. Meditative control of this flow is the making of a *mahāsiddha*. *Mahāsiddha*s therefore take the guise of Amoghasiddhi's Wisdom, which gives control of all attributes of *saṃsāra's* domain.

The Head centre is the arbiter of all the *prāṇic* flows in the body, once meditative discipline comes into play. It therefore controls the Garuḍa-*nāga* relationship in the Tantras, in relation to which Vajrapāṇi can be considered the director of the serpent power.

---

68 Nāgārjuna's name is derived from *'nag'*- serpent, 'arjuna' - bright, shining.

All who desire to ascend to higher spheres of being/non-being to gain liberation must comprehend the necessity of psychic protection and purity by cleansing all types of *saṃskāras*. Even the Buddha, despite his high level of purity as a Bodhisattva, was not absolved from having to battle the hoards of Māra.

With respect to the *maṇḍala* as a whole, Vajrapāṇi can be considered to toil in a manner similar to how a person will try to protect his body from disease-bearing agents. The 'heavenly food' that his consort carries does not just relate to the taste of liberation, but also to the fact that she will help in the proper vitalisation and nourishment of the *maṇḍala* (i.e., the body) by making sure that all energies vitalising it produce health. Everyone's quest for enlightenment depends upon this.

The north is the source of the energies and qualities of the *dharmakāya,* which exists in the form of the elixir of Life that Vajrapāṇi is said to be the guardian of. The 'bowl of heavenly food', or illumined consciousness, that his consort carries can also be said to embody attributes of this immutable body of *dharma*. The *dharmakāya* is held in a *kapāla* (skull cap) by deities, but here we see that it is also contained in the vessels held by the Bodhisattvas with whom Vajrapāṇi forms a triad: 'Amitāyus,[69] who holds the ambrosial vase, and Padmapāṇi, who carries a *kalaśa*'. Both of these Bodhisattvas take Amitābha as their Dhyāni Buddha. His Discriminating Inner Vision projects the full potency of Mind via the western gate of the *maṇḍala* of the Jinas. The importance of this is found in the fact that Vajrapāṇi has been ascribed the role of the Mahāchohan. He wields the potency of the greater third Ray that governs the purpose of the five Rays of Mind. (Rays three to seven.) Being expressions of Mind the Bodhisattvas who are the reflex of Amitābha are chosen to help dispense the *amṛta* to human units that can be nourished by it.

The quality of the *dharma* for the northern direction is given as 'causes of deliverance'. Deliverance here refers both to awakening to

---

69 Amitāyus: meaning 'eternal life', can be considered the Bodhisattva form of Amitābha. Getty states; 'he may be termed either a 'crowned Buddha' or a Bodhisattva, and is therefore richly clad and wears the thirteen ornaments. His hair is painted blue and falls on either side to his elbows, or may be curiously coiled. He is seated like a Buddha, and his hands lie on his lap in *dhyāna* (meditation) *mudrā*, holding the ambrosia vase, his special emblem.' (*Gods of Northern Buddhism*, 39.)

śūnyatā (the inwards direction) and to the Bliss-Identifications that the *dharmakāya* accords.

The *virtuous root of the Bodhisattva* given is 'acceptance of existence through origination by their own will'. The utilisation of the *will* here is of the highest virtue, as it alone can properly help liberate one from *saṃsāra,* and to raise consciousness to the subtlest states of revelation and bliss. Of necessity such a will requires a developed Heart (the active manifestation of *bodhicitta*), otherwise it demonstrates as the black or grey self-will of the sorcerer.

In concluding this section on the Mahābodhisattvas, it should be noted that the third, fourth, and fifth Rays have a special relationship in that they form a triangle of Initiation-accomplishment that sets the stage and testings for revelation of the mysteries of enlightened Being. This necessitates mastery of all aspects of *saṃsāra,* which principally happens in the southern portion of the *maṇḍala.* It demands control of the material domain. Mañjuśrī's wisdom must be brought right down into the concrete world via the compassionate undertaking of Nīvaraṇaviṣkambhin in the southwest direction to produce proper comprehension of what attachment to material objects entails. Mañjuśrī is depicted holding a sword and the book of the *prajñāpāramitā,* the transcendental wisdom, wherein the teachings concerning *śūnyatā* are exemplified. This is the middle between extremes that the fourth Ray also confers. Ākāśagarbha, in the southern fixed cross position, oversees all forms of material activity whereby people gain their base experiences and expand their consciousness-spaces into new domains of awareness.

Nīvaraṇaviṣkambhin helps people to collate the gain of their undertaking in a logical fashion so that proper comprehension is gained. Once the path of the *yogin* has been discovered and meditation becomes the forte of the individual, then the orientation of perception moves away from the lower three of the form and upwards to revelatory vistas obtainable through the higher dimensions of perception. The greater third Ray purpose associated with Vajrapāṇi then swings into focus wherein the perspicuity of the *dharmakāya* becomes an object of aspiration. The Bodhisattva path, as veiled by Avalokiteśvara, then becomes the way of achieving the full revelations afforded by Vajrapāṇi's direction. The potency of the *vajra* comes to be wielded in the form of the fusion of the power of wisdom and compassion in all domains of meaning, as the *yogin* is Initiated into its full expression. Liberation then becomes possible via the gate offered by Samantabhadra, as the purpose of the *maṇḍala* of the Mahābodhisattvas has reached its fruition. Nothing more can be gained by the Initiate further residing in their sacrificial domain and so he/she moves out of it. Hallelujah! Another victor has gone 'beyond', moved 'to the other shore' (of the time-space continuum).

10

The Numerology of the Maṇḍala

Why all Tantras are knotted with veils and blinds

Numerological considerations lay at the heart of any thesis on *maṇḍalas* and the way that *chakras* function. Tantric texts are eschatological dialectics utilising yogic and mythic symbolism dealing with the ontology of the *maṇḍala* of the human *nāḍī* system, and of the way to liberation through a thorough control of its properties. The related *chakras* are the hypostasis of all yogic processes associated with such ontologies. Their forces and qualities are quantified or anthropomorphised in terms of the interrelationships between theriomorphic entities, deities, Bodhisattvas, *ḍākinīs* and Buddhas. Because of this, and because of the difficulty of conveying the true import of the subtleties and complexity of a subject matter not perceived by the normal senses, *all* Tantric works contain veils and blinds in them. (Veils allow one to partially see the truth; blinds are designed to conceal the truth.) The doctrines are also purposely garbled for other very good reasons. Otherwise, those desirous of psychic power for (often inadvertently) selfish reasons could use such information to develop *siddhis*, and thereby create much misfortunate *karma*.[1] That *karma* will then fall upon the teacher and practitioner alike, as the teacher is responsible for the effect of his teachings, if students earnestly (albeit selfishly) utilise them.

---

1 For example, they might masquerade in their minds subtle desires as things directly pertaining to the *dharma*, or wish to influence others or events for their own purposes.

For this reason the true inner Tantras have always been secret, and shall remain 'ear-whispered' truths given by guru to disciple when the disciple has been proven worthy to apply them by having passed the tests required. The tests are similar to those met by Naropa, Milarepa, Padmasambhava, and a host of other enlightened beings. Their severity depends upon the degree of initiation concerned. The symbolism concerning the lives of these saints has never been correctly deciphered mainly because the nature of initiation into the mysteries of being/non-being has not been comprehended.

By providing a proper grounding of the nature of the *chakras*, as well as a succinct presentation of the way their energies manifest, the correct esotericism relating to the teachings of the abovementioned saints can be given. Many formerly hidden aspects of these Tantras now need to be presented to eliminate much of the ignorance and misrepresentations of symbolism concerning them. The *karma* has ripened for such revelations in this modern era of information explosion, and spiritual education must keep apace with the developed needs of the enquiring minds of the most advanced seekers. It is a western orientation of esoteric information that must be utilised for today's disciples. Earnest practitioners need a source of valid information that will better assist their quest for enlightenment than was hitherto possible.

The teachings need to reach a widely dispersed global audience, rather than being relegated to only a few centres (or countries) specialising in esoteric yogic practices. (Which was all that was possible in past epochs.) Thus the *buddhadharma* evolves, unravelling some of the knots binding it, allowing comprehension of formerly veiled teachings. As a consequence, greater knowledge can be presented to earnest students to accelerate their path to enlightenment, however, the risks of wrong usage of presented information by the foolish also persists. Appropriate safeguards will thus still be found, mainly because of the sheer bulk and esoteric nature of what is presented. Also, teachings concerning *bodhicitta* (and the power of Love) have been presented in the past millennia preparatory for the new revelations, when a considerably larger number of advanced thinkers than ever before possible need to be catered for. No practice along the right hand path can be accomplished without a proper ethical foundation. Those who disregard the ethical safeguards demanded by the teachings then follow a path of karmic reprobation not shared by the teacher.

Before elaborating upon some of the basics of the *chakra* system, some information shall be provided concerning the way these veils and blinds manifest in Buddhism. This allows illustration of the relative truth of what had been presented by the wise in the past.

Geshe Kelsang Gyatso's book delves into the subject of Tantric *mahāmudrā*, which he describes as 'the profound and swift *anuttarayogatantra* method for achieving the fully awakened state of a buddha'.[2] Therein it is stated:

> The heart channel-wheel is of particular importance and is therefore described in more detail as follows. Its eight spokes, or petals, are arranged in the cardinal and intermediate directions (with the east in front) and in each spoke mainly flows the supporting wind of a particular element as indicated in Chart 3.

Chart 3 *The spokes of the heart channel-wheel*

Direction	***name of spoke***	***supporting wind***
east	the triple circle	of the earth element
south	the desirous	of the water element
west	the householder	of the fire element
north	the fiery	of the wind element
southeast	channel of form	of the element of form
southwest	channel of smell	of the element of smell
northwest	channel of taste	of the element of taste
northeast	channel of touch	of the element of touch

> From each of these eight petals, or channel-spokes of the heart, three channels split off. These twenty-four are the channels of the twenty-four places. They are divided into three groups of eight: those called the channels of the mind are blue and through them mainly wind flows; those of the speech are red and contain mostly blood, or the red drops; those of the body are white and contain mostly white drops.[3]

2 Geshe Kelsang Gyatso, *Clear Light of Bliss, A Commentary to the Practice of Mahāmudrā in Vajrayana Buddhism*, (Wisdom Publications, Boston, 1982). Quoted from the inside front cover summary of the book. The book is chosen because it is widely available and presents the generally accepted teachings of the subject in an accessible and pertinent manner. Controversy related to his doctrinal dispute with members of his Gelugpa order is irrelevant to his erudition in this field.

3 Ibid., 22-23.

If we look to the eight qualities given in chart 3 and *omit* the directions assigned to them, then we see that they correspond to the listing of the eight *vijñānas* of the Yogācāra explained in chapter 9. (There the correct esoteric view is presented for the directions.)

The channels of touch, taste, and smell, obviously have reference to the *prāṇas* of the associated sense-consciousnesses, which they channel. The 'channel of form' relates to the hearing sense-consciousness, hearing being the most limiting of the senses. Its main concern therefore is channelling Earthy *prāṇas* through the *nāḍī* system. That which is depicted here as 'the fiery' can be considered to symbolise the qualities of sight, which provides input into the mind of the Fiery *prāṇas* that directly feed the production of all types of images. The 'householder' concerns the resident of the 'house' of the mind, namely the intellect, which coordinates all of the qualities of the sense-consciousnesses incorporated by the mind. The channel denoted 'the desirous' corresponds to *kliṣṭamanas,* whose main function involves channelling the Watery *prāṇas* of desire and the emotions, and integrating them with the qualities of mind. It is therefore concerned with the defilements of mind (desire-mind), representing the most problematic *saṃskāras* that people must deal with. Finally, 'the triple circle' refers to the *ālayavijñāna*, which interrelates the impressions coming from the spheres of body, speech, and mind. The appellation also has subsidiary references to the triune circles of petals of the Sambhogakāya Flower, which coordinates the impressions from the *ālayavijñāna*, as well as the three levels of the abstract Mind.

The supporting winds listed in chart 3 do not correlate to all of the five senses, or to the five Elements that all Tantric, and indeed, general *sūtrayāna* utilise. Provided are; smell, taste, and touch, leaving 'form' to refer to either sight or to hearing. Two of the sense-consciousnesses are missing, and also the subtlest of the Elements, Aether. Concerning this Element, Govinda states:

> The Brain or Crown Centre, is represented by a blue flaming drop (*bindu*; Tib.: *thig-le*), the symbol of the element 'Space' or 'Ether' (ākāśa; Tib.; *nam-mkhaḥ*). Its Lord is Vairocana, who embodies the 'Wisdom of the Universal Law' and who is embraced by the 'Mother of Heavenly Space'.[4]

4 Govinda, *Foundations of Tibetan Mysticism*, 183-184.

Having stated this, the paradigm which the author utilised can be revealed, namely the dynamics of the swastika, plus that of the fixed cross. Only four Elements are presented here, as earth, water, fire and wind, as well as four of the five sense-consciousnesses (form, smell, taste and touch). The expression of sense-contact with the objects of *saṃsāra* is always active, whilst the four Elements constituting the objects contacted via the senses, are relatively fixed. They are really the substance of the developing consciousness, hence the exact nature of the *prāṇa* contained in each channel is veiled. The most esoteric Element (Aether), and sense-consciousness (in this case, sight) are omitted, but are effectively found at the hub of the *maṇḍala* of the interrelated crosses.

The utilisation of this veil allowed the integration of the key doctrine of the eight *vijñānas* to be incorporated throughout the *nāḍī* system. (Despite the fact that each *nāḍī* is constituted of combinations of five types of *prāṇas*.) This is an important point for the Buddhist mind-set, and offsets the need to accurately portray the actual form of the *chakras* and the accompanying *nāḍīs*. (Which is more akin to the Hindu mind-set.) We therefore get the dynamics of the flow of various consciousness-states, which supplements the teaching of the way that the *chakras*, petals, and *nāḍīs* actually exist.

Now, if we look to the eight *vijñānas* and the order they appear in the list with respect to the eight-armed cross, then we see that the order is correct esoterically, from the point of view of the way that the attributes of mind can be converted to *bodhicitta*. This necessitates *ālayavijñāna* (the triple circle) to be placed upon the eastern position of the fixed cross. The Heart centre's potency is then utilised to bring about the necessary conversion from mind to Mind. Here the sum of the *manasic saṃskāras* can be utilised in the transformation process, by virtue of *ālayavijñāna* being the store of all such *prāṇas*. The *saṃskāras* to be processed at any time can then be directed via this eastern gate. *Kliṣṭamanas* (the desirous) takes the southern direction because that is the orientation of the field of desire in people. It must be turned around and away from 'self' involvement upwards towards liberation, via the many transformative battles to happen in the southwest direction.

Intelligence (the householder) represents the western direction that governs human civilisation. They must battle therein with all aspects of mind and bring them to meaningful resolutions. The eye (the fiery) takes the northern direction, because it stands in the guise of the all-seeing Eye. It can thereby direct the necessary energies and gain insights to wherever in the *maṇḍala* it desires.

The fixed cross position just described then doubles up as being the integral conveyor of the four main Elements in the *maṇḍala*.

With respect to the swastika of the intermediate directions, here touch is situated at the northeast position because it is the sense-perceptor that unifies all contacts with phenomena into one body of experience. Hearing (channel of form) takes the southeast position because it melds the sense-experiences from *saṃsāra* into a form that allows them to eventually be appropriately understood. The sense of smell takes the southwest position where the subtlest discernments obtained from all experiences in *saṃsāra* can be realised. The sense of taste is attributed to the northwest position because the grand results of all experiences will eventually produce that taste of enlightenment that will produce the generation of emanatory good will, and then the Will-to-Love for all sentient beings.

One can also view this in terms of the relation between the Yogācāra doctrine based on the 'eightness' of the *vijñānas,* and the mode of their transmutation, verses the 'fiveness' related to the Jinas. This 'fiveness' becomes the twelve when they and their consorts, plus the Ādi Buddha and consort are integrated into one great *maṇḍala* of expression—that of the heart in the Head centre.

The eight petals attributed to the 'heart channel-wheel' (or *chakra*) represents a veil, as the *chakra* in reality has twelve petals.[5] If we reinterpret Gyatso's information to understand why the veil has been used, we could attribute the relationships as follows. Three groups of eight channels are said to split off from the Heart centre. They are concerned with the way that the eight *vijñānas* eventually come to be integrated into consciousness and how they are converted into the attributes of enlightenment. This necessitates the symbolic (or rather, effective) aspects of the Mahābodhisattvas, their consorts, and the Herukas. The entire *maṇḍala* (of liberation from *saṃsāra)* can then be incorporated in the process of transforming the *vijñānas*.

To the first group of eight, the blue channels of the mind, can be

5 Shown in the diagram on pages 144-145 of Govinda's *Foundations of Tibetan Mysticism.*

ascribed the eight Mahābodhisattvas, who reflect the qualities of the divine prototype into the dynamics of the *nāḍī* system. They represent the major fixed cross attribute of the Heart of Life, embodying the compassionate attributes *(bodhicitta)* of the Heart centre's function. The Heart directs *saṃskāras* of the consciousness-winds through the channels either towards storage in the *ālayavijñāna*, or towards transformative expression in *saṃsāra*. The overall purpose of this process is to direct consciousness towards enlightenment.

The second group of eight channels, said to be the mainly blood red channels of speech, is embodied by their consorts; *dākinīs* who direct the winds of the *skandhas* and the process of their alchemical refinement. This concerns the *karma* of the substance of which the *saṃskāras* are constituted. Here we see that there is a correlation between their role and the activities of the senses which are *karma*-forming, which constitutes the swastika of intermediate positions on the eight-armed cross.

The third group of the channels said to be of body, white in colour, consists of the Heruka forms of the Bodhisattvas. They are concerned with the transformative directives of the cardinal cross associated with any of the *prāṇas* of the eight consciousnesses in the various *chakras* in the body these *prāṇas* come to be expressed. The Herukas are the guardians of the outer gates to enlightened awareness for the personality. The Bodhisattvas serve to present the blue *dharma* (Love-Wisdom) expressing the inner awareness of the direct revelation of the *ālayavijñāna,* and thence *śūnyatā*. The *ḍākinīs* qualify the substance that is transformed from one state to another. The Herukas must be first contacted to engender the *will* required to transform *saṃskāras* into the consciousness-attributes of the *bodhisattvas* utilising the substance *(karma)* conveyed by the *ḍākinīs*. The drops both red and white are thus 'drops' of *karma* or *saṃskāras*. The *bodhisattvas* represent the compassionate 'middle ground', whilst the Herukas guard the gates into the inner mansion of a *maṇḍala*. They represent the actual wilful (first Ray) transformative forces acting upon the substance of the *prāṇas* conveyed by the *ḍākinīs*. The Herukas are thus positioned to proscribe and reject anything that is not appropriate for the Heart centre's domain. The entire process of transforming the base *saṃskāras* happens within the mind of the meditator, necessitating the use of the directive will and the power to visualise.

Everything concerning yoga in Buddhism has its veils, and the qualities associated with this triad are no exception. The Tantras were never meant to be used as meditation texts without an enlightened preceptor to untangle the knots. So far we are considering:

Body—Herukas	Earthy Element—white
Speech—*ḍākinīs*	Watery Element—red
Mind— *bodhisattvas*	Fiery Element—blue

When observing this triad we must first understand that we are really analysing the attributes of mind. The 'body' thus refers to the immediately perceptive, formed attributes of the input from the sense-consciousnesses. 'Speech' refers to its active expression to affect *saṃsāra* in some way. The 'mind' then refers to its intrinsic expression containing its inner directives. The proper colour of the attributes of mind, however, is the orange-red of the fiery flames seen surrounding the fierce dancing Herukas. The colours 'white, red and blue' then symbolise the general attributes associated with the *prāṇas* conveyed in the *nāḍīs.* They are symbolic only and do not represent the actual colours, qualities or expressions. They are exoteric, thus the 'red' attributed to the feminine is taken from the colour of her menstrual discharge, the 'white' to the colour of the seminal discharge of males, the 'blue'[6] is the correct attribute for the energy of compassion. From this we can quite clearly see that the wise ones that formulated the Tantras thus had no intention to allow the unworthy using the texts to develop *siddhis,* starting with Tum-mo, the 'inner fire'[7].

Of the three principal channels, the left is the lunar feminine *iḍā* channel, the right is the solar masculine *piṅgalā* channel, and the central one is the integrating *suṣumṇā* channel. With respect to the colours,

6 Gyatso, *Clear Light of Bliss*, 52, presents *bodhicitta,* as white, another veil.

7 Ibid., 34, where it is said that 'the Tibetan word Tum-mo means 'the fierce one' and is generally used to refer to heroines (Skt. Virini; Tib. Pa-mo). These heroines, who are slightly wrathful in appearance, bestow simultaneous great bliss upon their consorts, the heroes'. It can therefore also be considered the Fiery potency of certain *ḍākinīs,* such as Vajravarahi and Nairatma, enacted during the completion stages of the highest yoga Tantras (*anuttarayogatantra*).

Gyatso, utilising the *Hevajra Root Tantra* stemming from Vajradhara as his source states that:

> The right one is red and the left one is white. (Note that the inside of all three channels is red. The colours mentioned before only refer to the outside of the channels. In inner fire meditation the outside of the central channel itself is slightly blue.)[8]

We can see here, with respect to the teaching provided so far concerning the multifarious hues (qualities) of the *prāṇas* and *saṃskāras* conveyed by these channels, that we have a veil in the central red colour. This veil is justified from two perspectives:

a. Exoterically the *nāḍīs* are likened to veins and the red blood conveyed by them.

b. Esoterically it is the colour of the first Ray of Will or Power that must be utilised to awaken the *siddhis* via yogic prowess. Without the right generation of the will naught can happen. Both the left and right hand practitioners must utilise this energy. There is a difference, however, in motive, in the first case it is for intensification of the power of the self-centred ego, and in the second case it is for compassionate grounds. There is also a hint as to the generalised colouring of the Fiery expression of the *prāṇas* of mind, which conditions all being.

The white colour has reference to the generation of the white *dharma* that is promulgated by the wise, whilst the blue is the colour of the Love-Wisdom that must be expressed if enlightenment is to ensue. This energy must effectively line walls of the *nāḍīs* to safely contain the Fires when they are liberated, if the Fire is not to burn holes in the psyche, spelling disaster for the practitioner.

In Gyatso's presentation the colourings of the *iḍā* and *piṇgalā nāḍīs* have been reversed from what they should be. The white energy could be said to convey the energy of *bodhicitta* and, contrary to his presentation, is conveyed by the right hand channel. However, the nature of this energy is more correctly the deepest, most intense blue. The *piṇgalā* channel is the bearer of the consciousness-attributes (which is coupled

8 Ibid., 43.

to the Watery-Airy emotions and the principle of Love). The left, red coloured channel represents the bearer of the Fires of the intellect *per se*. However, having said all of this, the general colouring of the *prāṇas* is golden-yellow, or orange-yellow, but will show the dominant subsidiary colour of the main type of *prāṇa* conveyed, which will be one of the colours of the Rays of Mind. The *prāṇa* itself could be of a brilliant hue, or be dull, greyish, depending upon whether it conveys a loving disposition (*saṃskāra*) or a selfish, sensual one.

As well as helping to prevent psychically impure practitioners from prematurely developing uncontrollable *siddhis*, such reversal of important functions also prevents a meditation teacher that has not been Initiated into the mysteries of the Tantra to amass too much *karma* through promulgating the text in the fashion of a recipe book to earnest students. To factually teach the way to the liberation of *kuṇḍalinī* much awakened Vision is needed.

Veiling techniques were specifically important in the culturally yogically orientated societies of India and Tibet, where the oriental mind facilitates the development of *siddhis*. The Western psychic constitution necessitates more fact based intellectual stimulation for the awakening of similar impressions, thus the information provided in this treatise. It is a great mistake to treat the Oriental and Occidental student as if their psyche's are identical. They are not, and different approaches in their education *need* to be promulgated by the wise teacher. Mantric potency, for instance, is nowhere near as important for the enlightening of Western practitioners as for their Oriental brothers, but correct facts are.

If one tried to correlate the colours, symbolic representations of entities, and seed syllables provided in the various Tantras, as visualisations for meditation, then it would produce a confusing complexity. The Tantra, the perspective from which one analyses, as well as the nature of the veils and blinds used, must be taken into account. To illustrate, one only needs to compare Kelsang Gyatso's account to Lama Anagarika Govinda's. Gyatso states:

> First visualise within the vacuole of the crown a round flat moon shaped crescent made of white light. This cushion is in the shape of the circular surface formed when a pea is cut in half. Upon this moon cushion is the letter *haṁ*...In the vacuole at the throat is another moon

> cushion upon which is the letter *oṁ*. This is also the size of a mustard seed, but is red in colour and stands upright...In the vacuole of the heart is another moon cushion, upon which is the letter *huṁ*. It is standing upside down, blue and symbolises the indestructible drop... in the vacuole of the naval clearly visualise another moon cushion. Upon it, again the size of a mustard seed, is the red letter short a...the short a should be visualised in the nature of fiery heat.[9]

Govinda, quoting from the Demchog-Tantra, gives us differing colours associated with these centres. Here the Naval (Solar Plexus) Centre is depicted

> as a white disc or sphere (the form of a drop), corresponds to the element 'Water'...the Heart Centre, is represented as a red triangle [that] contains the sacrificial fire-altar, the sacred flame of which transforms and purifies, melts and integrates the elements of our personality'... the Throat Centre, is dedicated to the element 'Air', symbolised by a semi-circular bow or a hemispherical body green in colour...the Brain or Crown Centre is represented by a blue flaming drop.[10]

The Head centre in Gyatso's account provides a 'moon shaped crescent made of white light', Govinda's account provides 'a blue flaming drop'. The Throat centre in Gyatso's account is associated with the colour red, whilst that of Govinda's is green, etc. Clearly the true colours, symbols, and so forth, of these centres are not represented. Rather, what is useful as aids for the meditation sequence of the Tantras is provided. It is all a process of *dhāraṇīs* and *maṇḍalas* formed in the mind by the meditator, and if guided by an enlightened preceptor who can wisely unveil the symbolism and unbind the soteriological knots at the appropriate time, then the meditation tools can assist in providing the objective of the Tantra.

Mantrically, the sum of the meditation 'commands' are synthesised by the Tibetan short '*a*'. The practitioner is asked to visualise this at the base centre, to awaken the vital energy. The syllable *Haṁ* is generated at the Head lotus, and necessitates the full awakened powers of this

9 Ibid., 50-51.

10 Govinda, *Foundations of Tibetan Mysticism,* 182-183.

lotus to do so. This connotes the generation of a wealth of esoteric knowledge, or years of study, and development of the needed intensity and 'specific gravity' of the Fires of the mind/Mind. When this has been accomplished then the potency of the energy can be driven down to the base centre, which when integrated therein gives us the emanation of the *sa* sound, causing the appearance of things, of that which can be identified. Together the three seed syllables produce the sound *ahaṁsa,* which would normally intensify the I-concept, or *ahaṁkāra,* the I-am-ness, selfhood.

There is, however, a higher version of this concept of 'selfhood'. This concerns the drawing down of the qualities of the highest principle within the person, the Father or Monadic aspect (the Buddha within, or *tathāgatagarbha*), for the purpose of awakening the highest spiritual possibilities, making the divine 'individuality' of the Master, Arhant, or Adept possible. Thus to prevent the disaster of the manifestation of the black path, it is important that the *Haṁ* sound comes from the domain of the *tathāgatagarbha* through the process of purity of lifestyle, and compassionate undertakings. This coupled with the generated intensity and 'weight' of the Fires of the Mind, automatically travels to the base centre to unite with the feminine forces stored there at the appropriate time. The field of conveyance of this seed syllable therefore is the *Oṁ,* which generates the blue of *bodhicitta.* (The personal will, therefore, is needed not, the Will-of-Love suffices.) It demonstrates as the expansiveness of consciousness-space that only the awakened Heart can express. When the *Oṁ* and the *Haṁ* syllables are combined through the livingness of the Bodhisattva path, and emanated via the transformative Love of the Heart centre, then we get the *Hūṁ* of all-embracing compassion. It has the Void as its base and drives forth the liberation of all sentient beings. Thus we have the three seed syllables *Oṁ, Āḥ, Hūṁ,* the epitome of the qualities of 'body, speech, and mind' of Tibetan Buddhism.[11]

11 See Govinda, *Foundations of Tibetan Mysticism*, 185, for a good explanation of this mantra. He states that the 'three principles of 'Body' *(kāya);* (Tib.: *sku),* 'Speech' *(vāk;* Tib.: *gsuṅ),* and 'Mind' *(citta;* Tib.: *thugs),* which – after the unification of all psychic qualities and forces of the meditator – are transformed into: 1. The principle of the all-embracing universal body ('OṀ'), realized in the Crown Centre; 2. The principle of all-embracing, i.e., mantric speech (Tib.: *gzuṅs)* or creative sound ('ĀḤ'),

Kālahamsa (a form of Brahmā, or Parabrahma) is the swan that wings out the entire duration of space and time, thus represents the expression of the mantra *ahaṁsa*. It is that which causes the appearance of the universe of phenomenon, as conditioned by time *(kāla)*. It, however, flies in the space of consciousness represented by the *Oṁ*. The feathers of this bird moves the substance of the Airy Element through which it flies, and which conveys it to far distant cosmic vistas.

The *ḍākinīs* and the *chakras*

The *ḍākinīs* embody substance and thereby control everything underlying empirical constructs, other than what is manipulated by human will. They are the coherent forces governing the processes conditioning the sum of Nature. They build the vehicles through which consciousness must manifest, and thus help direct the *karma* associated with the flow of consciousness. *Karma* is only possible if consciousness has a vehicle that allows it to affect phenomena in any of the ways that produce tangible effects in *saṃsāra*. The *ḍākinīs* work to redefine the various images and formed ideas created by human consciousness in such a way that their effects will eventually harmonise with the general outpouring of Nature's flow. They endeavour to offset any chaotic or destructive trend against the general equanimous well being of the whole. This represents the way that *karma* flows. They are the great recycling agents in Nature, continuously recycling forms (the 'containers' of sentience) according to the vicissitudes of group *karma*, so that those forms can better adapt to new environmental conditionings, and meld with the new. They work with the Plan of the Buddha or Bodhisattva to whom they are affiliated.

The sentience and consciousness-bearing units of the various classes of beings in *saṃsāra* technically evolve from the substance of the wombs of the *ḍākinīs*. By manifesting the collectivised thought constructs of the *rūpa* (formed) and *arūpa* (formless) levels they are thus the governing forces in Nature. There are many levels and subdivisions of these feminine forces (which can also be termed *devas*), which cannot

---

realized in the Throat Centre; 3. The principle of the all-embracing Love of the Enlightened Mind *(bodhi-citta;* Tib.: *byaṅ-chub-sems)* of all Buddhas (HŪṀ'), realized in the Heart Centre.'

be detailed here. A bare outline only can be provided here concerning their role in building the *chakras* in Nature. Consideration of the minor *chakras* (the Inner Round) shall be omitted.

It should be noted that there are two categories to the main *chakras* in the body. One set above the diaphragm that finds their expression in Nature through channelling and embodying the energies of the *arūpa* realms. The other set are the *chakras* below the diaphragm, which similarly channel and embody the energies of the formed realms that incorporate the three worlds of human livingness. (The mental, astral and physical domains.) Their governing centre is the Solar Plexus (Naval) centre, and the Wrathful and theriomorphic deities of the Bardo Thödol represent their embodiments.

The consorts of the Dhyāni Buddhas and Bodhisattvas, the Vidhyādharas (knowledge-holders), and the Guardians of the four directions of space, function similarly for the *arūpa* levels, where we find the Head and Ājñā centre duo, the Heart centre, and the Throat centre. We therefore have three levels of *chakras* represented.

The *chakras* governing the *arūpa* levels are:

a. The combined Head centres, governing the principle of directive Will. All Peaceful Deities are represented with their consorts, under the auspices of the Dhyāni Buddhas. The Element processed is Aether, and Vairocana's All-accomplishing Wisdom is developed through its functioning. The Head lotus can be considered the macrocosm, and everything below represents the reflected microcosm, whose qualities come to be expressed in it after due processing.

b. The Heart centre (*anāhata chakra)*; governing the role of consciousness in organising Life, and its drive to liberation. Principally the consorts of the Bodhisattvas and Dhyāni Bodhisattvas govern this function in *saṃsāra*. The consorts of the Bodhisattvas that govern the seven Rays build the qualities of the seven sacred petals of the Heart Lotus, whilst the consorts of the Dhyāni Bodhisattvas govern the five non-sacred petals. They manifest seemingly lesser roles because these *ḍākinīs* preside over the transformation of the five sense-perceptions into the corresponding Wisdoms of the Dhyāni Buddhas throughout the sum of Nature. The associated Element is Air and Akṣobhya's Mirror-like wisdom is its outcome.[12]

c. The Throat centre *(viśuddha chakra)*; governing the dissemination of the Fires of mind that dissect, analyse, and instigate separative changes. Thus the active *saṃskāra*-creating forces are represented. Here we have the active role of the Vidyādharas, the Fiery representatives of the consorts of the Mahābodhisattvas, and the Guardians. The Element expressed is Fire, and Amitābha's Discriminating Inner Vision is developed as a consequence.

The *chakras* governing the *rūpa* levels of *saṃsāra* are:

d. The Solar Plexus centre (*maṇipūra chakra*). This *chakra* manifests in the form of a dual pentagram, one pointing upwards (towards the consorts of the Jinas), and the other pointing downwards (to vitalise the theriomorphic deities). They project the power of the Jina-Consorts into the sum of manifest Life, thereby being the forces that shape the physical attributes found in Nature. This centre is also the centre of the personal will in the individual. The governing Element is Water, controlled by Ratnasambhava's Equalising Wisdom.

e. The combined Sacral/Base of the Spine centres. Vajrā-Kīla Heruka and the five Jñāna-Ḍākinīs are integral to the functioning of this unit, as will be explained later. The Element controlled is Earth, courtesy of Amoghasiddhi's All-accomplishing Wisdom.

It should be noted that *force* is the impact of energy that bears fruit. Force is needed to manifest a change in substance, the characteristics of forms, or to move something which is lethargic, inert, or which is resistant to change. *Energy* is an emanatory quality that manifests in a pervasive manner upon all (things) and which allows them to perform

---

12 Note that the Elements corresponding to the Jinas presented in this *Treatise on Mind* are different than that traditionally given. The view here relates to the actual plane of perception and the associated *chakra* that the respective Jina embodies. The traditional view presents a veil, where the correlation has some validity with respect to the direction assigned to the Jinas. Both Gyatso and Govinda provide Amoghasiddhi as the Element Air for the direction north, Akṣobhya—Water for the direction east, Amitābha—Fire for the direction west, and Ratnasmbhava—Earth for the direction south.

functions and do work. It is organised by directed will to manifest a force that does work of some type. (Such as the transformation of *saṃskāras,* the building of *maṇḍalas.*)

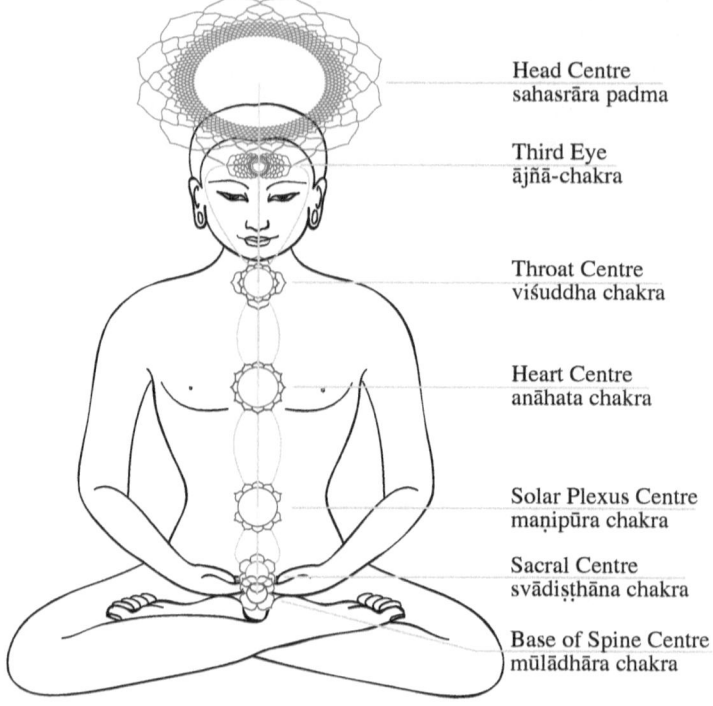

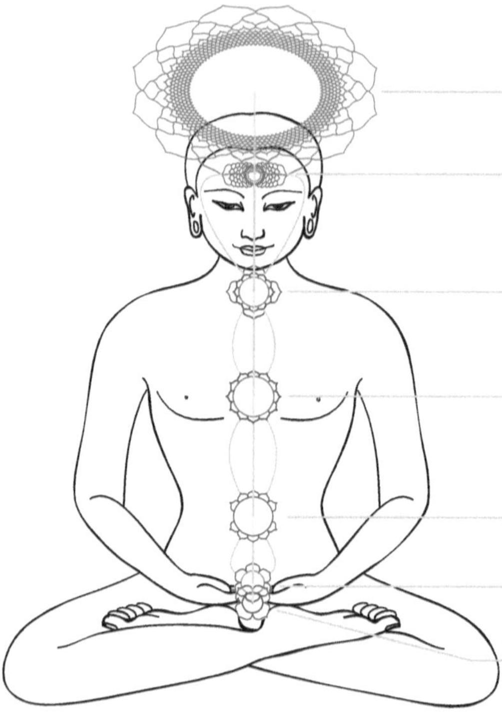

Figure 26. The seven major *chakras*

Astrologically, twelve zodiacal energies are brought to bear in building the forms relating to the evolution of consciousness via the twelve petals of the Heart centre (*anāhata chakra*). Ten (planetary) forces then condition the ten petals of the Solar Plexus centre (the *maṇipūra chakra*). This statement presents a basis to comprehending the nature of the science of astrology. The idea can then be extended to the physical universe and applied to the motions of the stars and planets with respect to our earth, wherein human consciousness evolves. The twelve astrological constellations therefore relate to the expression of the heart in the Head centre in that portion of a cosmic *maṇḍala* represented by the visible stars in the night sky. The ten planetary rulers are the expression of the petals of a *maṇipūra chakra* that the solar system functions in terms of. Such a solar system contains Ḍākinīs, Bodhisattvas, and Buddhas that had evolved from past aeons of solar and cosmic evolution long before the earth was formed. The energies and forces associated with these cosmic entities are the Real. When reflected into the domain of the human personality and viewed in terms of a human natal chart they become part of the illusionality of *saṃsāra*.

The inner and the outer universes are reflections of each other, as symbolised in the yin-yang. For this reason one can go inwards to find the mysteries of being/non-being, and comprehend the nature of outer phenomena, or one can go outwards to consider cosmos in their endeavour to comprehend the inner universe. From this perspective Buddhists are only half right, as they have really only thoroughly explored one half of this *maṇḍala* of Life, that of the inward contemplation. This allows them to see all phenomena as the product of 'mind only', as the product of human consciousness. There is also an externalised Mind that conditions consciousness and carries it in its embrace. The movement of the stars and planets in the heavens are aspects of that Mind in motion. Most thinkers have yet to contend with this concept and to incorporate the related considerations into their ontology. Hopefully, this book will assist Buddhist thinkers to see the natural extension of their inward-focussed ontology outwards towards a scientific appreciation of how the external universe is actually constructed. The vast scale of levels of relativity need to be comprehended in terms of dimensions of perception, and the way of evolution of 'thus-gone' ones in cosmos.

This dual process is incorporated in the constitution of the Eye of direction, the all-seeing or 'third Eye', the Ājñā centre. The awakening of the petals of the left lobe of this centre allows one to focus upon the external universe, and the awakening of the right lobe allows observation of the internal universe. The central disc unifies the two lobes. It conveys the integrated *prāṇas* of both lobes together, allowing *śūnyatā* to be a base for *dharmakāya*. This Eye processes the dominant *prāṇa* of consciousness manifesting at any one time. As that *prāṇa* becomes clarified it allows vision in the subtle realms at the level relative to the *prāṇa* concerned.

The *ḍākinīs* seed the qualities of the Elements, via which all sentient forms come into manifestation, and from which are derived the *skandhas*. Their representatives are the *devas*; the creative nurturing forces embodying all phenomena. The difference between the two is that the *ḍākinīs* are a form of *deva* that directly embody the substance and therefore guide the expression of massed human consciousness, plus those streams of sentience that will evolve into human units. The term *deva* on the other hand, is generic for all of the governing forces in Nature. They are the agents for the Intelligent Design that govern the evolutionary process. The *devas* are the feminine counterpart to the masculinely polarised human kingdom. The relation between the two kingdoms is symbolised by the yab-yum position of a Buddha and consort. What is signified here is more than just mastery of sexuality, but the complete integration and fusion of the two evolutionary streams (as the masculine and feminine forces in the subtle body, *prajñā* and *śakti*) within the consciousness of the *yogin*.

Consequently, the Void signifies more than just the elimination of all consciousness-attributes, because the *devic* forces constituting the form and *nāḍī* system must be found and married at every step of the way. At first the process is automatic, but at the stage when the Tantras need to be pursued, then the merging consummative process must be conscious. The process is symbolised by the rubric of raising the goddess (*kuṇḍalinī*).

Because the work of the consorts is consequently far more esoteric (from the human perspective) than that of the Bodhisattvas, little has hitherto been revealed concerning them. This book hopes to provide some detail of this important subject, including for instance, their role in building the *tathāgatagarbha* attribute of all humans.

Numerological considerations concerning *chakras*

The petals of the *chakras* govern the appearance of a human form (technically a *nirmāṇakāya* expression), and paradigms of the associated *chakra* constructs are based upon two numbers; four and six. The number four, or multiple thereof, relates to form and the processing of the four main elements. That relating to consciousness (desire-mind) are conveyed by the number six, and its multiples. (The petals therefore express the *prāṇas* of the five sense-consciousnesses plus the intellect.)

The number four can represent:

a. The four arms of the swastika.
b. The four main Elements and associated *skandhas.*
c. The main *ḍākinīs* constructing the aspects of form.
d. The main *chakras* below the diaphragm,
e. The four petals of the Base of Spine centre.
f. The deities embodying the four arms of the fixed cross, or the swastika.
g. The four main directions in space, quadrants of the *maṇḍala,* or Doors of Initiation.

Mind represents the fifth or central point that integrates the four into a unity. The *chakras* existing at the *sambhogakāya* level are constructed on the paradigm of the abstract principles (e.g., Father-Son-Mother) symbolised by the number three. (Thus we have the 3 x 3 main petals of the Sambhogakāya Flower.) Each petal of any *chakra* stores the associated consciousness-quality (*saṃskāra*) manifested by the individual, symbolised by the attributes and functions of the various deities attributed to them.

There are twelve major petals to consider as the basic paradigm for the *chakras* relegated to the gaining of enlightenment. Here the perfection of consciousness is attained via transmuting the five poisons into the five Jina Wisdoms and then integrating the results into the qualities of the seven Rays.

The number twelve also integrates the symbolism and potencies associated with the numbers three, four, and six. This is one reason why the Heart centre is the heart of the *maṇḍala* of Life, allowing it to generate the vitalising and liberating *prāṇas.* The full expression of all the attributes of the human persona whereby *bodhicitta* can rule is thus possible. As a reflection of the Head lotus, the Heart integrates the *sambhogakāya* level with the *nirmāṇakāya* form, and is the basic *maṇḍala* that allows the *dharmakāya* to effect the world of forms. The Head lotus is based upon the geometry (multiples) of twelve, as was previously explained in relation to the numerology of this centre. We saw also earlier in this

Treatise on Mind how the qualities of the five *prāṇas* were processed by the *chakras* and ultimately abstracted into the Head centre.

There are only five major *prāṇas* possible, or multiples of five, such as 'branch winds', because they are the expressions of the five Elements that are seeded as meditative emanations of the five Dhyāni Buddhas. Their Wisdoms (*prajñā*) represent the distilled expressions of the qualities associated with the *prāṇas*. These flow through the *nāḍīs* that join the petals of one *chakra* to another. The influences of the five Dhyāni Buddhas are pivotal in understanding the Head centre, and the transmutation of the consciousness-attributes of which it is the receptacle.

The veil in the Buddhist texts that present only eight petals to the Heart centre (*anāhata chakra)* rather than twelve can now be lifted. The eight consciousness-attributes or directions of space embodied by the Mahābodhisattvas and their relationship to the twelve petals of the Heart centre means there are 96 channels stemming from the Heart centre to be accounted for.[13] We thus do not have the 72 quoted in the texts, as per instance provided by Gyatso, where we shall continue from the earlier quote:

> From each of these eight petals, or channel-spokes of the heart, three channels split off. These twenty-four are the channels of the twenty-four places. They are divided into three groups of eight... Each channel goes to a different place in the body...Each of these twenty-four channels splits into three branches differentiated in terms of the elements—wind, red and white drops—mainly through them. Each of these 72 then splits into a thousand so that there are 72,000 channels permeating the body.[14]

As the number 72 here has its foundation in the number eight, so the statement has a validity only in terms of the way that the flow of the *nāḍīs* are organised, according to the nature of the eight directions in space. This has validity in the basic functioning of a Heart centre, which directs *prāṇas* of the eight consciousnesses via the eight spokes of the

13 There are in fact 96 minor petals to this chakra, which are synthesised by the twelve major petals. When we add the two numbers together then we obtain the sacred number 108.

14 Gyatso, *Clear Light of Bliss*, 23.

cross of direction in space. (Here the petals relating to the cardinal cross are effectively dormant.) The number 72 also provides the number 6 x 12, relating to the philosophy of the six sense-consciousnesses and the processing of their *prāṇas* by means of the twelve petals of the Heart centre. For this reason the Buddhists kept the Hindu concept of 72,000 *nāḍīs* alive in their own systemisation of yoga philosophy.

The foundational eight petals, each of which processes three major forms of *prāṇa* (wind, or red and white drops) fits well with the doctrine of the eight Mahābodhisattvas, but does not account for the full properties of the Heart centre, which necessitates twelve petals, so that all twelve zodiacal potencies and what they represent can be expressed. The zodiacal wheel conveys all of the potencies of Life, of which the Heart centre is the distributer. The Zodiac is the Heart centre in cosmos, of which all Heart centres are the reflection. The twelve petals of the Heart centre therefore incorporate the eight directions of space, plus an additional four petals that are needed to account for the directions that the swastika can move. (To the left or to the right, and also in terms of energies coming into the *maṇḍala* from an external source, or leaving the *maṇḍala* bearing its energies with them.) The arms of the fixed cross position (of the directions north, east, south, and west) do not move so. They convey the fundamental energies integral to the *maṇḍala,* such as that of the four principle Elements, the purpose of the four main quadrants of the *maṇḍala*. Their purpose remains fixed, whilst the rest of the *maṇḍala* of the Heart is mutable, in accordance with the nature of the evolution of consciousness. At a later stage upon the Bodhisattva path, the left hand motion of the swastika is no longer active and is replaced by the cardinal cross of resolute one-pointed purpose.

Astrologically, this cross of one-pointed purpose is represented by the signs Aries, Cancer, Libra, and Capricorn. They represent the source of Life to the *maṇḍala*—Aries; the place of repeated incarnations (or cycles of activity)—Cancer; the regulation of the law, the *karma* that guides it all—Libra; and finally, the place of liberation, representing the gain—Capricorn. These signs also have secondary characteristics in terms of the evolution of consciousness, thus in the form of the fixed cross of normal human expression, we have the gates for the processing of the *prāṇas* of Fire (Aries), Water (Cancer), Air (Libra), and Earth (Capricorn).[15] In Tantricism these gates are represented by a special class of deities, the Herukas that guard the gates in terms of the transmutation of consciousness-attributes. The other eight petals are needed to demonstrate the mutability of the interplay between Bodhisattvic and *saṃsāric* activities in transforming the eight *vijñānas*.

The number twelve also allows for:

1. The twelve zodiacal potencies.
2. The 2 x 6 expressions of the *saṃskāras* of the five sense-consciousnesses plus intellect, whilst they are being transformed from defiled streams into liberated qualities.
3. The interplay between the energy qualifications of the seven Rays and the five consciousness-attributes that are being transformed by interrelating with the Rays.
4. The four main Elements multiplied by the three qualities conveyed by the *iḍā, piṇgalā* and *suṣumṇā nāḍīs*.
5. The mode of expression of the five Dhyāni Buddhas via three groups of four petals, taking the central point of the *chakra* into account as Vairocana's position. These three groupings represent the way their energies affect *saṃsāra,* the domain of the Jina Bodhisattvas, and the four cardinal positions (taken by the Jinas themselves).

One can then clearly see that eight petals are insufficient to demonstrate all of the functions necessitated by the Heart of Life. Twelve petals, however, adequately convey this purpose.

The number 24 that Gyatso provides as 'the channels of the twenty-four places' does have a representative truth here in the mechanics of the Heart centre in that 24 = 2 x 12, which represents the two directions of the flow of *prāṇas* of the Heart *chakra,* of the reversed and rectified wheels.

Having clarified the nature of this veil, we therefore need to substitute the number twelve for the number eight in the teachings

15 We can see from the above description that the nature of energy circulation within the *chakras* is not straightforward, and that much depends upon the degree of attainment of the person concerned.

provided and compare the results. The premise being that the number twelve refers to the actual number of petals and related *nāḍīs* to the system concerned, thus with all the processes of Life, whilst the number eight on the other hand, focuses upon Bodhisattvic activities (the generation of *bodhicitta*). Thus the statement provided, relating to three groups of eight channels splitting into three branches each, would become 3 x 3 groups of twelve, making the sacred number 108 (9 x 12) altogether. Next it is stated that 'each of these 72 [branches] then splits into a thousand so that there are 72,000 channels permeating the body'. One could also consider 108 major channels above and below the diaphragm, each which can then be multiplied by the number 1,000 when related to the Head lotus.

The number 1,000 when multiplied by another number presents another blind, as the number 1,000 simply means 'a very large number'. The presentation of such blinds, however, are a valid technique to conveniently simplify thought in terms of large round numbers that approximate truth. The number 1,000 is also based upon multiples of the number 10 (10 x 10 x 10), which for many reasons represents the perfect number, the number of completion. For instance, it is the number of the five Dhyāni Buddhas and consorts in their perfect *yab-yum* state, therefore symbolising the domain of their actuality, plus that which expresses their reflected attributes in *saṃsāra*. The entire transmutative process of deriving the actuality from the reflection in the mind is veiled here. (The petals of the *maṇipūra chakra,* from which much of this activity is accomplished, are therefore based upon this number.) Also, it represents the Tetractys. Here all phenomena is said to emanate from the One (or Unity), which manifests as dual, male-female principles in the One. The duality produces birthing of the middle principle, the Son (i.e., consciousness). The quaternary of form (seen also in the Base of Spine *chakra*) is the foundation that the entire process stands on. Its mutability makes it unstable, as it tends to move back towards the trinity. The ten stages of the evolutionary process shall be explained in Volume 5 of this series. Esoterically, the number 10 may also be viewed as 7 plus 3, for instance, the seven *chakras*, plus the three synthesising tiers of petals in the Head lotus.

The number 10 x 10 x 10 places the symbolism of everything

associated with it upon three levels of expression:[16]

a. The number 10: referring to the *dharmakāya* (the domain of the Real*)*, wherein perfection is seen in its simplest terms. This represents the domain of the Spirit, the Father, the *chakras* in the head, the forces pertaining to the *suṣumṇā nāḍī.*

b. The number 100 (10 x 10): referring to the *sambhogakāya* level, wherein consciousness categorises the appearance of all phenomena. This represents the domain of the Son, the Soul, the *chakras* in the chest cavity, the forces pertaining to the *piṇgalā nāḍī.*

c. The number 1000 (10 x 10 x 10): referring to the *nirmāṇakāya* level of the phenomenal appearance. Thus we have the domain of the Mother, the Body, the *chakras* below the diaphragm, and the forces pertaining to the *iḍā nāḍī.*

We can see from this that veils hide much symbolic, plus factual truth, and must be carefully analysed by the student to derive maximum benefit as to why they are placed there by the wise.

The derivation of number 72,000 given by Gyatso is outlined below, presenting relevant symbolic truth. The symbolic truth has it's own import, however, the number 96,000 is the numerically correct arrangement of the petals.

The number 96 represents the number of subsidiary minor petals to the twelve major petals of the Heart centre, allowing it to properly channel all energies in terms of the eight directions of space (96 = 8 x 12). Each direction channels the *prāṇas* associated with either the eight Mahābodhisattvas, or else with the eight *vijñānas.* Each of the major petals therefore sorts out any of the *prāṇas* projected into it according to the way of expression of any of these directions. (With respect to the number 72, there is a similar philosophy, but here only the qualities of the 'six senses' are involved, 72 = 6 x 12.) Therefore, the major petals can also act as alchemical retorts, transforming the 'poisonous' attributes of the consciousness-states into Bodhisattvic attributes.

The number ten is obtained by adding the qualities of the five Dhyāni Buddhas and their consorts. (We also know that four of these

16 The actual ordering of numbers can be reversed, depending upon the perspective one is viewing from.

Jinas are orientated according to a north, south, east, or western orientation.) They can be considered the originating sources of all the phenomena contactable by means of the senses and then correlated and comprehended by the intellect. Next, for each of these ten there is said to be 72 subsidiary channels for their energies to flow. Thus we get the number 72 x 10 = 720. These 720 can then be multiplied by 10 for each of the 'ten doors' that are said to be 'located along the central channel'. They are doors of access to all the *prāṇas* conveyed by the *nāḍīs,* according to the qualities of the centre they symbolise. This presents us with 7,200 forms of *prāṇic* qualification. Their mode of manifestation then involves the ten directions of time and space (relating to the eight above mentioned directions, plus the projection of *saṃskāras* from the past through the present to make the future). Therefore, we have arrived at the number 72,000. These directions allow gaining the sum of experiences possible in the external universe, in a similar manner as the Heart centre relates to the internal universe. Technically, the concern here involves phenomenal experiences—the outward projection of consciousness.

Gyatso refers to the *chakras* (doors) as follows:[17]

1) The upper tip of the central channel: the point between the eyebrows. (The Ājñā centre.)

2) The lower tip: the tip of the sex organ. (This is another way of referring to the *suṣumṇā nāḍī*. It symbolises the lowest place of expression of this energy, and the need to control the sexual function before its Fires can be liberated.)

3) The centre of the crown-channel wheel: located in the apex of the cranium. (The Head centre.)

4) The centre of the throat-channel wheel: located near the neck of the throat. (The Throat centre.)

5) The centre of the heart-channel wheel: located between the two breasts. (The Heart centre.)

6) The centre of the naval-channel wheel. (The Solar Plexus centre.)

7) The centre of the secret place channel-wheel, which begins four

17 All quotes are from Gyatso, *Clear Light of Bliss*, 19. My notes are in parenthesis.

finger widths below the naval. (The Sacral centre.)

8) The centre of the jewel-channel wheel, located in the centre of the sex organ near its tip. (The Base of the Spine centre.)

9) The wheel of the wind: the centre of the forehead channel-wheel, having six spokes. (This is another way of referring to the functioning of the *piṇgalā nāḍī,* as that which bears the consciousness-principle. Five *prāṇas* (winds) of the sense-consciousnesses are admixed to produce the sixth, the intellect.)

10) The wheel of fire: the centre of the channel-wheel located midway between the throat and the heart channel-wheels, having three spokes. (This is another way of referring to the functioning of the *iḍā nāḍī,* which bears the attributes of Fire in terms of the three *guṇas*[18]*:* *sattva*—sublime and intense energy, *rajas*—kingly or strong, sometimes forceful energy, *tamas*—slow or inert energy.)

Observing the overall picture with respect to this philosophy, and substituting the number 96 for 72, we see that there are necessarily five levels of expression for all of the channels and their energies. They therefore have a relation to the way of dispensation of the five wisdoms of the Dhyāni Buddhas throughout the embodied form.

1. The Dhyāni Buddhas and consorts — 10
   The Dharmadhatu Wisdom of Vairocana
2. The Heart *chakra* — 96
   The Mirror-like Wisdom of Akṣobhya
3. The 96 x 10 channels — 960
   The Discriminating Inner Vision of Amitābha

---

18 *Guṇas:* positive quality, virtue, a property of all things. Literally 'fundamental quality', all objects in the manifest world (*prakriti*) are structurally composed of the three *guṇas: sattva, rajas,* and *tamas.* In the physical world, *sattva* embodies what is pure and subtle (e.g., sunlight), *rajas* embodies the activity (e.g., a volcano), and *tamas* embodies heaviness and immobility (e.g., a block of granite).

From the point of view of human development, *sattva* (rhythm or balance) is the nature of that which must be realised; *tamas* is the obstacle that opposes this realisation; and rajas (activity) is the force that overcomes *tamas* (darkness, inertia). In terms of human consciousness, *sattva* is expressed as peace and serenity; *rajas* as activity, passion, and restlessness; and *tamas* as laziness, lack of interest, and stupidity.

4. The 10 doors — 9,600
   The Equalising Wisdom of Ratnasambhava
5. The 10 directions — 96,000
   The All-Accomplishing Wisdom of Amoghasiddhi

The above presents a general description of the distribution (not accurate detail) of the way *prāṇas* are directed in the *nāḍīs* through five levels of their expression. Starting from the major channels, and ending with the minutest *nāḍīs*.

Each major petal has effectively the capacity to admix *prāṇas* internally in accordance with karmic directives, so that any of the qualities of the eight directions can be focused upon. This necessitates 96 minor petals to accommodate the *prāṇas* that are evoked as a consequence. This number is also seen when the *chakra* is drawn geometrically to indicate the placing of the petals. The twelve petals of the Heart centre also incorporate the energies, or rather, processes, associated with the twelve signs of the zodiac. Indeed such a process is inevitable in relation to all of the five points presented above concerning the twelve petals. Thus when we add the number twelve to the number 96 we get the number 108, presenting us therefore with some major reasons why this number is considered sacred.[19] Another reason lies in the fact that the Sambhogakāya Flower is the true entity directing the *karma* determining the way the Heart centre is to unfold, and when we account for each of its nine major petals and the possibilities of their influencing the twelve petals of the Heart (in the Head centre), then again we have 9 x 12 = 108. This is the way of manifestation of the *saṃskāras* stored in that Flower to express the karmic propensities of the individual.

The internal structure of each of the major *chakras* similarly possesses subsidiary minor petals based upon the number 96. These minor petals also interrelate the major *chakras* to the next level or layer of *chakras* and *nāḍīs* in the human body, as they represent their major petals. Each Flower seeds the petals of the *chakras* of the personality

19 It is for instance the number of beads assigned to the *malā*, which the devotee uses to help in keeping track of the number of times a sacred mantra or invocation has been recited. It is also the number of charnel grounds surrounding a Tantric *maṇḍala*.

with refined *prāṇas* by means of the nature of the eight directions of space in accordance with the way that *prāṇa* must flow. The 96 minor *nāḍīs* are directed to their correspondences in the other *chakras*. The specific focus in the Heart centre, or the Heart in the Head, is the generation of *bodhicitta*. The Heart, therefore, is Life, and this Life sustains the consciousness of the personality.

The focus of the number 72 is actually upon the Diaphragm centre, which is a minor *chakra* possessing eight petals situated below the Heart centre. Its prime concern is the redirection of the *prāṇas* in the body, directing those from below the diaphragm to above and vice versa, in a cross-over fashion. In many ways this *chakra* acts as a Heart centre for the average person, because they are not able to utilise the powerful transmutative processes associated with the Heart centre's true purpose. This is another reason why the number 72 was used as a veil for the Heart centre.

Numerically, the number 96 can also be divided into 4 x 24 and 2 x 48, and these numbers are also important. The meaning of the number 24 = 8 x 3 has been explained above in terms of the eight Mahābodhisattvas, their Consorts, and Herukas. When multiplied by four we have the projection of their qualities into the four cardinal directions of space. This then interrelates them with the Jinas that rule those directions.

The number 96 (2 x 48) is also important because it relates to the number of petals of the two lobes of the Ājñā centre. They integrate the sum of the qualities of the Heart *chakra* into the main corpus of the *prāṇas* from the other main *chakras* (not counting the Head lotus). They therefore interrelate the *prāṇas* of the two main divisions of the body, those from the *chakras* above the diaphragm, and those from below. When we count the petals of each of the major *chakras* below the head then we see that there are 48 petals in all (Throat 16, Heart 12, Solar Plexus 10, Sacral 6 and Base of Spine 4). The *piṅgalā prāṇas* in the form of the symbolism of the 'white drops' are processed in the right lobe of the Ājñā centre, whilst the left lobe processes the 'red drops' of the *iḍā nāḍī*.

The *chakras* that deal specifically with the energies of the personal-I during normal human functioning, thus with the *prāṇas* associated with the generation of the desire-mind and all of its attributes, are the Throat centre, Solar Plexus centre, Sacral centre and Base of Spine centre (the energies of the Heart centre are omitted here). They are responsible for the creation of the *saṃskāras* that bind one to the trammels of *māyā*. Thus we have 36 major petals represented, one half of the number 72.

The number 72 is derived by adding together the two groups of paths that these desire-mind *prāṇas* move along. First, 36 types of *prāṇas* can be generated to manifest the way of the left hand or *iḍā* path. Then there are the 36 *prāṇas* that can be generated to manifest the way of the right hand path, of the *piṇgalā nāḍī*. This then produces the 72 x 1,000 *nāḍīs* presented in exoteric accounts. They account for the sum of the major types of *saṃskāras* developed via normal human development.

The Heart centre allows the energy of *bodhicitta* to manifest, it converts the *prāṇas/saṃskāras* of the unenlightened personality into enlightenment-attributes. We therefore must add the twelve petals of the Heart (to the 36 petals mentioned above) to make 48 petals. These associated *prāṇas* can be processed by the Ājñā centre in either the left or right lobes, according to the nature of the *prāṇas* present.

When the sum of the *prāṇas* of both lobes of the Ājñā centre are incorporated into the functioning of the twelve major petals of the Head lotus, then again we get the number 108. There is a complicated arrangement, as each group of *prāṇas* processed by the Ājñā centre is incorporated into one of the major petals of the Head lotus at a time. There are 400 subsidiary petals altogether to each major petal, and the *prāṇas* fed into it by the Ājñā centre condition any grouping of these petals according to the quality of *saṃskāras* conveyed by the *prāṇas*.

It is also possible to add the 96 petals of the Ājñā centre to the number 400 previously established to be associated with any of the twelve major petals of the Head lotus, because the two centres are conjoined. (The Ājñā centre works with only one of these major petals of the Head lotus at a time.) This then makes 496 petals altogether. Now, if we add the three petals with which a major petal forms either a fixed or mutable cross (swastika) in the overall *maṇḍala* of the Head lotus, then we get the number 499.[20] When this activity is incorporated into

20 Such 'fourness' is the *modus operandi* of this Lotus, as it interrelates it to the four main petals of the Base of the Spine centre, which is the foundation for the activity of all other major centres. It integrates the activity of the *prāṇas* of the four main Elements at any time. Accordingly, the highest and lowest centres are yogically integrated by the seed syllables 'a' and 'ḥāṁ', as previously explained.

the completeness of the Head lotus as a unit, then the number 500 is obtained, which is the number representing the great perfection of Mind. (One can therefore see its relation to the five sense-consciousnesses, five Jinas, etc.) If this number is doubled, to take into account the yin-yang, male-female, *iḍā-piṅgalā* duality, then the number 1,000 is produced, which gives credence to the number of petals that the Head centre is generally said to possess.

This number then also depicts the number of arms (transformative Rays of *prāṇic* direction) possessed by Avalokiteśvara. They represent his compassionate endeavour to save all sentient beings. The 'sentient beings' in this context represent all of the wayward *saṃskāras* below the Head centre that need to be converted into the attributes of Mind.

In the discussion of the number 72 verses 96 we can see the relation of the exoteric to the esoteric. This gives the reader an idea as to the way that veils incorporated into the Tantras can serve the dual function of both: assisting the worthy candidates for Initiation with pertinent information, and preventing the foolish from gaining too much ground in any rash programme for premature gaining of *siddhis*. They provide the uninitiated and casual reader sufficient material to work with until they are ready to properly adhere to the precepts of the gurus, with respect to their ability to transform unruly *saṃskāras*.

Avalokiteśvara and the Sambhogakāya Flower

The major esoteric significance of Avalokiteśvara's Tibetan name as Padmapāṇi, the holder of the lotus, relates to his embodiment of the entire kingdom of the Sambhogakāya Flower. Quoting from legend, Govinda says this about Avalokiteśvara's compassion:

> *Avalokiteśvara*, looking down upon this suffering world with his all-penetrating eye of wisdom, was filled with such profound compassion, that in his overwhelming desire to lead beings towards liberation his head burst into innumerable heads,[21] and from his body sprang a thousand helping arms and hands, like an aura of dazzling rays. And in the palm of each hand an eye appeared; because the compassion of a Bodhisattva is not blind emotion, but love combined with wisdom. It

21 Iconographically represented by eleven heads.

> is the spontaneous urge to help others, flowing from the knowledge of inner oneness. Thus wisdom is the pre-condition of this compassion and is therefore inseparable from it; because wisdom consists of the recognition of the inner identity of all beings – and the experience of this solidarity results in the capacity of feeling others' sufferings as one's own.[22]

In Tibetan representations the eleven heads of the standing Avalokiteśvara are arranged in five levels. The lower three levels consist of three heads each, above which sits the head of the fierce Bodhisattva Yāma (the Lord of death) which is surmounted by that of Amitābha Buddha.[23] Avalokiteśvara takes the guise of Yāma because the entire purpose of his manifestation is to assist in overcoming the death-like attributes of *saṃsāra* by those he has vowed to serve.

Here Avalokiteśvara symbolises how the Head centre integrates with the Sambogakāya Flower. The five levels can be related to the levels of expression of the five Jina qualities; to the input derived from the five sense-consciousnesses. Accordingly, both the Flower and the Head centre are also based upon the paradigm of this 'fiveness', as previously explained. The 1,000 arms are the petals of the Head centre which see into *saṃsāra,* and the tiers of heads are the petals of the Sambhogakāya Flower. The fierce head of Avalokiteśvara represents the bud-like tier of the Sambhogakāya Flower, and the pupil of the Śūnyatā Eye (the central sphere in Figure 27 on page 361) is represented by Amitābha's head.[24] He thus symbolises the conquering of the cycles of birth and death at the fourth Initiation when the Sambhogakāya Flower explodes into the light of *nirvāṇa*. One thus becomes liberated, a Bodhisattva of the higher *bhūmis,* who now manifests the prototype qualities of the Bodhisattva ideal in full. The head of Amitābha signifies the boundless light that qualifies the domain of Mind wherein the Sambhogakāya Flower resides.

---

22 Govinda, *Foundations of Tibetan Mysticism*, 232.

23 Ibid., 233.

24 In the book by Tove E Neville: *Eleven-Headed Avalokiteśvara Chenresigs, Kuan-yin or Kannon Bodhisattva: Its origin and Iconography* (Munshiram Manoharlal, New Delhi, 1999) 12, Avalokiteśvara is spoken of as being the sun (Sūrya), an extension of the fact that Amitabha is the Buddha of infinite light. Also, the Sambhogakāya Flower is in fact a sun-like source of illumination to the incarnate personality.

Avalokiteśvara is the absolute master of *saṃsāra,* thus Lord of death and karmic transformations within *saṃsāra*. Each triad of heads manifests the symbolism of the three times for their respective level (of the physical, astral, and mental planes respectively), and of the qualities of the Hindu *trimūrti*,[25] Brahmā, Vishnu, and Śiva. The most important attribute of the symbolism, however, alludes to the three main triads of petals of the Sambhogakāya Flower, which exists within the domain of the abstract Mind.

We saw above how the number 1,000 is produced in relation to the integration of the Ājñā centre with the Head lotus, and when the two main *nāḍīs* are integrated into this interrelation. From this perspective, therefore, the 1,000 arms of Avalokiteśvara represent the way of integrating all of the *prāṇas* incorporated by the evolving personality into the Head lotus. If we look to the main subdivisions of these arms, which according to Govinda, quoting from *Tsao Hsiang Liang-tu, a Chinese Lamaist text,* we see that the 'thousand arms are divided into eight belonging to the Dharmakāya manifestation, forty belonging to the Sambhogakāya and nine hundred and fifty-two to the Nirmāṇakāya manifestation'.[26] Now all of these numbers are multiples of eight, referring to the mechanics of the nature of energy distribution of the eight-armed cross of direction. We thus have 1 x 8 for the *dharmakāya* level, 5 x 8 for the *sambhogakāya* level, and 119 x 8 for the *nirmāṇakāya* level of manifestation. If we add an additional 8 to the last level, then we would obtain 120 x 8. These additional 'arms' relate to the way of projection of the necessary refined *saṃskāras* from the head lotus to the Sambhogakāya Flower. From this perspective then we will have 1008 'arms' altogether, which is but another version of the symbolic number 108.

In the numbers 1 x 8, 5 x 8 and 12 x 8 we again have groupings of 5 and 12, signifying the relation of mind/Mind to the dynamics of the twelve-petalled lotus explained above. From this we can easily discern how the interrelation of the Sambhogakāya Flower to the Head lotus is veiled by the myth of the compassion of Avalokiteśvara. Concerning this myth, Getty states:

---

25 The three forms or faces of Deity in One, in Hinduism; Brahmā, the Mother/Creator, Vishnu the Son/Preserver, and Śiva the Father/Destroyer.

26 Govinda, *Foundations of Tibetan Mysticism*, 234.

> There are several versions of the legend explaining his eleven heads, but they all resolve themselves into the following: Avalokiteśvara, the All-Pitying One, descended into hell, converted the wicked, and conducted them to Sukhāvatī, the paradise of his spiritual father, Amitābha.
>
> He discovered, however, to his dismay, that for every culprit converted and liberated, another instantly took his place, and legend claims that his head split into ten pieces from grief and despair on discovering the extent of wickedness in the world, and the utter hopelessness of saving all mankind. Amitābha caused each piece to become a head, and placed the heads on the body of his spiritual son Avalokiteśvara, in three tiers of three, with the tenth head on top and his own image above them all. Thus the 'On-looking Lord' was endowed with twenty-two eyes instead of two, to see all suffering, and eleven brains instead of one, to concentrate on the best means of saving mankind.[27]

There are a few interesting implications to the numerology supplied here. First we have that there are actually ten heads to Avalokiteśvara, which relate to the significance of the perfect number ten mentioned above. Next, we saw that one of the heads actually was that of Yāma, which leaves nine heads altogether that are specifically those of Avalokiteśvara, arranged in three tiers of three heads each, namely as depicted in the constitution of the Sambhogakāya Flower, where 'heads' become petals of a lotus. Yāma then refers firstly to the mechanism of interrelation with the Head lotus, where base *saṃskāras* must be properly converted, eliminated from their 'death-like' qualities before being integrated into the constitution of the Sambhogakāya Flower. Secondarily, he refers to the petals of the bud lotus of that Flower, where there is a need to eliminate all *saṃsāric* qualities altogether before the remainder can be abstracted into the Śūnyatā Eye.

The constitution of the Sambhogakāya Flower (the *tathāgatagarbha)* has been explained in Volume 3 of this series. There we saw that this Flower has three main groupings of three petals, plus a bud-like grouping of three petals shielding the central Śūnyatā Eye. All aspects of this Flower is triune, thus the Śūnyatā Eye consists of a dark 'pupil' part, and a surrounding 'iris' part, that has a series of radial lines

27 Getty, *Gods of Northern Buddhism*, 67.

(*antaḥkaraṇas*) passing through it. The 'white' of this Eye is constituted of the portion comprising the groups of three major petals, as shown on the following page in Figure 27.

The Sambhogakāya Flower exists as a refined form of consciousness not distorted by the defilements of the material domain. It contains the store (*ālayavijñāna*) of the sum total of what has been derived consciously from material involvement by embodied units of consciousness (personal-I's). It also directs the accumulated streams of *saṃskāras* of all past incarnations of that unique evolving entity. It does this through its function of being a container in the field of consciousness that is organised in such a way that forwards their organised progression and retrieves the gains, perfumes and nectars of enlightenment. The process is achieved through the mechanism of three major whorls of energy, taking the form of petals. They consist of the substance of the higher abstract Mind, and each of these whorls are also triune, making nine whorls altogether.

The quality of these three whorls of petals are expressed in terms of Sacrifice-Will (Power), Love-Wisdom, and Knowledge.

The 3 x 3 petals can thus be described as follows:[28]

1. Sacrifice-Will—Sacrifice-Will
2. Sacrifice-Will—Love-Wisdom
3. Sacrifice-Will—Knowledge
4. Love-Wisdom—Sacrifice-Will
5. Love-Wisdom—Love-Wisdom
6. Love-Wisdom—Knowledge
7. Knowledge—Sacrifice-Will
8. Knowledge—Love-Wisdom
9. Knowledge—Knowledge[29]

---

28 The dominant energy or quality is given first and the subsidiary one is given second.

29 See also Alice A. Bailey, *A Treatise on Cosmic Fire*, 823, where a similar diagram is presented from a different perspective, and from which the information of the attributes of the nine petals provided here was derived.

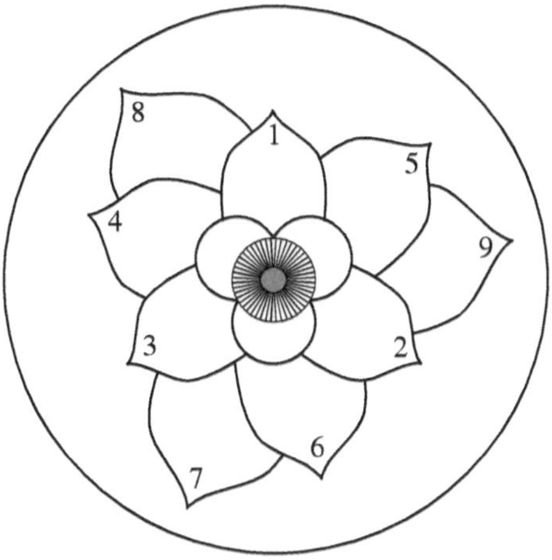

Figure 27. The Sambhogakāya Flower

The five levels of heads to the standing Avalokiteśvara can be explained in terms of receptivity to the emanations of the five Dhyāni Buddhas and their consorts via Amitābha. Avalokiteśvara presents to the world the purpose of the Dhyāni Buddhas via the qualities of his special mantra Oṁ Maṇi Padme Hūṁ. This assists in helping to free the residents of the Six Realms in the manner explained by Govinda in *Foundations of Tibetan Mysticism.*[30]

With respect to the arrangements of Avalokiteśvara's heads, the topmost head is that of access to the *dharmakāya* via the special dispensation of Amitābha. The focus of the *maṇḍala* depicted here is centred upon Amitābha because the energisation of the domain of Mind is being expressed. He stands therefore in the guise of Vairocana, as the central integrating dynamo. The kingdom of the Sambhogakāya Flower is really the embodiment of Amitābha's paradise realm, Sukhāvatī.[31] The Element represented here is Fire-Aether. Yāma's head then directs the Fiery-Airy *prāṇas* from Akṣobhya's domain.

---

30 Govinda, *Foundations of Tibetan Mysticism*, 234 *et seq.*

31 Sukhāvatī: the blissful pure land of Amitābha the Buddha of infinite light, the western paradise (of the setting sun). Here devotees are said (according to the Pure Land sect of Buddhism) to be born, never to be reborn again in any land of suffering until they are ready to gain enlightenment.

The topmost triad of heads channels the Fiery-Earthy *prāṇas* of Amoghasiddhi, manifesting in the form of the Power or Will attributes of the highest triad of petals of the Sambhogakāya Flower. The most refined and abstracted *saṃskāras* are processed here, viewed in terms of the manifesting potency of the All-Accompishing Wisdom of this Jina. The second group of heads symbolises the Love-Wisdom triad of petals. It channels the Fiery-Watery *prāṇas* of Ratnasambhava, where the magnetic potency of the energy of Love integrates the most refined *piṅgalā prāṇas* abstracted from the incarnate personality. In this way the Equalising Wisdom of this Jina comes to condition the activity of these petals. The bottom grouping of heads symbolise the Knowledge triad of the Sambhogakāya Flower, that abstracts the most refined forms of *iḍā nāḍī prāṇas* from the Head lotus. It channels the Fiery-Fiery *prāṇas* of Amitābha. The Discriminating Inner Wisdom of this Jina thus rules the qualities of these petals.

Amitābha appears twice in this list because the focus is upon the abstract levels of Mind. It is also upon the way of the integration of the Sambhogakāya Flower with the Head lotus of a human unit, symbolised esoterically by means of the standing figure of the 1,000-armed Avalokiteśvara. The hands are the charitable, liberating, guiding principle of the Sambhogakāya Flower caressing and directing the petals of the Head lotus to help stimulate the required qualities of the developing mind of the personality.

Avalokiteśvara stands (symbolically) on the lotus of the Heart centre, his standing body stretched long like the *sūtrātmā* (literally 'thread self') linking the Sambhogakāya Flower to this centre via the thousand-petalled lotus of the Head. The Heart is the lowest point of contact for the Sambhogakāya Flower, and is its focus of expression. From it derives the compassionate stance of Avalokiteśvara. The *sūtrātmā* is important in another sense, because the *prāṇa* external to an individual (such as obtained in food or through breath) must be channelled to the Heart centre and admixed with this energy from the *sutratma*. The *praṇa* then becomes uniquely (karmically) an aspect of that individual, known as *jīva*, the individual Life force. The *jīva* incorporated in a human form is what makes that form vital, 'alive'. It is the Life force of the individual that gives a person individuality.

Avalokiteśvara symbolises the Bodhisattva activity of the kingdom of the Sambhogakāya Flower. Each Flower expresses the qualities of a Bodhisattva upon the *sambhogakāya* level of expression. It fulfils this function until a human unit (being its incarnation at the time) takes the *śūnyatā* Initiation. The Bodhisattva path then becomes the role of that Initiate to direct. There is no need for an intermediary Soul form (Sambhogakāya Flower) because the Initiate is then sufficiently impelled by the Will-of-Love to direct all future lives to their conclusion in Buddhahood.

The eight principal arms of Avalokiteśvara represent the mode of activity of the eight-spoked wheel of direction in space. The turning of this wheel is the mechanism in each *chakra* whereby any of the energies within the *nāḍī* system are projected through one or other of the petals of that *chakra*. With respect to the arrangement of the groups of arms, Govinda presents the following summation[32]:

Innermost circle	....	8 arms	(*dharmakāya*)
Second circle	....	40 arms	(*sambhogakāya*)
Third circle	....	142 arms	(*nirmāṇakāya*)
Fourth circle	....	166 arms	
Fifth circle	....	190 arms	
Sixth circle	....	214 arms	
Seventh circle	....	240 arms	
Total		1,000 arms	

The actual number of arms is symbolic only; they represent the mechanism by which the Sambhogakāya Flower communicates with the 1,000 petalled lotus that is the Head centre. (The actual number being 1056 petals.) The important thing to note in this arrangement is that there are seven levels of arms depicted, in three main categories. They thereby relate to the seven Ray expressions. This is symbolised by 'a thousand helping arms and hands, like an aura of dazzling rays', plus also the fact that in the palm of each hand an eye appears. The eye is a mechanism for multidimensional vision, allowing downward-focussed visioning from above for each helping hand. Also esoterically, each

32 Govinda, *Foundations of Tibetan Mysticism*, 234.

is a source of the energy of light that is dispensed via the downward focus; the source of the 'gift wave' of energy, for instance, of a guru's gaze upon his disciple. We can see here that the five levels of heads and seven tiers of hands have a direct relation to the 5 + 7 petals of the Heart centre described earlier. We can also look to the Head centre, with twelve main petals and three main tiers of petals that have a relation to the three main circles of hands, according to a similar exoteric doctrine as that of the '72,000 channels' explained previously.

Thus from the innermost circle of hands emanates the first Ray of Will or Power, expressing the potency from the *dharmakāya*. The second tier of hands distributes the energies of the second Ray of Love-Wisdom that pours forth from the *śūnyatā-saṃsāra* nexus. The remaining five tiers of hands come under the auspices of the third Ray of Enlightening Mathematically Exact Activity, and are known collectively as the Rays of Mind. The third circle thus disseminates the qualities of the third Ray itself. The fourth circle disseminates the energies of the fourth Ray of Beautifying Harmony in overcoming Conflict. The fifth tier of Bodhisattvic compassion disseminates the energy of Intelligence, correct Scientific Reasoning. The sixth tier disseminates the energy of Devotion to noble causes. The seventh tier disseminates the energy of Ceremonial and Cyclic Activity-Demonstrable (spiritual) Power.

The coloured Rays are also symbolised by the bands of colour that radiate downwards, painted on the clothing in artistic representations of this Bodhisattva.

From the above, we see that the complexity and overall beauty of the symbolism of numbers should become apparent to the reader. The way they come to be expressed esoterically depicts the reason why the third Ray, under whose general auspices they fall, is described in terms of 'Mathematically Exact Activity'. Their proper comprehension is the means to understanding the nature of the economy of activity of Mind.

11

The Great Bodhisattvas and their Consorts

The *maṇḍala* of the eight Mahābodhisattvas

Further notes on the major characteristics of the Eight Mahābodhisattvas can now be presented. As before, I shall assign the Mahābodhisattvas to one or other of the ruling positions of the eight directions of space. The accompanying *maṇḍala* is important because it signifies the way that the Lords of Life, the Council of Bodhisattvas from the precincts of Shambhala, energise *saṃsāra* from the domain of the Heart (in the head). It represents the process whereby the energies of the *dharmakāya* are projected into physical manifestation via the dynamo of interrelating Mahābodhisattvas and *ḍākinīs*. They are the propelling force behind the evolution of all sentience and consciousness upon this planet so that enlightenment for all becomes the inevitable result.

It should be noted that the Dhyāni Buddhas embody the adamantine power of a *vajra* (Tib.: Dorje). The *vajra* projects the energies of enlightenment outwards into four directions of space (*ākāśa*). This emanation does not actually move of itself, as it is consistent with *śūnyatā*, which is its base support. The Buddhas remain quiescent in dynamic rapturous *dhyāna*. What moves the energies of the Buddhas (channelling of their qualities with respect to the variances needed in *saṃsāra*), are the swastikas embodied by the Mahābodhisattvas and their Consorts. The *vajras* (or rather *viśvavajras*) organise space according to the 'five-ness' of the Jinas that they bear. The *dharmakāya,* therefore, is the base of their potency, and the Flowers (*chakras*) of conscious, expansive, meditative experience are their mechanism of expression. For this reason Buddhas and Mahābodhisattvas are depicted seated upon their petals.

The Mahābodhisattvas direct the movement of the petals of the *chakras* that come to wield their forces in the form of swastikas of activity. This takes the style represented by Figure 28, which contains a wealth of information, of which only the major outlines shall be explained. Mahābodhisattvas are therefore primarily concerned with the growth and expansion of the petals of these Flowers, and their overall radiance in the fields of Life. The swastikas are not static and turn according to the way that the associated *prāṇas* need to flow to produce a specific effect at any time. Therefore, the interrelation between the Consorts provided indicates their most congenial position. Other variations may also be deduced. The information is presented within the context of the constraints of the symbolism of the Buddhist philosophy. My purpose here is to show that the deities represented are not just Mind-born entities, but are also liberated beings and their feminine *deva* counterparts that play an active role in effecting the course of planetary evolution. The mode of their interrelating is shown by means of moving swastikas because the *deva* Consorts embody the substance of mind/Mind, hence the expression of the mind/Mind.

Swastikas indicate how energies (*prāṇas*) are transferred from one part of the *maṇḍala* to the next, by moving from arm to arm of the swastikas as the gyrations come to contact each other. As they are transferred they become coloured by means of the intrinsic qualities of the area of the *maṇḍala* they pass through. The patterning can repeat itself endlessly to fill the confines of any Logoic form, or manifest entity. This constitutes the 'blueprint' of the fabric of space, of which the present analysis concerns the psycho-spiritual attributes, as presented in Buddhist philosophy. In reality, we have depicted here only one portion of the etheric grid (*nāḍī* system) of space.

The focus, as mentioned before, is from the perspective of above-down, and therefore of the way that Shambhalic potency can come to properly organise chaos/*saṃsāra.* These Lords of Life therefore concretise or reify their energies in such a way that the resultant forces can be appropriated by sentience and the minds that must utilise them.

The tabulation below represents the Dhyāni Buddhas, the Mahābodhisattvas and Consorts, as derived from the information in chapter 9, and which forms a basis to the *maṇḍala*.

Dhyāni Buddha	Mahābodhisattva	Consort	Direction
Amoghasiddhi (north)	Vajrapāṇi	Nṛtyā	north
	Samantabhadra	Mālā	northwest
Akṣobhya (east)	Kṣitigarbha	Lāsyā	east
	Mañjuśrī	Ālokā	northeast
Ratnasambhava (south)	Ākāśagarbha	Dhūpā	south
	Maitreya	Puṣpā	southeast
Amitābha (west)	Avalokiteśvara	Gitā	west
	Viṣkambhin	Ghandā	southwest

In the *maṇḍala* we see the forces of the various Mahābodhisattvas and their Consorts manifesting in the form of swastikas (which can turn either from the left to right, or vice versa). The swastikas indicate the way forces flow from the centre to the periphery of the *maṇḍala,* thus into outward service for humanity via the functioning of the various Mahābodhisattvas, as already described. The evolution of the four kingdoms of Nature also come into perspective via the work of the Consorts. Each swastika consists of four arms manifesting via two axis crossing at a central point (of immutable serene poise), around which they revolve. This point represents the central vivifying Jina. Four swastikas are thereby represented in the four directions of the fixed cross. They are integrated in one overall motion by a larger swastika turning on the mutable cross position. This swastika is turned by the overall purpose of the central Dhyāni Buddha Vairocana. Effectively, this is formed through the combined arms of the other swastikas. The overall qualities of the *maṇḍala* of the five Jinas are therefore incorporated into the following diagram.

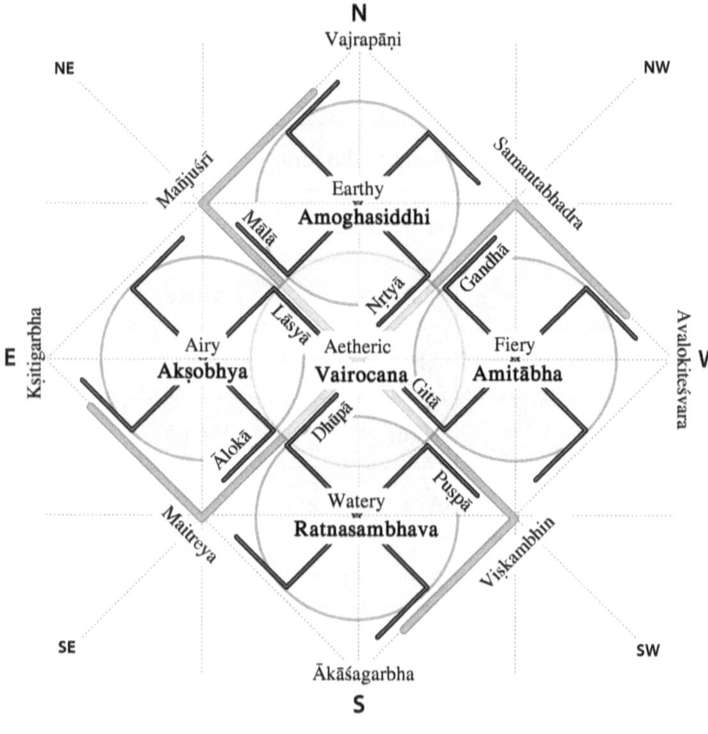

Figure 28. The activity of the eight Mahābodhisattvas

Each axis of the subsidiary swastikas represents the dynamo of the moving purpose of a specific Mahābodhisattva and Consort. There are thus four main pairs of such revolving vortices of energy producing the entire diamond-like lattice of this *maṇḍala*. Not represented here, but over and above the entire construct will sit the *maṇḍala* of the Ādi Buddha and Consort.[1]

1 Samantabhadra's dual role of being both a Bodhisattva and also an Ādi Buddha could also be incorporated here if desired.

Mahābodhisattvas are indirectly concerned with developing the levels of sentience of the various kingdoms in Nature.[2] Their major purpose is with respect to humanity, to help people build thought-forms that will inevitably produce enlightenment, and ensure the wise development of liberating human civilisation. They work to elevate gross, sensual, base, selfish and separative thoughts of people into a higher more compassionate level of ideation, and the eventual transmutation of such thoughts. Mahābodhisattvas are thus focussed upon assisting humanity to cleanse the defiled *saṃskāras* they have created over the millennia, so that they too can tread the Bodhisattava path. They thus work to refine people's consciousness. Their Consorts embody the process of transformation of the substance of *saṃskāras*.

The meditations of the Dhyāni Buddhas overshadow the transformation of mind for humanity as a whole. The Jina most directly associated with the attainment of *śūnyatā* is Akṣobhya. This requires directing the action of transmuting the most refined thoughts and aspirations of the world's disciples into Void attributes. The three remaining Dhyāni Buddhas; Amoghasiddhi, Ratnasambhava, and Amitābha, cleanse the base defilements of the substance constituting all attributes of human consciousness. They deal with the qualities of body, speech and mind of humanity respectively.

The swastikas set the conditions whereby humanity can learn from the folly the emotions created, and will help to propel the cleansing *karma* that will rectify the energy imbalances created by humanity. All this happens within the zone of governance of the Buddhas and Mahābodhisattvas that hold humanity within their compassionate embrace. People then move from the mutable cross (swastika) to the fixed cross of poised Bodhisattvic purpose. All perturbed mind-spaces must become tranquil and serene in time through the action of the compassionate ones that remain steady in the Heart's clear embrace. Inevitably, humanity will come to reside in the Clear Light of Mind. Their heavens and hells will then be a thing of the past. The swastikas associated with Amitābha (Fire) and Ratnasambhava (Water) integrate

---

2 This is a generalisation, however, and it may depend on the qualities embodied by any particular *Bodhisattva*. For example, the fifth Ray Lord (Viṣkambhin), who governs scientific reasoning, is also considerably focussed upon such development.

the regulation of the desire-mind of humanity, the most problematic factor of all human considerations. The factors incorporated into all of humanity's heavens and hells are drawn from the store substance governed by the Jina and Mahābodhisattva Consorts. They therefore embody the *karma* of whatever is to be, and their Lords focus upon how it must be best dealt with by the perpetuators. Everything concerning the imbroglio of passionate desire, hatreds, envy, spite, jealousy, etc., that cause so much pain and *karma* to rectify, can thus be appropriately transformed into enlightening qualities.

As the swastika oriented in the western direction of Amitābha directs the Fiery Element, so all that concerns the development and control of mind comes under his control. Those within Amitābha's department work first with building edifices and constructs for the development of mind by humanity, then with purifying and transmuting the associated Fires. He directs the thought-forms of humanity in such a way that they can be refined, rightly expanded and elevated with the cleansing, transforming energies of *bodhicitta* (from the Heart) and by the refreshing, enlightening breezes from the domain of the higher Mind. The Mahābodhisattvas Viṣkambhin and Avalokiteśvara are assigned to Amitābha, forming a triad with him. We thus have Fiery Power (Amitābha), enflamed Love-Wisdom (Avalokiteśvara), and Divine Fiery Activity (Viṣkambhin), seeding all attributes of mind and of its development into Mind in manifest space. The Mahābodhisattvas embodying the Fiery swastika are responsible for the development of the inner vision, wisdom, and power that manifest through a properly controlled mind, which is the leitmotiv of the higher consciousness states associated with the lofty concepts of the enlightenment gained from the Clear Mind.

There is also a direct interchange between the Fiery and the Earthy Element through the connection between Gandhā and Nṛtyā shown in the Maṇḍala of the eight Mahābodhisattvas. The interchange happens between the arms of their respective swastikas as they approach each other. (As each swastika is spinning.) This connects Vajrapāṇi's purpose with Viṣkambhin, allowing the factors of mind to come to be fully expressed in the Head lotus of an incarnate personality. We thus have the Throat centre–Head centre interrelation (the Fiery *iḍā nāḍī* line) exemplified.[3] (Gitā and Nṛtya can similarly interrelate, depending upon the rate of turn of each wheel of motion.[4])

Next, through the interrelation between Gitā and Puṣpā, the important Fiery-Watery interrelation comes into play. Thus the forces of Avalokiteśvara (the Solar Plexus centre) and Maitreya (the Sacral centre) become integrated, allowing the full panoply of desire-mind, admixed with the emotions to manifest.

In the swastika centred upon Ratnasambhava we find a Watery triplicity orientated in a general southern direction. In overseeing the activity of the Watery principle Ratnasambhava's swastika works to cleanse the astral emotional murk created by humanity. All turbulent Watery streams are pacified through refining the muddied colourations, thus allowing the formation of an integrated harmony of colour and clarity of vision. The Mahābodhisattvas assigned to him are Maitreya and Ākāśāgarbha. We thus have Ratnasambhava (Watery Power), Ākāśāgarbha (fluid Love-Wisdom) and Maitreya (Divine fluidity and integrating activity merging all into the oneness of Universal Love; the keynote of this future Buddha). They are directly concerned with the appropriate regulation and positive transformation of people's emotions, helping them to cleanse their defilements through emotional control. Through the development of clarity of thought on all issues, vibrant emotional harmony between all human relations can develop. The Mahābodhisattvas help the development and refinement of the sense-consciousnesses. The base attributes of mind that entwine the emotions, leave people blind to higher reasoning and revelation of the nature of enlightenment. Emotions obscure, distort, circumvent and deny reason. They thickly glaze over the mind with glamour, colouring thinking according to the object of desire. Rightly directed, however, they can assist in the development of the five virtuous qualities.

Despite their negative features, the emotions are necessary because they present the foundation upon which the basic lessons of the nature of Love can be gained. Love supersedes base desire because it is the

3 See Figure 25 for the relationship of the *chakras* to the Mahābodhisattvas.

4 There are similar interrelations between all other pairs of Consorts in the *maṇḍala*, which the earnest student can analyse if desired.

driving impetus towards the aspiration to serve others. Love is a highly refined form of the Watery Element, and in its direct form is Airy, the development of which necessitates the proper control of the emotions. The Dhūpa-Ālokā relation in the *maṇḍala* facilitates this development.

The arms of Ratnasambhava's swastika draw from the Fiery and Airy segments of the *maṇḍala*. Love and Mind can then be utilised to discipline and transform the emotions via comprehension of their effects. The Dhūpa-Ālokā interrelation facilitates the general *prāṇic* flow of the entire *nāḍī* system towards the Watery pool. Emotions can thus be intensified, or else the principle of Love can produce an equilibrating harmony. This assists conversion of the emotional-mental defilements into wisdom principles. The energy of the Heart centre (Kṣitigarbha) can then be integrated into the formed realms via the grounding activities of the southernmost Mahābodhisattva (Ākāśagarbha). Without emotional control and right understanding, the influx of Fiery energy can make the emotions far more volatile, aggressive, fanatical, etc.

The swastikas of the upper portions of the *maṇḍala* are embodied by the qualities of Akṣobhya (Air) and Amoghasiddhi (Earth). Here Air refers specifically to the most refined of the *prāṇas* incorporated in the *nāḍī* system, whilst Earth refers to the *prāṇas* directly conditioning the corporeal realm, wherein all forces and energies must be expressed. This means that Amoghasiddhi and Akṣobhya work to ground all that transpires upon the emotional-mental realms so that they can be brought to fruition; refined and cleansed of defilements. (A product of the general driving force of the Airy Element from Akṣobhya, and his accompanying Mahābodhisattvas.)

Akṣobhya has Kṣitigarbha and Mañjuśrī as accompanying Mahābodhisattvas. The resultant Airy triad signifies the transmutative potency of *śūnyatā* mirrored into manifestation by Akṣobhya. The wind of *bodhicitta* fans the purifying *prāṇas* of Love throughout the *nāḍīs* (Kṣitigarbha); and the divine activity of the two-edged sword of Mañjuśrī cleaves asunder the defilements of mind from the attributes being transformed. Kṣitigarbha fans the Airy *saṃskāras* to intensify all *saṃskāras* of liberation, and brings to the surface of humanity's experiential life that which needs refining. The energy of this wind thus helps to transmute the gross defilements. The resultant attributes of wisdom (Mañjuśrī), become ever more radiant, to be recycled upon ever higher arcs of experience.

The remaining pair of Consorts needing to be discussed; Mālā and Lāsyā ensure that all the *karma* and related processes that need to be experienced in the form occurs via the driving impetus of the Airy Element (Lāsyā). Lāsyā sweeps *saṃskāras* into activity at the most opportune time so that they can be properly processed by the attributes governing consciousness (Mālā). Here the Heart and Splenic centres are linked to assist in the proper processing and recycling of all *prāṇas* so that they can eventually accommodate the activity of the way of the Heart.

The triad associated with the northern direction is centred upon Amoghasiddhi's power to convert all elements of the embodied form into weapons of Light. Amoghasiddhi ensures that all subjective processes inevitably find right and proper expression upon the physical plane. The effect of his energy works to transmute all Earthy defilements. This naturally includes the sublimation of the five *skandhas* found throughout Nature and their elevation northwards to liberated realms. Vajrapāṇi then incorporates them as potencies of the Head centre's delight. Samantabhadra demonstrates the activity to project them to external *maṇḍalas* of unified sight. As an expression of the Earthy Element, this northern direction also represents the lowest reflex of the *dharmakāya*. The specific role of Samantabhadra's Consort, Mālā is to ensure that the moving weft and warp of *karma* works its way throughout the tapestry of Life in such a way that the purpose of liberation is achieved. Exoterically, the term *mālā* refers to a string of 108 beads upon which mantras are counted. This can symbolically represent the thread of *karma* manifesting through one's life in such a way that defilements are cleansed of their impurities.

Vairocana, at the heart of the *maṇḍala,* transmutes all forms of consciousnesses into the higher abstracted states of the *ālayavijñāna*. The effect of his energy helps project all Life out of the domain of *saṃsāra*. This becomes the basis for later receptivity to the *dharmakāya*, allowing human units to travel to the far reaches of cosmos. His Consort integrates the work of all the inwardly focussed *ḍākinīs*.

The Bodhisattvas and the Solar Plexus centre

These great Bodhisattvas represent the mechanism of active compassion in domains wherein they no longer possess integral *karma*. An important relationship exists between the five Dhyāni Bodhisattvas and the eight Mahābodhisattvas. The five Dhyāni Bodhisattvas represent the active compassion of the Dhyāni Buddhas. Three of the Mahābodhisattvas are included in both lists and have been presented in the list of the eight Mahābodhisattvas in chapter 9. Therefore, if we integrate them all into one list then effectively we could consider ten Mahābodhisattvas altogether. (Viewing the term 'Mahābodhisattva' here simply as a great Bodhisattva that is essentially at the highest *bhūmi* level.[5]) It is better, however, to analyse them in two groups of five, relating to the five Dhyāni Bodhisattvas who are helpers of the respective Dhyāni Buddhas, and the five remaining Mahābodhisattvas who work at a slightly lower level of the *maṇḍala* of our planetary expression. This numerology allows the Bodhisattvas to extend the purpose of the Jinas from the Head lotus (Shambhala) to below the diaphragm of our planetary expression. The 'diaphragm' here represents the line of demarcation between *saṃsāra* and the liberated realms. They positively influence the ten petals of the Solar Plexus centre of humanity, facilitating the transformation of mental-emotional *saṃskāras* into enlightened attributes of Mind.

The Dhyāni Bodhisattvas project their forces via the right or left lobe of the planetary Ājñā centre, to the *piṇgalā* or *iḍā nāḍī* flow of human consciousness, depending upon the focus or need. They can also work directly upon the ten petals of the interrelated Base of Spine/ Sacral centres of humanity. Their energies thus need to be evoked by a direct utilisation of conscious Will-to-Love, specifically through yogic discipline with the view of liberating *kuṇḍalinī*.[6] Their influence then

---

5 In reality they are active Buddhas that have not relinquished ties with earth's activities, hence karma with it. They thereby still manifest Bodhisattvic roles upon our planet.

6 Such liberation should be analysed in terms of the process of the transformation of planetary *saṃskāras*, though viewed above in relation to an individual's psyche. The reflexive attributes of the Dhyāni Buddhas are also expressed in the transformative processes of *saṃskāras* in the dual Splenic centre, according to the symbolism of the four directions of space. (There being a combined number of twenty [4 x 5] major petals involved.)

automatically flows down in the form of a Fiery Will-of-Love.

For the Buddha-Mind to influence all of the attributes of consciousness it must be able to reach down to where the emotional and desire impulses are generated, namely, the Solar Plexus centre. As the attributes of mind are five, the five *prāṇas* of the sense-consciousnesses, so a Ray of five energies must be projected at any time to affect any specific *saṃskāra* being processed. Personifying the concept allows one to envision the entire process upon a vast (planetary, and even cosmic) scale, so the Dhyāni Bodhisattvas spring into existence.[7] Bodhisattvas are needed, not Buddhas, because Buddhas are 'thus gone', therefore remain aloof, ensconced in the *maṇḍala* of the Head lotus. This is the threshold of their consciousness and everything below this point can be compared to the autonomous function of our physical body requiring no application of awareness.

The potency of *manasic* compassion may be viewed in terms of groups of five *prāṇas* at a time. This differs from the expression of the eight Mahābodhisattvas, who work automatically as a function of the Heart centre, being the directive forces of the principle of Love-Wisdom.

Below is a list of the Dhyāni Bodhisattvas and the positions they occupy on the respective *maṇḍala* of the Dhyāni Buddhas.

Position	**Bodhisattva**	**Buddha**
Centre	Samantabhadra	Vairocana
North	Viśvapāṇi	Amoghasiddhi
East	Vajrapāṇi	Akṣobhya
South	Ratnapāṇi	Ratnasambhava
West	Avalokiteśvara	Amitābha

As the major battles with unruly *saṃskāras* occur in the Solar Plexus centre (the abdominal brain), so the role of these Bodhisattvas with respect to these battles can be explicated. Such work occupies by far the greatest amount of time for all practitioners, and therefore should be elucidated. The focus for the disciple is upon emotional control and the elimination of glamours and illusions. The focus of the Dhyāni

7 They are also embodied integral beings, as explained previously with respect to the teaching concerning the Chohans.

Bodhisattvas, therefore, is similarly directed as positive liberating forces acting upon the world's Solar Plexus centre.

Of the two pentads that the two groups of Bodhisattvas can be incorporated into, we will see that one pentad (the five Dhyāni Bodhisattvas) projects the transforming forces from the Logoic Mind to control the Solar Plexus *prāṇas*, and another pentad composed of the remaining Mahābodhisattvas works more specifically with cosmic Love.

With respect to a pentagram we look at the projection of forces in terms of the symbolism of a head (the central organising principle), two hands (directing the *iḍā* and *piṇgalā nāḍīs*) and two feet, which ground these two types of *prāṇa* in the material domain. Also, the hands express the general Watery functions of the *piṇgalā nāḍī,* and the feet the general Fiery disposition of the *iḍā nāḍī.* The head represents the *suṣumṇā* disposition.

The Dhyāni Bodhisattvas are orientated in a general north-south direction, because they are concerned with the projection into the matrix of *saṃsāra* the energies from the enlightened realms, as well as the redirection of *prāṇas* from *saṃsāra* towards the centres of enlightened perception.

We can also consider a triad represented by the Ādi Buddha (Samantabhadra), Vairocana, and Samantabhadra (the Bodhisattva). They overshadow a quaternary of four Dhyāni Bodhisattvas, making a septenary of Power altogether. Esoterically, their work manifests via the expression of seven types of liberating Fires.

These Dhyāni Bodhisattvas manifest a role within Shambhala, as far as our planetary Hierarchy of Bodhisattvas is concerned, when we take them to represent existing entities rather than abstract concepts. We have the three departmental heads, termed the Manu, or Lord of Life (the first Ray department), then the one known as the Christ (the second Ray department), finally the Lord of Civilisation, the Mahāchohan (governing the third Ray department). There also are two additional great Ones that have stayed with our planetary dispensation rather than becoming 'thus gone ones'. They have played important roles in Tibetan history: Padmasambhava and Tsongkapa. Detail as to the nature and relation of these great Bodhisattvas, as well as the makeup of the entire Council of Bodhisattvas, will be provided in Volume 7, *The Constitution of Shambhala*. It suffices here to present the philosophical background that has been veiled in the doctrine of the Dhyāni Bodhisattvas.

Under these great Ones stand the Lords of the Rays of Life (the Chohans) that have been described above in terms of the functions of the Mahābodhisattvas. As the interpretation concerning the *maṇḍala* of the Dhyāni Bodhisattvas is at a higher Shambhalic level than that of the Mahābodhisattvas, so we see, for instance, that Vajrapāṇi was formerly associated with the Lord of Civilisation and the Head lotus with respect to the *maṇḍala* of the Dhyāni Bodhisattvas, however, his potency represents the lowest expression. (The Earthy quality.) As such, his true function as holder of the power of the *vajra* in the pentad of the Dhyāni Bodhisattvas is Viśvapāṇi. He represents the power of the extended *vajra* in the formed domain, which he bears. Another Bodhisattva therefore takes the symbolic role of the holder of the single *vajra*. The roles are complimentary, and simply reflect shifting focus at different levels of expression. We need to note also the difference between the idealised Bodhisattva and the actual embodiment. The embodied Bodhisattva can therefore take different roles, depending upon the way the ideal can be interpreted.

The other Dhyāni Bodhisattvas represent the transmuted qualities of the higher Elements. Consequently, when viewing Ray qualities here, we must interpret them as being sub-Rays of the first Ray of Will or Power for our planetary manifestation. The third Ray quality of Samantabhadra (Bodhisattva) therefore needs to be interpreted in its first Ray potency, conditioning the overriding Purpose of the remaining Rays—as they are really the sub-Rays of this Ray of Mind.

However, rather than the Rays of Light, which the Mahābodhisattvas actively disseminate into the planetary system, the Dhyāni Bodhisattvas express forms of rarefied Fire. This Fire manifests in terms of the five aspects of the first level of *dharmakāya*. They are veiled in terms of the five Elements and can also be viewed as the *prāṇas* of cosmic Mind. They can therefore be considered as specialists in the expression of the five types of Buddha-Mind, as denoted by the qualities of the five Dhyāni Buddhas. They have been qualified in terms of the five Buddha families. These are symbolised by the *wheel*— the emblems of Vairocana and Samantabhadra, next is the *vajra*—the emblems of Akśobhya and Vajrapāṇi, then the *lotus*—Amitābha and Avalokiteśvara; the *jewel*—Ratnasambhava and Ratnapāṇi; and finally the *viśvavajra*—

Amoghasiddhi and Viśvapāṇi.

One must be careful not to interpret such symbols as 'wheel' and 'jewel' in common terms. What is meant by 'wheel' is literally that Fire that establishes the entire *maṇḍala* of the eight-spoked wheel of cosmic direction in time and space, from whence all forms of motion and energy directions originate. It is the establishment of the central point of power of each *chakra*, and the eventual radiation out from the centre to the periphery of the spokes of energy that will inevitably turn the wheel. It thus manifests onwards to fulfil its appointed purpose, being the expressed *dharāni* of the cosmic Thinker. What is meant by the *vajra* is the emanation of the five Rays of Mind (a central Ray and four radial Rays) that empower all of space with the fundamental Wisdoms of the four Dhyāni Buddhas.

At first the orientation of the *vajra* is north-south in order to generate the divisions of space as the forms of Mentation impact and interrelate with primordial substance matter *(mūlaprakṛti)*. Later the east-west orientation of the *vajra* is added (thus we have the orientation of the Ājñā centre), making the *viśvavajra,* when there is an enlightened response from the streams of consciousness that have evolved from the *mūlaprakṛti.* This east-west direction represents the generation of the way of Heart and Mind and delineates the liberation of the type of substance that was once 'darkness'. The *viśvavajra* thus becomes the power of the awakened Base of Spine centre orienting and transmuting substance in such a way that it expands into a fully awakened Head lotus. The *jewel* then represents the matrix of the energy field that is organised by Mind wherein all this is accomplished. It is seen in terms of the *nāḍī* system, and when rightly purified and transformed into the Mind of a Jina, so then we have the *cintāmaṅī,* the 'diamond-Mind', the wish-fulfilling jewel of enlightenment.

The above presents an outline of an evolutionary process that is explained in different ways throughout this *Treatise on Mind.*

Dhyāni Bodhisattvas direct the Fiery qualities of cosmic Mind into planetary manifestation according to the degree that humanity can bear the Fires. By contrast, the Mahābodhisattvas distribute the Waters of cosmic Love to invoke the Bodhisattva ideal. These two energies (Love and Mind) combined express the potency of what is known as *bodhicitta*. We thus have:

1. Samantabhadra as the Ādi Buddha embodies the directive force of the first Divine aspect, which can best be described as Fiery Will or Power. Here the overall energies of the entire Head lotus of our planetary expression (Shambhala) are brought into play.
2. Vairocana (incorporating the qualities also of the remaining Jinas) manifests the second Divine aspect as Fiery Love-Wisdom from the domain of the Heart in the Head Lotus of Shambhala. Here the combined Compassion of all 'thus gone ones' directed to our planetary malaise is properly incorporated so that it best suits humanity within the conditioning evolving cyclic time zones. Our entire solar evolution is governed by this Ray of Love-Wisdom.
3. Samantabhadra as Bodhisattva expresses the third form of *dharmakāyic* Fire that turns all of the Wheels of Life upon our planet in the form of Mathematically Exact Activity. He thus dispenses attributes of cosmic Mind into manifestation, to direct the overall patterns of the *maṇḍalas* of Life. This energy emanates from the outermost activity tier of the Head lotus that is Shambhala. This Lord (the Manu) thus actively directs the Lives of our planetary dispensation. He plays the reflexive role of the above two Buddhas, bringing their potency into active manifestation.
4. Vajrapāṇi bears the fourth form of *dharmakāyic* Fire, that vitalises the fabric of space. The *vajra* directs the energies of the above triad via the power of the remaining three Dhyāni Bodhisattvas. (It thus embodies the function of the Ājñā centre.) It helps empower transformative activity in the three worlds of human livingness. This Lord acts as a Contemplative, a mediator integrating the energies directed from one group to the other. The *vajra* aptly controls the dispensation of the entire *nāḍī* system of all forms. Vajrapāṇi (Tsongkapa) thus comes to bear the reflexive potency of Akṣobhya's mirror-like Wisdom, in that he mirrors the *maṇḍalic* expression of Shambhala into the activity of the Council of Bodhisattvas. The Shambhalic energies are thus toned down, being incorporated into the matrix of the *maṇḍala* of evolving human consciousness (our focus here) by means of the remaining Dhyāni Bodhisattvas. They represent the 'Body' (Viśvapāni), 'Speech' (Ratnapāṇi) and 'Mind' (Avalokiteśvara) of this *maṇḍala*.

5. Avalokiteśvara manifests via the attributes of the direct Fires of Shambhala, becoming a Liberating Flame to help overcome all illusional thinking amongst humanity. Rationality and wisdom must inevitably guide human civilisation rather than emotionality. The steady stream of logical Thought directed from above will eventually overcome the glamour-forming attachments that the Solar Plexus of humanity forms. Avalokiteśvara therefore rightly vitalises those in *saṃsāra* that aspire towards aspirational thought. Here the Solar Plexus is viewed as the 'abdominal brain', which represents the sum of the streams of Lives that are evolving, or who bear consciousness. In this guise Avalokiteśvara (as the Christ[8]) takes the role of the Head of the Hierarchy of Bodhisattvas upon this planet. Engendering compassionate activity through the wise use of the Mind for humanity at this time is the main purpose of this prototype Bodhisattva, and all those Bodhisattvas he works with. The function of Avalokiteśvara's energy is specifically the conversion of the Watery energy of humanity. Their glamours and distorted perceptions must inevitably vanish via the translation of devotion into high aspiration towards the fruits that enlightenment brings. The murky Watery ocean created by humanity must be converted by those that utilise the power of the Mind of enlightenment, thus of appropriately explicated logic. The Watery substance will then be evaporated so that the Clear Light of Mind stands in its place. The concept of 'prototype Bodhisattva' refers to that which embodies the general population of Bodhisattvas. Their combined energies are utilised to assist in this task. Here the reflexive potency of Amitābha's Discriminating Inner Wisdom comes into expression.
6. Ratnapāṇi, demonstrating the power of the wish-fulfilling Jewel of compassionate thought, empowers the esoteric function of the Watery dispensation as a cleansing Fire. The glamoured perceptions

8 In the *New Testament* this one incarnated via the consecrated vehicle that Jesus provided (thus he was effectively a Tulku), to fully anchor on the earth a cosmic Principle of Love. Hence we have the Biblical term Christ-Jesus. No position in the Hierarchy is absolutely fixed. There is a continuous movement upwards and out of our cosmos as a 'thus gone one', once another has gained the qualities to take a senior's place. The Buddha, for instance, once held this position, now it is the role of the Christ, who once held an incarnation as the Buddha's disciple Śāriputra.

of humanity inevitably vanish via the translation of devotion into high aspiration towards the fruits that enlightenment brings. The murky Watery ocean created by humanity must be controlled by those that utilise the power of the Mind of enlightenment, thus of appropriately explicated logic, as was provided by the incarnation of this Lord as Padmasambhava. The energy of aspiration must be utilised in the application of meditation and yogic prowess utilising *dhāraṇīs* to invoke the powers desired, producing full mastery of the Waters. Ratnasambhava's Equalising Wisdom is thereby expressed into the Planetary manifestation.[9] Once the Watery perturbations have been stilled and clarified only the *nāḍī* system remains as a conduit for vital energies. The powers of the *chakras (siddhis)* can then be awakened producing mastery over all phenomena. Such was the path demonstrated by the 'lotus born one' (Padmasambhava). Consequently, the energies coursing through the Sacral centre (the distributer of energy) must eventually be mastered by humanity, assisted by the work of this Dhyāni Bodhisattva.

7. Viśvapāṇi, demonstrating the potency of the *viśvavajr*a—has the power to convert all aberrant *saṃskāras* in *saṃsāra* into enlightened attributes by grounding the potency of the *vajra* into the four directions of space. The Base of the Spine centre automatically begins to reveal its potency upon the physical domain of human livingness through the new edifices of civilisation that are brought to the fore, once people have been rightly orientated to Hierarchy and Shambhala. This conversion process of the formed realms manifests via the function of the seventh form of Shambhalic Fire, which cyclically regulates the activity and demonstrable Power of Mind to transform the landscapes of self-focussed mind. It rules the forces manifesting through the *chakras* via the pre-ordained originating patterns of Mind seeded into the *bījas* of what is to be by the Ādi Buddha. This exemplifies the role of the Mahāchohan. He incorporates all five attributes of the Divine Wills of Mind, reifying them so that they can be utilised by humanity. The inevitable

9 That Padmasambhava is seen to be an embodiment of Amitābha is because of the potent Fiery dispensation of all these Dhyāni Bodhisattvas. It is their fundamental energy of expression. Fire is the Element ruled by Amitābha.

purpose is to externalise the kingdom of Shambhala on earth in such a way that human civilisation emulates its qualities. Eventually the paradigm must be made concrete. This necessitates the application of the *viśvavajra,* through the organising power of the seventh Ray of Maitreya. He plays a subsidiary role of anchoring the power of the all into manifestation. The 'grounding' work of the Base of Spine centre veils an esoteric reason why Maitreya is considered as the next human Buddha, as well as being viewed as a Mahābodhisattva. In the above we have the reflex of the All-accomplishing Wisdom of Amoghasiddhi demonstrated.

The Dhyāni Bodhisattvas manifest in the form of a cardinal cross for the purveyance of the energy of the Divine Will into manifestation. We saw earlier that this is the cross of dynamic steadfast purpose that drives onward to (cosmic) fulfilment the entire *maṇḍala* of expression towards any direction that is the present Logoic purpose. This cross thus bears the Power of the forces borne by these Bodhisattvas directed towards effecting changes upon our planet.

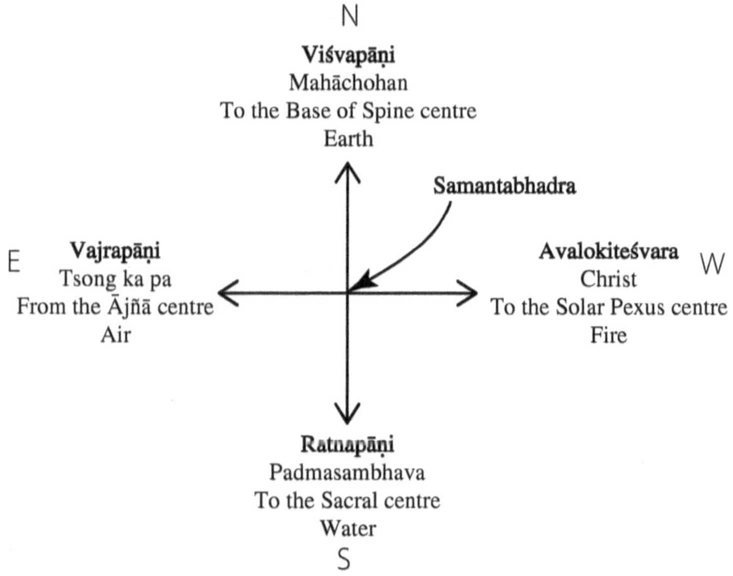

Figure 29. The Dhyāni Bodhisattvas

In this cross we see that Viśvapaṇi holds the northern position, disseminating the potency of the Earthy Element, from a cosmic perspective, for our planetary manifestation. He thus anchors what is for the 'thus gone ones' of cosmos their most concretised energy. This translates as the Divine Ideations regulating the *maṇḍala* of the higher mental plane. Ratnapāṇi takes this Fiery Energy and integrates it into the Watery dispensation of the world's disciples to assist in the rightful development of *siddhis,* and to counter the effects of the left hand practices promulgated by the wayward ones.

Vajrapāṇi takes the eastern position of directing Airy energies from the cosmic astral domain to feed the *nāḍīs* of the etheric web of humanity with the fundamental quality of Love-Wisdom that governs our solar system. Avalokiteśvara draws this Love-Wisdom energy (integrating it with the Fiery cosmic Mind) and projects it via the western orientation of the cross to rightly stimulate the Fires of the minds of humanity with the impetus of Love, so that inevitably wisdom is the gain. This is the fundamental energy that impresses and is utilised by the entire Hierarchy of Bodhisattvas as they progress along their Bodhisattva stages *(bhūmis)* serving humanity all along the Way.

The Dhyāni Bodhisattvas do not technically manifest as a swastika because they are contemplatives. They stand dynamically poised in meditation, directing planetary affairs from their high places within the Shambhalic domain. The Mahāchohan (Viśvapāṇi), however, rules the way of the swastika for the planetary system. This outpouring impresses upon people's minds via his left foot function (of the pentad) and stimulates material activity. The Dhyāni Bodhisattvas may also be represented as a pentad of expression. The focus here is from the point of view of the functioning Head centre (Shambhala) of the Logos of our planet via Vairocana. We thus have:

1. The Head of the pentad of the Dhyāni Bodhisattvas is Samantabhadra. He represents the directive potency stemming directly from Shambhala. From him the integral transformative power of the entire *maṇḍala* is directed. It represents the point of projection of Fiery energies at an advanced stage of meditation.
2. The objective of the right hand of the pentad, Vajrapāṇi, is the empowering of good will of humanity and its conversion to the Will-

of-Love. He therefore projects the forces effecting the transformation of *piṅgalā prāṇas* so that they can be directed to the Heart in the Head. He reflects the power of Akṣobhya's Mirror-like Wisdom into the Solar Plexus's domain. It should be noted here that the Solar Plexus in an ordinary individual is the source of the personal will, and similarly for the collective Solar Plexus of humanity. An important task, therefore, for the Dhyāni Bodhisattvas utilising this right hand energy is to try to overcome the potency of this will (such as which drives nations to make war, and their insensate selfishness).

3. The left hand of the pentad is held by Ratnapāṇi. The name means 'holder of the precious jewel', referring here to the 'jewel' of the Mind. A person's mind must come to dominate the emotions and field of desire via the imposition of any current intelligent project. Then it must aspire upwards via the power of Love to the domains of its abstraction before that jewel can be found. Ratnapāṇi thus embodies the power of the entire *maṇḍala* to convert the Watery *saṃskāras* of humanity so that the Eye of multidimensional discernment can be opened. He directs Ratnasambhava's Equalising Wisdom into manifestation by projecting the transforming *iḍā-nāḍī prāṇas* so that all energies can then be mastered. The radiant jewel of the *nāḍī* system will then be revealed.

4. The pentad's right foot is taken by Avalokiteśvara. He directs the power from the Heart of Life outwards into the field of service. The aim is the conversion of *kāma-manasic* propensities of humanity by washing them with the general *piṅgalā prāṇas* from the Heart in the Head centre. The entire field of Bodhisattvic activity must therefore be rightly directed to appropriately tackle the most important tasks of conversion in the most skilful manner. He directs the purpose of Amitābha's Discriminating Wisdom into manifestation. The focus therefore is upon rightly impressing the domain of the Sambhogakāya Flower (ruled by Amitābha) with the right seed thoughts so that they direct their incarnate personalities according to the overall Plan.

5. The left foot, Viśvapāṇi (the name means 'the holder of the *viśvavajra*', the extended *vajra* empowering all four directions of space). This position concerns the ability to project *manasic prāṇas* via the Throat centre into the fields of mind so that the

empirical mind can eventually be converted into Mind. Accordingly, Viśvapāṇi directs the imagery from the Knowledge tier of petals of the Shambhalic lotus to convert the *saṃskāras* of erroneous thought-streams of humanity. He therefore wields the most tangible, germane integration of the work of all the above Bodhisattvas designed for human consumption. Enlightening ideas are thereby produced in a way they can hopefully best comprehend. Through the potency of the imprint of his 'footsteps', the entire course of human civilisation should be able to turn its focus away from the material domain and upwards to the domains of liberation. He directs the All-Accomplishing Wisdom of Amoghasiddhi.

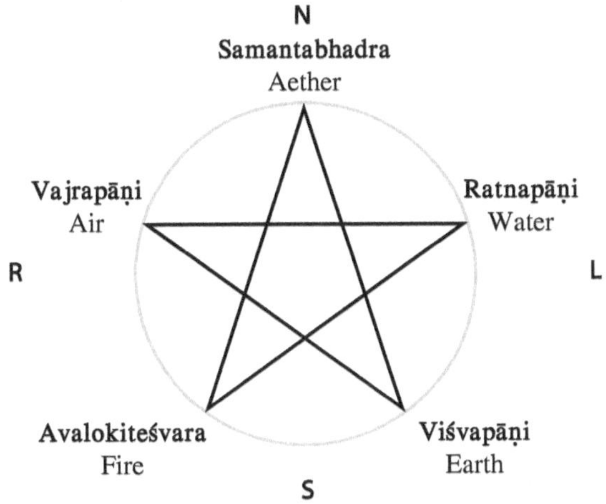

Figure 30. The governing pentad of Dhyāni Bodhisattvas

The left and right feet of this pentad play an interesting role in that they bring the full potency of the *iḍā* and *piṇgalā nāḍīs* of the entire Shambhalic Purpose actively into planetary manifestation. The cadence of the cycles of impressing the minds and hearts of humanity with their next step onwards towards evolutionary purpose represents the left and right steps of these feet. Avalokiteśvara bears the compassionate stream of the principle of Love via the rarefied Fires of Mind to engender Love-Wisdom in humanity via the domain of the Sambhogakāya Flower, hence his Tibetan name of Padmapāṇi, the wielder of the lotus. This right foot specifically steps onto the domain of these Flowers via the cosmic ethers (*śūnyatā*), to impetus this purpose via his stance as the downward-looking Lord. Viśvapāṇi bears the *manasic* stream, the principle of Mind into the planetary manifestation via the downpour of cosmic Waters directed by Ratnapāṇi. He thereby engenders Love-Wisdom in humanity by effectively stepping right down into the material domain the reified cosmic principles of Love and Mind.

The two 'hands' assist in the work of energy direction of Shambhalic Purpose. (Each 'hand' bears five fingers of *prāṇas* of energy.) Thus there is a direct line of interrelationship between Ratnapāṇi and Viśvapāṇi, Vajrapāṇi and Avalokiteśvara.

It should be noted that because this view is from the perspective of the Head lotus (of part of the constituency of Shambhala), so the downward focus of Avalokiteśvara (for instance), is from the domain of Mind into the agitated sphere of the world's Solar Plexus, upon which he is compassionately focussed. Our view is that the domain wherein humanity resides (*saṃsāra*) is the Solar Plexus centre of the planetary Logos, so then the above pentad of expression becomes inverted. The reason for this is that this domain represents the field of incarnation for the energies of these Dhyāni Bodhisattvas. Avalokiteśvara uses both the Fiery Throat and Heart centre energies to help convert those awash in the world's emotionality. The earlier listing of the eight Mahābodhisattvas was from the view of the Heart centre as a conversion principle, and included the function of the Splenic centre. If we subtract the three Bodhisattvas that have a dual function from the listing of the eight (Dhyāni Bodhisattvas), then the remaining five Mahābodhisattvas have specific relevance, in being able to enlighteningly transform one or other of the five sense-consciousnesses of the generalised *prāṇas* developed by humanity. They help refine these *prāṇas* and direct them upwards so that they can be absorbed into Shambhala. They therefore manifest in the form of an upward pointing pentad.

It is important to note the different representations of Avalokiteśvara. They are as follows:

1. As the head of the Council of Bodhisattvas, here called 'the Christ'.
2. The entire Hierarchy of Bodhisattvas, who collectively manifest the qualities of this downward looking compassionate Lord. It should be

noted that as such they work principally via inspiring the kingdom of the Sambhogakāya Flower. This is the 'right foot' expression. The 'left foot' expression involves actual incarnation into the *māyā*.

3. The Chohan symbolically taking this role, becomes the embodied vehicle of the Christ-principle in manifestation. This manifests via a sixth Ray dispensation, hence the term Christ-Jesus of the Christian Bible.

Another incarnation of this great One was Milarepa. Jesus founded a religion wherein Devotion became the mainstay of its expression, and Milarepa played a similar role for the Tibetan dispensation. Those who played a prominent role in the Biblical Story karmically had to incarnate in relation to him. The role of this Mahābodhisattva is significant, in that his main focus is the training of aspirants to overcome the Watery allurements of the astral plane. Because the emotional and desire principle (governed by the sixth Ray) is the major source of trouble, the cause of all types of defilements that mar the path to enlightenment for all seeking liberation, so this great One has a herculean task to offset the massed effect of humanity's emotional mire. Effectively then he plays the symbolic role of Avalokiteśvara in the form of the compassionate Buddha within each of the spokes of the wheel of the Six Realms. As such, compassion is the focus of the entire Council of Bodhisattvas, wherein cosmic Fire (*dharmakāya*) must come to liberate the Watery ones (emotional-desire based humanity) by providing them with the wisdom to overcome their woes. All Mahābodhisattvas work to assist in this onerous task. Samantabhadra, the apex of the downturned pentacle of Figure 32 then sets the conditionings for such activity. The *maṇḍala* of these ten Mahābodhisattvas represents the overlooking Lord of Compassion, and the wheel of the Six Realms represents the zone of shedding the tears of active compassion. It is what must be mastered by means of the Fires of Mind if enlightenment is to ensue and suffering overcome.

The five Mahābodhisattvas that form a pentad of expression when we remove those denoted as Dhyāni Bodhisattvas from the list of Mahābodhisattvas are responsible for the general evolutionary direction, and thus gradual purification of the five sense-consciousnesses, collectively developed by humanity. They represent the forces of the

Heart centre working via the Solar Plexus centre in conjunction with the work of the Dhyāni Bodhisattvas to transform *saṃskāras.* They then direct them to the centres above the diaphragm. Other *saṃskāras* need to be reprocessed in the Splenic centre, or sent to the Inner Round that energises the sum of the internal organs. (The constituent parts of a civilisation or nation.) The Bodhisattvas working within their various departments (thus are along the same Ray lines) assist in the general work of conversion of the associated *saṃskāras.*

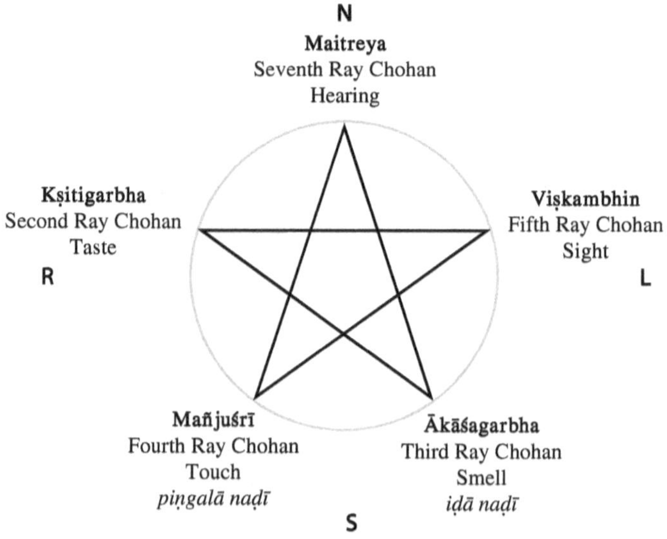

Figure 31. The pentad of Mahābodhisattvas

The head of this upward pointed pentad is Maitreya, the seventh Ray Chohan. He is responsible for the hearing sense-consciousness, wherein the sounds of all the *saṃskāras (karma)* generated via the physical incarnation of human beings are heard. They must be appropriately purified of noisy effects and made to harmonise with the 'music of the spheres' before they can be directed away from *saṃsāra,* and upwards to Shambhala. This work therefore includes the ability of humanity to eventually correctly intone the right mantras through ritual and purified living styles to produce magical effects in the formed domains. Maitreya thus governs the general expression of the cleansing of the aberrant *saṃskāras* of humanity via the cyclic impulses of the seventh Ray. This effect will become increasingly more predominant during this oncoming Aquarian epoch, which will be ruled by this Ray.

The right hand is represented by Kṣitigarbha (the second Ray Chohan). His purpose is to help generate the subtle discriminations within humanity associated with the taste sense-consciousness. These discriminations relate to the engendering of the energies of good will and the Will-to-Love, the *prāṇas* of the awakening of *bodhicitta* within the Solar Plexus's domain, which he directs to the Heart centre (Hierarchy). He is thus directly involved with the training of all who are developing Bodhisattva capabilities.

The left hand is taken by Viṣkambhin, the fifth Ray Chohan, who is concerned with helping humanity to rightly develop the *saṃskāras* associated with the sight sense-consciousness. We thus have the development of right mental discriminations, wisdom, from out of the projections of concrete-minded *saṃskāras*, which is the basis to all wisdom teachings.

The right foot is taken by Mañjuśrī, the fourth Ray Chohan, who directs the course of the *piṅgalā nāḍī* generated by humanity upwards to higher planes of perception. The generally Watery *saṃskāras* are therefore processed by his department. Here the touch sense-consciousness, of all generally loving attributes and feeling-perceptions of humanity pass through the alchemical process of upward moving essences that are continuously refined as they move to higher chambers of the still. The baser substances are recycled and redistilled, until all essences meet the required grade. The purpose is to incite compassion through right devotion.

The left foot position is held by Ākaśagarbha, the third Ray Chohan, that manifests a similar function with respect to the *iḍā nāḍī* stream (the development of *manas* in humanity). He specifically works with humanity's smell sense-consciousness, making sure that only the most abstracted, refined thoughts of right understanding within the elementary *manasic* fields of desire-mind can eventually reach the domains of Shambhala. The awakening of the attributes of Mind is the main reason why the sense-consciousnesses exist, as the human consciousness-stream perpetually manifests upon the physical domain to learn its most material lessons.

Figure 32. The Bodhisattvas and the Solar Plexus centre

When the two pentads are integrated into one *maṇḍala* we get Figure 32,[10] showing the mode of cleansing the petals of the planetary Solar Plexus centre by utilising the vivifying *prāṇas* from the Heart centre, the domain of the Council of Bodhisattvas. Collectively their actions manifest the tears of the Watery *prāṇas* from the cosmic astral plane, which is the demonstrated expression of the Love of all the Jinas in cosmos. Together they also symbolise the downward looking Lord of Compassion, shedding tears (purifying *prāṇas*) to enlighten and liberate the suffering ones.

Further information could be gleaned by the astute reader if the directional *prāṇas* to and from the various *chakras,* which the petals of the Solar Plexus centre interrelates with, such as the Liver and Stomach centres, are analysed. The qualities earlier associated with these *chakras* need to be assigned to the general population of humanity that have developed them. Thus, some human groups manifest primarily Stomach centre qualities, others Liver centre qualities, etc. We see therefore the respective target arenas that the various Mahābodhisattvas are focussed

10 This Figure can also be inverted, depending on the angle of vision.

upon via the Ray directives they embody. Their disciples incarnate to try to rectify these in a positive manner. In Figure 32, Samantabhadra is viewed as the first Ray Chohan, who is upon the line of development of the Lord of Life.

The role of the Consorts

Vairocana's Consort is Ākāśadhātvīśvarī. She therefore is the active embodiment of the substance of his *dharmadhatu* Wisdom. Technically, the Consort is a śakti, a force projection demonstrating the purpose of her Lord via the substance of the embodied form. This allows the expression of the power of the Wisdom of the Jina into *saṃsāra*. Hence we have the concept of the *prajñā* in Buddhism, the wisdom aspect of enlightenment, to best describe the nature of the Consort. Her role thus is similar to that of the Dhyāni Bodhisattvas, except that she embodies the reflexive substance via which the compassion of the Bodhisattva is carried out. In doing so both carry the Wisdom component of the Jina, however, the Bodhisattva expresses the compassionate action, seeded in *dhyāna,* and the Consort is the mechanism of delivery. All happens via her agency, which is the substance of the *māyā* wherein it is carried out. Thus the *karma* of the action is seeded, and inevitably the *karma* is rectified in the process of harmonising the movement of the *māyā* of being.

Ākāśadhātvīśvarī is the main source of *prāṇas* from *dharmakāya* which the Mahābodhisattva's Consorts (of the cardinal directions) draw from. The Consorts also draw energies from one another depending upon the energy source that is most purposeful at any time. The Consorts assist in setting the stage (the karmic conditionings) that allows the transformation of attributes of consciousness via union with their respective partners. This transformative process is illustrated as the symbol of sexual union where the 'white drops' (semen) of consciousness are admixed with the 'red drops' of the mind (*ḍākinī* substance) in their womb that may produce the 'child' of enlightened perception or liberation.

The activity of each Mahābodhisattva of the four cardinal directions of the *maṇḍala* of the eight Mahābodhisattvas uniquely distributes the qualities of the Dhyāni Buddhas in their own way. (The cardinal directions being the orientation of the Dhyāni Buddhas.) We thus have

Avalokiteśvara—the overall elimination of suffering in the normal world of human relationships; Kṣitigarbha—through the seeding of *bodhicitta* so that humanity can follow the way of the Heart; Vajrapāṇi—to bring immutable spiritual power to those aspiring to gain enlightenment, and Ākāśāgarbha—the awakening *chakras* of those who correctly follow yogic pursuit.

Each Consort integrates the energies from a pair of Dhyāni Buddhas along the northeast—southwest or southeast—northwest axis of the diagram. They thereby project the background environment for the transformative process of consciousness associated with the qualities of the Buddhas whose *maṇḍalas* they are part. This occurs in accordance with the contemplative focus of these Buddhas upon the Bodhisattvas and their Consorts. The Dhyāni Buddha at the centre of each swastika integrates all of the associated *prāṇas*. The Dhyāni Buddha assists in the conversion of all consciousness-attributes into that of his primary Wisdom. He also incorporates the transmutative potency of the Void Element associated with him to assist the work of the Bodhisattva Consorts in the field of substance and associated *karma*.

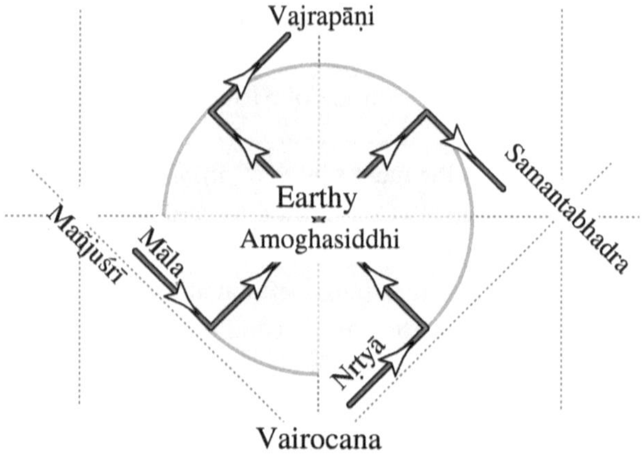

Figure 33. The energy flow of the *maṇḍala*

The Figure above represents one segment of the *maṇḍala* of the Mahābodhisattvas which illustrates the way the *ḍākinīs* direct *prāṇas* from one level of expression to the next higher, like an alchemical retort. There are two tiers or spheres of activity within the *maṇḍala* in which the *ḍākinīs* function. An inner tier that relates to the processing of transferring *prāṇas* from a lower to a higher level. An outer tier which integrates the *prāṇas* from an external source so that it can be processed. (Each arm of a swastika, associated with one or other of the *ḍākinīs* therefore manifests this dual function.) We see that all energy flows become properly admixed in the centre, and redirected according to the purpose of the associated Jina.

Each of the *ḍākinīs* work directly with their corresponding sister. One directs *prāṇas* from the centre of their portion of the major *maṇḍala* (Figure 28) in accord with the four inner Consorts (Lāsyā, Dhūpa, Nṛtyā and Gitā). The other integrates the various qualities of the Consorts associated with the outer tier of the *maṇḍala*. The *prāṇas* reticulate around the outer tier of the *maṇḍala*, as well as to and from the inner tier of the *maṇḍala*. The flow of *prāṇa* is regulated by *karma* within the body of manifestation of each *ḍākinī*. Each arm therefore manifests in the form of a yin-yang, and their interconnectedness assists their ability to direct the *karma* governing all manifest forms. One spiral of the yin-yang is inward focussed, and the other outwards.

With respect to the *ḍākinīs* governing the outer, activity sphere of the *maṇḍala*, we see that they govern the evolution of the forms via which the appearing lives incarnate.

1. The *ḍākinī* of the southeast direction, Ālokā, is concerned with building the forms occupied by human consciousness, and the consequent evolutionary push for this kingdom. The illuminating light that will enlighten all thoughts can then develop, causing eventual liberation (*śūnyatā*). This brings into manifestation the qualities of the Mirror-like Wisdom of Akṣobhya. The ensuing process allows humanity to enter a superhuman kingdom constituted of Bodhisattvas and Buddhas. Ālokā is paired with Lāsyā, who clarifies the substance of the Heart that is the Mind so that it manifests in the form of a mirror. This allows the candidate to visualise Life in the realm of enlightened being as a precursor to entering it.

2. The *ḍākinī* of the northwest direction, Gandhā, builds the evolving forms of the animal kingdom in such a way that they can develop a human-like intellect, and eventually enter the animal version of

śūnyatā. The Fiery energies of Amitābha are therefore incorporated into the world-sphere. With respect to humanity, Gandhā is concerned with the substance of human intellects, helping them to build a better thought life. This process continues until humans develop enlightened perceptions and are liberated from *saṃsāra*. Gandhā is teamed with Gitā (being two arms of the same swastika) who as previously stated 'enlightens all perceptions', allowing humans to develop the inner hearing, to listen to all liberating sounds, the mantras from the higher domains. They can thereby attain more desirable rebirths.

3. The *ḍākinī* of the southwest direction, Puṣpā, directs the *devas* who build the forms of the plant kingdom, and is also concerned with the evolution of their sentience. As these plant lives evolve, their sentience eventually enters the plant *śūnyatā*, preparatory to becoming members of the animal kingdom. Her corresponding responsibility with respect to the human kingdom is to build the human *chakras*. The 'Mother of Pearl' and 'white lotus' Puṣpā carries are symbols of the *chakras*, whilst the mother of pearl colour symbolises the rainbow hues of the *prāṇas* in the *chakras*. In later completion stages of yogic development she will help with the awakening of *siddhis*, such as that of past-life vision and remembrances. The Watery Element, of whose substance she and her *devas* embody, must be fully mastered in this process. Her work therefore is to help purify the *prāṇas*, making them esoterically white, a colour containing the sublime potencies of all the Rays of light. She is paired with Dhūpa, whose 'sweet smelling essences' represent the qualities of the purified *prāṇas*. The *siddhis* thus involve mastery of everything incorporated in the astral domain created by humanity from Puṣpā-Dhūpa's Watery substance.
4. The *ḍākinī* for the northeast direction, Mālā, directs the Earthy quality of Amoghasiddhi via Samantabhadra's virtue of universal kindness. This means that Mālā is concerned with building the mineral forms and directing the aeonic course of the evolution of the elementary lives embodying all forms. They can then eventually enter the mineral *śūnyatā* and consequently become a member of the plant kingdom. This *śūnyatā* thus represents the zone of transition

for the sentience of a mineral unit into that of a plant form. The point of transition happens at a microbial level.

Mālā also works to help build and to vitalise the forms of all liberated lives via the *nāḍī* system, symbolised by the 'garlands of flowers' attributed to her. This incorporates the higher, transmuted correspondence of the mineral kingdom in cosmos (the *manasic* substance of the *tathāgatagarbha*) that eventually evolves to Buddhahood. This Earthy quality represents the transmuted, refined *saṃskāras* of the *yogin* who is in the process of developing the All-Accomplishing Wisdom of Amoghasiddhi. She is paired with Nṛtyā, who prepares the candidate to enter cosmos by offering heavenly food; the visions of what will transpire in that liberated state of great bliss. They represent the visions provided to those upon the first three Initiation levels. This concerns the way of being appropriately incorporated into the domain of the cosmic plant kingdom (*chakras*).

The Elements associated with the intermediate positions are Airy-Earth for the northeast; Watery-Air for the southeast position; Firey-Water for the southwest direction; Earthy-Fire for the northwest direction. The dominant Element in any pair depends upon the nature of the *saṃskāra* governing an individual, or aspect of the world-sphere, at any time.

Having built the substance of the various sheaths that are the embodied qualities of the Elements constituting a human persona, it is natural, therefore, that the *ḍākinīs* appear in the consciousness of a *yogī* or *yoginī* at various important stages of their spiritual development. This happens when they are transmuting the attributes of a specific important obscuring *saṃskāra,* and thus must move to the next stage of the refinement of substance, hence of development towards the production of the Void Elements. Mastery of the elemental substance into which one has incarnated produces the associated *siddhi.* It is therefore of great benefit both to the *yogin* concerned, and the *deva* Life (embodying the substance) that is elevated thereby. The *ḍākinī* often then indicates what must be developed or done next (for the purifying of those sheaths, or the rectification of *karma*). This is illustrated in the many stories of visualisations and appearances of *ḍākinīs* at important times in the lives of the great Bodhisattvas.

Sometimes a *ḍākinī* appears at an early stage of a *yogin's* development to direct him/her to One who can instruct in this yogic alchemy. The imagery of the lives of various Mahāsiddhas veils the many steps of this process.

The evolution of mind in Nature

The *ḍākinīs* are characterised as expressions of the Mahābodhisattvas to which they are bonded, but their focus is upon the karmic attributes of embodied forms, thus upon the way of evolution of sentience. Sentience is the precursor of the human mind. This is the key for further analysis when endeavouring to extrapolate what is possible from the considerably veiled characteristics assigned to them in the texts. In analysing the function of the eight Consorts we are effectively enquiring into the mode of evolution of the five sense-consciousnesses, as developed by the major classes of the animal kingdom, rather than as perceived in humanity.

It is easy to perceive, for instance, that dogs and their kin have developed a heightened sense of smell (it is in effect their speciality), eagles and other stalking animals a heightened sense of sight. The intention here however is not to draw a list of the various members of the animal kingdom to note their predominant evolutionary characteristic. These are fundamental principles that will allow later researchers to form a comprehensive analysis to be made regarding the way the sense perceptions are developed in Nature, and are finally incorporated in a humanity that has evolved out of the animal kingdom.

Three further qualities of the five sense perceptions can be presented. They represent the precursors of higher sense-faculties possessed by the human kingdom. They are:

1. Elementary mind
2. Devotion
3. The expression of dominance

These qualities will eventually become transmuted in humanity. Elementary mind is the foundation for the development of the astute abstract Mind that is the basis of all wise action. This is governed by the third Ray of Mathematically Exact Activity. Devotion becomes the matrix that allows the awakening of Love (*bodhicitta*). Here we have the foundation of that which is ruled by the second Ray of Love-Wisdom. Dominance develops at first the self will that largely differentiates humanity from the lesser kingdoms in Nature. We then have the development of the Will-to-Good which pierces all barriers on the road to enlightenment and eventual liberation. Thus is the qualification of the first Ray of Will or Power.

These three qualities are the basis to the formation of the three major groups of petals of the Sambhogakāya Flower:

1. Elementary mind—the Knowledge petals.
2. Devotion—the Love-Wisdom petals.
3. The expression of dominance—the Sacrifice petals.

In terms of the eight *vijñānas* of the Yogācāra philosophy we see that elementary mind is translated in terms of the *manovijñāna* (intellect), *kliṣṭamanas* in terms of devotion and all associated emotionalities and dominance as the general purveyance of the *ālayavijñāna*.

When analysing the *maṇḍala* of the eight Mahābodhisattvas with respect to the above there are two groupings of *ḍākinīs*.

1. The four of the inner circle, associated with Vairocana's purpose.
2. The four of the outer circles associated with the activities of the corresponding Mahābodhisattvas.

The four inner *ḍākinīs* are responsible for the development in Nature of qualities related to the mind and its expression, rather than merely the functioning of the sense-perceptors. Thus the qualities of elementary mind, devotion, and the expression of dominance, are assigned to them. To this listing we must add the sense of vision to complete the quaternary, as vision is the sense-perceptor that most directly stimulates the mind and its development.

The quality *devotion* is an expression of the Watery Element, governing the general expression of the emotions, thus Ākāśagarbha's Consort, Dhūpā, is responsible for its development in Nature.

The quality *elementary mind* (the Element governing the mind) is a Fiery expression that Avalokiteśvara's Consort, Gitā, is responsible for developing.

The quality *dominance* is an Earthy expression (the physical plane being the domain that needs to be dominated). We therefore have Vajrapaṇi's Consort, Nṛtyā, in control of its development in Nature.

From this perspective the quality *vision* is an Airy expression, which enables the ability to perceive far into the distance, and to gauge perspective, the shape and nature of forms. Therefore Kṣitigarbha's Consort, Lāsyā, is responsible for its development.

Together these four Consorts also develop the fifth Element, the Aetheric, which can be considered the subtlest essence or 'perfume' of the previous four Elements. These essences are both seeded by the five Jinas and reaped as evolutionary gain. Eventually the various forms of animal sentience are transmogrified into the factors incorporated as human intelligence.

Note that the qualities assigned to the Elements here may differ to that presented earlier in Volume 3, chapter 5, of this series. For instance, vision (or sight) being assigned to the Airy Element rather than to the Fiery.[11] The reason for this is twofold. The first being that here we are analysing only the groups of four generally found in Nature, as the fifth Element is most refined and barely represented therein. Secondarily, the qualities of the sense-perceptors (*skandhas* and *saṃskāras*) attributed to them formerly apply only to the human kingdom. They are factors of mind, or intelligence that the animal kingdom has not yet developed.

We now need to look to the Elements assigned to the four remaining Consorts of the Mahābodhisattvas guarding the intermediate directions or gates of the *maṇḍala*. The relations are more or less the direct correlations of the physical attributes of the qualities touch, taste, smell, and hearing to that of the four Elements. Sight is omitted here because it is the major sense related to the development of the mind, as treated above. The other sense-perceptions play an auxiliary role, but may be dominant in one or other animal species.

The sense of *touch* (sense of body) consequently is Earthy in quality, as physical things are what are touched in order to experience and to

11 From the perspective of the expression of the instincts within a human unit the instinct of self assertion relates to the sense of smell and to Aether. The group or herd instinct relates to the sense of taste and to Air. The instinct towards knowledge relates to the sense of sight and to Fire. The sexual instinct relates to the sense of touch and to Water. The instinct of self preservation relates to the sense of hearing and to Earth.

survive in the material world. Samantabhadra's Consort, Māla, therefore regulates the development of this sense in Nature.

The sense of *smell* is Airy because the olfactory apparatus needs the perfumes and odours in the air in order to function. Mañjuśri's Consort, Ālokā, regulates the development of this sense in Nature.

The sense of *taste* is Watery as one must masticate with saliva in order to taste anything. Maitreya's Consort, Puṣpā, performs the function of seeding this Element in Nature.

The sense of *hearing* is therefore (from the present perspective) Fiery, as of all these four sense-perceptors, hearing necessitates the most developed sense of discernment as to where the sounds are coming from and what they mean. Also, this sense leads inevitably to the function of speech, which is one of the specific qualities possessed by humans that signify their intellectual faculties. This is not possessed by animals, except in the most rudimentary fashion. Viṣkambhin's Consort, Gandhā, regulates the development of this sense in Nature.

From the northeast direction Māla works with the *'sense of the body',* principally to develop the general forms of interrelated species, and the integrated interrelation of the social structures between species. This concerns the perfection of balance and harmony in all of Nature.

We see here that the means of physical existence whereby all species can come to interrelate through the forms they have incarnated in is seeded via this northeast direction, which represents the originating source of all *maṇḍalic* activity. Māla directs their activities via the 'garland of flowers' that is one of her symbols. The garlands symbolise *chakras* that organise all manifest life, through which the animal kingdom incarnate, according to the inherent characteristics possessed by the *chakras.* Once scientists properly understand the *chakras,* then the true mode and lines of evolution of the various kingdoms of Nature can be understood.

Māla's other symbol, the bell, refers to her command of sound that directs the movements of all manifest life via the *nāḍī* system in the Body of the great Mother.[12]

Ālokā's southeast direction assigns her to the development of the sense of *smell* in Nature, being part of the Airy swastika. Smell refers

12 The Mother of the World. All *devas* and *ḍākinīs* are part of Her body of manifestation.

at first to awakening to the awareness of direction, then of belonging to a group, pack, or herd, within the expanse of territorial boundaries. This also produces an awareness of enemies, and imparts knowledge of sexual pheromones, fear, and other subjective tangibles. Inevitably we have the development of subjective perceptions, with the clairvoyant and clairaudient abilities of animals effectively being their prime means of communication. These faculties are a non-intellectual sense of knowingness, coupled with the instinct that drives them to eventual fulfilment. They represent the highest of the developed animal qualities. It is the animal's version of the enlightened thought-awareness conveyed to humans by Ālokā. Such development then indicates the way whereby many animals move in unison, such as schools of fish and flocks of birds. In the more advanced animals, such as dogs, we can observe how sympathetically attuned they become to the wishes of their masters.

In humanity such inner perception becomes the basis for *siddhis* in later stages of development. People can then gain the experiences they need for further empirical development and evolution on the road to the illuminating light that will eventually produce release from all bondage.

In the southwest direction, Puṣpā, by being part of the Watery swastika, works at the development of the sense of *taste* in the animal kingdom. This is the least developed of the senses, and is more specifically associated with the subtle discernments obtained through close social interactions, than the eating of food. The tongue is used to bond the higher animals of a family group. It concerns the processes related to finding a mate and building a nest, den, etc., to produce offspring and their upbringing. It also involves the nature of the developed relations in group, herd, or family interrelations and affectionate interplay (specifically amongst young mammals), such as between a pride of Lions. The statement formerly given concerning Puṣpā's ability to listen to all sounds and cries of suffering of the needy translates here to the mother animal's keen psychic sense of responsibility for the welfare of her offspring, which Puṣpā works to foster. The implication also concerns the strong relation between the Fiery and Watery Elements (taste and hearing) via such herd and family relationships and the use of the mouth. It lays the foundation for the development of speech, one of the distinctive human attributes.

Puṣpā integrates her energies with those from the northwest Fiery swastika of Gitā and Ghandā. The integration assists her work for the development of the sense of *hearing* in Nature. This concerns hearing the sounds and intonations of formed being; the warnings for defence or flight, the sounds of the prey, the general sounds of the environment, and cries of suffering. It also involves hearing instructions from the higher guiding and manipulative intelligences, such as *devas* and humans. This allows the most important advanced form of sentience to be developed by the animal kingdom, the elementary mind that represents the way out of the animal kingdom and into the human. Therefore, instead of working to 'overcome all presently-occurring intellectual activities', which is the keynote of Gandhā's work with humans; in the animal kingdom her function is to instate such abilities. Gandhā is said to carry 'incense', (which is smelt), which here represents the nascent *manas*, that when lit by Fiery development will awaken animal sentience to rudimentary thought.

The inner circle of *ḍākinīs*

In the above account we can see that the way of evolution concerns Intelligent Design, governed by the guiding principle of the *ḍākinīs,* rather than the Darwinian concept of natural selection via survival of the fittest. Darwin's theory has been discredited in many ways, such as the lack of missing links in the fossil evidence. Competitiveness is of course important, and does have a role to play in the development of nascent intelligence, but does not guide evolutionary change from one species to the next.

Having established the foundation for the development of mind within the general constituency of animal evolution, (later to evolve into the four out of the five basic groupings of human *saṃskāras*), we can now look to the workings of the inner circle of Consorts.[13] Their work specifically concerns the fanning of the flames of mind, enthusing devotion, and the sense of dominance in the members of the animal kingdom that are being prepared as candidates to enter the human kingdom. This perspective will focus upon the broader activities of

---

13 The focus of this inner circle is upon the Consorts of the Mahābodhisattvas, rather than on the Consorts of the Dhyāni Buddhas, because the latter play a similar role specifically with human *karma,* which is not our concern here.

these *ḍākinīs* rather than the specific details of human awakening.

Nṛtyā, incorporating the Earthy Element, produces development of the sense of *dominance* in Nature. This form of competitive spirit allows natural selection to take place upon the physical domain, as a form of Darwinian theory but by Intelligent Design, not chance. We therefore have for instance the masculine rivalry over breeding rights and the fight for territorial dominance in many animal species. (In humanity this quality manifests as the desire for power over others, and the many wars by nations for territorial possession.) Once having conquered the territorial zone for breeding purposes, the animal unit then experiences its version of the 'foretaste of bliss' delegated by this Consort. Also, through the achievement of dominance, an animal form can individualise from its group experience into singular individual *karma;* that esoterically differentiates human beings from animals.

Lāsyā, working via the Airy Element, assists in the development of the sense of *vision* in Nature. This concerns the ability of animals to gauge depth, and to rightly discriminate the different characteristics between objects. They can then move forward to forage, attack prey, etc. The development of the sense of sight facilitates the awakening of the discriminative abilities of a mind structure that will elevate the animal kingdom out of its domain, and into an animal śūnyatā preparatory to incarnating into a newly forming group of animal-men. This necessitates the formation of the Sambhogakāya Flower for each animal unit. From this perspective the mirror that Lāsyā carries projects the developing primal animal-mind into the domain of Mind, wherein the Sambhogakāya Flower *(tathāgatagarbha)* can be incorporated around the elements of that animal-mind.

Gītā, utilising the Fiery Element, works at quickening the development of the nascent *elementary mind* in Nature. (Instigated because of Nṛtyā's foundational work.) Sentient lives can then eventually individualise into the forms of containment of mind known as humans, whose sequence of unfolding lives are governed by a newly formed overshadowing *tathāgatagarbha*. She does this by closely interrelating target members of the animal species in this western direction (such as dogs, cats, horses) with humanity.[14] Through this close association with

14 The context for this close interrelation between humans and animals is in relation

human (manasic) activity, and by mimicry, animal sentience can then be fanned by the Fires of mind. Karmic ties are thereby established with humanity, producing a sense of aspiration or companionship and, of sharing activity with individual members of humanity.

Specifically, human speech is 'obeyed' (by domesticated animals), with the articulation of its sounds and related meanings being somewhat comprehended and then remembered. This produces *saṃskāras,* remembrances that are carried through to successive generations of the animals concerned. They gradually become skilled in this faculty, necessitating eventual incarnation in human forms as the next evolutionary step for them. Gītā is therefore said to 'enlighten all perceptions of tone with the sound of heavenly music', meaning here that her speciality concerns the direction of sounds in Nature, so that eventually human articulation can be established as a natural outcome of evolutionary gain.

Dhūpā works to intensify the forms of animal companionship with humans through the quality of *devotion* in domesticated pets, and between animals that have developed social traits, such as wolves. The foundation for the much later development of love and wisdom in humanity lies in these affectionate ties. We therefore have the adding of the Watery principle to the nascent Fiery qualities so far developed amongst animals. This produces concepts of attachment and 'belonging' to a human master, within the contexts of the related cycle of activities, and formation of further qualities to be added to the *saṃskāric* 'remembrances' earlier developed. (Further incarnations of the animal species into this southeast direction of the *maṇḍala* thereby consolidate the generated qualities.)

Through close companionship with humans, as evidenced in household pets such as dogs and horses, a way out of the limitations of animal sentience is found. The animal kingdom's form of *nirvāṇa* is thereby attained. We also have the exemplification of what may be viewed as heroic activity of certain animals to assist humans, where they engender characteristics beyond the bounds of normal animal behaviour. For example, the dog that jumps into a river to try to save a

---

to the future evolution of the present animal kingdom. There was a different process involved in the past because humans were not then incarnate.

drowning person, or a horse with an uncanny sense of prescience with respect to its human master.

The 'sweet-smelling essences' that Dhūpa carries refers here to the highly developed devotional and emotional *saṃskāras* that the animal kingdom have developed amongst their own species, especially with respect to companionship with their human 'owners'. With respect to their animal origins these are the easiest qualities to recognise in humans. They become the basis for the theriomorphic entities that shall be analysed in the next volume of this series, *An Esoteric Exposition of the Bardo Thödol.*

Another perspective concerning the *ḍākinīs* can now be presented, related to their overall work in Nature. The four outer *ḍākinīs* are responsible for the purveyance of the Elements because by the time the substance has flowed to them it has become sufficiently concretised to manifest as *saṃsāra*:

Mālā: (touch)	Earth
Gandhā: (hearing)	Fire
Ālokā: (smell)	Air
Puṣpā: (taste)	Water

Each of the four inner *ḍākinīs* are concerned with the welfare and evolution of a specific kingdom of Nature. The view is from two perspectives. Firstly, that relating to the downward drive of substance (*skandhas*) into objective manifestation and the early genesis of *saṃskāras* by the kingdoms concerned. Next, that related to later evolutionary development.

1. Nṛtyā: (dominance) Earth—*humanity.* We view the human domain here in terms of the Earthy Element, rather than the Airy, because of the level of expression upon which we are focussed. The physical form contains the instincts that by now are below the threshold of consciousness for humanity, which were developed via physical incarnation. With respect to humanity this concerns the development of the 'self' concept, of individualistic competitiveness that drives the personal-I to manifest its selfish attitudes. The 'earthy' domain then becomes the place of ascent, wherein the human factor takes over from the elemental *deva* forces of Nature, to be responsible for its own

evolutionary development. Hence we have the entire path to liberation necessitating the complete mastery of all the factors associated with *saṃsāra,* within the context of being incarnate in a physical body.

With respect to the mineral kingdom, the term 'dominance' represents the basic substance that dominates the forms into which all lives must incarnate. The purpose of the evolutionary process is for the reincarnating lives to eventually dominate this substance, which happens once a human kingdom has developed the science of yoga.

The *chakras* concerned for the human kingdom is at first the Solar Plexus - Sacral/Throat centre interrelation, and later the Heart centre. The mineral kingdom (in its etheric and concrete manifestation) manifests via the Sacral/Base of Spine centres. The four petals of the Base of Spine centre are also responsible for the dissemination and cohesion of the formed nature of all the four kingdoms in Nature.

2. Gītā: (elementary mind)—*animal kingdom,* Fire. This involves the general development of the basic qualities needed for animals to evolve into a humanity. There are two levels of expression. The first relates to the development of the basic sense-consciousnesses. The second is associated with the interrelation of higher domesticated animals to humans. The *chakra* involved is the Solar Plexus centre, and the entire Inner Round. The 'mind' here developed is the desire-mind, governed by the 'abdominal brain'.
3. Dhūpā: (devotion)—*plant kingdom,* Water. This concerns the general energisation that feeds all kingdoms in Nature. 'Devotion' is here viewed as an intensified form of energy projected towards a specific project or agenda. This view concerns the way plants provide sustenance to all forms of life. Plants utilise energy directly from the sun and from dissolved mineral compounds, combining these in the form of the substances (vitamins, chlorophyll, etc.) that the animal kingdom can utilise. Esoterically, the energy currents (*prāṇas*) in Nature are channelled through the externalised *nāḍīs* to the floral attributes of the *chakras* that embody the sacred locations in Nature. The various groups of plant sentience (*devas*) manifest as externalisations of the archetypal *chakras*. The *chakra* involved is the Splenic centre, and associated minor *chakras* of the Inner Round.

4. Lāsyā: (vision)—*mineral kingdom*, Air. The Airy focus here is with the etheric component of the mineral kingdom, rather than the atoms of substance. We are therefore concerned with the energy fields upon which all depends. The physical form is the automatic concretion of these energies. It is difficult for most to think in terms of these energy fields and what pertains to the real, so ensconced are they in thinking of the concretions of *saṃsāra* all around. For the mineral kingdom 'vision' concerns the nature of the upward march of this most basic sentience, the atomic essences of things (occultly termed 'the blinded lives') towards arenas of light. This upwards march to light is the reason why the next highest kingdom needs light to sustain its existence. Therefore crystals that refract light, and the beautiful colouration of many ores, represent the highest stage of development of this kingdom. The development of vibrant colouration represents the mechanism of 'enlightenment' for this basic level of sentience in this hylozoistic universe, whilst radioactivity presents their means of liberation. All other kingdoms in Nature evolve from this foundational kingdom, producing increasing sensitivity to and the need of the response to light, and eventually the development of sight. Sight then becomes the essential sense that develops the Fires of mind.

   For humans, vision implies more that just the extended animal function obtained by the eyes, but also the development of inner vision, the Clear Light of Mind, associated with the awakening of the Heart and Throat centres, in combination with those of the Head. Indeed, the meaning of the significant word 'enlightenment' is based upon the extension of the concept of 'light' obtainable only from reaching supernal domains.

   The mineral kingdom also grounds the influence of the subtlest of the five Elements (Aether), which is all-pervasive and too subtle to be expressed at this level of consideration of the *maṇḍala*. The laws of energy interrelationships governing atoms veil the nature of the laws emanating from *dharmakāya*. The influence manifests in the form of the 'five-ness' already discussed. We can therefore add the kingdom of the *devas/ḍākinīs* (inclusive also of the domain of liberated being) to the four abovementioned to complete the picture of the nature of manifestation.

The above essay has presented a concept to Buddhists as to the scientific application of their philosophy that has hitherto been veiled. This can now be further developed by later advocates of the religion to help bring to the fore a new scientific understanding, where the subjective inner universe concerning the laws governing mind can be applied to investigate the outer world of phenomena. The information here presented can then be amended or further developed according to results accrued through investigative deduction. The complete panoply of the Head lotus can then awaken upon this enlightenment path.

12

Cells of Time

The experience of time

Having analysed the functioning of the Dhyāni Buddhas, Mahābodhisattvas and Consorts, we can now continue our focus on the theme of consciousness, and to the way it evolves. We saw that the Eightfold Path indicates the way this progression happens in the eight directions in space. Consciousness grows (like any other membrane in a cellular structure) from the territory wherein the originating seed (*bīja*) was planted to the domain of the fully grown tree of knowable awareness in the eight directions. All associated lives move together, from the originating territory to a domain that exists in some vast unknown space.

Implicit in this theme then is the growth of what can be termed *cells of time*. Time is experienced within the membrane surrounding consciousness. Such a membrane exists at the surface of any thought-sphere (thought-form), which first makes contact with any new sense-impression. This experience represents the present cognition of experiential growth. As that experiential growth moves in time so we have the production of the cellular structure. All that is held within it represents the past, whilst the sum of the activity of the structure represents the eternal Now. All outside of it is the relative future. The past, the present and the future are experienced sequentially in the growth of consciousness. The cell is alive, continuously moving, expanding and broadening its scope for response to any stimuli coming from any of the eight directions. Therefore it grows, expanding all of its membranes and organelles. It grows whenever a being incarnates into an experiential form. Each being can also be seen to collectively manifest an aspect or mechanism for the growth of a vaster cell of time into which they are integrated. Such collectivised units are then incorporated into vaster units, and so forth, until the vast stretches of a universe come to be manifest in the form of one integrated cellular unit. This is the basis for the understanding of our universe to be hylozoistic, as well as by extension to be inclusive of a 'God' concept. A being progresses with the culmination of experience, adding to the collective storehouse of consciousness of the cellular unit. The cell accumulates consciousness-*bījas* in the form of units of knowledge (of experience, movement and change) once unnamed, then named. The *bījas* then develop *saṃskāras* that will govern the generation of future activity.

Conscious life grows and eventually moves beyond the confines of the form that contained it. It expands until it is apparently extinguished in a particular life, and then is reborn. This happens because the inherent instinct to gather knowledge is ingrained in the very nature of consciousness. Lack of comprehension of what lies 'outside' the consciousness-space compels consciousness to manifest the appropriate form via which it can come to know. The rebirthing principle is therefore integral to this function of consciousness. This produces comprehension of a fundamental law of Life, the ever-spiralling unit that grows and expands until the path is known from the seed's territory to the full extent of the consciousness-tree's domain. New seeds are then produced, based upon the empirical gain of the past cycle, and adapted to accomplish a greater capacity to know more. Everything moves from the progenitor's territory to be ever more inclusive of vaster consciousness-spaces, and beyond. Thus the vast domain of a universe inevitably comes to be.

From this perspective *śūnyatā* can be viewed as that which is represented outside the circumference or ring of experience of the consciousness of the cell. It represents the 'all' which could be experienced, but which is presently not known. In purely physical terms, therefore, it represents the vacuum of space. It can also be veiled by the central *bīja* 'point' from whence all originated.[1]

As *time* is experienced on the surface of the membrane, with respect to the exterior phenomena that the conscious unit contacts, so consciousness, or conscious expansion of thought, is made by the passing of time via this 'membrane'. (Physically manifest as our brain awareness, represented as the mechanism of neurons and their synapses.) The influx of energy from the past into the future would cause the body that was informed to expand until it could no longer contain the expansion. However, it is met by a resistance to the internal pressure by the impact of what is to be. This represents the pressure of new experiences from sense-contact upon the membrane.

It also presents a view to be taken into account by present physicists exploring the logic of a 'big bang' universe, that such a universe has an implied limit to its expansions brought about by an implied resistance of a primeval substance (elemental mind) within which it is expanding, and which it is seeking to come to Know by means of incorporating that substance into its cellular structure. From this perspective we have a consideration of 'dark matter'. There is a natural boundary, a 'ring-pass-not'[2] to every incarnating unit, a skin of delineation containing the sequence of consciousness-expression for that cycle. The entire process is predetermined by the nature and content of the originating *bīja*. It contains a potency of energy (propulsive momentum) according to the qualities of the *saṃskāras* that must flow from it. These *saṃskāras* can be of a predominantly Earthy, Watery, Fiery, or Airy expression. The evolution of our universe is based on low grade thought substance developing into the intensity of enlightened substance.

Form is constituted by that which is assimilated from the past, in relation to its resistance to the impact of what the future brings. Despite the manifestation of such forces there exists a mechanism of balanced expansion to record the past events that were once part of the unlimited future.

---

1 If it is at all possible for *śūnyatā* to be represented as a point-like expression of that which is and is not, it cannot then be considered as void of everything, simply as void of the consciousness-space one resides in.

2 A term coined by H. P. Blavatsky in *The Secret Doctrine.* (Vol I, 187-189. The Sixth [Adyar] Edition, of the six volumed version.)

The flow of consciousness manifests in a similar way to how a cell maintains its internal pressure.[3] It has organs and a wall lining, and each membrane has a certain permeability, allowing entities (molecules, or information) to flow through,[4] so that the cell structure maintains its levels of balance with an inside pressure and processes that meets the outside pressure (of information) from the larger environment of which it is a part.

The concept of 'pressure' is of importance. It refers to the amount, quality, and type of information that needs to be processed at any time. All types of pressures, tensions, boundaries, walls of accommodation and of exclusion, are maintained just to function normally in a society. The process continues in every sub-category within that society, such as is found in a Buddhist monastery. When we look to the level of the manifesting personal-I, then we view that which is 'outside' the membrane of consciousness to be an expression of the *dharmakāya* type of *karma* that governs the all. It is 'outside' because the *dharmakāya* governs the environment of which the personal-I is a part, whilst the personality manifests conscious volitions of its own accord that segregates a cellular structure apart from the *dharmakāya*. The *dharmakāya* has no direct input into the general working of the separated structure. The entire process of the path to enlightenment consists of breaking down the cell wall of the constructed structure so that it no longer manifests its own internal pressure resisting the impact of that which is external to it. The internal and external have melded into a unity in such a way that the enlightened consciousness still retains control of the way that the resultant impressions are processed. Also, that which no longer has the necessary potency of energy (pressure), such as coarse ideas, cannot enter into the domain of the expanded structure. The *maṇḍalic* unit that had formerly been built with respect to concepts of 'self' no longer suffices, but is integrated into the pathways of pressure flow of the vaster structure that represents the universal whole.

The Sambhogakāya Flower sustains the internal pressure of the separated unit of consciousness (the personal-I). It consists principally of the *skandhas* and *saṃskāras* needed by the personality to maintain equilibrium in life. The pressure of the external environment, of one's

3 Osmotic pressure in the case of a cell wall.

4 A plant leaf contains stomata, used for gas exchange.

habitat and societal conditionings, forces the internal environment to adapt and rightly respond to external conditionings. New *saṃskāras* are developed and old ones are modified to meet the needs of ever-changing scenarios. Consciousness evolves through continuous adaptation and readaptation to externalised *saṃsāric* pressure. Such adaptation creates new *bījas* of expression within the respective petal of the Sambhogakāya Flower responsible for the absorption of the associated quality.

Note that the pressure of *saṃskāras,* such as violent passions, temper, and strong emotions, may be intense at any time, producing a strong predisposition to violence, etc. This predisposition may be the result of many lives of engendering such violence. The accumulated weight of what is developed in these lives produce *saṃskāras* expressing the nature and intensity of the pressure involved. A pressure can be intensified for a period of time, or made broad and expansive, governing the entire life's concourse. The overcoming of *saṃskāric* pressure over any particular aspect or aspects of one's life, and which tend to produce the wrong outcome (such as a coarse emotion), constitutes the way of becoming enlightened. Also, the pressure of the *bodhicitta* developed through former lives of striving and through right renunciation makes one pursue Bodhisattva activities. Such activities can also suddenly manifest during any period of one's life, or else be evident throughout the general course of that life.

People often live out the pressures of any particular past life during a portion of their life. The pressure changes when aspects of another past life comes to the fore. Other *saṃskāras* flow into consciousness to be cleansed. (This happens, for instance, when one takes on a new lover who appeared in a different life than the lover they previously had a relationship with.) If people note the various *saṃskāric* pressures of their lives with care they may get a glimpse as to the nature of the past life (or cultural situation of the past) that they may be reliving at any time. There is always something valuable to learn and to develop during such re-experiencing, recycling, processes. Hopefully consciousness modifies itself in such a way that gross or lethargic qualities are transformed, allowing one to consequently work upon higher, subtler levels.

The external pressure from the *dharmakāya* is, however, brought to bear upon the domain of the Sambhogakāya Flower existing upon the abstracted realms of Mind. This is a way that the *dharmakāya* helps their growth. The *dharmakāya* also manifests the energy of liberation and transcendental Wisdom in the form of pressure directly upon the Sambhogakāya Flower via the Śūnyatā Eye. Its potency manifests with increasing intensity as the various stages of the Bodhisattva path progress.

Each cell processes various categories of information that are sequestered into various departments inside it, serving their many functions. They fill it up with functional unities that grow. These organelles manifest the storage capacity (patterns of activity within the *maṇḍala* of the cell) generating a vital, healthy tensile strength. Such strength is based on the cell's response to the outer environment, and is organised by the directive information coming from its nucleus. (The Śūnyatā Eye in the case of the Sambhogakāya Flower.)

The process conditioning each cellular unit is similar to the way information in the mind is processed. The surface area of each structure of consciousness processes what is experienced, and everything within each structure holds a memory of what transpired in its experiential sphere. To maintain its existence the mind has to keep its assertions of reality under the pressure of the substantial environment within which it resides.

The experiential contact of the cell's surface then becomes the memory of the past, buried within the content of various organelles. As the cell's containment of experience grows, so its surface of possible contact with further experience also expands, increasing its surface area. Consider the nature of the true surface area, the expansion of the experiential contact, developed by a Buddha as his enlightenment grows to embrace the universal Infinitude of cosmos. Regardless of whatever his effect in cosmos may be, with respect to human minds a Buddha's aura is of immense transcendental propensity, manifesting an intense pressure of *bodhicitta.* A lesser unit of enlightened consciousness represented by a Bodhisattva-Mind manifests a similar radiance, but with a weaker consciousness-intensity. *Bodhicitta* is being expressed, because it alone can manifest the subtle potency of experiential growth known as 'radiance'. Such radiance will reach far beyond the immediate spheres of contact of the cellular structure. It carries with it a plethora of transmuted consciousness-bits (defined in terms of 'pressure' or 'intensity' above), which is implied in the definition of the Sanskrit term *prajñā* (transcendental wisdom).

This definition of enlightenment allows an immediate conveyance of information to the cell (mind) in question of the nature of these interrelated 'others', concerning content and mode of categorisation far beyond what a normal cell has obtained. (It has not yet produced the necessary transformations of base *saṃskāras* to produce the consciousness-density to properly fathom the full context of the radiance manifesting upon it.) The quality of the radiance reveals it all via its colourations, intensity, and density of information-bits. Without the manifestation of an adequate consciousness-density the emanation of a penetrative radiance is not possible. Consciousness-density is dependent upon the quantity and quality of the information stored in the organelles of the cell. When developed over many lives, becoming increasingly highly refined, then fully clarified, the consciousness-density eventually becomes the diamond-Mind of a Buddha.

A radiant aura manifests from a place of intensity of associated energies and qualities, and then radiates out from an expanded sphere of containment, the bounds of which are delineated by the extent of the internal pressure of the cell. Its permeability has facilitated the outpouring of lighted substance, which is propelled by the potency of the internal pressure. Thus we have the appearance of what are esoterically known as Sons (suns) in the universe. The expanding effect of the radiatory activity of the enlightened Minds (the Son-suns) it contains ultimately pushes forward the bounds of a formed universe in all directions in multidimensional space. Our universe is also bounded by the delineation of expansive inclusive Reason, but because of its relative vast bulk, storage capacity and 'surface area', its rate of expansive growth is far slower than that of the 'spheres of containment' (units of Consciousness) that are its constituent cells. Expansive growth comes from within, but there is a limit to the capacity of any form to maintain accelerated growth. The radiatory energy it emits, however, manifests a boundless path upon which to travel.

Ultimately, the formed universe will submit to the pressure needs of the generated consciousness-density. When the form can no longer withstand the pressure of that which it contains then units of consciousness will vacate. When sufficient Life force (*jīva*) leaves, then old age has set in stifling growth, its cellular structure ruptures and the cell dies. The essence of the Life that it once contained is then released into a vaster, unbounded consciousness-space. For humans it is the astral or mental plane, for the Son-sun we have the universe. At an advanced state of evolution it can enter into the *ālayavijñāna* environment of the Sambhogakāya Flower (at this cosmic level of expression) prior to rebirth. This happens because of the regulatory nature of *karma* coupled with the pressures within the Flower that forces an integration of the elements needed to be contained within the new form, thus moulded to include the gain of the past.

There is no entropy for what consciousness embodies, except at the attainment of *śūnyatā*—even then Life persists. Regulating order is an intrinsic nature of consciousness, the relative intensity of Fire increases as that consciousness evolves. Energy is generated from within-without, and accumulates that which is gathered from without to within. The evolution of consciousness concerns the generation of increasing intensity of Fire. It manifests as a flux of various energy stratum and on the empirical (dense) domain generates an electric cosmos,[5] plasma fields, and a microscopic universe based on quantum uncertainty, wave-like fluctuations of streams of photons, the appearance of particulate matter, and finally the geometrisation of cellular forms. Consciousness works to bring order to space, and overcomes the effects of the second Law of Electrodynamics, which demands that entropy[6] increases as time evolves in any enclosed system. What is observed in the phenomenal universe is, after all, the 'great illusion', *māyā*.

Chakras as the basis to it all

It can be said that consciousness is real from the perspective of it being the field for the *dharmakāya*. *Śūnyatā* is the ground (energy field) that supports its existence, and the *dharmakāya* is the domain that establishes the validity of its purpose. The *dharmakāya* is the Mind of the All that IS. The *dharmakāya* impacts upon *mūlaprakṛti* (the

5 The reference here is to the theories of physics known as Plasma Cosmology, instigated by Nobel Prize winner, Hannes Alfvén, Eric Lerner, Halton Arp and others, to replace the problematic, though mainstream, 'Big Bang' theory. The theories of Plasma Cosmology, though not yet finalised, should be adapted to the philosophy of consciousness as presented in this *Treatise on Mind* to best explain the nature of the universe as it is.

6 This is defined as the degree of disorder or randomness in a system.

primeval substance of space) so that it can be utilised to produce the forms that allow consciousness to evolve. Phenomena appears when from the *dharmakāya* is projected a Ray of light by a Creative Logos to incorporate *mūlaprakṛti* into forms that will eventually allow consciousness to evolve. The projected Ray is constituted of the five Void Elements that are stored in *śūnyatā*. They then organise chaos. There is no other purpose for the appearance of a sun. Each sun betokens that a cosmic Son of Consciousness-endeavour has delineated a cellular structure to contain and convert its portion of the dark matter of space. The entire universe of countless galaxies evolves thus with mathematical exactitude.

Cells have a valid reality on all levels of expression, from *dharmakāyic* levels down, though they are temporal in nature. All living cells emanate auric fields of radiatory energy. (Though in the case of defiled human minds such auras are murky, generally consisting of many swirls of dulled colourings, until cleansed of defilements upon the Bodhisattva path.) Such a body of radiatory energy necessitates a mechanism for its incorporation in the embodied form in such a way that consciousness can gain through its expression. The *chakras* and *naḍī* system are therefore necessary mechanisms to convey the qualified energy fields of Life if consciousness is to evolve. They exist to contain and properly regulate the flow of all integrated energy (what is sometime described as 'bio-fields') in a living system. Without their existence consciousness would have no true way to interrelate with the form. They are the effects of the laws governing the expression of mind as it utilises energy to condition substance. Consciousness delineates the curvature of space (the space-time continuum explained earlier in this treatise) and of the petals that come into existence to encapsulate the substance of mind.

The nervous system, the neurons and synapses in the head, suffice not to develop consciousness, contrary to what medical specialists wistfully suppose. Neither will they allow continuation of consciousness after the death of the body. There is more to Life than just the physical apparatus.

Chakras are flowers of energy reception that are formed when the *naḍīs* cross. Each *naḍī* is a channel of energy conveying the gain of conscious expression (the consequence of wilful volition) by means of the five senses. There are five types of energy (*prāṇas*) consequently formed, and when incorporated into consciousness as a force-potential they are termed *saṃskāras*. *Saṃskāras* produce tendencies for future action. A major *chakra* is formed when 21 or more *naḍīs* cross, where seven or more cross then the minor *chakras* come into existence. The *chakras* and *naḍīs* constitute a containment mechanism of consciousness. They are the sum of the form whereby *saṃskāras* can be incorporated by consciousness and further processed. We thus have the manifestation of an individualised 'self', a cellular unit, that delineates the field of application within which to work.

Each *chakra* is the expression of a different quality of energy, according to the law that delineates the septenary nature of the octaves of light. Seven major *chakras* are thus formed, each being the container of one or other of these octaves of energy. From a *bīja* point, lines of energy radiate out, based upon a twelve-fold underlying force-field. This field is delineated by an overall impress from forces originating in *dharmakāya* that reflect the qualities of the twelve great constellations of the zodiac into manifestation. They represent the conditioning forces of all manifested Life, and are the basis for the formation of the Heart centre, from which comes the rhythms and pulsations of Life.

Śūnyatā is veiled here by means of its encompassing form. The basic unit of this expression is the four petalled lotus of the Base of the Spine centre, and when multiplied by the expression of the three types of crosses (mutable, fixed and cardinal), representing the three main types of energy expression *(guṇas)*, which the Hindus have termed, *sattva, rajas* and *tamas* (rhythm, mobility and inertia), then we get the petals of the Heart centre.

The four petals of the Base of the Spine centre exist to convey the qualities of the four main Elements *(bhūtas)*, and when multiplied by the three *guṇas*, they form the most basic function of the Heart centre. The Heart centre also exists to transform the gross form of these *bhūtas* into the Void Elements by means of the effect of the energy of *śūnyatā*, whose energies it exists to appropriately convey. The Head centre manifests a similar function with respect to all knowledgeable factors directed to it by means of the consciousness-engendering Life process.

Even the ten petalled lotus of the Solar Plexus centre is based upon the paradigm of the twelve petals. It is minus two petals because they are not needed in its prime function of the transformation of pentads containing the base qualities of the *saṃskāras* of the five sense-consciousnesses into the more refined attributes that can be incorporated into the Heart centre for further purification according to the way of the Heart, as was earlier explained in this *Treatise on Mind.*

Also, the *skandhas* and *saṃskāras* from the consciousness states from former lives (directed by the Sambhogakāya Flower in conjunction with the *deva* hierarchy) pass through the *chakras,* in order to regulate the expression of the manifesting *karma* governing the evolution of the consciousness-stream of the being. In this way also, the substance of the past is integrated into the body corporeal. The past and the present thereby eventually come to be transmogrified into the enlightenment that the future provides.

Ultimately, once the properties of the *chakras* have been harnessed, they will rightly control and transform all expressions of the forces coming in from external sources to the cellular units that are to be incorporated into them. The ability to do so consciously is developed through the practice of yoga, and one who does this is called a *siddha.*

We can also analyse that state of identification with the all which is 'empty of self' (*śūnyatā).* It can be realised via the Heart centre, being that which integrates all spaces between forms. That the Heart *chakra* exists principally to convey the potency of *śūnyatā* is a true enough statement, however, this *chakra* actually lies at the centre of two universes of 'self', the microcosmic world (an expression of the *maṇipūra chakra*), and the macrocosmic realm of the 'Universal Self', an expression of the *sahasrāra padma.* That which is the 'non-self' stands in between, and is a necessary transition from one to the other. This is a basic truth. All of the other *chakras* in the human system are concerned with the coming and going of the consciousness-states and sentience associated with these two universes. Without *saṃsāra, śūnyatā* would have no reference point. It is the ending, or else the beginning, neither ending nor beginning, or both ending and beginning, as all of these are possible expressions of its existence/non-existence.

One line of investigation relates to *śūnyatā* being the 'jewel in the heart of the lotus' of each of the *chakras.* It is therefore the base substance of each of the *naḍīs* leading from one *chakra* to the next.

Our perception here concerns more than just the *chakras* constituting each human unit (the microcosm), but we must also look to their macrocosmic correspondences. We must therefore perceive the *naḍīs* that exist universally in Nature, which are expressive of the *dharmakāya*.

Each *chakra* found in Nature is really an integrated reservoir of consciousness or sentient state. When relegated to the *dharmakāya* cosmos they convey the potency of superhuman states of evolution: *devas*, Bodhisattvas, *ḍākinīs*, Buddhas and Logoi. Together such great ones constitute the petalled structure of vast *chakras*, in *maṇḍalas* of great power in cosmos. If these *chakras* are organised in a corresponding manner to that found in a human unit, then the kingdoms of Nature will be conditioned in terms of them. The minor ones in the macrocosmic body will be shown to express all of the forces and attributes governing the manifestation of phenomena. These forces and qualities will be collectivised, blended, sorted and redistributed by the three major *chakras* found below the diaphragm. The qualities relating to the domain of the abstract Mind and beyond to the *dharmakāya* will be controlled by the major *chakras* above the diaphragm. We can then better comprehend what truly constitutes the Logos of a Planetary system, such as that governing the earth, or on a vaster scale, of a solar system, right up to the Logoi governing the constellations of stars.

In the case of Logoi, the *prāṇas* conveyed by the *naḍīs* represent the Lives and groupings of lesser lives incarnated as their Bodies of manifestation. This concept of Logos needs to be thoroughly investigated by future Buddhist philosophers for their religion to advance to its next step of enlightened expression. Humanity as a whole would benefit accordingly.

The *chakras* in each human unit are localised in the etheric (energy) body, as indicated by the diagrams in yoga texts, whilst their correspondences in Nature have been briefly noted above. Each Flower integrates the qualities of the others, and regulates the Element or sub-Element it is the custodian of, allowing the predominant *saṃskāric* pressure (*prāṇa*) to be experienced in the realm of consciousness. The integration and interrelation of these energies is determined by numerological considerations of the petals, as earlier described. The *naḍīs* allow the *skandhas* and *saṃskāras* associated with all phenomenal Life to be conveyed from one flower to the next, without distorting or modifying what is conveyed in any way. We can see, therefore, that they are constructed out of the substance of the Void Elements. They are an expression of *śūnyatā* manifesting via the fully integrated jewel that is the *naḍī* system. The *prāṇas* flowing through the *naḍīs* are streams conveying the *karma* of consciousness, because the manifesting *saṃskāras* represent the impetus of past karmic activity. The karmic processes therefore cannot be modified whilst they are being conveyed through the *naḍīs*, but when expressed through a *chakra* they affect the consciousness to act in some way. The will of the thinker can suppress the emerging *saṃskāra,* act according to its energy directives, or modify it, either positively towards liberation from that karmic stream, or negatively. In either case new *saṃskāras* are engendered.

The general Element contained in the *naḍīs,* allowing them to function as they do is Air, which symbolises what can be denoted as the *śūnyatā* of the Void Elements. *Prāṇa* is the wind of Voidness tainted with defilements. By its characteristic of being 'empty', only *śūnyatā* will not colour or mar what the *naḍīs* convey. (An absolute vacuum is not possible within these vessels for this would be equable to saying that nothing at all exists.) This, however, does not mean that *śūnyatā* does not act upon these energy flows. It acts with respect to *prāṇa* in the following ways:

a. By conveying the energy flows, thus facilitating their movement in the direction to which they must go, i.e., from flower a to flower b.

b. By working in conjunction with the action of the *chakras* in manifesting a type of *prāṇic* filtering system. As the *prāṇas* (*saṃskāras*) are filtered the more refined extracts flow to a higher *chakra*, and the residue (and residual depressed 'pressure') finding outlet in the lower *chakras* where coarser energies are processed.

   This happens because *śūnyatā* is a form of intensified energy that exerts an effect upon unrefined energies. Its effect upon the general flow of the forms of energy that are too lethargic to find opportunity for expression in the *chakras* ahead is for them to be diverted to a more base *chakra*, or to be transformed into a subtler form that more closely approximates the Void.

c. Because *saṃskāras* are refined and rarefied, so eventually only those that produce liberation of consciousness remain. All *prāṇas* therefore inevitably find their refined expression in the Head lotus. *Śūnyatā* then exists to integrate the Void Elements for that cycle, and to convey the transmuted attributes of consciousness to *dharmakāya.*

These effects are possible because *śūnyatā* necessarily has grades associated with it. It is not merely of uniform consistency, of absolute homogeneity. One way to examine this is to posit the question: is the type of *śūnyatā* experienced by a sentient being liberated from the mineral kingdom different from that experienced by a being liberated from the sentience of the plant kingdom, and different also from that of the liberation from animal sentience? We can ask such a question because each different level of sentience can be considered a quantum leap ahead of its predecessor, in a similar way that human consciousness is to animal sentience. Also, the state of awareness of a Bodhisattva that has entered *śūnyatā* can likewise be considered a quantum leap above that of normal human consciousness.

In the above we have five *śūnyatā* states indicated:

1. The mineral *śūnyatā.*
2. The plant kingdom *śūnyatā.*
3. The animal kingdom *śūnyatā.*
4. The human kingdom (*arhat*) *śūnyatā.*
5. The *śūnyatā* of Mind, the vehicle of *dharmakāya,* experienced by a high level Bodhisattva or a Buddha.

The above is a reason why it can be said that each tiny *naḍī* is the conveyor of five different *prāṇas*, and why there are five *skandhas*, senses, and their perceptors, as well as ultimately the five Wisdoms of the Dhyāni Buddhas. In fact, we have the reason why there are five, and not six or eight or thirteen of them. By the very nature of being a Buddha of meditation each Jina can be said to embody a different type of *śūnyatā* as his particular medium of expression. These differences are depicted in terms of the five Wisdoms, colours, Buddha emblems, etc., but they are all interdependent, expressive of each other, and also *śūnya* (Void) with respect to the things of *saṃsāra*. These different *śūnyatās* and Wisdoms reticulate down throughout the entire order of Nature in such a way that eventually sentience, and gross consciousness-states, can evolve to attain the awakening of a Buddha.

The way of ascent incorporates a filter system, otherwise there could be no ascent for any entity. Only *śūnyatā* can incorporate such a system, for it cannot be sullied by that which comes in contact with it. Also, its effect automatically eliminates all forms of *saṃsāric* stains. The entire *chakra* and *naḍī* system therefore acts as a distillation unit. As *prāṇas* come to ascend in the system, so consequently that which 'defiles' is discarded, i.e., filtered through into the lower and minor *chakras* constituting the rest of the system, where these energies might find a use. Thus that which is considered 'evil' to one higher upon the scale of evolutionary being is considered 'good' to another.

Everything is relative, therefore the most virtuous attribute of a person normally engrossed in basic normal human actions may be the least virtuous quality of a high level Bodhisattva, a defilement to be discarded. Thus the least virtuous 'defilement' of such a Bodhisattva may be a ray of beneficence to another. In the overall energy balance of the universe there is no wastage, everything is ultimately recycled and elevated.

The Dhyāni Buddhas and the 'five-ness' of things

The growth of experiences is an expanding cellular membrane moving through time towards the future. Each new experience constitutes the beginning of another cycle of activity for mind. The *future* is also:

1. The unrealised potential of the past.
2. That which is not manifest, but yet to appear.
3. That which acts as a matrix that has established the potential for all possible experiences (to be), according to a prearranged categorisation. This can be conceptualised in the fashion of library shelves, where books are arranged according to a coded system (e.g., the Dewey Decimal System) that has places for existing books as well as being able to accommodate all future expansions of the library. Every book desired can be easily and speedily retrieved for the information content needed, and also new books can be easily placed in the right category when they arrive. Also, any book in the library can be accessed for the information contained within it,

the information stored then being the future potential of what can be revealed. (If not having been previously read.)

As this cell grows, it records the imprints of that which is manifest around it, or appears to be manifest (because of the reaction mechanism of surface happenings). Thus that which was recorded in the past becomes a mechanism for determining future imprints.

4. That which is necessary (or is availed upon) to cleanse *saṃskāras*. (The reference here is to the gain of the 'filtering' system associated with the *chakras*.) There are many levels of expression (cellular constructs) that can be envisioned here. The basis to this view relates to the fact that the *saṃskāras* of past volitions are karmically carried forward to a future potential. (As manasically envisioned by Lords of *karma*.) When all of the *saṃskāras* that are contingent upon the manifestation of a complete picture or scenario of happenings are projected towards their future interrelation then the picture of the future potential already exists. Enlightened beings work with such images to plan their service work.
5. A guarantee for the eventuality of Buddhahood for all.

The *Dhyāni Buddhas* are integral to the process of manifesting future occurrences so that Buddhahood is eventually attained. With every new experience the (human) cell revivifies and again finds its source *maṇḍala*, its point of contact with the future, where all Buddhas reside, for the small limited memory-space of a cell must expand continuously to inevitably contain what is veiled by the *maṇḍala* of these Jinas. The way of manifestation from Vairocana to Amoghasiddhi is thus a process that inevitably includes the unfolding of consciousness from the past pristine state to the future all-accomplished state.

The Jinas seed the qualities of the five Elemental *śūnyatās* throughout Nature, and the paradigms of their immaculate Wisdoms are built into the human *naḍī* system by the *tathāgatagarbha*. When the new personality is born and matures, so then *saṃskāras* from the past life's activities are carried forth in the *naḍīs,* via the agency of the Void Elements according to the type of energy (i.e., numerical) affiliation with the *saṃskāras* concerned. These are then modified by the evolving consciousness through a prearranged karmic pattern (the five types of pressures of varying degrees of *saṃskāras*) established by the Sambhogakāya Flower as the *maṇḍala* for that life. The objective of each *maṇḍala* for a particular life that is established by this Flower is that it follows a sequential pattern that will inevitably produce receptivity to the *dharma* for a future personality. The Bodhisattva path and consequent Buddhahood is then a natural expression for that one to follow. Resisting this is the natural lethargy of the consciousness that is attached to age-long habit patterns of grasping for the sensations associated with ephemera.

As the influences of the Jinas are found manifest throughout Nature, so their sublimely aromatic, yet potently intensified meditative states find their reverberated and reticulated expression in all liberating forms of *saṃsāric* involvement. As we descend down the *lokas* of *saṃsāra* the five types of emanations of the Dhyāni Buddhas congeal and become increasingly coarse. This is necessarily so as we move from the *arūpa* to the *rūpa* levels, and thence from the subtler types of forms created upon mental and emotional levels, until we finally have the grossest forms seen in the world of physical plane interactions.

In this way every atom, form, sentient being, category of human activity, human civilisation, comes under the sway of their combined meditative power. All are conditioned and organised by the five Rays of Mind, by the five-fold differentiation of their collective Meditation; all come to be gradually refined by the inherent filtering system that is built in the *maṇḍalic* structure of the All. For this reason the pinnacle of evolution in Nature's domain—the human unit, is fivefold in constitution. This 'five-ness', symbolised by the pentagram: the human torso, two arms and feet; five digits to the hands and feet, as well as the five spokes of the *dorje,* is the guarantee to one's eventual mastery over the entire natural world. The domain of consciousness is conditioned by this number, and then the liberated states of the Dhyāni Buddhas.

If we think all this out clearly, then we shall see that the pressure to manifest comes from the *dharmakāya*. One mantric Sound, one *bīja* from therein, as uttered by a Buddha, reverberates manifold in *saṃsāra* to produce a multitude of 'things' which appearing different, are tied through a similarity or thread to that particular Sound. By the time it has reached the grosser *saṃsāric* spheres the note has become a voluminous cacophony of sounds. The idea presented is similar to the Buddhist statement that the entire many-volumed *prajñāpāramita* has emanated from the single letter 'A'. We can extend the idea to all of Nature, where each Jina has emanated one such syllable to make the complete Word of manifestation, of the appearance of manifested space, and of everything we know within it. One must also take into account that this process is facilitated by their consorts who clothe that word with form.

The *dharmakāya* is the source of primal causative *karma*. Therefore everything must ultimately be abstracted back into it, once a conscious unit has discovered the base of that Word and can properly decipher its sounds, the mantras and mantric sentences. (As a Bodhisattva, that unit then inevitably carries an entire world-sphere with them, as that is a part of the long vision of their vow.) Here is wisdom indeed, and such knowledge is the most guarded of secrets in the Halls of Liberation. For only those that are worthy can be entrusted with such keys to the creation or destruction of the order of all that is. They have demonstrated that they possess sufficient purity of motive (the necessary compassion), and the proper auric cleanliness. Not in textbooks, therefore, can such Words be found. The selfish, self-centred, prideful, separative, or malicious ones have found other words of power, following a similar line of reasoning, which leads them deeper into the ensnarement of *māyā* and karmic bondage, not liberation into the future, but further encasement into the materialism of the past.

Beware, therefore, as to what your true motives are when you aspire for psychic power, as the way delineates sharply at a particular point of the path: the left-hand way into materialistic might, verses the right-hand way into liberative delight. Be warned and beware, for only on the path of Love, guided by wisdom serene, can liberation be achieved.

The 'five-ness' mentioned above is really part of a pattern of 'ten-ness' when the consorts of the Dhyāni Buddhas are included. We also have the previously explained *maṇḍalas* of eights of the Mahābodhisattvas. There is also a veiled septenaric manifestation within each grouping of ten (7 + 3) relating to the seven Ray differentiations of all Life that come to be abstracted into a primordial triad (of Father-Son-Mother). In these numbers we have veiled the true Esoteric (Dewey)

Decimal System well worthy of study for all serious students of wisdom for future enlightenment.

The influence of these Buddhas throughout Nature produces the *dharmakāya* type of *karma* in such a way that all elementary forms of life, sentience, and units of consciousnesses, are eventually led to liberation. Buddhahood thus comes as a consequence of:

a. The normal progress of evolution, because it is guided by the inherent Love and Wisdom of the Jinas that govern the sum of its manifest expression. Everything evolves in accordance with the rhythms and cycles accorded to its kind, species, or grouping. Every category in Nature has its evolutionary goal, transmuted affiliation, *nirvāṇa* state, and consequent rebirth, a recycling as a new category of entity, which is interrelated with all the others. Each new cycle manifests upon a higher, more embracive aspect of the entire *maṇḍala.* The cycles of events are pre-planned according to the progress of a desired outcome upon the evolutionary time scale. The view here concerns kingdoms in Nature other than that of the human. The human kingdom has the added factor of conscious volition, necessitating free will, which can radically alter what was planned for them to achieve within a specific cycle or *yuga.* Consequently, they actually determine the length of a cycle, or the nature of the repetitious perpetuation of these cycles.

b. The hastening or slowing of the normal evolutionary progress of any entity because of human karmic interaction with it. We can see here that the originating Plan developed by the Jina concerned must be modified, if and when necessary, to take into account the modifying factor of human free-will and karmic action. It should be noted that human karmic defilement of normal evolutionary patterning concerns a relatively temporary union with a specific category of sentience, waylaying that sentience to serve the purpose or function of the human self-will. The person's will has integrated that sentient unit as part of his/her *karma,* and consequent *saṃskāras.* Hence, units of sentience are tied to a consciousness-stream during the time it takes for the *saṃskāra* to be properly resolved. Such interrelation can be either good or bad, depending upon the way the human unit has developed his/her *saṃskāra*. For instance, is it a *saṃskāra* of hate or violence that is involved, or one of loving interrelationship with an animal unit?[7]

By further reasoning we will see that such human *saṃskāric* interactions with Nature as a whole is part of the planning of the Dhyāni Buddhas. It is designed to generally assist the lesser kingdoms in Nature by integrating them into human consciousness states. They can then learn somewhat by means of sympathetic mimicry what human consciousness is. In fact, evolving into a human kingdom signifies progressing past the *śūnyatā* level for them, as explained above.

It should also be noted that the Council of the Bodhisattvas regularly convene in order to appropriately modify the Plan developed by the Dhyāni Buddhas so that the necessary outcomes happen in *saṃsāra*. Human units are co-creators of *saṃsāric* conditionings, though few are consciously aware of the significance of this fact.

The Jinas and the future

The five aspects of the future presented earlier can also be elaborated and related to the Dhyāni Buddhas. It should be noted that this section could be greatly expanded as the Jinas reside *entirely* in the future, from the perspective of where humanity presently stands. They have developed consciousness states humanity have yet to awaken to, but inevitably will when the five processes indicated below are carried through to conclusion. They represent the processes sequenced over time via the filter system of the dimensions of perception, starting from the most limiting (the dense physical) and progressing to the subtlest (the *ātmic*). Each level of future activity requires the elimination of the grosser forms of *saṃskāras* preceding it.

1. *Amoghasiddhi. The unrealised potential of the past.* This refers specifically to the physical interrelationships and interactions from the past where the breadth and depth of the entire world play of past actions is seen in the scope of the vision. All diverse separative factors must be interrelated and brought into a harmonious future by the All-accomplishing Wisdom of Amoghasiddhi.

---

7 From another perspective we can say that because it *is* human consciousness of some type that the sentience has been wedded to, so there is always some evolutionary gain for it.

2. *Ratnasambhava. That which is unmanifest.* This refers principally to the subjective astral, emotional energies (of the higher *rūpa* levels of Buddhism) that must come into manifestation. All disincarnate lives residing here in the various Bardo states, and their comings and goings into physical incarnation, or to the more sublime realms, must be visualised. This Buddha determines how all who experience Bardo can best gain from their types of identifications, thus can consequently be brought to more wholesome rebirths and consciousness states.
3. *Amitābha. That which acts as a matrix* that has established the potential for all future possible experiences. As the cell grows, it records the imprints of that which is manifest around it, or appears to be manifest (because of the reaction mechanism of the surface areas). Thus that which was recorded in the past becomes a mechanism for future imprints. The reference is to past consciousness *bījas* and the ramifications of their effects in the future. Amitābha works in a way that allows all attitudes of mind, consciousness states, doctrines and philosophies, to be better harmonised through discriminative inner visioning. Enlightenment *saṃskāras* are thereby produced.
4. *Akṣobhya. That which is necessary to cleanse saṃskāras.* This specifically concerns drawing upon the Airy qualities of the Heart centre, and *bodhicitta*, which 'cleanses' the defilements of past actions and wrong patterns of mind. This process involves sacrifice, and the pain of relinquishing cherished aspects of the past that were once held dear. It necessitates the gaining of investiture into new awareness states, new identifications, with enlightened perceptions revealing beings formerly unseen and unknown. The process of mastery of the entire path of Life is involved. Akṣobhya thus helps produce the way of Initiation into the mysteries of all categories of Life, introducing that step or level of attainment immediately ahead of one. The Initiation process into the mysteries of being/non-being is a vast esoteric science.
5. *Vairocana. Buddhahood is guaranteed.* Here we look to the ultimate attainment of the entire evolutionary purpose. It involves all the enlightened and enlightening forces and factors in evolution that bend backwards to help cleanse the grosser qualities of those aspiring

to achieve their future inheritance. Perception essentially comes to be directed towards the spaces between incarnate states, to the interlude state between the in and out breathing process of meditation. It produces the revelations acceded to *dhyāna*, instigating visions of the future, of the reality that will eventuate in the realms of form. The rhythms and patterns of the past are thus altered to produce a new design more in accord with the imprint of the Divine. It concerns the way of abstraction into the transcendental, where processes once difficult are now mastered, and then recede below the threshold of awareness. The liberated of any cycle are dressed in new garb, and educated into a higher order of being/non-being, before manifesting again in a new cycle bearing qualities not previously possessed. The integrated liberation process of the entire *maṇḍala* for all kingdoms of Nature is meditated upon by this Buddha.

The flow of *saṃskāras*

As the cell *expands*, it adds to itself, continuously delineating its self definition. A cell is likened to a person, because as people receive information they both record and add it to their concept of 'self'. The categories of information deemed worthwhile then come to mould the persona of the individual concerned.

This recording process is the mechanism whereby past experiences (which are the categories that both cells and humans make to define the living entity) are developed to become the future, and as this happens the process becomes the past mechanism. The process can be visualised in terms of *saṃskāras* moving onwards and outwards along a moving, expanding time line that is *curved*. The curvature happens because the line is shaped by means of a moving consciousness that relegates time in terms of cycles of events known only to its experiential awareness.

This awareness is also curved, because that is the way it has developed from the child to the adult stage. Many influences have come and altered consciousness. As they come in they shape it this way and that, and consciousness consequently moves accordingly. Its progress is thus not a straight line, but moves according to the way the thought-stream moves as buffeted by all extraneous forces. When the to's and fro's of the buffeting is smoothed, then the curvature of expansive consciousness is seen.

We can look to *linear time,* as an ordered sequence of events, such as the march of history. Or we can look to *curved time,* which is the way that *saṃskāras* influence consciousness, as any *saṃskāra* from any part of any past life can come in and sway the track of conscious direction or motivation from what may have been linear into a different way; a different past continuum becoming the present-future.

In other words, the thought-stream tends to move in a straight line, but then *saṃskāras* and stored images come to the surface of consciousness and impact upon the moving stream from an oblique angle, which then alters the movement of the thought, deflecting its motion. As the images and *saṃskāras* attracted to the thought-stream are of a like nature to the thought, they tend to deflect its motion in a given direction, producing, therefore, a spiral motion. The process can be visualised in the following manner:

1. The motion of the originating thought.

2. The *saṃskāra* impinges upon the thought.

3. Thus deflecting its motion with that added effect of its momentum.

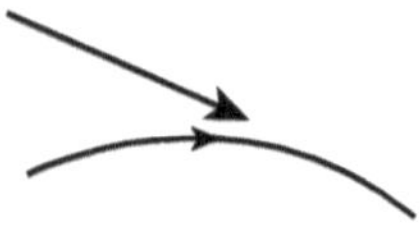

4. Another *saṃskāra* manifesting similarly to the above further accentuates the spiral.

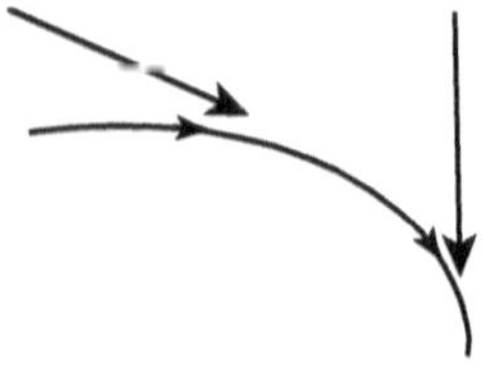

5. The continuing effect of such action is to produce a spiral, which eventually develops into a time-space continuum as the *saṃskāras* develop into consciousness-attributes over time.

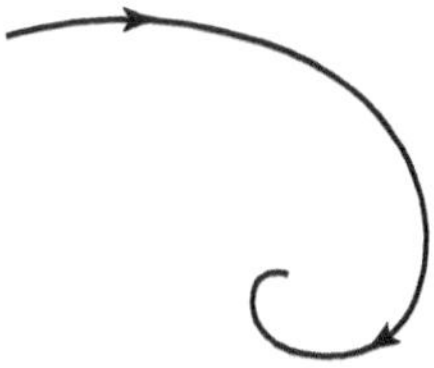

The above is an idealised depiction, presuming that thoughts come to produce a progressive outcome. Negative or sloppy thinking can produce a wobbly line, but overall most thought-streams are sequenced to produce conclusive deductions based upon progressive thought. Therefore, in those thoughts that are illogical or inconsistent, vague and inchoate, the spiral motion may not be applicable. However, the overall effect over time is that all thought structures will find their placing within such a spiral time-line. The impact of awakening *saṃskāras* pushes the entire thought structure in this manner. Ideally, the spiral manifests according to the proportions of the golden mean, if the thought-stream is well thought out and not erratic. Thus evolution proceeds.

What about *the future?* Does it not also shape the consciousness of the cell? The past patterns may produce the shape of future happenings, however, this future is moulded by Lords of *karma*, which the five Dhyāni Buddhas and their Bodhisattvic expressions can also be considered to be. Future karmic disposition is also guided by the impulses from the Sambhogakāya Flower, and specifics by all members of the *deva* kingdom. Thus we effectively have past and future influences upon the present consciousness trend, which affects the way consciousness views time. The way *saṃskāras* manifest to modify present consciousness is actually the measure of time, for they determine the way we experience things, and the 'timeless spaces' wherein such things are processed.

All past life *saṃskāras* are:

1. Ways to predict the future, e.g., premonition of likely repetitions in cycles due to the law of *karma*.

2. A memory assisting the future synthesis of experience, a moving momentum of consciousness unfolding according to a predetermined pattern constructed for their rightful unfolding.
3. The product of many cycles of sensory contact in a consciousness-stream reincarnating continuously to learn the lessons of all modes of living. The cycles inevitably teach what not to do, by transmuting the base *saṃskāric* potencies into subtler forms more conducive for the development of enlightenment. Thus the perfection of Buddhahood and liberation from all materialistic *saṃskāric* ties is eventually attained.

From this perspective we can then ask 'What is a Buddha?' We find that such a One is a master of the life process. He has transmuted consciousness derived from the known past of humanity and their *saṃskāras*, and develops new *saṃskāras* that lead him to higher spheres of contact away from the realms of human experience and consciousness. We must recognise here that the urge to meditate is a *saṃskāra* leading to higher fulfilment, as is the development of *bodhicitta*, and the walking of the Bodhisattva path. Without such developed *saṃskāras* (representing the future for the bulk of humanity) nobody could walk the path to liberation in a consecutive, progressive manner from life to life. A Buddha's cellular bubble has burst, he has reached the spaciousness of the vaster 'cellular structure' (*maṇḍala*) within which his former consciousness bubble was entrapped. (Which was but one of milliards similarly constrained.)

A cell exerts pressure on the outer environment as it evolves, collecting and storing information from all past movements and expansions. It stores energies from the outer environment from which it feeds. These energies add to its bodily consciousness, supporting its activities. The influx of energies is a natural process, where the pressure caused by the outer environment of the cell can be just as active but far more refined than that coming from the cell itself. If this is the case, then the outer environment could be said to help feed the cell with future purpose. The propensity, therefore, is for the cell to grow towards the outer universe to form its body of experience, rather than to contract towards a central point. (The movement is from a state of relative lethargy to greater refinement and broader scope of experiential awareness.) Indeed, the energies propelling the unit towards future expansiveness are inherently more intense than those which keep the unit attached to the rigor mortise of the limitations of the past.

Thus if the future is considered to consist of the outer energy (that which the cell has not yet experienced) then the evolutionary progression of the cell is made mostly by means of contact with it. This is the basis to comprehend the nature and efficacy of the actions of Bodhisattvas upon all sentient beings, because the Bodhisattva's conscious comprehension represents the future for those acted upon. The entire course of each Bodhisattva's accumulated action towards enlightenment for all, and their united striving towards the future, produces outward pressure on individual cells. It makes them expand out of the confines of their limited minds.

The expansion of the cellular structure

That which emanates from the inside of the cellular structure represents the culmination of the past for the individual, as the central nucleus contains the (genetic) seeds for the future expansive growth of the cell. It also contains the inherited imprint of the collective awareness of the entire vaster *maṇḍala* of which the cell is a unit, of their united movement towards the all. We can therefore see that the cell's expansive growth involves coordination between that which lies outside and inside the cell's structure. That which lies outside exerts a gradual pressure towards future expansiveness via refinement of consciousness, whilst that within the nucleus consists of the major evolutionary impetus, if heeded.

The outside contains the sum total of the pressure of the past momentums and future striving of all cells of the system. They are all at differing stages of consciousness expansion, some lie in the future for the cell, others lie in the past. This, plus the general effect of the push from the Lords of Life, helps to produce a future expansion for the entire *maṇḍala*.

If the level of energy outside the cell can be measured to be more than the inner resistance of the cellular membrane, then there are two perspectives possible. First, if the external environment is constituted of murky Watery substance, then the individual gets swamped in a sense of hopelessness, ennui, depression, etc. Here the individual has failed to master life. The external forces overpower and misery ensues.

However, if the external environment is liberating then there is a lessening of the grip of the personal-I, of its egotism, concepts of 'self'. (Remembering here that energies go in and out of the cell if it is a living functional entity, and we are analysing a sphere of consciousness.) This mergence with the external universe is possible only if that inside the cell is progressing towards the future. We have a contraction or disintegration of the formerly rigid structure of the cellular walls because the individual has done the necessary meditation to master the life processes, to bring the cell structure to an elevated energy zone. The disintegration allows for a vast expansion of a highly refined 'remainder' of the cell wall that disappears from its former habitat. It must die to allow for a future vehicle that can better accommodate the potency of the *prāṇas* contacted. Thus, as the qualities inside a cell become commingled with those from the outside, the cell wall becomes more permeable and less resistant. Eventually it is altogether gone, producing a unity with the exterior all. The concept of 'self' consequently is eliminated for that cellular unit, but the united pressures of all other cellular 'unities' still bear upon the integral consciousness. It consequently is fully aware of the sum total of their need, their united cry of pain, all sounds, and movements, as they contract or expand according to the way they respond to external and internal pressures.

The awakened one fully experiences this and consequently arises to meet the challenge of assisting all in terms of where the need is greatest, having developed the vision and subjective hearing to encompass the total extent of the *maṇḍala* of which that one is a part. Such a one has specialised along any of the specific qualities of the five Jinas that course strongest in consciousness. Here lies the seed thought answering the mystery to understanding what constitutes enlightenment.

The purveyance of the Jina's Wisdoms is that which organises the outside of the cell wall upon the level of the abstract Mind. Whilst inside the cell only the nucleus is left to control the internal activity. This nucleus is effectively the *bīja* of the Sambhogakāya Flower. We saw earlier how this Flower is organised and functions with respect to the Dhyāni Buddhas. The inner and the outer then interrelate face to face, without the third party (the personal-I) intervening. The conjoining of the Buddhas (masculine) and the Flower (feminine) produces the appearance of the *Sambhogakāya* of a Bodhisattva in the subjective realms. This then takes the semblance of an 'I', when expressed into the Head or Heart lotus of an incarnate person, and so we have the appearance of a *nirmāṇakāya.*

At a later stage of evolutionary development, when we have a condition of absorption into *śūnyatā*, the *bīja* of the Sambhogakāya Flower no longer exists. The eventual focus is then upon the *dharmakāya.* In this case the building of a *nirmāṇakāya* happens, with the base being *śūnyatā* and the qualities of a particular Dhyāni Buddha being the emanative expression in the Head lotus of a person. (To the extent such qualities have been developed.) That Head lotus then contains all of the transformed former *saṃskāras* that still manifest attributes of 'Individuality' and uniqueness, but the separative ego no longer exists.

The condition governing the bulk of humanity, however, is their exaggerated forms of self-concern and self-centred activities. Here the general constitution of the internal structure of the cell is conditioned by *saṃskāras* from the past that are intensely resistant to the momentum of the future encroaching in. We then have an intensification, a strengthening of the cell wall, thus the concept of ego. Here the personal-I is concerned purely with its own internal movements, converting everything from the outside quickly with its own form of 'self-ish' emotional mental activity. The intensified resistance to the external pressure to evolve (plus resistance to that from its own nucleus), prevents rarefied liberating energies from entering. The cell wall hardens and the internal structure builds reinforced attitudes of 'self'. Such ego is most evident in those with static, rigid idealisms and concerns; the religious bigots, fundamentalists, those engrossed in cupidity, and conservative pedagogues. We also have the selfish reifying materialists, who hold no other opinion but their own to be sound or to be valid. They shower disdain or ignore serious investigations in other lines of thought. Unfortunately, these ones, who will only interpret that around them in terms of what they wish to believe, presently educate our societies.

The intensification of 'self' is thus a major obstacle to further growth. It represents a disease or malfunctioning in the scheme of things. It rigidly adheres to the past when everything else is moving to the future. Thus there is a type of backwards motion that is antagonistic to evolutionary progress, to lightening changes overcoming entrenched attitudes. Such structures are inevitably broken via a jack-hammering effect by both the Sambhogakāya Flower working internally with conscience-volitions, and the Lords of *karma* manifesting the effects of *karma* externally, to mitigate the destructive impact of the resistant unit on the general flow of the structure which it is a part of.

Both internal and external forces work together to produce the karmic consequences that cause materialistic empires to be shattered, and the corresponding internal convictions to be severely shaken. Many lives of undertaking are often required to produce the destruction of such concreted belief patterns. This may necessitate incarnation into completely different religious streams and social conditionings to which the materialist formerly adhered, to soften the viewpoints relating to the 'other'. Eventually, internal resistance is broken through painful turmoil, the progressively directed 'new' is grasped, and the cellular unit moves outwards to embrace another aspect of the future.

We can even build a case for a contraction if there is a weakening of internal resolution and at the same time movement towards the past. This happens in the case of fears of all types. The individual reacts negatively to impacts from the external environment. He withdraws into himself and will not look outside, with regards to any one, or of any of the issues concerning the future perspective. The stronger the fear or fears, the greater the contraction of the cell wall of 'self'. The experience intensifies the rigidity of the wall, and at the same time undermines it by incorporating much consciousness-mud. This is the opposite of the case given above, where the cellular unit is moving towards the future. There the elimination of resistance to external pressure produced liberation, here instead we have increased bondage to the object of the fears. They become the overriding passion of consciousness. Their substance becomes the encasing wall, coupled with Watery defensiveness in anticipation of future events. The object of the fear/s becomes a jail or cocoon binding the personal-I into walls of limitation.

Next, we can analyse the quality of *pride* that reinforces the cell wall by the consciousness, through intensifying the internal pressure of the properties of the cell. The cell takes from the external environment that which feeds the select internal attributes that are focussed upon as meaningful. Pride can be viewed as an endeavour to include the external as part of the unit's constitution so that only building blocks of reifying 'self' can manifest. It allows no reciprocal motion other than what is designed to attract further flattering substance, or to destroy that which opposes its expansion. Pride is thus an intensified form of separative critical action towards other similarly expansive units. The empire of the prideful one is built on much Watery stuff. It glamourises being different, more important than the 'other', increasing the intensity of the cell wall of the prideful one. Seeking only that deemed worthy if it can feed its self-esteem, the cell thus grows in an expansive, cancerous manner with respect to the community of cells that it is a part. It feeds off qualities of the others to increase the potency of its own structure. Others view it in terms of a glamour or glaze of its own making. The nucleus of the cell is pampered with glamour—images of self-worth created by itself, and oft propped-up with other's opinions.

The prideful one consequently acts to drain energies and resources from others, giving little in return, except if the others stay attached to the bubble the prideful one has created. The fact that the universe of the prideful one is empty of substantiality is discovered in time, when the cell wall implodes to the point of the real worth of the evolutionary characteristics possessed by the cell. This happens when the Sambhogakāya Flower endeavours to assert its authority upon the personal-I that is travelling in the opposite direction to the Flower's own intrinsic purpose. *Karma* is chosen to manifest in such a way that the prideful one loses the empire of his/her making. In any case death often intervenes, and there is a consequent rebirth into situations that are definitely non pride-invoking.

Intensification of selfish thinking, pure avarice, malice, personal power, and even intensely lustful activities, all will produce a cancerous situation of the cellular constitution. It involves a reaching out to directly control or manipulate others purely for the benefits of the individual cell or 'self'. So the cellular unit then reinforces its attributes of self-worth and identity, which single it out from all others in its consideration of purpose. The cellular structure can then enlarge to the extent it wishes to manifest its self-image. This produces an increased intensity, or pressure of its internal substance. Such intensified substance then reaches out to grasp the cells around it, to chain them to it through lines of interrelationship that it uses to control their movements and activities. It then ruthlessly takes whatever it wants to feed its own power, and uses the pressure of its own substance to keep others under its personal will. Such action continuously weakens all other cells, allowing it to maintain its strength over them.[8]

We can also extend the imagery to depict the way that our entire world civilisation is governed. For instance, we have unprincipled, villainous plutocrats masterminding their financial empires and multinational organisations, that make a handful of individuals extremely wealthy, with the masses of people, and whole countries serving as economic slaves to feed their gross over-bloated cupidity and perfidious lust for material power. The entire environment of the planet is devastated as a consequence and convulses with waves of pain under the weight of their rapine.

Above we have cursorily depicted a mode of activity of the forces of evil (the dark brotherhood). Many more examples could be provided, but would digress us too far. When the wilful manipulation of psychic power (*siddhis)* for the intensification of 'self' is added, then the picture is complete. Those who practiced the black arts yogically in one life, can be found to have reincarnated as the above mentioned financiers and the politicians assisting them, for instance. *Maṇḍalas* (covens) of such dark ones incarnate together to produce their nefarious effects during any epoch. They may not be engaged in occult practices in that life, but the *samskaras* generated in their former lives manifest concretely in the way indicated today. Just as not every Bodhisattva remembers their past lives of yogic training, so also it is with their dark brothers.

The garnering of *siddhis* for self-aggrandisement can be so intense that it can completely eliminate all influence from the Sambhogakāya Flower. Its purpose has died and a severance of the link has occurred, but the cancerous cell has produced such a momentum of energy and resource drainage from the cells that it manipulates and preys upon that its ensuing perpetuation in *saṃsāra* is assured. As long as *saṃsāra* persists with foul conditions/*prāṇas* for it to work, so it will, and does

8 See also Balsys, *Karma and the Rebirth of Consciousness,* 209-211.

everything in its power to perpetuate that in which it thrives. This leaves the *dharmakāya* type of *karma* to educate it, and this takes aeons, those (Buddhas and Bodhisattvas) whose purpose involves the education of such miscreants must generate incalculable patience to bring them back upon the evolutionary path.

The above mentioned cellular states are governed by the meditative unfoldment of the five Dhyāni Buddhas:

1. *Vairocana*, the Dharmadhātu Wisdom, embodying the central point of the *maṇḍala*. He works with the liberating aspect of all cellular consciousnesses that are working to cooperate with the Plan for evolution and to merge with universal consciousness. He acts specifically with the *dharmakāya* type of *karma*, to ensure that the various diversifications of Nature work according to a Plan. Here we have evolving patterns in Nature producing evolutionary gain. The general effect of Vairocana's energy upon an individual assists that personality to overcome the delusions of 'self', the concepts of an 'I', through a gradual process of identification with that which is not 'I'.
2. *Akṣobhya*, the Mirror-like Wisdom embodying the *eastern* direction works to counter the faculty of pride in humanity. The mirror shows to the *prideful* the nature of their self-concepts via images depicting the grotesque ways their activities manifest. It depicts the truth of what is parodied as pride. The posturings of 'self' are revealed with respect to its worth in the realm of the Real. Akṣobhya thus ensures that the paradigm of the Real overrules the self-aggrandisement of the prideful. Residing in the regal sovereignty of the Heart's domain, this Lord of all-embracive Compassion roars the Sound of the intrinsic emptiness of all phenomena. It shatters the egoistic bubbles of those that try to compete with it. The Hūṁ of universal potency speaks from the Heart of all that is, requiring humbleness from those who seek its domain. The ego is shattered through a painful self-effacement effected through *karma's* hand and by inwards contemplation upon the nature of reality. The practitioner thus learns to express the all-embracive entitylessness seen in the mirror of the All held in the hand of Akṣobhya.

   The true nature of the humbleness of the Heart is thereby instated upon all seekers of truth. This is expressed in terms of the united plan of the community of the Bodhisattvas meditating upon the welfare of all sentient beings. As the prideful one learns to attune to their united Heartbeat emanating from the enlightened realms, so the expeditions that once glorified a personalising aura dissolve into the austere blue radiance of the unifying non-ego.

3. *Amitābha*, the Discriminating Inner Vision embodying the *western* direction. His Wisdom counters best the most hardened rocks of mind, of fundamentalist, concrete, or materialistic beliefs. Right discrimination as to which item of information to select out of the host offered is the key here. This is the roadmap to the highest truths, in a similar way as a twig leads to a limb, thence branch and finally to the main trunk of the tree of Wisdom. Amitābha's Wisdom knows where to cleave asunder the most convoluted thoughts, causing the producer to start anew, along a more logical, revelatory, and sometimes esoteric, fluidic line. Fluidity of thought paves the arenas for the inner visions to screen. The task is to eventually nullify the concreted mental-emotional *saṃskāras* of humanity, replacing them with the unsullied mind in its natural state, open to impressions from the *dharmakāya*.

   Amitābha's specific effect, however, is upon the Sambhogakāya Flowers, to instill into them the detailed vision of the interrelated activity of their domain, and the immediate and inevitable purpose of the human civilisation that they create together. The proper ordering and progression of the *ālayavijñāna* is therefore the focus of his Discriminating Vision. Here is found *sukhāvatī,* the blissful Pure Land, or paradise realm that many Buddhists aspire to, which is presided over by this Jina. From the domain of the Flower then can come inspiration and ideations, the illumination flooding the minds of receptive incarnate humans. The entire world of ideas can thereby be stimulated to produce beneficent advancement for human civilisation.

4. *Ratnasambhava*, the Equalising Wisdom embodying the *southern* direction governing the Watery Element. Fears of all types represent acquiescence to the most Watery of all emotional qualities. Images of hell states and of things fearful to face then dominate, and when taken to be real, the person retreats into an emotional shell.

Ratnasambhava works to calm the massed fearful reactions of humanity, and consolidates sound opinions wherewith fears can be rightly reasoned and understood as the mirages they really are. How can fears stand if the inner and outer portions of the cell are equalised, where one is made to appear as if the other? How can fears and other intense emotions stand if all is equalised in the becalming, unifying Waters of Love? How can the emotions stand if the truth as to their illusional, all-deceiving, glamoured, 'self'-establishing, distorting nature is revealed? Once pacified, therefore, the fears give way to an acceptance of what must be, the sense of the equality of all things because of their true transitoriness, and that *śūnyatā* is at the heart of all. There is nothing really to fear in *saṃsāric* turmoil other than the fear itself arising in response to any situation.

Emotional *saṃskāras* and fear can also be whipped up by mantras of fright and scorn by the lords of dark face, and those that emit lying propaganda. We can see here another avenue of service for those working in Ratnasambhava's department to counter. Many are the meditative paths to be taken to overcome the evil intent of those manipulating the emotions of the masses. Much equalising power needs to be asserted, if *siddhis* of enlightened accomplishment are to arise from the woes of maligned emotional focus.

The future is the revelation of truth pertaining to enlightenment, and the inner fearful state is then made to embrace the course of enlightenment through the development of the steps of the Eightfold Path and right knowledge, whereby the transitoriness of all types of emotional phenomena are eliminated. The fearful one is shown the image of his or her fear in its true nature, and then the steps to be undergone to overcome such fears. Hell states are thus shown to be the illusions they intrinsically are. Lying propaganda can also be shown for what it is by revelation of the undeniable truth. The processes associated with overcoming fearful states for a human unit also find application with respect to the course of evolution of a nation, and ultimately to a civilisation. The little emotionalities, serpents, and demons of imaginative constructions, the interrelatedness of other's fears, worries, anticipations, and false beliefs find application in our cities on a massive scale. It is often what motivates and controls the way groups generally behave. All fearful states and situations in our societies must eventually be equalised through calming techniques and right information of the causes of people's lack of emotional control. Eventually trust and right loving relationships are built up between all humans and nations in the world. Eventually all is made equanimous in Love.

Ratnasambhava's activity will thus inevitably counter the various images created by humanity upon the fluid astral plane throughout all of the millennia of their emotional, religious, and societal activities. His energy will instate the true beauty of enlightened perception into the world, thus surmounting the desirous, reactionary, and lust-conditioned images of humanity.

5. *Amoghasiddhi*, the All-Accomplishing Wisdom embodying the *northern* position of the *maṇḍala*. Amoghasiddhi's task is perhaps the hardest because he must counter the self-centred iron will of the most cancerous materialists, and also cleanse the blight caused by the avaricious, egotistic, and separative members of humanity. We see that his task is almost exclusively focussed upon the worst miscreants of humanity, overturning the basis of their egoistic stance into the enlightened attitude that loss of ego provides. We thus have the production of true selfless activity for the common good. The task involves weaving the most materialistic types of *karma*, and their transformations, so they eventually reflect *dharmakāyic* constructs in such a way that the bearers of evil intent do least harm to humanity. As such his work is the summation of that of his brother Jinas, grounding their various forms of meditation.

The *dharmakāya karma* involves more than just our earth sphere. It generally necessitates visualising the trend of entire solar evolutions, and of their interrelatedness in the cosmic landscape, because of the vast number of rebirths of those espousing the most intense, hardened, egoistic forms of consciousness. Ultimately, even the greatest sorcerer will become a Buddha, but the transformation process may take more than one solar incarnation to achieve. Amoghasiddhi must keep track of all the changes that karmic education has made upon such a one, and to always be ready to apply the next disciplinary action, so that cancerous threads are severed one by one, and the released souls that were attached to the threads are led to tread the path to light supernal.

The most intense forms of light must be utilised to counter the blackest beams of mind, and there are myriads of shades of grey to account for. This is a most esoteric form of work, and those working inside of Amoghasiddhi's department know well how to counter all schemes woven by sorcerers of the most evil might. Thus grey and black forms of darkness are eventually transformed into brilliant luminosity.

Note that the accounting here of the antidotes attributed to the Jinas differs from the traditional presentation, where for instance Ratnasambhava's Wisdom is said to be the antidote to pride, and Akṣobhya's is that for anger or hatred. There may be some basis for such reasoning, but this book presents an expanded view, where the effects of developed *siddhis* are taken into account. The traditional account given is in reference to the Six Realms, where Ratnasambhava's antidote is to pride, the main fault of the Gods. Amoghasiddhi's antidote is directed mainly to the main fault of the *asuras*, being envy or jealousy. Vairocana's antidote to ignorance overcomes the main delusion of the animal kingdom. Amitābha's antidote to selfish lust overcomes the main delusion of the *pretas* (also given as 'unsatisfied passions'[9]). Akṣobhya's antidote to anger or hatred overcomes the main quality of the denizens of hell. Humans take on all of these attributes and therefore have a Manuśi (human) Buddha manifesting the antidote for all of their fetters to enlightenment.

In Govinda's account, we have the Bodhisattva Avalokiteśvara taking on various attributes and bearing gifts in each of the Six Realms for the salvation of the respective residents. We can surmise that the attributes taken are aspects of the Jinas mentioned above, plus that of Śākyamuni for humanity.[10]

---

9 Govinda, *Foundations of Tibetan Mysticism*, 240.

10 Ibid., 239-241. Thus the lute provided for the Gods, so that they can hear the heavenly sounds of the *dharma*, represents the function of Vairocana; the flaming sword of discriminating knowledge to assist the *asuras*, represents the Wisdom of Amitābha; the spiritual food provided for the *pretas*, manifests as an attribute of

The interrelated *maṇḍala* of Jinas, the Dhyāni Bodhisattvas, Mahābodhisattvas, and their consorts has been shown in this book to represent a plethora of cause-effect interrelations that conditions all domains and attributes of being/non-being. The presentation has developed far further into the field of causes of all natural phenomena in cosmos than what traditional views have proferred. This should prove valuable to future seekers of truth. Hopefully this presentation will assist future meditators that possess a scientific leaning to appropriately integrate these higher esoteric understandings into the deductions of the present scientific materialistic community so that a more wholesome science is obtained, one that incorporates the subtle domains and those of liberation.

Oṁ

---

the Equalising Wisdom of Ratnasambhava; the book of knowledge read out to the animals, so that they can evolve into humans, represents the Mirror-like Wisdom of Akṣobhya. Finally, the purifying flame needed to transform the conditions of the hell realms, represents the function of the All-accomplishing Wisdom of Amoghasiddhi. Humans are presented the alms bowl of Śākyamuni, so that they can learn to follow in the footsteps of this *Mānuśi* (human) Buddha.

Bibliography

Bailey, Alice A. *A Treatise on Cosmic Fire.* New York: Lucis Publishing Company, 2005.

Balsys, Bodo. *I-Concept.* Kathmandu: Vajra Publishing, 2009.

Blavatsky, H.P. *The Secret Doctrine. Vol. 1,* Adyar: Theosophical Publishing House, 1971.

Brauen, Martin. *The Mandala: Sacred Circle in Tibetan Buddhism.* London: Serinda Publications 1997.

Coleman, G (ed). *The Handbook of Tibetan Buddhism.* New Delhi: Rupa & Co., 1995.

Dalai Lama (Tenzin Gyatso) & Hopkins, J *Kalachakra Tantra: Rite of Initiation.* London: Wisdom Publications, 1989.

Ferris, Timothy. *The Whole Shebang.* London: Phoenix, 1997.

Ganguly, Swati. *Treatise in Thirty Verses on Mere-Consciousness.* New Delhi: Motilal Banarsidass, 1992.

Garfield, Jay L. *The Fundamental Wisdom of the Middle Way: Nāgārjuna's Mūlamadhyamakakārikā.* New York: Oxford University Press, 1995.

Getty, Alice. *The Gods of Northern Buddhism.* Oxford: Oxford University Press, 1928.

Govinda, Lama Anagarika. *Psycho-Cosmic Symbolism of the Buddhist Stūpa.* Berkeley: Dharma Publishing, 1976.

——. *Foundations of Tibetan Mysticism.* London: Century Paperbacks, 1987.

Gregory, Peter N. (trans.). *Inquiry into the Origin of Humanity: An Annotated Translation of Tsung-Mi's Yüan Jen Lun with a Modern Commentary.* Honolulu: University of Hawai'i Press, 1995.

Griffiths, Paul, J. *On Being Buddha.* Delhi: Sri Satguru, 1995.

Gyatso, Geshe Kelsang. *Clear Light of Bliss, a Commentary to the Practice of Mahamudra in Vajrayana Buddhism.* Boston: Wisdom Publications, 1982.

Hakeda, Yoshita S. *The Awakening of Faith Attributed to Aśvaghosha.* New York: Columbia University Press, 1990.

Hopkins, Jeffrey. *Meditation on Emptiness.* London: Wisdom Publications, 1983.

Leidy, Denise Patry, and Robert A. F. Thurman. *Mandala: The Architecture of Enlightenment.* London: Thames and Hudson, 1997.

Makransky, J. *Buddhahood Embodied.* Sri Satguru Publications, 1997.

Muller, F M (ed). *Sacred Books of the East. Sacred Books of the East. Vol. 10,* Delhi: Motilal Banarsidass, 2004.

Perkins, James S. *A Geometry of Space and Consciousness.* Adyar: The Theosophical Publishing House, 2004.

Ramanan, K. Venkata *Nāgārjuna's Philosophy: As Presented in the Maha-Prajñāpāramitā-Śāstra.* Delhi: Motilal Banarsidass, 1978.

Reynolds, J.M. *The Golden Letters.* Ithaca: Snow Lion, 1996.

Richelieu, Peter. *A Soul's Journey.* London: Thorsons, 1996.

Rinpoche, Dujom. *The Nyingma School of Tibetan Buddhism: Its Fundamentals and History.* Boston: Wisdom Publications, 1991.

Rucker, Rudolf v. B. *Geometry, Relativity, and the Fourth Dimension.* Dover Publications, 1977.

Schumacher, S., and G (eds) Woerner. *The Encyclopaedia of Eastern Philosophy and Religion.* Boston: Shambhala, 1994.

Snelling, John. *The Buddhist Handbook.* London: Rider, 1998.

Snodgrass, Adrian. *The Symbolism of the Stupa*, New York: SEAP Cornell University, 1985.

Sparham, G (trans). *Ocean of Eloquence, Tsong-Ka-Pa's Commentary on the Yogacara Doctrine of Mind.* Delhi: Sri Satguru, 1995.

Stcherbatsky, Theodore. *The Central Conception of Buddhism.* Delhi: Motilal Baranasidass, 1994.

Suzuki, Daisetz Teitaro. *The Lankavatara Sutra.* London: Routledge & Kegan Paul Ltd, 1973.

Tucci, Guiseppe. *Theory and Practice of the Maṇḍala.* London: Rider and Co., 1961.

——. *Tibetan Painted Scrolls.* Bangkok: SDI Publications, 1999.

Wayman, Alex. *Untying the Knots in Buddhism, Select Essays.* Delhi: Motilal Banarsidass, 1997.

Index

A

Abstract Mind, 17, 434
  Aether, 22
  awakening via third initiation, 165
  illustrated, 16
  Mādhyamika description, 77
Ādi Buddha, 368, 376, 379
  definition of, 6
  formation of world sphere, 79–80, 84–85, 169, 217
  in relation to a Logos or God, 34–41
  inward vision of a, 36–38
Aether
  abstract mind, 22
  fifth element, 330–331
Afflictive emotions
  the four, 73–74
Ākāśagarbha, 298–302, 325, 389, 392
Ālaya, 23–28
  definition of, 26
  maṇḍalic structures within, 36
Ālayavijñāna, 162, 165–166, 188, 189, 320, 330, 360, 415, 440
  attribute of mind, 22, 26–29
  definition of, 9, 82
  in relation to eight directions of space, 276, 331
  in relation to eightfold path, 252, 253, 256, 273, 274
  in relation to Head centre, 103, 230
  nature of the, 36, 311
  of a world-sphere, 35
  Yogācāra perspective on, 76–77
Ālokā, 284, 285, 367–368, 372–373, 393, 399, 399–400
Amitāyus
  definition of, 324
Animal kingdom
  evolution into human kingdom, 81, 396–397, 401–406
Antaḥkaraṇa
  conscious building of, 74, 89–90, 248–249
  definition of, 34
Anuttarayogatantra, 162
Arhat
  definition of, 19
Astral body, 140
Astral plane, 140–143
  as hell realm, 145
  higher levels of, 143
Astral projection, 137–138
Astral substance, 136
Astral travel, 139

Ātman
definition of, 186
relation to tathāgatagarbha, 28
Aura
definition of, 140
Avalokiteśvara, 307–314, 325, 383, 384–385, 443
different symbols of, 386–387
in relation to Shambhala, 380–381
in relation to the Sambhogakāya Flower, 356–364
Avatar
definition of, 95
Awareness
expansion of, 54–55
threshold of, 39–40

B

Bardo, 117, 134–135
Bardo Realms, 138–139
Being/non-being, 418
mysteries of, 32
upper strata of, 40
Bhūmi, 282
definition of, 114
Big Bang theory, 7
Bīja
as zero-dimensional object, 125
definition of, 1
from dharmakāya, 71
in relation to mūlaprakṛti, 75
of a maṇḍala, 167, 183, 213, 253, 256
Bījas
accumlulation of, 409
activation of, 248, 262, 265
refinement of, 11
storage of, 11, 15, 41, 275
Bindu
definition of, 3
Bodhi
definition of, 11
Bodhicitta, 19, 92, 378
definition of, 15
expression of, 27, 212–213, 256, 413
generation of, 210, 254, 271
in relation to śūnyatā, 65, 372
teachings concerning, 328
transforming astral substance, 145
Bodhisattva
educators of humanity, 113–114, 151, 207, 212–216
expansion of mind, 33–34
path, 225, 253, 254, 261, 264, 267, 270, 271–272, 307, 325, 363, 369, 432–433
use of the Will-to-Love, 210–212, 220, 255
Bodhisattvas
evolution of, 114
in Heruka forms, 333–334
Buddha
as Logoic Lord, 46–47
what is a, 432–433
Buddha field, 61–62, 79, 96
of a Logos, 38–40, 99
Buddha-gotra, 16
Buddha Maitreya
bringing new revelations, 62
Buddha-Mind, 377, 413
domain of the, 35, 375–376
evolution of, 99, 115
in relation to human thought, 43–44, 221
Buddhas
appearance of, 114–116
Burning ground, 163–164

C

Cakravāla, 20
Cardinal cross, 169, 333, 347, 382
directions of four noble truths, 249–251
Caryātantra, 162, 164
Catuṣkoṭi
definition of, 68

Cells
expansion of, 429–439
in relation to chakras, 100–101, 416
in relation to maṇḍala, 184
sentience of, 98–99
Cellular evolution, 98–100, 187–188, 238
in relation to time and experience, 408–415, 422–423
Chakras
Ājñā Centre, 183
as a maṇḍala, 191
as expression of energies, 417–422
awakening of, 169, 246–247
Base of Spine, 21
primordial substance, 71, 378
definition of, 46
formation of, 191
governing the arūpa levels, 340–341
governing the rūpa levels, 341
head centre, 95, 157–158, 201
petals of the, 221–233
Heart centre, 95, 103, 224, 243, 331, 332–333, 417–418
in relation to cellular structure, 100–101
in relation to eight directions of space, 281, 287, 300
in relation to eightfold path, 252, 254, 260, 262, 265–266, 267, 272
in relation to eight Mahābodhisattvas, 281, 283, 287, 294, 301, 305, 309, 313, 316–317, 323, 366–374
in relation to the eight consciousnesses, 101–103
in relation to the five senses, 102–103
Logoic correspondences, 46–47
minor, 192
Sacral centre
significance to nāḍī system, 102
Solar Plexus, 47–49
in relation to Mahābodhisattvas, 374–391
Splenic centre
function of, 103
Chakra system
colours of the, 337
composition of, 107, 416–421
in relation to astrology, 342–343
in relation to numbers, 344–356
maṇḍala of, 245–246, 298
Chaos, 92
as disorganised thought-structures, 63
as mūlaprakṛti, 66
bubbles of, 67
definition of, 66
in relation to evolution, 133
void interrelation, 68–69
Chela, 266
Chohan, 387–390
definition of, 282
fourth Ray, 286, 389–390
Christ, 376, 380, 386
Circumambulation, 175
Citta
as principle of Life, 76–77
attribute of mind, 22–23, 73–74
definition of, 23
evolution of, 85, 88
five grades of, 85–87, 95
role in formation of saṁsāra, 80–81
Cittamātra. *See* Mind-only
Cittavṛtti
control of, 33
Clairvoyance, 131
basis in solar plexus, 102–103
Clear Light of Mind, 7, 15, 69, 165, 307. *See also* Nexus, śūnyatā-saṃsāra
within the abstract Mind, 16

Concrete mind
definition of, 15
domain of the, 36–39
Consciousness, 13
contraction of, 436–437
dimensions of, 130
evolution of, 75–76, 125, 170–171, 190–191, 197, 244–248, 255
in relation to cellular structure, 433–438
in relation to Divine will, 216–217
in relation to saṁskāras, 429–433
in relation to time, 408–415
expansion of, 10, 184
fourth dimensional, 130, 157
gap in, 74
I-consciousness, 12, 70, 72–74
in relation to numbers, 155–158
in relation to śūnyatā, 69
in relation to the human mind, 200
manifesting phenomena, 69–70
spheres of, 19, 20, 45, 58–59, 88–89, 238–239
spirals of, 20, 158
storehouse of, 9
stream and rebirth, 217–218
threshold of, 31–33, 45
Consorts
directing prāṇas, 393–398
in evolution of animal kingdom, 401–403
in evolution of consciousness, 404–406
in evolution of instinct, 397–400
role of, 391–396
Cosmic Mind. *See also* Mahat
nature of, 56
Cosmos
as maṇḍala, 238, 240
definition of, 94–95
Council of Bodhisattvas, 18, 34, 165, 254, 264, 282, 320, 365, 379, 390, 427. *See also* Hierarchy

D

Ḍākinīs, 37, 39, 80, 107, 333
as Buddha-germ, 170
as units of intelligence, 168
definition of, 166
directing prāṇas, 392–395
in evolution of animal kingdom, 401–403
in evolution of consciousness, 339–340, 344, 396, 404–406
in evolution of instinct, 397–400
Dark brotherhood, 97, 216, 322, 438–439
Dark matter, 54, 410, 416
Darkness, 9. *See also* Ignorance
Dependent Origination, 6
formula of, 67–68
sequence of events, 75–83
Desire
transmutation of, 250
Desire Principle, 84, 254
Devas, 37, 39, 107, 133, 239
as form, 166
definition of, 80, 344
watery, 133, 164
Dhāraṇī/s
as elements of thought, 179–181
compared to mantras, 180
definition of, 170, 179
influenced by the will, 199–200
role in the creative process, 180, 181, 210, 378
substance of, 182
Dharmakāya, 17, 62, 222, 230, 324
as source of karma, 425
definition of, 3, 415–416
exerting evolutionary pressure, 412–413, 417, 424–425
expression of, 60, 167, 377, 411, 419
foundation stone of the, 44
in relation to eightfold path, 253, 258, 261, 264, 269, 273, 274

logoic expression via, 42, 44–47
numerology of, 358
pathways toward, 33, 115, 165, 212
relationship to maṇḍala, 173
space as expression of, 63
way, the, 255, 273, 320
Dharmakāya Eye, 173
Dharmas
definition of, 186
Dharmatā, 153, 167, 271
definition of, 17
Dhūpā, 299–300, 300, 367–368, 372–373, 393, 394, 397, 405
Dhyāna
definition of, 6
in relation to eightfold path, 255, 258, 260–261, 271–272
Dhyāni Bodhisattvas
governing pentad of, 385
in relation to chakras, 374
in relation to solar plexus centre, 374–391
Dhyāni Buddhas, 18, 52, 160, 165, 172, 181, 226, 275, 348, 349, 374–375
Akṣobhya, 87, 384, 393, 428, 439–440
Amitābha, 87, 200, 231, 314, 357, 361–362, 384, 394, 428, 440–441
Amoghasiddhi, 87, 200, 231, 323, 385, 394, 427–428, 442–443
as a creative Logos, 239, 423–426
in relation to a vajra, 365–366
in relation to eight Mahābodhisatvas, 285, 289–290, 304, 313, 316, 320, 324, 367–373
in relation to the future, 427–429
meditations of, 369
minds of, 94
Ratnasambhava, 87, 201, 231, 362, 384, 428, 440–441
role of consorts, 391–395
Vairocana, 87, 165, 167, 172, 379, 383, 428, 439
consort Ākāśadhātvīśvarī, 391–392
wisdoms of, 93, 96, 352, 421–422, 439–444
Dimensionality
nature of, 124–125
of a one-dimensional zone, 125–126
of a three-dimensional object, 128–130
of a two-dimensional object, 127–128
of a zero-dimensional object, 125
Discrimination
five criteria of, 122
right, 147, 211, 440
Discriminative process
as partner to enlightenment, 121, 150–151
development of, 119
Discriminatory mind, 149
recomprehension of 'things', 121–122
Divine Will, 215–216
Dorje
manifestation of, 71
Dreams
as astral experiences, 137

E

Ego
death of, 152, 165
Eight consciousnesses
in relation to eight directions of space, 276–278, 331–332
in relation to eightfold path, 252, 254, 257, 260, 265, 267, 272, 274, 276–278
in relation to elementary mind, 397–398
in relation to the chakras, 101–103

Eight directions of space, 245–249
in relation to eight Mahābodhisattvas, 280–326
in relation to eight qualities of the dharma, 279–280
in relation to eight virtuous roots of the Bodhisattva, 280
in relation to the eightfold path, 251, 254, 256, 258–259, 262, 265, 266, 267, 269, 271, 273, 274, 276–278
in relation to the heart channel-wheel, 329–330
Eightfold Path, 242, 251–275, 276–278
in relation to Mahābodhisattvas, 285, 289, 291, 299, 303, 311, 315, 320
Eight Mahābodhisattvas, 280–326, 333
consorts of the, 246, 284, 285, 333, 401–406
in relation to evolution of humanity, 369–374
in relation to motion of swastikas, 365–373
in relation to solar plexus centre, 374–391
in relation to the chakras, 366–375
Eight qualities of the dharma
by the Ratnagotravibhāga, 279–280
Eight virtuous roots of the Bodhisattva, 280
Elementary mind, 396–397
Elements
in relation to evolution of instinct, 397–400
in relation to evolution of mind, 104–105
in relation to processing of prāṇas, 221–224, 229–230
Elements of mind
Fiery-Aetheric, 26
Fiery-Airy, 25–26
Fiery-Earth, 23
Fiery-Fiery, 24–25
Fiery-Watery, 23–24
Emotions, 73, 203
animal-like, 118–119
as watery element, 29–30, 133, 164, 262, 440
control of, 164
dried by fire, 50
transcending, 145
transformation of, 371–372
via the Solar Plexus centre, 47–49
Empiricism
relationship to enlightenment, 13
Energy
definition of, 341
of a radiant aura, 414
Enlightened Mind, 122
no-thought, 123
Enlightened thoughts
as multidimensional, 147
benefit of, 59
intensity of Will, 200–201
Enlightenment
a definition of, 60
process of, 13, 109–116, 182–184, 211–212, 243–244
relative to level of evolution, 119
Etheric body, 140
definition of, 136
Event horizon, 8
Evolution
as cycles of numbers, 156–157
expressing fiery element, 76
of a community, 151
of cells, 98–100, 429–433
of logic, 148
patterns of, 120–121
via experience of time, 408–415
via Logoic thought, 76–79, 216
via the physical plane, 39–40
way of Logoic, 47

Expansion
of awareness, 54–55, 184
Experience, 57
evolution over time via, 408–415
Eye
all-seeing, 331–332

F

Five
significance of the number, 422–427
Five Jinas. *See* Dhyāni Buddhas
Five principal atoms, 41–42
Five sense-consciousness, 38
Five Senses
in relation to chakras, 102–103
Five Void Elements, 63, 67, 70–71, 95, 416
Fixed cross, 167, 331, 332, 333, 347, 369
Flowers
as spheres of containment, 157–158
Force
definition of, 341
Four Noble Truths, 242, 249–251
Fourth dimensional matter
as watery element, 131–132, 135–136
Fourth dimensional visioning, 131–132
Free will, 208–209, 426

G

Gandhā, 303, 305, 367–368, 370, 393, 399, 401–402
Garuḍa, 323
definition of, 322
Ghaṇṭā
definiton of, 287
Gitā, 309, 312, 367–368, 371–372, 393, 394, 397, 401, 402–403, 405
Glamour
of pride, 437
God
nature of, 79
Goodwill, 209–210
development of, 224–225
Guṇas
definition of, 352
Guru paraṃparā
process of, 40–41

H

Harmlessness
in relation to eightfold path, 256
Head centre
as a flower, 157–158
petals of activity, 221–233
Heart
channel-wheel, 329–330, 332
energies of the, 211
way of the, 287, 292
Heart centre, 331, 332
activity of, 243
function of the petals, 95
in relation to numbers, 346–351
in relation to zodiac, 347–348
Heavenly realm, 142
Hell realms, 141–142
Hierarchies
deva and human, 107
Hierarchy
of enlightened beings, 18
Humanity
as group-Buddha, 115

I

I-concept, 21
Identity
in relation to enlightenment, 152–154
Ignorance. *See also* Darkness
in relation to the Void, 88–89, 91
origin of, 82
zone of comparative, 8
Illusional void, 92
Indreya-jñāna, 24

Initiation, 170
- 1st, 163
- 2nd, 164
- 3rd, 165
- 4th, 167
- 5th, 167
- maṇḍalic structure of, 161

Intelligence, 331
Intelligent Design, 401–406

J

Jinas. *See* Dhyāni Buddhas

K

Kālachakra
- Maṇḍala, 52, 160
  - definition of, 109

Kālahamsa
- definition of, 339

Kalaśa
- definition of, 288

Karma. *See also* Saṃskāras
- as group law, 36–37
- four types of, 13
- in relation to a Buddha, 98
- in relation to evolution, 88, 98, 217, 227, 235, 420
- in relation to Love, 94
- in relation to selfish will, 204–205, 206
- in relation to the Logoic thinker, 76
- law of, 168, 170, 218, 219, 240
- production of, 134–135, 152–153
- psychic, 164
- unit of, 7

Karmic purpose
- equilibrium, 133

Kleśas, *See also* afflictive emotions
- definition of, 154

Kliṣṭamanas, 71–73, 145, 313, 330, 331
- definition of, 48

Knots of thought, 58
Knowledge, 92
- in relation to the Void, 92

Kriyātantra, 162, 164
Kṣitigarbha, 287–291, 310, 389, 392
Kuṇḍalinī, 317, 374
- definition of, 228

L

Laṅkāvatāra Sūtra
- D.T. Suzuki, 23–28

Lāsyā, 287–288, 367–368, 373–374, 393, 398, 402, 406–407
Liberation, 18
Life-flux, 217, 219
- definition of, 156

Light
- in relation to all realms of perception, 137–138
- speed of, 53–54

Livingness
- definition of, 49

Logic
- evolution of, 148

Logoic body, 40
Logoic eye, 40
Logoic maṇḍala, 62
Logoic Mind, 38, 238
- organising principle, 68
- void within the, 67

Logoic thought
- and dharmakāya, 44–47
- moving citta, 75–76
- structure of, 38–42
- use of dhāraṇīs, 179, 181

Logos, 34–42
- Buddha-field of a, 38–40
- expressed Will of, 37, 42
- way of evolution, 47, 97

Love, 93
- in relation to the Void, 92
- principle, 371–372

M

Mādhyamaka
  view of time, 55–56
Mādhyamā pratipad
  definition of, 233
Mahābodhisattvas, 243, 275, 280–283. *See also* Eight Mahābodhisattvas
  in relation to eight directions of space, 280–326
  in relation to eightfold path, 285, 289, 291, 299, 303, 311, 315, 320
  in relation to evolution of humanity, 369–374
  in relation to motion of swastikas, 365–373
  in relation to solar plexus centre, 374–391
  in relation to the chakras, 366–373
  pentad of, 388
Mahāchohan, 282, 324, 376, 381, 383
Mahāmudrā
  central element of, 166
  concept of, 169
  definition of, 94
  tantric, 329–330
Mahāsiddha
  definition of, 171
  great bliss of, 107
Mahat
  definition of, 45
Maitreya, 291–299, 388
  as Buddha, 297–298
Mālā, 315, 316, 367–368, 373–374, 394, 399
Manas, 5
  attribute of mind, 22, 24–29
  colouring and vibrancy of, 44
  creative aptitude of, 48
  definition of, 25
  double-nature of, 74–75
  ordering of saṃsāra, 85
Manasic substance, 5
Maṇḍala
  as a bee hive, 191–197
  as a mirror, 60
  as cellular unit, 150–151
  as motion of consciousness, 51–53
  as sphere of limitation, 59–62
  centre of the, 166–167
  definition of, 1, 158–160
  elements of, 160–166
  evolution of via will, 199
  expression of via dhāraṇīs, 179–181, 220
  function of, 181–184
  of a chakra system, 245–246
  of mind, 33–34
  orientation of major directions, 197–198
  patterning of, 7, 17
  symbolism of the, 167–169
  unveiling process of a, 182–183
Maṇḍalas
  construction of, 30, 147, 150–151, 220
    via numbers, 156–157
  correct visualisation of, 149
  cycles within, 55
  macrocosmic, 34–42, 159–160
  to categorise thought, 14
  within consciousness, 32–33
Mañjuśrī, 283–287, 325, 389
Manovijñāna
  attribute of mind, 22–25
  definition of, 24
Mantra, 107
Mantras, 258
  as empowering word, 35
Manu, 376, 379
Māyā
  as part of a maṇḍala, 182
  definition of, 13
  in process of evolution, 182, 214–215, 260

Māyāvirūpa
definition of, 145
Meditation, 115–116
purpose of, 216
Meditation-Mind, 32, 243
Mental realm, 143
Milarepa, 387–388
Mind, 4
abstract level of, 14
activity aspect, 19
Love-Wisdom aspect, 19
Will or Power aspect, 19
after death, 117–118
attributes of, 8, 73–75
ālayavijñāna, 22, 26–29
citta, 22–23
manas, 22, 24–29
manovijñāna, 22–25
vijñāna, 22–29
categorising function of, 123, 190
characteristics of, 118
clear light of, 7, 123–124, 165, 307
conscious aspiration, 33–34
created by, 9
development of, 82–84, 109–116
discriminatory, 108, 121–124
domain of, 68
dual functioning of, 14
elementary, 396–397
essence of the, 70
evolution of, 396–401
expansion of, 11, 31–33
fires of, 83–84, 130, 265
five elements of, 22–30
in relation to numbers, 345
in relation to the Void, 89–90
laws of expanding, 54–55
layers of, 4, 21
maṇḍala of, 33–34
maṇḍalas as, 14, 237
organising chaos, 106–107, 133
registering phenomena, 64–65
relative to motion, 50–52
seven Ray aspects of, 119
definitions, 203–204
sphere of limitation, 21
spheres of activity, 14
spheres of thought, 31–34
telepathic communication, 34
threshold of awareness, 39–41
Mind-only, 28
Mineral kingdom
appearance of, 80
Monad, 171
Moon, 305, 312
Mount Meru, 20, 177
Mudrā
definition of, 293
Mūlaprakṛti, 68, 378
abstraction of, 70–71
as chaos, 66
definition of, 65
Mutable cross, 168
as swastika, 244, 369

N

Nāḍī
definition of, 25
iḍā, 168, 295
definition of, 223
in relation to eightfold path, 275
pairs in relation to chakras, 283
piṅgalā, 168, 313–314
definition of, 223
in relation to eightfold path, 275
suṣumṇā
definition of, 283
in relation to eightfold path, 275
system, 41, 102–103, 163, 192, 298, 416–417
cleansing of the, 169, 222, 265, 302, 323
element Air, 420
in relation to colours, 334–337

in relation to head centre, 223–232
in relation to the eight vijñānas, 331
Logoic correspondences, 46–47, 378
of the Void, 95

Nāga
definition of, 321

Nāgārjuna
catuṣkoṭi, 68, 108
on nirvāṇa and saṁsāra, 64–65, 89

Nexus
mandala expressing nature of, 159
śūnyatā-saṃsāra (saṃsāra-śūnyatā), 12, 64–66, 162, 169
as domain of enlightened mind, 122, 182, 241
re Nāgārjuna, 64–65
via the Sambhogakāya Flower, 17
zone of, 8, 159, 230

Nirmalā tathatā
definition of, 79

Nirmāṇakāya, 435
definition of, 107
numerology of, 358

Nirvāṇa. *See* śūnyatā

Nīvaraṇaviṣkambhin, 302–307, 325

Nṛtyā, 320, 324–325, 367–368, 370, 393, 395, 398, 402–403, 404–405

Numbers
as symbols, 155
in relation to consciousness, 155–158
mystery of, 154
sequences of, 155–157
sound of, 155

Numerology, 124

P

Paean
as mantric songs, 46

Parinirvāṇa
definition of, 114

Pentagram
symbolism, 376–377, 424

Perception
astral plane of, 140
fifth-dimensional, 137
first-dimensional, 136
fourth-dimensional, 131–132, 137
in relation to saṃskāras, 190
lower mental subplanes of, 144
multi-dimensional, 131–132
of objects, 184–190
realms of, 137
second-dimensional, 136
seven dimensions of, 20
third-dimensional, 136

Perfection
relativity of, 111–112

Personal-I, 15, 165, 260, 360, 411. *See also* I-concept
domain of the, 36–37
evolution of, 104–105, 189, 191, 235, 434
formation of, 32
inward focus, 50, 435–436

Phenomena
absence of in śūnyatā, 63
as numeric sequences, 156
denial of, 153
nature of all, 32
of saṃsāra, 66
ontology of, 65–66
production of, 13

Phenomenal world
formation of, 79–80

Physical matter
as empty space, 129–130

Prajña
definition of, 166

Prajñāpāramitā, 285
definition of, 232, 284

Pralaya, 62, 157
definition of, 70

Prāṇa, 163
definition of, 21
in relation to chakras, 192–196, 244, 346
in relation to the nāḍīs, 334–336
processing of via the head centre, 221–224
Pratītyasamutpāda, 168. *See also* dependent origination
Pratyakṣa, 18
Pressure
in relation to evolution, 411–412
Pride, 439–440
pitfalls of, 436–437
Primordial Buddha, 36, 318–319. *See also* Ādi Buddha
Primordial substance. *See also* chaos
four levels of expression, 71
in relation to Base of Spine, 71
Psychic karma, 164
Psychic powers, 6, 18, 171, 425
Psychics, 136
Puṣpā, 291, 293, 367–368, 371, 394–395, 399, 400

R

Ratnapāṇi, 380, 383, 384–385
Ray, 325
1st, 319, 364, 376, 377
2nd, 310, 364, 376, 389
humanity conditioned by, 168
3rd, 168, 300, 302, 320, 324, 325, 364, 376, 377, 389
Ḍākinīs representing, 168
4th, 286, 325, 364, 389
5th, 305, 389
6th, 308, 387
7th, 294, 295, 388
rDzogs-chen tradition, 69–70
Rebirth, 183
cycles of, 234, 241
in relation to head lotus petals, 222–226
principle of, 409
process of, 217–221

S

Sādhana, 210
definition of, 199
Samalā tathatā, 81
definition of, 79
elimination of impurities, 84
Samantabhadra, 315–319, 326, 368, 376, 379, 383, 387, 391, 394
Śamatha
definition of, 145
Sambhogakāya, 165, 166, 435
definition of, 33, 117
numerology of, 358
Sambhogakāya Flower, 15, 18–19, 26, 29, 139, 218, 224, 247, 345, 353, 384–385, 415, 431, 437–438
as a cellular unit, 37–38, 40
as Son of Mind, 16, 19
as tathāgatagarbha, 29, 78–79, 218, 235
driving rebirth process, 234–238, 424
in relation to animal units, 402
in relation to Avalokiteśvara, 356–364
in relation to eightfold path, 252, 253, 254–255, 256, 258, 261, 273, 274–275
in relation to Oṁ Maṇi Padme Hūṁ, 311
in relation to the Will, 233–237
petals of the, 397
relationship to mind, 84, 222
relationship to soul, 29
relation to pudgala/ātman, 29
use of dhāraṇīs, 180
Saṃsāra, 49
definition of, 5, 89
formation of, 79–80, 181
foundation of, 71
manipulating aspects of, 260
phenomenon of, 66
relationship to śūnyatā, 12
Saṃsāra-śūnyatā. *See* nexus
Saṃsāric activity, 33

Saṃskāra. *See also* Karma - unit of
definition of, 7
Saṃskāras, 13, 154, 157, 217, 409
and development of mind, 84, 259
evolutionary flow of, 429–433
manasic, 165, 259
pressure of, 412, 435
purification of, 103, 164, 165, 214, 226, 236, 247
via head lotus, 221–223
relationship with chakras, 417, 418, 420
Saṃskāric stream
of reincarnation, 55
Samyaksaṃbodhi
definition of, 119–120
Satya, 14
Self
as obstacle to growth, 435–436
denial of, 208
Selfhood
distorting a maṇḍala, 151–152
Separativeness, 250
Shambhala, 376, 379, 383, 388
definition of, 212
Sickness
in relation to evolution, 236–237
Siddha, 18, 50, 418
Siddhis, 6, 99, 323, 438–439. *See also* Psychic powers
Silence, 107
Silver cord, 138, 139–140
Six Realms, 138–139, 141, 309–310, 387
in relation to Oṁ Maṇi Padme Hūṁ, 312–313
Sixth sense. *See* Manovijñāna
Skandhas, 157, 163, 373, 411–412, 418
definition of, 72
Solar Plexus centre
controlled by the Heart, 48–49
emotional thinking with, 47–49
Soul
relationship to Sambhogakāya Flower, 29
Sound, 106–107
Space
as expression of dharmakāya, 63
between atoms, 130–131
eight directions of, 245–249
Space-time
concept of, 7
continuum, 8, 183
Stūpa
as a maṇḍala, 172–178
definition of, 171
symbolism of, 172–178
Substance
forth-dimensional, 131–133, 135
refinement of, 11, 163
Solar Plexus watery, 49
Sun, 300, 312, 416
Śūnyatā, 69, 150, 318, 372, 394
and emptiness, 65
definition of, 12, 63, 152
direction of prāṇas, 420–421
in different levels of evolution, 421–422
in relation to dharmakāya, 415–416
in relation to eightfold path, 254, 273
in relation to the Heart centre, 417
relationship to saṃsāra, 12, 152–154
sixteen types of, 91
within the abstract Mind, 16, 17
Śūnyatā Eye, 18–19, 284
expression of the, 38, 235–236
of the Sambhogakāya Flower, 42, 253, 274, 289, 357, 359–360
Śūnyatā-saṃsāra. *See* nexus
Sūtrātmā, 18
Suzuki, Daisetz Teiraro
the Laṅkāvatāra Sūtra, 23–28

Swastika, 20, 168, 178, 331, 333
motion of the, 244–248, 347
in relation to Mahābodhisattvas, 365–373
Syllogisms
in relation to spheres of thought, 57–58
Synthesis
of viewpoint of self, 59

T

Tactical adversity, 97
Tantric mahāmudrā, 329–330
Tantric texts
definition of, 327
Tapas
definition of, 244
Tārā, 314
Tathāgata
definition of, 6
Tathāgatagarbha, 29, 81, 165, 218, 220, 235–236, 248, 271, 423
as perceived by a Logos, 40
creation of, 99
in relation to Love, 168
nucleus of, 78–79
relationship to Ālaya, 28, 29
Telepathy, 123–124
Theory of Relativity, 52–54
Theriomorphic deities, 29
Thought
abstract vs empirical, 53
and motion, 50–52
bubbles of, 46
colourations of, 43
high vs low quality of, 43
human vs Buddhic, 43–44, 170
knots of, 58
law of attraction, 48
laziness of, 57
multidimensional, 147, 149
observation of, 69–70
one-dimensional, 126
patterns of, 46
process of construction, 44–45
relative spheres of, 31–34
speed of, 54
transient nature of, 61
Thought-constructs
dhāraṇīs, 179–181
fiery, 43
watery, 43, 47–49
Thought-form/s
concretised, 148
discerning aspects of a, 2
emotional, 49
intensity of, 200–201
relative to astral realm, 142
Thought-streams, 430–432
Three Dimensional rules and limitations, 129
Time, 75
as expression of third dimension, 130, 137
cycles of, 50–51
evolution via experience of, 408–415
illusion of, 52–55
Mādhyamaka view of, 55–56
production of, 55
relativity of, 97–98
universal, 7
Turning-back, 27–28

U

Universal time, 7
Universe
as maṇḍala, 238
multidimensional, 238, 240, 414

V

Vajra
definition of, 20
in relation to the Dhyāni Buddhas, 365–366
manifestation of, 52
Vajrapāṇi, 320–326, 379, 383, 392
Vajrayāna, 274
definition of, 267

Vāsanā, 219
 definition of, 93
Vijñāna. *See also* Consciousness
 attribute of mind, 22–29
 definition of, 23
 in relation to rebirth, 217–218
Vijñānas
 transformation of, 332
Vipassanā
 definition of, 145
Viṣkambhin, 389
Viśvapāṇi, 381, 383, 384
Viśvavajra, 378
Void, 8, 63, 67, 84–85, 87–95, 344. *See also* śūnyatā
 as a mirror, 91
 Buddhist view of the, 56
 chaos interrelation, 68–69
 element, 68

W

Will
 as conscious projection, 201
 Divine Will, 215–216
 driving rebirth process, 218–221, 234
 free will, 208–209, 225
 goodwill, 209–210, 225
  development of, 224–225
 group, 205–207
 influencing dhāraṇīs, 199–200, 220–221
 lack of, 199
 nature of the, 201–202
 re evolution of consciousness, 199, 219
 re maṇḍalic evolution, 199–200
 selfish will, 202–207
 seven forms of, 202–217
 strong desire, 202
 Will-of-Love, 212–216
 Will-to-Love, 199, 210–212, 224, 374
Wisdom, 92
World-sphere
 formation of, 35
 origination of, 77

Y

Yāma, 357, 359, 361
Yidam
 definition of, 306
Yogācāra school, 10, 227, 276, 332
Yogatantra, 162, 164
Yogīn
 definition of, 16
 in relation to eight directions of space, 306–307, 322
 in relation to eightfold path, 253, 259, 260, 266

Z

Zodiac, signs of
 in relation to eightfold path, 251, 254, 256–257, 260, 263, 266, 269–270, 273–274
 in relation to evolution, 232–233, 417
 in relation to Heart centre, 347–348

About the Author

BODO BALSYS is the founder of The School of Esoteric Sciences. He is an author of many books on subjects centred on Buddhism and the Esoteric Sciences, a meditation teacher, poet, artist, spiritual scientist and healer. He has studied extensively across multiple traditions including Esoteric Science, Buddhism, Christianity, Esoteric Healing, Western Science, Art, Politics and History. His advanced esoteric insights, gained through decades of meditative contemplation, enable him to provide a rich understanding of the spiritual pathway toward enlightenment, healing and service.

Bodo's teachings can be accessed via the School of Esoteric Science's website: http://universaldharma.com

For any other enquiries, please email
sangha@universaldharma.com

About Universal Dharma Publishing

Universal Dharma Publishing is a not for profit publisher. Our aim is make innovative, original and esoteric spiritual teachings accessible to all who genuinely aspire to awaken and serve humanity. The books published aim in part to provide an esoteric interpretation of the meaning of Buddhist *dharma* with view of reformation of the way people perceive the meaning of the related teachings. Hopefully then Buddhism can more effectively serve its principal function as a vehicle for enlightenment, and further prosper into the future.

A further aim is to provide the next level of exposition of the esoteric doctrines to be revealed to humanity following on the wisdom tradition pioneered by H.P. Blavatsky and A.A. Bailey.

Cover Design by
Angie O'Sullivan & Kylie Smith

www.ingramcontent.com/pod-product-compliance
Lightning Source LLC
Chambersburg PA
CBHW031701230426
43668CB00006B/68
* 9 7 8 0 9 9 2 3 5 6 8 3 5 *